FIVE ELECTIONS
IN AFRICA

A GROUP OF ELECTORAL STUDIES

EDITED BY

W. J. M. MACKENZIE

PROFESSOR OF GOVERNMENT IN THE
VICTORIA UNIVERSITY OF MANCHESTER

AND

KENNETH ROBINSON

DIRECTOR OF THE
INSTITUTE OF COMMONWEALTH STUDIES
AND PROFESSOR OF COMMONWEALTH AFFAIRS
IN THE UNIVERSITY OF LONDON

OXFORD
AT THE CLARENDON PRESS

Oxford University Press, Amen House, London E.C.4

GLASGOW NEW YORK TORONTO MELBOURNE WELLINGTON
BOMBAY CALCUTTA MADRAS KARACHI KUALA LUMPUR
CAPE TOWN IBADAN NAIROBI ACCRA

X765134038

ᶜ

FIRST PUBLISHED 1960
REPRINTED LITHOGRAPHICALLY IN GREAT BRITAIN
AT THE UNIVERSITY PRESS, OXFORD
FROM SHEETS OF THE FIRST EDITION
1961

6002104322

FIVE ELECTIONS
IN AFRICA

PREFACE

THE contributors to this volume have separately acknowledged help received from many quarters: it remains for us as editors only to reiterate that studies of this kind (if they are judged to be worth while) depend on generous support and collaboration from governments, political parties, administrators, and universities. We have received such support in full measure.

In July 1957 the Warden and Fellows of Nuffield College most generously arranged a small conference which was attended by the contributors to this volume and by a number of other scholars interested in the study of elections or of African affairs. The East African Institute of Social and Economic Research made it possible for the only one of the contributors to this book who was not in England at the time of the conference (Mr. Engholm) to fly there for the purpose, and we are most grateful to Professor L. A. Fallers (then Director of the Institute) for such generous help.

We are also greatly indebted to members of the staff of the Institute of Commonwealth Studies of the University of London: Miss M. Eyre and Mrs. N. Marsh for much assistance in the preparation of the manuscript for publication; Mrs. M. Bull for compiling the index; and Mr. A. R. Hewitt for reading the proofs.

W.J.M.M.

K.E.R.

CONTENTS

LIST OF ILLUSTRATIONS

MAPS

PLATES

Acknowledgement for permission to reproduce the plates is gratefully made to the following: *West African Pilot* (Plate 1a), *Daily Service* (Plate 1b), *Daily Times* (Plate 2), Western Region Information Service (Plate 3a), J. H. Price (Plate 3b) and *Paris-Dakar* (Plate 4).

I

INTRODUCTION

THIS book is concerned with a phase of political development which has been in progress for about twelve years and has not yet been the subject of much academic study. Throughout what was once the colonial world, new political units are being created following the withdrawal of European control. A few of these have inherited the territory of ancient states, but in most places the new entity is an artificial one, defined mainly by the accidents of European diplomacy during the phase of colonization.

In such territories there is seldom any native tradition of unified government that can be revived; each new state must create its own tradition of political authority. What ideological basis is available except that of free elections under a wide franchise? This is the principle recommended by the West as the true pattern of sovereignty within the state; those seeking independence aspire to it; Western opinion (in so far as the West is anxious to facilitate transition) thinks of new states as legitimate only if they are framed in this Western image. Elections are, accordingly, an important device in facilitating the transfer of power: they provide a basis for a new legitimacy acceptable in theory both to the 'colonialists' and to their 'nationalist' opponents. Agreement in theory may conceal great and increasing divergence in practice: nevertheless, a study of the practice of elections is an important point of entry into an extremely complex and diverse subject, that of political development in non-Western countries under Western influence.

Although the reports here presented are modelled on studies of British elections since 1945, made under the auspices of Nuffield College, Oxford, our object has been wider than that of the Nuffield surveys. 'Political development' is a subject which seems to invite comparative study. There are at present a surprisingly large number of 'emergent states' in the world—the total depends on what basis of reckoning is used. Their circumstances are very diverse—ranging (for instance) from Laos to the British West Indies—yet there is enough similarity between them to tempt the political scientist to seek general conclusions, as economists studying a very similar field have sought general conclusions about economic development. The temptations are great, but the difficulties are forbidding. Each

B

political unit has a very complex life of its own, the situation changes rapidly, the number of independent observers is very small, and they work under great difficulties. The method of electoral survey at least allows some beginning to be made, in face of great practical and theoretical difficulties.[1]

First perhaps is the problem of time. How can academic observers secure and publish material of objective value in time for it to be of relevance in a rapidly changing situation? One advantage of studying an election is that it comprises much, yet happens quickly. There is a standardized electoral routine or drill, which passes through all its stages in a relatively short time. Yet (where elections are taken seriously) this routine is of central importance in politics, and compresses, as it were, the whole stream of politics into a narrow channel, in which it moves fast and with great intensity. No human observer can ever grasp the whole life of a political system in action, but more can be learnt in a space of about three months during an election than in any other comparable period.

Secondly, there is the problem of comparison. The method used by the contributors to this book is one familiar to all political scientists trained in British universities, so that it does something to establish a common procedure and point of view. Our contributors did not go into 'the field' to examine specific hypotheses derived from a general theory of politics. Nevertheless, they all look at elections in Africa from a single standpoint, that of direct experience of British elections; and this experience has been crystallized by academic study so that there is a familiar 'check list' of points important to elections, based on common criteria of relevance. There may well be a certain insularity about our approach: but it makes comparison possible without enforcing over-simplification.

Thirdly, the onus is on the research worker to show results, and the method of electoral survey has in this respect two concrete advantages. It preserves a careful contemporary record of events important in history; and it offers to administrators (both public administrators and party managers) an independent analysis of practical problems which have been faced in one election and must be faced again. For some readers, general conclusions may be of greater interest, and an attempt is made to present these in the last part of Chapter VIII. But such generalities are of necessity tenuous. They do inadequate justice to the complexity of events in the countries studied, and are no more than tentative hypotheses in relation to the great question at issue, that of the domestication of a political institution in settings

[1] A further discussion of methods of study is to be found in W. J. M. Mackenzie, 'The Export of Electoral Systems', *Political Studies*, vol. v (1957), p. 240.

drastically different from that in which it grew. The political scientist cannot but be fascinated by such a problem, but he knows how thin his conclusions must seem, and he is reassured if he can offer, as we do here, some 'hard news' for historians and administrators.

Our choice of five territories for study was in one sense fortuitous; the over-riding factor was that these elections all took place within a limited space of time, and qualified observers could be found to study them. In one sense, our subject extends beyond Africa, because the question of the 'domestication' of Western elections is not by any means only an African question. But even if we had not been limited by our resources, we should still have wished to restrict the range of study (for the present) to elections in Africa. As readers will find, there are even within Africa very wide gaps between the experience of different territories; to extend our studies further at this stage would certainly have made comparison illegitimate.

Within Africa, it would be absurd to talk of 'sampling'; diversity is too great for that. But our studies offer at least the opportunity to compare French methods with British, large units with small ones, the absence of 'settlers' with the presence of 'settlers' of very different types, in Senegal, Sierra Leone, and Kenya. And each of the elections marks a stage of decisive importance in political development for the territory concerned.

It may perhaps be helpful (finally) to add a brief note, intended for readers not familiar with recent electoral studies, about certain lines of thought common to all the reports which follow. The main theme of electoral research during the last forty or fifty years in Britain, France, and the U.S.A. has been that nineteenth-century reformers over-rated the part that has been or can be played by rational choice in national elections. This trend began in Graham Wallas's time[1] and patient collection of facts in many countries has tended to show that voting is largely a 'habit'.[2] It is 'habit', not rational reflection, which induces most of us to vote steadily for one party or another, to be (at least relatively) uncorrupt, and to respect electoral results. Further analysis is possible. Differing 'habits' can be correlated statistically with variations in other factors, such as age, sex, economic status, education, social class, religious affiliation, and so on; the whole national structure of 'habit' (or tradition, or ideology) can be related to the material tradition and structural integration of a self-perpetuating political community.

---

[1] Graham Wallas, *Human Nature in Politics* (published 1908), in particular chapters 3, 4, and 5.

[2] A. H. Birch, 'The Habit of Voting', *The Manchester School*, vol. xviii (1950), p. 75.

How far can such analogies go? Some hope thus to obtain a complete 'explanation' of voting behaviour, so that the problem of individual reason in politics disappears. Probably there is a gap in logic here, since all methods of investigation at this level deal with stabilized universes and not with individuals; a prediction about a universe, however iron the laws on which it is based, does not relate to the action of individuals. But, logic apart, no explanation of voting as yet comes near to covering the whole universe of voters. The margins of error leave groups of voters unaccounted for, and in most systems small groups are important, both as balancing votes and as leaders of opinion. There is plenty of room still for the element of rational choice within the world of habit.

Twentieth-century research does not therefore wholly 'de-bunk' nineteenth-century optimism. It merely sets the theme of habit alongside the theme of reason. So far as politics is concerned, a link between them is offered by the study of political parties; bodies which depend for their existence on familiarity, loyalty, and solidarity, yet make an appeal to reason by offering to the voter a choice of purpose and a choice of means in the affairs of state. In the West we do not feel inclined to give the name of party except to bodies which present programmes, debate them, and enter the electoral arena to attract votes by argument: but a party is of course also a focus for tradition, mythology, and sentiment.

This triple theme—habit, reason, and political parties—is directly applicable to the variety of situations in Africa; so clearly applicable that one of our objects must be to avoid the temptation of too easy parallels. Observers not intimately acquainted with Western politics may find politics in Africa very strange; we are perhaps too apt to find it familiar, and therefore strain to emphasize also the factors which are not present (or are of trivial importance) in Western elections—such factors as tribal organization, the extended family, and mass illiteracy. But it is not unfair to stress also what is common to Africa and to Europe, because to some extent the formal structure of elections dictates forms of political organization. Indeed, if there are factors which prevent political organizations from thus adapting themselves, elections can only survive (if they survive at all) as something detached from political reality, a trivial part of the national structure.

In what respects must political organization adapt itself to elections? To discuss this in detail would anticipate what follows, but there are three recurrent themes. First, elections and administrations are interdependent. The electoral process is administratively complex; it can be managed with success only by a body of officials tolerably advanced in standards of honesty and routine competence; the existence of such an administration creates and steadies public confidence in electoral procedure—but unless it is supported by public confidence this particular task is beyond it.

Secondly, if elections on a national scale are to make sense politically there must be some national system of 'mass communications'. It is impossible to define a minimum; certainly mass illiteracy is not in itself a bar, if there are channels other than the printed word through which the voices of politicians at the centre can reach the extremities. But there must be some common points of contact, some common political language, for the political unit as a whole; without communication no entity exists. Our attempts to measure communication are of necessity crude; but our reports all seek for signs of its presence or absence.

Finally, there must emerge a new category of 'political persons', working in and through the electoral system and the party system. The concept is a vague one, most easily defined by negatives. This is not necessarily an *élite*, because the political 'middle-men' may prove to be relatively subordinate as against older and greater powers governing through them. It is not necessarily a matter of new classes against old, new education against tradition; the intelligent traditionalist can set himself to learn the game, and may hold better cards than the smart young men. It is not necessarily limited to political leaders and candidates; the new political world may include newspaper men and broadcasters, the leaders of trade unions, the leaders of business interests, religious groups, and other organized pressure groups, in so far as they work in and through a unified political system at the centre of which is an assembly based on free elections. Indefinite though all this is, the emergence of such a category is fairly easy to recognize. They are the people who know how to work the new system. They will certainly pull against one another, seeking as rivals to extract their own advantage from it; yet, once established, such people have a common interest in stability, and may collectively have wisdom enough not to push rivalry to the point of mutual destruction.

II

NIGERIA: AN INTRODUCTORY NOTE

THE Western Nigerian election of May 1956, reported in Chapter III, and that in Eastern Nigeria in March 1957, reported in Chapter IV, were two of a series of three elections in preparation for the Constitutional Conference originally planned to take place in September 1956 but held eventually in London in May and June 1957.[1] It was, unfortunately, impossible to arrange a study of the third of the series, the Northern Nigerian elections of November 1956, the first direct elections to the Northern House of Assembly; this leaves an important gap in our picture of Nigerian politics at a critical stage of its development. The politics of the Eastern and Western Regions are interrelated and each is also affected, though less directly, by the problems of the North.

As a political entity, Nigeria is an artificial creation, the boundaries of which were defined as a result of the partition of Africa in the years following the Berlin West Africa Conference of 1885. But in spite of its variety and internal conflicts, Nigeria has a certain unity because no part of it can hope to attain its fullest economic and political development except in association with the others. Constitutional controversies have turned on the clash between the facts of diversity and the expediency of unity: the problem of self-government is confused because of the variety and vitality of indigenous societies; the problem of federal unity is confused because there is no general agreement about the boundaries of the states which should form the component units of the federation. The present division into three Regions dates from 1939 when Southern Nigeria was divided into two groups of provinces, Eastern and Western, each, like Northern Nigeria, under a Chief Commissioner. Its basis will become clearer in the light of a brief survey of the main social and economic characteristics of Nigeria and of its political history.[2]

[1] See *Report by the Nigeria Constitutional Conference* (Cmnd. 207 of 1957).
[2] Some general works about Nigeria are: K. M. Buchanan and J. C. Pugh, *Land and People in Nigeria* (London, 1955); Sir Alan Burns, *A History of Nigeria* (London, 5th ed., 1955); International Bank for Reconstruction and Development, *The Economic Development of Nigeria* (Baltimore, the Johns Hopkins Press, 1954); G. B. Stapleton, *The Wealth of Nigeria* (London, 1958); J. Wheare, *The Nigerian Legislative Council* (London, 1950); D. Forde and R. Scott, *The Native Economies of Nigeria* (London, 1946).

Social and economic factors. The northern part of the Northern Region, which is the focus of power there, consists of a relatively dry pastoral zone, the southern fringe of the Sahara, which is also the southern fringe of the Muslim world. Its economy is based on the cultivation of grain as a food-crop, the use of cattle, and the export of ground-nuts, cotton, and hides and skins. Although there are many areas which are not Hausa in speech (notably the large Kanuri-speaking province of Bornu), the dominant language is Hausa and the pattern of social life is characterized by a fusion of Hausa custom and Muslim law and belief. The political structure of this part of the Northern Region is based on an ancient monarchical state organization, with a developed system of administration and taxation, generally taking the form of an emirate headed by a ruling dynasty of Fulani origin. Hausa and Fulani together constitute about half the population of the Region.

'Hausaland' gives place to the 'Middle Belt', extending roughly along the line of the middle Niger and Benue rivers, and in many respects intermediate, in social and economic conditions, between North and South, though at present almost wholly included in the Northern Region. No one ethnic group is dominant in this very diverse area, and, while many have been affected by Fulani con-quest and Muslim belief, they are not Hausa-speaking and much of earlier social institutions survives. Largely as a consequence of physi-cal conditions, neither Northern nor Southern cash-crops are grown, though the food-crops of both are widely cultivated. Agricultural incomes are correspondingly lower.

There is no clear break in social and economic conditions between the area north of the Niger and Benue and the area just south of them: similarly the line of the Niger dividing Eastern and Western Regions does not mark a clear frontier, and its wide delta, in parti-cular, is placed ambiguously between them. Nevertheless there is a rough demarcation between the rich cocoa-growing areas of the West and the less rich palm-oil areas of the East, between territory dominated by Yorubas and that dominated by Ibos. In contrast with 'Hausaland', the subsistence agriculture of both East and West is the cultivation of root crops for food under a system of bush fallowing, but their differences in social organization and in the development of export crops overshadow this basic similarity. The indigenous political units of the East (with the exception of Onitsha, and certain coastal towns) were small and political authority was widely diffused; in the West a series of large and loosely connected chiefdoms charac-terized the major ethnic group, the Yorubas, who have in some cases established a similar pattern of rule over formerly diverse groups.

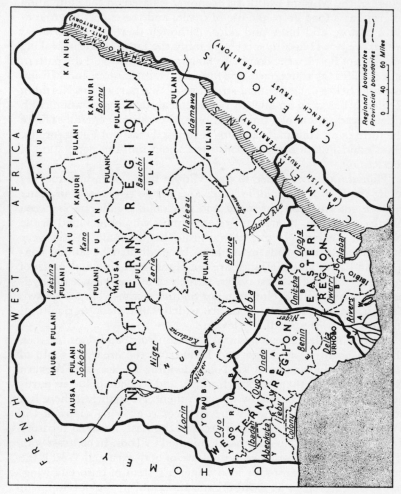

MAP I. NIGERIA. TRIBES AND ADMINISTRATIVE BOUNDARIES

One of the marked features of Yoruba society was the concentration of population in the political capitals, which became the centres of British administration and have continued to grow: large towns and a high proportion of town-dwellers are salient features of Yorubaland.

There is thus a very rough correspondence between the river boundaries and the social and economic structure of Nigeria. The lack of complete correspondence, as well as the variety within each of the three areas so delimited, is a main cause of political friction, but even though the present regional boundaries do not coincide with the river boundaries, the social and economic differences just outlined are evident enough to explain, if not to justify, the present political division of Nigeria into three Regions: the Northern dominated by the Muslim emirates and by the Hausa and Fulani peoples; the Western, of which the kernel is Yorubaland; and the Eastern, in which the Ibos are the largest group.

The main features of the ethnic composition of the Regions are illustrated in Table 1.

TABLE I

Ethnic Composition of Nigeria by Regions

Ethnic Group	Northern Region	Western Region	Eastern Region
Fulani . . .	3,023	7	. .
Hausa . . .	5,488	41	11
Ibo	167	342	4,917
Yoruba . . .	536	4,302	11
Others . . .	7,597	1,385	2,271
Non-Nigerians . .	24	3	5

(Figures in thousands)

SOURCE: Population Census of Western Region, 1952; of the Eastern Region, 1953; and of the Northern Region, 1952.

The major groups together contribute only about three-fifths of the population; but their contrasting social and political institutions and economic activities determine the shape of Nigerian politics. The economic contrasts are indicated by the calculations reproduced in Table 2.

The formation of Nigeria. Southern Nigeria has for long been part of the Atlantic world, linked to it by the slave-trade, by missions, and by the growth of 'legitimate trade' in the nineteenth century. A British consul for the Bight of Biafra and Benin (with headquarters in Fernando Po) was first appointed in 1849, and Lagos was annexed as a British colony in 1862 (in the course of action against the slave-trade). To the Colony of Lagos was gradually added a Protectorate in its immediate hinterland; parts of the Niger delta were declared an 'Oil Rivers' Protectorate in 1885 and were renamed the Niger Coast Protectorate in 1893; in 1886 a Royal Charter was granted to a commercial company formed in 1879 to develop trade in the Niger hinterland. Under its new title, the Royal Niger Company extended British influence inland until 1900, when its charter was revoked and a Protectorate of Northern Nigeria declared. The southern part of the company's territory was linked with the Niger Coast Protectorate to form the Protectorate of Southern Nigeria. Lagos Colony was joined with this in 1906 as the 'Colony and Protectorate of Nigeria'.

TABLE 2

Gross Product per Head, 1950-1

	£m.	Per head of population
North . .	246·3	£14·6
West* . .	200·5	£32·9
East . .	149·9	£20·8
Totals . .	596·7	£19·8

*Including Lagos, which is now federal territory.

Source: A. R. Prest and I. C. Stewart, *The National Income of Nigeria, 1950–51* (London, 1953), p. 61.

The amalgamation of Southern and Northern Nigeria was begun in 1912 by Lord Lugard, who had been appointed Governor of both and who became, on its formal completion in 1914, Governor-General of Nigeria. The main object of the amalgamation was to extend to the south the Native Authority system established by Lord Lugard as High Commissioner in the North from 1900 to 1906, and to provide certain technical services on an all-Nigerian basis. Lieu-tenant-Governors were appointed for Southern and Northern Nigeria and these remained largely separate units. Lord Lugard created in 1913 a wholly advisory 'Nigerian Council'. It was intended to cover all Nigeria, and its 36 members included 6 unofficial European and 6 unofficial African members. It was not considered a success, and in 1922 was replaced by a Legislative Council for the Colony and southern part of the Protectorate. This new Council also superseded the Legislative Council of Lagos, which had had a continuous existence since 1862. It included 10 unofficial African members (out of a total of 46) of whom 3 were elected by Lagos and 1 by Calabar on a franchise limited to men with a gross income of at least £100 a year, British subjects or natives of the Protectorate. The legislative powers of the new Council were restricted to the Colony and Southern Nigeria (the Governor legislating directly for the North); it acquired a measure of *de facto* control of Northern Nigerian affairs since there was a single annual budget for Nigeria as a whole which required its approval, and much of its legislation (e.g. relating to customs duties) inevitably affected the North. Its official members included the Lieutenant-Governor and certain senior officials from the North, but it had no African unofficial members from that part of Nigeria. Even after amalgamation, Northern Nigeria thus remained a substantially separate administration within the new Nigeria. Under the Native Authority system, its strong indigenous authorities remained largely self-governing in their internal affairs, subject to the advice and ultimate control of British Residents.[1] Although after 1931 there were a number of conferences of Emirs and senior British officials, designed to bring the former together to consider problems of common interest to Northern Nigeria, there was not even a beginning of an indigenous government of the region as a whole until a Northern House of Assembly and House of Chiefs were created as part of the constitutional reforms of 1946 introduced by Sir Arthur Richards (later Lord Milverton).[2]

The constitutional arrangements initiated in 1922 remained substantially unchanged until 1946, but towards the end of the Second World War increasingly vigorous criticism of them came from African organizations outside the Legislative Council. The reforms effected in 1946 were, however, essentially the work of the Governor, whose avowed purpose was 'to promote the unity of Nigeria, to provide adequately within that unity for the diverse elements which make up the country and to secure greater participation by Africans in the discussion of their own affairs'.[3] A Legislative Council whose competence and membership covered the whole of Nigeria was established, 28 of its 41 members were to be unofficial, of whom 4 would continue to be directly elected by Lagos and Calabar (though on a £50 franchise), 20 were to be selected by Regional Councils established in each of the three Regions which had resulted from the division, in 1939, of Southern Nigeria into the Eastern and Western

---

[1] The classical discussion of the Native Authority system is in M. Perham, *Native Administration in Nigeria* (London, 1937). An instructive contemporary criticism is in W. R. Crocker, *Nigeria: A Critique of British Colonial Administration* (London, 1936). The most detailed assessment of its achievement in practice is by Lord Hailey, *Native Administration in the British African Territories*, Part III (London, 1951).

[2] The texts of the 1922 and 1946 Orders in Council setting up the legislative councils are in J. Wheare, op. cit. For the 1946 Constitution see *Proposals for the Revision of the Constitution of Nigeria* (Cmd. 6599 of 1945). [3] Cmd. 6599.

Provinces. Richards argued that a central legislature was not enough. 'Nigeria falls naturally into three regions, the North, the West and the East, and the people of those regions differ widely in race, in customs, in outlook, and in their traditional systems of government.'[1] He considered that some bodies for the discussion of public affairs were needed on a plane less narrow than the purely local and less wide than the Nigerian, and that these should also provide a link between the central legislature and the Native Authorities. In addition to the bicameral Regional Council in the North, he accordingly established single chamber Councils in the East and the West, called Houses of Assembly. In all the Regional Houses of Assembly there were unofficial (and African) majorities, but they consisted of members selected by the Native Authorities. The Regional Councils had no legislative powers and only limited financial ones. Executive power remained in the hands of British officials, at the centre as well as in the Regions.

The modern development of politics. Although its roots can be traced much farther back, the modern development of politics in Nigeria dates essentially from the latter part of the Second World War and the reactions to the enactment of the Richards Constitution. The earliest political organizations grew up in Lagos where the Nigeria National Democratic Party was created by Herbert Macaulay to contest the 1922 elections; this was followed in 1937 by the Nigeria Youth Movement, a largely Yoruba organization which succeeded an earlier Lagos Youth Movement, and, under the leadership of H. O. Davies, successfully contested the Lagos municipal elections of 1938 against the Democratic Party. A Legislative Council by-election in 1941 produced dissensions within the N.Y.M., and in the Lagos Town Council elections of 1943 the Democratic Party resumed control. In 1942–3, largely under the impetus of Nigerians who had returned from study overseas, attempts were made to create a 'national front', but without success until the National Council of Nigeria and the Cameroons was founded in August 1944 under the leadership of Macaulay and Nnamdi Azikiwe,[2] an Onitsha Ibo educated in America who had become a prosperous business man and newspaper proprietor. Its aim was to set up a broadly based political movement

---

[1] Cmd. 6599.

[2] Born 1904. Educated in Nigeria, then Storer College, W. Va., U.S.A., Howard Univ., Washington, D.C., Lincoln Univ., Pa., Univ. of Pennsylvania, Columbia Univ., N.Y.; M.A., M.Sc., LL.D. (Hon.), D.Litt. (Hon.). Instructor in Political Science, Lincoln Univ., 1931–4. Edited *African Morning Post*, Accra, 1934–7, *West African Pilot*, Lagos, 1937–47. Managing Director, Zik Enterprises Ltd., 1937–53. Member of the Legislative Council, 1946–51; of Western House of Assembly, 1952–3; of Eastern House of Assembly since 1954. Premier of the Eastern Region.

(including such bodies as tribal improvement unions, trade unions, and political parties) to promote Nigerian self-government within the British Commonwealth. The Democratic Party was one of its associated members and continued to be active in Lagos politics. The N.C.N.C. attacked the new Constitution because of the failure to enlarge the electorate and extend the principle of direct election, and also because of the inclusion of chiefs as 'unofficial' members of the legislature and the new regional assemblies. It contended that in reality chiefs had become subordinate officials appointed and controlled by the British administration. It conducted a widespread campaign for funds to send a deputation to the Colonial Office. This was led by Dr. Azikiwe.[1] The Colonial Secretary (Mr. Creech-Jones) advised its members to return to Nigeria and give the new Constitution a fair trial, but agitation against it (and other actions of the administration) nevertheless continued. An undertaking had been given that the Constitution should be reviewed after nine years, but in 1948 the new Governor (Sir John Macpherson) recommended that changes should be introduced after three years. One of the principal complaints against the Richards Constitution had been that it had not been the outcome of consultation with leaders of Nigerian opinion. Special arrangements for ascertaining the views of all sections of the population were accordingly proposed, and these took place throughout 1949 and much of 1950.[2] The new Constitution enacted in 1951[3] established legislatures in each of the three Regions, empowered to legislate on specified subjects (e.g. agriculture, social services, and local government). Members of the central legislature were elected from their own numbers by the regional legislatures (sixty-eight by the Northern Region and thirty-four by each of the two Southern Regions). The proportion of nominated and ex-officio members, both in the central and in the regional legislatures, was reduced. In each Region and at the centre there were African 'ministers' who formed the majority of the appropriate excutive councils, but their administrative responsibility was not clear cut and the Governor (or Lieutenant-Governor) continued to preside. The power of the centre was limited because both central ministers and the central legislature were chosen by the regional legislatures (each having an equal number of the elected 'ministers'). But regional powers were limited because their legislation was

---

[1] Herbert Macaulay died shortly before its departure from Nigeria.
[2] See *Proceedings of the General Conference on the Review of the Constitution, January 1950* (Lagos, Government Printer, 1950).
[3] *The Nigeria (Constitution) Order in Council, 1951* (U.K. Statutory Instrument No. 1172 of 1951).

restricted to specific fields and could be disallowed by the central
executive.

Methods of election to the new legislatures varied, but, except in
Lagos where direct elections by secret ballot continued, they everywhere took the form of primary elections to a series of electoral
colleges. In the two Southern Regions all male taxpayers were entitled to vote in electing the lowest level of the pyramid of electoral
colleges; in the Northern Region there was an elaborate system of indirect election, through five stages, based on the Native Authorities.
But even these indirect elections (and perhaps also the system of
nation-wide consultation preceding the Macpherson Constitution)
helped to promote the development of political parties.[1] In the
Northern Region those elected subsequently formed the Northern
People's Congress, the dominant party at the first direct elections in
November 1956. In the South those chosen were mainly the leaders
of the agitation for a new constitution. In the Eastern Region they
were organized in the N.C.N.C., to which there was at first no opposition in the new legislature except for a few 'independents'. In the
Western Region a new body, Action Group, had by now taken
shape under the leadership of Chief Awolowo, who had been one of
the leading members of the Nigerian Youth Movement until his
departure in 1944 to study in Britain. Its origins are described by
Dr. Whitaker;[2] it was essentially a Yoruba party, emerging from a
Yoruba cultural organization, the *Egbe Omo Oduduwa*,[3] and supported
by a number of men of substance, chiefs, lawyers, business men. It
obtained a majority in the Western Region legislature in 1951,
partly by gaining adherents after the election, partly by astute
management of the second stage of the elections (there was as yet no
effective party organization at the first stage). Dr. Azikiwe, who had
been one of the elected members for Lagos under the Richards Con-

---

[1] For Nigerian political movements, see J. S. Coleman, *Nationalism in Nigeria*
(Los Angeles, 1958); R. Perry, *A Preliminary Bibliography of the Literature of Nationalism in Nigeria* (London, n.d.); and N. Azikiwe, *The Development of Political Parties
in Nigeria* (London, 1957).   [2] See below, p. 21.
[3] The name means roughly 'The Association of the Descendants of Oduduwa'
(the mythical ancestor of the Yoruba people). The Constitution of the Egbe, as
quoted by Hodgkin (*The New West Africa*, ed. B. Davidson and A. Ademola,
London, 1953, p. 95) included among its objects:
'To unite the various clans and tribes in Yorubaland and generally create and
    actively foster the idea of a single nationalism throughout Yorubaland.
'To recognise and maintain the monarchical and similar institutions of Yoruba-
    land: to plan for their complete enlightenment and democratisation, to
    acknowledge the leadership of the Yoruba Obas. . . .
'To accelerate the emergence of a virile modernised, and efficient Yoruba state
    with its own individuality within the Federal State of Nigeria.'

stitution, was again elected for Lagos in 1951. This meant, however, that he was not a member of the Eastern Region legislature (where his party was in control) but of that of the Western Region, and he was not among the members whom its Action Group majority sent to the central legislature. Towards the end of 1952 the N.C.N.C., at his instigation, called upon its central and regional ministers to cease co-operating in working the Constitution and to resign. As a result, a number of them left the N.C.N.C. and formed the United Nigeria National Independence Party, which became the main opposition party in the Eastern Region from 1953 to 1957.

Although the N.C.N.C. and Action Group were not on friendly terms, both continued to press for more effective powers for African ministers, and in May 1953, in opposition to the N.P.C. members of the central legislature, they joined in supporting a demand for self-government in 1956. This resulted in a Constitutional Conference held in London in June[1] which eventually led to a new constitutional settlement, in force from 1 November 1954.[2] The Regions now assumed the aspect of States within a Federation; the Lieutenant-Governor (now called Governor) of each Region ceased to preside in the legislatures, there were no longer any *ex officio* or nominated members except in the North, the members of the Executive Councils became responsible ministers, headed by a 'Premier' (though the Governor remained President of the Executive Council), and separate regional judiciaries and public services were created. At the centre there was a Council of Ministers, three from each Region (and one from the Cameroons). It also included three ex-officio members, and there was no 'Premier'. The centre became at once stronger and weaker than under the 1951 constitution: stronger because the central legislature was now directly elected, and 'ministers' were charged with executive responsibility and could be dismissed after a resolution of the central legislature supported by not less than two-thirds of its members; weaker in that it was for the first time a 'federal' government with limited powers (residual powers now fell to the Regions). After some controversy, Lagos was excluded from the Western Region, to serve as federal territory and capital. A further constitutional review was to be held in 1956, and any Region that wished it could then become fully self-governing in respect of all matters within the competence of the regional governments. It was

---

[1] *Report by the Conference on the Nigerian Constitution held in London in July and August 1953* (Cmd. 8934), and *Report by the Resumed Conference on the Nigerian Constitution held in Lagos in January and February 1954* (Cmd. 9059).

[2] *The Nigeria (Constitution) Order in Council, 1954* (U.K. Statutory Instrument No. 1146 of 1954).

made clear, however, that there must be safeguards to insure that
the Regions did not prejudice the Federal Goverment in discharg-
ing its agreed functions or make the maintenance of federation
impossible.[1]

The first federal elections, those of 1954, were held under arrangements prescribed in regulations made separately for each Region by
the Governor-General (under paragraph 8 of the Order-in-Council).
Those in the North were indirect, those in the Eastern Region were
direct and based on universal adult suffrage; in the Western Region
the rule was that all men aged twenty-one or over might vote if they
were *either* 'natives' of the Division in which they sought to vote *or*
residents and taxpayers for a period of twelve months at the qualifying date. Women could qualify on the same basis, provided that they
had themselves paid a tax of over £1.[2] In the Northern Region the
N.P.C. won the election with 84 out of 92 seats; in the Eastern
Region the N.C.N.C. had 30, Action Group in alliance with the
United National Independence Party had 7, and others 5; in the
Western Region the N.C.N.C., in favourable circumstances and by
better organization, won 23 seats to Action Group's 18 (the 'Commoners' Liberal Party' secured 1 seat). The first federal Cabinet consisted of 6 N.C.N.C. ministers and 3 N.P.C. ministers, together with
the 3 official members, and a member from the Southern Cameroons.

The background of the elections of 1956 and 1957. This set the stage for
the elections of 1956 and 1957, which were essentially preparatory
to the Constitutional Conference planned for 1956 to settle the next
stage (including regional self-government) but eventually held in
1957. In the Western Region there had been no direct elections for
the regional House of Assembly, which was still (though much
changed by by-elections) that of 1951, and it was essential to Chief
Awolowo's authority as Premier of the Western Region at the Constitutional Conference to show that, in spite of the N.C.N.C. victory
in the Western Region during the federal elections, a majority in the
West was still behind him. These were the circustances which led him
to advise a dissolution in April 1956. The resulting elections are
reported by Dr. Whitaker in Chapter III. In the Northern Region
there was little uncertainty about the result. Southerners attacked
the North for its 'reactionary' adherence to indirect elections, a
procedure abandoned in 1956. They also hoped that opponents of
the N.P.C. might achieve sufficient success in the towns and in the
'Middle Belt' to weaken somewhat the negotiating strength of the
N.P.C. and to make a case for narrowing the boundaries of the North

[1] Cmd. 8934, para. 28.
[2] *The Nigeria Elections (House of Representatives) (Western Region) Regulations,* 1954.

and perhaps creating new states. Their success was very limited. The N.P.C. won 100 of the 131 seats, as compared with 11 for the United Middle Belt Congress, 6 for the Northern Elements Progressive Union (plus 2 more won by a party in alliance with it), and 4 for the Action Group alliance in Ilorin.[1]

After the 'non-co-operation' policy had been adopted by the N.C.N.C. in 1952, the ministers in the Eastern Region had refused to resign and eventually the House was dissolved in May 1953; Dr. Azikiwe thereupon resigned one of the Lagos seats in the Western Region legislature, which he had held since 1951, and contested Onitsha, his home town. The result was an overwhelming majority for the N.C.N.C., which won seventy-two out of eighty-four seats. In August 1956, however, the Governor (Sir Clement Pleass) and the Secretary of State (Mr. Lennox-Boyd) decided that there must be an inquiry into allegations that Dr. Azikiwe had, as Premier of the Eastern Region, misused his position to further the interests of the African Continental Bank of which he was the founder. (Much public money had been invested or deposited in the Bank, and Dr. Azikiwe had been attacked in this connexion by a member of the regional House in a motion tabled in April 1956.) This decision led to the postponement of the Constitutional Conference, which was to have been held in September 1956.[2] The Commission of Inquiry, presided over by the Federal Chief Justice, Sir Stafford Foster-Sutton, reported in January 1957; its Report[3] (as might perhaps have been anticipated) found certain facts established which were, on the whole, regarded by African opinion as favourable to Dr. Azikiwe; and the regional legislature was then dissolved. The ensuing election is described by Mr. Price in Chapter IV.

[1] *West Africa*, 1 Dec. 1956, p. 975; Cmnd. 505, p. 56.
[2] It was eventually held in 1957. See *Report by the Nigeria Constitutional Conference* (Cmnd. 207).
[3] Cmnd. 51 of 1957.

III

THE WESTERN REGION OF NIGERIA
MAY 1956

1. *The Character of the Region*

THE Western Region is three-quarters of the size of England and Wales,[1] and has a population of just under 6,100,000.[2] It is divided into seven provinces, the five most westerly of which have an overwhelmingly Yoruba population.[3] With the exception of the Colony, each of these five provinces was intended to represent the territory of a section of the Yoruba people—clans or groups of clans—some of whom were engaged in armed conflict as late as the end of the last century.

In the two other provinces, Benin and the Delta, the Yorubas form a very small minority,[4] and there is a considerable proportion of Ibos.[5] In Benin the majority of the people belong to a grouping loosely known as the 'Bini'. The Delta is inhabited by a number of tribes; half the people are Urhobos and about a quarter Ibos. The remainder are principally Itsekiris, Ijaws, and Itsokos. While the Benin–Delta tribes feel little affinity with the Yorubas, they are also conscious of their own differences: their languages are mutually incomprehensible. English, or at least pidgin-English, is generally understood in Southern Nigeria; in this particular area it serves as a *lingua franca*.

There is thus a major difference between these two parts of Western Nigeria, Yorubaland and the Benin–Delta area. Indeed, in the early days of the British administration, the latter, together with an adjacent area now in the Eastern Region, was governed as the Central Province. There is now a movement for the setting up of a Mid-West State, but this would be economically dependent on the

---

[1] 45,000 square miles.
[2] The Eastern Region has an area of 29,484 square miles and a population of 7,200,000, and the Northern Region, covering some 270,000 square miles, nearly 17,000,000.
[3] Abeokuta 90·8%, Colony 72·8% (9·1% Ibo), Ibadan 97·7%, Ijebu 95·5%, Ondo 96·4%, Oyo 96·4%
[4] 1·2 and 0·9 per cent. respectively.   [5] 16·7 and 23·5 per cent. respectively.

other Regions. Benin and the Delta export large quantities of hardwood, rubber, palm oil, and palm kernels, through a number of ports, principally Warri, Sapele, Forcados, and Burutu. All of these are modern towns, built up on the export trade, and serve a large area of Nigeria, both for importing and exporting.

Most of Yorubaland is in the cocoa belt, and the bulk of the cocoa produced in Nigeria comes from this area. In 1954 nearly £40 million worth of cocoa was exported, but in 1955 the world price of cocoa dropped from £400 to £280 a ton. The Cocoa Marketing Board, until 1957 an agency of the Federal Government, operated a guaranteed price policy. During the years prior to 1955, owing to the large and sustained rise in the world price of cocoa, it was able to accumulate large reserves; the excess of the world price at which its cocoa was sold over the guaranteed price it paid to producers.

The fall in cocoa prices emphasized the need for a more diversified economy for the Western Region. The Western Region Production Development Board (an agency of the regional government) has encouraged the establishment of new light industries, and has conducted agricultural and industrial research on a limited scale. It has also set up industries of its own, including a fruit-canning factory near Ibadan. Large areas, cleared of cocoa in an attempt to eradicate disease, were planted with pineapples and citrus with the assistance of the Board, and the produce canned or bottled at this factory. In general, however, the policy seems to be to encourage private enterprise, the Board helping with technical advice. The Regional Loans Board lends money for the setting up of new enterprises. These tend to produce for the home market and show little interest in exporting.

The Yorubas are characteristically dwellers in large towns;[1] each section of the tribe has its own town, divided into sections or compounds, each of which is (in principle, though the practice is not strict) inhabited by a single patrilineage. Agricultural work is based on the towns and on dependent villages each within the orbit of a town; there is a strong sense of attachment to the ancestral town and village even among individuals born elsewhere who have never visited them, and this loyalty is at least in part associated with loyalty to chiefly families, and to the institution of chiefdom as a symbol of unity. This system may be contrasted with that of the Ibos, who are

[1] Burns (op. cit., p. 53) states that nine of the ten largest towns in Nigeria are Yoruba. These are: Ibadan (pop. 460,000), Lagos (272,000), Ogbomosho (139,000), Oshogbo (123,000), Ife (111,000), Iwo (100,000), Abeokuta (82,000), Ilesha (72,000), and Oyo (72,000). The tenth is Kano, a Hausa town in the Northern Region with a population of 132,000.

village-dwellers,[1] organized in smaller social units, and cohering (in spite of many divisions) through an equally complex but less hierarchical system of tribal organization. In the Delta (as was said above) most of the towns are new and not traditional, and their political importance is rather different from that of the Yoruba towns.

Members of both tribes are scattered throughout West Africa, but Ibos are more noted for enterprise and the desire for advancement. In Western Nigeria they are perfectly willing to take on work of a kind which Yorubas will avoid if they can. Thus it is rare to find a Yoruba houseboy or 'steward'; many of these are Ibos, who also form a large percentage of the police force. Ibos are also important in various trades, particularly as motor mechanics. Yorubas are traders *par excellence*, and, partly at least because of land-tenure customs, provide the majority of the farmers in the West.[2] There are a number of traditional Yoruba crafts. Professional men, doctors, lawyers, and the like, tend to practise in their own country.

Trade unionism is not strong in Nigeria, which is still primarily a peasant country. Total membership for the whole country was, in the year of the election, put at 165,130. Only seven unions had a membership of over 5,000,[3] and many others were house unions, consisting of the employees of one particular firm. Of the 177 unions registered, 68 had a membership of 51 to 250. There was little affiliation between the unions and the political parties; an opportunist approach seemed to be generally preferred. Some of the senior office staff of the parties received their early training in organization with the trade unions, but the latter do not appear to have provided many candidates at elections.

2. Parties, Politics, and the Press

Parties. Since the early 1920's, Lagos has had an active political life, even if only amongst a small and sophisticated minority of the

[1] There are only two large Ibo towns, Onitsha (pop. 77,000) and Enugu (pop. 63,000).

[2] For practical purposes, land is the property of the tribe or clan rather than the individual. Hostility between Yorubas and Ibos would make it very difficult for the latter to obtain the use of land for farming. Cf. H. L. Ward-Price, *Land Tenure in the Yoruba Provinces* (Lagos, Government Printer, 1932).

[3] Railway Workers' Union of Nigeria (10,899), Public Utility, Technical and General Workers' Union of Nigeria and the Cameroons (11,085), Nigeria Union of Teachers (31,213), Nigeria Union of Local Administrative Staff (5,934), Cameroons Development Corporation Workers' Union (10,220), Nigeria Civil Service Union (6,488), Nigeria African Mine-Workers' Union (13,210). (*Nigeria Year Book*, 1956, pp. 93–101.)

population. Much attention was devoted to the affairs and welfare of Lagos itself, and very little notice was taken of what was going on inland. Even the small 'nationalist' groups which sprang up before the Second World War appear either to have been concerned with abstract principles alone or at best to have seen themselves as heirs to the British rulers. Two ·of them, however, the Nigerian National Democratic Party and the Nigeria Youth Movement, were to provide the foundations for later developments, since the N.C.N.C. descended from the former and Action Group from the latter.[1] As has been described in Chapter II, Dr. Azikiwe emerged as leader of the N.C.N.C. on the death of its first president, Herbert Macaulay, in 1946, and he led its deputation to London in 1947 to protest against the Richards Constitution.

In the meantime, a number of Yoruba leaders in Lagos had continued to work through the N.Y.M., but this did not spread its influence very far afield. During the war years it had a branch in Ibadan, with Mr. Obafemi Awolowo as its secretary. Mr. Awolowo later went to London to read for the Bar, and shortly after his return to Nigeria in 1947 he published a book[2] reviewing critically, from a nationalist point of view, constitutional progress in Nigeria and making suggestions for future developments. While building up a flourishing legal practice in Ibadan, he became General Secretary of the *Egbe Omo Oduduwa*, an organization for the 'culture and advancement' of the Yoruba people. It is stated to have been formed in London in 1945, and inaugurated in Nigeria in 1948. Initially its membership was influential rather than large; early in 1950 the full-time Administrative Secretary, Mr. Delano, went on a tour to popularize *Egbe* in Nigeria.

At the end of March 1950 Mr. Awolowo called a meeting to which six people came in addition to himself.[3] The purpose of this was to discuss the desirability of forming a political party, in view of the probability that the revised Constitution would provide for some form of parliamentary government. From the beginning the need for organization was stressed, but the party was in the first instance

---

[1] For the early history of the Nigerian political parties, see R. L. Buell, *The Native Problem in Africa* (New York, 1928), vol. i, pp. 743–5; N. Azikiwe, *The Development of Political Parties in Nigeria* (London, Commissioner for the Eastern Region of Nigeria, 1957); and P. C. Lloyd, 'The Development of Political Parties in Western Nigeria', *American Political Science Review*, vol. xlix (1955), pp. 693–707.

[2] *Path to Nigerian Freedom*, London, 1947.

[3] These were: Abiodun Akerele (Barrister, Ibadan), S. O. Shonibare (U.A.C. Manager, Lagos), Ade Akinsanya (Manager, African Press, Ibadan), A. O. Adigun (Editor, *Morning Star*, Ibadan), Olatunju Dosumu (*Daily Service* reporter, Ibadan), S. T. Oredein (Secretary, Gen. Tobacco Workers' Union, Ibadan).

formed privately, contacts with Yoruba leaders being made through *Egbe Omo Oduduwa*. By the end of 1950 there were only sixty-seven members, living mostly in Ibadan and Lagos. Committees were set up, and a 'shadow' cabinet was formed to prepare to take over the government if called upon to do so. A membership subscription of 10s. was decided upon.

Early in 1951 a circular was sent out to influential people in the West under the heading:

THE ACTION GROUP (WESTERN ZONE) NIGERIA
Motto: 'FREEDOM FROM THE BRITISH RULE'[1]

This stated that a group of responsible men in the West had been organizing privately for a year, and was now ready to come forward publicly to form a political party. It stressed that membership was open to all, and gave as its political creed:

The Group believes first and foremost in the unity of all people of Western Nigeria as stepping stone to the unity of Nigeria as a whole.

It also believes that opportunity of comfortable living, medical attention and free education should be given to all people in the West.

There followed an announcement that a Provincial Organizer would be touring the Province concerned. A copy of his itinerary was attached, and it was suggested that mass meetings should be arranged to meet him. It was also suggested that where a Town Union existed this could be made the nucleus for the meetings, which were to be open to all.[2]

These tours were undertaken, and by the middle of 1951 a secretariat had been set up with a paid staff; the Group had also acquired the use of two vehicles, a car and a kit-car. Loans were sought, to be repaid by donations, subscriptions, and a 10 per cent. levy on the salaries of any Action Group members who might be elected to the House of Assembly. A programme and policy pamphlets were produced.

Though the *Egbe* and Action Group have always been quite distinct bodies, relations between them are close. The two headquarters are near to each other in Ibadan. Dr. Maja, the president of *Egbe*, is even today termed the 'father of the Action Group', although he did not play any official part in the formation of the party; his photograph is given a prominent place on the Group's calendar

---

[1] This was soon to be changed to 'Freedom for all and Life More Abundant'. The early badge of the Action Group—a mosquito—is still to be seen occasionally in the Western Region. This, later replaced by the 'palm-tree' symbol, was intended to symbolize the driving out of the European from Nigeria.

[2] For the town unions, see Lord Hailey, *Native Administration in the British African Territories* (H.M.S.O., 1951), Part III, p. 19.

together with those of the seven who attended the first meeting. Mr. (now Chief) Awolowo, leader of Action Group, and now Premier of the Western Region, is still *Egbe*'s General Secretary. Membership, of the *Egbe* has, however, never been a prerequisite of membership of Action Group.

At the 1951 election Action Group was relatively new to most Nigerians, who were far more familiar with the N.C.N.C. It concentrated its activities on the Yoruba parts of the country, and it managed to win a slender majority in the Western House of Assembly. When that House met, more members immediately joined the Group, giving it a comfortable majority. These happenings caused some unpleasantness, since the N.C.N.C. believed that it had won a majority at the first stage of the three-tier system of indirect election,[1] and Action Group's enemies were not slow to suggest that these accretions were due to bribery. There can be little doubt, however, that the organization of the N.C.N.C. at the time of the election was so nebulous that many of those who had flown the N.C.N.C. banner did not know for what they were standing. There was no question of their being 'official' candidates in any true sense of the word. Action Group concentrated its propaganda on the intermediate electoral colleges, where they brought the delegates face to face with political doctrines and realities for the first time. The chance of supporting an organized political party, with a policy that was designed to appeal to Yoruba interests, was enough to bring many of them into the Action Group fold.

This chapter is concerned only with the two parties as they operate in the Western Region, but both claim to be 'national' parties, and to have a 'national' organization. Apart from one member in the Eastern House of Assembly, Action Group was in 1956 represented only in the West. The N.C.N.C., which dominated the Eastern House of Assembly, had a small organization in the Northern Region and was in alliance with the Northern Elements Progressive Union, a minority party in the North. In the West, of course, the N.C.N.C. provided a substantial opposition.

As a point of departure in our attempt to outline the nature of political divisions in the West, we can consider the assumption that the Action Group is a Yoruba party, and the N.C.N.C. composed of non-Yoruba elements. The first part of this is substantially true, but a glance at a map showing the areas won by the two parties shows

---

[1] The method of voting in Primary Elections and Intermediate Colleges varied; it was often by a show of hands. In the Final Electoral Colleges it was by secret ballot. The Electoral Officer, generally the District Officer, could assist illiterate members to mark their ballot papers.

that the proposition frequently breaks down.[1] The eastern part of the Region, where there are few Yorubas, is fairly solidly N.C.N.C., but even this area has its internal divisions, some of which will be discussed later.

There are also strong N.C.N.C. pockets in the midst of Yoruba country, where their support is drawn substantially from Yorubas. Mr. Lloyd[2] has given examples which show that these frequently arise from chieftaincy disputes. Other instances have arisen since he wrote. He points out that traditional machinery exists for the settlement of these disputes, but popular feeling is often aroused by them, particularly since the declaration and modification of local customary law rests with Local Councils,[3] and this may include customs relating to chieftaincies. Frequently, if a chief is at loggerheads with a section of his people, and also in bad odour with the Western Regional Government, he may receive the aid and succour of the N.C.N.C., and may well go into its camp. Two recent examples of this are the Alafin of Oyo and the Olobe of Ilobe. Both of these were driven towards the N.C.N.C., and both of them were deposed less than three months after the 1956 elections, Action Group sympathizers being put in their places. Party-affiliated groups also tend to grow up around contenders for vacant titles.

Attitudes to traditional rulers can affect party allegiances in a variety of other ways. In Ilesha, for example, there is a feeling that to support Action Group is to acknowledge the rule of the Oni of Ife, a prominent Action Grouper. There is also resentment around Ife against the payment of *shakele*, a tax levied on those who have not the traditional right to the use of land. This gains the N.C.N.C. not inconsiderable support. Payment of a similar tax in Oyo, and the method of its collection, were among the causes of hostility to the Alafin, but in this case Action Group benefited because of his alleged connexion with the N.C.N.C.

Although Ibadan is the capital of the Western Region, it is an N.C.N.C. stronghold; six of its eight seats went to that party in this election, all with substantial majorities. The most important reason for this is a long-standing feud between the Ijebus and Ibadans, both Yoruba groups, principally over the 'ownership' of land. This was raging when the British first entered the area.[4] Chief Awolowo is an Ijebu, born at Ikenne, and some of his lieutenants come from the same area. It is still very easy to persuade many of the Yorubas of

---

[1] See map on p. 97. [2] Lloyd, op. cit., pp. 703, 704.
[3] W.R. Local Government Law, 1952, para. 60.
[4] See S. Johnson, *A History of the Yorubas* (London, 1921), *passim*, particularly pp. 41, 608, and 609.

Ibadan not to vote for a 'party of Ijebus'; they would even prefer a 'party of Ibos' like the N.C.N.C. Town societies like the Majeobaje, which exist to foster the welfare and traditions of the Ibadans, thus become important N.C.N.C. recruiting and propaganda agencies. The N.C.N.C. in Ibadan was led by Mr. Adegoke Adelabu, an extremely able politician who knew well how to sway a crowd.[1] He and Dr. Azikiwe are probably the only two men at the national level of Nigerian political life who can win a significant number of votes by their oratory and personality. Until early in 1956 Mr. Adelabu was chairman of the Ibadan District Council, which was dissolved after a Commission of Inquiry had found certain of its members, including Mr. Adelabu, guilty of corruption.[2] This Council was N.C.N.C. dominated; during its existence, it went to some trouble to give employment to non-Yorubas. There is a widespread belief that the better-paid jobs in the public service of the Western Region go to Yorubas regardless of merit, and this attitude tended to win support for the N.C.N.C. Mr. Adelabu was one of the relatively few Muslims in West Nigerian politics, and this gained him the personal support of many of his co-religionists (it has been estimated that as many as 60 per cent. of Yorubas are Muslims). On the other hand, Chief Awolowo, a keen Methodist, is also a strict teetotaller, and this fact inclines some Muslims in all parts of the Region to his party.

In the eastern parts of the Region Yorubas are in a minority, and there is a multiplicity of smaller tribes, with a considerable proportion of Ibos. In the main, these tribes fear Yoruba domination, of which they believe Action Group to be the exponent, and therefore tend to support the N.C.N.C. Notably in Warri, however, tribal differences can lead to one of the sides aligning itself with Action Group. Tribal unions play an important part in the politics of this area, and a feeling that they belong neither to the West nor to the East has produced separatist tendencies. The Benin–Delta Peoples' Party has thus won a good deal of support in its demand for a separate State. Both the major parties have subscribed to this idea; perhaps because of a feeling that the area has not received as many benefits as the Yoruba part of the Region, the B.D.P.P. threw in its lot with the N.C.N.C. just before the 1956 elections.

This brings us to the minor parties. In the elections under review, none of them achieved any success; in fact, all their candidates forfeited their deposits. Three parties have grown up in opposition

---

[1] For a pen-portrait of Mr. Adelabu, see *West Africa*, 12 May 1955, p. 221. He was killed in a motor accident in 1958, after this passage had been written.

[2] Mr. Adelabu was subsequently acquitted.

to the whole idea of immediate self-government. The reasons for this
are not far to seek. In the words of Chief Awolowo himself:[1]

Given a choice from among white officials, chiefs and educated Nigerians
as the principal rulers of the country, the illiterate man today would exercise his preference for the three in the order in which they are named. He is
convinced, and he has good reason to be, that he can always get better treatment from the white man than he could hope to get from the chiefs and the
educated elements.

Almost certainly this is less true today (1957) than it was ten years
ago, when it was written, but there is still a great deal of substance
in it. The writer has been disagreeably surprised at the treatment
sometimes given to waiters, servants, and the like by their fellow
countrymen.

Both the Dynamic Party and the Nigerian Self-Government Fiasco
Party sought to arrest what one of their leaders termed 'the mad rush
towards self-government'. Before the 1956 election they coalesced.[2]
Dr. Chike Obi, the leader[3] of the Dynamic Party, was a lecturer in
mathematics at University College, Ibadan, a London M.Sc., and a
Cambridge Ph.D. On the basis of his 'studies in mathematics, biology
and military history', he concluded that self-government was impossible in a country where, in his opinion, apathy and ignorance
were widespread. His answer to all this was 'Kemalism' or 'Dynamic
Collectivism', presumably with himself in the role of the Turkish
dictator. The help of Europeans and Americans was to be sought for
economic and cultural progress. There was an earnest attempt to
make the party appear to be as well organized as the Action Group,
with such organs as a 'Department of Propaganda and Spiritual
Education'. What lay beneath this surface can only be conjectured.
Some stress was laid on the party's having been 'born' under the
constellation Aries, and for this reason the ram was adopted as its
symbol.[4] A subsidiary part of the Dynamic Party's programme was
the division of Nigeria into fifteen states.

---

[1] Op. cit., p. 32.

[2] Since the Fiasco Party appears to have been afraid of domination by the
intellectuals, this coalition with the party of 'Kemalism' was, to say the least of it,
strange.

[3] In August 1956, when the Colonial Secretary odered an inquiry into the affairs
of the African Continental Bank, Dr. Obi declared his support for immediate
self-government. Apparently he believed that the object of this inquiry was to
protect British banking interests in Nigeria. For this change of outlook he was
removed from the leadership of the Dynamic Party.

[4] See *Our Struggle—A Political Analysis of the Problems of the Negro Peoples Struggling
or True Freedom*, by C. Obi (Ibadan, 1956).

The Nigerian Commoners' Party, led by Mrs. Adumi Oluwole, was also concerned with the dangers of a too precipitate move towards self-government. As its title implies, it was critical of too much power getting into the hands of the Chiefs and the intellectuals. It had little or no organization.

Mr. Awokoya's Nigerian Peoples' Party was the result of his break-away from the Action Group a few days before the dissolution. In the short time at his disposal he did not formulate any clear policy but stood principally in opposition to what he considered to be dictation from the centre in the Action Group.

Programmes. The considerations mentioned above, tribal feeling and local politics, serve to explain the predominance of a particular party in any given area; illiteracy, and the overriding problem of earning a living, preclude the majority of the people from having less immediate interests. Party programmes as such can appeal only to the small proportion of the population which has some measure of education. Even if we make the exaggerated assumption that all literate persons of voting age are likely to be influenced by them, this would not comprise the margins by which the majority of seats were won. The class-structure, if such a term can be allowed, does not correspond to that which exists in Britain. The most unlikely people become rich very rapidly, and fortunes are equally quickly lost. Family and tribal obligations do much to ensure 'welfare' services, and the majority of the people respect traditional institutions. Setting on one side the question of self-government, there is thus very little in the way of fundamentals that a political party can seek to change with any hope of support; parties tend rather to vie with one another in promising the same things—hospitals, educational facilities, roads, and the like. Taxation is always a pressing grievance. There can be little doubt that the N.C.N.C. won a great deal of support in the Western Region in the 1954 Federal Elections because the Action Group Government had just imposed a 10s. education tax. However, there is an increasing realization that taxes have to be imposed to pay for benefits. It is now generally known that taxes in the N.C.N.C.-controlled East are also high—higher in fact than in the West for the majority of people —so that neither party can win many votes on this score. The fact that the rich are relatively lightly taxed seems to worry very few; they have to do a lot to support their 'families', which may include quite distant relatives.[1]

[1] The argument has even been advanced that Africans who are entitled to a house by virtue of their jobs in government service should receive larger quarters than Europeans, at the same rent. This is because their prosperity is likely to lead to numerous poorer relatives, whom they cannot send away,

A period of thoroughly bad government would probably change this pattern radically, and cause many people to pay attention to the actual policies of the parties. As it is, the parties have their programmes, partly in order to discipline themselves, and partly in order to attract the intellectuals who can provide leadership and, indeed, ministers. These programmes differ from one another largely on issues which touch the ordinary man remotely. They are conditioned by the different background of the two parties. Although it might wish it otherwise, Action Group was at this time to all intents and purposes a party of the Western Region, and even there it faced a strong N.C.N.C. opposition. Whether it likes it or not, its strength in its own Region is based almost entirely on Yoruba 'nationalism', which it must foster or perish. The N.C.N.C., on the other hand, appeared to be firmly entrenched in the East, and to have a strong foothold in the West, this latter depending largely on anti-Yoruba sentiment and on internal Yoruba divisions. In the Eastern Region election of 1957, described in the next chapter, the Action Group played the same game against the N.C.N.C. with some success: but in 1956 it was bound above all to attempt to consolidate its hold in its own territory. If it lost this it could play no part in the future of Nigeria.

The two parties had therefore radically different proposals to make about the new Constitution which must come with self-government. Action Group wished to see as much power as possible remaining with the regional governments, partly at least in order to have the maximum amount of control over the West. Because, at any rate while cocoa prices remained high, the West was the richest of the three Regions, the Action Group wished to see federal revenue allocated 'by derivation', that is to say, that federal grants should be paid to Regions in proportion to their contributions to federal revenues. The N.C.N.C., conscious of the difficulties of the East in financing social services, would like to see the revenue distributed 'according to need'. The N.C.N.C. had also declared that regional self-government would have little meaning if the Federation as a whole were still under British control, while Action Group put regional self-government at the head of its programme.

For similar reasons the question of the status of Lagos created differences. In 1954 it had been excised from the West to form the federal capital. The Region thus lost Nigeria's most important sea-

coming to live with them. Others have told the writer that increases in salary mean little to them, because their family obligations become correspondingly greater. But it appears that in many cases this particular custom is losing its hold in face of modern conditions.

port, together with its revenue, and potential control over the com-merce of a great deal of the country. Although for some time after the 1953 Conference this issue caused a great deal of clamour, it was not prominent in the 1956 elections.

Both parties subscribed to the creation of a Benin–Delta State. This would mean the removal from the West of an area which sends an almost solid block of N.C.N.C. members to the House of Assembly, and would make Action Group's position in the remainder of the West as secure as the N.C.N.C.'s in the Eastern House. From the N.C.N.C. point of view, it would strengthen the party's position in the federal second chamber if the Constitution included a 'senate' constructed somewhat on the American or Australian model.

In the internal politics of the Western Region, Action Group had the support of most of the traditional rulers. Partly because of its economic policy, many business men were active workers for the party. At least in Yorubaland there were few places where it lacked local leaders of proven ability. On the other hand, the N.C.N.C. in the West, though it numbered many able men among its leaders, appeared to have few reserves of real talent to fall back upon. At the local level, some of its leaders were semi-literate, often mere mal-contents, without any clear political objective. This situation appeared to be improving.[1]

Without defining what it means by the term, the N.C.N.C. cites as one of its aims 'to set up [a] Socialist Commonwealth'. Several of its leaders are men who, as students in Great Britain, were attracted by the Labour Party there, but it is difficult to discover from them how any real measure of socialism could be grafted on to West Nigerian society. The term 'Tory' is sometimes used in N.C.N.C. propaganda in abuse of 'imperialist' actions, but it is doubtful whether it evokes anything in the minds of the majority of those who hear it.

At its Benin conference held in December 1952, Action Group considered the question of adopting an 'ideology'—Socialism, Con-servatism, or Liberalism—but decided that the time was not ripe to do so.[2] Probably more because of its faith in good party organization than any political affinity, Action Group has tended to draw on the example of the organization of the British Conservative Party.

Organization. Both the parties have a national organization, repre-senting the three Regions, and at the federal level each party is governed by an Annual Meeting. These are stated to be the 'supreme authority' of their respective parties; both elect officers and a

[1] See Lloyd, op. cit., p. 705. This criticism of N.C.N.C. politicians does not apply to Warri or Oyo.
[2] *Daily Times*, 23 Dec. 1952.

National Executive Committee.[1] Action Group's National Congress consists of the members of the National Executive and thirty members from each Region. In practice it seems to be concerned mainly with the discussion of matters brought up by the Executive Committee, or more particularly by the President, Chief Awolowo, and has little to do with the initiation of policy. Its powers are not specified in the party constitution; those of the Executive are, and they are very wide. The Executive is the final court of appeal in most party matters.

The N.C.N.C.'s Annual Convention, composed of the members of the National Executive Committee, two members from each affiliated branch, and all parliamentarians of the party, is specifically empowered to control all aspects of the party's activities, though, naturally enough, the day-to-day work is left to the Executive Committee. In practice, the principal personalities appear to be firmly entrenched, and to have their way in most matters. At present Dr. Azikiwe's personal gift of leadership, reinforced by his occasional threats of resignation, seems to be the main guiding and cohesive force. Nevertheless, lively and sometimes acrimonious discussion can take place at Convention meetings, and even 'Zik' himself has on occasion come under heavy fire.

At the regional level, Action Group has a Regional Conference and a Regional Executive. There is also provision for a Parliamentary Council, consisting of the members of the Regional House of Assembly. This is concerned only with parliamentary business, and is subordinate to the Regional Conference and Executive. These in their turn are responsible to the National Congress. Below these again are the Divisional Committees and the Branches; the Committees must contain at least two representatives from every Branch in the Division.

There is a large headquarters in Ibadan, with a big staff. Much of the organization is in the hands of professionals, who rarely appear on platforms, and who take a considerable pride in their work. The Principal Organizing Secretary, Mr. S. T. Oredein, who was one of the founder-members of the party, had already had organizing experience as the secretary of the Nigerian General Tobacco Workers' Union in Ibadan. He went to the United Kingdom at the time of the 1955 General Election, and on his return presented a report to his party which showed him to be a keen observer. Many of his recommendations appear to have been put into practice in the election reported here.

The N.C.N.C. also has its Regional Conference and Regional

[1] They may be summoned to special meetings in an emergency.

Working Committee, but they do not enjoy the same measure of autonomy as those of Action Group. The National Executive Committee is empowered to suspend any Regional Working Committee which 'by its activities threatens the unity and harmony of the National Council', and it can then order a new election. Appeals against suspension can be lodged with the Party Convention, which is also empowered to decide appeals on a variety of other questions. There is provision for a parliamentary party in each Region.

Moves were being made in 1956 to set up an N.C.N.C. regional headquarters in Ibadan, but at the time of the election little had been done in this direction, and control was exercised from the national headquarters in Lagos. Even in Lagos there are few, if any, full-time officers with administrative powers. The National Secretary, Chief Kolawole ('Kola') Balogun, was then Federal Minister for Research and Information; the Elections Secretary, Dr. Sanya Onabamiro, an eminent parasitologist, can have had little time to spare from his ordinary work.

The consent of the National Executive Committee is required for the creation of a local branch of the N.C.N.C., and it is empowered to close down any branch which it considers unnecessary or prejudicial to the welfare of the party. Annual reports and statements of accounts are supposed to be sent by Branches to the National Secretary. Headquarters has therefore in theory a very strong control over the day-to-day affairs of the party, but in practice it would be folly to exercise this except in extreme cases. Much time has often to be taken by members of the National Executive in smoothing over local difficulties.

Central control over the N.C.N.C. is further weakened by the admission to corporate membership of various tribal unions and local associations, which may be affiliated to local branches on payment of a fee of one guinea. The Oyo Parapo and the Urhobo Renascent Convention[1] are examples of bodies which constitute a large part of the N.C.N.C.'s support in a particular area. There are many other instances. While the National Executive has power to expel such a union, to do so would have the most serious consequences. This means that a great deal of local autonomy can exist.

Individual membership of both parties is on payment of an annual subscription of 6s., payable either as a lump sum or by monthly instalments of 6d. Action Group also charges an admission fee of 1s., upon payment of which a party card is issued. Intending members of Action Group have to take an oath of allegiance to the party.

Explicit provision is made in the constitution of the N.C.N.C. for

---

[1] See below, pp. 77 and 90.

youths' and women's organizations, and these commonly exist. Dr. Azikiwe has all through his life been interested in sport, and has a private stadium at Yaba, a suburb of Lagos. He also gives his patronage to an important football club.[1] While this side of 'Zik's' interest is undoubtedly altruistic, sport is frequently a cohesive influence in the N.C.N.C.'s youth organizations. Chief Awolowo is also a patron of sport, particularly tennis, but not on Dr. Azikiwe's lavish scale, and Action Group, though it does not ignore either women or young men[2], pays less formal attention to their organization. In practice, neither of the youth organizations works as it is supposed to work on paper. Young people tend to be attached to local organizations, and to supply a reserve of messengers and the like. Regrettably, some of them form gangs of 'toughs', who can cause disturbances and sometimes bloodshed at meetings; and young children also get involved in party contests. At many meetings children scarcely able to talk were seen in organized groups singing the offensive songs of one or other of the parties. It is to be feared that some schoolmasters are not above indoctrinating their charges.

Both parties claim to be financed from the subscriptions of members and from donations. There is considerable difficulty in collecting subscriptions, and the majority of members appear to enjoy most of the privileges of membership without making regular payments. The N.C.N.C. rules lay it down that holders of offices shall be 'financial members', thus tacitly admitting this situation. The bulk of Action Group's money certainly comes from 'donations'. This is partly because, as we have seen, many wealthy traders and business men consider that their prosperity depends on maintaining Action Group in power. There is also a widespread belief, probably without real foundation, that the Regional Loans Board will grant money more readily if the applicant is in good odour with the party. Many members of the House of Assembly pay a proportion of their salaries to the party, which, they feel, has given them the chance of an increased income. The same applies to the members of the various boards and other public bodies, most of whom are Action Group supporters.[3]

[1] He was President of the Lagos and District Amateur Football Association until 1954. He is now Vice-Chairman of the Nigerian Boxing Board of Control, President of the Amateur Athletic Association of Nigeria and of the Nigerian Table Tennis Association, and a member of the Nigerian Olympic Committee.

[2] In the election under review it probably mobilized the women's vote better than the N.C.N.C.

[3] This one-party composition of the boards seems inevitable at present, since party feeling is in many ways far stronger than it is in Britain. There is a natural tendency to believe that 'he who is not for us is against us'. Evidence of percentages

For all these reasons, Action Group has far more money at its disposal than the N.C.N.C. There is plenty of evidence of this in the organization of the two parties, and in the way they conduct elections. The N.C.N.C., for instance, was seriously short of cars in the election of May 1956.

It is sometimes maintained that the differences in the organization of the two parties originate from Ibo and Yoruba traditions; the small social units of the former and the large towns and more centralized tribal organization of the latter. Action Group has, however, many potential leaders, while the majority of those attracted to the N.C.N.C. in the West are of the wrong type for this task. Moreover, the N.C.N.C. is not primarily concerned with the Western Region. Neither of the central organizations has in fact as much control over its party as it appears to have, and within wide limits local branches can act as they please. Dr. Azikiwe's personal hold over his party is an important factor in the cohesion of the N.C.N.C. Were he to be removed from the scene, it is easy to envisage all sorts of confusion and struggles for power within the movement. While it would be foolish to underrate the importance of Chief Awolowo to the Action Group, it is difficult to point to any 'key man' in the party. Its dependence for so much of its support on the tribal myth helps to ensure its continuity so long as there is any widespread loyalty to that myth.

The Press. Three 'national' daily newspapers are published in Lagos in English, and circulate in the Western Region. These are the *Daily Times*, *Daily Service*, and the *West African Pilot*.

The *Daily Times* is a subsidiary of the British *Daily Mirror*, and ·; one of a chain of such newspapers published throughout British West Africa. Its editor is an African, and there is little evidence that there is any European control over its policy; it rarely reflects views commonly held in Britain, let alone those which might be expected from the *Daily Mirror* itself. On occasion, however, it does give quotations from the *Mirror* on subjects likely to be of interest to Nigerians. It is sometimes difficult to discover what its editorial policy is, but it is frequently attacked by both the main political parties, perhaps the best tribute to its impartiality. On the whole, it appears to give the benefit of the doubt to the government of any particular Region, though its editorials are often outspoken on what are considered to be abuses, whoever may be responsible for them. Considerable care seems to be taken to maintain a balance between

of salaries being paid by members of the House of Assembly and of the boards to Action Group funds is contained in the annual report given to the Warri Conference of the party (*Daily Times*, 18 Dec. 1953).

the parties in the news items; most of this reporting is done in a factual, 'dead-pan' style. Contributors of articles of general interest appear to be given great freedom of expression. Cameros Helios,[1] with his 'Cameroons Comments', and Ebenezer Williams, who contributes articles on a variety of topics, are both free in their criticism of what they see—perhaps more critical than constructive. They are quite prepared to take sides on particular issues, but this partiality does not align them with a political party. Articles from a variety of other sources, including students from overseas, are generally lively, often informative or stimulating. There are two strip cartoons, one of Danish origin, and the other an advertisement inserted by the United Africa Company. Sport is well covered, particularly boxing, and there is a lively and controversial correspondence column. It must be said, however, that the paper is not without its modicum of misinformation.

Both the *Daily Service* and the *West African Pilot* are avowedly party organs; more so than any newspaper published in Britain, with the exception of the *Daily Worker*. They have their origins in Lagos politics, and in their early days reached levels of vituperation and rhetoric which must be read to be appreciated.[2] From time to time both have had to pay considerable damages for libel, but in recent years their tone has moderated and their style has become more orthodox.

The *Daily Service* dates from 1933. In the early 1940's it was connected with the Nigerian Youth Movement, going on to support the Action Group. It is published by the Amalgamated Press of Nigeria Ltd., whose managing director, Mr. S. O. Shonibare, is also publicity manager of the Action Group. While it mentions most events of importance in Nigeria, it devotes most of its space to the successes of the Western Regional Government and the failures of that in the East. There is a daily 'horoscope' feature, and articles for women and children. Sport receives considerable attention.

The *West African Pilot* is owned by Dr. Azikiwe's 'Zik Enterprises Ltd.' First published in 1937, it became an important instrument in Dr. Azikiwe's rise to power and fame. It is as strongly partisan as its rival the *Daily Service*, and like it it is given to the use of sensational headlines. It commonly consists of four pages, sometimes more. These are larger than those of the *Service*, but the type is also bigger, and a considerable proportion of the space is given over to advertisements. Sport is well covered, and a religious article and cartoon, both

---

[1] His real name, not a pseudonym.
[2] For a further analysis and a notable quotation, see Wheare, op. cit., pp. 59 and 60.

of American origin, appear daily. Often there is also a political cartoon, drawn by the paper's own artist, 'Lash'.

None of these newspapers devotes much space to news from outside Nigeria, though the *Daily Times* is better than the other two in this respect; even affairs in other British West African colonies receive scant attention. Even the most intelligent and politically active Nigerians show little concern for what goes on outside their own country. Some would say that they have enough on their hands at home.

The three Lagos newspapers are distributed in their respective lorry fleets, and reach all principal towns in the Western Region by the late evening.[1] It is difficult to obtain a reliable estimate of their readership in the Western Region, but that of the *Daily Times* and *Service* is probably of the order of 40,000, and the *Pilot*'s rather less. The number of people reached is much greater than this, since newspapers pass from hand to hand, and are shared among families.

Some years ago there was a small provincial press, but this has declined almost to nothing. There are two Ibadan dailies, consisting of only four pages, the *Nigerian Tribune* (Action Group) and the *South Nigeria Defender* (N.C.N.C.). Both are completely partisan, and their standard of production and printing is low. Although they sell for a penny, as compared with the twopence of the Lagos newspapers, their circulation is small.

There is a small vernacular press. Two weeklies published in Lagos appear in Yoruba, but their importance is negligible.

3. Events Leading to the Election

The stages of constitutional development since 1951 have already been summarized, and it is necessary here only to explain briefly the political history of the Western Region during this period, emphasizing the immediate antecedents of the election.

The election of 1951 naturally provoked recrimination between Action Group and the N.C.N.C. After the election, however, the Action Group ministers pressed for vigorous use of their new powers, and this led to a period of friction between Action Group and the Governor (Sir John Macpherson) and the Lieutenant-Governor in the Western Region (Sir Hugo Marshall), and so to a temporary *rapprochement* between Action Group and the N.C.N.C. At the Action

---

[1] The *West African Pilot* only organized its own lorry service early in 1956. Before that it made use of haulage contractors.

Group conference held at Benin at the end of 1952, a resolution was passed pledging members not to 'fraternize' socially with Sir John Macpherson 'until such time as there is clear evidence to the satisfaction of the party as to his change of attitude'. This same meeting voted a donation of £100 to the African National Congress in South Africa and £50 to the Kenya African Union.[1] In the central legislature in 1953 Action Group and the N.C.N.C. joined in supporting a motion demanding 'self-government in 1956'. Four Action Group ministers in the central government were withdrawn by the party,[2] and the Northern members were thus isolated.

This period of pressure led up to the London conference, which met on 30 July 1953: Chief Awolowo supported Dr. Azikiwe in pressing for adequate representation of the N.C.N.C., and a preliminary agreement about membership of the conference was reached between these two and the Northern leader, the Sardauna of Sokoto. At the conference itself this unity broke down over the question of the exclusion of Lagos from the Western Region, a matter on which the Northern Region and the N.C.N.C. combined against the West; Action Group accepted this division with great reluctance, and it was equally displeased by the decision which took the choice of federal ministers out of the hands of the regional governments.[3] Dr. Azikiwe, on the other hand, spoke buoyantly of having been offered 'self-government on a platter of gold'. This pressure on Action Group continued during the Lagos Town Council election of November 1953 and the first federal election of 1954: in the former, Action Group and its allies defeated supporters of the N.C.N.C., in the latter the N.C.N.C. succeeded in securing a majority of federal representations from the Western Region, as well as in dominating the Eastern Region both in the regional election, decided in January 1954, and in the federal election.

Three other series of events during this period are worth mentioning. First, progressive legislation in the Western Region. Much of

---

[1] *Daily Times*, 23 Dec. 1952. On the N.C.N.C. side, when H. O. Davies went to Kenya to assist in Jomo Kenyatta's defence, Mr. Kola Balogun accompanied him, but was not admitted to the Colony under security regulations, since he had not been retained as Counsel, and therefore had no specific business there. It must be borne in mind that the Mau Mau atrocities had not then aroused the horror they were later to do.

[2] The Oni of Ife (Without Portfolio), Chief Bode Thomas (Transport), Chief Arthur Prest (Communications), and S. L. Akintola (Labour).

[3] They were to be nominated by the leader of the party having an absolute majority in the House of Representatives, or, if none existed, by the leaders of the parties securing most seats in each Region. Three were to be chosen from each Region, and one from the Cameroons.

the friction with the Governor and Lieutenant-Governor arose over the Local Government Ordinance, which eventually received the Governor's assent at the end of February 1953.[1] This was a bold step forward from 'indirect rule' to local government of the British type: it transferred considerable powers to elected local authorities, and reduced the authority of District Officers in charge of Divisions, who were renamed early in 1956 'Divisional Advisers'. The change also increased the scope for political patronage and party organization, central and local.

In September 1952 the regional government introduced a free medical service for those under eighteen: and early in 1955 it abolished fees in primary schools and envisaged large expansions in the system of secondary education. This scheme was to be financed in part by a 10s. 6d. Capitation Tax, begun in 1954, and some observers attributed Action Group's poor showing in the federal election to this new tax. Opponents of Action Group did not deny the reality of economic development, but alleged that it was so managed as to increase the patronage of the ruling party and the funds at its disposal.

Secondly, there were events which drew Nigerian politicians into larger affairs, and underlined the position of Nigeria as an 'emergent state', potentially of great importance. In May 1954 Dr. Azikiwe and a party left on an economic mission to Europe and the U.S.A.; and he was in the U.S.A. again for six weeks in October and November 1955. He was attacked by Action Group for ulterior motives and unrealistic plans, but there was no doubt about the popular appeal of a drive for industrialization, even if based on foreign investment, and Action Group responded in March and April 1956 by a mission to Europe, the U.S.A., and Japan, led by Chief Awolowo. He had already visited India in 1952, and perhaps his visit led to some of the similarities to Indian electoral law which are to be found in the *Western Region Parliamentary and Local Government Electoral Regulations* of 1955. Above all, there was the Queen's visit to Nigeria, which was very successful, in spite of examples of the sort of friction about social relations from which royalty is seldom free. There was a truce in party warfare from 21 January to 23 February 1956, on the whole remarkably well kept; the whole country contrived to put on a brave show in a period of national holiday; and rivalry in display perhaps helped to emphasize national greatness and unity. But this was holiday-time, not work-a-day politics.

[1] See W. Fowler, 'Some Observations on the Western Region Local Government Law, 1952 (No. 1 of 1953)', *Journal of African Administration*, vol. v (1953), pp. 119–23.

Thirdly, there ran through this period a series of inquiries into troublesome cases of political disturbances and corruption, culminating in the Foster-Sutton inquiry into the affairs of the African Continental Bank at the end of 1956, which involved Dr. Azikiwe himself. Some of these cases will be referred to again later, as they provided much material for the electoral campaign: the following were the most important. In February 1953 Mr. Bernard Storey, the Town Clerk of Norwich, reported on the conduct of Lagos Town Council in such terms that the Council was dissolved on the following day. Few of the leading members of the Council emerged with credit, and specific allegations against certain supporters of the N.C.N.C. were held to be proved.[1] This led to new elections for the Council, in which (as has been mentioned) Action Group was more successful than the N.C.N.C.

In September 1954 there was political rioting at Oyo in the Western Region. The report of the Commissioner (Mr. R. D. Lloyd) who conducted an inquiry was published in June 1955,[2] and found, inter alia, that the Alafin of Oyo, who shares with the Oni of Ife the most important place among Yoruba traditional rulers, had been guilty of several acts of misrule, though many of the accusations made against him were not justified. The Commissioner stated, however, that he could see no reason why the Alafin should continue to live in voluntary exile. Chief Awolowo's government, however, did not accept the Commissioner's conclusions; in consequence, the N.C.N.C. rallied to the support of the Alafin against Action Group, and assumed the role of supporter of the institution of 'natural' rulers.

In January 1956 appeared two other reports which had political significance. In the Eastern Region the Ikpeazu Commission found Mr. Mazi Mbonu Ojike, Eastern Minister of Finance, and Mr. Michael Agwu, Minister of Land, guilty of abusing their offices by accepting bribes.[3] In the Western Region the Nicholson Commission into the conduct of the Ibadan District Council[4] found that four members of the N.C.N.C., Messrs. Adelabu, Ade Bello, Amoo, and Bandele, had been involved in corrupt dealings.

In the Ibadan case the Western Region Government gave the Ibadan District Council an opportunity to remove those found

[1] Report of the Commission of Inquiry into the Administration of the Lagos Town Council (Lagos, Govt. Printer), 1953.
[2] Daily Times, 8 June 1955; 'A Crown Falls', West Africa, 25 June 1955, pp. 583-4.
[3] D.T. 19 and 20 Jan. 1956; West Africa, 28 Jan. 1956, p. 87.
[4] D.T. 17 Jan. 1956; Report of the Commission of Inquiry into the Administration of the Ibadan District Council (Abingdon, 1956).

guilty in the Nicholson Report. This it refused to do. The Governor-General wrote to Mr. Adelabu, requesting him to follow British practice, resign his federal ministry, and defend his integrity outside the Council of Ministers.[1] The N.C.N.C. Federal Parliamentary Party made a statement which included the following remarks:

Mr. Adelabu was given to the service of the nation by the N.C.N.C. It is the N.C.N.C. that will withdraw Adelabu by resignation from the nation's service if circumstances warrant such withdrawal, and will not allow dictation by any parties.
. . . The N.C.N.C. will make its stand, and when it has spoken the nation will take note.[2]

Eventually Mr. Adelabu did in fact resign his Ministry of Social Services, but it is not certain which of the forces acting on him made him decide to do so.

During the royal visit which followed, even the Ibadan District Council affair had been shelved to avoid unpleasantness, but when it was taken up again, Mr. Adelabu still refused to resign the chairmanship of the Council. In this decision he was supported by the majority of the N.C.N.C. councillors, who genuinely believed that he was being 'framed' by the Western Region Government. They did not, however, go so far as to say that Mr. Nicholson was a party to this conspiracy. Criminal proceedings were brought against Mr. Adelabu, and he was eventually acquitted, though not until after the election. As will be seen later, this did not affect his public life seriously, apart from the loss of his portfolio.

In an attempt to persuade Mr. Adelabu to resign, six leading members of the Western Region N.C.N.C., including his counsel before the Nicholson Tribunal, Mr. Fakayode, wrote a letter to him, which does not seem to have met with any result.[3] On 5 March, therefore, the Western Region Government dissolved the Council. In this they were supported by Dr. Azikiwe, who declared that they had done the right thing.[4]

All these events during 1954 and 1955 meant that Action Group had gained some ground politically in anticipation of the election

[1] D.T. 20 Jan. 1956.
[2] D.T. 21 Jan. 1956.   [3] D.T. 2 Mar. 1956.
[4] D.T. 7 Mar. 1956. In spite of Dr. Azikiwe's support of the Western Region Government over the dissolution of the I.D.C., Mr. Adelabu was one of the principal speakers for the N.C.N.C. in the May elections, and was subsequently made Leader of the Opposition in the Western House of Assembly. Only after this was he cleared of the charges of corruption in the courts of law. This tends to reinforce the view that strong local groups can 'call the tune' in the party.

which it was assumed must either take place during May 1956, or be postponed for some time.[1] It was for the Premier, Mr. Awolowo, to choose his moment for dissolution, but his choice of date was somewhat restricted because the new register would not be available till 1 May, and the rainy season made electoral activity almost impossible from June until mid-October. At the end of October 1955 the N.C.N.C. announced some grandiose plans for the conduct of the campaign when it took place. The N.C.N.C. campaign was to be called the 'Fifth Freedom Crusade', and it was to be directed by 'Zik' himself, from a prefabricated house, equipped with radio communications. This was to be moved about as and where required.[2] In fact, neither the title of the campaign nor the house were used. It was also announced that £50,000 had been set aside for the cost of the election.[3] During November, electoral registration was in progress, as described in the next section. At the end of November Dr. Azikiwe returned from his second tour in the U.S.A., in January came the reports of the Ikpeazu and Nicholson Commissions, followed by the Queen's visit. From 12 March Chief Awolowo was abroad on his economic mission, and he returned on 15 April to a triumphant reception in Lagos and Ibadan. A somewhat sinister sign in Ibadan was the presence of a number of youths, carrying whips, and wearing black shirts and berets with the Action Group badge. The writer heard several reliable reports that they had occasionally caused trouble in the crowds.

On 19 April there was news of a minor crisis in the Eastern Region. In Calabar, it appears, some rating authorities had failed to raise sufficient funds to pay grants-in-aid for voluntary agency schools. It was reported that, if these schools had to close 25,000 children in 120 institutions would be affected. The *Daily Times* blamed the Ministries of Local Government and Education for each attempting to make the other responsible for the deficit.

At this stage began the political manœuvres which led directly to the election. These can be reported here only on the basis of published information, which is naturally very incomplete. On 21 April

---

[1] Chief Awolowo had claimed that since the original Western House of Assembly had not sat until Feb. 1952, the Constitution did not demand new elections until early in 1957, and he had declared his right to remain in power until then. The N.C.N.C., on the other hand, maintanied that the original elections had been completed by the end of Sept. 1951, and that new elections would therefore have to be held before the last quarter of 1956.

[2] *D.T.* 21 Oct. 1955.

[3] Evidence before the Foster-Sutton tribunal of inquiry into the affairs of the African Continental Bank suggests that some of this money may have been borrowed from that bank. (*D.T.* 6 Sept. 1956.)

Mr. Awokoya, the Western Minister of Education and author of Action Group's education schemes, resigned. He was followed by Mr. Babalola, Minister of Works, and by Mr. Oladipo Amos, the Publicity Secretary of Action Group.

In his letter of resignation to the Governor, Mr. Awokoya said:

For some considerable time now the relationship between the Premier and myself leaves very much to be desired.

... In particular, I feel that unless some public declaration is made before it is too late, this Region will be ruled by a totalitarian Government dominated by the personality of Chief Awolowo, and thereby doomed for at least one generation to a dictatorship that may drag us to the most dreadful depths of human degradation.

Chief Enahoro, Minister of Home Affairs, who had been acting-premier during Chief Awolowo's absence abroad, replied by accusing Mr. Awokoya of refusing to serve under any other person as acting-premier, of running a bus service while a minister, and of spending his time buying second-hand buses while overseas on a Government mission.

It was also alleged that he had failed to repay 'monies expended by the Government on the woman whom he wrongly holds out to be his wife', and that he had refused to attend certain functions in honour of the Queen 'because he had been told that he could not present the woman in question to Her Majesty'. He was further accused of having requested the party to force him on his constituency, which had refused to readopt him.[1] Subsequently, it was said that Mr. Awokoya's acceptance of the C.B.E. was embarrassing to Action Group.[2]

Mr. Babalola gave as his reason for resigning that 'For some time it has become very trying for me to continue in a political situation in which the Premier regards himself as the autocrat who must bully his colleagues into submission'.[3] Mr. Amos merely accused Action Group of having denied him 'fair play'.

Action Group claimed that both the ministers had been asked to resign earlier.[3] The N.C.N.C. was thus able to retaliate that Action Group, for all its calls on them to purge themselves of dishonest politicians, had in fact been harbouring them itself.

At first there were rumours that the three who had resigned would join the N.C.N.C., but Mr. Awokoya began to try to form a party of his own. Its political outlook appeared to be not very different from that of Action Group, but its title of Nigerian Peoples' Party

[1] *D.T.* 24 Apr. 1956. [2] *D.T.* 23 Apr. 1956.
[3] *Sunday Times* (Lagos), 22 Apr. 1956.

was intended to imply that it stood for internal democracy. The new party went off to a bad start, and the writer did not come across anybody who showed any enthusiasm for it. Many Action Groupers felt that, even if the accusations of dictatorship were true, yet their party gave them all they wanted. The more cynical viewed the whole affair as a personal struggle for power. As it turned out, the new party had less than a fortnight to publicize itself before the election was announced, and most people had not the time to form any worthwhile opinions on it.

On 27 and 28 April the N.C.N.C. held a Convention at Oshogbo. Much of the debate was on the subject of the new Constitution. It was decided that Lagos should remain federal, and that the Nigerian police should also remain the responsibility of the central government. A Mid-West state was to be created. In a speech at the Convention, Dr. Azikiwe accused the Western Region Government of plotting secession from the Federation. Inevitably there was a call on that government to resign in view of the recent happenings.

This Convention had been the subject of some controversy. For some weeks before there had been a ban on political meetings in Ibadan and Oyo Provinces, because of disturbances which were not unconnected with the Ibadan District Council dispute. The N.C.N.C. maintained that their Convention was a private gathering. There were some unfortunate threats that, whatever the view of the authorities, the meetings would be held. Since the Convention was in no sense a political demonstration, no administrative objection was made to the holding of it, but after the N.C.N.C.'s plans had been made known, Action Group threatened to hold a conference, also at Oshogbo, on the same days. Conflict between the supporters of the two parties would have been almost inevitable, and fortunately wiser counsels prevailed over this show of bravado. The Action Group gathering was postponed, and in fact it did not take place, at least in its original form. Before it could do so, the dissolution of the House of Assembly was announced. The N.C.N.C. Convention had not concerned itself very much with election matters, so that the party had not taken advantage of the opportunity to prepare itself for the fray. In all probability it had come to the conclusion that at that stage Action Group would not 'go to the country'. But the new register came into force on 1 May, and next day Chief Awolowo announced an immediate dissolution, leading to an election on 26 May, the first Saturday after the three-week period required by law between dissolution and polling.

4. *The Franchise and the Register*

The franchise. The first election to the Western Region House of Assembly took place (as has been explained) in 1951, under regulations[1] for indirect elections made under Section 63 of the Nigeria (Constitution) Order in Council of that year. The basic franchise in the lowest tier of elections was then that all male taxpayers might vote in the place in which they paid tax.

The first direct elections of a 'Western' type in the Region were those for local government bodies under the Local Government Law, 1952, which received the Governor's assent in February 1953. The qualification was now payment of tax and in addition *either* one year's residence in the area *or* being a native of the area. The term 'native' was undefined, and was construed in practice by reference to patrilineage and compound: a man could vote in his 'ancestral place', irrespective of residence and actual place of birth. Only men could vote, and the tax register therefore served adequately as an electoral register.

This was followed by the regulations governing the federal election of 1954 in the Western Region.[2] The rules were virtually the same, but gave the vote to women who had paid a local rate (exclusive of water and electricity rates) of more than £1. Women do not pay the ordinary direct tax, and the tax registers could therefore no longer be used as electoral registers, which had to be specifically prepared.

After the federal election new regulations were made for elections in the Western Region under Section 37 of the Nigeria (Constitution) Order in Council of 1954[3] and Section 33 of the Western Region Local Government Law, 1952.[4] The new regulations[5] took effect from 15 August 1955. It may seem curious that fundamental provisions regarding the franchise should be contained in regulations made by the Governor on the advice of his Executive Council, not by regional or federal law, or even by regulations made in the Western Region. In practice this no doubt meant that the government of the Western Region had a large say in the making of the regulations, subject to limited control by the federal government, which was partly 'expatriate', partly representative of all Nigerian Regions. The

---

[1] *The Western House of Assembly (Elected Members) Electoral Regulations, 1951*, as amended.
[2] Above, p. 16.
[3] United Kingdom Statutory Instrument No. 1146 of 1954.
[4] Western Region Law No. 1 of 1953.
[5] *The Western Region Parliamentary and Local Government Electoral Regulations, 1955* (Western Region Legal Notice 260 of 1955), hereinafter cited as *P.L.G.E.R.*

procedure was thus a safeguard against abuse of power by a majority in any regional House to alter the franchise in its own favour.

The franchise was in principle universal, but subject to some important complications. These were derived from the regulations governing local government elections under the 1952 Ordinance; and reflected the very strong attachment of the Yoruba to the compound of their patrilineage, the place in which most would wish to vote in local ward elections. The franchise was, however, now substantially extended, and the new rules were briefly as follows:

Reg. 10. (1) A person shall be registered as an elector
　　　　(a)　(i) Where he/she has resided in the Division for two continuous years preceding the election;
　　　　and (ii) has paid tax for two years or has been exempt therefrom.
　Or:　　(b)　(i) Is a native (defined with reference to place of birth or father's birth) of the Division;
　　　　and (ii) is 21 years of age or has paid tax in the preceding year.

To this Reg. 12 adds that a person resident in the Division *must* register in the ward in which he or she resides: a person resident outside it *must* register in the ward of which he or she claims to be a native.

These regulations created a widespread belief, even among educated Nigerians, that women would be virtually disenfranchised, although they were not radically different from those under which the federal elections had been fought. Even after the preliminary figures had been published, showing that rather more women than men had registered,[1] a number of people made this complaint to the writer. A better founded rumour was that the registration would force women to pay tax if they were to have the vote. This gained sufficient currency for Chief Awolowo to make a broadcast pointing out that non-taxpayers could vote in their 'native' Divisions.[2] Nothing was said on the subject of women who were not 'natives' of the Western Region, and the N.C.N.C. telegraphed the Colonial Secretary, protesting that women from outside the West would not be able to vote unless they paid taxes. This was in accord with the intention of the regulations, and nothing came of their protest, or of a second objection in their telegram, made on the grounds that the regulations for local government and parliamentary elections were merged. It was pointed out from many quarters that this was

[1] See Appendix II.　　　　　[2] *Daily Service*, 5 Oct. 1955.

the practice in the United Kingdom, and complaints on this score subsided.[1]

Organization and administration. Arrangements for conducting registration for the federal election had worked well. Then the voters' lists had been compiled by the administrative officers in charge of Divisions, under the general supervision of a Chief Electoral Officer. It was natural that some changes should be made in the Western Region in 1955, if for no other reason than that the next elections were expected to take place either just before or soon after the attainment of self-government in the Region.

Under the 1955 regulations, central direction and control was strengthened by the appointment of an Electoral Commissioner, without any intermediate administrative link between him and those responsible for the conduct of the actual registration and election in the constituencies. As far as registration was concerned:

It shall be the general duty of the Electoral Commissioner to ensure that registers of electors are prepared and elections are conducted in accordance with the provisions of these Regulations, and for that purpose he may:

(a) require information from any officer appointed under this part with respect to any matter relating to the functions of such officer under these Regulations;

(b) subject to the provisions of these Regulations issue general instructions to any such officers with respect to the performance of their functions under these Regulations.[2]

The natural choice for the post of Electoral Commissioner was Mr. P. H. Balmer, who had been D.O., Ijebu Remo, the first area to introduce local government elections under the law of 1952, and subsequently Chief Electoral Officer of the Western Region during the 1954 federal elections. He had the assistance of one administrative officer[3] and a senior and a junior clerk. No doubt the elimination of Residents and District Officers from any mandatory part in the electoral machinery sprang from the policy of 'Nigerianization'. Administrative officers were, of course, always in the background ready to be consulted when difficulties arose, but their advice was not always sought.

In each constituency the Electoral Commissioner was required to appoint a Registration Officer. It was laid down that, unless he thought it inexpedient, the Commissioner should choose the

---

[1] There were also complaints on other matters, such as the drawing of constituency boundaries.

[2] *P.L.G.E.R.* 6 (i) and (ii).

[3] In actual fact, before registration was completed he had had no less than three of them in succession, due to postings, &c.

secretaries of Divisional or District Councils for these posts.[1] Where he thought it necessary, he could divide constituencies into two or more parts, each under its own R.O.

Objections to this arrangement came from the N.C.N.C. on the grounds that 'This is wrong in principle, as it is known that many local government secretaries have party affiliation, and do not even bother to cover their party sympathies and aspirations'.[2]

The party suggested that administrative officers ('who are no politicians') should be made both Registration Officers and Electoral Officers. This plea was not answered, and in the great majority of cases there were no serious complaints against Registration Officers on the grounds of partisanship.

Registration Officers were empowered to appoint Assistant Registration Officers in their constituencies, and, subject to the regulations and the instructions of the Electoral Commissioner, to direct their activities.[3] These A.R.O.s were to be in charge of a Registration Office, a suitable number of which were to be set up by the R.O.s.[4]

The actual registration was to take place during the month of November 1955, but there was much preliminary work to be done. The cost was to fall on regional funds, and this was one reason why it was decided to distribute the necessary stationery and equipment from Ibadan; the central distribution of forms and the like was also a convenient check on local administration. Local distribution, generally through administrative officers, was largely done in September. In the latter half of that month Mr. Balmer went on tour to meet Registration Officers.

In the registration for the federal election, preliminary lists were prepared from 'nominal rolls, any lists of electors used in local government or other elections and such other information as may be available'. Claims and objections could then be decided and the preliminary lists revised to form the register.[5] The complexity of the qualifications for voters had made this procedure difficult to carry out, and in 1955 the onus was thrown on to the would-be voter to take the initiative in registering. He (or she) was required to attend at the Registration Office and submit a written claim on a prescribed

---

[1] *P.L.G.E.R.* 3.

West African Pilot, 4 Oct. 1955.

[3] *P.L.G.E.R.* 4 (1) and (2).

[4] The place of residence of any person in a registration area was not to be more than three miles from a registration office; nor was a registration area to contain more than 500 voters (*P.L.G.E.R.* 18 (ii) (*a*) and (*b*)). There were some 7,500 A.R.O.s in all.

[5] *The Nigeria Elections* (*House of Representatives*) *Western Region Regulations, 1954*, Part II, *passim*.

form (Form 'A'). Illiterates were entitled to bring with them a literate person of their choice. Where the qualification depended on the payment of rates or taxes, the receipts for these had to be produced.

Form 'A' called for a statement of name and address, and the nature of the qualification on which the claim was based. It was so designed that this could be for one qualification only, and included a statement that the applicant had not had his claim accepted in any other constituency. The provision that illiterates could be accompanied by a literate person of their choice inevitably played into the hands of the parties, especially where illiteracy was widespread. They were only too willing to provide the necessary scribes. In point of fact, the forms did not have to be filled in at the Registration Offices, and in any case Action Group had printed its own copies before the end of October. There was nothing in the regulations to say that the officially printed forms had to be used, and the Electoral Commission had to make it clear that any form of the prescribed pattern would be accepted.[1] Needless to say, it was not long before the N.C.N.C. was also in a position to distribute copies of the form. Generally, of course, these completed forms were presented by the persons named on them in a perfectly regular manner. There were precautions in the regulations to see that this was so; A.R.O.s were required to read out the name and address of the person about to register before accepting his form. The parties were permitted to have Registration Agents present to check on irregularities. Nevertheless, there is a strong suspicion that in some cases forms were handed in by those who had already registered on behalf of people who were not present.

Obviously, it was to the advantage of the political parties to register as many as possible of their supporters, and a large part of the credit for the success of the registration must go to them. They both made great efforts all over the Region, but especially in those areas where the political struggle was at its bitterest. In Warri, for example, two tribes, Urhobos and Itsekiris, dispute the 'ownership' of the town. The Urhobos mostly support N.C.N.C., and the Itsekiris, Action Group. Consequently, a large number of persons, reputedly about 13,500, were brought in from outside to claim native qualifications. Many of them made long journeys by canoe from the Creeks to register, having been led to believe that the Government wished to know which of the tribes was the more numerous in the town.[2] In no other case were similar numbers involved, but

---

[1] Cf. *Nigeria Tribune*, 28 Oct. 1955.
[2] Cf. P. C. Lloyd, *Tribalism and Politics in Warri*. Proceedings of the W.A.I.S.E.R. Conference, 1956 (Ibadan, 1956).

there are many instances where the return of would-be voters to their 'native' constituencies was organized by one or other of the parties.

Nevertheless, much of the cost of propaganda was borne by public funds. All available resources were mobilized for a campaign which lasted throughout October and well into November. A pamphlet called *Voting in the Western Region of Nigeria* had been prepared well in advance. This was colourful and well presented. In addition to a simple text, diagrams and cartoons carried the message. It was issued in Yoruba and English versions. Other pamphlets, though none so striking, were printed or cyclostyled, many of them in the minor languages of the Region. Altogether, some 100,000 pieces of propaganda of one kind or another were distributed. Mr. Balmer delivered a series of ten-minute talks on the radio. These explained the procedure for registration and its importance in terms which seemed simple, though a number of people interviewed by the writer told him that they had not been able to understand all that was said. Tape recordings of these broadcasts were made by the Western Region Information Services, which sent out its loudspeaker vans to play them in most of the towns and villages—in fact wherever an audience could be gathered. Further explanations were given by information officers travelling in the vans. Songs on the theme of registration were also composed and recorded; these were played at the same time. The press played its part, publishing advertisements and reporting Mr. Balmer's speeches. The weekly *Western News*, published by the regional Information Service, gave a great deal of its space to registration.

Administrative officers were able to help greatly in this work, addressing village meetings while on tour, and taking advantage of their contacts with local notables to impress on them the importance of registering.

Registration.[1] Procedure for registration fell into four stages: first, the presentation of Form 'A' at Registration Offices and the issue of Receipt Cards; secondly, the preparation of Preliminary Lists, which was to be completed by the end of December; thirdly, the lodging and hearing of claims and objections, to be completed during January; fourthly, the preparation of Final Lists and issue to printers for return and checking before publication on 1 May.

The first stage, with one exception, went smoothly. At first people came in slowly, but by the close of registration nearly three-fifths of

[1] See also P. Whitaker, 'The Preparation of the Register of Electors in the Western Region of Nigeria, 1955–6', *Journal of African Administration*, vol. ix (1957), pp. 23–29.

the estimated population over fifteen had registered;[1] the proportion of qualified electors registered must therefore have been much higher, though it cannot be exactly stated. This can be regarded as very satisfactory, in a country with a low literacy rate, where the onus of registration was thrown upon individuals, the system was new, and party organization was not highly developed.

Each voter whose Form 'A' was accepted was given a Receipt Card.[2] This was meant primarily as a check upon objections to the Preliminary Lists: a voter whose name was not on the list could, if he produced a Receipt Card, get the error put right with very little trouble. Perhaps unfortunately it was suggested in one of Mr. Balmer's speeches that voters should keep their Receipt Cards and note their registration numbers on them when the final register was published; they could then help polling officials to find their names quickly by producing the card with the number on it. In consequence the idea got round, and had to be energetically corrected by further propaganda, that the Receipt Card was in fact an Elector's Card, and had to be produced on polling. This was wholly incorrect: the practice at polling was the British one, that no identity documents are needed and the elector need only claim unambiguously to be a specified person named on the register. But before this had been made clear the two parties had begun to take custody of Receipt Cards as electors left Registration Offices, and the writer has seen stacks of many hundreds of them in the house of more than one local politician.

The second stage, the production of the Preliminary Lists, raised no problems except those to be expected in the circumstances. The registers were subdivided into the wards used in local council elections.[3] In most cases individual addresses could not be given; the ward lists showed, besides names, only the compounds covered, which were usually large and not numerous. The regulations prescribed that the family name was to be entered first, the personal or Christian name second: but the clerks at registration very often simply followed whatever order was given by the applicant in his (or her) Form 'A'. Hence Receipt Cards might well be helpful as a means of finding individual names in the register.

There were difficulties of a different kind during the process of claims and objections.[4] On this occasion (unlike that of the federal

---

[1] The census figures were divided into the age-groups '15–49' and 'over 50'. The total of these two for the Western Region was 3,534,892 (1952 census), including Lagos. 1,945,644 of these registered.

[2] P.L.G.E.R. 10 (6) mentioned the issuing of Receipt Cards, but left their form to the discretion of the Electoral Commissioner.

[3] P.L.G.E.R. 14.   [4] P.L.G.E.R. 23.

register of 1954, which was compiled administratively from tax lists and other records) claims could be made on the grounds that someone who had actually registered in November had either been omitted or entered in the wrong ward (this was when Receipt Cards might be decisive evidence). Objections could be made by any person on the Preliminary Register to any other on the widest possible grounds, either lack of qualification or entry in the wrong ward. In theory claims thus ought to be a routine matter, objections might prove more formidable.

Over the Region as a whole objections were not numerous: the parties seem to have fallen asleep after their earlier efforts, and in many areas people appeared on the register who were certainly not qualified. On the other hand, where political conflict was bitter, as in Warri, Ibadan, and Oyo, the parties showed great zeal in 'attending to the register', and there were scenes reminiscent of registration courts in nineteenth-century England. The extreme case (a unique one) was that of Warri, when some 12,000 names had been objected to in a list which originally included about 26,000: obviously names had been objected to simply because they belonged to a different tribe—blocks of a hundred or more names were objected to by the same person.

Under the regulations claims and objections should normally have been heard by the Registration Officers; these were clerks to local authorities, and their impartiality was not above attack. The Electoral Commissioner therefore had power to appoint someone else if necessary, and in most cases a schoolmaster was the obvious choice. In Warri six barristers were brought in from Ibadan, to deal with about 2,000 cases each, in a period of about a fortnight. There is no shortage of legal talent in Warri, counsel were briefed by both parties[1] and toured from hearing to hearing, conducting a few cases in each and then handing over to the party agents.[2] It was the rule that persons objected to must appear to answer when called on, and in the end some 8,200 names were struck off, many of them on the ground of non-appearance (mainly a result of the inefficiency of the parties). In the hearings at Warri observed by the author decisions were arrived at without much uniformity of rule or procedure, amidst suggestions of perjury,[3] and in most difficult physical

---

[1] When Revision Courts were held in Britain, it was not customary to hear Counsel.

[2] The most notable were Chief Arthur Prest (Itsekiri) for the Action Group, and Mr. Ovie Whisky (Urhobo) for the N.C.N.C.

[3] In conversation, many Warri people of both political parties expressed the opinion that certain local 'juju' oaths, now illegal, would have been held rigidly binding by those prepared to disregard the Bible or a matchet.

conditions. But the business was got through even here: and it must be repeated that Warri was an extreme case. Almost everywhere else most cases could be put right quickly by the Registration Officer by reference to Form 'A' and the Receipt Card.

The last stage, in principle a formal one, presented difficulties which were more striking, perhaps, to a student fresh from England than to a West African. It is a formidable administrative task to build up a register from ward lists locally compiled by about 7,500 different Assistant Registration Officers, and then to get the resulting list of about 2 million names printed accurately and checked for issue by a specified date. The task is not easy to do well, even when competent clerks and typists are readily available,[1] printers are experienced in the business, and the routine is well known. In Western Nigeria a new organization faced all the difficulties for the first time: much of the printing had to be done outside the country by printers in Europe ignorant of West African names and places: and there were never enough competent clerks. The job was done, one day ahead of time, but only by heroic feats of administrative extemporization, and overwork. It should be simpler in future because the register is a 'permanent' one. Those whose claims have been accepted remain on it, and if they move they can transfer their registration: only those newly qualified, or previously neglectful, will have to make fresh claims. The number to be dealt with will therefore be much smaller, even if the parties become more active; much of the type of the register can be kept standing and used again; and with the burden of printing reduced it may be possible to have all the work done within Nigeria.

Delimitation of constituencies. The constituencies (all single-member constituencies, voting by simple plurality) were set out in the First Schedule to the Regulations. These had been framed in accordance with the following rules. Each of the twenty-four administrative Divisions was to have at least two seats; the boundaries of local council areas were to be followed in demarcating constituencies; there were to be eighty constituencies in all. The population of Divisions as shown in the census of 1952 varies considerably, the smallest have only about 6 per cent. of that of the largest: after two seats had been allocated to each Division the thirty-two seats left over were allocated between Provinces on the basis of population, and were then allocated between Divisions so far as possible in

---

[1] This is not to suggest that there are not many excellent Nigerian clerks and stenographers, but they are at a premium; hence most of them do not stay long in local government service; they tend to migrate to Lagos or Ibadan to become Civil Servants or work in business houses.

proportion to resident adult population. There was a proviso that
not more than twenty seats should be allocated to the mid-West
area (Benin and Delta provinces). There were not nearly enough

MAP 2. NIGERIA, WESTERN REGION

seats available in this way to equalize the population of constituencies, especially as demarcation was cramped by the need to follow
local government boundaries. Differences in the percentage of the
population registering introduced further variations.[1] A register of

---

[1] See *Report on the Holding of the 1956 Parliamentary Election to the Western House of
Assembly, Nigeria* (Western Region Government Printer, 1957), p. 4.

about 1,950,000 yields an average of 24,375: in the end the registered voters per constituency ranged from 8,304 to 69,670. The last figure is exceptional, but there was a fairly even range of sizes from about 8,000 to about 40,000.

These variations do not seem to have told in favour of one party or the other, and were certainly not due to deliberate 'gerrymandering'. But they naturally gave rise to a good deal of complaint: and, as explained in section 10, the system had a small bias of a different kind against the N.C.N.C., owing to the relatively even distribution of their supporters.

5. *The Campaign*

To many political observers in Nigeria the dissolution came as a surprise, but others had realized for some time that a more propitious moment was unlikely to occur. As Chief Awolowo stated at a press conference on the afternoon of the day of dissolution, Action Group had some important proposals to make at the forthcoming Constitutional Conference.[1] It was obviously desirable that it should be able to go to London with a 'fresh mandate'. Also, the Western Region Government's Trade Mission to countries overseas had just published its report. This made impressive reading, with its contracts for the setting up of new industries, and the promise of new channels of trade. Any doubts about it on technical or economic grounds would not easily be impressed on the electorate by the party's rivals in the course of less than four weeks. The cost of new social and educational services would inevitably soon have to be reflected in new fiscal measures.

There is reason to believe that Action Group had called for a canvass of the divisions some weeks before the dissolution, and that the results had been satisfactory to them. Nothing of the nature of a door-to-door canvass was, or could have been, attempted, and in most cases, local party leaders were only able to base their forecasts on the number of Receipt Cards which had been handed to them, and the estimates of officers in the wards. In more than one instance the leaders of both main parties in the same constituency showed the writer data from which they each formed the opinion that they would win. But there is no reason to disbelieve that Chief Awolowo's claim that Action Group would win 54 seats (they won 48), made at a meeting at Igbeti on 9 May,[2] was given in good faith.

Dr. Azikiwe, who had only just returned to Enugu after spending

---

[1] *D.T.* 3 May 1956.   [2] *D.T.* 10 May 1956.

some days in the Western Region, commented when the dissolution was announced that it had not come as a surprise. The N.C.N.C., he said, would fight all eighty seats, and he would return to the West to lead the campaign in person.[1] But if he was prepared for the election, many of his followers were not, and a number of the more important members of the N.C.N.C. were quite ready to admit it. Arrangements had been made to set up a regional headquarters in Ibadan, and premises for these had been rented from the beginning of April, but little more had been done. The N.C.N.C's Convention at Oshogbo was only just over when the election began. The official headquarters of 'Operation 80'—as the N.C.N.C. named its campaign, in allusion to the number of seats to be contested—were at Oshogbo. This was fairly central, and was, incidentally, Mr. Kola Balogun's home town. Nothing was heard of the elaborate mobile headquarters which the party had earlier let it be known would be used in the Western elections.[2] A great deal of organization was done from Lagos, and Dr. Onabamiro, the Elections Secretary, undertook much of the administrative work from his house at Ibadan, as well as carrying on his professional duties.

Action Group appeared to be better organized, but it did not seem that the party organization had been forewarned of the exact date. For some months previously, supplies of printed material had been accumulated, and early in the year delivery had been taken of a large number of Land Rovers and other transport. From about the end of February the tempo of activity at the party headquarters was manifestly increasing, but many local organizing secretaries were caught virtually unprepared. However, the superior organization and greater wealth of the party as a whole meant that it was in a better position to begin work than its rivals. In most Divisions Action Group had had cars for some time, but the N.C.N.C. organizers commonly had to collect theirs from Lagos early in the campaign.

Registration of symbols. Subject to certain conditions as to their nature, parties could register their symbols with the Electoral Commissioner on payment of a fee of £25.[3] This conferred on their official candidates the exclusive right to use them. It was left to the Commissioner to decide who were the 'official' candidates, after consultation with the leader or secretary of the party concerned.[4] The symbols to be affixed to the ballot boxes were in the form of transfers, which had had to be prepared well in advance. It was possible to foresee a demand for the palm-tree of the Action Group,

[1] *D.T.* 3 May 1956.
[2] *D.T.* 21 Oct. 1955.
[3] *P.L.G.E.R.* 123.
[4] Ibid. 44(3).

the cock of the N.C.N.C., or the ram of the Dynamic Party, but others, like Mr. Awokoya's Nigerian People's Party, formed just before the dissolution, had in practice to select their symbol from the range offered by the Commissioner.[1] This registration of symbols closed at midday on 5 May, but nominations could be received until the 14th, so that Independent candidates did not have to choose their symbols until then. Where symbols had not been registered it sometimes happened that the same one was used for candidates in different parts of the Region without any party connotation.[2]

Preventing violence. Immediately the dissolution of the House of Assembly had been announced, the Electoral Commissioner called a meeting of the leaders of the two principal parties. Both called on their followers to keep the peace and fight cleanly.[3] An agreement was reached between them that they would not campaign in the same place on the same day. Where there had been bans on the holding of political meetings, arising out of earlier disturbances, these were lifted, though restrictions were retained on the use of offensive songs, and sometimes on drumming. Local agreements were very generally made to the same effect.

The candidates. Nominations closed on 14 May. Up to the last, the N.C.N.C. had difficulties in completing an agreed list of eighty official party candidates. In Asaba South, Mr. C. A. J. Nwajei, a member of the National Executive Committee of the N.C.N.C., and one of its principal legal advisers, tried unsuccessfully to wrest the nomination from the sitting member, Mr. F. H. Utomi, and eventually stood as an Independent. In Warri East, there was a sharp division over the N.C.N.C. candidature, the solution to which did not satisfy everybody. Here also, this gave rise to an independent candidature. There was trouble in a few other constituencies, but the party was able to put forward its full list of candidates. Mrs. F. Ransome-Kuti did not return from a women's conference in China in time to sign her nomination paper for Egba East, and at the last moment Mr. J. A. O. Akande, who was already member of the Federal House of Representatives for Egba North, had to be put up in her place. She was the only woman whom either of the two major parties sought to nominate.

Unfortunately, the N.C.N.C. lost two candidates, in Ondo North-

[1] Apparently the Fiasco Party would not settle on a symbol at the time of registration. The issue was deferred, but lapsed when the party joined forces with the Dynamic Party.

[2] e.g. the Independents in Oshun North, Oshun West, and Ondo North all chose the key. In Western Ijaw North, Ekiti South, and Okitipupa South, the Independents chose the hurricane lamp.

[3] *D.T.* 3 May 1956.

West and Egba North, through a technical irregularity in nomination. The nomination forms issued were not a perfect copy of 'Form G' prescribed in the regulations, in that no space was provided for the signatures of the requisite two nominators. When this was realized, on 11 May, Mr. Balmer gave a warning that these signatures were needed. It appears that the forms were not amended in time by these two candidates, nor by two Independents in Ondo North-West. The N.C.N.C. declared that the corrected forms had been handed in in time by the Ondo candidate, but that the Electoral Officer had refused to return the old one. This fact was endorsed on the form by the candidate. Dr. Azikiwe led a deputation to the Governor on the matter, but nothing was done to interfere with the normal procedure. Motions were filed by the party against the rejection of the forms. At the Ado Ekiti High Court on 23 May, Mr. E. O. Fakayode, an Ibadan lawyer, and a leading light of the N.C.N.C., withdrew the motion concerning Mr. S. O. Omonubi, would-be candidate for Ondo North-West, in favour of an election petition to be filed later.[1] He is reported to have said that he did this on the advice of Mr. Geoffrey Bing, the British Q.C.[2] On the following day the Chief Justice of the Region dismissed with ten guineas costs a motion asking the High Court to quash the disqualification of Mr. Kuforji, N.C.N.C. candidate for Egba North. Thus, at the eleventh hour, 'Operation 80' had become 'Operation 78', in fact if not in name.

Action Group was not without its troubles over candidates, though these only became public after nomination. In Badagry East, Mr. S. A. O. Fadun resigned from the party, and stood as an Independent.[3] Action Group forthwith adopted Mr. Idowu, who had been nominated as an Independent. In Asaba South, the Action Group candidate, Mr. Nwaka, declared himself an Independent, and the party was not able to put up a candidate in this constituency in his place. The underlying reasons for these two changes are confused. Discontent with the party and local feeling both played a part. In Asaba South, this local unrest affected the candidature of both parties, and at one time an additional Independent stood nominated but he withdrew shortly before polling day.

Altogether, thirty-seven Independents stood for election. Four of

---

[1] This petition was rejected.
[2] *D.T.* 24 May 1956.
[3] In the *Report on the Holding of the 1956 Parliamentary Election to the Western House of Assembly, Nigeria*, p. 17, it is stated that Mr. Fadun notified the Commissioner that he no longer intended to stand and that the 215 votes cast for him were credited to the Action Group in the summary of the results there printed.

them[1] were Action Group ex-members of the Western House of Assembly who had not been renominated. Others, like the two mentioned in the preceding paragraph, had differed from their parties, and stood on matters of principle. Some stood because they believed that they had a strong local following. All, or nearly all, those who were nominated by the Nigerian People's Party were ex-Action Groupers; the N.C.N.C. gained the support of the old Benin–Delta People's Party on the strength of its pledge to set up a Mid-West State.[2] The former Independent member for Kukuruku West, Mr. J. A. Ogedengbe, was also returned under the N.C.N.C. banner. Action Group renominated twenty of its sitting Members, the N.C.N.C. ten.[3] The four minor parties which remained in the contest on polling day put forward a total of twenty-one candidates, making with thirty-six Independents a grand total of 213.[4] In thirty constituencies there was a straight fight between Action Group and the N.C.N.C.

Lack of information makes it impossible to give details of the occupations of the candidates, but the great majority were drawn from one or other of the professions. This is inevitable where only a small proportion of the population has as yet enough education to carry on parliamentary business. Many lawyers and schoolmasters were nominated. There were also traders, contractors, and industrialists; the N.C.N.C. made political capital out of the fact that several Action Group candidates in these categories had received government loans for their enterprises. Mr. O. Akenzua, the unsuccessful Action Group candidate for Benin Central, is a son of the Oba of Benin. Dr. Chike Obi, leader of the Dynamic Party, who lost his deposit in Ibadan North-West, was the only member of the staff of University College, Ibadan, to seek election. Mr. S. A. Dada, a medical student of that college, was the only undergraduate to stand. He lost his deposit as the N.C.N.C. candidate for Ekiti North. Mrs. A. Oluwole, leader of the Nigerian Commoners' Party, was the only woman candidate. She also lost her deposit in Ondo North. She was, incidentally, the first woman to contest any Nigerian parliamentary election.

[1] Mr. Fafunmi (Egbado East), Mr. Babola (Ekiti North), Mr. Edu (Epe East), and Mr. Hassan (Epe West).
[2] Action Group has also declared for this cause, but had apparently failed to win the B.D.P.P's confidence (see above, p. 29).
[3] Seven of these Action Groupers were defeated, as well as two of the N.C.N.C. candidates.
[4] The two Action Groupers who were unopposed are not here regarded as 'candidates in the election' since they did not figure in the campaign or the polling.

The manifestos. The party manifestos did not play as important a part in the campaign as in Britain, and most of the principal issues only emerged as the conflict progressed. The Action Group manifesto appeared on 4 May. After an introduction of some 150 words claiming that the party had fulfilled the promises it had made in 1951, it went on to outline a programme of social and economic development for the Region under twenty-one headings.[1] One plan was to establish at a cost of £200,000 a factory for the manufacture of exercise books and school textbooks. The amount to be spent on each project was stated, often, curiously enough, to the nearest thousand pounds. Nothing was said about the time in which this money was to be spent. The manifesto ended with a reiteration of an earlier pronouncement of Chief Awolowo's on policy with reference to foreign capital. The N.C.N.C. was not even mentioned, and there was no statement of the philosophy of Action Group.

The N.C.N.C. manifesto did not appear until six days later; presumably its publication had to wait until Dr. Azikiwe had arrived in Lagos and conferred with the *ad hoc* 'Strategic Council' charged with the planning of the campaign.[2] Its scope was outlined in the preamble:

. . . Firstly to outline what the N.C.N.C. stands for; secondly to examine critically some of the doings of Action Group in the last four years, and lastly to set out what an N.C.N.C. Government in the Western Region would do if voted to power.

The first section which, with the preamble, formed over half of the manifesto, attempted to contrast the two parties. The N.C.N.C. was stated to be the party of the common man, Action Group of the wealthy. The appointments of a Hausaman as Mayor of Enugu, and of Yorubas as chairmen of public corporations in the Eastern Region were contrasted with the alleged 'tribalism' of Action Group. N.C.N.C. was the party of a United Nigeria. Policy-making in the N.C.N.C. was democratic, whereas Chief Awolowo was represented as the dictator of Action Group.

Of the remaining space nearly half was occupied by a 'critical examination of the work of the Action Group government'. This

---

[1] These were 'Agriculture', 'Forestry', 'Veterinary', 'Department of Industries', 'Department of Trade', 'Co-operatives', 'Social Welfare', 'Community Development', 'Medical and Health', 'Education', 'Cultural Research', 'Public Works', 'Electricity', 'Survey', 'Land and Town Planning', 'Information Services', 'Exercise Book Factory', 'Western Region Production Development Board', 'Local Government Councils (Special Grants)', 'Local Government Councils (Loans)', and 'Policy of [sic] Foreign Capital'.

[2] The holding of this meeting is mentioned in *D.T.* 8 May 1956.

again covered the same ground as the first section, alleging favouritism on tribal grounds, and the failure of the Government with regard to loans, agriculture, and education.

The rest of the manifesto—less than a quarter—dealt with policy. It began with a general statement of principles, liberally interspersed with innuendoes about the corruption of the Action Group Government. There followed fourteen specific headings, some of a negative kind such as the stopping of 'jobbery' in public corporations, and some of them giving general plans for future developments. These headings began with a promise to repeal the order exiling the Alafin of Oyo.

Dr. Obi's Dynamic Party was the only minor party to produce a widely publicized manifesto. It began with a promise to 'arrest the mad rush of the Action Group towards self-government for the Western Region'. It declared its intention of pressing at the Constitutional Conference for a unified Nigeria. 'National' loyalty was to be encouraged. Co-operation with Europeans and Americans was to be sought for the improvement of the country. Communications were to be improved, beginning with the Ishan, Kukuruku, Egbado, and Ekiti Divisions (it should be remembered that four of the five Dynamic Party candidates stood in the Ishan and Kukuruku Divisions). Two giant reservoirs were to be built to serve 'the parts of the Region which obviously need water'. 'Above everything' the creation of a Benin–Delta State was to be opposed unless there was a constitutional guarantee that revenue would be allocated according to need for at least the next twenty-five years.

Campaigning: the leaders. Both major parties began their regional campaigns in earnest at about the same time, a week after the dissolution. The two leaders each went out with a group of vehicles, including Volkswagen vans and 'minibuses', some equipped with loudspeakers. Many of the N.C.N.C. vehicles were brightly painted in the party colours. Dr. Azikiwe addressed a great many large meetings, over forty in all, in every part of the Region. Chief Awolowo, while not rejecting this technique, appeared to devote more of his time to 'whistle stop' meetings along his route than did his rival. These often lasted only a matter of minutes. Topics of local importance were touched upon, such as the building of new roads or farmers' loans. Analogies were sometimes drawn from the party symbols. Chief Awolowo, for instance, would point out that the palm-tree provided food, fuel, money, thatch for housing, and palm wine for luxury and relaxation. It was firmly rooted to the ground. The N.C.N.C. could extol the virtues of the cock. On at least two occasions, the writer came across instances of the ritual slaughter of a cock at or after Action Group meetings. (Chief Awolowo was almost certainly unaware that this was going on.)

Meetings were generally held in market places; those addressed by the leaders often had audiences of more than 5,000. It was at these, naturally enough, that the more important pronouncements were made. Commonly, the local traditional leaders would preside; sometimes they did this out of sympathy with the particular party, but sometimes as 'fathers of their people' they appeared at both N.C.N.C. and Action Group gatherings. Unless a chief was known to be hostile, courtesy calls were generally paid on him. Needless to say, when the N.C.N.C. team was passing through Ilesha, where the exiled Alafin of Oyo was living, they made a point of visiting him with all possible publicity.[1]

Lack of time, and the enormous distances to be covered, meant that it was impossible for the leaders to speak in every constituency. Both tended to devote most of their time to those areas where they had most support. This was important in view of the low poll which many anticipated; it seemed desirable to work up as much popular enthusiasm as possible. In most instances, it was a case of 'preaching to the converted'; nearly all those present at meetings wore the badges of the relevant party, sometimes even clothes printed with its slogans. Hence, hostile questioning of the speakers was uncommon. Whenever the party leaders appeared they were greeted with cries of 'Zee-ee-k' or 'Awo-o-o'. The receptions accorded to them reinforced the view that Dr. Azikiwe had more of a charismatic hold on his followers than had Chief Awolowo. Nevertheless, Chief Awolowo seemed to play a larger part in the meetings than did his rival. This was undoubtedly due to the latters' inability to speak Yoruba, at least fluently. Chief Awolowo was able to taunt him with this in Yoruba-speaking areas: 'If Dr. Azikiwe came here, he would have to speak to you through an interpreter.' Frequently, 'Zik', speaking in English, would do little more than introduce 'some of my friends', and leave them to do the talking. His mere presence at the meeting was, however, a tremendous asset. Of course, the language difficulty did not help Chief Awolowo everywhere in the Region.

Much of Action Group's strength lay in Yoruba country, so that Chief Awolowo was able to do practically all his campaigning by daily journeys from Ibadan. In the middle of the campaign he went north to Bauchi and Oyo; in the latter area there was an Action Group pocket which was to yield the party six seats—N.C.N.C. won two more only by narrow margins.

[1] *D.T.* 22 May 1956.

Dr. Azikiwe was in a more difficult position, in that his support, which was most solid towards the East, was also scattered in pockets all over the Region. Thus Ibadan, Benin, Oshogbo, and Lagos had to serve in turn as bases for daily excursions. An exception to the rule that campaigning was generally most intense in friendly territory was the large number of important meetings held by the N.C.N.C. in Ijebu and Remo, Chief Awolowo's home country. Unless the party had grossly over-estimated its strength there, this extreme effort can only be construed as an attempt to carry the war right into the enemy's camp. It was at Ikenne, where Chief Awolowo was born, that 'Zik' announced that he was 'optimistic' of his party winning 'more than a comfortable majority'. All the six seats in these two Divisions were won by Action Group, none with a majority of less than 3,000.

Particularly on the N.C.N.C. side, other party notables, especially federal ministers, addressed large campaign meetings, and were stationed at strategic points throughout the Region. Mr. Kola Balogun was in charge of 'Operation 80' headquarters at Oshogbo, and worked energetically in the centre of the Region, although his party was not able to win any large number of seats in that area. A delegation from the East was based on Warri. The principal role in the N.C.N.C. campaign around Ibadan was played by Mr. Adegoke Adelabu. His presence and his eloquence never failed to produce at the same time extremes of loyalty and hatred. For years he had been at the centre of controversy; throughout the period of the election he was on bail awaiting trial on charges of corruption in connexion with his chairmanship of the dissolved Ibadan Town Council.[1] When he went to make a political speech, he was almost invariably accompanied by two or more lorry-loads of youths, sometimes armed with matchets. There may well have been some justification for his claim that he needed a 'bodyguard', but the size and nature of his retinue tended to cause unrest. During the campaign, this 'bodyguard' came into conflict with some Action Group supporters in Ijebu Ode, and bloodshed resulted. Mr. Adelabu was charged in connexion with this occurrence, and released on bail.[2] This was the only incident of its kind in which he was involved, but there were a considerable number of minor scuffles between supporters of the two parties all over the Region, including Ibadan and Oyo. Fortunately, none of these was serious enough to poison the atmosphere for long.

On 9 May Action Group headquarters posed 'Ten Vital Questions for the West Region' to Dr. Azikiwe. By implication, these accused

[1] As already stated, he was subsequently acquitted.
[2] D.T. 16 and 17 May 1956. He was subsequently acquitted.

the N.C.N.C. of favouring the Eastern Region in federal affairs, by appointing three Easterners to two Westerners to the Council of Ministers. The allocation of Colonial Development and Welfare funds was another alleged instance of this. It was suggested that the taxation of cattle entering the East from other Regions and the special licensing of newspapers published outside the East were a denial of the party's professed policy of 'one Nigeria'. Other insinuations were that the N.C.N.C. was afraid to dissolve the Eastern House of Assembly before the Constitutional Conference; that it had changed its policy on regional self-government because of the near-bankruptcy of the Eastern Region, and that it had failed to purge its ranks of corruption.

Speaking on the same day to a meeting at Igbeti—a town in the Oyo North constituency some forty miles off a tarred road—Chief Awolowo contrasted social services in the West with those in the East, and referred particularly to the threatened closure of schools in the East for lack of funds. He also spoke of the fruits which, he claimed, would result from the Economic Mission.

On the following day, Dr. Azikiwe, at Ibadan, took notice of the 'ten questions'. Some of the insinuations he denied; in other cases, while accepting the facts, he questioned the interpretation put on them. In this encounter the honours appeared to be about equal. Speaking in Iseyin and Oyo, Chief Awolowo declared that the Eastern Region had been 'dragged to the brink of financial collapse because of the indolence and planlessness of the N.C.N.C.'; he alleged that women were being heavily taxed in the East, and mentioned the relatively high level of taxation there. On 11 May, continuing his tour of Yorubaland, he promised that the salaries of traditional rulers would be increased, quoting from the minority report of the N.C.N.C. representatives at the 1953 Constitutional Conference to the effect that the institution of traditional rulers was 'a return to the dark ages'.

'Zik', meanwhile, had moved to the Delta, and was accusing Action Group of 'vindictive acts against the Urhobo people'. He pointed out that no Urhobo had been made a Cabinet Minister in the West, and suggested that the Government had reduced the number of seats in Urhobo Division from six to three because the Urhobos had not supported the Action Group. It was reported in the *Daily Times*[1] that the Ovie of Oghara, in an address of welcome to Dr. Azikiwe and his party, remarked that in the past Nigerian politicians had 'done nothing for Urhoboland, in spite of promises made at such campaign meetings'. He stressed that, as a natural

[1] 12 May 1956.

ruler, his duty was to co-operate with the Government in power. As has been suggested above, this was the common attitude of those chiefs who had for one reason or another not become committed to a political party.

It would be tedious and unnecessary to recount in detail the speeches of the leaders throughout the campaign. In different guises, the same sort of topics were brought up again and again; maladministration in the Eastern and Western Regions, tribalism, and living conditions. A recurrent theme of Action Group's was the allocation of federal revenue. Largely because the West is the wealthiest of the three Regions, it supported the idea of allocation by derivation. N.C.N.C. supported allocation according to need. Undoubtedly the 'one Nigeria' ideal here coincided with the needs of the East; Action Group termed it 'Pillage and Plunder'. On the whole, the two parties tended to ignore each other's remarks, rather than to waste time in trying to refute them. Probably this policy of pursuing an independent line was the wisest one, but in any case it would have been difficult for either of the leaders to obtain full reports of each other's speeches, even if the hard work they had to do each day had allowed them time to read them. There were, of course, occasions when some notice had to be taken of the remarks of rivals. Dr. Azikiwe made frequent allusions to the banishment of the Alafin of Oyo and the Olotta of Otta as examples of the attitude of Action Group to natural rulers.[1] On one occasion,[2] Chief Awolowo denied responsibility for the two acts, and said that they were removed because they did not agree with their people. Practically everybody had made up their minds on these issues long ago, and little that anybody could say would have altered them. Speaking at Agege, Chief Awolowo had to refute an allegation by Dr. Azikiwe that he had called the Ibos half-naked cannibals.[3] Earlier, he had stressed that he did not hate Ibos, but at the same time he made what seemed a gratuitous attack on the numerous Ibo officers and N.C.O.'s in the Nigeria Police.[4]

Very little was said on international topics. Self-government was

[1] As a matter of fact, the ex-Olotta of Otta appeared on several Action Group platforms, and declared that he had no animosity towards the party.

[2] *D.T.* 23 May 1956.

[3] In his broadcast speech of 19 May, Dr. Azikiwe said that 'in numerous articles he has insulted the Ibo people by calling them "jungle dwellers", "half-naked cannibals", and "other uncouth epithets" '. Chief Awolowo coupled his denial with a suggestion that these were the sort of remarks made by certain anthropologists and the London *Times*. Few people who read that newspaper would consider this likely. But most of Chief Awolowo's hearers would not have done so.

[4] *D.T.* 19 May 1956.

occasionally used as a rallying cry, but the great majority of the electorate were interested only in matters which affected them more immediately.

Campaigning: the local organizations. In spite of their tremendous efforts, the party leaders were able only to reach a small proportion of the electorate, and the bulk of the work of contacting voters rested with the local party organizations. Owing to the size of many of the constituencies[1] and the state of the roads, they were faced with a very big problem. As has been remarked, Action Group had been supplied with cars well before the campaign started, while the N.C.N.C had to collect theirs from Lagos in its early days. Action Group had at least one official car, often a Land Rover, in most of the constituencies, the N.C.N.C. had far fewer, but both parties were usually able to supplement these from local sympathizers. Both parties had generally nursed their constituencies for some time past, and had carried on an intensive campaign at the time of registration. Nevertheless, during the election teams often set out before dawn and returned after dusk. As has been said, agreements had been made that the two parties should not campaign in the same areas on the same day. Commonly the division was made between the large town of the constituency and the more rural parts of it. The writer was present on two occasions when one party, doing a little 'unofficial' campaigning in 'bush' areas, ran into those who had the right to be there. There was tension on both occasions, but good sense prevailed, and the 'intruders' withdrew. Of course, the chances of collision were remote. The campaign teams might or might not include the candidate; they invariably contained party officials and local speakers; often there was a prominent local figure who had 'crossed the floor', and was ready to give a testimony to his new political faith.

In the towns, the parties generally contrived to hold meetings in every quarter, and even in every large compound. These took place in any available open space, preferably under a large tree. Audiences were frequently a hundred or more. Here, more often than in the villages, women's meetings might be held, particularly where there was a strong women's section of the party. As often as not, these meetings would be addressed by a man, but there was no lack of vigorous female politicians in most areas—market women's organizations provide a good training ground for politics. In some towns, many of the innumerable societies which exist in every community invited the politicians to address them.

---

[1] The mean size of the constituencies, 668 square miles, was four-and-a-half times that of British constituencies. Those in Divisions such as Oyo and Western Ijaw were twice this size, and communications were far from good.

Campaigning in the rural areas could be arduous. Many miles might have to be travelled between villages, often on roads that could scarcely be described as such. Sometimes it was necessary to walk or go by bicycle along roads that could not take a car. In the coastal belt, canoes had to be used to reach the numerous villages which were only accessible by water. Having spent some time with them in their campaigning, the writer has nothing but admiration for the stamina and determination of the politicians. They can have missed very few communities of any size or importance.

The general techniques adopted were the same in the small town meetings and in the villages. Here, even more than in the big meetings, it was unlikely that any hostile person was in the audience. The most important thing was to persuade the people to vote. Frequently, the party leaders in the locality had been warned of the approximate time when the teams would arrive. The cars would drive up, and their occupants begin to shout party calls as they approached, or simply 'Zee-ee-k' or 'Awo-o-o'. These calls would be answered from all sides, and a meeting would assemble, which might last anything from a few minutes to an hour or more. A good deal of the time was often taken up with the vilification of the opposite party; in spite of general agreements to the contrary, provocative songs were frequently sung with relish. Occasionally questions were asked by doubters; more often some of the audience would get up and speak in support. Ward captains and other local party leaders would generally join the itinerant speakers. Where loudspeakers were available, they were generally used, though they were usually not necessary and often seemed to hinder intelligibility, since humidity, dust, and the shaking caused by rough roads tended to put the equipment out of action very quickly. When larger pre-arranged meetings were held, audiences were often summoned by teams of drummers, playing for as long as half an hour. They could be heard from a distance of half a mile or more.

Action Group campaigners, and to a lesser extent others, would very commonly take with them on their journeys a dummy ballot box, bearing the party symbol. At the end of a meeting, this would be produced, the symbol on it being carefully pointed out. Several members of the team, bearing pieces of paper, would then line up, and, after demonstratively checking the symbol, insert their folded 'ballot papers'. Experience of past elections showed the need to point out that the paper had to be inserted into the box, and not left on top of it. The members of the audience would then be formed in a line, handed pieces of paper, and made to go through the motions of voting, including taking a careful look at the symbol before doing so. Sometimes the process would be repeated two or three times.

Independent candidates and those of the minority parties were not able to campaign on so lavish a scale. The amount of money they had to spend depended on their personal wealth and that of their followers, but it was never more than a small part of that available to the two major parties. Generally cars were found and loudspeakers obtained; Dr. Chike Obi, leader of the Dynamic Party, was often to be seen fighting Ibadan North-West with a bicycle plastered with the posters of his party, though he sometimes used a car. He went on a tour in support of the other candidates of his party in the course of his campaign. None of the other minor parties campaigned so flamboyantly; possibly none of them shared the Dynamic Party's confidence of complete success.

6. Press and Radio

The Press. The party newspapers played their part to the full in the campaign. The two Ibadan papers, the *South Nigerian Defender* (N.C.N.C), and the *Nigerian Tribune* (Action Group), with their small size, were devoted almost entirely to the election. Zik's *West African Pilot*, and the Action Group *Daily Service* did not go quite so far. The *Pilot* still frequently appeared with only four pages, evidence of the N.C.N.C.'s lack of funds. On 21 May (a four-page issue), the whole paper was given over to the election, with the exception of one three column-inch news item about an aeroplane crash in Canada, eight column-inches of a religious article, the radio programmes and, of course, advertisements. Even the week-end's sport was ignored. More than half the news space consisted of the text of a political broadcast by Dr. Azikiwe. On no other occasion did this paper go to quite these lengths. The *Daily Service*, because of its greater size, was always able to print a certain amount of news, though never very much. It also retained its 'features'.

The *Pilot* printed a political cartoon by its artist 'Lash' every day, though the same ones were generally reprinted at intervals. This was presumably due at least in part to the realization that the majority of its readers would not see the paper every day. The cartoons portrayed such subjects as a man labelled 'Nigerian Unity' being dealt a blow on the back of the neck by a fist labelled 'Action Group'. Two figures, entitled 'N.C.N.C.' and 'N.P.C.' look on in horror. Another showed a gorilla,[1] one of the artist's symbols for Action Group, pointing a pistol labelled 'victimization' at a line of Obas with shouldered

[1] See Plate I.

PLATE 1

a. A *West African Pilot* Cartoon

b. A *Daily Service* Cartoon

NIGERIAN POLITICAL CARTOONS

rifles. The caption was 'anyone of you not toeing the party line?'
The *Service* published cartoons sporadically; one by 'Mike' showed a
man, Action Group, guarding a house labelled 'Western Nigeria's
Treasure House', while a masked face, the N.C.N.C., peered round
a corner.[1] A 'balloon' carried the words 'If I can only get in here I
shall burgle the money for use of my govt. of the E.R.' [*sic*]. In all
these cartoons there was rarely an attempt at humour, but simply
the representation of some point or other.

The *Pilot* published a series of articles and quotations from speeches
featuring such subjects as education and the comparative records of
the governments of the Eastern and Western Regions. Its editorials
were generally split into three parts, each dealing with one topic of
this kind. Occasionally, they broke into mild vituperation, as for
instance when reference was made to 'the Action Group and its
filthy organs',[2] but the language used never reached the levels
common during the federal elections.

On the whole, the *Daily Service* appeared to concentrate rather on
the passing scene of the Action Group campaign, by means of brief
quotations from speeches. While the *Pilot* printed all the N.C.N.C.
election broadcasts in full, the *Service* only did this for Chief Awolowo's
address. A series of articles on individual candidates was clearly
intended to show that Action Group had the 'men for the job'. The
editorials each discussed one major topic; for instance, Dr. Azikiwe's
dictatorship over the N.C.N.C., the finances of the Eastern Region,
or welfare measures in the West. Another column, similar in character to the editorial, appeared on an inside page. On the revenue
allocation question, the *Service* published daily one or more slogans
such as 'Reject National Council of Crooks. It is your money they
want.' Short articles on the subject were headed 'Now it must be
monkey work, baboon chop' (i.e. food), the implication being that
if revenue were allocated between the Regions according to need,
labour in the West would not reap its full reward.

Both newspapers took pains to show that their side was not the
instigator of the minor disturbances which broke out from time to
time during the campaign. Both also indulged in 'scare' tactics,
under such headlines as 'N.C.N.C. Fanatics Plan Election Day
Invasion', or 'A.G. Intends to use Foul Methods to win Election.'
Some of the alleged 'plots' sounded, to say the least of it, improbable.

Owing to the writer's ignorance of Yoruba, it is impossible to
discuss in detail the contents of *Irohin Yoruba*, the vernacular weekly
published under the same auspices as the *Daily Service*, but its policy
seems to have been akin to that of the *Service*.

[1] See Plate I.   [2] W.A.P. 12 May 1956.

The *Daily Times* maintained a cross-bench attitude; perhaps a measure of its success in this is the fact that it was a target for the attacks, and the occasional praise, of both sides. It reported the most important parts of the speeches of the party leaders, and any other statements or happenings of interest of which it was aware. In its news columns, it seemed to avoid expressing any opinion, even on such a subject as the size of a meeting. Editorial comment on the election was forthright; praise was given where it was felt to be due, malpractices were roundly condemned. The paper never lost its interest in matters unconnected with the election; indeed, several of the editorials during the campaign period were on normal subjects. On 24 May, two days before the polling day, the editor devoted his attention to the large number of public holidays, which, he claimed, the economy of Nigeria could not afford. On the eve of poll, there was a solemn homily on the responsibilities of the voter. 'Ebenezer Williams' was given a very free hand to comment on what he saw on a tour of the Region during the campaign period. Consciously or otherwise, his style seemed to be modelled on that of an Old Testament prophet. Much of what he said was to the point, and his articles aroused considerable attention and controversy. Signed articles on different aspects of the election by other writers appeared frequently.

There was one regrettable incident in connexion with the *Daily Times* which it could not, perhaps, avoid. Not long before the election, it had begun to print a series of articles on the activities of the Western Region Production Development Board. Since these also appeared in the *Daily Service*, they were obviously a publicity 'hand out' issued by the Board; the *Pilot* naturally had nothing to do with them. Further articles in this series continued to appear in the *Times* during the campaign. Since Action Group was continually harping on the good work it had been able to do for the Region through the Board, this gave the party extra space for propaganda without charge to its funds. Equally to be deprecated was an advertisement of the Western Region Information Service which appeared in the *Daily Service* on 21 May. Under the heading 'It's a Revolution', information was given on the success of the West's primary education scheme. This tended to reinforce the claims made by Action Group during the campaign, many of them in rebuttal of the accusations of the N.C.N.C. Since this advertisement did not appear in the *Daily Times*, it can reasonably be assumed that it declined to accept it. To the credit of all concerned, it was not published a second time.

During the last three days of its campaign Action Group published a two-page advertisement in the *Daily Times* and *Daily Service*. This gave a statement of the achievements of the Action Group Government, and a twenty-two point summary of the party's programme. The N.C.N.C. did not spend money on propaganda of this sort, but it received help from outside. The 'Association of Yoruba Students in London' published a 'Message to the Voters of Western Nigeria'. This was signed by a President and Secretary, and twelve 'Executive Members', the home Division of each being given. There was an accommodation address in London. It attacked the activities of the Action Group as 'rule by terrorism, propaganda, riots and bloodshed'. It did not directly invite people to vote for the N.C.N.C., but ended:

> We will not bother you with more facts. The opportunity you now have comes once in five years. Please think well before you use your vote. *Let Nigeria remain one.* Remember that when you vote, Premiers, Ministers, Candidates and our respected Obas will not be there. You will stand alone, with no one but God to see how you cast your vote, and with no one to fear. Please use your vote wisely. May God guide you aright.

Nobody would be likely to miss the inference. Nothing was said about the standing or membership of the Association; indeed, other Yoruba students in London wrote declaring their support for Action Group, and claiming that the Association was insignificant. However, the 'Message' made an impression on quite a number of people. In conversation with the writer, several seemed to assume that he would have come across the Association while in London, though nobody in Nigeria seemed to have heard of it before. Whether the full-page reprint in the *Daily Times* on the eve of the election was paid for by the London body or N.C.N.C. is not known; a day or two before, it had been circulated by N.C.N.C. agents as a handbill printed in London.

Other printed propaganda. In whatever form, printed propaganda could only reach a very small proportion of the electorate, so that the quantity used in the election was small. Action Group placed considerable faith in the Report of its Economic Mission abroad, which had been published just as the campaign opened. The Tribune Press and other Ibadan printers were kept busy printing election addresses for those candidates who used them, as well as a number of pamphlets on local issues such as the Benin–Delta State question. Some candidates had literature printed or duplicated locally, and a small number of handbills were issued by the N.C.N.C. It was quite clear, however, that the great majority of electors, literate or otherwise, had not seen a handbill of any sort, except for the slips bearing a palm-tree or cock symbol and the injunction to vote for the relevant party. These were ubiquitous.

Although it did not circulate widely,[1] one leaflet deserves special mention. It read as follows:

N.C.N.C. MANIFESTO

WHAT WE NCNC PLAN TO DO

1. In enable us finance our free education no woman shall be a trader unless such is prepared to pay tax as men as we do in the East [sic].
2. In order to have better crops, no one will be a farmer unless he can read and write English.
3. In order to slandardise [sic] the position no one will be an Oba unless he can read and write English.
4. In order to have better status no one will be a Chief unless he can read and write English.
5. In order to save money paid to clerks no one will be a native Court judge or Assessor unless he can read and write English.
6. In order to prevent accidents, no one will be a driver unless he can read and write in English.
7. In order to improve the standard of debate no chief will go into the House of Chiefs unless he can read and write English.
8. In order to use scientific methods, no one will be a fisherman unless he or she can read English.

NCNC National Headquarters,
Commercial Avenue,
Yaba

This was distributed so near the end of the campaign that the N.C.N.C. were not able to point out to all that it had reached that it was a blatant forgery.[2] It was a sufficiently good parody of the declared policy of the N.C.N.C. for some people to be half-inclined to believe it, and fear accordingly. There is no evidence that local Action Group organizations had to do with its distribution, although in that case it is difficult to see who could have undertaken it. It seems best to regard it in the same light as the 'ration book' pamphlet of the 1955 British General Election.[3] This is the only pamphlet of its kind that the writer found; had there been others his attention would almost certainly have been drawn to them.

The Nigerian Broadcasting Service. Radio reception in most parts of the Western Region is poor, so that, apart from their cost, it is not worth most people's while to possess sets. In eleven of the large towns in the Region, however, there are rediffusion networks which

---

[1] The writer has only evidence of its distribution in the more backward parts of the Delta and in Ilesha.   [2] Even the address was wrong.

[3] Cf. D. E. Butler, *The British General Election of 1955*, pp. 93, 100.

are widely patronized;[1] it would not be difficult for anybody there to find somewhere to listen to a programme. More of the electorate was therefore likely to be reached by broadcasts than by the printed word, but still only a small proportion of it.

Excellent news coverage was given to the campaign, important speeches being well summarized and happenings of note reported. Great care was taken to see that a reasonable amount of attention was paid to all the minor parties, and that neither of the major contestants received more of the limelight than the other. In spite of the meticulous neutrality of the N.B.S., it managed to catch a good deal of the excitement of the campaign.

It had been decided that only those parties which put up a minimum of 20 per cent. of the maximum possible number of candidates should be allowed broadcasting time. When nominations were completed, it was obvious that only the two major parties would qualify. On 14 May, after nominations had closed, it was settled at a conference with the Electoral Commissioner that each was to have three half-hour evening broadcasts. A recording was to be played earlier the following evening. One speech of each party was to be heard on the National programme, the others only in Western Region transmissions. Naturally, the parties gave their leaders the Nigeria-wide broadcasts. The programme was as follows:

16 May: Chief Rotimi Williams (Action Group), Minister of Justice and Local Government.
17 May· 'Discussion' between Chief Kolawole Balogun, national secretary of the N.C.N.C., Federal Minister of Research and Information, and Dr. Sanya Onabamiro, the party's elections secretary.
20 May: Dr. Azikiwe (N.C.N.C.).
21 May: Chief Awolowo (Action Group).
22 May: Mr. A. Adelabu (N.C.N.C.).
23 May: Mr. S. L. Akintola (Action Group), Chairman of the Western Region Finance Corporation.

There is no means of assessing the effective coverage of these broadcasts. So far as could be judged from discussion, those of Chief Awolowo and Dr. Azikiwe made the greatest impression. This was not only because of their personal standing; illiterates in particular seemed to find that the way in which they concentrated on and reiterated a few points made them easier to understand. The reputed firebrand, Mr. Adelabu, permitted himself some rhetoric about the

[1] Abeokuta, Ede, Ibadan, Ife, Ijebu-Igbe, Ilesha, Ijebu-Ode, Iwo, Ogbomosho, Oshogbo, and Oyo. The total number of 'boxes' (loudspeakers) hired out was 26,789 in May 1956.

'four years' reign of terror in the Western Region'; but on the whole his speech was, like the others, a moderate enough statement, if judged by the standards of Nigerian campaigning.

Between them, the speakers covered most of the familiar arguments on each side pretty thoroughly, but there were no new issues or special incidents. It was noticeable that only Dr. Azikiwe made any attempt to meet and answer points made by opponents.

7. Polling

Administration. Some of the more important administrative arrangements for polling were announced by the Electoral Commissioner at a press conference on 3 May. Between 5,000 and 6,000 polling stations were to be set up, and these were to be kept open from 9 a.m. to 5 p.m. on the polling day, 26 May, a Saturday but not a public holiday. The ballot papers were printed outside Nigeria, and were not distributed to Electoral Officers until just before election day. There were slight differences in the form of the papers issued in each Province, as well as secret marks in the design known only to the Electoral Commissioner and the printers. Repeated warnings were issued that the use of forged ballot papers would inevitably be detected. Before being handed to the voter, the papers were authenticated by being punched with a pattern of holes.

Before issuing a ballot paper, the Polling Officer could ask the applicant if he was the person named on the register, and if he had already voted. He was obliged to do so if requested by a candidate or polling agent. The Polling Officer was also empowered to require that a voter should submit to a search to see that he did not already have a ballot paper on his person.[1] This was because in the federal elections it had been suspected that voters were taking their papers out of the polling stations to hand them to party agents, possibly for money. These agents could then see that these votes went to the 'proper' party. The power of search was not used extensively, if at all.

Immediately before voting, the elector's left thumb was marked with an indelible ink, on the ball of the thumb and the base of the nail. In the latter position, it would be difficult to remove, and would also show up very clearly.[2]

The preliminaries completed, the elector retired to a screened polling booth, where he inserted his ballot paper in a box bearing the name and symbol of the candidate he wished to support. Elaborate precautions were taken to see that the boxes were equidistant from the door. They were screwed down to a secure base in order to

---

[1] *P.L.G.E.R.* 50 (1) (*a*) (ii) and (iii).   [2] *P.L.G.E.R.* 50 (1) (*g*).

prevent a recurrence of what had happened during the federal elections. Then there had been cases of voters bringing a ballot box out of the polling booth and voting publicly. This might have been in order to claim a cash reward. Before polling began, the ballot boxes had to be shown empty to 'such persons as may lawfully be present' (i.e. the polling agents) and sealed.[1]

Reference has been made to the problem of Receipt Cards. For some days after the register became available, workers could be seen at almost any party office in the Region filling in electoral numbers on the cards they had collected at the time of registration. This indirectly gave rise to an unfortunate incident. Action Group produced cards which effectively duplicated the Receipt Cards, carrying personal particulars and the electoral number of the voter, but also bore a small palm-tree symbol. The tendering of such a card at the polling station clearly contravened the regulations forbidding 'wearing, exhibiting or tendering any notice, sign, token, symbol, slogan, badge, photograph, or party card referring to the election' inside or within 200 yards of a polling station.[2]

Two days before polling day, the Electoral Commissioner, having apparently got wind of this development, stated in a 'final warning to voters':

It is possible that cards upon which are printed party emblems or party names may be used for this purpose [i.e. presentation at polling stations].

It is illegal to tender or exhibit party cards at polling stations.

If this is done the person who tenders the party card will commit an offence—the punishment for which on conviction is a fine of £100 or imprisonment for one year.

Printed cards or pieces of paper upon which no party name or party emblem appears can be tendered or exhibited at polling stations.

This at once brought a host of protests and accusations against the Commissioner. Action Group spokesmen declared that the threat of heavy punishment would deter many from voting. Immediately after the election, influential members of the party were prepared to ascribe the loss of several seats to this occurrence. To its announcement of the results, the *Daily Service*[3] added the following 'Editor's note':

It is understood that the eve-of-election broadcast by Mr. Balmer, the Western Region Electoral Commissioner, threatening that voters who carried party cards would be sentenced, scared a lot of voters more prounnounced [*sic*] is the Egba Central Constituency, where the Action Group candidate.

---

[1] *P.L.G.E.R.* 49.   [2] *P.L.G.E.R.* 103 (2) (*e*).
[3] 28 May 1956.

Chief Akitoye Coker, was defeated by a narrow margin by his N.C.N.C. opponent.

At the meeting of the Action Group Parliamentary Party held on 2 June, Chief Awolowo made a somewhat grudging attempt to put things right. After praising the Commissioner for his part in organizing the election, he said:

> His eve of election announcement about polling cards caused some alarm and has been widely criticised. I am satisfied, however, that the Electoral Commissioner acted in good faith; and we should treat the incident as one of those accidents of life that even the most meticulous of mortals cannot sometimes avoid.[1]

Some space has been devoted to this incident because of its implications for the status of an Electoral Commissioner after the grant of self-government. It seems incontestable that only two courses were open to Mr. Balmer: either to allow this irregularity to take place on a very large scale, with the inevitable prosecutions, or to state the law clearly, as he did. It is unfortunate that Mr. Balmer was not able to issue his warning earlier, but the writer could find little evidence that the warning frightened people from voting, even in the more backward areas. It did cause party officials to withdraw the illegal cards. It is indeed strange that Action Group, which is served by so many lawyers, should ever have issued them.

Official propaganda to persuade people to vote was not so important as official propaganda for registration, but the resources of the Regional Information Service were mobilized to the full. Many of the official pamphlets issued at the time of registration had a bearing on voting. Mr. Balmer made broadcasts outlining the procedure to be followed, as well as the 'final warning' that caused so much trouble. In practice, however, the work of persuading people to vote was done largely by the political parties.

The organization for polling was analogous to that for registration. Where Registration Officers had not lost the confidence of the people, they were generally appointed Electoral Officers, but in a minority of cases others had to be chosen. After the experience of the registration, it was laid down that Electoral Officers should be appointed by the Governor, and not by the Electoral Commissioner, as the regulations had stated.[2] The writer knows of one incident in which an Electoral Officer, the Secretary of the Etsako District Council, was replaced shortly before the election, as a result of charges of

[1] D.T. 4 June 1956.
[2] Supplt. to Western Region Gazette Extraordinary (No. 21, Vol. 5), 30 April 1956.

partisanship.[1] If there were other cases of this kind, they were not numerous.

Polling officials were appointed by the Electoral Officers. Considerably more clerks were required than at registration, because of the number of duties to be performed at each polling station, even though there were considerably fewer polling stations than there had been registration offices. It was not important to keep wards separate, and the registers gave an accurate statement of the number of electors in any one ward. It was thus often possible within the framework of the regulations covering distance and numbers to combine areas covered by more than one registration office.

Voting papers, ballot boxes, and other equipment were in general distributed through administrative officers, and released only on the eve of poll. In the course of a long motor journey on that day, the writer often saw schoolchildren with the boxes on their heads, or men, presumably Presiding Officers or poll clerks, with them on the carriers of bicycles. The symbols were fixed to the boxes before they were delivered to the polling stations.

During the last few days before polling both the administration and the politicians were kept busy. The former had to mark and distribute ballot boxes, mark polling stations, in some cases build them from a wooden framework covered with matting; local party officials were using spare moments to return to their owners Receipt Cards marked with the number of the voter and his polling station.

Police were drafted into the Region from Lagos, and all available men were stationed at points where trouble was expected. On the eve of polling day, parades of police could be seen in towns everywhere. In spite of N.C.N.C. protests, it had been decided that police should not be placed in polling stations. This was partly because of the shortage of men, and probably also to forestall any possible suggestions of police pressure on voters. Instead, police were assembled at strategic points. In the event, this policy was justified.

Voting. Voting was orderly and good-humoured. There were no reports of any disturbances, apart from occasional jostling in queues. Amongst a people who have not, perhaps mercifully, acquired the habit of forming queues, this was in itself remarkable. Undoubtedly, much of the credit for the orderliness of the day's proceedings must go to the sense of responsibility which seemed to seize everybody concerned. Party leaders reiterated their appeals for calm, and there was also a speech from the Governor in the same cause. Mr. Balmer's reminder that election offences could meet with heavy penalties undoubtedly had a sobering effect upon some who heard it. It

[1] *D.T.* 21 May 1956.

must also be remembered that, although the election campaign had only been running properly for less than a fortnight, during that time it had been very intensive. It was possible to detect among both politicians and people a feeling of having had nearly enough, and that it was best to get things over decently and quickly, and to return to the normal tempo of life.

Very few people can have been shut out of the polling stations when they closed at 5 p.m. 'Vote early' was the order of the day. There were a number of complaints, some of them no doubt justified, that some stations had opened late and closed early.

On the whole everybody could be well pleased with the way things had gone all through the period of the election. There were, however, some real grounds for complaint, even for bitterness. Irregularities had occurred, blood had been shed and bones broken. It may in the long run be fortunate that Action Group won by so large a margin as to make it evident that its majority was not due to these minor incidents.

8. *The Election in Two Constituencies: (a) Oyo East*

This section and the next may serve to suggest how local issues fit into the pattern of regional politics, and what the day-to-day problems are which the politicians have to face in carrying out their tasks. But these two constituencies were selected purely for practical reasons, because they were reasonably accessible to a student working single-handed: it is not suggested that they are in any objective sense 'typical'. Each constituency has its own character and problems.

Antecedents. The constituency of Oyo East consists of the town of Oyo, having a population (1952 census) of 72,133, together with a large but sparsely populated area lying to the northward. Oyo itself is some thirty miles due north of Ibadan, on a tarred road leading from Lagos to Ilorin and the Northern Region. Nearly all the constituency is at least a thousand feet above sea-level, and the countryside is largely savannah. The soil is moderately fertile. Nearly all the people are Yorubas, and many of them make their living by farming, growing maize, cassava, yams, and similar food crops. The great majority of the farmers live in Oyo township, and move out into the small outlying villages during the farming season. The permanent population of the 'rural areas' is therefore small. There is a serious lack of roads of any sort to serve the farms, so that the crops have often to be carried long distances before they can be put on lorries. As a result, a great deal of food sometimes rots before it can be taken away. Much has been done by community effort to remedy this situation, one village clearing a roadway to the next, perhaps ten miles, and so on until the main road is reached. The District Council has given considerable help in surfacing these roads with laterite, but even so the springs of vehicles using them are put to a severe test. Many of them would be useless during the rainy season. At the present rate of road-building it will be many years before communications reach a satisfactory standard.

The town itself consists mostly of single-story houses, with a fair number of two-storied buildings. It is dominated by an imposing town hall. The market opens only at night, and is an important one. Apart from the farmers, there are numerous traders, and there are co-operatives of weavers, carvers, and leather-workers. While Oyo is by no means a poor town, it could not be described as prosperous. Until well into the present century, Oyo was the capital of Yoruba-land, in fact as well as in name. The Alafin of Oyo is the paramount chief of the Yoruba,[1] and around him much of the politics of the constituency revolves. The gate of his palace, the Afin, confronts the town hall at the other end of the main street. In recent years Ibadan has grown into the largest town in West Africa, and has completely eclipsed Oyo, to which it once paid tribute. Many Oyo people resent this, and feel that their town has been completely neglected by 'officialdom'. It lacks electricity, and the water-supply is barely adequate. When Action Group emerged as a political party just before the 1951 elections, its status as a Yoruba party and its position with regard to *Egbe Omo Oduduwa* naturally recommended it to Oyo people. It is not surprising, therefore, that all the five members returned to the House of Assembly in 1951 by Oyo Division were Action Groupers.

Many Lagos residents, who traced their descent from Oyo, and therefore regarded themselves as first and foremost Oyo people, became worried about the decline of their town. In the early 1950's the Oyo Parapo, or Oyo People's Party, was formed, not so much to enter party politics as to act as a pressure group to bring the claims of Oyo before those in authority. For some time, attempts to create an active branch of the Parapo in Oyo itself seemed abortive, and its driving force remained in Lagos.

In 1953 friction developed between the Alafin, Adeyemi II, and the newly formed Oyo Southern District Council, which was dominated by Action Group. The Alafin was an old man, and probably neither willing nor able to adapt himself to the new institutions of

---

[1] See S. Johnson, *A History of the Yorubas, passim.* pp. 41 et seq. deal particularly with the status of the Alafin.

local government. The main allegations against him were that his envoys were persecuting the people in the collection of tax, the appointment of more than one person to the same chieftaincy, receiving money to settle chieftaincy disputes, interference in cases being held in Native Courts, holding private courts in the Afin, and opposing the collection of the capitation tax.

The rights and wrongs of these accusations do not concern us here. The District Council discussed and protested against some of these alleged happenings, but felt that its advice was being ignored and its decisions overridden by the Alafin. It will readily be imagined that the town, and indeed a much wider area, became divided into two camps; those who stood behind the old traditions, symbolized by the Alafin, and those who supported the new, embodied in the District Council. Other alignments also arose; the District Council and the line it had taken became associated in men's minds with the Action Group. Similarly, the Parapo, in its role of guardian of traditions, found itself bound up with the cause of the Alafin. The N.C.N.C., as the adversary of the Action Group, was willing to give all aid and succour to the Parapo and the Alafin.

While this friction was mounting, a Mr. Johnson was sent by the Lagos branch of the Oyo Parapo to be a full-time organizer in the town, a sign of the importance that was attached to what was going on there.

In the latter half of 1954, when preparations were being made for the federal elections, tension was strong. On 5 September the Oyo Parapo arranged to hold a big meeting in the principal market place to celebrate its formal alliance with the N.C.N.C. It appears that from the middle of the day there were a number of incidents in which blows were struck and missiles thrown between members of this coalition and the supporters of the Action Group. Finally, the meeting was broken up, and a major riot ensued, with the loss of six lives and many injuries. Those killed and the owners of the worst damaged property were all Action Groupers. Political meetings and drumming were immediately banned, and the Alafin went into semi-voluntary exile at Ilesha. As was mentioned earlier, a commission of inquiry was set up, with Mr. R. D. Lloyd, a barrister, as sole commissioner.[1] He spent some weeks conducting hearings, and returned to England to prepare his report. On 17 September, ten members of the Oyo Parapo were each sentenced to 2½ years'

---

[1] Most of the facts of the riot and the earlier unrest can be gleaned from the evidence given before Mr. Lloyd (*D.T.* 27 Sept. 1954, et seq.), and from his Report (*D.T.* 8 June 1955).

imprisonment; on 16 October, ten Action Groupers were similarly found guilty.

Meanwhile, the results of the federal election for Oyo South, which comprises the House of Assembly constituencies of Oyo East and Oyo South, had given the victory to the Action Group. Its candidate, Mr. E. O. Omolodun, obtained 6,919 votes, and his rival, Mr. P. A. Afolabi, President of the Parapo, 5,477. The Parapo/ N.C.N.C. alliance fought under the name and lion symbol of the Parapo. At the end of March 1955 the elections to the Oyo Southern District Council were fought with some bitterness, Chief Awolowo and Mr. Adelabu lending their support on opposite sides.[1] This resulted in Action Group winning twenty-five seats, and the Parapo twenty-four. One of two further seats which had to be recontested because of irregularities went to each of the two parties. Both Mr. Akerele, the Action Group member of the House of Assembly, and Mr. Laniregun, the local Action Group Organizing Secretary, were defeated.

Considerable impatience began to be shown because, although it was known to have been submitted to the Western Region Government, there was no sign of Mr. Lloyd's report being released. The reason for delay became clear when it was published on 7 June 1955. After a discussion of the unrest in Oyo, and of the riot, for which he put most of the blame on the Parapo, Mr. Lloyd turned to the Alafin:

I have already stated many allegations against the Alafin—in my opinion were not justified.

There is no doubt that the Alafin has not always seen eye to eye with the Oyo Southern District Council or the Oyo Divisional Council, but he must remember that it is his duty to do all in his power to see that their decisions are carried out.

I therefore see no reason why the Alafin should continue to remain in voluntary exile.

At the same time as this Report was released, Chief Rotimi Williams, Minister of Justice and Local Government, read a statement to the press, in which he gave his reasons for disagreeing with the Commissioner on a number of points. He also said:

It is true that matters raised by the Commissioner should be taken into consideration by the Government in coming to a decision on the issue (the return from exile of the Alafin) but it should not be overlooked that Government has also to consider generally all the facts and circumstances relating to the peace, order and good government of Oyo Division.[2]

[1] Mr. Adelabu was related to the Alafin by marriage.   [2] See *D.T.* 8 June 1955.

It was clear that the Government had no intention of allowing the return of the Alafin to Oyo, at least for some time. The N.C.N.C. made this into a major issue; within ten days it had sent a team into the Region to campaign against the decision.[1] The Oyo Parapo/ N.C.N.C. alliance became to all intents and purposes one body— the N.C.N.C.—although there are many influential people in Oyo who appear to consider themselves first and foremost Parapos, and look to the day when they can resume their separate identity. For the time being, at least, they found complete unity in working for the return of the Alafin.

Party organization. The Action Group organizing secretary, Mr. D. Laniregun (otherwise Olaniregun), is a fairly prosperous farmer, probably below middle age. He is a member of one of the chieftaincy families of Oyo, and has taken an active interest in politics for many years, having originally been a member of the N.C.N.C. The party has a small office staff in Oyo, serving the Division as a whole. Some time before the campaign began, the constituency was provided with a Land Rover, equipped with loudspeakers, and with a full-time driver.

Mr. Akerele, the sitting member, was readopted as the candidate. He is Chief Awolowo's partner in a firm of solicitors, and a member of the Western Region Production Development Board. Born in 1914, he is a native of Oyo and has a large house there. The stoning of Mr. Akerele's car as he entered the town was the first act of violence in the riot of 1954.

In addition to Mr. Johnson, who has been mentioned above as having been sent from Lagos to help organize the Parapo, the N.C.N.C. in the constituency had the services of two other full-time secretaries. These, Mr. C. O. John and Mr. S. F. Abatan, are also from Lagos, but trace their descent from Oyo. They are both young, while Mr. Johnson is probably past middle age. The N.C.N.C. did not have a car until some days after the dissolution, when a large private car and driver came up from Lagos. On its arrival, the loud-speaker system was found to be defective, and it had to return for this to be repaired. This car had to be shared with the other four constituencies in the Division, but spent a great deal of time in Oyo East.

While there is no direct information on this point, it seems reasonable to infer from the fact that the N.C.N.C. did not normally spend money on three paid officers in a constituency that a great deal of the responsibility for the party organization rested with the Parapo. The car lent from Lagos had the appearance of being the property of a private person, presumably a well-wisher there.

[1] *D.T.* 17 June 1956.

The party had a small office just off the market place, large enough to contain a table where a few helpers, mostly volunteers, could do clerical work without the advantage of much privacy. The residences of the secretaries of both parties seemed to play a more important part than the office of either of them.

Mr. Afolabi, the N.C.N.C. candidate, was headmaster of a Lagos secondary school. He once taught Mr. Akerele. He was an early member and president of the Oyo Parapo, and had played an important part in the politics of the town.[1] In the federal election he was defeated by Action Group, in spite of the vigorous campaign then going on in Oyo over the capitation tax. It will be remembered that this election took place after the riot, but before the publication of the Lloyd Report and Action Group's declaration of its attitude towards the Alafin.

At the time of registration, the N.C.N.C. claimed to have brought in nearly a thousand 'natives' of the town, mainly from Lagos, and to have registered them successfully. Transport was provided in the lorries of well-wishers. A number of these certainly returned to vote, but it is not known how many.

To sum up, the parties were, in their different ways, well equipped to fight an election. All the secretaries were able and intelligent men, dedicated to their cause, but capable of approaching their task realistically. Although the N.C.N.C. lacked such things as adequate transport, it was blessed with a larger organizing staff, and was campaigning on one burning issue. Both parties were well aware of the importance of the female vote, and had women's organizations. The N.C.N.C. women's leader, Madam Peters, was a most colourful personality. The writer only heard her speak in Yoruba, but it was evident that she had a great gift for carrying an audience with her.

Campaigning. Because of the background of violence in Oyo great care had to be taken in arranging meetings so as to avoid inter-party clashes. Detailed arrangements were made with the District Adviser, setting out the precise place and time of each party's meetings, on the general basis that on alternate days one party should campaign in the town while the other worked in the rural areas. Probably through a genuine misunderstanding, this arrangement broke down on at least one occasion known to the writer. One of the parties went into a village where it had a permit to hold a meeting, to find the other's car there. An unpleasant situation might have developed; supporters of the two parties confronted each other, and there were many heated words; blows seemed about to be struck.

---

[1] Like Mr. Laniregun and Mr. Akerele, he gave evidence at some length before Mr. Lloyd.

Fortunately, there was a meeting of secretaries, and the intruding party agreed to withdraw into another part of the village while the meeting was going on. Not long after the campaigners had left, the rival car also departed, and those who had withdrawn themselves came back into the centre of the village, still in a belligerent mood. There was further shouting, but this gradually died down. The whole incident was a reminder that feeling was not far off boiling-point.

Within the town itself, the leaders of both parties held big meetings, drawing audiences which filled the principal market place—certainly over 5,000 persons. In each case, the audiences consisted almost entirely of supporters. Police were much in evidence on both occasions, but their services were not required. Chief Awolowo, speaking on 10 May, devoted most of his attention to economic questions, alleging that the Eastern Region was on the 'brink of collapse'. The original date of Dr. Azikiwe's meeting had to be changed, because 20 May, when his published itinerary said he would be speaking in Oyo, was a day reserved for Action Group. It is not known how often similar occurrences happened elsewhere. The problem was an awkward one for the N.C.N.C., as Dr. Azikiwe's plans had to be made to fit the itinerary of his tour; Chief Awolowo, working largely from Ibadan, was not so restricted. In the event, 'Zik' spoke in Oyo on the 19th. This was one of those occasions when he did little but introduce 'his friends' in English, the rest of the meeting being held in Yoruba. Both Mr. Afolabi and Madam Peters spoke. Needless to say, the Alafin question loomed large.

On its own initiative, the local N.C.N.C. arranged another market-place meeting to be addressed by Mr. Adelabu. It was perhaps fortunate that on that day he did not appear; a warrant was out for his arrest in connexion with the disturbances in Ijebu Ode, and the police did not find him to serve him with it until the following day.[1] There was an element among the younger Action Group members in Oyo who would not have objected to Mr. Adelabu appearing and speaking, but threatened to do violence to his 'bodyguard' if it appeared, as it undoubtedly would have done. Numerous police and the Divisional Adviser were present to deal with any possible trouble, but after waiting for over two hours the crowd finally dispersed when it was clear that Mr. Adelabu was not going to appear that day.

The politicians appeared to have very little doubt that most people

---

[1] See *D.T.* 18 May 1956. There were demonstrations against the issue of the warrant, and an appeal to the Governor. His deputy said that it was not the place of the Governor to interfere with the course of justice and the normal processes of the law. Mr. Adelabu surrendered to the police, was released on bail, and subsequently acquitted on all counts.

PLATE 2

a. Chief Awolowo

b. Dr. Azikiwe

NIGERIAN LEADERS ADDRESSING MEETINGS

had made up their minds which side they supported, but nobody seemed to be sure how large a proportion of the electorate would vote. Although it was the farming season, a traditional festival brought a large proportion of the people from the farming areas into the town for the better part of a week. During that time many of the smaller farming villages were practically deserted, and their inhabitants could be 'got at' in the town.

Town meetings followed the usual pattern; groups of perhaps fifty meeting in a vacant piece of ground, and being addressed by two or three local politicians. In the rural areas, the method of campaigning of the two parties differed, largely on account of their different resources. Action Group, with the exclusive use of a Land Rover in the constituency, was able to go from village to village, starting at dawn and returning at dusk, holding 'whistle stop' meetings. Because of the sparse population, more time had to be taken travelling than in actual speaking. Often roads were traversed which seemed to be almost impassable. Messrs. Akerele and Laniregun were sometimes joined by two prominent local people who had left the N.C.N.C. in the previous few months. At most of the meetings, a practice ballot box was produced, and the audience were invited to go through the motions of casting a vote.

For some days towards the end of the campaign, Mr. Akerele went with the Land Rover to the northern part of the constituency, known as Ikoyi, while Mr. Laniregun held the fort in Oyo and concerned himself principally with administration.

The N.C.N.C.'s relative lack of transport was largely compensated for by its having three responsible officers, who amongst them could supervise a wide area. It appears that the party believed that the die had been cast long before the campaign opened, and Mr. Johnson, at any rate, did not seem much perturbed at delays such as that caused by the loudspeaker being defective.[1] He appeared content to go on with the marking of electors' names on their Receipt Cards, a large number of which had been collected at the time of registration. This is not to suggest that the party did not also campaign vigorously.

Meetings in the outlying villages aroused considerable interest amongst those who were at leisure to attend them, though the numbers seemed invariably to be small, usually thirty or less. On one occasion (and one only), the writer saw money being passed to an audience 'to buy some palm wine'. Almost certainly, this would not have bought a single vote, nor was it intended to, but it might have created that little extra goodwill which would induce people

[1] The Action Group's loudspeakers also gave trouble, and were out of action for some of the time.

to go to the trouble of voting. Allegations of bribery were frequently made by members of both parties, but no real evidence of it was ever produced. No doubt instances of improper influence did occur, but the official party organizations were almost certainly not connected with them. There was one regrettable incident during the campaign. On May 12 a minor disturbance broke out in which five people were injured, one seriously. This was not directly connected with the campaign; it appears to have resulted from a private quarrel in which politics was involved.

Polling day. A journey by road from Ibadan to Oyo before the polls opened made it clear that great interest was being taken by the electors. There were large queues outside every polling station and by 9 a.m. many of these queues appeared to contain practically all the 500 people of voting age for whom each station was supposed to cater. Women were out in force, attended, of course, by numerous children. Many shops were shut, and the atmosphere somewhat resembled that of a fête. Outside the police station were two lorries, back to back, loaded with steel-helmeted police armed with batons and wicker shields. About 9.30 a few of them were called upon to deal with a disturbance in one of the queues at a polling station in the market place, caused by the fact that people at the back were not satisfied with the speed at which polling was taking place. This was soon settled. Later on in the morning, one of the police lorries disappeared, presumably to 'show the flag' in other parts of the constituency; it soon returned. About midday, one lorry was left unmanned, and some time later the crew of the other also retired to the police station, where they were doubtless ready if called upon.

A tour of some of the outlying villages during the morning showed that those where there was no polling station were practically empty. The roads were almost devoid of lorry and other traffic and it was not surprising that the polling was as heavy as it was.

About half an hour before the close of poll a storm hit Oyo town, but did not extend over much of the constituency. Where it occurred, it effectively stopped the day's proceedings, putting some of the temporary polling stations out of action completely. By that time, however, practically everybody had voted, and there were no vocal complaints. There were some who averred that a few polling stations had opened late, but nobody seemed very much perturbed about this.

On polling day, of course, the activities of the politicians were severely limited, being virtually restricted to watching for irregularities. Both the N.C.N.C. and the Action Group offices had to be closed because they were within 200 yards of polling stations. Signs on them were obscured or removed. The regulations forbade the use of cars to convey voters to the poll, so that this traditional occupation of British politicians on polling day was denied them. In fact, nothing was done on the day itself to 'get out the vote'. Possibly the administrative problems of so doing are too great, otherwise this might pay dividends in a future election.

The result. The result of the election was:

P. A. Afolabi (N.C.N.C.)	.	20,280
A. Akerele (A.G.)	.	17,570
N.C.N.C. majority .	.	2,710

A close result was not unexpected. With 48,676 voters on the register, the poll was just under 78 per cent., a tribute not only to the intensity of feeling in the constituency, but also to the hard work of the politicians. Nothing is known of the canvass figures of Action Group, but at the beginning of the period the N.C.N.C. believed it had just under 10,000 supporters, and felt reasonably confident of winning on the strength of this. Thus the poll was at least twice as large as they had expected, and this provides an example of how difficult it is as yet for a political party to keep its finger on the pulse of the electorate.

In Oyo Division, two of the other four seats went to each of the parties, tending to follow the pattern of traditional allegiances.[1] The most substantial Action Group majority was in Oyo South, the terrain of the Bashorun, the Alafin's principal adversary.[2] This lends strength to the view that in Oyo East the Alafin issue was also the key factor.

Needless to say, the N.C.N.C. construed the result in Oyo East in particular, and Oyo Division as a whole, as a 'mandate' for the return of the Alafin, but Action Group replied, reasonably enough, that the majorities were not significant. The aggregate N.C.N.C. poll in Oyo Division was 54,460, and Action Group won 53,188 votes: 76 per cent. of the electorate voted.

Thus the election failed to solve the problem which many people in Oyo hoped it would solve. On 6 July the Action Group Government declared the exiled Alafin deposed, and a week later six of the eight traditional kingmakers chose a successor. Probably the quarrel is not yet at an end, but the manner in which the people of Oyo conducted themselves during the election marks a great advance over the happenings of September 1954.

[1] Oyo C. (N.C.N.C.); Oyo N. (A.G.); Oyo S. (A.G.); Oyo W. (N.C.N.C.).
[2] A. O. Adeyi (A.G.), 8,364; S. K. Aiyegore (N.C.N.C.), 2,644.

9. The Election in Two Constituencies: (b) Warri East

Antecedents. The constituency of Warri East lies in the Niger Delta. It consists of the township of Warri, at the head of the mouth of the Forcades River, and of two other District Council areas, Ode-Itsekiri and Ogbe-Ijaw. Warri Town is almost entirely a growth of the past forty years, and its livelihood depends on its being an important seaport. Timber, palm kernels, palm oil, and rubber are the principal exports, miscellaneous goods are imported. The road virtually ends at Warri, access to the rest of the constituency being by water. The common mode of transport is by canoes, ranging from small dugouts to boats 50 or 60 feet long. Warri Town has a population of about 20,000, many of whom are traders, either wholesale, or distributing imports on a smaller scale. Many of the 10,000 or so Creeks people in the constituency are fishermen. The nature of the countryside makes agriculture on a substantial scale impossible; only a few crops are grown, mainly for family consumption. Contacts with European traders have gone on for a very long time; cannon and other relics of ancient trading stations are to be seen in many of the Creek villages.[1]

The population of the town is roughly 38 per cent. Urhobo, 28 per cent. Ibo, and 15 per cent. Itsekiri; the other 19 per cent. are members of various small tribes, with a few Yorubas. The Itsekiris are mainly a Creeks people, and comprise the majority in that part of the constituency, while the Urhobos have their roots inland. Warri Town is on the boundary of the lands of both tribes, and the politics of the town largely hinge on this fact. These have been well summarized by Mr. Lloyd,[2] and are briefly as follows. The Itsekiri, because of their geographical distribution, were the people who came most into contact with European traders, and acted as the go-between between them and other tribes, notably the Urhobos. This gave them a position of superiority which they continue to assert, especially since a part of their ancient traffic was in Urhobo slaves.[3] In 1932 a case heard before the Privy Council led to a ruling to the effect that the land on which the town stood was part of the Itsekiri domain. In 1955, when the Warri Urban District Council (one of the very few U.D.C.'s in Nigeria) was set up, the Olu of Warri, the Itsekiri paramount chief, was made chairman *ex officio*.

These factors, none of which has any great practical significance in

---

[1] See K. O. Dike, *Trade and Politics in the Niger Delta* (Oxford, 1956), *passim*.

[2] See P. C. Lloyd, *Tribalism and Politics in Warri* (Proceedings of the West African Institute of Social and Economic Research Conference, Ibadan, 1956).

[3] Most of the slaves were not Urhobos, but came from the slave markets farther inland, Urhobos acting as additional middlemen.

itself, have tended to make the Urhobos anxious to fight against what they feel to be a lack of recognition of their true status.[1] In September 1952 an attack was launched on an Itsekiri demonstration to welcome Chief Arthur Prest, then a federal minister, who is regarded—at least by the Urhobos—as the champion of the claims of the Itsekiri. Fighting ensued, and Itsekiri houses were sacked. The memory of this tended to bring tribalism to the fore in the politics of the town and constituency, so that now the Itsekiris can almost be equated with the Action Group, and the Urhobos with the N.C.N.C. There are exceptions to this, however, largely on the Itsekiri side. Chief Festus Okotie-Eboh, for example, is an Itsekiri[2] but a member of the N.C.N.C. He is federal Minister of Labour. At the election to the Warri Urban District Council, held in 1955, 14 Urhobos were chosen (13 N.C.N.C., 1 A.G.), 3 Itsekiris (1 A.G., 2 Independent N.C.N.C.), and 4 Ibos, all N.C.N.C. The Ibos, incidentally, are not involved in the local tribal conflict in any way. The Olu of Warri is a wholehearted supporter of Action Group.

The three predominant languages, Urhobo, Ibo, and Itsekiri, are so different from each other that English, or at any rate pidgin English, is universally spoken. This greatly simplified the work of following what was happening.

Registration. Some reference has been made to this earlier. Whether it was that the politicians realized that they could exploit tribal feeling for their own ends, or whether the tribes more or less spontaneously realized that the register could be used as a trial of their relative strength is not known; probably the former. However that may be, the idea gained currency that the register would be an indication of who 'owned' the town, probably with a view to its use in local government rather than parliamentary elections. Many Itsekiris were brought in to claim 'native' qualifications from Sapele and other areas where they were in a small minority, and the Urhobos retaliated by bringing in members of their tribe from outside also. Altogether there were some 13,000 such importations. Such a large-scale enterprise was remarkable in itself, but it was not backed by an equally efficient organization. Naturally enough, each party objected to the other's 'native' voters, and tended to submit a form of objection to any member of the opposite tribe they did not know.[3] The result, which has been described earlier, was that in the

---

[1] Mr. Lloyd has found that the Urhobos own 47 per cent. of the house property in the town, the Itsekiris 41 per cent.

[2] Some Itsekiri Action Groupers profess to doubt this. A pen portrait of Chief Okotie-Eboh is in *West Africa*, 12 Feb. 1955, p. 221.

[3] This could easily be done, since Urhobo and Itsekiri names are distinctive.

end nearly 9,000 names were struck off the register, which then comprised 17,301 names.

The candidates. Action Group seem to have agreed on the candidature of Chief Reece Edukugho sometime before the election. He is an Itsekiri, a prosperous trader, probably not yet middle-aged. Although when the writer was in Warri at the end of January Chief Edukugho was generally assumed to be the candidate, a rumour, probably N.C.N.C. inspired, arose at a later date that Chief Prest had been considered and rejected; it is in fact unlikely that he would ever have allowed his name to go forward, since he was already a member of the Federal House of Representatives.

The N.C.N.C. were not so fortunate. In January everyone seemed to take it as a foregone conclusion that Mr. Ovie Whisky would be its candidate. He had played a large part in fighting the party's cause at the hearing of claims and objections, and appeared to be generally popular in its ranks. The story of what happened subsequently is confused, but the main points seem to be beyond dispute, and are as follows.

In spite of their unequal size, the three district council areas making up the constituency each sent six delegates to the selection meeting. It was assumed that these delegations would contain a proper proportion of the minority tribe in their area. Warri and Ogbe-Ijaw both did this, but Ode-Itsekiri sent six Itsekiris. Protests were unavailing, and finally the Urhobos boycotted the meeting. The 'rump' of Itsekiris that were left selected Mr. M. Kubenje, an Itsekiri lawyer. Appeals against this were made to Dr. Azikiwe, who went to Warri just before nomination day. According to the report in the *Daily Times,* which agrees substantially with the writer's own information,[1] 'Zik' was at first inclined to order a new selection to be made. Chief Okotie-Eboh, who was chairman of the selection committee, and is, it will be remembered, an Itsekiri, took this as a reflection on his integrity. He threatened to resign his federal ministry and his seat in the House of Representatives. Obviously, the N.C.N.C. could not afford to allow tribal feeling to have too much publicity in its affairs. Lawyer Whisky (an Urhobo barrister) saved the day by announcing his support for Mr. Kubenje—a pledge which he most certainly kept.

The Urhobo tribal organizations also decided not to carry the matter further, but some members of the tribe were still disgruntled. Two of them announced their intention of standing as Independents,

---

[1] *D.T.* 14 June 1956. This refers to 'the N.C.N.C. candidate for Urhobo', meaning, of course, Warri East.

but finally Mr. I. Okandeji, an Urhobo lawyer, stood alone as the protest candidate. His symbol was the lion.

Party organization. Action Group had maintained an organization in Warri for a considerable time before the election, under the chairmanship of Chief Elliott Begho, a schoolmaster and manager of an important Warri school. Since 1953, the Division, which contains the two constituencies of Warri East and Warri West, had had a paid organizing secretary. Direction of the campaign was shared between the Divisional and Constituency Committees, the membership of which overlapped considerably. During the campaign, the party claimed to be employing about a hundred messengers and junior clerks. Within the wards, there generally appeared to be an efficient *ad hoc* organization.

The party was not issued with an official car; Chief Kubenje's own car, painted a brilliant red and yellow, was pressed into service for the campaign on land. A portable public address system was used. Action Group also used a large canoe flying the party's flag.

The N.C.N.C.'s organization was in many ways a contrast. Some attempt had been made to set up a Divisional Committee, but this had never done more than appoint organizing secretaries and the like. The campaign was run by a Constituency Committee. Nearly all those concerned were part-timers; the two Secretaries were employees of Messrs. John Holt's transport department, and were given no time off for electioneering.[1] Thus, they were only able to do this in the afternoons and evenings. This defect was largely compensated for by the presence during the last week of the campaign of the Eastern Regional Minister for Health, Mr. D. I. Okpara, together with his private secretary, Mrs. Ekpo, who campaigned in the Delta generally.

This delegation had transport of its own. Apart from this, the N.C.N.C. was equipped with a loudspeaker van, which arrived from Lagos on 11 May, and with an outboard motor for a canoe. These were for the use of the Division as a whole, including Warri West. One of the loudspeakers was damaged in an accident *en route* from Lagos, allegedly through the fault of the driver. He was dismissed, and the van was driven by local volunteers.

Campaigning. Very little excitement was detectable in Warri at the time of the campaign. There seemed to be two reasons for this. There had been mild disillusionment because the result of all the excitement over registration had been slight and many had been turned voteless away. After this came the affair of the N.C.N.C. candidature.

[1] The position in Warri reinforces the view that the Parapo had something to do with the staffing of the Oyo N.C.N.C.

The great issue was no longer that of tribal supremacy, on which the politics of the area had for so long been based.

When Dr. Azikiwe came to Warri he was first confronted with the dispute in the party. He held his meeting in the sports stadium on 11 May, before the question of the candidate had been decided, so that he was not able to be specific even on the tribal question. He did challenge Chief Awolowo to produce the list of Action Group candidates, presumably to forestall any questioning as to why he himself did not introduce an N.C.N.C. candidate for Warri East. Rain brought the meeting to a premature end. Mrs. Ekpo held a more successful meeting in the Town Hall on 22 May. This was generally admitted to be full. Some very large claims were made for the number in the audience, but to judge from the size of the building it was probably 800 at the most. At a meeting held at Oghara, in Urhobo West constituency, twenty-five miles or so from Warri, 'Zik' made some remarks which had some relevance to the Warri campaign. He accused the Action Group of 'vindictive acts against the Urhobo people', and suggested that no Urhobo had been made a minister in the Western Cabinet because Urhobos do not support the Action Group. He went on to imply that the number of seats in Urhobo Division had been reduced from six to three for the same reason.

Chief Awolowo came to Warri on 15 May. Taking up Dr. Azikiwe's point, he reminded his audience that there was only one Urhobo in the Action Group Parliamentary Party, Mr. J. G. Ako. He had been made a Parliamentary Secretary as soon as he had crossed the floor from the N.C.N.C., 'even though his sincerity to the party was being tested'. Earlier, the Premier had remarked, 'You cannot make a man a minister unless he is a party member.' He also said that if anybody hated the people of Urhobo, it was Dr. Azikiwe. In the Federal Government, Chief Okotie-Eboh had been made a minister, but, he alleged, no Urhobo had received recognition.[1]

Campaigning in the town produced nothing unexpected. Action Group claimed that 200 Delta people working in the Eastern Region had returned to help them in their campaign.[2] Certainly, the Action Group team contained a number of them. Action Group meetings were often summoned by a team of drummers, playing at an ever-increasing tempo. Theirs were not the 'talking' drums of the Yoruba.

The tribal question having been put out of court by events, life in the Eastern Region became an important topic. It must be remembered that the Delta is in almost as good communication with the Eastern Region as with the West. Social services and the Economic

[1] *D.S.* 14 June 1956.   [2] Ibid.

Mission were discussed; this latter subject gained in interest because, in the previous few months, the prosperity of Warri had shown a decline, most clearly marked by a reduction in the number of people attending the various places of amusement in the town.

Many people felt that both parties made a mistake in allowing their meetings to cover too many topics at once, instead of dealing with only one or two in a distinct manner. There was also a tendency to use too involved language. English may be the *lingua franca*, but it is most definitely pidgin English.

For the Creeks campaigning, the candidates certainly needed all their youth and stamina. It meant setting off at dawn, and returning at dusk. The Creeks villages were thoroughly covered. Action Group teams were generally led by a Chief, and a circular letter, signed by Chief Begho, was sent in advance to the local leaders asking them to see that 'their' people were ready to receive the delegation. The date was given, and it was stated whether the team was expected to arrive in the morning or the afternoon. There was no evidence of such careful organization on the part of the N.C.N.C., though campaigning seemed to be carried out efficiently enough. Apparently local party organizations existed almost everywhere.

Lawyer Okandeji's campaigning was much more happy-go-lucky. After the first excitement over the candidature, many Urhobos had had second thoughts, and abandoned the idea of supporting an Independent. He was quite frank about the fact that he had little idea of the size of his support. When the writer visited him, he was keeping almost an open house, and made no bones about discussing the situation before anyone who might be there. The most important part of his campaigning impedimenta was a large megaphone.

The Olu of Warri did not do any active campaigning, but he is reported to have stated publicly, in the course of a strongly pro-Action Group speech, that it would be impossible for the N.C.N.C. to come to power in the West. 'Anyone who holds that idea should discard it.'

Campaign literature. The campaign in Warri was remarkable for the amount of literature produced. Here and elsewhere in Benin and the Delta, Action Group circulated a pamphlet, printed in Ibadan, about the Benin–Delta State question. It suggested that the N.C.N.C. had won the federal election in the area by promising to set up such a state, but accused it of failing to support the motion to create it which was later passed in the Western House of Assembly. It ended:

The Action Group would like to call the attention of these people to the fact that as the N.C.N.C. has never redeemed any of its promises, the people of Benin and Delta Provinces cannot hope for a Succour from the N.C.N.C. Party of which Festus Okotie-Eboh is the National Treasurer. THE SALVATION OF THE BENIS, IJAWS, ITSEKIRIS, THE URHOBOS, ETC., IS IN THE HANDS OF THE ACTION GROUP.

Vote for the Palm Tree
Vote for Action Group.

In some of the Creek villages, but not in the town itself, the 'mock N.C.N.C.' pamphlet[1] was distributed towards the end of the campaign, so that the N.C.N.C. scarcely had time to do anything to counter it. Possibly its reference to the compulsory use of English would not have caused as much worry in this part of the world as it would have done elsewhere, but its suggestion of a literacy test would. It certainly disturbed not a few.

Chief Edukugho produced a 10 in. × 7½ in. handbill, locally printed, bearing a photograph of himself. A summary of developments in the Western Region ended:

YET THIS VAST PROGRESS IS JUST A BEGINNING.
VOTE FOR PALM TREE.

Then came a promise to demand greater facilities for the constituency:

You need a man with the Practical Experience of your needs to fight your battle.
I AM SURE YOU WILL AGREE THAT SUCH A MAN IS CHIEF R. EDUKUGHO.
Vote for Palm Tree.

If you vote for Palm Tree you are asking for better Medical Facilities.

If you vote for Chief Reece Edukugho, you are asking for better standard of living.

If you vote for Palm Tree you are ensuring for better Communication Facilities.

If you vote for Chief Reece Edukugho, you are ensuring the use of a Latent Political Talent that will bring you progress that will make life worth living.

If you vote for Palm Tree you are voting for Self Government in 1956, and Freedom for All and Life more Abundant.

VOTE FOR PALM TREE.

The N.C.N.C. distributed a large (20 in. × 28½ in.) poster:

VOTE FOR THE COCK
Z – E – E – K.

The members of the Urhobo Renascent Convention[2] have implicit trust in the ideology, manifesto and the leadership of the N.C.N.C.

[1] Above, p. 70.
[2] This is not to be confused with the Urhobo Progressive Union, which P. C. Lloyd (op. cit.) describes as 'having as its main aim to foster Urhobo unity, and to

As long as the NCNC does not depart from its ideology there will be no thinking otherwise.

We are confidently NCNCers.

The Urhobo Action Groupers in Warri are trying to deceive the Urhobo NCNCers with FALSE SLOGANS to caricature their senses with sentiments.

THEY HAVE PRESENTED A BARRISTER WHO IS A GROUPER TO CONTEST THE ELECTION ON THE PRETENCE THAT ALL URHOBOS SHOULD VOTE FOR THE URHOBO CANDIDATE WITH A VIEW TO SPLITTING THE NCNC VOTE FOR THE ACTION GROUP CANDIDATE TO WIN THE ELECTION IN WARRI EAST CONSTITUENCY.

The Urhobo Renascent Convention on behalf of the entire Urhobo NCNCers object to be used as a tool by brainless Groupers.

Urhobos who are NCNCers will vote for the NCNC candidate no matter from what tribe they may emanate.

ALL URHOBOS WILL THEREFORE VOTE FOR THE COCK
THE SYMBOL OF THE NCNC

The Lion is a private symbol of the Action Group

Therefore do not be deceived.

YOU MUST NOT, REPEAT NOT VOTE FOR PALM TREE
,,   ,,   ,,   ,,   ,,   ,,   ,,   LION

VOTE FOR THE COCK.
Long live Dr. Azikiwe

URHOBO RENASCENT CONVENTION
Publicity Office, Warri.

Mr. Okandeji circulated a small (8 in. × 5¼ in.) handbill. Above a representation of the 'lion' symbol was the injunction:

VOTE FOR THE LION
Champion and Defender of your Rights and Liberties.

And underneath it:

VOTE Solidly for IROLIKI OKANDEJI And Be Sure That The Many Problems Facing This Great Metropolis Will Be Solved.

Polling. The writer was in Oyo on the polling day, but reports indicate that nothing unusual happened in Warri. The distribution of the ballot boxes and other material was undertaken by the District Office, and much of the transport was by canoe. Some of the steel ballot boxes had suffered damage in transit to Warri, and the lids were difficult to remove and replace.

Because of ill feeling created at the time of registration, and a number of subsequent unsubstantiated attacks on his integrity, the Clerk to the Urban District Council was replaced as Electoral Officer.

ensure that in the race for progress the Urhobos are not left solely with the crumbs dropped from the table by other tribes'. It would appear to be simply an agency of the N.C.N.C.

Polling officers in some of the more remote parts of the constituency had to proceed to their posts on the day before polling day, but the collection of the ballot boxes was so well organized that the results were out on the 27th.[1]

Action Group sent out a cyclostyled 'Instruction to all Polling Agents'. This gave an indication of the more important points which the agents had to watch, and laid down that they were to 'follow up the Polling Officer' each time he entered the polling station. They were also to accompany the ballot boxes to the 'place of safety' after the close of the poll. Agents in the Creeks area were to be at their stations at least twenty-four hours before polling began, presumably a precaution in case they were delayed *en route* there. In the Urban District Council area, they had to be on duty by 7 a.m.

It shall be the duty of the Agent to see to it that all Action Group Party Members and sympathisers line up orderly at their Polling Stations long before voting begins, so as to ensure easy and timely voting.

Nothing suggests that the N.C.N.C. were in a position to organize their agents so thoroughly, but they announced their intention of paying them for their services at the regional minimum wage of 5s. for the day.

The result. The result of the election was:

R. D. Edukugho (A.G.) . . .	5,810
M. Kubenje (N.C.N.C.) . . .	5,376
T. Okandeji (Ind.) . . .	121
A.G. majority	434

The most interesting thing about these results is the smallness of Mr. Okandeji's support, in so far as it is a measure of unalloyed Urhobo tribalism in the constituency. It is almost certain that nearly all the Urhobos voted N.C.N.C.; nevertheless, they saw their interests as being represented by a party, even when its candidate was a member of the rival tribe. Clearly, there had been some rethinking.

10. *The Election in Retrospect*

The results. In tabular form, the results of the election were as follows:[2]

SEATS WON

Action Group	48
N.C.N.C.	32
Others	0

[1] The result for Warri West was a day later than this, but the problems of organization there were even greater.   [2] Derived from *D.T.* 30 May 1956.

VOTES CAST

Action Group	.	.	.	.	.	623,826	48·3% of total
N.C.N.C.	.	.	.	.	.	584,556	45·3% ,,
Independents	.	.	.	.	.	64,388	5% ,,
N.C.L.P.	.	.	.	.	.	5,401	0·4% ,,
N.C.P.	.	.	.	.	.	5,133	0·4% ,,
Dynamic Party	.	.	.	.	.	4,841	0·4% ,,
N.P.P.	.	.	.	.	.	3,029	0·2% ,,

The most obvious result was the complete eclipse of the Independents and the minority parties. To a great extent this can be explained by the greater facilities available to the principal parties, both during and before the elections. Most of their branches had been open and active for some time, their organizations had often a hard core of full-time workers, and the people had been exposed to their propaganda for at least five years.

A glance at Map 3 will show that there is an almost complete correlation between the seats won by each of the parties and the factors referred to in Section 1 above. The non-Yoruba areas in the east of the Region voted almost solidly for the N.C.N.C., and Yorubaland for Action Group. Exceptions such as Warri and Oyo, Ibadan or Ilesha could readily have been expected. What was surprising was tha t local victories should generally have been so clear-cut. Only 23 out of the 78 contested seats were won with majorities of less than 3,000, although the mean poll was smaller than 16,500 per constituency. By British standards few even of these smaller majorities could be regarded as 'marginal'; all close contests were in areas where there were strong local issues.

Tribal feeling was therefore the main influence in determining party allegiance, but it must be borne in mind that many who might have voted did not do so. The poll for the whole of the Region was 68 per cent. of the registered voters, but there were many who did not take the trouble to register. It may safely be said that only about half of those who might have registered and voted actually did so. Forty-eight of the seventy-eight constituencies where voting took place polled between 58 per cent. and 78 per cent. of their registered voters. There were few extreme departures from the average; in Okitipupa South less than 37 per cent. of the electorate voted; in Okitipupa North the poll was only 46 per cent., in Aboh East 41 per cent. At the other extreme, the poll in Ishan East was 87 per cent.; in Ishan West it was 81 per cent. Benin West polled 82 per cent. of its electorate, as did Oshun South. It is difficult to find satisfactory reasons for the exceptional percentages. In Ishan, strong local and tribal feeling was involved, while in Okitipupa communications were bad and party organizations were apparently not all they might have been, though a large proportion of the population had registered. Intensity of local feeling seems to have been a major influence on the size of the poll; good party organization was also important. Often these were interrelated. Except in Okitipupa, there was little correlation between the heaviness of polling and the 'developed' or 'undeveloped' state of the constituency concerned; five of the eight Ibadan constituencies, in one of the most 'developed' parts of Nigeria, had a poll of less than 60 per cent. Nor does the literacy rate seem to have had much bearing on the heaviness of polling. In several of the areas where there was a low poll, markedly fewer women than men had registered. This suggests that inefficiency on the part of the party organizations was a contributory cause; however, polling was heavier than the average in Ilesha, where the number of women registered was very low.

For the future, the very large number of people who did not vote, or even take the trouble to register, must be of great importance to the parties. In the absence of thorough local studies, it is not possible to do more than give impressions of the reasons for abstention, and the value of these is reduced by the fact that it was easier to discuss such matters with some sections of the community than with others. Many non-voters with whom the writer spoke were reasonably content with their lot, and felt that government by either party would suit them equally well. Others believed that what went on in Ibadan would affect them very little; they were much more concerned with District Council politics, and many of them may be expected to vote in local elections. A few were far from sure of the secrecy of the ballot, and were frankly afraid of the consequences of voting. Some of these were surrounded by neighbours of the opposite party who knew their politics, and they thought it better to be able to swear that they had not voted, in order to ensure future peace and quiet. There were also some, mainly of the older generation, who felt that they could not vote for candidates who, by tradition, were too young to lift up their voices in council. Others had prospered under the old régime, and were not ready to show any support for the new. Two of the most bitter of these with whom the writer talked had been made Warrant Chiefs under the British administration many years before. It was to such elements that the parties opposed to self-government made their appeal. There were some who endorsed the aims of these parties, but did not vote for them because they distrusted their motives.

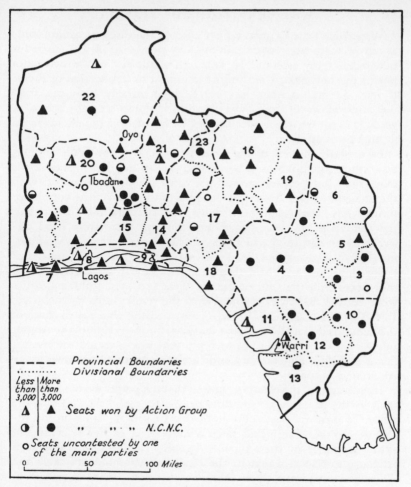

MAP 3. ELECTION RESULTS IN WESTERN NIGERIA

No.	Division	Province	No.	Division	Province
1	EGBA	} ABEOKUTA	14	IJEBU	} IJEBU
2	EGBADO		15	IJEBU REMO	
3	ASABA	} BENIN	16	EKITI	} ONDO
4	BENIN		17	ONDO	
5	ISHAN		18	OKITIPUPA	
6	KUKURUKU		19	OWO	
7	BADAGRY	} COLONY	20	IBADAN	} IBADAN
8	IKEJA		21	OSHUM	
9	EPE				
10	ABOH	} DELTA	22	OYO	} OYO
11	WARRI		23	ILESHA	
12	URHOBO		24	IFE	
13	WESTERN IJAW				

Were some issue to arise which affected the interests of any large group of these non-voters, they could clearly have an enormous influence on any election. In 1956 the 'platforms' of the two main parties did not make a real effort to appeal to any section of them; it may be that neither has yet decided on any 'vote-catching' measures. However, in future elections it would seem to be worth while to enlist whatever support can be found, and the efforts to do so may be interesting.

Particularly in view of the small proportion of the adult population which voted, it would be unwise to read into the overall result more than has been suggested above: a general satisfaction with things as they were. In the eastern part of the Region the voting appears to have confirmed the wish for a Benin–Delta State, but of this the politicians are well aware. For the rest, there were local differences, the nature of which has already been indicated. Members for Ibadan were chosen (at least in part) because of memories of battles long ago with the Ijebus, and those for Ilesha because of differences with the Oni of Ife. In these two cases solid majorities were secured, but in Oyo and Warri the results were inconclusive. In the former case the N.C.N.C. construed the winning of three of the five seats in the Division as a mandate for the return of the Alafin, but Action Group was able to reply that this reflected an insignificant majority, and did not indicate a reconciliation between the Alafin and his people.

If the results of the election showed that the possession of particular seats by the parties was generally secure, they also showed that the tenure of them by particular individuals was not. Apart from last-minute changes, there had been a number of earlier rejections of sitting members by their parties. In some cases this was due to a tendency to regard a seat in the House of Assembly—or often the salary and perquisites that accompany it—as a benefit in the gift of the electorate. In return, visible improvements in the constituency such as roads and water-supplies are expected. Some individuals may look for government loans or even jobs. When these are not forthcoming, the sitting member is liable to be saddled with a considerable share of the responsibility. Many battles were therefore fought out within the local party organizations before they could be made campaign issues. All this makes politics local in character, but for all that they do not lack vigour.

The conduct of the election. It must be said at the outset that the writer was deeply impressed by what he saw in Western Nigeria. Even a decade ago, few thinking men, even Nigerians, would have dared to believe that such an election could have taken place. Not only was it held, but, after fair hearings, only one of the petitions against its results was upheld.[1] These facts alone far outweigh any criticisms that may be made. The greatest credit is due to all concerned; the Electoral Commissioner and his staff, the Electoral Officers, police, politicians, and people.

Nevertheless, there are certain prerequisites for the satisfactory conduct of an election, and the fact must be faced that they were missing in some cases. The most important of these is a belief in the fairness and impartiality of the administration. This was all too generally absent. Much of the trouble was due to ignorance of the machinery for conducting the election, and of the safeguards which were incorporated in the regulations. The mechanism for reporting alleged irregularities and having them investigated was all too rarely used, and it must be placed on record that some politicians who undoubtedly knew better were prepared to foment and exploit distrust. In Ibadan, for example, the rumour was widely current that certain Action Group ballot boxes had been 'stuffed' with papers before polling began. Many of those who sincerely believed this were intelligent enough to realize when it was explained to them that this could only have happened if the polling agents of the N.C.N.C. had been utterly incompetent. Unfortunately there were many to whom this was not explained. Similar happenings took place in other areas. There were several official complaints by party officers that more people had polled in certain stations than the number on the register. Records of the number of votes cast at each station had been kept,[1] presumably to guard against innocent or wilful complaints of this nature. The Commissioner was thus able to satisfy those concerned that the alleged irregularities had not in fact taken place.

Much good could certainly be done if, before another election, organizations such as the Regional Information Service could make everybody familiar with the precautions taken to ensure fairness. For this to have its maximum effect, it is essential that government agencies, such as the Development Corporation or the Information Service, should themselves avoid giving rise to suspicions that they are liable to be used for party propaganda. There is, however, little hope that future elections will create a sense of stability and popular consent unless the politicians play a greater part in creating public

[1] This was in Ekiti South. The High Court found that there had been irregularities in one polling station, part of whose records were missing. It had been kept open well after 5 p.m. In the General Election Action Group had a majority of eighty-nine, but in the by-election which followed, with no Independents and the same candidates from the two major parties, this was substantially increased.

[2] Under *P.L.G.E.R.* 61 (2).

confidence in the way they are run. In this election, the N.C.N.C. as opposition party were the principal offenders, but Action Group often showed hostility towards the clerks of N.C.N.C.-dominated Local Councils when these were employed as Electoral Officers.[1]

Fortunately, there was no loss of confidence in the Electoral Commissioner, though there were occasional attacks on him over matters of detail, notably that by Chief Awolowo in the matter of the Action Group cards. This was due partly to the high standard maintained in making hundreds of administrative decisions under great pressure, partly to his position as an 'expatriate'. The days when a European can preside over Nigerian elections, or even act as an umpire, are clearly numbered, and the only hope of a satisfactory answer lies in the emergence of a body of Nigerian officials trusted by the community at large. The greatest hope seems to lie with the expanding local government service, but it has been noted in the preceding paragraphs that irresponsible statements made during the campaign tended to undermine the beginnings of public confidence.

It would also be valuable if the political parties would co-operate to strengthen good administration by forming, by agreement, an Electoral Commission of some sort. Until now, there has been a tendency for inter-party compacts to be broken or tacitly repudiated; unfortunately this has happened not only at the local level.[2]

There were other fears besides fears of dishonesty. There were a few cases of traditional rulers expressing their condemnation of those who voted against the party they themselves supported, but these were rare and were far outnumbered by those of Obas who genuinely respected the freedom of choice of their people. It is difficult to estimate the effectiveness of the political pressure of a traditional ruler; much would depend on his popularity.[3] More sinister was the fear of physical violence, illustrated by the absence of members of the rival party at political meetings, and in a reluctance to ask hostile questions. There are welcome indications that the danger of members of a crowd taking the law into their own hands is diminishing. The quietness of Oyo and Warri, both towns with a record of

---

[1] Dr. Azikiwe in his broadcast attacked Electoral Officers appointed by Action Group, and Chief Awolowo's pronouncements suggesting that political pressure might be brought to bear on the voters by the Nigeria Police, with its predominance of Ibos, did not help to increase public confidence.

[2] This state of affairs might be contrasted with the reception given by all parties to Mr. Bevan's implicit attack on the integrity of the Boundaries Commission in the British General Election of 1955. Cf. Butler, op. cit., pp. 77 and 157.

[3] e.g. the resistance of the people of Ilesha to the Oni of Ife, which expressed itself in opposition to his party, the Action Group. The Oni certainly did not abuse his traditional status for political ends.

violence, bears this out. Nevertheless, there were real grounds for fear; the number of persons injured more or less seriously as a result of the elections must certainly have run into three figures, and casualties might have been more numerous but for police precautions.

In quite another category from mob violence was the use of gangs of 'toughs', which sometimes took place with at least the connivance of local party organizations. It is also beyond doubt that some of them, if not actually paid, received generous allowances. Some had been imported into the Western Region from the Lagos waterfront. Members of local party youth organizations occasionally adopted a menacing attitude, and a few politicians sometimes took with them gangs of retainers. The excuse that these were necessary as a 'bodyguard' was (to say the least of it) unconvincing, since even the threat of their appearance was enough to start preparations for counter measures. The majority of itinerant speakers, including ministers, relied on the good nature of the people and the protection of the police, and were not molested in any way; the opposite practice was rare, but might easily prove infectious if not checked in its first stage of development.

Allegations of bribery were widespread, but no cases were proved. There can be little doubt that it was occasionally practised, but the sums involved were probably not large. In any case the secrecy of the ballot box afforded no guarantee that a 'bought' vote would be given to the right candidate, and there were regulations to prevent the public casting of votes and the sale of ballot papers. It is impossible to say how far these were successful in securing their objects, but no instance of a successful prosecution has come to the writer's notice. 'Treating' in a mild form was certainly widespread, but it is doubtful whether it had any significant effect on the voting; gifts of small sums by local politicians 'to buy some palm wine' to those who gathered to hear them appeared to be taken as a gesture of benevolence, and were not complained about by rivals.

In the circumstances, it would be impossible to impose any limitation on expenditure similar to that obtaining in Great Britain. It would, however, be an advantage that someone other than the candidate should bear legal responsibility for the proper conduct of the campaign, such as is borne by the candidate's agent in Britain. It would then be in the agent's interest to see that the law was kept, and it would be reasonable to expect him to do so. In most cases, local organizing secretaries would be well able to undertake this responsibility.

The sort of small-scale bribery and 'treating' that have been mentioned can never be eliminated by law; as has been said, they are not of any great political significance. 'Cola', 'dash', and other synonyms for tips and 'rake-offs' still play a very large part in public and private life. Sometimes the dividing line between them and outright bribery and corruption is obscured. This is an evil of which people in all walks of life are aware, and efforts are being made by various private associations to stamp it out. 'Leagues of Bribe Scorners' and similar bodies often make their presence felt.

A more serious matter was the prevalent attitude towards candidates facing major criminal charges. At least two successful candidates fought the election while on bail, and one of them (Mr. A. L. Ade Bello in Ibadan Central) only a few days after polling day lost an appeal against a sentence of six months' imprisonment for assaulting a Native Court Judge. Many Ibadan electors firmly believed that Mr. Bello's trial and sentence had been a political 'frame-up', and in the second case, that of Mr. Adelabu, his party maintained that he was innocent of charges of corruption made against him by the Commission of Inquiry into the affairs of the Ibadan Town Council. Mr. Adelabu was subsequently acquitted, but such cases indicate a dangerous distrust even of the superior courts (which maintain the highest traditions) and also a lack of squeamishness within the parties and among the electorate about offences of certain types thought to be 'political'.

The campaigns. Few accounts of speeches by political leaders during the campaign would ever have suggested that they had originally come before the public eye as nationalists. Federal politics and plans for the new Constitution received little attention except in the written manifestos which can only have reached a small proportion of the people. Even the 'One Nigeria' call of the N.C.N.C. appears to have been rarely used as a rallying-cry at campaign meetings, and explanations of its meaning were even less frequent. The writer's Ibo house boy remarked on hearing of the Action Group victory that 'there will never be one Nigeria now'. Pressed further, he had no idea of what the term really meant, but he appeared to be convinced of its importance.

In any community it is one of the functions of the politician to educate the electorate on political matters, and this would seem to be extremely important in an area such as Western Nigeria. It is also in his long-term interest to bring forward new issues, since it is these which help him to attract more attention than his rivals. In this election, both the main parties seem to have neglected these functions, though their capacity for giving constructive leadership was shown at the time of registration. How long the impetus given by tribalism and a somewhat threadbare nationalism will last is a matter of opinion. With the keen interest in politics manifested by the electorate it cannot be for very much longer. The added responsibilities of self-government will call for more serious thought, and for the evolution of policies to meet them.

These comments apply with even greater force to the party newspapers than to manifestos and speeches. The *Daily Times* is not every man's meat, and would never seek to be so. In any case it has its shortcomings. In West Africa there is even more scope than in many other places for a 'sensational' press, but there is also a great need for mass education. If Nigeria is to fulfil her ambitions and occupy a place of importance in Africa and the world, it is essential for her people to have some idea of the great issues they will have to face. As things are at present, only a small minority, even of literate Nigerians, have information on which they can even begin to form judgements. Much of this information is derived from the overseas press, particularly British newspapers, and these are few and far between.

In these circumstances Nigeria is a fertile ground for the spreading of false rumours. Occasionally, unscrupulous politicians were prepared to take advantage of this during the election. Even the more responsible of them seemed ready to make statements which their audiences were for the most part unable to check. Dark hints of irregularities taking place in other parts of the Region, or of gross mismanagement in the East, could therefore assume a quite disproportionate importance.

The electoral regulations. One of the first reactions to the result of the election was a renewal of N.C.N.C. protests against the allocation of seats. An article in the *West African Pilot*[1] quoted figures which tended to give substance to their claim that some of the areas where they were strongest had fewer representatives in relation to their population than other parts of the Region. In terms of seats won in the House of Assembly, Action Group's majority in the Region as a whole certainly exaggerated its electoral support. There are some analogies between the position of the N.C.N.C. and that of the Labour Party in Great Britain. Looking at the regional result, and making the rough assumption that in most areas the N.C.N.C. vote could be equated with non-Yorubas, Action Group's support was concentrated in one area—Yorubaland—which included large numbers of N.C.N.C. supporters who were, however, not numerous enough in most places to win the seat. In those areas, particularly Benin and the Delta, where N.C.N.C. victories were won on largely tribal grounds, the party often polled several times the number of

[1] 29 May 1956.

votes given to the Action Group candidates.[1] Circumstances thus caused Action Group's strength to be much better deployed for an election than the N.C.N.C.'s.

The system of constituencies described in Section 4 was in some places unfair, but it is difficult to imagine any other system of allocation which would have served as well. Founded as they are on existing differences, provincial and divisional boundaries are at least as sacrosanct as those of British counties. The only provision which might be called in question is the allocation of two seats as opposed to one as the minimum for a Division, but there are good precedents for the practice which was adopted. Short of a system of proportional representation, which is scarcely possible in Nigerian conditions, there is little more that can be done to improve the representation of substantial minorities. Certainly there is no evidence to support charges of 'gerrymandering', and the N.C.N.C. appears to have been the victim of circumstances rather than of malice.

It may be argued that the present electoral regulations gave rise to no serious difficulties at the time of the registration except in the Delta, but it is possible that in future a political party may employ similar tactics elsewhere. It has been stated on countless occasions that the principle underlying the electoral regulations is 'universal adult suffrage', and the results of the registration show that this was attained to a remarkable extent. The doctrine of a 'stake in the country' has much to be said for it, but in most countries where there is parliamentary government, the assumption is that citizenship alone is sufficient to provide that stake. In the Western Region the House of Chiefs is a recognition of the existence of tribal loyalties; the 'native qualification' in elections to the House of Assembly seems to represent the same factor again.

Improvements in communication and an increasing tempo of economic life mean that more and more people are having to move out of the areas where they traditionally live. Any reminder that they 'belong' elsewhere may serve to detract interest from the place where they are, and from which they draw economic benefits. 'Rootlessness' brings with it great evils, and it is reckless to destroy traditional loyalties without reflection: but these loyalties are at present so strong in the Western Region that they scarcely need

[1] e.g. Urhobo C.   N.C.N.C.—25,336   A.G.—7,081
    Urhobo E.   N.C.N.C.—12,747   A.G.—5,729
    Urhobo W.   N.C.N.C.—30,629   A.G.—10,698
    Benin C.   N.C.N.C.—13,345   A.G.—6,836
    Benin W.   N.C.N.C.—13,852   A.G.—6,671
    Benin E.   N.C.N.C.—21,841   A.G.—9,081
Action Group had also a few comparable majorities.

legislative encouragement. The need is rather to encourage new loyalties alongside the old, loyalties without which representative government can scarcely function well. It is argued in some quarters that this change will inevitably take place; a generation is growing up which was not born in the traditional 'family house'. Local authorities, it is pointed out, will increasingly use their permissive powers to levy rates. These will almost certainly be on a *per capita* basis in most instances, so that more and more people will qualify for the vote as ratepayers. If this is so, there is still less point in preserving the 'native qualification', a 'fancy franchise' destined to die but causing much trouble and expense in the meantime. At present, Action Group derives some advantage from the difficulties placed in the way of 'non-native' voters, but this is an added reason why those difficulties should be removed.

Another problem is that of young people under twenty-one registered as voters because they are taxpayers. Interviews with a number of these do not suggest that the 16–21 age-group has any great sense of responsibility or of 'stake'. Indeed, it appeared that their voting intention was influenced by little more than the attitudes of their elders or their friends, or by the rival merits of the local party youth movements. Nothing suggested that the Nigerian youth of sixteen is any more mature mentally and emotionally than his contemporary in other countries of the world. If people in their teens are, by implication, deemed unfit to vote under the rules of the 'native qualification', there seems no reason why the franchise should be given to others merely as compensation for having to pay taxes.

On both counts therefore it seems administratively and politically preferable to substitute for the present system one of straightforward adult suffrage with a simple residence qualification and a minimum age, presumably twenty-one. This would simplify the conduct and improve the fairness of parliamentary elections: the same rules need not apply to local council elections, an equally difficult problem of which the writer has had no direct experience in Nigeria.

ACKNOWLEDGEMENTS

THE author wishes to express his gratitude to the University of Manchester, University College, Ibadan, and the West African Institute of Economic and Social Research, for financial and material assistance which made this study possible; to the Premier of the Western Region, Chief the Hon. O. Awolowo, for approving its initiation; to the Electoral Commissioner of the Western Region, Mr. P. H. Balmer, O.B.E., and his staff, to Registration Officers, Clerks of Councils, and others engaged in electoral administration, who spared him their time, often when they were busy with more important things; not least to politicians at all levels, who almost without exception gave him every facility to see what they were doing in the election campaign.

IV

THE EASTERN REGION OF NIGERIA
MARCH 1957

1. *Introduction*

THE Eastern Region of Nigeria, with a population according to the 1953 census of about 7,200,000[1] and an area of 29,484 square miles, is the smallest and most densely populated of the three Regions into which Nigeria is divided. As a result of this, there is very great pressure upon the land in most parts of the Region, and a great deal of emigration to other parts of Nigeria and of West Africa, particularly by the most numerous tribe, the Ibo. The breakdown of the population by tribes is as follows:[2]

Edo	4,027
Fulani	757
Hausa	10,288
Ibibio	737,118
Ibo	4,916,734
Kanuri	2,151
Nupe	2,811
Tiv	5,121
Yoruba	11,377
Ijaw	258,962
Other Nigerian tribes	1,261,614
Non-Nigerian Africans	4,289
Non-Africans	2,578
	7,217,827[3]

[1] This figure is arrived at by subtracting the population of Bamenda and Cameroons Provinces, which at that time were a part of Eastern Region, from the census total (see *Population Census of the Eastern Region of Nigeria*, 1953, Lagos: Department of Statistics).

[2] The tribal categories into which the population was divided for the 1953 census are far from satisfactory for our purpose, as they are based upon the major tribes of Nigeria as a whole, and not of Eastern Region in particular. The category 'Other Nigerian Tribes' includes in Eastern Region such important groups as the Annangs (435,210) and the Orons (123,404), both in Calabar Province, and the Ogonis (156,118) of Rivers Province. The Kalabaris (who do *not* live in Calabar) are included amongst the Ibibio.

[3] One interesting feature which the census reveals, and which can be taken to

The Ibo, whose society is organized on a clan basis, are themselves subdivided into seventeen major groups, each of which speaks its own dialect of Ibo; but from the point of view of regional politics the major significant division is between those Ibos centred on Onitsha and the rest, who are for convenience referred to as 'non-Onitsha Ibos'. The non-Ibo tribes are ethnically and linguistically quite different from the Ibo, and are themselves derived from several different ethnical and linguistic groups. They live mainly in a narrow crescent covering the eastern, south-eastern, and southern sections of Eastern Region.

The regional constitution is similar to that of the other two Regions, except that there is no Upper House in the Legislature.

The administration is headed by a Governor (at the time of the election Sir Robert de S. Stapleton, K.C.M.G., C.B.E., who had only recently been transferred from Tanganyika), who presides over meetings of the Executive Council. The Executive Council consists of the Premier and all elected ministers: the Governor has only a casting vote. There is also a Privy Council, which includes certain non-political figures, the main responsibility of which is to advise His Excellency on the exercise of the Royal Prerogative of mercy.

The Regional House of Assembly, which includes no *ex officio* or nominated members, has a membership of eighty-four. At the time of the dissolution (ignoring the fact that one member had recently died and a by-election was therefore pending), the membership by parties was as follows:

N.C.N.C.	.	.	.	.	72
U.N.I.P.	.	.	.	.	10
Action Group	.	.	.	.	1
Independent	.	.	.	.	1
					84

The solitary Action Group member, a former Parliamentary Secretary,

be of some significance in the light of the heavy female poll described later, is the sex structure of the population. Taking the overall figures for Eastern Region and the Southern Cameroons, the number of males per thousand females in the different age-groups is as follows:

All ages	.	.	.	945
Under 2.	.	.	.	934
2–6	.	.	.	974
7–14	.	.	.	1,163
15–49	.	.	.	880
50+	.	.	.	864

named A. G. Umoh, had not been elected on the Action Group ticket, but crossed the floor of the House after a disagreement with the N.C.N.C. leaders.

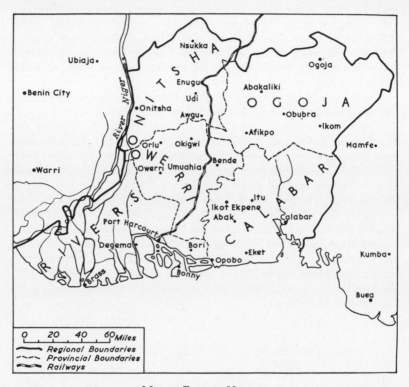

MAP 4. EASTERN NIGERIA

The career of Dr. the Hon. Nnamdi Azikiwe, the Premier, has been referred to in Chapter II. He has a remarkable hold over the masses, both Ibo and non-Ibo,[1] but his one great failing, as the leader of a political party, as opposed to a national movement, is

---

[1] Even the Police (a Federal service) have succumbed to Azikiwe's *charisma*. Inside the police sentry box outside the Premier's Lodge in Enugu can be seen a series of pencilled *graffiti*, presumably scribbled there by policemen when bored with the long hours of night duty. Amongst them we find 'Zik is a Lion and our King', 'Zik is the Black Star of Africa', 'Zik is sent by God to lead us', and 'The Police must not fail Zik'.

indicated in the comment of someone who had worked close to him for several years: 'a temperamental *prima donna*, who cannot stand any other person of ability close to him'.

2. *Background to the Election*

In the opinion of most observers, official and unofficial, before the election, there were four important factors which it was believed would be decisive in its conduct and in the result. They were:

(*a*) *The Foster-Sutton Tribunal.* The circumstances in which the Commission of Inquiry under the chairmanship of Sir Stafford Foster-Sutton was set up have been explained in Chapter II. Its report was not released until 16 January 1957 but it had been obvious from the evidence given publicly that Dr. Azikiwe could not escape censure. During December 1956 the one problem which had exercised the minds of all politicians and officials in Nigeria had been what his course of action would be when the report was eventually released. He could accept the censure and retire gracefully from the scene, but that seemed a most improbable course for a person of his character. He could, on the other hand, ignore it and carry on as if the Tribunal had never sat—though that would have brought him into direct conflict with the Governor of the Region. His only other course was to fight a general election, and to try to secure a vote of confidence from the electorate of the Region.

At a meeting in Port Harcourt on 6 January 1957, the N.C.N.C. ministers, realizing that the report was bound to be unfavourable to Dr. Azikiwe, passed a resolution that he should not resign after the report came out, but should if necessary hold a general election. The ministers were not apparently unanimous, since Dr. M. I. Okpara, the Minister of Health and Chairman of the N.C.N.C. Eastern Working Committee, was reported in the local press to have urged the Premier's resignation.

After the report had been published a meeting of the Executive Council was held with the Governor in the chair, and Dr. Azikiwe announced that he would not resign but would advise the Governor to dissolve the Regional House of Assembly, thus forcing a general election.

In the event, the effect of the Tribunal's report was not unfavourable to Dr. Azikiwe. In the minds of many Nigerians he became a martyr who had been sacrificed to British banking interests. Typical of the reaction was the editorial comment in the *Eastern Sentinel*: 'Support Zikist rallies—they are but a warning to British Imperialism that the land belongs to Nigerians, and no one can stretch a dirty hand from across the seas to humiliate the country's No. 1 Leader under the cloak of a legal fault finding set-up.' The *Nigerian Spokesman*, referring to the report of the Tribunal in the biblical language which is so favoured in Nigerian journalism, said: ' "Touch not my Anointed and do my Prophets no harm", saith the Lord.' On the other hand, the Opposition *Eastern States Express*, crying in the wilderness, referred to '. . . the attempt of the N.C.N.C. to mislead ignorant people that the issue between Zik and the Colonial Secretary is not one of wrong versus right but that of so-called British imperialism against African nationalism'.

The N.C.N.C., as might have been expected, made such political capital as it could out of particular findings by the Tribunal. Phrases from the report (in particular, from para. 192), were freely quoted out of context to suggest that the Tribunal had whitewashed Dr. Azikiwe, and in *The People's Mandate*, the election manifesto of the N.C.N.C., it is stated: 'We are happy to note that the Tribunal believed that Doctor Azikiwe's primary motive was to make available an indigenous bank with the object of liberalizing credit for the people of this country.' (This was a direct quotation of part of para. 192.)

Expatriate officials in the Eastern Region thought from the first that the N.C.N.C. would win the forthcoming general election (and possibly with an increased majority), because of, and not in spite of, the findings of the Tribunal. Why then did the Secretary of State play directly into Dr. Azikiwe's hands by setting up the Tribunal? The most natural explanation is that given to the writer in conversation by a senior British official: 'One could take a completely cynical view of the matter, arguing that after all the country was going to get self-government very shortly, and that if Azikiwe chose to play ducks and drakes with the country's money, it was after all the country's own money, derived from the taxpayers of the Region. The taxpayers had the remedy in their own hands if they did not like what Azikiwe was doing. On the other hand, it must be remembered that the United Kingdom is still technically responsible for the Eastern Region of Nigeria, and it would be morally wrong for such activities as Azikiwe's to be condoned or overlooked merely because the United Kingdom Government was shortly going to withdraw its responsibilities. The United Kingdom has a moral responsibility in the matter as the trustee for the inarticulate masses, and it would be failing in its trusteeship if it did not expose to the public gaze what was being done with the public's money.'

(b) *The impending London Conference*. It had originally been intended that the Nigerian political leaders should meet in London in 1956 in order to discuss the future of their country with the Secretary of State for the Colonies. This conference had been postponed in order that the result of the Foster-Sutton Tribunal should be known. Whoever won the general election in the Eastern Region would therefore be the person to speak on behalf of the Region at the conference. As the conference was of great significance to Nigerian electors, since it would decide the form and nature of regional self-government, and (it was hoped) the date of the final granting of independence to the Federation, it was believed that the issue would become an important one in the election campaign.

(c) *'U.P.E.'* The primary schools of the Region are for the most part managed by the Missions, and naturally tend to recruit their pupils from the children of their own parishioners. In 1956 the Eastern Region Government announced its plans for 'Universal Primary Education', under which the school building programme would be immensely accelerated, and all schools would be eligible for government grants. £300 (barely enough to provide a thatched roof on cement block pillars, with a surrounding wall about 1 ft. 6 in. high) was allocated for each school to the local authorities of Eastern Region, in order that building could take place during 1956 in readiness for the introduction of Universal Primary Education in 1957. The Missions, and in particular the Roman Catholic Missions, also started to build new schools during the latter part of 1956, in order (it was hoped) to qualify for the government grants. These schools were built at the Missions' own expense, and very often with the aid of voluntary labour and contributions from local villagers. Towards the end of the year, however, it was announced by the Ministry of Education that the management of all schools was to be vested in the local authorities, and a completely secular system of primary education was to be established in the Region.

The Roman Catholic Mission, which is by far the largest of the Missions in Eastern Nigeria (it has a total membership of 1¼ millions, including 1 million confirmed Catholics and ¼ million catechumens, with 600,000 school children in the primary schools) resisted this move, partly for fear of the loss of the heavy sums already committed to new school building, and partly through a genuine disapproval of a universal system of secular education.

On 3 January 1957 all the Roman Catholic members of Enugu Municipal Council walked out of the council chamber in protest, after the Finance Committee's recommendation that all primary schools in Enugu should be maintained by the Municipal Council had been passed by thirteen votes to twelve. (It is interesting to note that the religious composition of the Enugu Municipal Council, which has since been suspended, is 12 Protestants, 12 Roman Catholics, and 1 Muslim—the N.C.N.C. Mayor, who has a casting vote.)

On 23 January the Roman Catholic bishops of the Onitsha Archdiocese met at Onitsha. It was immediately rumoured that the Roman Catholic Mission had decided to contest the election against the N.C.N.C. on the issue of Universal Primary Education. On 25 January, however, Mr. J. Anyansi, the Chairman of the Eastern Nigerian Catholic Council, announced that the Church was not contesting the elections, but merely instructing Roman Catholic voters to vote for 'God-fearing capable men and women who will defend the right of parents to train their children according to their beliefs'. This, of course, to anyone on the spot looked like direct political intervention.

A prominent member of the Catholic Church in Onitsha was of the opinion that about 80 per cent. of the Roman Catholic vote would go to the N.C.N.C., and only 20 per cent. against, despite the religious issue which had been raised. He blamed the muddle over Universal Primary Education on the two expatriate officials (the Director and the Deputy Director of Education), both of whom were Protestants and one of whom was an Ulsterman. He was anxious to show that the Mission did not believe that any of the blame rested with the minister; evidence from other sources was that the minister's attitude was much the same as that of his advisers.

The Mission was also perturbed by N.C.N.C. allegations of 'Irish Imperialism'—based on the fact that the majority of the priests in the Archdiocese are from Southern Ireland.

The Church Missionary Society (Anglican), on the other hand, which had formerly supported the Roman Catholic Mission in its stand about educational liberty, now supported government policy. The Church Missionary Society's Senior Supervisor of Schools gave as his reason that the rank and file parishioners were bitterly hostile to the Roman Catholics and to their opposition to the Government, and had passed a resolution which made it obligatory for him also to oppose the Roman Catholic stand. Supporters of the Church Missionary Society also accused the Roman Catholic Mission of trying to 'jump the gun', and get themselves into an unfair competitive position by accelerating their 1956 building programme in anticipation of Universal Primary Education. It seemed, indeed, that the Church Missionary Society had slipped into the position of nonconformists in England in the nineteenth century; they would sooner have secular education for all than allow the dominant church to run its own schools.

The official view of the Roman Catholic Mission, when the election campaign started, was that it wished to continue to administer its own schools, and to open the schools which it had built in 1956; but at the same time it was perfectly willing to make its schools completely open to government inspection before any grants were received from public funds.

(d) *The Finance Law.* Hitherto, women had been exempt from direct taxation in Eastern Nigeria; severe riots ('The Women's War') had occurred at Aba in 1929 in consequence of an attempt by the British authorities to impose taxation upon women, who are in many places the wealthiest section of the community, since they are the market traders. The new Finance Law again proposed a direct tax; there followed mass meetings of market women in many parts of the region, and particularly in Aba itself, protesting against the decision and requesting the Government to reconsider it.

In the event, although the report of the Foster-Sutton Tribunal overshadowed the other factors in importance, and although Universal Primary Education became a focus of the propaganda and counter-propaganda of all parties, none of these factors had any real effect upon the result of the election.

3. *The Electoral Regulations*

The electoral regulations applicable in the Eastern Region at the time of the general election were extremely unsatisfactory both from the administrative point of view and in their political effects. This had already been recognized by the Executive Council, which had discussed a proposal to revise the regulations and to create single-member constituencies during 1957. This would have involved scrapping the twenty-seven existing multi-member constituencies, based upon the administrative divisions, with populations ranging from 45,760 in the case of Ikom to 560,673 in the case of Owerri, a major administrative undertaking which could not be contemplated in the short time available before the election. As a result, the general election had to be carried out under the provision of the Eastern House of Assembly Electoral Regulations, 1955[1] the details of which are as follows:

Qualifications of electors. Any male or female British subject or British protected person of the age of twenty-one years or more,

[1] E.R.L.N. No. 9 of 1955.

who was born, or whose father was born, in the constituency in which he seeks to be registered, or who is resident in that constituency on the qualifying date and has been so resident for a period of twelve months immediately preceding the qualifying date, and who applies to be registered in accordance with the regulations, is eligible to register and to vote, but he may only make application in respect of one constituency. Any person who owes allegiance to a foreign power, or who has been sentenced to death or imprisonment for a term exceeding six months, and has not suffered punishment or received a free pardon, or who is declared to be of unsound mind or judged to be a lunatic is disqualified from registering as an elector.

The procedure for registration and revision. The Electoral Officers (i.e. the administrative officers in charge of Divisions) are responsible for the maintenance of registers of persons qualified to vote in their constituencies. The Electoral Officer in each constituency is to set up polling areas as he thinks fit, and to appoint a Registration Officer to be responsible for registration in each polling area. Each would-be elector is to apply in person to the Electoral Officer or the local Registration Officer with a completed application form, on which is shown the basis of his claim to be registered. A separate register is kept for each polling area. Theoretically a running register is to be kept continually in existence, but in practice it was found necessary for a new register to be prepared before the general election.

Each registered voter receives a 'registration receipt' (actually a small and easily forged piece of coloured cardboard) which bears his registration number, and which is to be produced by him at the time of voting.

When the date of a general election or a by-election has been announced, each Electoral Officer prescribes a period during which the register shall be closed and no applications for registration may be made, and publishes in each polling area a notice giving the places and times at which the register may be inspected, the last day for making an application for registration, and the last day for making objections against the inclusion of names in the register.

There are no revising courts in the Eastern Region, but instead the Electoral Officer himself, during the fourteen days from the last day for making objections, may consider objections and if necessary hear evidence to decide whether the person against whom objection is made is entitled to be registered or not. Any decision by an Electoral Officer either to delete a name from the register or to allow it to stand part of the register may not be inquired into or questioned by any court.

When the lists for each polling area are finally settled, the Electoral Officer signs the register as proof of its accuracy and validity, and causes the names in each list to be recorded in a register provided for the purpose.

Elections and candidates. The method of election is by plural voting in multi-member constituencies, the number of seats per constituency ranging from two in the case of the smallest constituencies to six in the case of Owerri. Each voter has a number of votes equal to the number of seats in the constituency, but may not cast more than one vote for any candidate. This is ensured by giving each voter a perforated strip of ballot papers equal in number to the number of seats in the constituency, each paper bearing the same serial number.

Not less than five weeks before the election is due to take place, the Electoral Officer must publish in each polling area a notice giving the date of the election, the number of seats for each constituency, and the place and last date for the making of nominations, which must be not less than twelve days before the date of the election.

A candidate for election to the Assembly must be a British subject or British protected person of the age of twenty-one or more, who, or whose father, was born in the Eastern Region, or who has resided in the Eastern Region for a continuous period of one year immediately before the date of the election. No person may be a candidate for the Assembly who owes allegiance to any foreign power, is an undischarged bankrupt, has been sentenced to death or to imprisonment for a term exceeding six months and has not suffered punishment or received a free pardon, holds, or is acting in any public office,[1] or is a lunatic or of unsound mind. In addition no person is qualified to stand for election if he has, within a period of five years immediately before the date of the election, been sentenced by a court in Nigeria to death, or to imprisonment for a term exceeding six months, for any offence mentioned in the Third Schedule to the Nigeria (Constitution) Order in Council, 1954, and has not received a free pardon. All persons standing for election to the Eastern House of Assembly must be qualified to vote in the Eastern Region, and no candidate may be nominated for more than one constituency. Each candidate must make a deposit of £50, which is only returnable if he dies before the date of the election, if there is

---

[1] 'Public office' was not defined. In fact, no person was allowed to stand for election who was at the time of the election a civil servant, a government school teacher, or a local authority servant. Arrangements were made for 'temporary resignations' whereby a person not elected could be reinstated.

no contested election, if he withdraws his nomination before the date of the publication of the list of nominations, if he is elected, or if in a contested election he obtains votes equal in number to not less than one-eighth of the total number of votes cast in the constituency. That is to say, in a six-member constituency (the largest) a defeated candidate forfeits his deposit if he has not secured support from three-quarters of those voting—a result due simply to bad drafting. The Electoral Officer's decision that a candidate has been validly nominated cannot be questioned by any court.

Not later than twelve days before the election the Electoral Officer allocates a symbol to each candidate and publishes notices giving the full names of all persons nominated and their nominators, together with the symbols allocated to them, and if a candidate wishes, a photograph of himself supplied at his own expense. Where a candidate is the certified candidate of a political party, the symbol allocated to him will be the official symbol of the party.

Not less than nine days before the election, in the case of a contested election, the Electoral Officer is required to publish a notice in each polling area giving the day and the hours fixed for the poll (which must be a continous period of not less than eight hours), a list of valid nominations, the number of seats to be filled, and the situation of the polling stations in each polling area.

Polling arrangements. The Electoral Officer is to provide at least one polling station for every 500 persons registered as electors in each polling area (a recommendation for a standard layout of the polling station was circulated), appoint a Presiding Officer for each polling station and other polling officers to assist him, provide each Returning Officer with such a number of ballot boxes and ballot papers as may seem necessary, and provide a copy of the register of electors for each polling station.

Each candidate may appoint two persons, who must not be civil servants, as polling agents to attend at each polling station in the constituency, and must give written notice to the Electoral Officer stating who have been appointed and to which polling stations they have been assigned.

A ballot box is provided at each station for each candidate, and it must bear the name of the candidate, with the candidate's symbol, and where requested, a photograph of the candidate not exceeding in size 6 in. × 6 in. The ballot boxes must be screened from observation when in use. The Presiding Officer at each station seals the ballot boxes in the presence of the polling agents, &c., at the beginning of the poll, having first shown that they are empty.

Each voter, when he arrives, has to present his registration receipt to the polling officer, who checks his name in the register, and gives him a strip of ballot papers, all bearing the same serial number. If a voter has lost his registration receipt the polling officer is to detain him until all electors who have produced their receipts have voted, after which he must satisfy himself of the voter's identity before the ballot paper is supplied.

Before delivering the ballot papers to any voter, he is to mark or punch them with an official mark, record the number of the elector on the counterfoil, and mark the name of the elector in the register.

If a polling officer is not satisfied about the identity of any voter, he may ask at the time the voter presents himself the following questions:

(1) 'Are you the person whose name is in the register of electors as follows. . . .?'

(2) 'Have you already voted at the present election at this or any other polling station?'

The voter must not mark his ballot paper in any way, but must place it secretly in the box of the candidate of his choice. If he decides not to use all his ballot papers, he may hand the surplus back to the polling officer, who must keep the returned ballot papers in separate packets.

All voters, when supplied with ballot papers, have their left thumbs marked with ink sufficiently indelible to leave a stain for about ten hours.

At closing time the Presiding Officer is to allow no more persons to vote, and to seal each ballot box in such a way that no further ballot papers can be placed inside it. He then returns to the electoral office the ballot boxes, the unused and spoilt ballot papers, the returned ballot papers, the tendered ballot papers, the marked copy of the register of electors, the counterfoils of the used ballot papers and the tendered votes lists.

The count. The count normally takes place in the headquarters of the Division. Each candidate may nominate one person as a counting agent, to represent him at the counting of the votes. The count shall, as far as possible, proceed continuously until completed.

The Electoral Officer is to open each ballot box in turn, and after taking out the ballot papers, to examine the serial numbers to make sure that no two papers bear identical numbers. If any number is duplicated, one of the ballot papers only shall be counted. The valid votes in the box are then recorded. Ballot papers are also to be rejected which do not bear the official mark or which bear any writing or mark by which an elector can be identified.

When the count is complete the Electoral Officer seals up in separate packets the counted and rejected ballot papers. These, together with any other documents connected with the elections, stay in his custody for a period of six months after the election, and are then destroyed.

If a tie takes place between two candidates, a new election has to take place.

Finally, the Electoral Officer publishes a notice giving the result of the elections and notifies the Regional Electoral Officer and the Clerk to the House of Assembly of the names of the persons elected.

Election offences, petitions, &c. The usual provisions regarding election offences are included in the regulations. They cover corrupt practices such as personation, treating, undue influence, bribery, and aiding, abetting, counselling, or procuring the commission of personation. Election petitions are to be heard in open court by the Supreme Court. The only grounds on which an election may be questioned in the courts are as follows:

(i) that the Electoral Officer's decision that a candidate for election had not been validly nominated was wrong;

(ii) that the person whose election is questioned was at the time of the election not qualified or was disqualified from being elected a member of the House of Assembly:

(iii) that an election was avoided by corrupt practices or offences against these regulations; or

(iv) that the person whose election is questioned was not duly elected by a majority of lawful votes at the election. Where the courts declare that a person was not duly elected, a new election is to be held.

Indemnity is guaranteed to witnesses in election petitions who incriminate themselves in giving evidence.

One consequence of the loose drafting of these regulations was that it became necessary to amend them four times before the election. Three of the amendments became law within two months of the date of the election, the last of the amendments was only passed three days before it. The earlier amendments *inter alia* deleted referenees in the regulations to 'Chief Electoral Officers'. This was necessary owing to the abolition of the post of Resident of a Province, incumbents of which were to be Chief Electoral Officers under the original regulations. They also provided for the continuation of polling on the next day if proceedings in any polling station had been interrupted by a riot or open violence. The third and fourth amendments, issued on 11 February and 12 March 1957, will be described later.

4. The Administrative Organization of Registration and of the Election

As soon as Dr. Azikiwe's decision to advise a dissolution was known, a Regional Electoral Officer was appointed. This was the Acting Secretary to the Premier, the holder of a post which despite its title is comparable with that of Colonial Secretary or Chief Secretary in less advanced colonial administrations. If no special appointment of an Electoral Commissioner is made, as has been done in Western Nigeria, then the holder of the post of Secretary to the Premier is the obvious choice, responsible as he is for the co-ordination of the activities of all Ministries and of the administration in the Divisions. The Assistant Secretary to the Premier automatically became Assistant Regional Electoral Officer, but owing to the additional work in the Premier's office an additional Assistant Secretary was brought in temporarily from the Ministry of Internal Affairs.

The twenty-seven Administrative Officers in charge of Divisions were appointed Electoral Officers for the twenty-seven constituencies: they in turn set about appointing their registration officers according to the Electoral Regulations.

From then on all normal administrative work came to a standstill. The burden of registration and of preparation for polling day was such that administrative officers found it impossible to deal with any but the most urgent of normal correspondence, while the Premier's office took on the appearance of the battle headquarters of a beleaguered city. Owing to the lack of clear guidance in the Electoral Regulations on details of administrative procedure, and the lack of experience of many of the administrative officers in the organization of an election, queries and requests for guidance poured into the Premier's office by telephone, priority telegram, and letter at all hours of the day. It is impossible to exaggerate the dislocation that was caused to the Administration by the election period, particularly as more and more junior civil servants (clerks, &c.) were drafted in as registration officers and later as Returning Officers, Presiding Officers, &c. This is one of the most serious concomitants of a general election in an underdeveloped territory, where the inexperienced and often corrupt local authorities cannot be trusted to take upon their shoulders the burden of organizing an election.

The writer was not present in Eastern Nigeria during the registration period, which ended on 8 February 1957. An examination of registers and other records, however, and discussions with persons involved in the organization of the registration, give a good picture of what had happened. Since no specific forms had been prescribed in the Electoral Regulations for the registers, each Electoral Officer had relied upon his own ingenuity. In a few cases the final registers had been typed or cyclostyled, but in far too many cases they were merely written in pencil in school exercise books, duplicate copies having been made by putting worn-out carbon paper between the leaves. No attempt had been made to put the names in alphabetical order, though this was not necessary provided that all electors attended at polling stations with their registration receipts, which gave the number of each elector in the register. Owing to the low standard of education of the majority of the clerks who had been responsible for registration, many of the registers were virtually illegible, and it was hard in many cases to decide what any particular name was. As a result, all that really mattered in the registers on polling day was the number of the voter, which could be readily checked against the registration receipt.

Although Electoral Officers were constantly haunted by the thought—or rather nightmare—of what a re-registration or an invalid election would imply, there were several cases of electoral registers referring to particular areas having become temporarily mislaid (in one polling area for several weeks[1]) during the confusion of the registration period.

During the registration period, apart from the statutory notices which had to be published by the Electoral Officers, local announcements were made on the Nigerian Broadcasting Service network urging everyone to register, and the Eastern Nigerian Information Services inserted advertisements in the newspapers, distributed handbills, put up notices in the villages, and sent round Land Rovers fitted with loudspeakers to all constituencies in an attempt to persuade would-be voters to register.[2]

Of the 1,767,008 voters registered by 8 February, only 690,134—little more than one-third—had registered by 1 February. This may be due to the common human failing of always putting off until tomorrow what you do not have to do today: it may, on the other hand, be a reflection of the intense propaganda effort to secure the

---

[1] The police were called in to search for it, and it was eventually found embedded in a pile of accumulated debris in the D.O.'s office.

[2] Unfortunately the official handbills contained two mutually contradictory misstatements of fact about the age of eligibility for registration.

registration of their supporters which was undertaken by the political parties, and particularly the N.C.N.C., when they suddenly woke up to the necessity of securing the maximum possible registration of their own supporters.

As soon as registration was completed the Electoral Officers turned their attention to the revision and correction of registers. Because of the shortage of time, an amendment to the Electoral Regulations had been published[1] on 19 January 1957, reducing the revision period from fourteen days to seven days after the conclusion of registration. Owing to the character of the franchise regulations, under which a man or woman could establish his right to vote in a constituency if he was born there, or if his father was born there, or if he had been resident there for a period of twelve months immediately before the qualifying date—all of them very hard to prove in a country where registers of births are not kept and where, particularly in the towns, there is a great deal of mobility—a large number of objections was lodged *en bloc*. As time was so short the Electoral Officers had to deal pretty ruthlessly with these. If an objector did not appear at the proper time the objection was overruled; if, on the other hand, the person whose name was objected to did not appear, his name was deleted if it appeared to the Electoral Officer that the objection had some foundation. Despite this, a net total of only 663 names was removed from the registers, leaving a final total of 1,766,345 voters for the Region.

The next phase was that of preparations for polling, and perhaps the biggest single problem which Electoral Officers had to face was the physical difficulty of constructing in time sufficient polling stations and ballot boxes, and of organizing the transport of ballot boxes to and from the polling stations on the day of the election.

It had been decided that, since the Missions were believed to be playing an active political role in the election campaign, Mission schools would as far as possible not, as in previous elections, be used as polling stations (for which they were otherwise extremely convenient). Similarly, no clergymen or Mission school teachers were to be used as Presiding Officers, &c. This meant that thousands of polling stations had to be constructed for the occasion throughout the Region. As they were only required for one day, these polling stations were very flimsily constructed with a framework of bamboo or the trunks of palm-trees, a thatched roof, and thin screens made of woven palm leaves and grass. Where schools which were not under the control of the Missions were available, these were of course used,

[1] E.R.L.N. No. 20 of 1957.

and canvas, grass, or palm leaf screens were erected inside in order to provide a secret polling booth.

The ban on the use of buildings connected with the Missions did not apply to those belonging to the Muslim community, although— or possibly because—the Muslims were known to be pro-N.C.N.C. during the election period. One polling station seen by the writer was actually erected in the courtyard of the Mosque at Fagge, in Onitsha.

The ballot boxes were simple and crudely made wooden affairs, 1 ft. × 1 ft. × 1 ft. or 1 ft. × 1 ft. × 6 in., with a hinged lid in which there was a slot, and a padlock. Since the Eastern Regional Government had refused to accept responsibility for the storage of the boxes which had been used in the 1954 Federal Elections, most of those boxes had disappeared, and altogether less than 500 of them were used.[1] 32,712 ballot boxes were used altogether in the election, of which 32,353 had to be manufactured during the last few weeks. Most of this work had to be put out to local contractors, who, when they saw the urgency and the magnitude of the task, forced up prices disproportionately. A roughly made box of the type required would cost about 3s. 6d. before the election period began, but in the latter stages before the election contractors were charging 15s. each in many constituencies. The supply of padlocks was limited, as the large demand had not been foreseen by the importing firms. As a result, the Electoral Officers had to scour all the local markets in order to acquire any supplies that were available, and the price of padlocks soared accordingly. It was noticeable that, towards the end of the pre-election period, when it was widely known why the Electoral Officers were buying so many padlocks, locks were only available with one key each instead of the two keys which are normally supplied. Because of this, stringent precautions had to be taken to ensure that the missing keys were not used for corrupt practices.

Transport, too, had to be carefully planned. The Eastern Region Government is extremely short of motor transport, and very little is under the direction of the Administration. Transport from other Departments, such as the Public Works Department and the Agriculture Department, was therefore requisitioned for election day, and many local transport contractors were able to make substantial sums by hiring out their lorries. In most cases the lorries had to make two trips to each group of polling stations, the first (either

[1] A large number of the old boxes had been stored for a time in Owerri Prison, but the governor of the prison eventually refused to take further responsibility for them, as he complained that the prisoners were making piles of them and using them as ladders to climb over the walls of the prison in order to escape.

PLATE 3

a. Taking the ballot boxes to the polling station

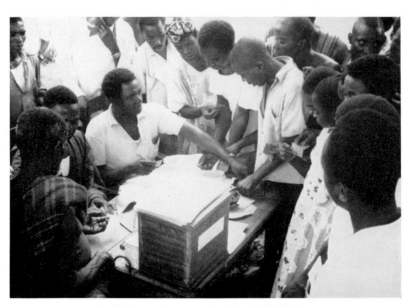

b. Polling assistants at work in Udi Division

BALLOT BOXES AND POLLING

late on the night before the election or very early on the morning of the election) to move the Presiding Officers, the police, and ballot boxes into position, and the second in the evening of polling day in order to bring back the staff and sealed ballot boxes. Stringent security precautions were necessary, and at least one policeman travelled on each lorry.

In the areas, such as the Rivers and parts of Onitsha constituency, where access to some polling stations was only possible by water, launches and motor-driven canoes had to be brought into use.

5. *The Parties*

The two national parties which were contesting the election, the National Council of Nigeria and the Cameroons, led by Dr. Azikiwe, with its National Headquarters in Lagos (though its centre of gravity was in Enugu), and the Action Group, led by Chief Awolowo, with its headquarters at Ibadan in the Western Region, have been described in preceeding chapters. It is necessary to add only that the Action Group had never previously contested an election in the Region, its only existing member in the Eastern Region House of Assembly having been a former N.C.N.C. man who 'crossed the floor' during the lifetime of the previous Assembly, and that the attitude of the N.C.N.C. and the Action Group towards mass membership was in practice noticeably different.

The N.C.N.C is in the true sense of the word a mass party, and its campaigning is designed largely to increase the number of members of the party, whether they keep up the payment of their subscriptions or not. The Action Group, on the other hand, while not despising mass support, is more anxious to secure the open support in each locality of the persons of influence, such as traditional rulers and professional men. Action Group campaigning is thus a rather more subtle process, although mass rallies in order to whip up support from the general public in each locality are not neglected.

Each of these parties had its own 'strong-arm gang', composed of the more hot-headed young supporters of the party. These groups were well organized, and seemed to have unlimited transport, relying in many cases upon the good offices of local taxi-drivers who were members. The N.C.N.C. organization was known as the 'Zikist National Vanguard' or 'Z.N.V.', a 'War Communiqué' of which is quoted later. The N.C.N.C. alleged that a large proportion of the members of the Action Group's 'Area Boys' had been imported from Western Nigeria, but the writer could find no proof of this.

Members of the Z.N.V. and of the 'Area Boys' frequently came into collision during the election campaign, but none of the disturbances was very serious. In fact, much of the hooliganism seemed to be intended rather to boost the morale of one's own side than to destroy the morale of the other.

The third party which contested the election, the United National Independence Party, was only active within the Eastern Region, and was in no sense a national party. Centred on Calabar, it was led by Mr. Eyo Ita, the Leader of the Opposition in the outgoing Assembly. Eyo Ita, who is in his early fifties, had been at one time the leading N.C.N.C. minister in the Eastern Region House of Assembly, and is a graduate of London and Columbia universities. Although he is a man of undoubted academic ability, he has not got the gifts required of a West African nationalist politician—popular oratorical appeal and a flair for organization. His party was formed originally by ex-N.C.N.C. ministers, six of whom were expelled from the N.C.N.C. in March 1953. It was from the first very poorly organized, if it can be said to have been organized at all, and secured little mass support even in the areas on which it was based.

The chief points of the U.N.I.P. were hostility to the Ibo elements, whose interests, it argued, were represented by N.C.N.C., and a demand for the creation of a separate state, known as the C.O.R. State, comprising the former provinces of Calabar, Ogoja and Rivers. These provinces, arranged in a crescent round the east and south of the Region, include most of the non-Ibo elements, but they have no ethnic unity of their own. Eyo Ita had obviously given very little thought to the constitutional form of this new state, or to its relationship with the rest of Eastern Region and with the Federation.

Both the national parties had prepared and issued their manifestos by the beginning of February 1957, but that of the U.N.I.P. did not appear till 23 February. An analysis of the main points in the three manifestos follows.

The *N.C.N.C. Manifesto*, which was entitled *The People's Mandate*, was a comparatively well produced booklet of 22 pages, printed by Zik Enterprises Ltd., Enugu. It was divided into four parts.

Part I, Preamble (1 page), referred to the findings of the Foster-Sutton Commission of Inquiry as if it had found Azikiwe blameless, and insisted that his actions in connexion with the African Continental Bank were in line with the N.C.N.C's policy as laid down in the 1954 Election Manifesto, where it said: 'The N.C.N.C. would found a State Bank to finance commerce and industry as a matter of business, such a bank to be controlled by a Board appointed by the Federal and State Governments.'

It went on to state that the National Executive Committee and the Eastern Parliamentary Party of the N.C.N.C. had decided that all private interests (e.g. Dr. Azikiwe's and his relatives') in the African Continental Bank should be transferred to the Eastern Regional Government.

It ended with the claim that it was because of the utmost confidence in the honour and integrity of Dr. Azikiwe which it cherished, and the belief that the people of Eastern Nigeria felt the same way, that the party had decided to seek a dissolution of the Eastern Assembly in order to ask for a fresh mandate from the people.

Part II (14½ pages), entitled 'What we have done', was a long and detailed review of the achievements of the N.C.N.C. while it had been in power in the Eastern Region. It had sections devoted to agriculture, commerce, industry and trade, education, health, internal affairs, local government, public finance, transport, welfare, works, and Nigerianization. The section concerned with education stated that 'the N.C.N.C. Government has guaranteed freedom of religious beliefs under the Universal Primary Education scheme by granting to parents: 1. the right to choose the schools which their children are to attend; 2. the right to choose the classes for religious instruction (in local government primary schools) which their children are to attend.'

Part III (2½ pages only) outlined an eight-point programme for future policy in the Eastern Region. It promised improvements in water-supplies, both in the municipal towns and in the rural areas, the tarring of more roads and the improvement of inland waterway facilities, the continuance and expansion of the U.P.E. scheme, the founding of a new university in the Eastern Region, the expansion and improvement of the health services, the handing over of greater responsibilities to the local government councils as 'our people gradually appreciate their duty, exhibit a sense of truth, probity and honesty in the discharge of their sacred duties', the 'self-realization of our peoples and communities in voluntary effort and communal labour', the commercial and industrial development of Eastern Region, the diversification of economic crops and the eradication of yam beetles.

Perhaps the most interesting feature of the N.C.N.C. Manifesto was its Part IV, in which 3½ pages were devoted to the N.C.N.C.'s proposals for constitutional reform. The manifesto announced that the N.C.N.C. would press for immediate self-government for the whole of Nigeria at the forthcoming Constitutional Conference, and that, since it considered the unity of the country to be of paramount importance, it would be prepared to come to an understanding with other political parties in the best interests of the country.

Its detailed proposals for the reorganization of the regional structure were as follows:

(a) *The Governor*. The Governor should be appointed by Her Majesty's Government, after consultation with the Regional Government, for a period of five years. He will represent Her Majesty's Government in the Region, open Sessions of the House of Assembly, assent to all Bills, and cease to be a member of the Executive Council.

The Governor's reserved powers, which shall be clearly written into the Constitution, should only remain for those instances where the machinery of Government has broken down and all possible constitutional processes are incapable of resolving the situation. The Governor should have power to disallow a Bill only where it is in the interest of the Federation that the Bill should be reserved or should be disallowed by Her Majesty's Government.

(b) *The Deputy Governor*. The Deputy Governor should be appointed in the same way and for the same term as the Governor, and should assist the Governor in the exercise of his duties, acting as Governor in the absence of the substantive holder of the post.

(c) *The Civil Service*. The N.C.N.C. proposed to establish an executive organ known as the Public Service Commission, which should have a chairman and four members, holding office for six years and appointed by the Governor after consultation with the Premier. It should be responsible to the Regional Government for all appointments to the public service of the Region, promotions, transfers, discipline, and conditions of service.

(d) *The Judiciary*. The N.C.N.C. was of opinion that the judiciary should be the responsibility of the Federal Government. If this ideal cannot be achieved there should be established a Judicial Service Commission with functions in respect of judicial officers similar to those exercised by the Public Service Commission in respect of the Civil Service. The membership of the Commission should comprise the Chief Justice and two other judges, one of whom may be a retired judge. The Chief Justice and other judges should be appointed by the Governor after consultation with the Premier, and should have security of tenure except on a resolution in the House of Assembly carried by a two-thirds majority of the total membership of the House.

The Attorney General and Solicitor General should be political appointments from among persons who are qualified to be appointed judges of the High Court.

(e) *The legislature*. The House of Assembly should consist of not less than ninety-four members with representation based on population.

A House of Chiefs should be set up on the lines recommended by the Jones Commission.[1] Elections should be by direct secret ballot based on universal adult suffrage in single member constituencies. The Cabinet system should continue, but the Premier should preside at meetings of the Cabinet instead of the Governor.

(f) *States*. The manifesto recommended that the States into which the Federation of Nigeria should be divided should be based upon present provincial boundaries, or alternatively fourteen States (which are listed in the manifesto) should be set up by subdividing the existing regions. The population of the recommended States ranges from 3·3 millions for Kano to 1·4 millions for the proposed Mid-West State. The N.C.N.C. would not support the proposed 'Ogoja–Rivers–Calabar'[2] State, 'because it is meaningless'. It therefore asked the electorate 'to reject the senseless proposal'.

(g) *Revenue allocation*. The existing revenue allocation by the Federal Government, based on derivation, was unfavourable to the Eastern Region, which contributed comparatively little to federal revenues and so received a comparatively small allocation. The N.C.N.C therefore supported a system of revenue allocation based on an otherwise undefined principle of independent revenues, needs, and the national interest.

The Action Group manifesto, which was entitled 'Operation Broom' —an allusion to the Action Group's hope of sweeping the N.C.N.C. out of the Region—was a much shorter document, occupying only five tabloid columns of newsprint, and was re-published in full in the *Daily Times* and the *Daily Service*.

The Preamble laid stress upon the necessity for the people of the Eastern Region to choose between two *national* parties, and claimed that the Action Group's plans, vision, and competence had been 'praised and plauded by Her Majesty the Queen, by political leaders and business men in U.S.A., by experts in Germany and Japan, and by His Holiness the Pope'. It contrasted the 'honest, dynamic administration' of the Action Group in Western Region, where free primary education for all had been achieved coupled with 'reasonably low' taxation levels, with the 'instability' and 'squandermania' of the N.C.N.C., which was guilty of 'corruption, graft, and nepotism'. In the Eastern Region, it claimed, 'morality has been banished from public life'.

The programme. In order that 'out of the existing chaos the East

[1] G. I. Jones, *Report of the Position, Status, and Influence of Chiefs and Natural Rulers in the Eastern Region of Nigeria* (Government Printer, Enugu, 1957).
[2] Note the changed order of the names, in order to avoid bringing the initials 'C.O.R.' to the voter's mind.

shall again emerge, under Action Group leadership, a prosperous, happy and contented Region in which all tribes, clans, and communities shall live together as happy members of a great family', the manifesto proposed an eighteen-point programme which may be summarized as follows:

(i) Economical administration, including the closing down of the 'wasteful and unproductive' Corporations, and the abolition of communal discrimination;

(ii) The creation of a 'happy and contented Civil Service', including 'the guarantee of attractive and stable service conditions to expatriates';

(iii) Amendments to the Eastern Region Local Government Law to strengthen the local authorities against the Regional Government, and to give greater standing to chiefs and other traditional rulers;

(iv) The revision of the Eastern Region Tax Law to remove the anomalies in the present income-tax system,[1] to exempt disabled and unemployed ex-servicemen and all men over seventy-five from direct taxation, and to abolish the recently introduced taxation of women;

(v) The stabilization of the prices of primary produce through Marketing Boards;

(vi) The stimulation of Nigerian business enterprises by expanding credit facilities, supporting all Nigerian banks without exception, provided they achieve the minimum standard of efficiency as laid down in the Banking Ordinance of Nigeria'[2]—'exploring all legitimate ways' to make the vast credit facilities of the British-owned banks available to Nigerian businessmen, and setting up through the Federal Government a State Bank for the whole of Nigeria;[3]

(vii) The establishment of a minimum daily wage of 5s. for all regional and local government labourers and the improvement of the salaries of local government officials and of teachers and nurses employed by the voluntary agencies to the levels enjoyed by the Civil Service, together with the implementation of the Davies Report[4] on increased salaries for civil servants;

(viii) Co-operation with local trade unions, provided that they recognize the need for a central trade union organization for the whole of the Federation of Nigeria;

(ix) The economic development of the Region, mainly by 'en-

---

[1] In fact, the system penalizes taxpayers heavily when they move up from one income-class to another; as a result of promotion, a man's *net* income may be reduced. Paradoxically, too, a man with a taxable income of £1 per annum pays £1. 10s. income tax.   [2] A dig at the African Continental Bank.

[3] Banking is a federal subject under the present Constitution.

[4] C. Davies, *Report and Recommendations of the United Kingdom Grading Officer* (Govt. Printer, Enugu, 1956).

couraging and supporting the efforts of private businessmen', and attracting foreign investment on mutually advantageous terms;

(x) The encouragement of modern farming and fishing through loans and subventions, particularly to those farmers and fishermen who unite together in producers' co-operatives;

(xi) The encouragement of the expansion of the co-operative movement, and the setting up of a Co-operative Bank of Eastern Region with an initial capital of at least £1 million;

(xii) The improvement of the status of chiefs and traditional rulers through adequate salaries, the granting to them of automatic membership of local councils, and the creation of an Eastern Region House of Chiefs;

(xiii) The improvement of communications within the Region, and in particular the tarring of a minimum of 200 miles of road each year;

(xiv) An educational programme which will 'guarantee that our educational institutions are thoroughly imbued with a Christian atmosphere'. Particular points of the educational programme are that the Action Group will launch a free universal primary educa-tion scheme, allow the voluntary agencies (i.e. the Missions) to open and run their schools under the scheme, guarantee the parents' right to choose schools for their children, encourage post-secondary school education by way of scholarships, bursaries, and studentships held both at the University College, Ibadan, and overseas, encourage worker students by providing evening tuition in Polytechnics, estab-lish well-equipped reading-rooms and lending libraries in the main towns of the Region, and expand teacher-training facilities in order to provide qualified teachers for the free primary education scheme;

(xv) The abolition of unemployment amongst ex-servicemen— 'the complete rehabilitation of our war heroes';

(xvi) The establishment of a free medical service for all under eighteen years and the provision of improved medical facilities, and mobile and floating dispensaries for the remoter areas;

(xvii) The extension of pipe-borne water-supplies in the main towns and deep wells in the rural areas; and

(xviii) Reafforestation to counteract soil erosion.

Constitutional proposals. The Action Group announced in its mani-festo that it would press at the forthcoming Constitutional Conference in London for the following:

(i) a strong and united Federation of Nigeria;

(ii) self-government for all Nigeria now, and in any case self-government for the Eastern Region now;

(iii) the creation of the Calabar–Ogoja–Rivers State, and any other states according to the wishes of the people of any given area;

(iv) residual powers to be vested in the Regions or States;

(v) revenue allocation to be on the basis of derivation subject to enough funds being made available to the Federal Government.

It will be noticed that both national parties refer in their manifestos to the vexed question of the allocation of federal revenues to the Regions, taking opposite viewpoints in the matter. This is the most important divergence in declared policy between the two parties, but it cannot be said that the average voter could comprehend the issue involved or that it affected his voting on polling day.

The manifesto of the United National Independence Party did not appear until 23 February 1957, and was the shortest and least detailed of all the manifestos in the election. Its proposals were as follows:

(i) *Constitutional.* In the manifesto U.N.I.P. stated that it was convinced that the splitting of the existing Regions into smaller units or states would conduce to Nigerian unity and make for a true federation. At the centre the party with an overall majority in the Federal House should form the Government and supply a Prime Minister. Given smaller units or states, U.N.I.P. accepted the thesis that residual power should be with the states. There should be written into the Constitution, however, guarantees against the right to secede.

U.N.I.P. believed that the present powers of the Federal Supreme Court on constitutional issues between the Regions should be enlarged to include original powers to deal with all infringements of individual freedom guaranteed by the Constitution. Except for the Federal Supreme Court, the Judiciary should remain a state responsibility. There should, however, be a Federal Appellate Court with unlimited jurisdiction over all matters within the competence of the state courts.

Each state should be responsible for its police force and for its civil service. University education and higher education at a comparable level should be a federal subject.

(ii) *Fiscal.* U.N.I.P. considered that the preservation of a due balance between federal and state considerations was not an easy achievement. It was, however, in favour of a judicious combination of the principles of needs, national interest, and derivation. None of these principles worked in isolation could, in the opinion of U.N.I.P., produce a fair and equitable result.

(iii) *The composition of the legislature.* U.N.I.P. wished to set up two Legislative Houses in each state as well as in the federal capital. 'We desire to see a bicameral arrangement at the centre, where the States would have equal representation in the Second Chamber.'

(iv) *The Eastern Region finance law.* U.N.I.P. promised to repeal this law (which *inter alia* includes a provision for the taxation of women) if it were voted into power. It condemned the excessively high schedule of taxation, which was weighted against the poorer classes and lower income groups. U.N.I.P. opposed the taxation of women, the 6*d.* per gallon tax on petrol in the Region, and the power to arrest without a warrant.

(v) *Trade Unions.* U.N.I.P. promised to encourage the trade unions to flourish and grow. It accepted the principle of collective bargaining as the inalienable right of all workers. 'Consultation and negotiation between labour and capital constitute the essence of economic democracy.'

(vi) *The farmers.* The party promised to encourage the creation of Farmers' Associations and to insist that the State Marketing Board should consult with their representatives before fixing produce prices.

(vii) *Health.* U.N.I.P. was resolved to throw every available penny and all available energy into the eradication of such menaces as yaws, mosquitoes, leprosy, and tuberculosis.

(viii) *Banking policy.* On the Foster-Sutton Tribunal report and the N.C.N.C. banking policy, which the party alleged to be the predominant electoral issue, U.N.I.P. accused the N.C.N.C. of making use of a smokescreen to veil the true issue involved in the inquiry—that of public morality. The manifesto stated: 'We have always supported the demand for the creation of a *genuine* State Bank and hereby reiterate that declaration.'

Despite its declared intention of fighting the election on the banking issue, U.N.I.P. was from the start identified in the popular mind and in the press with the campaign for the setting up of the separate 'C.O.R.' state, which would be free from Ibo domination.

6. *Mass Media of Communication*

It is obvious that in any predominantly illiterate community the conventional mass media of communication touch only a comparatively small proportion of the population, especially when wireless sets are beyond the means of the average man. At the same time, ideas and news spread very quickly in such communities by word of mouth, and it is important to analyse the mass media of communication which had an effect upon the election.

The press. There are four national newspapers which circulate in the Eastern Region, of which three are newspapers in the generally accepted sense and the fourth a religious weekly. All the other newspapers and periodicals are of purely regional interest and circulation. The national newspapers are as follows:[1]

[1] In both these tables circulation figures are estimated, and are certainly unreliable.

Name	Frequency	Circula-tion	Language	Proprietor	Political affiliation
Daily Times	Daily	79,597	English	The Daily Mirror Group	Non-party
Daily Service	Daily	18,000	English	Amalgamated Press of Nigeria Ltd., Lagos	Action Group
West African Pilot	Daily	18,000	English	West African Pilot Ltd., Yaba, Lagos	N.C.N.C.
Nigerian Catholic Herald	Weekly	12,000	English	Roman Catholic Mission, Ebute Metta, Lagos	..

The purely regional organs are:

Name	Frequency	Circula-tion	Language	Proprietor	Political affiliation
The Nigerian Spokesman	Daily	3,000	English	Associated Newspapers of Nigeria Ltd., Onitsha	N.C.N.C.
Eastern Nigerian Guardian	Daily	3,000	English	Associated Newspapers of Nigeria Ltd., Port Harcourt	N.C.N.C.
Eastern States Express	Daily	3,000	English	Ilemesit Co. Ltd., Aba	U.N.I.P.
Nigerian Daily Standard	Daily	2,500	English	Old Calabar Press, Calabar	U.N.I.P.
New Africa	Daily	2,000	English	Renascent Africa Press Ltd., Enugu	Doubtful but anti-Azikiwe
Eastern Sentinel	Daily	1,000	English	Zik Enterprises Ltd., Enugu	N.C.N.C.
Eastern Outlook	Weekly	13,000	English	Eastern Nigerian Information Services, Enugu	Pro-Government
Nigerian Observer	Twice weekly	2,000	English	Enitonna Ebul Stores, Port Harcourt	..
Nnewi District Telegraph	Monthly	1,000	English	G. Mojkwu, Onitsha	..
Niger News	Irregularly	..	English and Ibo	Church Missionary Society, Port Harcourt	..
Catholic Life	Weekly	..	English	Roman Catholic Mission, Onitsha	..
The Leader	Weekly	22,000	English	Roman Catholic Mission, Owerri	..

The *Daily Times*, which also has an evening edition circulating in the Lagos area and a Sunday edition (circulation 90,000) which, however, mainly contains 'magazine' features, is the best printed and best produced newspaper in Nigeria. Like its sister newspapers, the *Daily Graphic* in Accra and the *Daily Mail* in Freetown, which are also owned by the London *Daily Mirror* group, the *Daily Times* strives after a reputation for political impartiality. Unlike its sister newspapers, however, its method of achieving this seems to be by attacking each of the three major parties for approximately ten days each month, thus ensuring that two-thirds of its readers are satisfied at any given moment. According to its proprietors, it has a circulation in the Eastern Region of about 20,000. Many newspaper readers in Nigeria buy the *Daily Times* in addition to the newspaper which supports the party of their choice, because the *Daily Times* has by far and away the best news coverage of events both inside and outside Nigeria of any newspapers published in the country.

The *Daily Service* is the best printed of the newspapers published under local enterprise. Its news coverage both of home and foreign affairs is good, and it includes much more news about Ghana than any of the other Nigerian newspapers. The tone of its leading-page articles is violently abusive of the N.C.N.C., and fulsomely laudatory of Action Group personalities and policies.

The *West African Pilot* is also well printed, but contains much less overseas news than either the *Daily Times* or the *Daily Service*. As might be expected from one of Zik's many enterprises, it is very abusive about the Action Group, and devotes much space to the cult of Dr. Azikiwe's personality.

The *Nigerian Spokesman*, in common with the other privately owned regional newspapers, is very badly printed. It is pro-Zik, and its editorials have a strong republican flavour.

The *Eastern Nigerian Guardian* has as its slogan, printed across the front page of each issue, 'That universal brotherhood shall become a reality.' This does not prevent it from being vehemently anti-Roman Catholic: '. . . Roman Catholicism with its creed of gangsterism is riding to a fall.'

One Opposition newspaper, the *Eastern States Express*, which is very poorly printed, stands in an extreme left-wing position, and repeatedly accuses Dr. Azikiwe of being a Fascist. It gives strong support to the trade union movement. One curious report which it carried during the election campaign, for which there was no confirmation from other sources, was that a secret oath was taken at the Rex Cinema in Enugu by all the zonal leaders of the Zikist

National Vanguard. Each member present took an egg in his hand, it reported, held it to his chest, and then raised his arms in the air, while the oath was being sworn.

The *Nigerian Daily Standard* is comparatively well printed, and has an attractive type face on its outside pages, though the inside pages do not maintain this standard. As a U.N.I.P. organ, it strongly supports the proposed C.O.R. state, but its propaganda is very unskilful. It concerns itself mainly with local issues, and has very little news even of a regional flavour. Its editorial tone is, however, much more sweetly reasonable than that of most local newspapers.

New Africa, the motto of which is 'One God, one human race', is again very badly printed. As an Opposition organ in search of allies, it is strongly biased towards the Roman Catholic Mission, and during the pre-election period published a series of syndicated articles attacking freemasonry. It has throughout a strongly religious flavour.

The *Eastern Sentinel*, like most newspapers owned by Dr. Azikiwe, is comparatively well printed. Despite its leading-page slogan: 'That democracy shall continue to flourish', it frequently urges Dr. Azikiwe to follow a policy of dictatorship for three or four years, before 'putting on the garb of a democrat'. Its attitude over the report of the Tribunal was shrill.

The Eastern Outlook, as may be expected, since it is printed on contract for the Eastern Nigerian Information Service by the Government Printer, Enugu, is an elegant and well-turned-out publication. It gives an outward and specious appearance of impartiality, but actually it supports Dr. Azikiwe's government: for instance, after the announcement of the Foster-Sutton Tribunal's findings, it came out in strong defence of Dr. Azikiwe. This publication is discussed further when E.N.I.S. is examined.

The bi-weekly *Nigerian Observer* is the worst printed of all the newspapers in Eastern Region. It is also perhaps the most unbelievably unpolitical newspaper in Nigeria; the leading articles in the first two issues after the Foster-Sutton Report had been released dealt with rent control and with Soviet intervention in Hungary. It was not until 25 January 1957 that, after considerable equivocating, the leader-writer came out with 'After all, no man is perfect', in referring to the Tribunal's findings.

The *Nnewi District Telegraph* and the *Niger News* were too elusive to fall into the writer's hands.

The Roman Catholic newspapers, which are all excellently printed and skilfully edited, bore the hallmarks of syndication. They contained frequent attacks upon the alleged freemasonry of the

Eastern Region ministers, and constantly stressed the small number of expatriate Roman Catholic priests compared with the total population (the Roman Catholic Mission was frequently criticized as representing 'Irish Imperialism'). Even at the height of the election campaign, which they conducted with considerable skill, the Roman Catholic papers displayed none of the hysteria to which the more politically minded newspapers gave vent; instead, one got the impression of a huge, tireless, timeless propaganda machine in motion. Perhaps the most effective piece of propaganda in the whole of the election campaign was the front page of the *Leader* in its last issue before polling day. After having preached for several weeks past 'Your duty as a Catholic: to vote for honest and upright men', it bore on the front page a striking photograph of a pair of praying hands, reminiscent of the famous Dürer etching, underneath which was the caption: 'PRAY that there will be elected honest and upright men, who will respect the laws of God, and the rights of the Catholic Church.' The editorial in this issue reads: 'It is an incontestable fact that the main issue at stake in the election is that of education. The natural rights of Catholics have been violated, their protestations ignored. They and their Church have been the object of a lie-and-smear campaign. On March 15th the religious future of their children is in their own hands. After March the 15th it is in somebody else's!' At the bottom of the page was the Ibo slogan "NWA KA EGO, NWA KA AKθ'—'a child is worth more than money or riches.'

Finally, in order to give some impression of the bitterness of press comments during the election period, the following is an extract from the *Nigerian Spokesman* of 8 March 1957 (the *Spokesman* carried a front-page article every day during the campaign period describing in detail alleged Action Group corruption in connexion with the elections).

> *War Communique*
> *ZNV Supreme Command*
> *Bulletin 00226*
>
> *Onitsha Rivers Front.* . . . At 0010 hours on Tuesday morning, an Admiralty Convoy of destroyers, men of wars, covets, and squadrons, accompanied by Spitfires, V2, Jet Bombers, and fighters of the Fleet-Air Arm of a combined forces of the NCNC–ZNV Supreme Command attacked enemy posts in Umunachi, Umudioka, Nteje, Nkwele, and Ogbunike, after the surrender of enemy troops in Awka-Etiti, Nnobi, Oraukwu and Alor.
>
> At Ogbunike an enemy fifth-columnist was captured alive, and was brought before the NCNC War Council in Generalissimo Zik's camp where he made startling disclosures of enemy plans. . . .

It was decided to grant clemency to this spy by only cutting off his left ear and thenceforth to respect the territorial integrity and national independency of one Nigeria. . . .

The Nigerian Broadcasting Service. The N.B.S. is a federal service with its centre in Lagos, but its organization in each Region is under a Regional Controller, who has considerable discretion in the choice and presentation of local programmes.

Owing to the high cost of wireless sets, N.B.S. programmes reach the public largely through rediffusion. In the Western Region the rediffusion services are operated by a private company, but in the Eastern Region the Posts and Telegraphs Department are responsible for the facilities. There are about 4,000 rediffusion boxes in the Region, but although it is known that there is an unsatisfied demand for at least 12,000 additional boxes in the four main towns alone, the Posts and Telegraphs Department have decided not to extend the service, but only to maintain the existing number of boxes. Boxes are available only in Enugu, Port Harcourt, Onitsha, and Calabar, which are the four main towns of the Region. There are no boxes or public receivers in the market places of villages, such as are found in other parts of West Africa, particularly in Ghana.

Listener research has revealed that the audience pattern is rapidly changing in the Eastern Region. The commercial firms have given evidence of rapidly increased sales of the cheaper wireless sets (£6 to £7) since the introduction into the Region of cheap sets manufactured by Pye and a new cheap long-life battery ('Berec') which is very satisfactory in tropical conditions.

The normal peak-period listening public in the Region is about 200,000, but certain outstanding broadcasts have attracted an audience of up to a million listeners. As is common in predominantly illiterate countries, the secondary audience, that is the group to which information is passed by listeners by word of mouth, is very high. A controlled experiment in Enugu, where there are only 1,000 rediffusion boxes, revealed that an announcement of a mass meeting which was put out on the boxes, but was deliberately not broadcast over the air or reproduced elsewhere, produced an audience of 17,000 at the meeting.

Nearly all broadcasting is done in English, and vernacular broadcasts account for only about 10 per cent. of the broadcasting time. Only Ibo and Efik, the language widely spoken in the south-eastern corner of the Region, are used. Even so, the fact that there are seventeen different dialects of Ibo, which are to a large extent mutually incomprehensible, presents a serious problem to vernacular broadcasters.

The headquarters of the N.B.S. in Lagos keeps control of political broadcasts in its own hands. This attempt at remote control often leads to breakdowns in the detailed arrangements. The Lagos proposals for the political broadcasts in connexion with the Eastern regional election campaign were that three half-hour programmes each should be given to the Government and to the Opposition as a whole. The N.C.N.C. was thus allocated three half-hour periods, the Action Group two half-hour periods, and U.N.I.P. one half-hour period. There was to be one repeat broadcast of each talk. Of the N.C.N.C. talks, one was given by Dr. M. I. Okpara, the Minister of Health, who spoke for twenty minutes in English and for ten minutes in Ibo, one was given by Mr. Ameche, the Regional Secretary of the N.C.N.C., who spoke for fifteen minutes in English, after which a N.B.S. translator gave his speech again in Efik, and the last was given by Dr. Azikiwe, speaking for a full thirty minutes in English. Mr. Alvan Ikoku, the Deputy Leader of the Opposition in the old Assembly, broadcast for the U.N.I.P. in English. The first Action Group broadcast was half in English and half in Ibo, while in the second broadcast it had been planned that Mr. Ikoku's son should broadcast for fifteen minutes in Efik to introduce a fifteen-minute speech in English by Chief Awolowo, but when the time for the broadcast came Mr. Ikoku Junior insisted on speaking in English.

In addition to these special political broadcasts during the election period, the Eastern Region of N.B.S. has a weekly programme known as 'Government Hour', which was instituted in March 1955. This broadcasting time is made available to the Government to use as it wishes, but a set pattern has developed. For the first twenty minutes of the broadcast a minister gives a talk on the work of his own department; the next twenty minutes consist of a series of questions and answers; while the final twenty minutes is given up to 'public service broadcasting' (for example, a series of talks on dietetics by Dr. Azikiwe's niece). On the whole, Dr. Azikiwe has played fair with this programme, and when Mr. I. U. Akpabio, the Minister of Education, turned one of his talks into a political speech, the Premier allowed the Opposition to utilize time in 'Government Hour' for making a reply.

The influence of the N.B.S. during the election campaign was much stronger in the four main towns than in the rural areas, where there are no rediffusion facilities, but even there it made itself felt.

The Eastern Nigerian Information Service. Unlike the Federal Government of Nigeria and the other regional governments, whose information services are the responsibility of a government department, the

Eastern Region has a public corporation which is responsible for the dissemination of government information. The chairman of the Corporation is Mr. A. J. Disu, a Muslim journalist who has had wide experience both inside and outside Nigeria, and who is a strong supporter of the N.C.N.C. To an outside observer E.N.I.S. seems to be used to an alarming extent as an instrument of party political propaganda, but this provokes little comment or criticism from the general public, who tend to look upon the party and the state as one.

Reference has been made to E.N.I.S.'s weekly newspaper, *Eastern Outlook*, which takes as strong an N.C.N.C. line as any of Dr. Azikiwe's own newspapers. This attitude became more and more noticeable during the election period. The political broadcast by Dr. Azikiwe, alone of all the political leaders who had spoken, was reproduced in full, occupying a complete issue of the *Eastern Outlook*, and there were frequent photographs of N.C.N.C. rallies with captions such as 'A crowd acclaiming Zik's leadership by a show of hands'.

E.N.I.S. issues daily cyclostyled press releases to newspapers and to the N.B.S. These are for the most part purely factual, and include news from other parts of Nigeria supplied by the Federal and Regional Information Services.

The posters and handbills issued by E.N.I.S. during the registration and election period were of a uniformly poor quality. They would in any case have been much more appropriately issued by the Government itself.

During the election campaign the liaison between E.N.I.S. and the N.C.N.C. in the field was very close. Opposition politicians protested against the fact that the N.C.N.C. were using an E.N.I.S. Land Rover fitted with a loudspeaker for propaganda in bush villages. This Land Rover, which had been hired from E.N.I.S. by the N.C.N.C., still bore the E.N.I.S. markings when it was being used for party purposes.

7. *The Campaign*

The election campaigns of the main parties may be said to have begun on 8 February 1957, when registration ended. In fact, however, there was no formal division between the political campaigning during the registration period and that during the pre-election period; the one campaign merged almost imperceptibly into the other.

The parties. As described earlier, the issues before the electorate at the opening of the campaign appeared to be the Foster-Sutton

Tribunal, the forthcoming Constitutional Conference, Universal Primary Education, and the taxation of women. These issues were all laid before the public by spokesmen of all parties during the early stages, but despite the vociferous Roman Catholic Mission campaign on the issue of religious freedom and education, it soon became apparent that the electorate were really considering only one question: 'Are you for or against Zik, and therefore for or against Ibo rule?'

As might be expected, the N.C.N.C., wealthy, locally well established, and with the reins of Government and the power of patronage in its hands, was incomparably the best organized of the parties in the field. Dr. Azikiwe, ever keen on grandiose schemes which will attract public attention, announced that he would conduct his personal campaign by helicopter, claiming that this would be the first time that a helicopter had been used for such a purpose in the whole of the African Continent, and pointing out that this form of transport was the only satisfactory method for covering large areas of bush with poor communications. As the only helicopters in the Region are owned by the Shell–B.P. Development Company, which is sinking bore-holes in several parts of the Region in search of oil, the Public Relations Officer of Shell–B.P. issued an immediate denial that the Company proposed to lend a helicopter to Dr. Azikiwe. The project was finally killed by the Federal Department of Civil Aviation, which pointed out that under the Civil Aviation Ordinance it would be an offence for a helicopter to land except at an 'authorized landing ground'.

Because of this setback (but perhaps the scheme was never seriously intended), Dr. Azikiwe divided the ministers and parliamentary secretaries and other prominent personalities of the party into two groups, which were to campaign independently. Detailed itineraries, which read rather like army movement orders, were prepared and published for the two groups. These were circulated to all senior civil servants, in order that they might know where ministers could be reached in case of emergency during the campaign period, but in fact, owing to transport difficulties and the poor health of Dr. Azikiwe, the itineraries were not rigidly adhered to. The two groups travelled through the constituencies by road or by launch, whichever was appropriate, holding mass rallies in the larger centres and more informal meetings in smaller villages. On one occasion the Premier's launch ran aground on a sandbank and he was able to extract a great deal of personal publicity out of photographs of himself, stripped to his vest, pulling on the rope of the launch in order to free it. The *West African Pilot*, in an excess of hero worship, published a photograph of him standing in about eighteen inches of water, captioned: 'Zik swims to safety.'

Small propaganda teams, consisting of party organizers and sympathizers, travelled from village to village throughout the bush, and claimed to have covered practically every village in the Region by the end of the campaign. These teams, in hired canoes or Land Rovers, would on arrival in each village gather a crowd together by playing gramophone dance-music over the amplifier systems mounted on the Land Rovers or by beating drums, and would then give short pep-talks in the local vernacular, the main burden of which would be an exhortation to the villagers to support Dr. Azikiwe against the 'British Imperialists' and against the 'tribalists' from Western Region. Explanations were also given of the importance of voting and of how to do it, and it was often implied that the village would derive specific benefits after his return to power if it had solidly supported Dr. Azikiwe.[1]

Meanwhile, detachments of the Zikist National Vanguard roamed around the country in taxis loaned by members, whipping up enthusiasm, attempting to break up Action Group meetings, and on occasion threatening people with reprisals if they attended Action Group meetings or gave support to the Action Group. The Z.N.V. was, however, only conspicuous in the major towns which are linked by tarred roads, as the owner-drivers of the taxis were naturally reluctant to take them over bush tracks.

Much publicity was given during the campaign to the fact that Chief Hassan, the Regional President of the Eastern Muslim Party, had called upon Muslims in the Region to support the N.C.N.C., and had led prayers for an N.C.N.C. victory. As most of the Muslims in the Eastern Region are immigrants from the North, where in the past the majority party, the Northern People's Congress, had been hostile to the N.C.N.C., which had supported and been affiliated with the Northern opposition party, N.E.P.U., this seemed somewhat surprising, until investigation showed that at the time of the campaign the N.P.C. was having a quarrel with the Action Group over whether or not the Emirate of Ilorin, the population of which is largely Yoruba, should be detached from the Northern Region to join the predominantly Yoruba Western Region. The aim of the Muslims was therefore to prevent the Action Group from being successful in the Eastern Region. This intervention by the Eastern Muslim Party, although of considerable propaganda value to the N.C.N.C., which could use it to demonstrate that the party was

---

[1] An example of the propaganda put out by the N.C.N.C. for consumption at the bush village level is reproduced in Appendix I.

supported by non-Ibos, had a negligible effect upon the result of the election, since there are only about 50,000 Muslims resident in Eastern Region, and they are all concentrated in the large commercial towns, where their votes would be swallowed up in the large aggregates.

There was no reliable information about the source of the sums (over £70,000, it was said) spent by the N.C.N.C. during the election campaign; it was widely supposed that, apart from subventions from the African Continental Bank, considerable sums of money were received both as loans and as gifts from wealthy party supporters, who were either grateful for favours already received or hopeful of future favours if the N.C.N.C. were returned to office. It is certain that the subscriptions collected from paid-up members represented only a very small proportion of the total expenditure, especially as (even at election time) it has become the common practice in British West Africa not to pay one's subscription to the party which one supports unless one has to be a fully paid up member (or, as it is locally termed, a 'financial' member) in order to be eligible for office.

Action Group was campaigning for the first time in the Eastern Region, and had to build up its organization from scratch. A regional campaign headquarters was opened in a chalet at the Catering Rest House in Enugu under the direction of Mr. O. Agunblade-Bamishe, the party manager in the Region. This was a very convenient arrangement, as it meant that party leaders visiting the Region from the West and campaigners returning from the constituencies in the Region could be accommodated and fed in the Rest House in close proximity to their headquarters.

There is only one convenient crossing of the Niger from the Western Region, the ferry at Onitsha, and from the beginning of February 1957 large numbers of Action Group officials and supporters, together with twenty-five Land Rovers, came pouring over this ferry.

Chief Awolowo opened the Action Group campaign at Uyo on 2 February 1957 with a speech which set the keynote of the Action Group's campaign (Operation 'Broom'). In it he refuted the charges of tribalism levelled at him and his party by the N.C.N.C., alleged that the burden of taxation upon the poorer classes was much heavier in the Eastern Region than in the West, and stressed the low standards of public morality of the N.C.N.C. leaders, as evidenced by the report of the Foster-Sutton Tribunal. Two days later he and the other Action Group leaders conferred with U.N.I.P. in Aba with a view to setting up a coalition of the two parties under the title 'UNIPAG' for electoral purposes. This conference was only partially successful; the Action Group leaders were, it seems likely, somewhat unimpressed with the support which U.N.I.P. could offer them. It did, however, result in many candidates putting themselves forward in the earlier part of the campaign under the 'UNIPAG' aegis. The electoral agreement survived until the poll in a few constituencies, but only on a local basis.

Like the wise general of an invading army, Chief Awolowo did not allow his forces to be dispersed. Instead, the Action Group leaders moved together in a Land Rover cavalcade slowly across Eastern Region, holding large meetings in the major centres of population. These were much more formal and impressive than the majority of the N.C.N.C. meetings, and in every case an attempt, often successful, was made to secure the presence of traditional rulers and other local notabilities on the platform. A large part of the campaigning in fact consisted of making overtures privately to local leaders.

Owing to language difficulties Chief Awolowo and the other Yoruba Action Group leaders usually only spoke on these platforms for a few minutes in English, and then introduced some local notability who could address the audience in their own language. Although pidgin English is the *lingua franca* of the major towns of the Region, attempts to address the crowds in English for long periods were unsuccessful, since the standard English spoken by Chief Awolowo and his lieutenants was as unintelligible to the crowds as Yoruba would have been.

Groups of uniformed 'Area Boys' travelled with the Action Group cavalcade as bodyguards, and there were occasional clashes between them and the Z.N.V., particularly in Aba, a rapidly growing commercial centre, where political feelings have traditionally been very strong. Despite this, the allegation by N.C.N.C. newspapers that large numbers of hooligans were brought across the Niger by Action Group seems to have been unfounded.

Action Group showed its fighting spirit by concentrating its activities principally on the N.C.N.C.-dominated centres of population. Whether this was a sound electoral tactic it is hard to say, but greater dividends might have been achieved by giving more attention to the marginal areas and particularly to the villages, most of which were never visited by Action Group during the whole campaign. Action Group's propaganda in the bush was extremely ineffective, and will have to be improved considerably if the party wishes to enhance its position in a future election.

The party leaders, unlike their opposite numbers in the N.C.N.C.,

were handicapped during the campaign because government business was not at a standstill in the Western Region, and ministers
had therefore to return at frequent intervals to Ibadan to deal with
work piling up in their ministries. They were also hampered by a
lack of knowledge of the local vernaculars or of the local variety of
pidgin English, and by the allegation, which was repeatedly published in N.C.N.C. newspapers and from N.C.N.C. platforms, that
Chief Awolowo had called the Ibos 'half-naked cannibals'. This
allegation was never specifically denied by him during the campaign, but in an attempt to counteract its effects, the Action Group
newspapers frequently published photographs showing Dr. Azikiwe
and Chief Awolowo shaking hands with each other. This caused
repeated protests in the N.C.N.C. newspapers, which seemed to
think that to publish propaganda of this type was hitting below the
belt.

Whatever their other handicaps, the Action Group propagandists were not handicapped by shortage of money. The allegation in
the *Nigerian Spokesman* that in addition to the twenty-five Land
Rovers the Action Group had brought over a sum of £100,000 for
the election campaign in Eastern Region is certainly exaggerated,
but a very considerable sum must have been spent by them. There
were press reports that many leading business men and others in
Western Region had complained that they had not received the
favours which they had expected in return for the financial support
which they had given to Action Group during the Western Region
election; and it was universally assumed that Action Group raised
its funds for the Eastern election in much the same way as the
N.C.N.C. did, but from Westerners and not from Easterners.

Little can be said of U.N.I.P.'s campaigning methods. There
were a few desultory meetings addressed by Mr. Eyo Ita in Calabar,
but in most cases the campaign in the constituency was left to the
individual U.N.I.P. candidate concerned, and there were no attempts
to take the war into the enemy's camp. Organization was negligible,
and the leaders seemed to lack any drive or ability to settle down to
the arduous grind of campaigning. The leaders in their propaganda
tended to lay a great deal of stress upon their academic qualifications
and attainments, a point which, unfortunately, in modern West
African political conditions does not bring in the votes. Their
political utterances, like their manifesto, read rather like the essays
of a first-year 'Modern Greats' student, and showed no signs that the
implications had been realized or thoroughly studied. It is true that
the party suffered from shortage of funds, and everything had to be
done 'on the cheap'. The defeatism and lack of activity of the party

compared with Action Group may go a long way towards explaining the fact that the number of seats it won was only half those it held in the old Assembly, five instead of ten.

Symbols and photographs. Some friction was caused during the election campaign by the allocation of symbols to the candidates for fixing to ballot boxes and for use during the campaign. It was laid down in the electoral regulations that these should be 6 in. × 6 in., and a series of officially approved symbols was drawn by a commercial artist employed by E.N.I.S., specimens of which were run off by the government printer. Officially certified candidates of the parties were to use the officially approved symbol of the party, while independent candidates could choose any of the remaining symbols. Other symbols could be used by local independent candidates provided that they were officially approved, conformed to the electoral regulations in respect to the size, and were supplied by the candidate himself.

The N.C.N.C. took the red cock as its symbol. This symbol is also in use in other parts of West Africa for similar purposes, first of all by the Convention People's Party in Ghana, and recently by the U.P.P. in Sierra Leone. As Action Group had contested the Western Region elections with the oil-palm tree as a symbol, it naturally wished to do the same in Eastern Region, and the green palm tree supplied by the government printer was allocated to it. U.N.I.P. took a lion as its symbol.

After the 'UNIPAG' conference at Aba on 4 February 1957, representatives of the two parties approached the Regional Electoral Officer for permission to use a joint 'UNIPAG' symbol for all U.N.I.P. and Action Group candidates, to indicate that the two parties were allied. They proposed that the joint symbol should consist of a lion under a palm tree on one piece of paper. This request was refused by the R.E.O. partly on the ground that the two parties were separately recognized and registered, and therefore could not have a joint symbol, and partly because of the physical difficulty which would be involved in printing many thousands of these new symbols at such a late date. It was after this decision that the proposal for the joint candidatures of the two parties broke down, although in some areas, such as Calabar, the headquarters of the C.O.R. State movement, the two parties agreed not to nominate more candidates between them than the number of seats to be filled.

On 4 March 1957 representatives of Action Group called on the R.E.O. and complained that the palm-tree symbol drawn by the E.N.I.S. artist and printed by the government printer, which was an extremely crude and childlike drawing, hardly recognizable as a palm-tree, was an inaccurate portrayal of an oil-palm; if anything, it represented an *ubi* palm rather than an oil-palm. They therefore feared that illiterate voters in the farming villages might be confused by it if they were told to put their ballot papers into a box bearing the symbol of an oil-palm. The R.E.O., after taking the legal opinion of the Attorney General about this request, instructed the government printer to stand by to print 30,000 new symbols. Action Group, who were extremely worried, offered to print and distribute themselves symbols which would conform with the Electoral Regulations, the symbols which they had previously circulated for propaganda purposes in the constituencies being unacceptable since they exceeded the specified measurements of 6 in. × 6 in. Electoral Officers were instructed by the R.E.O. to use symbols supplied by Action Group if they arrived in time, and if not to carry on with the E.N.I.S. palms. An extremely good block of an oil-palm, which had been used by the Western Region government printer during the Western elections, was eventually used by Action Group, and in most constituencies the symbols were circulated by them at the eleventh hour.

The photographs which candidates were entitled to supply for affixing to ballot boxes also caused a great deal of trouble, since many of them did not conform to the regulation measurements of 6 in. × 6 in., and many also had extraneous matter inserted on them. For example, at Onitsha, where there were seventeen candidates for the five seats, about 3,000 boxes were required. Many of the photographs supplied by the candidates were not merely poor portraits, but included other features designed to make them electorally attractive. For instance, one Roman Catholic candidate[1] had a border of crosses round his portrait, while another produced a picture of a bulldozer with his own portrait in one corner of it. Most also bore the photographically reproduced legend: 'Vote for . . . .' In this constituency Dr. Azikiwe himself was the only candidate who submitted a genuine photographic portrait with no extraneous matter and of some artistic merit. The others were all badly printed block reproductions. As there is nothing in the electoral regulations expressly forbidding extraneous matter on photographs, the Electoral Officer at Onitsha allowed these photographs to be affixed to the ballot boxes, although in certain constituencies Electoral Officers, using their own discretion, forbade similar examples.

Events and incidents. Chief Awolowo's speech at Uyo, referred to above, was the first move in Action Group's campaign. On the

---

[1] This candidate was a woodworking contractor, who himself secured the lucrative contract for the ballot boxes used in this constituency.

same day, at Onitsha, a 'Convention of Protestant citizens in Eastern Nigeria' was inaugurated. It accused the Roman Catholics of 'abusing the pulpit', and of attempting to overthrow the Eastern Region Government. This was followed on 10 February by a speech by Dr. Charles Heery, Archbishop of Onitsha, in which he claimed that the Roman Catholic stand was being misrepresented by the Protestants. From that time onwards the attitude of the Churches towards each other was clear, but even the Roman Catholic leaders were aware that their attitude could not really affect the result of the election in any way.

The Women Traders' Association in Onitsha, Dr. Azikiwe's home town, announced on 17 February that they would sponsor a candidate against him because of the imposition of taxation on women, but this was obviously purely a bargaining move, since the candidate never actually stood. On the following day the Aba Women's Association—and no one has dared to ignore the opinions of the women of Aba since the women's riots of 1929—which usually supports the N.C.N.C. strongly, sent a message to the Premier asking him to repeal the Tax Law if he wanted the women's votes. As a result of these appeals, and the danger which the alienation of the women's vote would mean to the N.C.N.C., he made a somewhat vague announcement to the effect that the Eastern Finance Law would be reconsidered after the new Government came into office. This seemed to be sufficient to appease the women.

On 29 February 1957,[1] Mr. John Profumo, the Under-Secretary of State for the Colonies, stated, in reply to a question in the House of Commons, that Dr. Azikiwe would surrender his shares in the African Continental Bank and would 'freeze' £5,252 directors' fees which he had received from the Bank while he was Premier. This rather ambiguous statement was given wide publicity in the N.C.N.C. press, and was used by N.C.N.C. propagandists to clear away the last vestiges of any uneasiness which the general public might have felt about Dr. Azikiwe's banking interests, as a result of the confusion shown at first by the N.C.N.C. newspapers in their editorial comments on the Foster-Sutton Report.

The issues involved in the proposed London Constitutional Conference were very much simplified by the N.C.N.C. propagandists. They merely took the line: 'Zik, who has been pilloried by the Imperialist Capitalists, is the only person who can be trusted to speak on behalf of Eastern Region in London.' They consistently accused Action Group of being anti-democratic, tribalistic, and corrupt, and hinted that Chief Awolowo would sell Eastern Region

---

[1] *Parliamentary Debates, House of Commons*, 5th ser., vol. dxliv, col. 67.

to the Imperialists in London. The latter in his turn stated that he would not sit down at the same conference table with a 'crook' like Dr. Azikiwe, although when the conference took place his promise was forgotten.

All, however, was not well within the N.C.N.C. during the election campaign. There were several ministers and other leading members of the party whose continued political activity was an embarrassment to Dr. Azikiwe. It was impossible to refuse them the official nomination of the party at the election, so they were duly nominated as N.C.N.C. candidates, while hints were dropped in the constituencies by the Premier and his lieutenants that their candidature was not to be taken too seriously by local N.C.N.C. supporters. When the results came in, it was noticeable that several of these people, although elected, had received considerably fewer votes than their minor N.C.N.C. colleagues in the same constituency.

At Port Harcourt, the Region's busiest and most prosperous deep water harbour, the local N.C.N.C. Committee sponsored their own new candidates for election, despite the National Executive Committee's decision that all former members of the Assembly should be nominated. This led to a serious dispute with the leaders of the party, which was not resolved (in favour of the National Executive Committee's decision) until a few days before nomination day. Despite this, on a poll of 85·94 per cent. the N.C.N.C. candidates in Port Harcourt, who were the two sitting Assembly men, received 82·28 per cent. of the votes.

Contrary to experience in other parts of British West Africa, where ex-servicemen's organizations tend to be in the forefront of the more radical political movements, the Ex-Servicemen's Unions in the various towns of Eastern Region tended to be anti-N.C.N.C. They blamed Dr. Azikiwe for the heavy burden of income tax upon the low income groups, to which most of their members belonged, and the E.S.M.U. at Onitsha adopted a slogan: 'The Cock has stolen my palm-nut, but I will kill it'—a reference to the red cock which was the N.C.N.C.'s symbol.

Registration receipts. During the campaign the two major parties constantly and hysterically levelled charges of hooliganism, gangsterism, and corrupt electoral practices against each other, both in the press and from the platforms. But in fact, apart from the minor outbreaks of hooliganism described above, which were soon brought under control by the police and which were the subject of proceedings in the courts, and the possible intimidation of potential voters by the Z.N.V. and the 'Area Boys', which was hard to prove, the only serious electoral offences were connected with the receipts which had been issued to voters at the time of registration. The two national parties accused each other of forging receipts for issue to their supporters and of buying up for considerable sums of money receipts from supporters of the opposite party, thus hoping to prevent those persons from voting. It seems unlikely that buying up of registration receipts by the N.C.N.C. took place on any large scale, particularly in the Ibo areas, since the N.C.N.C.'s interest was presumably to get as many people to the polling stations as possible. Some Action Group supporters on the other hand certainly did indulge in this practice. Amongst many other such cases which came to the notice of the police were the following: 318 registration receipts were found in an Action Group Land Rover at Uyo on 2 March 1957; 864 registration receipts were found in the possession of eight men arrested in Onitsha; and 1,190 registration receipts were found in the possession of three persons arrested in Udi Division.

As at the beginning of the election campaign it was, owing to an oversight in drafting, perfectly legal to be in possession of registration receipts issued to other persons, it became necessary to issue an amendment (Amendment No. 3) to the Electoral Regulations on 11 February 1957 making it an offence punishable by imprisonment for a term not exceeding one year or a fine not exceeding £100 to be illegally in possession of such a receipt.

Later, when a certain Mr. Anthony Orakwusi was arrested at Onitsha for printing forged registration receipts, it was found that legally he had committed no offence, since the forged receipts were not receipts 'given to a person under the provisions of para. 4 of Regulation 10'. A further amendment (Amendment No. 4) was therefore passed on 12 March 1957 to make it illegal to be in possession of forged as well as of *bona fide* registration receipts. This was done by defining 'an election receipt' (a new term) as being a receipt which 'purports to be a receipt given to a person under the provisions of para. 4 of Regulation 10 whether such receipt has been given to a person under such Regulation or not, and whether such receipt is a valid receipt for the purposes of these Regulations or not'. As this amendment was only issued three days before the election took place, it was a case of shutting the stable door after the horse had gone.

Public order. The police force, which is a federal service locally controlled by the Eastern Regional Commissioner of Police, had a thankless task during the campaign period, as the total number of regular police in the Region is only approximately equal to the total number of polling stations (about 3,500), and, owing to a federal decision that it would be politically inexpedient to bring in reinforcements from Western Region (the most convenient area), it became impossible to increase their strength until just before polling day. The special constables were therefore called out, particularly for service on polling day, and additional men were recruited into a corps of short-term special constables whose period of liability for service only extended over the election period.

The police were indeed fortunate that the pre-election period was so quiet, apart from some hooliganism in the big towns. Indeed, the campaign was so peaceful that some senior civil servants were quite perturbed about it. They said that it was unique in their experience of the Eastern Region, and feared that it might portend serious disturbances on polling day.

Constituency impressions. In the course of a tour of constituencies, it became obvious that although the parties were working to an identical pattern in each constituency, the administration in its preparations for the election was not. This was due to the lack of precision in the Electoral Regulations, and it is obviously desirable that before another general election new regulations should be drafted, and that a detailed administrative brief should be circulated to all Electoral Officers, based upon pooling of their experience.

For instance, even in such a simple, though extremely important, matter as the numbering of ballot boxes, no two Electoral Officers were following the same system. In Aba, for example, ballot boxes bore a serial number which indicated the polling area, the polling booth, and the candidate's number: e.g.

$$\frac{20}{A} \frac{}{9}$$

would be candidate No. 9's box (there were only nine candidates, so the work in the numbering of boxes was comparatively light) at polling booth 'A' in polling area No. 20. This was a definite check, and eliminated the confusion which took place in many constituencies during the distribution of the ballot boxes in darkness on the night before the election. In Owerri, the biggest constituency, the boxes were numbered in three series. Those with simple numbers without a prefix were the old boxes left over from the previous election, and two other series bearing the prefixes 'A' and 'B' were manufactured by different contractors.

Again, despite the Regional Electoral Officer's instruction that at each polling station the ballot boxes for each party's candidates should be grouped together, at Aba, where Action Group and U.N.I.P. were in an electoral alliance, their boxes were grouped together, while at Onitsha the Electoral Officer decided to place the boxes in each booth in alphabetical order.

Standard VI boys, who are literate, comparatively well informed, and disciplined, can be very useful during the election period. Several Electoral Officers had decided to employ them at 5*s.* a day on polling day as ushers, and so on, but at Aba, the Electoral Officer, having used a similar technique successfully at the federal elections, was proposing also to use them to mingle with the crowds in the queues at the polling stations, partly to act as 'bell wethers' to lead the illiterate voters through the proper channels, and partly to explain informally to their neighbours in the crowds what the election was all about.

In Aba, as mentioned earlier, election fever was running higher than elsewhere. There had been some hooliganism in the constituency, especially in the town itself, where an Action Group meeting was broken up violently by the Z.N.V. The culprits had been charged; some were convicted, but some had been acquitted by an African magistrate on what the Senior District Officer and the police regarded as flimsy grounds. The police therefore intended to appeal, as they feared that otherwise a dangerous precedent might be set, and licence given for all manner of hooliganism during the campaign. The rural areas of the constituency were, however, completely apathetic, and there seemed to be a greater support for the Opposition there. As might be expected in Aba, the women had registered more heavily than the men. They are very conscious of their numerical strength at election time, and it was noticeable that the men were wooing their votes.

In Owerri, where the Roman Catholic Mission is very strong, there were 12 candidates for 6 seats—6 Independent and 6 N.C.N.C. Many of the Independents were unofficial N.C.N.C. candidates, who would immediately accept the N.C.N.C. whip if elected. The Independent candidates had adopted unorthodox symbols in this constituency. One man, who was obviously trying to woo the Roman Catholic vote, had a red Roman cross as his emblem, another had a woman and a child, and another had a black star reminiscent of Ghana's latest symbol. One of the Independent candidates had provided a photograph showing himself wearing a Homburg hat, and carrying a walking-stick and a fat brief case, the symbols of worldly success.

Mr. E. U. Eronini, a pharmacist and produce buyer in the area, who was the Chairman of the House of Assembly Public Accounts Committee and of the newly created Cinema Corporation, and who is married, with eighteen children, was so unpopular in the area that although he carried the N.C.N.C. ticket the leader of his own community was standing as an Independent candidate against him.[1] Because of this, the Electoral Officer was afraid that there might be trouble on polling day, and so, believing that the only way to control crowds is to keep them small, he had deliberately made separate polling stations for an average of 400 registered voters. He had also tried to keep every aspect of the construction of polling stations as local as possible, and wherever possible concentrated on one man. Where local authority schools existed, these had been used, with the headmaster of the school as Presiding Officer. Each headmaster involved had been given 10s. for erecting polling stations with schoolboy labour.

On the other hand, in Aba, where trouble was more likely than in Owerri, the Electoral Officer had sited a number of booths, usually three or four, in the same polling station. He thus ran the risk of a large riotous assembly on polling day, but simplified the tasks of supervising and policing, and of collecting boxes after the poll.

Several Electoral Officers informed the writer that they and their staffs had worked a twelve-hour day for seven days a week for at least three weeks before the election, and that during this period no normal administrative work could be attended to at all.

8. *Polling Day*

The police feared trouble on polling day, particularly at Aba, where there is always trouble; at Uyo, where Mr. E. O. Eyo, the former Deputy Speaker of the Assembly and Chief Whip of the N.C.N.C., who had precipitated the banking inquiry, was standing on the Action Group ticket; at Port Harcourt, which is a modern, detribalized, immigrant community; and at Onitsha, where Dr. Azikiwe was standing and the election was hotly contested by the Roman Catholics. To deal with expected outbreaks special constables would have been almost useless, and it was necessary for a reserve to be built up both at the regional headquarters and in the various divisional headquarters. The Commissioner of Police was eventually able to obtain small numbers of reinforcements of regular police from the federal territory of Lagos, and from the Northern Region, but these only arrived a couple of days before the election.

In order not to scatter his trained men, the Commissioner utilized ordinary and short-term special constables as far as possible at polling stations, and held back as many of the regular police as he could to form mobile reserves. A small reserve (usually about 25 to 30 men) was held at each divisional headquarters, while the main

[1] Mr. Eronini was elected.

reserve (about 200 constables) was held at Enugu, where a large number of constables were attending a refresher course at the Police Training School. There is no doubt that if serious trouble had broken out at scattered points throughout the Region, the police, unaided, would have been hard put to it to maintain order, despite these careful arrangements.

Meanwhile, the administration was preoccupied with the task of finding staff and transport for polling day. Owing to the ban on employing ministers of religion, teachers, and others on the staff of the Missions, which would normally have been a valuable source of recruits, the administration had to rely greatly upon junior civil servants in the areas where local authority schools did not exist. Not only were there hardly enough to go around, but their absence increased the strain on administrative officers.

The shortage of transport in Eastern Region, and the necessity to hire transport from local contractors and to borrow such as was available from other government departments, have already been mentioned. Partly for security reasons, and partly because the hired and borrowed transport could not be made available for election purposes until the last possible moment, it became necessary for Electoral Officers at divisional headquarters to load the lorries with ballot boxes and election stationery and to send them out with the polling-station staffs on the evening before polling day. This was a tremendous and confused undertaking, especially as at most divisional headquarters the loading of boxes on to the right lorries had to be undertaken by the light of hurricane lamps. It is remarkable that all the boxes, ballot papers, and so on, arrived with the staff at the right polling stations at the right time. Police transport was not used for this purpose, although it was used the next morning to relieve the policemen (in most cases special constables) who had been guarding the ballot boxes in the polling stations from the time of their delivery the previous night.

Polling commenced throughout the Region at 8 a.m. on 15 March 1957. It was the quietest polling day which the Eastern Region had ever seen. Orderly queues were formed at daybreak, and when the polling stations opened, practically the whole of the electorate of each polling area was outside, waiting patiently and in good order.

At most stations separate queues were formed for men and women. This was partly due to the arrogance of the menfolk, who objected to standing in the same queues as their women, and partly due to the necessity of admitting the men to the polling stations first in order to free them to go about their daily work. It was very unusual at any polling station for priority to be given to expectant mothers or mothers with small children strapped to their backs. The only cases of this which the writer saw were where a European officer was present at or visited the station.

The writer toured a number of polling stations in the Udi constituency during the course of the morning and afternoon. At none of the polling stations visited were more than a handful of male voters to be seen. This may have been due partly to the fact that the men for the most part voted early, and the women had to wait until they had finished, and partly to the fact that the women played a very significant part in the election. If reliable statistics of this could be compiled, they would probably show that considerably over 50 per cent. of the votes actually cast were cast by women. There must have been a great deal of laxity at the time of registration, because many of the women queueing to vote were obviously well under 21 years of age.

Although there were no major acts of violence on polling day, there were many minor disturbances at polling stations, mainly connected with queueing. The art of queueing is completely foreign to West Africa, as anyone who has ever tried to get on to an Accra or Lagos bus knows to his cost. Voters would queue one abreast in a straight line outside the polling station; gradually the pressure from the persons at the rear of the queue would build up, until the people at the front were hardly able to breathe. Something eventually had to give, and a woman would find herself squeezed out of the queue like a cherry stone squeezed from between the thumb and forefinger, having tried to turn sideways in order to prevent the baby strapped to her back from being crushed. Most brawls started when these women tried to get back into their rightful place in the queue. Willy nilly, the people who had been standing immediately behind her could not let her in, owing to the pressure on them from those at the rear of the queue. The most orderly polling stations were those at which the police constable on duty had made the voters sit down in long lines, thus preserving their proper order without any pressure building up.

The nerve centre of the administrative organization on polling day and on the days of counting that followed was the office of the Secretary to the Premier, in the new Secretariat building in Enugu. A roster had been prepared in order that at least one senior official and one clerk would be on duty at any hour of the day or night to deal with any queries which might arise and with possible outbreaks of violence.

In the office excellent arrangements had been made for oversea and local pressmen. A large board had been put up on which the results could be marked as they came in, and through telephone and teleprinter lines to Lagos had been engaged. Despite this, the press had in general been extremely unco-operative while the arrangements were being made; it had, for instance, been almost impossible for the Acting Secretary to the Premier to secure agreement amongst the pressmen on the allocation to the various newspapers of through lines, although this was obviously to their advantage. Despite the fact that large numbers of pressmen were present in Enugu on election day and immediately afterwards (the British and American newspapers had for the most part sent their representatives directly to Enugu from the Independence celebrations in Accra on 6 March) only one of them made any regular use of the facilities provided. Nevertheless, it is important that press facilities of this type should be provided on such occasions, especially as the press would be the first to complain if they were not adequately catered for.

9. *The Count*

There were 3,201,457 valid votes cast in the twenty-seven constituencies, and counting them within a reasonable time was from the administrative point of view the biggest single undertaking of the whole election period, since not only had the papers to be counted, but the serial number on every paper had to be checked, to ensure that two or more papers bearing the same serial number had not found their way into the same ballot box. In a few constituencies, such as Udi, Port Harcourt, and Awgu, counting started as soon as the ballot boxes began to arrive at the divisional headquarters, but in most cases counting was not started until 8 a.m. on Saturday, 16 March. It was felt that senior officials needed a breather after the exertions of polling day, and in any case, particularly in the more widespread constituencies, only a comparatively small proportion of the ballot boxes could be expected to arrive before about midnight on 15 March.

The counting staff, who for the most part were European senior officials, lecturers, secondary school teachers, and so on, were divided in each counting room into groups, usually consisting of five persons, each group at one table. One of the counters was put in charge of each team. All the ballot boxes from a particular polling booth were brought to one table, and were opened in turn by the counter in charge of the table, who had been given a list of the counterfoil numbers of the books of ballot papers which had been used at that booth. As each box was opened its contents were emptied on to the table in between the counters. The papers in it were then checked by the counters working in teams of two, one calling out the last three digits of the serial number of each paper, the other ticking off the number on special printed forms which had been provided for the purpose. It was thus possible to check immediately whether any particular number had occurred more than once in a particular box. The counter in charge of the table cancelled with a rubber stamp any papers which were invalid for this reason. Although the procedure was comparatively simple, the magnitude of the undertaking was immense in constituencies such as Onitsha, where 403,237 papers had to be checked and counted. In fact, after two continuous days of counting, the Electoral Officer at Onitsha telephoned to the Acting Secretary to the Premier to say that his European counters were all exhausted, and that he would have to engage more the next morning.

Many irregularities by presiding officers were revealed during the counting. At several polling stations in various parts of the Region, Presiding Officers had written the registration numbers of all the voters on their ballot papers, which thus had to be declared invalid at the count. In others, owing to a misunderstanding about the purpose of the indelible ink with which the voters' thumbs were marked, the presiding officers had made all voters put their thumbprints on the back of the ballot papers. Since this too made it possible to find out how a particular voter had voted, these papers also were disallowed. At one polling station in Onitsha constituency the presiding officer lost the secret mark with which he had been supplied to stamp all the ballot papers when they were issued, so he used the District Council rubber stamp. Later in the day the secret mark was found lying in the road outside the polling station, so orders were given to the Presiding Officer by the Electoral Officer that he should continue using the rubber stamp, and that if any ballot papers were found during the counting to bear the secret mark they would be declared invalid.

As in nearly all constituencies the verdict of the electorate was clear and indisputable, no recount became necessary except in Eket, where there were 12 candidates for 3 seats, and about 95,500 votes were cast. When the result was declared, it showed that Mr. D. U. Assam (Independent) had secured election as the third successful candidate. Mr. Assam therefore spent the evening entertaining his constituents at considerable expense. Some doubt arose in the Electoral Officer's mind about the result, and he ordered a recheck. On the first recheck, which was done by a comptometer operator (as the original totalling had been done), Mr. Assam's election was confirmed; but at the second (visual) recheck the next morning it was discovered that far from being elected, Mr. Assam had lost his deposit,[1] and that Mr. O. O. Ita, who on the previous count had forfeited his deposit,[1] was now elevated to the position of *second* successful candidate. This mistake was found to be due to the verbal calling of the figures to the comptometer operator. A total of 'six-two-eight' for Mr. Ita was recorded by her as 'sixty-eight'. On the check back she called 'sixty-eight' and that was heard as 'six-two-eight'. The same thing happened again at the first recheck, and it was only when the visual check was made that the mistake was detected.

As a matter of policy, it had been decided in the interest of fair play and speed of counting to engage predominantly European counting staff. There is a good case for completely Africanizing the counting at future elections, as the candidates and their agents are themselves present to see fair play during the counting. In many cases the speed of the European counters, who started off by looking upon the counting as a sort of picnic and ended up by regarding it as monotonous drudgery, left much to be desired; the cumulative waste in having a vast proportion of the available senior European officials doing a clerical job to the exclusion of their ordinary duties is tremendous; and if African counters were employed it would bring home to the country what an enormous undertaking an election is.

10. *The Results*

Two hundred and thirty-one candidates, of whom 80 were members of the former Assembly, contested the 84 seats in the election. When the results were finally available, it was found that the state of the parties in the new Assembly would be:

N.C.N.C.	.	.	.	.	65
Action Group	.	.	.	.	13
U.N.I.P.	.	.	.	.	5
Independent	.	.	.	.	1
					84

Although the N.C.N.C. headquarters in Enugu had been surprisingly modest before the election in its forecast of the results, Dr. Azikiwe claimed this as a sweeping victory. On a 46·78 per cent. poll the N.C.N.C. had secured 63·26 per cent. of the total votes cast—2,025,174 votes, as against 202,478 for the U.N.I.P., 344,153 for the Action Group, and 629,652 for the Independent candidates, making a total of 3,201,457.

[1] A consequence of the peculiar regulation referred to earlier: both candidates had about 10,000 votes.

Compared with the previous Assembly, in which Azikiwe had had seventy-three (towards the end seventy-two supporters), with an ineffective Opposition, his position was distinctly weaker. Not only had he lost eight seats, but he had for the first time to face in the Region an energetic, well organized, and wealthy Opposition party.

As the results came in to Enugu during the counting period, it became obvious that the former ministers and ministerial secretaries were not themselves faring as well as some of their back-benchers. This was perhaps partly because the party put it about quietly in the constituencies that they were not anxious for these men to be returned, but it seems more likely that the N.C.N.C. electorate are a little tired and mistrustful of certain leaders. At the same time, there was no sign of any decline in Dr. Azikiwe's personal popularity.

The most significant feature of the results was the discrepancy between the N.C.N.C. performance in the predominantly Ibo constituencies and in the predominantly non-Ibo ones. The latter, which for convenience may be referred to as the 'C.O.R. constituencies', number 15 out of 27, but as they are smallish constituencies they are only represented in the Assembly by 35 M.H.A.'s, as opposed to the non-C.O.R. constituencies, 12 in number, which are represented by 49 M.H.A.'s. In the non-C.O.R. constituencies the N.C.N.C. obtained 71 per cent. of the votes cast, while in the C.O.R. constituencies it only obtained 40·78 per cent. The detailed percentages by parties are as follows:

Party	C.O.R. constituencies (per cent.)	Non-C.O.R. constituencies (per cent.)
N.C.N.C. . . .	40·78	71·02
U.N.I.P. . . .	16·01 ⎫	1·86 ⎫
Action Group . .	27·91 ⎬ 59·22	5·91 ⎬ 28·98
Independent. . .	15·30 ⎭	21·21 ⎭
	100·00	100·00[1]

These figures seem to show unambiguously the nature of the electorate's reactions to the political parties. The people of the C.O.R. state area are so mistrustful of Ibo rule, with which they identify the N.C.N.C., that many of them would even prefer to be governed by an alien party from Western Region. In Ibo areas, on the other hand, tribe, party, and state are so closely identified that the only real contests are between official and unofficial N.C.N.C. candidates, divided primarily on local and personal issues.

[1] The results are analysed more fully in Appendixes II and III.

Nevertheless, the election gave Dr. Azikiwe the title to put himself forward as the democratically chosen leader of Eastern Region, and to go to the London conference as the spokesman of the whole Region.

11. The Aftermath

As after the Lord Mayor's Show, there is much to tidy up after an election of this kind.

The senior officials of the Administration, many of whom had had to postpone their leave on account of pressure of work during the election period, turned back to their normal duties, and caught up as best they could with the outstanding arrears of administrative work.

Expense. The election had to be paid for in cash too. The official cost was £107,474. 2s. in the financial year 1956/7, and £11,274. 2s. 3d. in the year 1957/8, making a grand total of £118,748. 4s. 3d. This breaks down into the following headings:

	£	s.	d.
Transport	16,375	6	9
Payments to staff	45,939	17	10
Equipment (including ballot boxes)	56,432	19	8
TOTAL	£118,748	4	3

This officially recognized expenditure (quite large by the standards of the Region—its annual revenue is about £12 million) was, however, not all. There were a number of concealed costs. For example, nearly every telegram which was sent out by the Regional Electoral Officer was circulated to about thirty addresses at the priority rate (double the normal rate). Postage, too, must have amounted to a considerable sum; although all the O.H.M.S. envelopes used by the Eastern Regional Government have a letter 'E' printed in the bottom left-hand cormer, the Federal Posts and Telegraphs Department have no machinery for computing the actual charge to the Region (nor have they for local telephone calls). The salary of every member of the senior or the junior staff of the Administration for at least the last two months before polling day could also be included in the cost of the election, as might several days' pay for virtually every senior official of all the other regional departments.

The high cost of the election was due partly to the fact that it had to be carried out as an emergency operation, and partly to the cumbersome system of plural voting in multi-member constituencies, which meant that special ballot papers had to be printed for each constituency and that excessive effort had to be devoted to the checking of the serial numbers of ballot papers during the count.

Administration. If elections are to be carried out in future without the 'panic' which attended the 1957 election, it seems essential that an Electoral Commissioner should be appointed, as has been done in the Western Region, in order to undertake the general planning of elections free from normal administrative duties, and to see that elections become a routine activity of the administration. It is too early in the development of the local authorities in the Region to hand over the administration of elections to them, and for some time to come it will be necessary for the administration to accept the burden.

If collapsible steel ballot boxes were obtained from the United Kingdom (as was done in the Western Region), and stored at convenient points in the Region, the initial cost would be high, but the expense of constructing approximately 30,000 new ballot boxes in a hurry, and therefore on a rising market, for every election would be avoided.

Again, if, as was visualized in the existing Electoral Regulations, a permanent register is compiled and revised annually, Administrative Officers will only be faced with a small flurry of work during the revision period each year, which they will be able to take in their stride.

New Electoral Regulations are essential, not merely because of expense and of the ambiguities and inconsistencies in the present regulations, which produced certain unfortunate results, such as the forfeiture of their deposits by nearly all defeated candidates, but also because the existing electoral system must be changed in order to ensure equitable representation. Apart from the fact that the number of seats allocated to each constituency (which has arbitrary boundaries based upon the existing administrative divisions) bears only an approximate relationship to the total population or the number of registered voters in each area, the existing system of voting is bound to be advantageous to the majority party and to under-represent minority groups. It is true that if the Region were to be divided into small single-member constituencies with the single non-transferable vote, the risk would still be run, as in the United Kingdom, of under-representing minorities. But in the Eastern Region, unlike the United Kingdom, the minorities tend to be concentrated almost exclusively in certain localities, and thus form a local majority. Comparatively small single-member constituencies would thus portray more closely the divisions among the electorate.

Since the division of the Region into single-member constituencies will mean a major administrative upheaval, involving a complete re-registration of the electorate, and since it is desirable that the demarcation of constituency boundaries should be done at a time when political feelings are not running high, it is essential that the redrafting of the Electoral Regulations, and the settling of the new constituencies and their boundaries, should be done immediately, in order that the decks may be cleared for an election at any future time.

It is desirable too that the Electoral Commissioner should be an expatriate, for the time being at least, in order that representatives of all parties may have confidence in his impartiality.

If present electoral trends continue, the breaking down of the existing constituencies would probably have an adverse effect upon the N.C.N.C.'s majority at a future election. But the fact that proposals for single-member constituencies had already been discussed by the Executive Council before the election, coupled with the existence of a permanent Ibo majority in the Region, suggest that the party would not find insuperable difficulties in the way of introducing the new system in the near future. As for the desirability of the proposal to establish a permanent Regional Electoral Commissioner, the successful example in the Western Region is clear for all to see.

The present Electoral Regulations prescribe no limits to the election expenditure of candidates, nor is it practicable without the appointment of official agents to the candidates for any accurate check to be made of what a candidate has actually spent. This not merely favours the wealthier candidates and parties, but can lead to obvious abuses. It is desirable therefore that the new Electoral Regulations should make provision for the appointment of official agents on the United Kingdom pattern, and for a limit to be imposed on election expenditure by individual candidates through their agents. Regulations might also be made restricting the use of cars and other forms of transport for conveying the supporters of particular candidates to the polling stations, but there was not in this election any indication that excessive transport was being used for such a purpose. However, it is as well to be prepared for future developments, and not to be caught unawares, with the consequent need to rush through frequent amendments to the Regulations in the period immediately before polling day, as happened at the last election.

Politics. The eyes of the world were on the Gold Coast General Election of 1951, partly because of the colourful personalities involved, but mainly because it was the first general election in any British African colony to be based, at any rate in most of the constituencies, on universal adult suffrage. The eyes of the world were similarly focused upon the Eastern Nigerian General Election of 1957, but in this case principally through anxiety to see what an African electorate would make of the findings of the Foster-Sutton Tribunal—although the election would not have had such good overseas press coverage had Enugu not been a convenient port of call for the European and American journalists who had been in Accra for the Independence celebrations on 6 March. Considerable disappointment was expressed, not only in the United Kingdom, but also in other parts of Nigeria, that what to an outsider appeared to be a flagrant breach of public morality had been condoned and endorsed by a majority of the electorate. It must again be emphasized, however, that the Foster-Sutton Tribunal report was never a real issue in the election, and if it filtered through to the illiterate bush villagers at all, it appeared to them as the pillorying by the capitalist imperialists of the great leader of Africa to protect the future profits of the London-controlled Bank of British West Africa Ltd. (Barclay's Bank (D.C.O.), the other British-owned bank in Nigeria, did not come in for the vehement political attacks which were levelled at the B.B.W.A.). The minority groups on the other hand were interested only in preserving themselves from Ibo rule, even to the extent of breaking up the Region or introducing Yoruba rule.

The electorate was thus neither condoning nor condemning the banking policy of Azikiwe; the issue was a tribal one—whether or not the Ibos should dominate the administration of the Region and monopolize the fruits of office.

APPENDIX I

An *N.C.N.C. Leaflet*

DON'T TAKE POISON

BEING a Warning to the People of Eastern Region against

ACTION GROUP/U.N.I.P. TRAVELLERS

For some time now, the tribalist Action Group has hired so many un-employed boys and ex-criminal convicts to travel from town to town, village to village in the Eastern Region to confuse and deceive the people.

Some of these idle boys will come to you in the night and in the day; they will speak to you about the heaven and earth which the Action Group will bring to you; they will make beautiful promises to you; they will condemn Zik and every nationalist in this country and present themselves and the Action Group as Angels from heaven. Fear them because they are agents of mischief. Drive them away and have nothing to do with them because they are not interested in your welfare but they simply want to deceive you and use you as a tool to accomplish their evil assignment.

This is a SERIOUS WARNING to every man and every woman who lives in the Eastern Region and in any part of Nigeria for that matter.

2. WHY YOU MUST DRIVE AWAY THE ACTION GROUP

We will now give you some of the reasons why you must drive away the Action Group and their friends—the U.N.I.P.—who are, in other words, known as the enemies of Nigerian Unity and Freedom.

1. You all know that when Zik came back from America, he declared a political battle with the British imperialists who had been cheating us for many years. He started to fight for our self-government. He called all the people of Nigeria to join together in this fight. You all joined with Zik and started the battle with greater force in the name of N.C.N.C. You all know the History of this battle and how many things we have won.

Workers are now paid better salaries; no white man will insult and slap any black man again; our traders can now trade direct with many countries of the world, hence they make profit and become rich; many of our sons can now go to England or America to study many things; we can now do many things by ourselves and therefore many white-men who were doing them before and refused to teach us are now going home.

You all know that the white people; known as imperialists, are not happy about our steady unity and progress; they do not want us to govern ourselves. So what did they do?

2. Listen now. They hired some of our black brothers to kick against Zik. They gave money and other help to them in order to carry propaganda against Zik and all of us who are known as the N.C.N.C.

This is the history of the beginning of the Action Group. We will tell you about their friends in the Eastern Region who are known as the U.N.I.P. later on.

3. HOW DO THE ACTION GROUP PEOPLE CARRY OUT THE WORK OF THEIR
MASTERS?

They are working very hard to divide our country, Nigeria. They incite one section of Nigeria to hate the other. They do this because their allies, the imperialists, have told them that if we are all united as one, we shall succeed in fighting them out of Nigeria. They support the imperialists to divide our country to make us weak.

4. The leader of the Action Group, Mr. Awolowo, wrote a book called 'Path to Nigeria Freedom', in which he described the people of the Eastern Region as the most backward and unprogressive people in Nigeria. You all know that this is a stupid lie. Again during the last election Awolowo referred to Ibo people as 'half naked jungle dwellers'.

5. Wherever the Action Group go they carry trouble with them; you know them by riots and bloodshed. We people in the East do not want riots and bloodshed; therefore you must not allow any of these Action Group rascals to come into your peaceful town or village.

6. Wherever the Action Group get power they try to punish and victimize innocent people. You all know how they wanted to put Adelabu into prison many times at Ibadan. You know how they banish Chiefs in the Western Region and send them out to die in exile.

7. They impose heavy capitation tax on poor farmers and if you cannot pay you go to prison. But you know that in the East here the N.C.N.C. has grouped rates with tax and reduced them for poor farmers in the villages but only increased taxation, after consultations, for workers who earn big salaries.

The Action Group is full of iniquities but we have only given you these few examples of their true colour in a very simple and mild language. We shall continue to give you more facts about the Action Group and their allies, the U.N.I.P., in other leaflets. Next time we shall tell you how they get the money which they spend like sand.

THE U.N.I.P.

The U.N.I.P. is an organization of those sit-tight Ministers who were pulled down by the N.C.N.C. in 1953. You will remember that they became Ministers and only went to the Governor's house to drink tea and forget the interest and welfare of the poor farmers who had voted them into power. Some of them went to England and drank Whisky and were about to 'sell' Nigeria when we pulled them down.

Since then, they formed themselves into an impotent organization, known as the U.N.I.P. The Action Group is supporting them to work against Zik and the N.C.N.C. The imperialists are supporting them because they help them to divide our country, Nigeria.

All these traitors, the U.N.I.P. and their brothers, the Action Group, supported by their imperialist masters are the greatest enemies of this country. They want to destroy all the good fight of the N.C.N.C. for the freedom of this country, they support the imperialists to see that we do not put money in African Banks, except in imperialist banks. They oppose the

N.C.N.C. Free Primary Education Scheme. They oppose every measure that will bring the unity, progress and freedom of Nigeria and in doing this dirty job they are supported by the imperialists.

CHASE THEM OUT OF YOUR VILLAGE

As we have warned you, be on the look-out. They will come to your village to try to deceive people, to incite every man against his brother. They are more dangerous than snakes; just as you fear leprosy and small-pox, fear them so. DO NOT HAVE ANYTHING TO DO WITH THEM.

If you allow them to bring their riot and confusion into your quiet village, it is just like taking POISON into a healthy stomach.

Tell them YOU BELIEVE IN ZIK AND THE N.C.N.C.

SUPPORT THE N.C.N.C. ALWAYS AND THE N.C.N.C. WILL LEAD YOU TO FREEDOM. MEET YOUR LOCAL N.C.N.C. SECRETARY FOR MORE ISSUES OF N.C.N.C. INFORMA-TION LEAFLETS.

Printed by Zik Enterprises Ltd., Enugu.

APPENDIX II

Registration Figures and Results by Parties

Constituency	Population	No. of seats	No. registered	Votes by parties					% by parties				% Poll
				N.C.N.C.	U.N.I.P.	A.G.	Ind.	Total	N.C.N.C.	U.N.I.P.	A.G.	Ind.	
A. C.O.R. Constituencies													
Abak	233,383	3	55,344	40,310	11,807	26,078	9,319	87,514	75·94	10·65	9·98	3·43	52·71
Ahoada	286,258	3	77,551	77,399		12,763	38,832	128,994	60·00		9·89	30·10	55·45
Brass	126,966	2	35,000	18,343	2,932	4,772	14,235	40,282	46·54	7·28	11·85	35·34	57·55
Calabar	140,975	2	50,999	28,640	24,249	24,697		77,586	36·91	31·25	31·83		76·07
Degema	117,937	2	54,370	33,222		14,367	5,852	53,441	62·17		26·88	10·95	49·15
Eket	238,786	3	91,698	27,216	20,065	24,828	23,455	95,564	28·48	20·99	25·98	24·54	34·74
Enyong	175,885	2	40,186	14,592	7,326	24,389	12,131	58,438	24·97	12·54	41·74	20·76	72·71
Ikom	45,774	2	12,817	9,368		8,193		17,561	53·35		46·66		68·51
Ikot Ekpene	282,771	3	38,421	25,349	12,055	19,266	6,731	63,401	39·98	19·01	30·39	10·62	55·81
Obubra	109,874	2	31,663	7,001	10,512	9,030	8,883	35,376	19·78	29·72	25·53	24·97	55·86
Ogoja	206,962	2	30,737	13,434		16,032	5,988	35,454	37·89		45·22	16·89	57·67
Ogoni	156,723	2	35,563	15,224		22,137	8,015	45,376	33·55		48·79	17·66	63·80
Opobo	172,091	2	41,815	17,778	17,501	2,879	2,413	40,571	43·82	43·14	7·10	5·95	48·51
Port Harcourt	59,512	2	14,797	20,928		2,249	2,257	25,434	82·28		8·84	8·87	25·94
Uyo	296,719	3	85,347	19,225	37,998	40,185		97,408	22·03	37·90	40·01		38·04
TOTAL	2,650,616	35	696,308	368,029	144,445	251,865	138,061	902,400	40·78	16·01	27·91	15·30	43·92
B. Non-C.O.R. Constituencies													
Aba	396,217	4	128,741	134,060	18,798	17,613	6,062	176,533	75·94	10·65	9·98	3·43	34·28
Abakaliki	472,891	5	35,193	38,041		5,812	9,374	53,227	71·47		10·92	17·81	30·25
Afikpo	246,827	3	31,879	21,629		4,785	13,839	40,253	53·73		11·89	34·38	42·09
Awgu	150,887	2	30,675	27,961		1,499	3,517	32,947	84·87		4·46	10·68	53·70
Awka	295,099	3	98,376	82,997		5,680	82,558	171,235	48·47		3·32	48·21	64·80
Bende	322,258	3	80,371	117,929		9,294	18,418	145,641	80·97		6·38	12·65	60·03
Nsukka	449,367	5	100,325	144,202		23,592	20,674	188,468	76·51		12·52	10·97	37·57
Okigwi	442,751	5	86,469	127,019			91,035	218,054	58·25			41·75	50·44
Onitsha	406,348	5	136,686	315,364	32,946	3,413	51,514	403,237	78·21	8·17	0·85	12·78	59·00
Orlu	356,282	6	90,776	114,909	6,289	13,178	41,607	175,983	65·30	3·57	7·49	23·64	48·47
Owerri	560,895	6	124,950	331,107			129,169	460,276	71·94			28·06	61·84
Udi	407,389	4	126,659	201,927		7,452	23,824	233,203	86·59		3·20	10·22	55·51
TOTAL	4,567,211	49	1,070,700	1,657,145	58,033	92,288	491,591	2,299,057	72·08	2·52	4·01	21·38	59·22
GRAND TOTAL	7,217,827	84	1,767,008	2,025,174	202,478	344,153	629,652	3,201,457	63·26	6·32	10·75	19·67	46·78

APPENDIX III

Population and Tribal Distribution by Constituencies

Constituency	Edo	Fulani	Hausa	Ibibio	Ibo	Kanuri	Nupe	Tiv	Toruba	Ijaw	Other Nigerian tribes	Non-Nigerian Africans	Non-Africans	Total
A. C.O.R. Constituencies														
Abak	6	..	34	2,200	5,222	..	..	3	1	..	225,883	12	22	233,383
Ahoada	244	26	280	1,701	253,270	..	1	26	331	3,324	26,996	26	33	286,258
Brass	46	..	41	1,181	1,070	..	6	..	607	119,233	4,760	8	14	126,966
Calabar	224	16	425	27,987	26,728	38	8	78	719	2,477	81,372	659	244	140,975
Degema	94	..	62	1,285	2,291	..	5	1	213	111,001	2,911	40	34	117,937
Eket	13	1	21	109,470	4,204	5	..	..	484	64	124,396	90	38	238,786
Enyong	3	10	7	91,156	50,494	4	2	..	43	67	33,386	177	36	175,885
Ikom	60	13	144	600	3,362	21	..	577	60	3	40,484	435	14	45,774
Ikot Ekpene	2	58	92	99,008	6,935	48	3	14	225	16	176,279	56	35	282,771
Obubra	9	12	31	312	6,653	..	1	207	32	11	102,572	30	4	109,874
Ogoja	4	170	667	297	10,826	52	12	3,825	122	41	190,421	488	37	206,962
Ogoni	..	1	11	402	3,062	..	..	..	7	1,582	151,648	4	6	156,723
Opobo	2	2	33	91,710	2,837	1	1	..	456	11,118	65,867	30	34	172,091
Port Harcourt	889	1	624	2,022	45,503	16	64	10	1,935	4,535	2,171	1,076	666	59,512
Uyo	14	..	34	288,257	5,844	56	1	..	59	16	2,315	69	110	296,719
TOTAL	1,610	310	2,506	717,588	428,301	185	105	4,741	5,294	253,488	1,231,961	3,200	1,327	2,050,616
B. Non-C.O.R. Constituencies														
Aba	184	19	273	10,928	378,065	..	15	3	723	2,880	2,766	255	106	396,217
Abakaliki	130	1	383	213	468,964	..	17	25	37	34	3,044	12	31	472,891
Afikpo	17	..	161	160	233,292	..	..	..	12	26	13,119	9	31	246,827
Awgu	10	..	7	..	150,808	..	..	3	12	1	14	13	19	150,887
Awka	26	87	265	21	294,384	1	13	3	51	41	119	37	51	295,099
Bende	58	119	690	6,816	311,713	1,882	61	14	187	123	436	46	113	322,258
Nsukka	21	16	576	17	446,948	..	370	30	276	68	1,008	14	22	449,367
Okigwi	14	2	101	75	442,247	1	1	8	81	64	107	6	45	442,751
Onitsha	820	75	3,558	179	448,812	26	2,103	73	2,802	804	6,764	177	155	466,348
Orlu	6	1	3	31	356,088	..	..	2	3	66	55	1	26	356,282
Owerri	262	3	195	281	558,721	47	..	..	290	592	242	40	222	560,895
Udi	869	124	1,570	809	398,391	56	79	219	1,609	775	1,979	479	430	407,389
TOTAL	2,417	447	7,782	19,530	4,488,433	1,966	2,706	380	6,083	5,474	29,653	1,089	1,251	4,567,211
GRAND TOTAL	4,027	757	10,288	737,118	4,916,734	2,151	2,811	5,121	11,377	258,962	1,261,614	4,289	2,578	7,217,827*

* Again the discrepancy of 2 creeps in from the census (see Introduction).

ACKNOWLEDGEMENTS

DURING my visit to Eastern Nigeria in February and March 1957 I received the greatest possible co-operation and help from all sides. It is impossible for me to acknowledge here the debt which I owe to all those who assisted me, but apart from the General Board of the University College of the Gold Coast, and the Colonial Social Science Research Council, without whose financial assistance the research would have been impossible, I must make particular mention of the following: the Hon. O. P. Gunning, C.M.G., Deputy Governor; Mr. B. H. Brackenbury, Acting Secretary to the Premier and Regional Electoral Officer; Mr. G. G. Briggs, Q.C., Attorney General; Mr. J. W. H. Kay, Assistant Secretary to the Premier; Mr. A. E. Eronini, M.B.E., Clerk to the House of Assembly; Mr. H. C. Byatt, Assistant Secretary, Ministry of Internal Affairs; Mr. G. W. Thom, Community Development Secretary; Mr. J. E. Hodge, C.V.O., Commissioner of Police, Eastern Region; Mr. D. L. B. Davies, D.S.P. (Regional Criminal Investigation Department); Mr. T. B. Radley, Controller, Eastern Region, Nigerian Broadcasting Services; and Mr. A. J. Disu, Chairman, Eastern Nigerian Information Service. In the constituencies I would like to make particular mention of the assistance and hospitality received from Messrs. D. Smith, R. Varvill, D.S.C., and P. L. Trevorrow, the administrative officers in charge of Onitsha, Calabar, and Abakaliki Divisions respectively.

V

THE SIERRA LEONE ELECTION OF
MAY 1957

1. *The Country and the People*

SIERRA LEONE'S population is about 2,000,000;[1] of these about 130,000 live in the 'Colony', the rest in the 'Protectorate', and the divergence in status and in sentiment between the two divisions runs right through the country's political life.

The Colony consists of the city of Freetown, the rest of the peninsula on which Freetown stands (the 'Rural Area'), and the Sherbro Urban District, formed by the town of Bonthe (on an island some 60 miles to the south-east along the coast) and the nearby island of York. Since it is a British territory, those born there and their descendants are British subjects, whereas the people of the Protectorate are 'British protected persons'. This legal distinction has only a limited practical importance, but their status is of great historical and sentimental importance to the people of the Colony. They represent a settlement of liberated slaves from Britain planted originally in 1788 and reinforced by later waves of 'settlers' rescued from some stage or other of the slave trade; and they thus cling to a form of the 'British way of life'. The earlier inhabitants had known it abroad and brought it with them, the subsequent arrivals had usually lost in captivity, however brief, their contact with their native societies and cultures and in their new life adopted British ways in their place. The numerous Christian sects which took root among them—together with some strange unchristian ones—fostered this as acceptable in the sight of God.

The Protectorate, established from 1896, knew the people of the Colony, the Creoles as they came to be called, as the colleagues and cultural fellows of the white men; they massacred them with the white men in the rising of 1898, deferred to them as to the white men

---

[1] *Sierra Leone Year Book 1951* (published by *Sierra Leone Daily Mail*, Freetown), p. 11, gives 2,005,000 as the 1952 estimate. The test enumeration of 1948 based, for the Protectorate, on the number of taxpayers (*Census of the Colony and Protectorate of Sierra Leone*, Govt. Printer, Freetown, 1949, Table A) gave 1,858,275. A fuller census, based, for the Protectorate, on a count of houses, was last taken in 1931, when the figure was 1,768,480.

in subsequent years. Within the Colony of Sierra Leone, to which throughout the life of the Protectorate, as before its establishment, people from the surrounding districts had constantly migrated, no distinction of status was recognized. To the Creoles within the Protectorate the same did not apply; the administrative arrangements of the Protectorate were at all times founded upon the tribal nature of the people's life, and the Creoles were not and never could be members of the tribes. One consequence of this was that any Protectorate person resident in the Colony could acquire land under the English law there prevailing, but no Creole—nor any other person— could acquire ownership of land in the Protectorate.

In practice, Creoles rarely settled in the Protectorate, for it was a poor country and had little to offer them. Their superior education turned them towards the more characteristically middle-class occupations, and if they migrated it was generally along the coast to the Gold Coast or Nigeria, rather than inland. In this the Creole resembled the European, and like the latter he rarely appeared in the Protectorate except on a short term of official service. It is not surprising that Creole politicians should liken the position of their people to that of the settlers in Kenya.

On the other hand, there is no conspicuous difference of colour to emphasize social differences; and there has been much intermingling because of the inflow of Protectorate people into Freetown, frequent intermarriage, and (at least in the days of Creole prosperity) the patronage and adoption of promising tribal children. Most educated people in the Protectorate have had experience of the Colony, at least as a place of education, and most socially eminent Protectorate families have some Colony blood in their pedigree. The two communities are now defined by sentiment rather than by descent, but the division is no less sharp for that. The Creoles are, roughly, the people who feel pride in their British citizenship, and find it distasteful to have to accept as equals (outnumbering them in a political situation where numbers have come to count) those who have affected to despise it and to prefer either the status of British protected persons—construing it literally, as recognition of a form of sovereignty —or some new status yet to come. They are those who feel pride in their non-recognition of chiefs—other than the annually elected village headmen—their ignorance of African tongues, other than the curiously transformed English dialect known as Krio, and their more than British external conformity to the requirements of Christianity; who resent the dancing and drumming and strange initiation ceremonies of the Protectorate secret societies—though their own societies dance and drum after their fashion—and the legally recognized polygamy which they believe to have paganized within living memory their once godly city and villages. Protectorate opinion, on its side, is prepared to put up with Christianity provided that it does not mean refusal to join the secret societies—and one of the American

MAP 5. SIERRA LEONE

missions is very acceptable on this ground—and to accept education, even education coming from the Colony, as a necessity for development. But it is profoundly suspicious of rootlessness, and has a peasant distrust of cleverness not allied to traditional virtues.

By the 1950's the prosperity formerly enjoyed by some at least of the leading Creole families had long been fading. Their eminence in the professions remained, though now challenged from the Protectorate, but much ground in the more lucrative fields of business had been lost within living memory to others—mainly to the Lebanese. In part this had been the result of the inferior business ability of the Creoles, but in part also it was due to the burden of expense imposed by certain aspects of their way of life, many of them laudable, such as the desire of families of substance to have their children educated abroad. Economic change and social pressure together had brought most Creoles by the 1950's to a state of demoralization comparable with, and exceeding in intensity, the contemporary state of the British whom they had so long imitated; they lost confidence in their own standards, and felt that they were in any case doomed because material circumstances had turned against them.

The Protectorate is by no means monolithic, as is shown in Table 1. Some sense of opposition exists between the Temnes, the majority people of the north, and the Mendes, the majority people of the south, commonly manifested in such forms as the abhorrence and fear expressed by the former of the practice of 'cannibalism'—actually ritual murder—revealed from time to time in parts of the territory inhabited by the latter, and in reflections by the latter upon the honesty of the former. The minor peoples of both parts also preserve their separateness. Susus commonly distrust Temnes; the cattle-keeping Fulahs of the north, with their tribal connexions and frequent intercommunication with French territory, are somewhat contemptuous of the parochial narrowness and incompetence with animals of the settled Temne, Kuranko, Yalunka, and Limba farming peoples among whom they move; the Konos of the east, a compact people living to the northward of Mende country, look with profound suspicion on their generally more enterprising neighbours. But towards the Colony and all whom they regard as Creoles, the Protectorate people show a fair degree of solidarity, especially when living among them. The political spokesmen of the extreme Creoles, wishing to break this front, sometimes claimed publicly that the Creoles had long been on terms of familiarity with the Temnes, from whom the original territory of the Colony was purchased, while both had always distrusted the Mendes. In the 1950's the leaders of the Government happened to be predominantly Mende, and there was in fact some resentment in Temne country about this. The situation was perhaps the more promising for Creole action in that the Temnes, long accustomed to accept patiently the autocracy of their chiefs, were at last following in the way of disobedience and deposition familiar to the Mendes, who traditionally set less store by the chiefly office; and there was a chance that the Temnes might become

TABLE I

Population of Protectorate by Tribes

Province	Tribe	District in which majority tribe	Other districts in which noticed (as population element 1931 or as members of a chiefdom or chiefdoms 1957)	Number in Province 1931
NORTHERN	Temne	Bombali, Port Loko, Kambia, Tonkolili	..	455,674
	Limba	Koinadugu (slightly more numerous than Kurankoes in 1931)	Bombali, Kambia, Tonkolili, Port Loko	135,639
	Loko	..	Bombali, Port Loko	64,363
	Kuranko	..	Koinadugu, Tonkolili	44,096
	Susu	..	Kambia, Port Loko	39,284
	Bullom	..	Kambia, Port Loko	19,471
	Yalunka	..	Koinadugu	16,066
	Fulah	..	Koinadugu	5,450
	Mandingo	..	..	2,176
	Mende	..	..	97
SOUTH-WESTERN	Mende	Bo, Moyamba, Pujehun	Bonthe	309,136
	Sherbro (Bullom)	Bonthe	Moyamba, Bo	125,930*
	Krim (related to Sherbro)	..	Pujehun, Bonthe	20,764*
	Temne	..	Moyamba, Bo	20,415
	Vai (related to Kono)	..	Pujehun	19,865
	Mandingo	..	Moyamba, Bo	8,020
	Gola	..	Pujehun	6,731
	Loko	..	Moyamba, Bo	5,179
	Susu	..	Moyamba, Bo	4,090
	Fulah	..	Bo	311
	Others (Banta, &c.)	..	Bo	239
SOUTH-EASTERN	Mende	Kenema, Kailahun	Kono	263,445
	Kono	Kono	Kailahun, Kenema	67,726
	Kissi	..	Kailahun, Kono	30,395
	Mandingo	..	Kono, Kenema	1,489
	Temne	..	Kenema	820
	Kuranko	..	Kono	189
	Susu	..	Kenema	179
	Others (Gola, &c.)	..	Kenema, Kono	526

* Including numbers in Sherbro Judicial District of the Colony.

SOURCE: *Sierra Leone, Report of Census for the year 1931* (Govt. Printer, Freetown). *Sierra Leone Protectorate Handbook* (Chief Commissioner's Office, Bo, 1957).

politically more ambitious. However, in the early part of 1957 the attitude of the northern peoples in general was clearly that though southern Protectorate leadership was in many ways objectionable it could be accepted until they could build up a leadership of their own, which for the time being they knew they were not in a position to do. Blandishments from the Colony evoked only a very meagre and localized response. In the Protectorate constituencies tribal divisions were important in determining support for individual candidates, but had little effect on party attachments.

The significance of the tribal factor was diminished because no tribe was a political unit. The Konos had an administrative district to themselves,[1] but they like all the other peoples were divided into a number of chiefdoms (seven in each of their two constituencies), and each chiefdom had its own paramount chief who recognized no superior. Some chiefdoms in other parts of the country, fashioned for administrative convenience by the amalgamation of a number of minute former chiefdoms, combined, not usually very harmoniously, people of different tribes. All chiefdoms were small, in contrast to those in parts of Ghana and Nigeria; no chief was in a position by mere traditional power to wield the votes of a whole constituency. Yet within their strictly local limits the chiefs were politically very influential. 'We are looking to the chief to whomever he will direct us', one villager in Kambia district was interpreted as saying at an instructional meeting on electoral procedure, and probably a great majority of the peoples of the Protectorate, including very many who realized that this was not the proper thing to say in the presence of the white man—as did the chief in whose presence these words were spoken—intended to do, and in fact did, the same.

Secret societies are a political force which defies analysis by the observer from outside the social system, and the life of Sierra Leone, at least of the Protectorate, is deeply penetrated by them. The ritual murders for which Kailahun and Bonthe districts are notorious are apparently the work of local but inter-related societies in those and neighbouring districts of the south. At least one official S.L.P.P. candidate in 1957 was reputed to have been involved with them in activities which led to a killing. In part of the south the Wunde society apparently takes precedence, in the status of its members and reputed efficacy of its 'medicine', over the general men's society, the Porro, and is reputedly more closely connected with such activities. In the north there is another restricted society, though a less notorious one, the Gbinle, the membership of which is apparently

[1] It included many strangers, but they came as individuals, not as communities, for diamond digging or other purposes.

open only to chiefs and those eligible for such office. The Porro, however, formerly the military organization, is country-wide, and its membership includes most of the adult male population. Membership of certain of the smaller Christian sects, of the Muslim faith in the stricter parts of the north, and of certain minor peoples such as the Mandingoes, is supposed to be incompatible with Porro membership, but in practice obviously is not. The seriousness with which the society is taken varies considerably; in parts of the south its ceremonies appear to be perfunctory and its obligations no more compelling than those of English freemasonry; in the middle north especially, but also upon occasions elsewhere, it can effectively hound to death a person who has incurred its displeasure. Potentially it is probably the most important political force in the country; in the state of the franchise and registration in 1957 the corresponding women's society clearly did not matter. How far electoral questions were fixed in the society's 'sacred bush' could not be determined. Colony politicians were apt to suggest, and probably to fear, that they were; Protectorate politicians, who were themselves almost without exception members and relied largely upon their occasional visits to the sacred bush back at home to maintain their standing there, suggested that they were not. One of the latter stated that it was usual to discuss political matters there and that in his district a decision had been taken there about the recent district council election. He suggested, however, that on a non-traditional matter such a decision was not binding, and claimed that he had defied the decision in question and won in spite of it. He suggested that the institution was politically most effective in keeping Creoles and other outsiders in the dark, and that the mere fact of non-membership would make it difficult for such people to get a sympathetic hearing in the Protectorate. The only case in which this seems to have been put to the test in 1957 appeared to support this suggestion. Certain of the sharper Colony politicians were popularly thought to have secured admittance to the lower degrees of Porro, though Protectorate politicians suggested that it would do them little good. There is probably no national organization of the society such as could be harnessed to any one party chariot.

One thing the whole country has in common: the impress of generations of poverty and failure. The combination of the leaching action of a rainfall exceptionally heavy even by tropical standards with a dry season long enough and complete enough severely to hinder the growth of much of the cover of vegetation which such rainfall might otherwise have promoted, have left the country with a quite exceptional proportion of laterite or lateritic soils, and consequently with a severe shortage of arable land and sizeable trees. The many meandering rivers which for centuries have been carrying its topsoil down to the sea have also made the development of communications a formidable task, and in the swamp areas with which they line the coast have made the building of an adequate network of roads almost inconceivable even now for many years to come. In return these processes had given much of the country a crust of iron of quite exceptional purity, a generous supply of other minerals, and highly favourable conditions for the growth of swamp rice. But the exploitation of the mineral resources, which require adequate means of transport for their exportation, has come late, beginning with the mining of diamonds and iron ore in the middle 1930's, and has only of recent years advanced beyond the pioneering stage to the point where the mining companies can usefully be squeezed for the general advantage. The agricultural richness of the swamps also was slow to be exploited because of the reluctance of the country's farmers to accept the inconvenience of working under such conditions, and is in any case insufficient to provide any very spacious conditions of life for the country as a whole, in view of the barrenness of the uplands. The land of the Colony is somewhat better than that of most of the Protectorate, but it is still poor, and life there has from the first been a grievous disappointment after the high hopes which the founders of the venture reposed in it. The sense that the world has in some way been unjust to Sierra Leone, almost universal among Colony people and found among many of those of the Protectorate as well, has become increasingly pronounced as the other countries of West Africa, in which Sierra Leoneans had been accustomed to find recognition of their superior education and leadership, came to surpass them in economic development, in educational facilities, in the reputed efficiency of their administration and latterly in political self-reliance and influence.

2. Constitutional Development

The Legislative Council dissolved on 8 April 1957 had been elected in October 1951 under the constitution of that year.[1] The 1951 constitution originated in proposals made in 1947 by the Governor of the day for reform of the 1924 Constitution, which by 1951 was the only constitution in British West Africa to retain an official majority

---

[1] S.I. 1951, No. 611, The Sierra Leone (Legislative Council) Order in Council, 1951 (made 9 Apr. 1951) and other instruments of that year listed, with amendments to 1955, in a pamphlet *The Constitution of Sierra Leone 1955*, p. 1 (Government Printing Department, 1955).

(eleven out of twenty-one) in the legislature: of the unofficial minority only three were elected, and all these came from the Colony. The 1947 proposals increased the membership of the Council to 30. They reduced the number of official members to 7, retained 2 nominated unofficial members to represent commerce, increased the number of members directly elected from the Colony to 7—without changing the existing restricted franchise—and provided for the election of 1 member of Legislative Council by the district council of each of the 13 administrative districts of the Protectorate from among its own members, and one by the unofficial members of the Protectorate Assembly from among the members nominated to it by the Governor to represent interests not represented on the District Councils—such as commerce, trade unions, and missions. The District Councils, instituted in 1946 as advisory bodies and in 1950 given executive functions mainly in connexion with development, were formed of all paramount chiefs, members elected by the tribal authorities—the officially recognized advisers of the chiefs, by whom they were usually dominated—and co-opted members. The Protectorate Assembly, which came into being at about the same time, contained, in addition to the Chief Commissioner for the Protectorate and nine *ex-officio* and six nominated members, two elected by each District Council. Its functions were purely advisory to Government, but its advice and grievances were taken seriously, and proposed legislation affecting the Protectorate was discussed with it well in advance of introduction.

These proposals were at first approved unanimously by the unofficial members of the old legislature, and were endorsed by the Secretary of State in July 1948; but rising discontent, mainly in the Colony, held up reform for three years and led in the end to the imposition of the proposals, virtually unchanged, without local agreement. As one of the Protectorate districts had in the meantime been abolished, and as it was desired to keep the new balance between Protectorate and Colony, the Protectorate Assembly was given a second member, to be chosen from among the members elected to it by District Councils. At the 1951 election eight District Councils returned chiefs and four, non-chiefs. The Protectorate Assembly returned two non-chiefs, one of them being a representative of the trade unions.

The period of the 1951 legislature was troubled not only by dissension over reform but by industrial riots in Freetown early in 1955,[1]

---

[1] *Report of the Commission of Inquiry into the Strike and Riots in Freetown, Sierra Leone during February 1955* (the Shaw Report) (Government Printing Department, 1955). Sessional Paper No. 1 of 1955 (the Government's statement on the report).

by the serious problem of illicit diamond mining in the eastern part of the Protectorate, and by a general rising against tax payment and corrupt and autocratic chiefs in the Western Protectorate in 1955–6.[1] In spite of these difficulties real political progress had been made, within the limits imposed by the country's economic resources. The appointment of ministers from among the elected members of the legislature had been envisaged from the first; six elected members were appointed to the Executive Council at once, and in 1952 five of these were invited to exercise a general watch, though without personal responsibility, over the business of groups of government departments selected and combined with regard to their personal experience. In December of the same year by an agreed resolution moved in the Legislative Council by Dr. Margai, leader of the majority party, it was decided that the time had come for the formal allocation of portfolios; in April 1953 all six representative members of Executive Council were accorded the title of ministers. One who was a paramount chief and was supposed to give much time to his duties as a local ruler became minister without portfolio, and the others were formally invested with ministerial responsibility for the groups of departments of which they had previously been gaining experience. In the following year Dr. Margai was granted the title of Chief Minister, but retained departmental responsibility as Minister of Health, Agriculture and Forests.

Despite the piecemeal method of formation this clearly had most of the essential characteristics of a cabinet system. While in legal form all ministers were appointed severally by the Governor, as in a system of the British monarchical type they must be, the evidence is that the future Chief Minister had a large part in their selection. The Governor of the time would, on the evidence of his own words, have preferred a coalition to a one-party government at that stage, had he had a free choice; and Dr. Margai's voice in the subsequent selection, though perhaps negative, was decisive. In Dr. Margai's own cautious words in the Legislative Council in January 1952:

It was simply natural that whatever doubt he [the Governor] had when he found that the group I was dealing with—call it a party, a small community or merely a number of people—was in a majority that he decided that I had to be consulted in selecting Executive Council. This does not

---

[1] *Sierra Leone—Report of Commission of Inquiry into Disturbances in the Provinces (November 1955 to March 1956)* (the Cox Report) (London: Crown Agents for Oversea Governments and Administrations, 1956); *Statement of the Sierra Leone Government on the Report*, &c. (Government Printing Department, 1956).

mean that I picked the people; he suggested names and I approved or dis-approved of them.[1]

The Government was small and there were·no junior ministers nor any possibility of providing them from the small legislature of the 1951 Constitution. The ministries were tailored to fit individuals and would ill have fitted any others; for lack of funds they had no staffs of their own, other than a secretary to the minister, and no separate office premises. The Secretariat continued in being, and set its stamp on all ministry work. It was not easy under the circumstances to build up an efficient working team with an individuality of its own. But the main limitation on party government was the continued presence within the Executive Council not only of the Governor but of four *ex-officio* members—the Colonial Secretary, who was in effect minister for defence, external affairs, internal security and the organization of the civil service, the Financial Secretary who performed the functions of a minister of finance, the Attorney General and, most questionably, the Chief Commissioner of the Protectorate; the last named is a sort of duplicate governor for the greater part of the country, through whom the three provincial Commissioners report to the Governor, and he is also a sort of duplicate minister of local government.

It was largely because of dissension over the nature of reform that the interim legislature of 1951 lasted six months more than its allotted span of five years, and at the end of 1956 the first element of a new Constitution, replacing the old Legislative Council by a new House of Representatives, again had to be imposed without local agreement.[2] In view of the lack of consensus in political life the Government had announced the intention of proceeding in two stages:

First, to ensure without delay the creation of a larger and more representa-tive legislature based on a wider franchise.

Second, to recommend as an early duty of the new legislature that it should consider proposals for changes in the composition and functions of the Executive Council and other related matters.[3]

The House of Representatives was to consist of a Speaker elected

---

[1] *Legislative Council Debates, Session 1951–52*, vol. i, p. 271 (proceedings of 31 Jan. 1952).

[2] S.I. 1956 No. 1893, *Sierra Leone (House of Representatives) Order in Council, 1956* (made 29 Nov. 1956).

[3] Sessional Paper No. 2 of 1956, *The Government's Proposals for Constitutional Reform*. Sessional Paper No. 1 of 1956 gives the Government's version of the forces which had delayed reform.

by the House itself by a two-thirds majority, from within its membership or outside, those four of the seven existing *ex-officio* members of the Legislative Council who were also of the Executive Council, fourteen directly elected members from the Colony and twenty-five from the Protectorate together with one paramount chief from each Protectorate administrative district. There were to be two non-voting nominated members to represent special interests; the Government's proposals, apart from providing generally for the second stage of constitution-making, had specifically reserved to the new House the right to reconsider the position of the nominated members.

The four *ex-officio* members of the 'cabinet' were to continue to hold office after 1957, at least pending agreement on further constitutional reform.

The degree of self-reliance to be attained was therefore less impressive than that achieved by the Gold Coast some years previously—let alone that of the new state of Ghana, which came into being during the election campaign and was much in people's minds. It was not even as high as the status reached by the neighbouring territory of French Guinea after its 1957 elections, though not much was known in Sierra Leone about this rather deceptive parallel. Yet much had been learned; some of the ministers had shown themselves efficient managers and able advocates of their departments. The legislature, sitting since December 1953 under an African Speaker with the title of Vice-President, was an impressive, and with a few lapses, a decorous body. But few citizens attended meetings, the press hardly reported them, the ministers attracted publicity mainly because of minor scandals. The whole performance was worthy, but was outshone by more showy achievements elsewhere.

3. *The Electoral System*

As in the other West African territories, a widespread franchise came before there was any general demand for it. National politics were by 1957 of very little interest to the generality of Protectorate people. Chiefdom politics were, as they always had been, very near to the centre of their interests. District Councils had developed since the 1940's out of conferences of such chiefs as were prepared to envisage co-operation with their neighbours, and in some areas a good deal of interest was taken in them as a means of pressure on unpopular chiefs. Once non-chiefly members were added to them, as soon happened, the councils became an alternative way to local eminence for those who could not hope for traditional office. But the central legislature was clearly something too remote from the concerns of the village for an interest in its composition to develop spontaneously. Yet as in the other West African territories the adoption of the ballot box was inevitable. Since other territories (including the Colony) had it and claimed it as an achievement, self-respect demanded it for the Protectorate; and since the Protectorate's case for achieving a larger representation as against the Colony rested largely in numbers, it was obliged to make use of the political process in which numbers showed to most advantage.

Elections had been known in the Colony since 1924. Until 1957 these were held according to the British system of marking ballot papers, literacy being a qualification for the vote. In 1951 2,438 persons voted in the three single-member constituencies given to Freetown in that year, and a further 869 were registered as entitled to do so out of a population of about 70,000. In the rural-area constituencies one member was returned unopposed, and two were elected in elections involving 550 and 288 voters. In the Sherbro Judicial District, where there was a possible electorate of about 1,100 in a population of some 7,000, there was an unopposed return. Elections had for a few years been fought on party lines, or at least under party labels.

In the Protectorate, however, elections were quite new, apart from the more or less traditional procedures applied in the election of chiefs. Most people were involved in these, in the sense of taking a lively interest and holding strong opinions, but decision was generally left to a small circle of elders 'hanging head'—consulting together—in private and seeking wherever possible a compromise, or at least an outwardly agreed settlement. In addition, informal types of election, usually by acclamation or by lining-up behind the favoured candidate, had been held by district commissioners to fill the places for non-traditional members introduced into the chiefs' councils since the 1940's. Elections to the District Councils and to the Protectorate Assembly and, under the 1951 constitution, from those two institutions to the Legislative Council, being indirect, were more subject to the influence of the chiefs than to that of their peoples, and were not complicated by parties. Direct popular elections first appeared in the Protectorate—under the franchise adopted for the subsequent House elections—for the District Councils between August 1956 and April 1957.

A commission under the chairmanship of Mr. Bryan Keith-Lucas of Nuffield College, Oxford, had been appointed on 1 July 1954, to make recommendations on the reform of the electoral system, including the franchise. The commission included both the Leader of the Opposition, representative of the principal objecting party, and four firm supporters of the Government, yet contrived to present on 9 September 1954, an agreed report,[1] which was with unimportant exceptions accepted by the Government. Unhappily, Dr. Bankole-Bright, the Leader of the Opposition, subsequently came to feel that the recommendations of the commission had been overthrown. This seems to have been because the pressure of events delayed effective action on the report for nearly a year and delayed the first national general elections for two and a half years, and in the meantime the circumstances of the country so changed as in effect to nullify the safeguard to which Dr. Bankole-Bright attached the greatest importance. Nevertheless in all essentials it was under the Keith-Lucas franchise that the elections of May 1957 were held.

This franchise was a complicated one. It differed for the Colony and for the Protectorate: in the former the vote was given to every man or woman of twenty-one years or more and at least six months' residence in the constituency who was the occupier of rateable premises of at least £2 annual assessed value or the recipient of a yearly income of at least £60. Joint occupiers might be included in such numbers that the annual assessed value divided by such number should not be less than £2, and in the process of drafting it was further provided that owners, as well as occupiers, and wives or husbands of owners or occupiers, should also be qualified on the basis of the same property. At the same time these franchise provisions were extended to the town of Bo in the Protectorate.

Elsewhere in the Protectorate a vote was given to every man of twenty-one years or more liable to pay the local head tax, other than paramount chiefs, for whose representation in the House special provisions were made, and those excluded by the usual disqualifications for unfitness; and to any woman of similar age who in fact paid tax, or who was 'entitled in her own right to the use or enjoyment of land or the rents and profits thereof' within the constituency, or who could satisfy the Registration Officer that she was literate. Except for women in the Protectorate not qualified under any other provision, literacy ceased to be a requirement. The commission recommended that this franchise should obtain only until, but not including, the second general election to the House of Representatives, which on the assumption then accepted that the first election would be held in 1956 would have fallen in 1961. From that date a franchise approximating to universal adult suffrage should replace it. In

---

[1] *Report of the Commission for Electoral Reform* (the Keith-Lucas Report) (Government Printing Department, 1954); *Sessional Papers* 2 and 4 of 1955 (successive government statements).

putting the recommendations into legislative form the Government did not commit itself specifically as to the future.

The complexities of the franchise were largely enforced by circumstances. No reliable census of the whole country had been taken, nor would it be possible to take one before 1956, the originally intended date of the elections. The public were largely indifferent to political rights, and outside Freetown there were no strong competing party machines to stimulate and organize mass interest and activity. It was therefore unlikely that any form of registration which required action by the voter himself would produce much result, and the subsequent response of women in the Protectorate confirmed this.

Occupation of property—though to the higher value of £6 in Freetown and £5 elsewhere in the Colony, and with a requirement of twenty-four months' residence in the Colony—had been the basis of the previous Colony franchise; there had also been a £60 income qualification, though residence and literacy qualifications had made the latter comparatively unimportant. Thus in the Colony the existing registers provided some basis on which to build. Bo town had not previously been a constituency for elections to the legislature and had only recently been constituted a local government unit, so there was no existing register, but it had already been decided to introduce there a local government franchise of the Colony type, as conditions were similar.

The tax-assessment lists were the only comprehensive register of names existing elsewhere in the Protectorate. Since the consolidation in 1954 of the settlers' fees payable by Colony-born persons and other non-natives resident in the Protectorate with the tax paid by the natives, and the conversion of this into a genuine head tax, these lists excluded few adult males—mainly those exempted from payment on the grounds of blindness or other physical incapacity. They included, however, only a few women, mainly sub-chiefs, and to compile similar lists of women at short notice would have been an immense administrative task; all the more difficult, because the tax lists were to be used as electoral registers for men, and this would deter women from coming forward lest they find themselves subject to tax.

But the exclusion of Protectorate women was also necessary as a support for the principle of two stages in the advance to universal suffrage, which played a large part in securing agreement within the Keith-Lucas commission. The roots of this concept lay in the Colony, where it was necessary to reassure conservative opinion that the existing electorate would not be swamped at once, but some appearance of consistency with Protectorate practice was politically essential. In the event there was hardly any exclusion in the Colony; the rising wages which followed upon rising costs between the commission's report and the registration, and which in particular resulted from the settlement of the industrial unrest of early 1955, meant that everybody could plausibly claim to have an income of £60. In Bo town where, uniquely, both property rate and chiefdom head tax were levied, the tax-assessment lists were in fact taken as a basis in the compilation of the list of £60 income voters, the two classes being regarded as virtually identical. Thus the universal adult suffrage of 1961 arrived in the Colony in 1957. The women of the Protectorate alone remained excluded, but did not appear to grieve at their exclusion, and their men (largely Muslim) clearly regarded it as right and proper.

The Keith-Lucas commission recommended the use of single-member constituencies throughout the country, and the Government adopted this except in the three wards of the city of Freetown and in the Sherbro Urban District, which had been single-member constituencies under the previous Constitution, and were now to have two members each, but could not be subdivided in time for the early election then intended. In these four constituencies each voter was to have two votes, of which he might not cast more than one for any one candidate. The representation of the Colony rural-area constituencies also was doubled, but each member under the old Constitution represented two local government units, and these were now separated as six single-member constituencies. The twelve administrative districts of the Protectorate, each of which consisted of from seven to fourteen chiefdoms, were each split along chiefdom frontiers into two single-member constituencies of roughly equal population. Bo town formed the twenty-fifth Protectorate constituency. All elections were to be direct and by simple majority.

The Government accepted the recommendation that voting should be by the placing of unmarked ballot papers in separate ballot boxes for each of the candidates, distinguished by the candidate's name and allotted symbol, together, if he so wished, with his photograph; but rejected as impracticable the suggestion that in Freetown and the rural area of the Colony, where voting had previously been by marking ballot papers and inserting them into a single ballot box, that system should be retained as an alternative for the use of literate voters, and that it should be introduced as such an alternative in any other constituency in which literates were more than 10 per cent. of the population.

There was one substantial departure from the recommendations of the commission which served to increase the asperity of the election campaign. In 1956 a Bill for the revision of the Freetown Municipal Ordinance came before a select committee of the Legislative Council and an amendment was there accepted refusing to implement a recommendation of the commission, and to remove the existing disqualification from membership of persons disciplinarily disqualified from the practice of their professions. The amendment in fact made the disqualification more severe than it had previously been, by omitting the previous limitation to a ten-year period, so that the electoral disqualification remained even when the period of professional disqualification had elapsed. At the same time the amendment made permanent the exclusion of persons sentenced to imprisonment for felony or for offences involving dishonesty; this had previously been for ten years, and the Bill, again following the commission, had proposed to limit it to five years. These amendments were not challenged at any later stage of the Bill's passage, and were subsequently copied into other local government legislation, in which they had previously had no place, and into the legislation governing central government elections, where the disqualification on professional grounds had not previously existed and the disqualification on ground of criminal record had been limited to five years. This change in regard to the central legislature was made by the United Kingdom Order in Council establishing the new legislature, published in Sierra Leone on 14 January 1957.[1]

There is little agreement as to who originally proposed these disqualifications, but it was common knowledge, and was never denied or questioned, that the exclusion on professional grounds had been aimed at Mr. Rogers-Wright, the very able leader of the United Progressive Party, an organization which very soon after its formation at the time of the arrival of the Keith-Lucas commission began to give concern both to the party in power, the Sierra Leone People's Party, and to the party forming the official opposition, the National Council of Sierra Leone, since it appeared to threaten their secure holds on the Protectorate and Colony respectively. In some degree everybody was involved in the affair. The Government and its supporters, whatever their part in its making, gleefully accepted the weapon when offered. The National Council was commonly believed to have played the main part, since the new party had profited by divisions within the National Council to gain a prominent founder member and spokesman in the Legislative Council, Mr. Wallace-Johnson. It was a cause of some malicious joy on the Government side, though small comfort to the U.P.P., that the amendment of the

---

[1] S.I. 1956 No. 1893, *The Sierra Leone (House of Representatives) Order in Council, 1956* (made 29 Nov. 1956).

clause on disqualification for criminal record, apparently introduced solely for consistency with that on professional disqualification, was subsequently found to exclude a leading member of the official Opposition. The U.P.P. itself was not free of accusations of complicity, for their principal recruit from the National Council, Mr. Wallace-Johnson, seemed to have done conspicuously little to promote the interests of his leader, Mr. Rogers-Wright, when the matter came before Legislative Council. After the 1957 election, in which he was successful, Mr. Wallace-Johnson was expelled from the party for an unspecified but declaredly serious offence and when the Government proposed to establish a commission of the new House to inquire into the exclusion clause he protested in vain that it was untimely.

4. The District Council Elections

The first experiment with direct elections on a wide franchise was made in the local elections held between August 1956 and April 1957. The polls in these elections were curiously varied, ranging from those of two wards in Moyamba and Port Loko districts, where candidates were elected by two and three votes respectively—in each case the only votes cast—to two wards in Pujehun and Koinadugu districts, where there were polls of 86 per cent. and 87 per cent., with a fairly even spread in between. The very low polls were due to abstention by one faction in areas which had recently been troubled, and to their more-or-less forcible dissuasion of their opponents. Extremely high polls arose from interest in a novel activity, stimulated in the most striking cases by energetic election staff in the District Commissioners' offices. A condition for their achievement was the readiness of whole villages to assemble at the polling stations at an early hour of the morning—which in view of the distances involved sometimes meant their coming the previous day—and to remain, if necessary, all day, since with the registers composed as they were it was only by calling in order of villages that voters could be sufficiently rapidly identified. These conditions made it improbable that similar results would be achieved again in the national elections, when the novelty would be tarnished and the issues less comprehensible.

The average poll in contested local elections seems to have been about 40 per cent. There was quite a high proportion of unopposed returns, mostly in the remoter chiefdoms, and almost always in those which had been most successful in preserving their traditional relations intact. The practises of voting were fairly well understood, largely as a result of intensive propaganda by Public Relations Office staff (who were limited to the range of the road system) and by the District Commissioners and their staffs (who were not). However, some voters in most polling stations failed to notice that the ballot box had a slit in the top, and consequently put their ballot papers on the box or under the box or, in one district, between the box and the label which, incorrectly, was loosely stuck to it. According to the regulations, these were all spoiled ballot papers, but in many stations the presiding officers on their periodic inspections of the voting room had recovered some of them and placed them in the box of the voter's apparent choice, or sometimes, it was suspected, in that of their own choice. It was also suspected that other voters had sometimes done the same. In order to give definite guidance in such cases it was provided in the regulations for the central government election that any paper found touching a box might be placed within it by the presiding officer and counted. Others were to be discarded.

Most voters seemed aware that a choice between persons was being made. In general it was understood that symbols were no more than distinguishing marks, but there were exceptions. The District Commissioner of Koinadugu district in the extreme north reported that some people thought that candidates using the symbol of a paramount chief's staff of office harboured ambitions to be chiefs. This seems to have happened elsewhere, and in the later stages of the election this symbol was withdrawn. Others thought that those who used the symbol of a cooking pot pledged themselves to feed their supporters and that those using the symbol of a hammock betrayed their lazy disposition. In such of the district council elections as it was possible to observe—those held in 1957—it did not seem that the order in which the boxes were set out in the voting rooms influenced the casting of votes. On the other hand, few voters gave much thought, or any, to the qualities desirable in a district councillor. The contest was thought of in strictly traditional terms as the making of rather minor chiefs. The voters seem to have looked for, and the candidates almost uniformly thought it well to offer, the qualities traditionally looked for in a chief—birth into one of the rival chiefly families which exist in most chiefdoms, local birth and residence, hospitality and readiness to give good advice to all who sought it. There was an almost complete absence among candidates of the animosity normally obtaining between rivals for a chiefly staff, a sign perhaps that the new office was not thought to be of much importance. Where relations between candidates were more strained there was generally some special factor; as in Koidu town, Kono district, where the contest was known to be a preliminary trial of strength for the central government elections, and in Samu chiefdom,

Kambia district, where the issue of the previous year's troubles had been kept alive by the restoration to office of a generally hated chief. For the twelve paramount chiefs who were to sit in the new legislature, the system of election remained as under the 1951 constitution. The constituency was still the District Council—itself now directly elected—and though the qualification for candidates was changed all members, whether chiefs or not, had the vote. The Election Regulations, as originally published on 7 March 1957 omitted the provision, contained in the previous regulations, that where only one candidate was nominated there should be a vote for or against, and by analogy with the direct popular elections provided for unopposed returns. When subsequently it came to be realized that this would produce some odd results in view of the requirement that all members of the new House should be literate (in two districts it would lead to the return of chiefs who were generally unpopular but alone possessed the literacy qualification), an amendment restored the old system. In the event, however, both unpopular chiefs were returned, one of them unanimously, apparently because other district councillors felt that not to return a member would bring discredit upon the district. Only Tonkalili district, in the Northern Province, returned no paramount chief; its only literate head of a chiefdom was a regent and not a substantive paramount chief, and it was ruled belatedly, that he was not eligible.

These chiefly elections seem to have produced a form of canvassing similar in duration to that of candidates seeking popular favour, but differing in kind. All that it is possible to say about this is that it consisted of a chief's letting it be known well in advance that he intended to stand, seeking to persuade possible opponents to stand down, commonly on promise of some equivalent service in another field, and making firm his friendship with his fellow councillors. The process was very close to traditional practice, and probably caused the public at large little concern. But there was obviously brisk competition within the councils resulting in some close contests.

5. *The Parties*

Two of the parties which fought the 1957 election first appeared during the preparations for the election of 1951. The National Council of Sierra Leone, originally called the National Council of the Colony of Sierra Leone until it was realized that this played into the hands of its rivals, was formed by the merging of Dr. Bankole-Bright's Sierra Leone Democratic Party with various other movements in the Colony, especially those connected with the former West Africa Youth League led by Mr. I. T. A. Wallace-Johnson. In 1952 Dr. Bankole-Bright's uncompromising and violently expressed refusal to recognize the accomplished fact of Protectorate political equality led Mr. Wallace-Johnson to part company from him.

The Sierra Leone Organization Society was created in 1946 out of an earlier organization founded originally by Dr. Margai and some other people of the Protectorate. The founders were mostly connected with the movement for chiefs' conferences and with other attempts at progress within the traditional scheme of things, and their aim was primarily educational. In 1950 this joined with the People's Party, formed in the Colony by the late Mr. E. N. Jones, who had taken the name of Laminah Sankoh as a gesture of renunciation of the European traditions of the Creoles in favour of solidarity with the peoples of the Protectorate. The amalgamation called itself the *Sierra Leone People's Party*. It nominated candidates for six of the seven Colony seats in 1951, and in the seventh constituency, Sherbro, the non-party candidate returned unopposed declared for it after the election and may have been in agreement with it from the outset. In one constituency, Wilberforce, its candidate withdrew before polling day, giving an unopposed return to Mr. Wallace-Johnson, then standing as National Council candidate. It won only Freetown East, where Mr. M. S. Mustapha, a Colony Muslim, was able to enlist the support of a number of voters of that community. The other five seats fell to the National Council, though later two were lost by the defections of Mr. Wallace-Johnson and Mr. J. C. O. Crowther, members for Waterloo and British Koya, of whom the latter joined the S.L.P.P. In the indirect elections in the Protectorate all candidates stood as individuals, in the manner of previous elections to the Protectorate Assembly.

The *United Sierra Leone Progressive Party*, generally known as the U.P.P., to avoid confusion with the S.L.P.P., was formed as a completely new movement in June 1954 by Mr. C. B. Rogers-Wright, the most successful practitioner at the Sierra Leone bar, who had previously taken no direct part in politics, by Mr. Wallace-Johnson, who had for some two years been without a party and could offer a voice in the Legislative Council, and by others mostly from the Colony. From the first, however, it sought to secure itself a following in the Protectorate; all parties put the unity of the whole country prominently among their slogans, but only the U.P.P. had much success in avoiding identification with one or other of the communities. It came into being in time to give evidence before the Keith-Lucas commission, and this was perhaps the immediate incentive for its foundation. It found itself obliged to rely on disillusionment with the established parties among the communities which they purported to represent. Among the Creoles such discontent was to some extent in existence from the first, for the leadership of the National Council was never fully accepted. Support could also be found among Protectorate people in the Colony, as Protectorate ministers once established in office came to seem very like any other group in power. In the Protectorate it was more difficult, but there were discontents, and in their work in the law courts and the Legislative Council respectively Mr. Rogers-Wright and Mr. Wallace-Johnson had made useful reputations as able champions. The principal opportunity came with the riots in the Protectorate between November 1955 and March 1956. The National Council gained some support there at the same time, but was hampered by its Creole associations.

Two other parties, without representation in the Legislative Council, presented candidates in the election of 1957. The first of these to appear, the *Sierra Leone Labour Party*, emerged from the industrial strike in Freetown in January 1955 which built up a strong personal following behind Mr. Marcus Grant, the most active of the trade union leaders in that incident. The party gained in prestige from what was widely considered to be the unfair treatment of Mr. Grant by the Commission of Inquiry presided over by Sir John Shaw reporting on the strike and on the destructive riots which followed from it.[1] Mr. Grant urged in his evidence before the Commission that the party had long been planned and was not an opportunist product of the moment of crisis, and he was probably right, but it could hardly have started at any other time with so much good will behind it. Yet it had no solid foundation of support. Its misfortune was that the trade unions were non-political and were kept so by the government Labour Department which fostered them; and that in so far as they had personal connexions with politicians they were divided among all parties, including that of Mr. Rogers-Wright, who was president of the railway workers. The Labour Party made little effort to appeal to workers in the Protectorate—iron and diamond miners and railwaymen—and where it did so it met with little success. Moreover, workers throughout the country were hardly aware of themselves as such rather than as members of their several tribes, and it was left to the new party to show them good reason why they should so see themselves. Mr. Grant took only the position of joint National Secretary of the party, that of President being given to Mr. Ronald Beoku-Betts, son of the Vice-President (i.e. the Speaker) of the

[1] See *Report of the Commission of Inquiry into the Strike and Riots in . . . February 1955* (Freetown, Government Printer, 1955).

Legislative Council, who had been one of the counsel for the unions before the Shaw commission—though on that occasion less spectacularly their champion than Mr. Rogers-Wright—and is an earnest man of mildly Fabian views.

The *Sierra Leone Independence Movement*, which appeared on the scene in November 1956, was the emanation of a single personality. Its founder called himself Edward Blyden—or sometimes Edward Blyden III—after his maternal grandfather, who through a career of conflict with educational authority and the Missions won recognition as a public benefactor for his work in the promotion of Muslim schooling; and he seems to have wished to re-enact in rather literal fashion the life of his distinguished ancestor. He laid great emphasis on education, and launched a national school fund for which contributions were taken at his meetings and from supporters; adopted an attitude of systematic defiance of authority, which had recently led to his dismissal from his post as extra-mural studies organizer at Fourah Bay College and in consequence to a protracted series of law suits; accepted from the more enthusiastic of his followers expressions of rather exaggerated discipleship, as well as his ancestor's title of 'Doctor', to which he was not himself entitled.

Though individual, the movement was not—and no movement could have been—entirely original. It owed much to other West African models, especially the National Council of Nigeria and the Cameroons, and perhaps even more to the National Unity Movement of Dr. Eric Williams in Trinidad; from the latter it derived much of its terminology and technique, although in its central thesis —the refusal to recognise any place for party politics in a society styled colonial—it was entirely at variance with the methods of that most systematic of parties. Its appeal was to the young, intellectual, middle-class Creole, to whom it offered an explanation for the failures of the past and the slipping of leadership from Creole hands, as Dr. Bankole-Bright could not do, being himself compromised by such failure. Mr. Blyden placed the blame squarely on colonialism and the infinite cunning of the Colonial Office.

The events of 1951, which led to the emergence of the S.L.P.P. as the party in power, are variously remembered and variously explained by those who participated in them. It is, however, a matter of record[1] that when the new Legislative Council met on 28 November 1951, the Governor, Sir George Beresford Stooke, said that there was no organized party structure such as would justify him in calling upon the leader of any one party to form a Government; and it

[1] *Legislative Council Debates, Session 1951-2*, vol. i, p. 89 (proceedings of 28 Nov. 1951).

seems clear that he had already discussed in some detail with one or more of the leading political figures of the Colony the composition of the coalition Executive Council which he then had in mind. By the following day he had changed his appraisal of the situation, possibly on the basis of instructions from London, but more probably because he had ascertained the attitude of Dr. Margai; some allegations connected the doctor's attitude with the advice of leading officials in the Protectorate with whom he had worked on close terms for a number of years. When the change of decision was challenged in the Legislative Council Dr. Margai was found, quite unexpectedly, to have the support and declared party adherence of an overwhelming majority of the Protectorate members, and subsequently they all adhered. Thus the country was committed to party politics. The National Council, the majority party in the limited field of declared party contest, was particularly aggrieved, and the militantly anti-Creole, or at least Protectorate-first, views expressed by the S.L.P.P. leader in the Protectorate Assembly during the preceding year left a large part of Creoledom resentful and suspicious.

This turn of events, though casual, was decisive. A party had been formed which appealed to, and quite manifestly obtained, the loyalty of the Protectorate peoples, on the basis of their resentment of the attitudes of superiority and of the supposed privileges of those whom they class as Creoles. In any future contest the cards were stacked against those who were attached to the way of life and the standards of social judgement of the Creoles, and they were faced with the choice, as often happens to communities so placed, of dying in the last ditch or aiding in the work of destruction by seeking favour with their new masters. One result was a flight from the National Council. Dr. Bright apparently decided for the last ditch and the small but certain vote which this meant. Others, though not many, went over to the S.L.P.P., where they were safe even if they could not hope to exercise much influence. Otherwise the Creole vote, such as it was, was on offer. The U.P.P., the Labour Party and the S.L.I.M. each at some time raised hopes among the Freetown intelligentsia of the emergence of a national cause adequate to end the communal feuding. All disappointed such hopes, though the U.P.P. did at least attempt organization on a national scale. Otherwise they were all bidding, together with the National Council, for the same body of support. Signs of discouragement appeared earliest and became most marked in the Labour Party, where dissension in the national executive in the latter part of 1956 lost it two of its minor leaders, one received back into favour in the S.L.P.P. and one snapped up by the S.L.I.M.

One candidate in the 1956 district council elections, a member of the U.P.P. standing in Moyamba district, seems to have presented himself as a party man, but he was probably unique. Otherwise, of the parties which came before the electorate in 1957, only the S.L.P.P. and the National Council had had any experience of fighting elections, and that on the most diminutive scale, in the Colony in 1951. That year's example was of little use in the new situation, and perhaps it suggested to intending politicians that bargaining among the victors after the election might again be possible. Certainly many seemed to work on that assumption.

6. *Events before the Election*

The period between the Keith-Lucas commission's presentation of its report and the appearance of the resultant legislation was politically very difficult. By the end of 1954 the process of preparing for elections had apparently gone no farther than seeking the advice of the Secretary of State on the procedure to be adopted. On 9 February 1955 negotiations over comparatively small wage demands by the two principal trade unions in Freetown, which had been in progress since September, broke down in a widespread strike which lasted for four days and was accompanied by looting and violence, some loss of life, and the intervention of the military. Both Government and public grew anxious over the ease with which violence could develop and the inadequacy of the country's security system; and from 11 March to 7 May the Shaw Commission of Inquiry was at work, distracting attention from other matters. The next stage of progress in the direction of constitutional reform came only on 22 July, when the Chief Minister invited the submission within the next two months of proposals by individuals and associations.

These proposals were laid on the table of the Legislative Council on 5 October, and a series of public meetings to discuss them was held at the beginning of November. In that month further debate in the Legislative Council on the reforms was promised, but the preliminary general discussion by a conference of representatives of all political parties on which the Opposition insisted proved impossible to call owing to the failure of the two sides in the legislature to agree about its composition. In the end the Government called a conference itself in April 1956, but this completely failed to satisfy its opponents. There had been further delay as a result of the tax riots which had broken out in the Northern Province of the Protectorate on 17 November 1955, and continued into March 1956. These were directed largely against chiefs, were called 'strikes' in imitation of the Freetown incidents earlier in 1955, and were, like them, of a quite unexpected and alarming violence. From the beginning of April to the beginning of July a Commission of Inquiry presided over by Sir Herbert Cox was in session. Its findings suggested extreme provocation on the part of some of the chiefs and inadequate mastery of the situation by the administration, both facts telling against the S.L.P.P., as the chiefs were among its founders and supporters and some thought that the administration had been seriously weakened by its policies.[1] In August 1956 the Government issued a statement accepting in the main the diagnosis and recommendations of the commission, but repudiating most of its suggestions of governmental responsibility; among other measures they undertook to hold inquiries into the conduct of certain chiefs. Accordingly, three commissioners experienced in judicial office in other territories began investigations in October, and published the main body of their reports on 20 February 1957, though certain inquiries continued into April. The Governor, whose term of office had been burdened by this succession of troubles, resigned in July 1956 owing to ill health, and his successor arrived in September.

Thus when the term of office of members of the Legislative Council came to an end in October 1956, the holding of immediate elections was not practicable, and extensions had to be granted. The events of recent months not only delayed the elections but left behind fears and resentments which affected them. The tax 'strike' of 1955–6, in particular, expressed and consolidated a division in the political life of the north and some districts of the south-east between chief's men and 'strikers', and Opposition parties could hope to insert a lever here for the demolition of the solid governmental following in the Protectorate, though it would clearly be a costly business, and those parties were not rich. The outcome of the Commissions of Inquiry into chiefs' conduct, which exonerated as many as they found substantially at fault, left almost equal discontent on both sides. One of the chiefs concerned was the minister without portfolio in the Government, and his colleagues were in consequence forced to induce him to resign; the report revealed also their lack of foreknowledge of the breakdown in social relations in the Protectorate. The centre of the troubles was in the traditionally docile north, the ministers all came from the south, except the minister censured for bad conduct in his chiefdom. The earlier Freetown strikes created the Labour Party, shocked public sentiment about the basis of public order in what had always been considered a well-conducted area, and accelerated the process of disillusionment with the S.L.P.P.

[1] See *Report of Commission of Inquiry into Disturbances in the Provinces* (*Nov. 1955 to Mar. 1956*) (London: Crown Agents, 1956).

among a section of the Protectorate population in Freetown. The principal leader whom they found in the strike, Mr. Grant, was himself a Creole; apparently few of the Protectorate working men realized this, but the Government certainly appreciated its significance.

The digging of diamonds by private African enterprise also proved politically important. This grew to vast proportions as a result of unfavourable agricultural conditions in the late 1940's and early '50's, and was then illegal by virtue of the monopoly concession held by the Sierra Leone Selection Trust. A modification of the Trust's concession was agreed in 1955, and it then became possible to regularize and so regulate this activity, which was unsafe, wasteful, and turbulent. On 7 February 1956 a scheme was brought into operation in five chiefdoms, to be extended later to others, by which individuals could obtain diggers' or dealers' licenses subject to certain conditions, including liability to inspection and the limitation of the right of exportation to three approved agencies. As the year 1956 progressed, it became apparent that there were still many illicit operators in the field—indeed it is possible that the new scheme increased their numbers by providing legal forms under which they could hide—and that many of them were unauthorized immigrants and aliens. Some were among the diggers but most were dealers in diamonds; nearly all were engaged in smuggling. The loss of revenue (though smuggling was by no means either new or due solely to recent immigrants) and the conditions under which many of the immigrants lived, moved the authorities to take action against them, but as they were moved out of one area after another they tended to bunch in those which remained, including notably those parts of Kono district in which diamond mining was by the revised agreement still left as a monopoly of the Selection Trust. In December 1956 a drive was instituted for the expulsion of these strangers, on the personal initiative of the newly arrived Governor. This met with success and general public approval at the time, but in the following months the strangers began to flow back over the many unguarded spots on the frontier, and diamonds continued to flow in the other direction.

This affected elections mainly by complicating the process of registration. Young men paid tax, and were so registered, at home, and then went off in search of diamonds; others paid tax at the diggings and reappeared at home at about election time to find that they were not on the register. Aliens paid tax on their own initiative, in the belief that this would give them a claim to remain in the country, and they thus got on the registers. There were also political effects in some places, particularly in Kono district. The Konos' habitual suspicion of others was aroused by the new agreement with the Trust; they suspected that not enough had been wrung from it for the benefit of their tribe—which did not itself take much part in the private digging—and their district. Apparently alone among the country's tribes, they formed at the beginning of 1957 a political organization of their own, the *Kono Progressive Movement*, which probably derived the last word of its title, as it certainly derived some of the political arguments of its leader, from Mr. Blyden, to whom the leader was apparently distantly related. It did not, however, maintain any close contact with the S.L.I.M., though Mr. Blyden did upon occasions include its membership, suitably inflated, with his own. It seemed to have no particular principles apart from Kono-firstism and a profound hostility to the sitting S.L.P.P. member, the Rev. Paul Dunbar, who was suspected, largely it seems on the evidence of his new house, of being in the Trust's pay. Attempts were made by the S.L.P.P. organization to arrange a deal between Mr. Dunbar and the Leader of the Movement, Mr. Mbrewa, on the basis of the assignment of one of the district's two seats in the new House to each, but animosity over such matters as the local chief's opinions of Mr. Dunbar's social standing and personal rivalries within the district's very small intelligentsia prevented success.

7. *Registration*

The central administration of the arrangements for both local and central elections was in the hands of an Elections Officer with a staff including two other 'senior service' (i.e. administrative class) officers. He was to work under the oversight of the Chief Minister, though subject also to the instructions of the Minister of Local Government in respect of local government elections. The registration officers were the District Commissioners, for both constituencies within their districts, the town clerks of Freetown and Bo and the clerk of the Sherbro Urban District Council, and for the rural area of the Colony the two assistants to the Elections Officer individually appointed. In the Protectorate the clerks of the chiefdom administrations were assistant registration officers for their chiefdoms. The District Commissioners were subsequently also designated returning officers for their two constituencies, as they had been for their districts in the local elections, while for each constituency in the three urban units and the rural area of the Colony a government officer was individually appointed to exercise that office. Each District Commissioner and the Freetown City Council were from April 1956 authorized to employ an elections assistant, a temporary official of superior clerical standing, to assist in, or sometimes organize, the clerical and propaganda work for the conduct of the elections; except in a few districts which found difficulty in obtaining suitable persons this was generally done. The vast but sparsely populated Koinadugu district in the extreme north of the country had no Assistant District Commissioner, and was given to help it in all election business a more senior government officer seconded from another government department and styled assistant returning officer. Elsewhere that title was not in use in the preliminary stages of the preparation for polling.

Registration was to be made initially for the local government voters' lists, since the elections at that level were to be held first. As the franchise was identical for central and local elections these lists would subsequently serve, after the correction of observed errors and the invitation of further applications, as the registers for the central elections also. Over the greater part of the country this intention was carried out.

The original regulations for the registration of district council voters, passed on 7 April 1956, provided for simultaneous registration throughout the Protectorate, but owing to the disturbed condition of many areas it was necessary to modify this by further regulations which allowed registrations at different times in different districts and chiefdoms. Nevertheless registration was everywhere complete in time for elections during 1956, except in the diamond areas of Kono district where extra time was required to deal with aliens wrongly placed on the register, and in Samu chiefdom in Kambia district where the tax assessment rolls had been completely destroyed or lost during the anti-tax troubles. The revision of the Kono registration was completed just before the end of 1956, though the local elections were delayed till January 1957, and the central election registration was opened there, as for the rest of the country, on 2 January. In Samu chiefdom a completely new register—to serve for both central and local elections—had to be made up on the basis of applications from those qualified, and by an intensive propaganda drive supported by the central Public Relations Office this was completed, and to a standard probably rather higher than elsewhere, only a week behind the central registration for the rest of the country.

The legislation governing registration and election in Freetown, Bo, Sherbro, and the rural area of the Colony was not passed until August 1956, so that it was not possible to complete registration in time to hold the local elections in that year. Bo town and the Sherbro urban district went to the polls in March 1957 but in Freetown and the rural area the local elections had to be postponed until after those to the House of Representatives. Nevertheless, the central election registration for all these areas was fixed for, and in fact began on, the same date, 2 January. Except in Freetown this worked quite successfully.

Registration in the Protectorate was comparatively easy to carry out, since from most of those entitled to vote, the male tax-payers, no application was required; in the absence of any reason to suppose them under age or aliens their names could be taken from the tax-assessment list. In quality, however, the result of this process was not high. The tax lists were themselves neither complete nor accurate in recording the names of taxpayers; the clerical work involved in turning them into electoral registers was more than the limited and relatively low-grade staffs of the District Commissioners' offices could well manage, even under strict supervision; and it was quite beyond the chiefdom clerks and the local literates with whom the drafts were deposited for public inspection and applications for correction. In many places little was done by these lowest links in the system to bring the process of registration and the action required by intending voters to the attention of the people, lest the even tenor of chiefdom administration be disturbed. The notices went up on 2 January, but few could read them, hardly any understood them, and many registers and application forms remained in the cupboard. Thus for one reason or another whole villages and many individuals were left off. Names of aliens probably remained on the lists except in the few areas where they were so numerous as to require special action for their removal, and persons offered themselves to vote and were traced in the registers who were manifestly well below not only voting age (21) but also tax-paying age (18). In many areas it seems to have been the practice for a boy to pay tax from the time of admission to the men's society, and this might be considerably below the legal age of tax-paying. Most of the errors could have been put right when applications were invited in January 1957—for the local elections had brought home their existence to many who could not themselves read the registers—or in February when claims were invited for the rectification of omissions or the deletion of those whom the applicants claimed to be unqualified. But in fact for lack of public knowledge of what was happening, and also, apparently, because it was not at the time felt by the public to be very important, applications in January were very few, though the opportunity was taken by the registration staff, including many of the chiefdom clerks, to correct all errors of which they were aware. The revision courts in the Protectorate were faced with not more than two or three claims of omission each, and had no claims at all for the deletion of names.

Women taxpayers, who were few, were required, like women claimants under the other qualifications, to submit applications; unlike the men, they must in fact have paid tax. In the event women applicants were very few, and almost all on the grounds of literacy; the other possible grounds for a claim to registration were not generally known, and by reason of the work involved registration officers did not press the matter. Few constituency lists contained more than two or three names of women, though a few candidates had organized those thought to be favourable to themselves, and one, in Bonthe North, had had thirty-six registered. A chiefdom in Pujehun district submitted some ten such applications, all on grounds of literacy, and all marked with a cross. At a gathering of local notables in Kailahun on the last day of registration the present writer was asked whether any woman could vote; the news that if registered they could, was received with interest, but nothing was done about it. A paramount chief's sister in Kono district, literate and apparently intelligent, was not to be persuaded that she could claim registration. The qualification on the ground of land use would probably have admitted many in some areas had it been used; one registration officer was of the opinion that he would have had to register without further question any woman so claiming. But the blow to masculine pride in that locality might have been rather serious.

In Bo town, where the franchise was as in the Colony, the task was hardly more difficult than in the districts, owing to the existence of the tax lists as a rough guide to the identity of the income voters. But in the Colony no tax was paid. The section of the electorate known from records already in existence was a small minority— those qualified by virtue of property ownership—while the occupiers and those qualified by income could be discovered only if they applied. In Freetown the number of applicants greatly exceeded what Creole opinion had expected or found acceptable, and since many of the application forms had of necessity been issued through representatives of the political parties, and since also it soon became apparent that many of the applications were in some way defective —particularly in the inaccuracy of the addresses given, but also in names, ages and grounds of entitlement—the suspicion at once spread that there was a plot by the Government and its party to swamp the Creole vote. It was in fact certain that under the new franchise the Creoles of Freetown would be outnumbered by residents of Protectorate origin with a legitimate claim to vote, but

there were also many fictitious names on the list, and it was emotionally comforting to believe in a plot by which these would come to
life on election day in the form of paid peasant S.L.P.P. supporters
shipped in bullom boats from the other side of the estuary, or in the
form of residents prepared to vote twice. The Town Clerk as registration officer became concerned at the evident irregularities, instituted
house-to-house checks, and began deleting the names of persons not
traced at the addresses which they had given, and then on 17 December the Minister for Local Government ordered him to desist. The
City Council, meeting two days later, decided to challenge the
minister's ruling as *ultra vires*, as it clearly was. A deputation waited
on the Governor, and on 31 December the resumption of the checks
was authorized on condition that there should always be more than
one checker and that the work should be confined to the hours after
3 p.m. and at week-ends, when people might be at home to present
their cases; times and places of checking were to be published in
advance, and persons not traced were not to be immediately deleted
but marked on the list and made liable to exclusion by the revising
officer at his court if they did not then put up a good case for their
retention on the list. A separate list was to be published of persons
whose applications for registration had not been allowed, and these
could claim reinstatement in the usual way at the same courts. The
fortnight, 2–17 January 1957, was set aside for applications for
inclusion in the supplementary list, which with the local government
list made up that for the House elections, and in the second week of
it there was a further rush, again predominantly of people of Protectorate origin, amounting to over 5,500 for the three wards. These
late applications could not be checked in the same way in time. The
lists in all other parts of the country except Samu chiefdom were
published on 1 February, those for Freetown not till the 25th, and
then under pressure from the Government. There were 7,565 claims
of omission, claims to reinstatement and notices of objection to be
considered on the local government list, and a further 678 claims of
omission and notices of objection against the supplementary list.

The Freetown revising officers' courts—one for each of the three
wards of the city—began to meet in the middle of March. After the
first meeting of the court for the east constituency on the 16th,
objection was raised—as previously to the house-to-house checks—
that many people were prevented by their work from going to defend
their claims to votes, and accordingly the courts were confined to the
hours from 3 p.m.—and subsequently from 5 p.m.—to 11 p.m., and
a second revising officer was provided for each court to share this
work. They completed their task on 28 March, largely because few

of the persons concerned appeared. Many of them probably did not exist, but those who did were not very favourably placed for making their cases. The business to be considered at each session of the several courts was not announced in advance, and it was hardly thinkable that many should attend all sessions in their constituencies on the chance of being present when their own cases came up; yet if they were not present they were struck off. Of those who by persistence or chance were in court at the right time some made good their cases, which given reasonable guile on the part of the applicant were difficult to disprove even if untrue. But a number of the simpler among them proved ignorant of the address at which they registered, the names of their alleged fellow residents, the date on which they came to live in Freetown or the means by which they earned their incomes of exactly £60; some even made statements which proved that their claims could not be true. This was sufficient to justify the Creole allegation that someone was briefing them for their appearance, and doing it badly. It may also be accepted that many names remained, especially on the supplementary list, to which no properly qualified persons corresponded. Certain houses were given as the addresses of far more people than they could possibly accommodate; in a number of cases it was proved, in others suspected, that names were those of children under age or of dead persons. On the other hand some persons whose applications were disallowed in the earlier stages on such grounds were manifestly alive and of full years, and for default of appearance in court not all of them were reinstated.

How the dead men and the rest got on to the register is not clear. There could be no adequate motive for the sort of plot by the Government in which many Creoles believed, but some government supporters may have supposed that they could aid the cause by registering a few absent friends and relations. In other cases illiterates were probably registered in haste by persons unfamiliar with their names and places of residence and not very careful to find them out accurately. Understanding between the communities was not helped by the readiness of some government party workers, including particularly one woman candidate, to stand up belligerently for the alleged rights of any Protectorate person, however absurd the claim. It was firmly believed by most Creoles that the same candidate had on the evening of 20 March, the third day of the courts' sittings, incited a meeting of Protectorate people against the Town Clerk who had been giving evidence, on the allegation that he was trying to prevent them voting. Attenders at the meeting were said to have threatened violence, but if so, delay in the reappearance of the Town Clerk and the presence of a police escort sufficed to cool tempers.

The only other sign of possible violence occurred on the previous day in the central constituency revision court, when the action of a conscientious court usher in removing the fez of a Muslim witness led to uproar and the withdrawal of the predominantly Protectorate audience. This movement was accompanied by the throwing of steel chairs, but fortunately not in any direction in which they could do more than make a noise, and after mutterings of 'no culture' and 'shape of coming events' and similar sentiments by a number of Creole matrons the proceedings continued to the accompaniment of a diminishing hum of disapproval from outside.

Only one constituency outside Freetown produced any excitement at the revision stage. In the neighbouring Colony constituency of Wilberforce the revising officer upheld 387 out of 399 objections entered by the National Council candidate, for the most part against the families of servicemen at the local barracks. This decision, given at the end of February, raised the spirits of the Creole militants and probably contributed to their belligerency in the subsequent Freetown revision.

The complications in Freetown played an important part in determining the date of the elections. The dates of registration for local elections settled it that registration for central elections could not begin before January 1957; and it was clear then that no polling date earlier than April would be possible because of the statutory intervals prescribed between the various stages of preparation of the registers, amounting in all to seventy-eight days. Some importance came to be attached to the idea of an April election as an index of the Government's good faith; ever since the expiration of the original term of the Legislative Council allegations had been directed at the Government to the effect that it was seeking to prolong its own life from fear of facing the electorate, or in the hope of concluding an advantageous deal with mining interests, or for whatever motives happened from time to time to occur to its critics. In the first months of 1957 officials were working to a schedule which set 12 April as provisional first polling day; this would probably have made it possible to fit in the later polling days—necessitated by the need to shift scarce polling staff over considerable distances from one constituency to another—within the same month. This, however, left little margin for manœuvre, and once it had been found impossible to get the Freetown registers published by 1 February it was certain that postponement would be necessary. In the middle of March the Government decided upon 26 April as first polling day, probably with a view to retaining the symbolic value of an April election—though in fact the election would even so have had to continue into the first weeks of May. A long Easter holiday, extending to Tuesday, 23 April, which was celebrated as the local public holiday of the Queen's birthday, precluded an earlier start, and it was subsequently realized that as the end of Ramadan, also a public holiday, would fall on 1 May little would be gained by starting the election period before these distractions were over. Consequently, when the Legislative Council was prorogued for the last time on 30 March, the dates announced were 3 May for the Colony and eighteen of the twenty-five Protectorate constituencies, the 8th for six more and the 13th for one of the remotest. These dates were adhered to, despite the presentation by the U.P.P. on 17 April of writs for injunctions to restrain the responsible officers from holding the elections, on the ground that no register of voters was available in the period—8–17 April—during which nominations were to be taken; proceedings on these received a first hearing in the Supreme Court and stood adjourned and undecided at the time of polling. The concentration of voting on the first polling day was due to anxiety to hold on one day all voting in constituencies within a reasonably convenient journey of Freetown, in order to set at rest fears of an incursion of unqualified voters from the provinces. Unopposed returns reduced the number of constituencies to poll on the first day by three and those polling on the second day by one, all four being constituencies in the central part of the Protectorate.

8. *Party Campaigns*

The uncertainty about the date of the election produced a corresponding indefiniteness about the opening of the campaign. Public meetings of the S.L.P.P., which had been held in Freetown every few weeks since the party's formation, were usually held weekly from the time of the Keith-Lucas commission, as also were those of the newly formed U.P.P. As polling day approached, teams of speakers began to go out into the rural area of the Colony and additional meetings in Freetown were fitted in, but there was no sharp change of pace. Mr. Blyden also began in November 1956, when his movement was founded, a regular routine of weekly meetings, which after the fashion of his Trinidadian model he called lectures, though unlike Dr. Williams he did not give them any particular cultural content. Meetings of the Labour Party and the National Council were less frequent, and they began no real campaign till the meetings of 7 and 12 April respectively, though the Labour Party did produce the first printed national manifesto at the end of January 1957.

Throughout the Protectorate developments were almost entirely out of the hands of the parties. This was largely due to the feebleness of their organizations, resulting from lack of experience and above all from lack of funds. Even the party in power, though it possessed a few rich ministers and other supporters prepared to dip into their pockets from time to time for such luxuries as loudspeaker vans, had not enough money to pay for the printing of its manifesto from its own funds, and this also had to be left to private subsidy. The U.P.P. had moments of relative affluence, due apparently to the support of Levantine and other business men and to contributions from troubled areas in the Protectorate at a time when it seemed capable of offering its supporters relief from the payment of taxes; but these sources proved less abundant as the campaign dragged on and there were no results. The National Council and the Labour Party were even poorer, and only the S.L.I.M. had no financial worries—it had only one man to support, and he never ventured into the expensive political world outside Freetown.

Local party organizations of the only two parties seriously involved in the Protectorate were few and existed more commonly on paper than on the ground. Though most people professed themselves S.L.P.P. men, few paid subscriptions, and hardly any paid them regularly. A prominent resident of Pujehun town counted himself an S.L.P.P. member in January 1957, because in October 1955, he together with a number of others paid a shilling into the bank to the party's credit, and delivered the bank-book to the paramount chief, who 'give us plenty pamphlet and something like card'. 'Since then,' he added, 'nobody pay nothing.' He had been made a trustee, with one other, for the money, but did not appear to know what, if anything, had happened to it. Tonkolili district organization of the S.L.P.P. decided upon a reduced subscription and sought authority for it from the central party organization. Receiving no reply, it continued to collect at its own rate and to use the money for its own purposes. Officials at the centre thought it unwise in the months before an election to remind local branches of their defaults, yet in some districts there was complaint that Freetown took too much of the contributions for itself. Local secretaries and other office holders were apt to pursue obscure purposes of their own which might have little relevance to those of the party. One local general secretary, whose appointment to elected office in local government the central authorities had vetoed, explained that his grief and perturbation at this situation had left him with little heart for party activities, and that the reduced effort to promote membership and collect subscriptions was a result of this. A local party president who had previously been a member of the U.P.P. admitted to having adhered to the S.L.P.P. to secure concessions from the Government for his town, and said that once provision for its electricity and water-supplies were in the year's estimates and a power house under construction he had become indifferent to politics and had ceased to call meetings. A provincial organizing secretary complained of the impossibility of securing the services of voluntary workers, and most other party workers confirmed this; one local secretary, he said, had written to demand pay on threat of return of the membership cards left with him for sale.

The position in the U.P.P. was no more favourable. It lacked the repute of being the Protectorate party, and had from the first been smeared by its opponents with the name of the 'Creole party' (the term 'Creole government' was also commonly used) and saddled with responsibility for all the supposed misdeeds of the Creoles in the past. It also lacked the advantage of being in power in a society accustomed to respect, or at least to keep on the right side of, constituted authority, and it could not, as the S.L.P.P. could, count on the safe votes of the loyal. Motives for adherence to it were as diverse as in the S.L.P.P. and as inadequate to keep a branch organization together. One leading local politician had apparently entered the party in the hope of securing legal aid against his rival for local eminence, and when difficulties were raised he left it. One chief was persuaded by a distinguished visitor to take a card, and only afterwards mentioned it to his chiefdom clerk, who explained that it was the 'Creole party'; whereupon, it was said, the chief threw away the card lest Dr. Margai should depose him. One District Councillor of the same district had made considerable use of the services of the same U.P.P. visitor during the local election—mainly, he suggested, as a means of transport, since the visitor, being ignorant of the local languages, was not of much use in other respects. He admitted to having taken a U.P.P. card, though claiming that he had never paid a subscription. At the same time he had held an S.L.P.P. card and paid his subscription, though subsequently it fell somewhat into arrears. He professed to be non-party in opinion, but speaking of his intention to stand for the House of Representatives, he said, 'If I am lucky to be successful I shall have a good idea of these parties.' He was not successful.

One of the few U.P.P. organizers in the southern provinces was found confident in the belief that he had an organization in a district where in fact it had long ceased to exist, and he named as the secretary of this body a man who a few days before had stated his intention of standing as an S.L.P.P. candidate, and who in fact did so.

A number of organizers for the north, appointed—apparently without much consultation of their wishes—from among the supposed recruits gained by a brief intensive campaign leading up to the party convention of December 1955, spoiled a promising situation by publicly announcing their resignation immediately on appointment, just at the time when the party's hand seemed strengthened by the tax riots. One, appointed National Organizing Secretary for the Northern Province—in intention a full-time paid post—declared his reluctance to abandon certainty and seniority in his profession as a chiefdom clerk in favour of a doubtful political venture, and asked to be assured that the remuneration would be adequate, and also that there would be funds for transport and the efficient running of the campaign. Apparently no satisfactory assurance was given, for the politician concerned remained outside the party, and while resisting the attempt of the S.L.P.P. to get him to accept terms of adherence to that party—or to pay a subscription—described himself in his subsequent campaigning for the House of Representatives (in the end he withdrew) as an S.L.P.P. member, because, he explained, the chiefs, on whom he relied, would otherwise suppose that he had gone Creole.

It was only in Port Loko West constituency, the part of the Northern Province nearest to Freetown, that the U.P.P. was able to maintain right through to the time of elections the control of the situation which it seemed to have won during the tax troubles, and it was only there in the whole of the Protectorate that regular meetings were held by any party, except perhaps for a brief earlier period when the U.P.P. had an energetic party organizer in Bo. Its strength in Port Loko seemed to depend almost entirely on the immense personal prestige won during the troubles by Pitier Kamara, one of the most active of the chief-spoilers and believed to be descended from a national hero of the Temnes. Being illiterate he was not himself eligible to the House of Representatives, but it was generally accepted that any candidate endorsed by him could expect to win. At the time of the troubles his leadership seems to have been recognized, though not perhaps effectively exercised, well beyond the boundaries of the Northern Province; by 1957 it was somewhat diminished, though he was still paraded about the country by the U.P.P. leaders, to whom he remained loyal. Within Port Loko he held sway very much after the manner of a chief, apparently collected tribute, and by his messengers summoned meetings, always, it seemed, under the direction of his party friends. There was no corresponding degree of political action there by the S.L.P.P. or any other party, and the U.P.P. itself had by the latter part of 1956 ceased any other than occasional and very small-scale activities in other parts of the north. Even in the neighbouring constituency of Kambia West, which had been at the centre of the tax troubles, U.P.P. activity had almost died out until the approach of the period for nominations in April 1957; there the S.L.P.P. strangely chose as its official candidate the ex-minister ex-chief of Kambia, and his unpopularity with most of his former subjects offered the U.P.P. a golden opportunity. Mr. Mahmoud Ahmed, the half-Syrian who had been principally concerned in organizing and escorting Pitier Kamara, moved over to Kambia, where he had family connexions, with as strong a force of party workers as the U.P.P. could raise, and brisk campaigning followed on both sides. But even at that late stage this was the full extent of U.P.P. activity in the north. In the other two provinces there had been only two major centres of discontent and so of promise for the U.P.P., and this promise soon faded. Personal quarrels within the U.P.P. and blandishments from the highest level of the S.L.P.P. had ended a hopeful U.P.P. beginning in Kono district in the last quarter of 1956, and there was continuous political activity only in Moyamba district, which like Port Loko had been a centre of the tax troubles, and also bordered on the Colony and was thus convenient for the visiting party workers from Freetown. For the U.P.P., being particularly deficient in local organization was, to a much greater degree than its opponents, forced to rely for its meetings on a travelling circus of speakers from the capital. Its leader, though a very busy man in his profession, was also exceptionally energetic, and managed to maintain a small staff of more-or-less full-time party workers.

The remaining parties, the National Council and the Labour Party, seem to have found the task of breaking into the Protectorate quite overwhelming, and the S.L.I.M. could not even begin to try. The National Council, traditionally arguing the benefits of Creole leadership, and so appealing almost exclusively to Creoles, had neither arguments nor support from which to work in the Protectorate. During the tax troubles the party's leaders held a few meetings in the north and managed to win the loyalty of a 'strike-leader' of some local influence in Samu chiefdom of Kambia West constituency. By the beginning of 1957, however, they clearly had no footing, and were making no effort to secure one, outside that one constituency, and even there they could not hold their ground. At a National Council meeting in Freetown on 22 March it was denied that their man in Samu chiefdom had been won over to the U.P.P., and an impressive account was given of his profession of loyalty to his old friends. But on 1 April, if not before, a U.P.P. team visited

his village, and at the close of nominations on the 17th it was found
that the National Council had no candidate; their man had apparently still not been fully won over by the U.P.P., but a further visit
and protracted discussion swung him and his followers into line by
polling day. The Labour Party was no better placed in the Protectorate, for what organized labour existed there was firmly in the
hands of other parties. Thus the workers in the Marampa iron mines
were believed by their union officials to be solid in support of Mr.
Siaka Stevens, formerly the leader of the United Mineworkers' Union
and at that time Minister of Lands, Mines, and Labour in the
S.L.P.P. government. A meeting organized there by the Labour
Party's principal trade unionist, Mr. Marcus Grant, in October
1956, seems to have met with a cold reception and was not followed
up. Mr. Stevens's successor in union office declared in January 1957
his intention of standing as a Labour Party candidate in Kono South
constituency, which contained the diamond mines of Yengema, but
in the event he was otherwise occupied at the time of the election; he
can hardly have been encouraged by the local elections in the area,
when the union machine placed itself firmly behind a candidate
who lost decisively. Industrial workers were not in a majority in any
constituency; if they were strangers to the area, as they often were,
they could not hope to influence anyone else, and if they were local
men they responded to the same influences as the rest of their people.
The labour vote was not worth canvassing, and the Labour Party,
being in the absence of any political levy—or even the habit of paying ordinary union dues regularly—probably the poorest of all the
parties, realistically did not try.

Attendance at party meetings in Freetown was throughout remarkably high. The S.L.P.P., the U.P.P., and the S.L.I.M. could
at any time from the latter months of 1956 to the elections draw an
audience of 300–400 to the town's principal meeting hall, considerably over its comfortable capacity. The National Council achieved
the same for the meeting advertised as the opening of its election
campaign, but therewith shot its bolt, and seems never again to have
drawn more than about twenty-five people to a series of dispirited
meetings in various schoolrooms. The Labour Party did even worse;
the opening meeting of its campaign in the same hall started with
an audience of thirty-three, which rose to fifty-five during Mr.
Marcus Grant's speech, and declined again as soon as he had finished;
thereafter it also retired to the schoolrooms, and at one meeting in
the last week before the elections had an audience of nineteen for a
platform of four. The first two parties early abandoned the hall for a
variety of open-air sites; at the most conveniently placed of them the

U.P.P. regularly claimed audiences for its weekly meetings of some 5,000, though they looked considerably smaller and in large part seemed to consist of bystanders rather than supporters or even listeners. S.L.P.P. open-air audiences seemed to be in general rather smaller than those of the U.P.P. and even less attentive; the party's less sophisticated following tended to be rather more parochial and not to move much outside its own part of the city. Political meetings of all groups habitually began an hour or so later than the advertised time, apparently as a matter of policy. Only Mr. Blyden regularly took collections, at each meeting one for his National Schools Fund, and one for general purposes which can hardly have covered more than the hire and lighting of the hall. Other parties, however, took collections from time to time for special purposes, as when the U.P.P. was sending a delegation to Britain. Conversations with attenders suggested that there was a large constant element in all audiences (at least for all meetings other than those of the S.L.P.P.) of people who attended at least some meetings of each party. These people were probably not so much politically open-minded as in search of entertainment, but they might perhaps have formed the material for a stronger united opposition if anyone had known how to organize it.

At first the S.L.P.P. probably made rather more use than did the others of such aids to receptivity as calypso bands and film shows, but as polling day approached their technique became simpler and they applied themselves more single-mindedly than any other party to the task of getting all available ballots, unspoiled, into the right boxes. Their last meetings consisted almost exclusively of demonstrations of the technique of voting, with practice for members of the audience who were left in any doubt, and applause for those who got it right, interspersed at very frequent intervals with the words—repeated by the audience—'palm tree', to familiarize all with the party's election symbol.

The U.P.P., holding its regular weekly meetings on Sundays, appropriately filled the time between its announced and its actual time of meeting with hymn-singing, besides having a hymn tune fitted with political words for use in the opening stages of proceedings, and it also opened the meeting with prayers for both Christians and Muslims. The speeches followed much the same pattern from week to week, opening with some of the party's Freetown workers, continuing with a contribution by Mr. Wallace-Johnson—distinguished by beginning with a scriptural text which did not always bear much relation to its context—and a report from a party worker in the Protectorate, and concluding with the addresses of the party's young

National Secretary-General, Mr. Nelson-Williams, and its Leader, Mr. Rogers-Wright. The U.P.P. followed a more stereotyped pattern than the S.L.P.P., which had a number of ministers to publicize and a more retiring leader; it was also less necessary for it, since it had a more sophisticated public, to provide simple repetitive and practical lessons in voting technique, though there was some of this. Its symbol was a red cock, and from an early stage of the campaign (well before the S.L.P.P. took to its 'palm tree' cry) it had been advertised at meetings and elsewhere with shouts of 'Koko-re-o-ko'.

The 'lectures' of Mr. Blyden were necessarily more nearly solo performances, though they lasted for about the same length of time —2½–3 hours, or longer as the date of election approached—as did those of other parties. In the earlier weeks there was an introductory speech by a leading supporter, an alderman of Freetown city council who became one of the S.L.I.M. candidates, and the rest of the time was filled by the leader himself. Later one, and finally another, supporting candidate, and the young people to whom Mr. Blyden particularly appealed, were given small allocations of time; the Leader's address (still by far the longest) was broken down into sections scattered throughout the meeting; and gramophone interludes were added. There was an odd, unplanned character about these later meetings, in which the allocation of time seemed to follow Mr. Blyden's momentary whims. Thus at a meeting on 15 April which began with the announcement that it would last all night there were two breaks for music in the first 1¾ hours, and then two within three minutes of each other; there was another at midnight, and twenty minutes later there was more music, and without warning the meeting ended.

Apparently until the latter part of 1956 the principal language of all meetings was English; thereafter it gave place almost entirely to Krio, the language of the common people of Freetown and in various forms the *lingua franca* of the whole country. Dr. Bankole-Bright continued to speak almost entirely in standard English, as also did Mr. Sawyerr, joint National Secretary of the Labour Party. Other speakers sometimes lapsed into it until asked from the audience to 'break it up'; Mr. Blyden, uniquely, made a practice of alternating a few minutes of English with an equal amount of Krio. All had in common a marked repetitiousness within speeches, between one speech and another at the same meeting, and from week to week, due perhaps partly to the need to drive points well home where the public cannot in general be reached by the printed word, but also to the obvious fact that the campaign had gone on for longer than anybody had expected, and there was not much left to say. With

Mr. Blyden it was rather different, for he had started later and unlike everybody else gained considerably from the delay; with him repetitiousness seemed to proceed rather from a curiously fugal manner of thinking. All, but perhaps especially the S.L.P.P., made much use of jokes; brief, acid, and strictly political with Mr. Blyden (as in his description of the senior expatriate civil servant's lot as 'C.M.G., O.B.E., plus physical disability'), warmer, involved and less closely relevant with the S.L.P.P. All demanded periodic audience participation, usually in the form of responses to half-slogans—'O.C.'— 'O.P.' for the S.L.P.P., 'Koko-re-o-ko, O.P.'—'O.S.' for the U.P.P. (O.C. = One Country; O.P. = One People; O.S. = One Sierra Leone). Blydenist audiences in the earlier weeks were subjected to the severer necessity of learning by heart passages from legislation, the work of Messrs. Wade and Phillips on constitutional law, and the periodical *Public Law*, and of giving the right answers to the leader's questions. On one occasion when they hesitated they were very angrily asked 'Nottoo so? Nottoo so? You are living human beings. Nottoo so?' and they agreed that it was so. Later they progressed to a slow chanting of the word 'SLIM' and a form of catechism—'The name is —', 'The slogan is —', 'The colours are —', 'The aim is —' (the aim was Independence).

At all meetings showmanship was much appreciated, and was of a particularly high order in the performances of Mr. Mustapha, Minister of Communications and Works, at S.L.P.P. meetings and in those of Mr. Blyden. With Mr. Mustapha and some others the technique often came very near to clowning; with Mr. Blyden it was in more heroic vein, applied to building up the image of the leader with such phrases as, 'I speak as one having authority', 'educating myself so that I can educate other people with lesser minds', or 'If one Blyden dies two continents will vibrate', or 'I have felt ashamed for you my countrymen because you have made yourselves slaves, because the white man has made you feel like slaves'. One of Mr. Blyden's candidates worthily seconded him by declaring that 'When God himself go send a man like this we go support him.' It is hard to say whether such performances had any effect in winning votes or whether they were merely appreciated as entertainment and exhibitions of technique.

In atmosphere the meetings of the S.L.P.P. were amiable and slightly smug, very markedly gatherings of the present holders of power. Despite the party's slogans of unity, which were much the same as those of other parties, its appeal was undisguisedly to the Protectorate people or 'countrymen'; it was ready to accept the support of others, but as was said at the meeting on the eve of

polling day, 'If they no gree we go on without them and we countrymen go save Sierra Leone.' The claim that the party 'gave you
power', heard at some earlier meetings, and a statement by the Chief
Minister that the party worked for the interests of 'Creoles as well as
ourselves' appeared to make the same assumption about the nature
of the typical S.L.P.P. member. On the whole, however, the language used by the S.L.P.P. about the Creoles was not as violent or
malicious as members of other parties commonly suggested—at least
at the large public meetings—though the taunt that the Creoles have
no country was heard. As with any party in power, a large part of
the argument was that things in general had been getting better and
better over the years of office, with particular reference to public
works in the Protectorate, and attention was drawn to the wisdom of
returning experienced men. It was also necessary to justify unpopular
legislative measures, such as a fisheries bill, and an essential services
bill which seemed to threaten the right to strike and which was
subsequently withdrawn. But there was also scope for attacks on
opponents. The suggestion was repeatedly made that the U.P.P. was
unscrupulous, particularly in suggesting that there could be a return
of the Protectorate head tax to a largely mythical traditional rate of
5s.; that they wanted power—as was of course true; and, as one
speaker said, that they would sell the country—to whom was not
specified. Towards the end of the campaign Mr. Blyden came in for
attack, as from all other parties. Mr. Mustapha described him as
'an educated fool' and wondered aloud—as did Dr. Bankole-Bright
—who held the cheque book for the National Schools Fund. A theme
of the later meetings of the campaign, together with the instruction
in voting techniques, was the need to be very careful to avoid
irregularities or incidents which would give openings for election
petitions. As at U.P.P. meetings, particular stress was laid upon the
importance of straight voting in the Freetown two-member constituencies.

Labour party meetings were rather too small to have any atmosphere at all. Apart from a man who at one meeting interjected the
comment 'Good talk' so loudly and so frequently as to be, apparently,
rather an annoyance than an encouragement to the platform, there
was so little reaction that the speakers seemed to be rather meditating
aloud than addressing an audience. This quality was particularly
marked in the most unpolitical candour of Mr. Beoku-Betts, whose
slow, gentle, unemphatic account of the difficulties of applying the
socialism which he had picked up in his student days to a situation
where 'the workmen themselves no sorry for themselves' and a large
proportion of the party's first executive had hurriedly moved out to

organizations offering better prospects of advancement, was a perfect illustration of the party's political incompetence. Mr. Grant's very different manner—one of the most violent in Freetown politics —was applied to saying much the same mild things. Unlike his President, he was given to damning the white man, but the course of his argument always suggested that the white man whom he particularly had in mind was Sir John Shaw, and that the only cause that was of real interest to him was the clearing of his honour unjustly besmirched by the Shaw commission. Recognizing that it had no hope of power, the party made hardly any effort to suggest what it would do if it got it. At most it spoke of getting a foothold in the new legislature.

Meetings of the other parties had a sharper edge to them, especially those of the U.P.P. after the publication of the Order in Council with the exclusion provision aimed at the party's leader. As the party of protest and of a champion of grievances, especially those expressed in defiance of the law, it was often obliged to use language which could be construed as implying the threat of violence. Thus in the beginning of his speech of 3 February 1957, which was typical of most, Mr. Rogers-Wright claimed that the people of Sierra Leone had been reputed law-abiding since the reign of Queen Victoria, but that it was for the Government to create the conditions which would allow the people to keep within the bounds of law and order. If provoked too far, he suggested, they would not be to blame. He went on to draw attention to the absence of fair play in the country's politics, leading up from the plight of a post-office technician discriminated against in his employment to (inevitably) his own exclusion from the House of Representatives. Mr. Blyden desired to have it reported 'that I have developed in this country an anti-European trend' and that the U.P.P. and Labour Party were following him, and he threatened that if he had any reason to suspect that the ballot boxes had been stuffed he and his followers would march on the counting station and turn the boxes out. He explained that: 'We no go for form government; we no go for form opposition. We are going there to cause trouble until we get good government.' One of his young men said of the Government, 'They have to give us new constitution within two years. If not, we shall force them to be free because it will be good for them to be free', and, apparently liking this Rousseauesque sentiment, worked it into all his subsequent speeches. The tone of National Council meetings was not one of violence, for they admitted their weakness, but of intense bitterness against Britain, through whose perfidy 'we go, loss we status' and, in Dr. Bankole-Bright, lamentation at the absence of men of spirit in the present generation of Sierra Leone politicians.

The opposition party audiences, however, were for the most part not caught up in this mood of anger, but rather enjoying with boisterous good humour a varied programme in which this was only one of the attractions. A large part of the fun was over incidentals: the setting of the open-air platform and the protracted testing of the amplifier system, the comings and goings of leading party figures, the evening cool and the coloured lights of the U.P.P. meetings, the party colours and waving flags and posters—'as in the Chicago convention', as Mr. Blyden said—and youth-club-rally high spirits of the S.L.I.M., Mr. Blyden's dramatic changes of voice, his screams of rage, his irreverences about the Governor, the Chief Secretary 'and the clerk work he's sent out here to do', and dignitaries generally, his intimations that 'buying and selling has been going on in the judicial department', that he knew 'what goes on behind drawn blinds on Hill Station', that he had in his pocket the letter written by one of his critics to a friend when seeking a job, that the files of the Secretariat and even the Colonial Office are not closed to him. The National Council, like the Labour Party, offered few such attractions and was soon deserted.

Such reactions do not mean that the politicians were unsuccessful; they held their audiences and probably affected their attitudes as much as they expected. Ministerial self-interest and the injustice of the exclusion of Mr. Rogers-Wright were kept very much in the public mind, and young men went about asking one another and anyone else who would listen whether party politics was possible in a Crown colony; those who replied that it seemed to exist were clearly considered to need a further course in Blydenism. This last lesson in fact was so well learned as to embarrass the teacher; when Mr. Blyden himself announced that he was putting forward candidates his more austere followers seem to have been shocked, and thereafter his progress was less smooth than it had been. When the names were announced, it was evident that not all accepted what he called 'the criteria I have applied in allowing my executive' to choose them, in subsequent meetings two of the candidates suffered some barracking, and in the attempt to defend them the leader's insults to his audience, which had previously been received with gratitude and devotion, seem to have incurred resentment.

Meetings held by Independent candidates did not appear until after the close of nominations on 7 April, since both men so standing were dissidents from the S.L.P.P.; one, in the central constituency, put up by a group of Temnes in protest against the selection of a somewhat uninspiring Creole for the official nomination, the other, in the west, put up by himself, in the belief that his abilities outshone those of one selected by the party. The latter attracted good audiences, but had apparently no arguments to offer apart from his qualities and his devotion to the area which he sought to represent and, strangely, to the party. Only one serious threat of a schism within the party occurred, when some of the leaders of Northern Province peoples in Freetown—a major element in the population of the east constituency—expressed to the Temne tribal headman in Freetown and two other Northern Province men among the leading office holders of the party their concern at the Government's action in deposing chiefs found substantially at fault by the Commissions of Inquiry. A general meeting of party members from the north was accordingly held in Freetown East on 3 March at which these three leaders explained the Government's policy. The threat of a split was averted, and the S.L.P.P. front in the constituency stood firm.

In the Protectorate, in contrast, most of the campaigning was done by individual candidates on their own initiative and in their own interest, and much the same was true in the outlying parts of the Colony. Party meetings were held rarely, and mainly on the occasion of visits by ministers or other leading politicians. Often, especially for meetings of the S.L.P.P., they had about them something of the quality of traditional chiefdom hospitality to the visiting great man. Apart from the greetings by the chief or other local notables, and replies by the politicians, the proceedings seem to have been, according to such few accounts as it is possible to obtain, much the same as in Freetown, with jokes and sometimes entertainment and more emphasis on past achievements or past wrongs than on plans for the future. There were probably only six constituencies in the Protectorate where the identity of the S.L.P.P. candidate was known before nomination, so that his merits could form a theme at meetings. In Moyamba North, where the sitting member of Legislative Council was to stand, a meeting on the evening of 23 February was introduced by the Chiefdom Speaker (the paramount chief's traditional lieutenant). The member then gave his account of the circumstances of his first election about which some unfavourable accounts had been circulating; and (according to the recollection of some who attended) explained what he had achieved in the legislature—electricity and water-supplies then being installed in Moyamba town, government scholarships awarded there and in his own neighbouring native village, and the development of roads and hospitals. He promised that if re-elected he would try to do more. There were speeches in his favour by the President of the District Council, the Chief Minister, who happened at the time to be in the town, and the paramount chief. In the afternoon of the same day he met representatives of the surrounding villages called in by the chief. Proceedings in Protectorate meetings were generally conducted in the local language, though often with Krio translation, and audiences were apparently apt to demand some knowledge of it from speakers as a test of tribal adherence, probably in general to the advantage of the S.L.P.P.

9. *The Press*

In a country with such a low proportion of literacy the press could do little to supplement public meetings as a means of making party programmes and purposes known to the people. The principal daily newspaper, the *Daily Mail*—one of a number of West African subsidiaries of the London *Daily Mirror*—had an average daily circulation of about 11,000. It alone of the Sierra Leone press was on general sale about the streets of the principal towns, and it reached some of the villages of the Protectorate as a subsidiary line of business for the drivers of mail contractors' lorries and other vehicles. Like the rest of its chain in West Africa, it was careful to avoid identifying itself with any one party, by praising and admonishing all in turn and by publishing signed articles by politicians of each whenever they had substantial cases to put. Some of these articles aroused much interest, notably one published on the 22 November 1956, accusing the S.L.P.P. of inciting narrow tribal loyalties and distrust of the Creoles among the tribal electorate, and hinting at the use of the secret societies to this end. A reply was allowed in a later number.

The only other newspaper of which the circulation may possibly have exceeded a thousand per issue—though certainly not by much—was the *African Vanguard*, published in Freetown three times weekly. This paper gave its support to the S.L.P.P., largely in the form of disclosures damaging to that party's opponents. The *Observer* of Bo, a weekly founded by Dr. Margai as the first official voice of the S.L.P.P., probably had in its best days a circulation of a little over a thousand per issue, though with the transfer of the centre of the party's activities to Freetown and the role of party spokesman to the *Vanguard* it had for a time ceased publication and had resumed only at the cost of some loss in circulation. It still gave fairly loyal support to the S.L.P.P. in the period preceding the elections, but probably no longer stood particularly near to its leadership. The U.P.P. had no official organ, for the *African Standard*, a weekly of which its Deputy Leader, Mr. Wallace-Johnson, had been the editor, had ceased publication some two years earlier, and the acquisition of a new printing press, long said to be imminent, had not happened by the time of the election. The *Daily Guardian* of Freetown, however, with a circulation of perhaps some 700 or 800 daily, though owned by a family with no obvious political bias, had for some time before the election had a strongly U.P.P. editor, and had come to reflect his views. Its columns remained open to writers outside that party, notably to a leading trade union secretary member of the Labour Party, but it made a speciality of reporting extensively all the main speeches at U.P.P. meetings. These ran on serially from day to day with a break in the speech where the paper's inflexible limit of four small pages (as for all papers other than the *Daily Mail*) dictated, rather than as the sense required. This and a somewhat individual style made its accounts rather difficult to follow, but as it was the only paper reporting any political meetings at all regularly or extensively it may have had some very slight influence on the electorate. The *Evening Despatch* of Freetown, with a circulation of 300 or 400, supported the National Council, whose Assistant General Secretary, Mrs. Bright-Taylor, half-sister to the leader, was its editor; its space, however, was largely devoted to advertisement, and its language was so cryptic and its printing so variable that it seems unlikely that it conveyed much information to any not long practised in its interpretation and presumably therefore already committed to the party. The Labour Party had the *Hurricane*, edited by Mr. Bamekole Sawyerr, one of its two National Secretaries; this, however, can hardly have had a circulation of a hundred, and in 1957 appeared only irregularly, on Saturdays at intervals of from two to six weeks. The *Advance*, a weekly of Bo, with an unknown but certainly small circulation, pursued an independent course, critical of all parties, sometimes violently and abusively so: it was well printed, but in style peculiar and unpredictable. The *Ten Daily News*, published rather more irregularly than its name suggests, and with a very small circulation, seemed similarly to be independent of the laws of newspaper finance, but it may have had some financial support as the journal of the Sierra Leone Women's Movement, an organization with a large trading side to its activities. Its political opinions were generally favourable to the Government.

A number of journals providing for the interests of the several religious communities had little or nothing to say about current politics; nor had one privately owned paper declaredly published as an act of family piety and certainly not a profitable venture, as it was well produced and had a very small circulation.

The readership of the newspapers was doubtless somewhat larger than the figures of their circulation suggest, but since illiterates tend to associate with illiterates rather than with those who might read out the news to them, the influence of the press among the people at large was probably not extensive. A small intelligentsia in Freetown and Bo perhaps read a number of the papers and weighed them up; a rather larger number heard something of the cautious *Daily Mail* point of view. For most the press might as well not have existed.

10. *Party Manifestos*

The Labour Party manifesto, a single page of about 400 words, was issued on 18 January 1957, and for some two months had the field to itself. The equivalent document of the S.L.I.M., 3,500 words long, called a charter and attached to the party's constitution, appeared in the latter part of March. In the middle of April came the S.L.P.P.'s election manifesto, of about the same length and accompanied by a 2,000-word declaration of the party's achievements and by messages from the Chief Minister as National Leader and from his brother as chairman. An earlier version of it had begun to appear on 2 April when the party newspaper got hold of a copy and started to serialize it, and had been recalled, to the sound of muffled explosions in the higher places of the party, when it was found to provide the opponents with some choice absurdities—notably a promise to provide 7,000 scholarships. The U.P.P., which since the beginning of the year had professed to have its manifesto ready, but to be keeping it secret lest the S.L.P.P. should steal it, produced it on 25 April. It was very slightly shorter than that of S.L.I.M. The National Council does not seem to have published a manifesto at all. At a meeting on 26 April, a week before polling day, Dr. Bankole-Bright summarized its main points and promised its appearance in a few days' time; possibly printing troubles prevented this.

The brief Labour Party manifesto was necessarily not very specific. The nearest approach to definite undertakings consisted in statements that the party would request the British Government by constitutional means to declare a date for the country's achievement of independence within the Commonwealth, that it would take immediate steps for the training of Africans to take over key posts in the civil service and that meanwhile they should understudy the present holders of these offices, that it would advocate free primary education throughout the country and endeavour to restrict by law the freehold purchase of property by aliens (which was already only

possible in the Colony), and that there should be old-age pensions
for all. Communications, mechanized agriculture, housing, social
services, full recognition of trade unions and democratic self-government were declared objects of the party's solicitude; industry was
mentioned only in the form of a declaration of intention to undertake the training of technicians. The aim 'to ensure the equitable
and fair distribution of the wealth of the country' was expressed
but not elaborated.

The other manifestos expressed much the same intentions, though
at greater length and with variations of emphasis which seemed to
bear little relation to the several characters of the parties as expressed
by their leaders in their meetings. Probably these variations proceeded from the interests of the persons, in all cases unnamed,
deputed to write the documents. In particular the S.L.I.M.
showed a marked, if rather amateurish, economic bias, and the
U.P.P. a medical, and rather conspicuously professional, one. The
former was most notable for the total absence of the characteristically Blydenist doctrine of the impossibility of party politics in the
country's circumstances, and hence also the necessity for the development of education by private enterprise. It was a typical party
pronouncement, setting out a programme of things to be done in
the event of the party's in some way coming to power. The S.L.P.P.
manifesto was less markedly biased in any one direction than those
of other parties, though in accordance with its traditions it gave
rather more space to education.

The S.L.I.M. was alone in indicating any specific fields for the
development of industry, and it exhibited a faith in detailed planning
by Government quite absent from the pronouncements of the other
parties. It was also unique in raising the question of the method of
financing economic development, though there was a certain unreality about this, as it looked to India among a wide range of other
countries to supply private capital; locally and internationally
raised loans, and grants from the United Kingdom were other
sources. It also seemed somewhat remote from observed fact, though
perhaps in agreement with general Freetown opinion, in supposing
that the country had large reserves of idle arable land and of timber.
It proposed a number of new forms of state action, among them
a Ministry of Production, a Planning Unit, a National Housing
Board and a Commission of Inquiry into the educational system.
The party was also unique in mentioning West African federation,
though only as a section heading; in fact its proposals did not go
beyond inter-territorial economic co-operation.

The U.P.P. proposals for the improvement of the medical services went so far into detail as to include, among other demands for the creation of specific posts, specifying the qualifications required for them. Other distinctive requirements, presumably connected with the party's bid for the support of the Muslim north, were the introduction and maintenance of the teaching of Arabic in all primary schools, the replacement of head tax by house-rating, and in general the assimilation of the Protectorate fiscal system to that of the Colony, and the provision by the state of minimum salaries of £1,000 a year for all paramount chiefs. Its economic proposals were particularly thin, consisting mainly of interest-free loans for farmers, and loan and credit facilities for business men and traders, loans to fishermen for the purchase of power-driven boats and equipment, increased minimum wages for government and local authority labourers, and parity of salaries with civil servants for local government staffs and for teachers in voluntary schools. In this economic field the S.L.P.P. manifesto, apart from promising a hydro-electric scheme to supply electricity to all rural areas, was fuller than that of the U.P.P., but scarcely more specific. It also promised financial assistance to Africans engaged in trading, particularly those dealing in local commodities, and though not offering loans to individual farmers it professed readiness to make grants to farming co-operatives. The National Council apparently envisaged the establishment of factories for craft work and, in some form not indicated, the development of rural areas.

These offers are not easy to compare. In certain fields, however, there was some obvious competitive bidding in terms of dates or otherwise. The U.P.P. promised independence in 1960, the S.L.I.M. by 1 January 1961, the S.L.P.P. during the life of the new legislature, which expires in 1962. In the interim the S.L.I.M. offered full self-government in internal affairs by 1958, with one fully elected chamber and one nominated chamber, which might include such *ex officio* ministers as remained, together with representatives of paramount chiefs and of religious denominations, and nominees of the Prime Minister. The S.L.P.P. and the U.P.P. offered immediate action to obtain a larger and all-African cabinet, linked by the S.L.P.P. to the abolition of the offices of Chief Secretary and Chief Commissioner of the Protectorate. The Labour Party manifesto, as mentioned, was vaguer on both stages, and the National Council would apparently have been vaguer still.

In another field of similar competitive bidding the S.L.P.P. offered 'free education to all of school age' by 1960, but without stating the age and apparently with only primary education in mind. All other parties also offered free primary education—and the

S.L.I.M. expressed the intention of making it compulsory—but did not say how soon. The S.L.I.M. further offered free secondary education within a ten-year period. S.L.P.P. and S.L.I.M. both demanded the development of Fourah Bay College into a full university college, the former specifying the provision of honours degree courses within five years. The S.L.P.P. gave more details than the others of its school-building plans; the U.P.P. alone professed interest in public libraries, and also in evening polytechnics, though all professed in general terms a concern for technical education. The S.L.I.M. alone envisaged governmental action to provide political education and a thorough review of the information services.

In the field of health and social welfare the U.P.P. offered free medical services for daily-wage workers and persons under the age of eighteen, children's allowances and homes for paupers and the aged, as well as grants to induce medical practitioners to practise in the remoter places and abolition of the restriction on government medical officers' private practices. The National Council also suggested an intention to demand free medical services for certain classes of the population. The S.L.I.M. proposed to promote instead a national health insurance scheme (as did the Labour Party), and to expand medical and dental services in schools; it also envisaged old-age pensions, unemployment insurance and a number of other benefits. The S.L.P.P. made no such bid but confined itself to suggesting in what places it would build hospitals, as also did the S.L.I.M.—and as the U.P.P. strangely did not—and to promising each chiefdom a health centre.

Housing was to be an object of every party's attention. So also was Africanization of the public service—and in the S.L.I.M. of 'all industries'—and the S.L.P.P. offered also the training of diplomats. On communications the S.L.P.P. offered a five-year plan of road building, including the provision of £5 million to provide all trunk roads with bridges and tarred surfaces. The U.P.P. undertook to build at least 200 miles of road a year and to modernize the telephone and telegraph systems. All were going to do something about the railway, none explained what, and the U.P.P. undertook to do it within three years.

11. Radio

The inadequate press and the belated manifestos were supplemented by the facilities of the Sierra Leone broadcasting system. At the end of December 1956 the Government announced its decision to grant broadcasting time, on a generous scale, to all parties presenting candidates for the election. Allocation of hours was made by a committee consisting of the Vice-President of the Legislative Council (the Speaker), a judge of the Supreme Court, and the Public Relations Officer (the director of the country's information services). Two quarter-hour periods a week at popular listening times were made available and assigned equally and in sequence to the National Council, the S.L.P.P., the U.P.P. and the Labour Party; a fifth period in each cycle was left vacant for assignment to any other parties which might be formed. This was continued from 12 January 1957 up to the elections. The S.L.I.M. (which at the time of the introduction of the arrangement and for some time afterwards was claiming not to be a party) was not assigned any time, and never sought any. The vacant periods were never filled. Moreover, the U.P.P. found it necessary, for reasons which it did not reveal, to withdraw from most of the broadcasts which it was scheduled to give, and apparently the S.L.P.P. and the National Council also missed one each. It seems that the parties most accomplished in the use of the mass meeting found difficulty with the very different technique of the broadcast talk. Even the parties which did participate did not present in this medium primarily the men who shone most on the public platform. All broadcasts were given in standard English, which almost certainly reduced their impact upon the public. Their audience was in any case probably not large. The power of the transmitters was not sufficient to provide a reliable coverage for the whole country, though evidently some of the broadcasts were heard at considerable distances inside the Protectorate. The talks were frequently mentioned in the press, though not reported at any length.

Despite the somewhat unrepresentative selection of speakers participating in it, this series of broadcasts expressed the divergence between the government party and the opposition parties rather more clearly and faithfully than did the manifestos, or anything to be found in the press, or even the speeches at the public meetings of the parties. On one side there was the argument that it would be unwise to abandon the team which had spent the last five years learning the business of governing the country. This form of argument seemed to come readily to the cautious and sober Chief Minister; with it he was able in the final talk in the series, on the eve of polling day, to enlist even the Government's mistakes in its favour, claiming in mitigation of such few as he admitted that on taking office he and his colleagues had had no predecessors by whose example and experience they could be guided. He asked: 'Do you honestly believe that any one of our opponents could have done better than we have done? And would you now be willing to run the risk of letting them take over the reins of government and begin all over again without the experience which we have gained over the past five years?' Another speaker for the party suggested, in the same vein, that the previous five years had been a period of sowing, with the harvest still to come, that 'patient dog eat fat bone'. On 20 March one of the ablest of the party's younger men, apart from repeating the Chief Minister's argument, had offered a bold, if somewhat dangerous, defence against the allegations of corruption by some ministers, which were the party's most vulnerable point—in Dr. Bankole-Bright's words, 'Ministers building mansions some of which cost over twenty thousand pounds with a two thousand pound allowance for five years, and trying to block an enquiry;' he asked, 'What party leaders would be guilty of bribery and corruption if you the people refused to offer bribes and to encourage corrupt practices for your own selfish and individual ends?'

Apart from this allegation of corruption and the other major charge of fostering communalism—Mr. Bamekole Sawyerr of the Labour Party drew attention to the difference between S.L.P.P. slogans of unity and the language of their loudspeaker vans going about the streets of Freetown—Opposition speakers directed attention to the limitations of the Government's achievements. They agreed in concentrating particularly on its ponderous and allegedly ineffective approach to the problem of the country's extreme educational backwardness. Mr. Sawyerr reflected on the fact that the party which used the palm-tree for its election symbol and gave itself the title of 'countryman party' had signally failed to promote the production of palm products or agriculture generally, and a party colleague observed that alone among the parties Labour had no politicians profiting by scarcity conditions in the rice trade. The Chief Minister rejoined that a democratic Government could not force farmers to grow rice when they would rather look for diamonds. To those who commented, as many did, on the shocking state of the country's roads he suggested that if they had travelled more outside Freetown they would have noticed the marked improvement over recent years. The National Council again made much of the practices of the S.L.P.P. in the Freetown registration—'capturing illiterate men and women from the high seas' (actually the passage across the Freetown estuary) 'and placing their names in the voters' list'. The basis of their own claim was the advice 'Look before you leap. Remember that old and tried friends are the best', and that only they had never broken their promises—a claim which in the subsequent skirmish of election posters was appropriated, strangely, by the Labour Party. Only the National Council, they claimed, had men of adequate calibre to run the country. Dr. Bankole-Bright, the leader, who spoke twice, was probably not much help to his party. His speeches were almost identical with one another and with those which he delivered at his meetings, evoking by name the giants of the Colony's past, lamenting the decadence of the present in highly metaphorical language which itself belonged to a past age and can certainly have done little to win the votes of the young. They were the speeches of a dogged fighter, but the mark of defeat was on them from the first.

Only the Labour Party had a manifesto before the public throughout the period of its broadcast talks, and the contributions of Mr. Beoku-Betts were devoted almost entirely to explaining his party's programme, though without adding much detail. Mr. Sawyerr was left to handle the knock-about of political abuse which was the main substance of the series, while Mr. Grant characteristically devoted himself to showing, with examples from British politics, that it was not wrong for trade unionists to take part in political action. Speakers of other parties, however, made incidental references to party programmes. The most notable feature of these was the importance given by all parties to the development of secondary industry, a subject which found conspicuously little mention in the printed manifestos.

12. *Individual Campaigns*

Systematic campaigning by the individual prospective candidates in the Protectorate seems in general to have begun early in January 1957. Persons whose jobs made heavy demands on their time, or required them to behave with particular discretion (such as those of schoolmasters or central native administration clerks), or to live outside their home areas where alone they could stand with much hope of success, were often not able to start until much later, when they could get and afford unpaid leave for the purpose. Several retired persons professed confidence that this would give them a great advantage, though in practice it seems to have been less than they thought. Some people who were otherwise occupied could in the meantime get relations or friends to initiate some action on their behalf. A minister who was nursing very carefully the constituency of Moyamba South had a paid agent, but probably men of less substance, as most were, found this quite beyond their means. In many places it was even thought unwise to campaign or to express any close personal interest in the election much in advance of nomination day, for fear of offending kinsmen who might have the same ambition, or, in a phrase that was frequently used, giving an opportunity to opponents to blacken one's character—presumably by holding up to public censure ambition unbecoming one who was not a chief. In Koinadugu district in the Northern Province the legend seems to have taken root that to campaign was a 'crime' and punishable as such. This extreme view seems to have arisen from misinterpretation of a warning by the District Commissioner against intimidation. Even there, however, the identity of the probable candidates was clear enough some months in advance of nomination day. A similar quotation by some politicians in the neighbouring Bombali district of the prohibition of riotous assemblies as a reason for not holding party meetings was declared by another to be a mere excuse for laziness, and probably this was so.

The usual pattern of early campaigning, according to candidates' accounts, was for them to go round the several chiefdom towns and the more important villages, visiting the chiefs—to one or more of whom the candidate was very likely to be related—and the village sub-chiefs, who in the opinion of some were more influential, exchanging customary greetings and asking that the people be gathered, usually in the open-sided court-house or *barri*. There the visitor would recount to the public his local origins or interest—and the king of arguments appeared to be that one had built a permanent house in the area a respectable number of years ago and kept it in good repair—and would ask for the favour of the listeners' votes. Few grounds seem to have been suggested in most places other than the general plea that 'I am best man for speak to Government', or as one said 'to crave the indulgence of Government', meaning in general that he was reasonably well educated, that he had some experience of the world, and probably of the ways of government, through former employment in the civil service or native administration, and that he was in favour with some important people. One candidate who used the phrase meant, among other things, specifically that he had on several occasions presented addresses to the Governor and Provincial Commissioner on the occasions of their visits. What happened if more than one person asked for support in the same place did not seem to be agreed; most prospective candidates seemed to think that having once given their pledge the people would not usually change their minds, so that it was of advantage to be the first solicitor. Others, mainly those who did not have the opportunity to canvass early, held that the latest visitor would leave the strongest impression. Most appeared to be rather shocked at the suggestion that they might have attempted to find out what rival candidates had been saying, or might have attacked them in their conversations with constituents; a few suggested that their opponents had done so. At later stages of the campaign candidates—mostly professional men —began to appear whose claim to be locally rooted was rather thinner, though they could usually point at least to local birth. They were not so conspicuously unsuccessful as the earlier campaigners had apparently expected them to be. The popular suspicion was that they had had to prove financially that their hearts were still in the old places, but such a rumour was natural and cannot be cited as evidence.

Methods in the Colony were similar, with the village headman in place of the chief; one Labour Party candidate was firmly convinced that his people would follow him because his father had on several occasions served as a much respected headman of the place.

In such local campaigning some mention, it seems, was generally made of the specific needs of the place—electricity and water-supply in all towns and Colony villages, and roads and schools everywhere. S.L.P.P. adherents, the great majority of all candidates, usually replied, when asked, that they mentioned, or would mention, the Government's achievements, but this seems to have been rather as proof of their possession of the basic qualification of loyalty than as an argument of substance.

It was repeatedly asserted, and never denied except by witnesses in election petition cases, that the approach to the local chief, whether or not the calling of a public meeting was desired, needed to be accompanied by the presentation of gifts of real, though not neces-sarily very high, value. It was generally stressed that little of this was bribery according to the popular understanding of the term, being rather a traditional gesture of friendship and respect, the omission of which would be highly resented. Clearly some of the gifts fell within the strict legal definition of the offence of 'treating', since they were intended by the prospective candidate who presented them to be spent by the local notable on food and drink for persons having the vote within the constituency. This was proved against one candidate on election petition, and might well have been proved against others in the Protectorate. Clearly also there was some giving of money and articles of value, and in one case it was alleged that threats and the offer of a scholarship for study abroad had been made by a minister to induce an inconvenient candidate to withdraw. This also was allowed for in native custom—as at the election of chiefs—and was probably not generally thought to be corrupt prac-tice, at least in its less extreme forms. The more pleasant parts of the traditional routine for securing a withdrawal was also observed. One person intending to stand as an unsolicited supporter of the S.L.P.P.

stated at the end of February that the campaigning of his opponent, whom for cabinet-building purposes the party wished to have returned, had so far consisted in visiting him and conceding that in any contest between them he would win. The hint was not taken and the unendorsed candidate did not then intend to take it; he intended to prove his opponent not a true son of the local soil and also to use against him all the influence of a chiefly office to which he hoped to succeed. The two men, however, had held some joint meetings. The same candidate was one of those who held most strongly that the most profitable method of campaigning was to visit 'just the heads of places', the influential persons to whom the generality of the citizens would usually turn for advice in any problem insoluble out of their own experience, such as that of the right candidate to vote for.

Privately produced campaign literature was very limited in amount. There was hardly any occasion for it in Freetown, where the campaign was from the first conducted by the parties, and in the Protectorate less than 5 per cent. of the population are literate. There may have been some private manifestos in the remoter constituencies of the Colony rural area, but probably even there the influence of the party organizations in Freetown and the communal conflict which they embodied was too strong. In Bonthe town in Sherbro constituency (the detached piece of the Colony where literacy is up to Colony standard, and communal sentiment, though seeming now to incline to the Protectorate rather than the Colony side, was not in most citizens very intense), party organization was, however, weak and there was scope in politics for the individual. One intending candidate so far misjudged the date of election as to produce his manifesto in August 1956, another had his manifesto printed at about the same time but cautiously withheld it from publication until after the local elections at the end of March 1957. Both manifestos stressed their authors' local birth and long residence. The earlier of the two was a polished and well argued but politically not very apt refusal to make rash promises of the unattainable, and it asserted the prime importance of education, in which field the candidates' experience lay. Possibly to his misfortune, it stressed the importance of not belonging to a party; by the time of the election its author had joined the S.L.P.P. The other manifesto consisted of twenty-two briefly stated and numbered points on the candidate's life and his achievements as member of the Urban District Council and active citizen; among them was the reopening of a bank in the town, which the bank itself was more inclined to attribute to the development of rutile mining in the area. No future course of action was suggested, and though the candidate was an active supporter of the National Council and later received its official nomination he made no mention of his party in his manifesto.

Shortly before polling day, other candidates in the Colony produced similar brief biographies in the form of handbills with photograph, supplementary to the manifestos of their parties. That of the S.L.P.P. candidate for the Colony rural area constituency of Wilberforce was a particularly queer product, because he came from elsewhere in the Colony. After a rather despondent attempt to make the best of some thin connexions with his constituency, it concluded with the observation that what really mattered was Sierra Leone as a whole and the candidate 'was born and brought up in Sierra Leone'—it having already been explained that he had spent a considerable part of his adult life in Nigeria. The independent candidate in Freetown West produced at about the same time an election address which exemplified the difficulties of a party supporter who insisted on standing against his own party. The address emphasized the necessity for a strong Government and had nothing to say about the role of independents. It urged the need for men of education, in which the candidate was clearly superior to his rival for the party nomination, and for 'fearless fighters', a title which the candidate claimed for himself. In policy it was individual only in urging the cessation of permanent employment of expatriates in government service in favour of contract service, loans to farmers and fishermen, and high import duties for the protection of Sierra Leonean products.

Before polling day most candidates in Colony and Protectorate alike produced and displayed some form of poster, with their photographs, election symbols and names and sometimes a brief text. Apparently all such texts were in standard English, except some of those of Mr. Marcus Grant, which were produced in Krio on the theme of 'gentry for gentry, poor for poor'. The photograph of one of the candidates for Kenema South showed him in the practice of his trade as a druggist giving an injection. It was the general opinion that this was more likely to win votes than to lose them.

How official party adoption would help them or their opponents few candidates in the Protectorate seem to have considered far in advance. Most of them appreciated when the point was explained that only one person could have the party symbol—though as late as March 1957 some stoutly denied that party symbols would be used at all outside Freetown—but thought that such a symbol, even if it were the S.L.P.P. palm-tree, would mean no more to most voters than the personal symbols with which they were familiar from the previous year's district council elections.

13. *The Candidates*

There were in all 121 properly nominated candidates for 39 seats. The S.L.P.P. alone had validly nominated candidates for all seats. The U.P.P. had 12 in the Colony, 6 in the Protectorate; the National Council 11, the Labour Party 6, S.L.I.M. 4, all in the Colony. This leaves 43 Independents, 10 of them in the Colony.

The field from which these candidates were selected could in the circumstances of the country only be a very restricted one. The legal requirement that all members of the House of Representatives should be literate in English excluded almost all the peasants in this peasant country; and since the general quest for security and respectability made the civil service traditionally the most attractive profession the service rule excluding from membership all in the direct employ of the state debarred many of the most able among the limited intelligentsia. Lawyers remained eligible in fair numbers because they were mostly in private practice, though professional necessity had moved most of the Protectorate-born among them from their native districts and the almost absolute popular insistence on local candidates prevented them from standing anywhere else. Doctors were mostly in government service and so excluded; of the three who stood two were retired and one did not practice.

The government-licensed druggists, on the contrary, who in the absence of sufficient trained medical practitioners were the country's principal curers of the sick, were available and were generally interested in a political career; their professional activities often caused them to travel widely in the villages and gave many of them large personal followings which they could hope to turn into votes. Central native administration clerks, the officers chosen among the clerks of the several chiefdoms to serve in the District Commissioners' offices co-ordinating the activities of their fellows, were also available, since they are paid from chiefdom funds, not from those of the central government. As they had shown in the district council elections, they are actively interested in politics: furthermore, they also travel widely, they have influence over men of local influence, and they derive prestige from their near-governmental status. In the event only three of the twelve in the country stood, one of them having given up his post before nomination, the others still serving. Staffs of local authorities were not excluded by any general instruction, and among the candidates were two junior clerks of District Councils, a health inspector, an agricultural supervisor, two supervising teachers (local school inspectors), and two of the three provincial education secretaries (school inspectors at a higher level), all paid directly or indirectly, from District Council funds. The first three stood not in the areas of their authorities but in their home districts, where they had connexions with chiefly families.

Some District Councils, however, had apparently advised teachers in their schools that they would not be allowed to stand without resigning their posts, by analogy with the position of teachers in government schools. The exclusion of the latter seriously reduced the range of educated persons available for election, though the mission-school teachers, most of those of the District Councils, and the few serving in private educational institutions were in a position to stand. One teacher who resigned from government service to stand and was declared elected was subsequently unseated on election petition, on the ground that his resignation had not become effective at the time of nomination; a government agricultural instructor who narrowly failed election would apparently have suffered the same fate had he won. The council of Fourah Bay College, the country's only institution of higher education, decided early in 1956 that no person elected to the new House might hold a full-time teaching post during his term of election. There was some doubt as to how this was to be applied, but it subsequently became apparent that it was less comprehensive than the exclusion of civil servants, in that it did not necessitate full resignation or loss of seniority; one member of the College staff, a sitting member of the Legislative Council, stood and was elected, though he subsequently resigned his seat without contesting an election petition brought against him on other grounds. Most missions seem to have left their clergy free to stand, and five did so, in addition to the Fourah Bay College lecturer who was also in holy orders.

There was a limited range of other professional and analogous posts from which candidates might be drawn, and among those who stood were the general secretaries of a major trade union and of the government-sponsored Ex-servicemen's Association. Clerks and other employed persons were another possible source, but in fact only three stood, and of these one was very near retirement and another likely to be out of employment in the next few months owing to the closing of his office; it seemed that a political career did not look worth the sacrifice of secure employment. Thirty of the candidates were traders and other self-employed business men, most of them in a rather small way of business. Retired persons, young men not yet employed, and men of independent means, were almost as numerous, if one reckons among them those describing themselves as farmers— for literate persons in West Africa do not farm as their regular way of life, and, on the other hand, nobody in rural areas ever retires completely. For such people politics was an interesting new field of opportunity.

Within this field of possible candidates there was general agreement as to the considerations defining the class of those who might reasonably hope to succeed. Good education and, in the Protectorate, chiefly connexions were great assests. Local birth was, as noticed, generally considered an essential in the Protectorate, and this was probably so in most of the Colony also; it applied in Freetown, but perhaps only because party policy so decreed. To avoid increasing communal tension more than was necessary, and to win some Creole favour, the S.L.P.P. declared well before the election that it would not adopt as its official candidates in the Colony any persons not of Colony birth except those who had lived there for thirty years. This last exception was probably dictated by the impossibility of refusing to adopt in the East Ward of Freetown Kande Bureh, recognized by the Government as headman of the Temne community in Freetown and a figure of immense prestige among all the northern Muslim communities in the city—and of conspicuously short patience with the more extreme wing of Creoledom. In fact he was the only person covered by the exception. In return the party adopted for the Protectorate constituency of Bo town a long-established and popular druggist of Creole birth, but this was a concession of less value, since party discipline there was less firm, and in making it the party had deeply offended the president of Bo town council, a man of local birth who had attained that office in rivalry against the newly endorsed candidate. The local man again opposed him in the 1957 election, was generally believed to have brought the Porro network into play against him, and won. Since active S.L.P.P. Creoles were comparatively few except in the peculiar conditions of Sherbro, and the Protectorate vote was small in the Colony outside Freetown, the official S.L.P.P. nomination was to be had cheap in the rural area, and in at least one place it was apparently accepted only under pressure.

In the Protectorate, on the contrary, there was no lack of takers. Endorsement was given to the four sitting S.L.P.P. Legislative Council members who were available—that is, to all who were not paramount chiefs—even though it was clear from the first that one of them had not such a following among the new wider electorate as would give him a reasonable hope of success. Each of them chose one of the two constituencies in the district for which he sat; the Chief Minister actually chose the half of his district with which he had been less closely associated, possibly because it was the less accessible, little canvassing would be required and he might hope for an unopposed return. There were also two sitting members elected by the Protectorate Assembly, who were ministers in the Government; one of them, the Chief Minister's brother, was placed in that half of Moyamba district from which his family came, the other half being bespoke for the sitting member. The other case, that of Mr. Siaka Stevens, was more difficult. He also came from Moyamba district which was closed to him, and he therefore turned to the Port Loko East constituency, in which he had worked for some years as a trade union secretary at the iron mines. But this was desired by one of the party's vice-presidents, who had useful connexions there and was one of the leading spokesmen for the north within the party's leadership; and perhaps in any case the party would have preferred to be rid of Mr. Stevens. There was apparently an idea of inducing him to fight one of the less inviting Colony seats, but this was defeated by the party's reservation of Colony seats to Creoles, and in the end he was allowed Port Loko East, whereupon his rival resigned his party office, though not his membership, and stood against him unsuccessfully as an Independent. About that constituency and also about Bo town the decision of the party's national executive originally went the other way, and it was only after further meetings and much pressure and recrimination that it was reversed.

Where the seat was not thus pre-empted the party's purpose seems to have been to pick among candidates who were already in the field and might be prepared to accept S.L.P.P. nomination— in most cases all of them—the one who seemed to have the best chance of winning. The choice of the deposed chief in Kambia West was strange, but was probably determined by the lack of other contenders, his persistence, and his powerful connexions within the party. There was also a miscalculation in the two Kailahun constituencies, in one of which perhaps there was a false estimate of the balance of forces between the two rival chiefly families and the decision went against the currently ruling family whose champion was thought to incline to the U.P.P. Otherwise, the party's choice was not far out.

In the East constituency of Freetown adherence to the Muslim faith was generally considered essential for election, and the S.L.P.P. was in any case bound to choose Kande Bureh and Mr. Mustapha, the sitting member, a member deemed to be representative of the

Colony Muslims. In the other two wards two energetic ladies who seemed fitted to appeal to the new illiterate feminine vote were obvious first choices. The one chosen for the Central constituency, Mrs. Cummings-John, was a leading officer of the Sierra Leone Women's Movement which on one side of its activities was a market women's purchasing co-operative, and though herself a Creole she had also established herself, in her capacity as a government-nominated member of the City Council and otherwise, as a vociferous advocate of any claims of the Protectorate people. The other, chosen for the West ward, had come over from the U.P.P. and, though less well known, was similarly established with the women traders. Of the other seats in these two wards one—which proved to be that in the West constituency, which probably looked the safer—obviously had to go to the party's very able National Secretary-General, H. E. B. John. Only the second seat in the reputedly conservative Central constituency remained vacant, and this was assigned, to the surprise of most people, to a loyal but obscure party supporter who had been nominated (but did not stand) for another Colony seat in 1951.

The U.P.P., where it stood in the Protectorate, had rather a different problem from its rival. The smear of 'Creole party' which had been effectively laid upon it made its endorsement seem rather a liability than an asset, and though it approached at least one candidate who had been unsuccessful in the contest for the S.L.P.P. nomination it could not persuade him to accept the Party's label. It had in fact only six candidates in the twenty-five Protectorate constituencies. Relying on 'anti-chiefism' rather than local standing, and on political effort from the centre rather than the personal initiative of the candidate, it was perhaps freer to move its people about than the S.L.P.P., but it could not depart far from the general Protectorate pattern. In the tax-trouble area, which had seemed promising, it enlisted in the end only one candidate, a little-known village politician in Bombali East. The departure for Kambia of Mr. Ahmed, who had been popularly thought of, though possibly not by his own party, as a candidate for Port Loko West, left only one possible—or literate—candidate for the latter, a former motor driver who during the tax troubles had been a sort of secretary to the strikers, 'a very tactful young man' as his opponent described him, who had helped to give the rising some authority by the letters of support which he claimed to receive from various persons of influence, and who after some hesitation between parties had opted for the U.P.P. and become a regular participant in its Freetown meetings. In the chief-dominated and comparatively unpromising constituency of

Port Loko East one of the party organizers for the province was put up. In Moyamba district the available U.P.P. forces consisted of two full-time party workers; both lived within the northern constituency, one in Moyamba town, the other on the coast, but both in their political activities covered the whole of the district, the former appealing particularly to the substantial Loko minority—with whom the S.L.P.P. candidates were unable to speak in their own language—the latter to the Temne fishermen whom he had from time to time served as a petition-writer. The latter, however, was thought to be disqualified from seeking election by virtue of a past criminal conviction, and the U.P.P. nominated to stand in his place in Moyamba North his wife, daughter of a former paramount chief in the area. The other candidate, who was thought to be the stronger, was switched from Moyamba North (where he had been expected to stand) to Moyamba South to oppose Mr. Albert Margai, the Minister for Education and Local Government, who was the more important and was reputed to be the weaker in popular favour of the two S.L.P.P. candidates. Otherwise the Protectorate and Sherbro offered no opening, though party workers professed, and may well have had reason, to hope that if they could make a good showing some of the uncommitted candidates would join them after the election.

In the six rural area constituencies of the Colony Mr. Wallace-Johnson had a clear claim to the nomination at Wilberforce, and there was apparently no difficulty in finding five other citizens of local repute to take the U.P.P. symbol. In Freetown also there was no lack of material. Unlike the S.L.P.P. but like the National Council, the U.P.P. ran in Freetown East one Christian and one Muslim candidate; it chose for the former place a generally respected druggist and city councillor. The only nomination to arouse general excitement, with some confusion, was that of Mr. Rogers-Wright himself to stand for Freetown Central, together with the party's young professional General Secretary, Mr. Nelson-Williams. Coming directly after the Secretary of State's refusal to consider the suit of a U.P.P. delegation for the removal of the disqualification of Mr. Rogers-Wright, this nomination was apparently based on the hope that the hand of authority might be forced by such an overwhelming demonstration of popular support as in 1951 brought Mr. Nkrumah from prison to be Leader of Government business in the Legislative Assembly of the Gold Coast—a precedent which Mr. Rogers-Wright himself quoted in his public speeches. Meanwhile the acceptance of his nomination was itself celebrated in U.P.P. speeches as a victory, though in fact the regulations gave the returning officer no power to refuse a nomination which was formally in order; this was generally pointed out by the other parties, with the inference that a vote for Mr. Rogers-Wright would be a vote wasted. But the U.P.P. probably had the better of this argument, in the judgement of a public unlearned in legal subtleties.

The National Council had two members of the old legislature eligible for the new; its leader in Freetown Central and another in Freetown West, its third member, previously sitting for a constituency in the rural area, being disqualified on account of his criminal record. For the East constituency a widely respected Muslim city councillor was an obvious choice, and another councillor and an alderman were conveniently available for the second seats in East and West respectively. To one of the Sherbro seats a town councillor who had been very active in the party's cause had an unmistakable claim. The second seat in Freetown Central, however, had been an object of controversy for some time. The leader was known to wish his half-sister, Mrs. Bright-Taylor, Assistant General Secretary of the party, to run with him there, and it was generally believed that this threatened to antagonize an active Muslim supporter resident in the constituency who had been a useful pamphleteer in the party's interest, and who wanted the seat for himself. As the period for nominations approached all three began again to appear on party platforms together, and it was deduced that agreement had been reached. It proved indeed, when the party's list was announced on 12 April, that the Assistant General Secretary had, against all expectation and apparent reason, been sent to Kambia West in the Protectorate, while her rival had the nomination in Freetown Central. Surprisingly, there were National Council candidates for only five of the six Colony rural area seats, and of these one had already been nominated for the same place by the Labour Party and chose to stand under that symbol.

Candidates were named for four of the Protectorate constituencies nearest to the Colony in addition to Kambia West, and the names of further candidates were promised. But this promise remained unfulfilled, as did a similar one made by the Labour Party at a meeting on 7 April. Those selected for the Protectorate were an oddly assorted set, the candidates for Kambia West and Port Loko West having no known connexion with their constituencies or even with the Protectorate, and the candidate for Kambia East being a barely literate former chiefdom clerk from the west of the district, who could hardly have hoped for many votes in the other half. But when nominations closed, it was found that none of them had been duly nominated. The candidate in Moyamba South had been objected to by the S.L.P.P. on the ground that his nominators were not registered voters of the constituency, and the two Kambia candidates on the ground that their nominations were not handed in by 4 p.m., the prescribed closing time. The two Port Loko candidates apparently failed to arrive in time owing to a breakdown of transport. Mrs. Bright-Taylor immediately afterwards complained to the Governor at the rejection of her nomination in Kambia West. The substance of her complaint seems to have been that she and her party colleague in the other constituency of the district had been unable to pay in their deposits when they wished to do so, owing to the absence of the proper members of the returning officer's staff, whom she suspected of having been bribed to obstruct them; and further that the papers and deposits were in fact in the hands of the returning officer's assistant when the objection was raised, and it was then only 3.50. But why, when there were ten days assigned for nomination did the National Council candidates in the Protectorate take no action until the last day—and in Kambia district until after 3 o'clock on the last day? In Kambia district they apparently had to spend some time collecting from their local supporters the money for their deposits, but this hardly seems an adequate explanation. They were not, of course, alone in their procrastination; members of other parties who should have been well informed also left matters late; some confusion may have been caused by the fact that the final day for nominations was referred to in government pronouncements about the election as 'nomination day'.

The Labour Party and the S.L.I.M. probably had no difficulty in the selection of candidates, but put up all that they could find. The former relied mainly on its office holders, having its President standing alone in Freetown Central, its two National Secretaries in Freetown West and its Vice-President in the rural area constituency of Kissy; in two other rural area constituencies its symbol was accepted by residents of the locality, a retired civil servant and a former handicraft teacher. For the S.L.I.M. its leader put up himself in the central constituency of Freetown, a young lawyer in the East, and in the West a druggist and city alderman and a young transport contractor who had been a member of the executive of the Labour Party. This last explained from the platform at a S.L.I.M. meeting on 29 April how, a few weeks after his resignation from the Labour Party in protest against what he considered its equivocal attitude to the exclusion clause directed against Mr. Rogers-Wright, he had been called to Mr. Blyden who explained that he needed an influential person in the West constituency.

14. *Administrative problems*

In respect of the mechanics of its first popular election Sierra Leone could build on the experience of other West African territories. Legislation was adapted from that used elsewhere, and the instructions issued for the guidance of returning officers, presiding officers, polling assistants, and candidates were taken almost verbatim from those of Ghana.

Symbols. Experience of the use of symbols had been gained in the district council elections of a few months previously, when designs representing in black outline on a white ground objects familiar in local life had been used in place of the differently coloured boxes bearing the candidates' photographs, which were used by the electing bodies in the previous indirect elections. None of these symbols had any party significance, though the candidate in Moyamba district who advertised himself as the U.P.P. candidate also sought in his propaganda to relate his symbol, the cutlass—though it is in West Africa an agricultural tool rather than a weapon—to the 'warrior' Pitier Kamara, whom he brought in to help him and who was and remained a leading argument of the party. For the election here described new symbols were produced, in colour and generally showing solid figures on a white ground; and for the first time in Sierra Leone the parties were allowed to give their official candidates symbols of their own design, duplicated at public expense. The S.L.P.P., like the Nigerian Action Group, had chosen the palm-tree for its symbol, produced in green within a green outline shield. The U.P.P., like the N.C.N.C. in Nigeria and the C.P.P. in Ghana, chose a red cock, the National Council a design in black outline of a pair of clasped hands with above them a lighted torch with flame in red outline, the Labour Party a blue crossed pick and shovel. Fourteen other designs were produced for allocation among independents. The S.L.I.M., which was late in announcing its intention of putting up candidates, agreed to produce its own symbols and chose its party flag of black, red, and green.

Two difficulties became apparent before polling started. One was the necessity of deciding, if party symbols were to be used, which of several S.L.P.P. candidates offering themselves in some constituencies was the official one. The Chief Minister was said to be in favour of leaving this to local decision, and of obliging all to stand under independent symbols if no local decision could be secured. In the end firmer, though less realistic, views of party discipline prevailed, and the party national executive set itself to the difficult task of drawing up an official list. An instruction issued by the Elections

Officer to returning officers, again following the practice of other West African territories, authorized them to issue the party symbols only to candidates in possession of letters of appointment from their parties, signed by the appropriate party officers, whose names were given in the instruction. But such was the state of organization that candidates who were not allowed the party symbol were not distressed by this in the least.

Secondly, though there were four double-member constituencies, no provision had been made for a symbol to differentiate the second party candidate from his running mate while still indicating his party adherence, nor apparently did this point occur to the party leaders until a change was made shortly before nomination day; until then they had been assuring voters at their meetings in the four constituencies concerned that they had only to look for the party symbol. The elections office was aware of the difficulty, but by reason of the production problem involved took the view that second candidates would have to take symbols as independents. In the end, however, the matter came to official attention in the Chief Minister's office, and it was arranged that the party symbols should be produced in a different form for such candidates. The S.L.P.P. design was produced in yellow as well as in green, the U.P.P. design in black as well as in red, the Labour design, for the one constituency where that problem occurred, in red as well as in blue, the National Council design in a version with a green flame as well as the one with a red flame, the S.L.I.M. tricolour against a blue, as well as against a white background—also for one constituency only. Mr. Blyden took the occasion to point out at his meeting that this development showed the party system in a crown colony to be a sham, since the voting was for individuals—as of course it was, there or in any other British territory. Fortunately the change came just before the parties began their intensive campaigns to teach the technique of voting, so at the cost of a little confusion they were able to amend their instructions.

In addition to the symbol and name placed on the box at the public charge, candidates were permitted to have a photograph attached if they provided it themselves, and many did so. No form or maximum size of photograph was prescribed, and Mr. Blyden used those of his election posters (which he claimed had been printed for him by his friends in America), although they were several sizes larger both than those of other candidates and the ballot boxes to which they were affixed.

Publicity. Recent experience of district council elections strengthened the case for publicity to make the nature of the general election clear to the voters. It was generally suspected, in some cases proved, that the quite numerous unopposed returns in local elections were due to misrepresentation or suppression of information by chiefs autocratically inclined, and low polls in contested elections were probably caused by less successful attempts to prevent a contest. Such tactics would be more difficult in the House of Representatives election, as each constituency included several chiefdoms, and the stakes in the contest were larger: but the risk was present. In Tonkolili East an unopposed return was from the first taken for granted, and the election turned merely on the question of which of his sons the paramount chief of Kunike Barina—not the richest chief in the constituency, but the highest in personal prestige—would persuade to assume the burden of representation. In the two divisions of Bo district, also, there was never any question of a contest against the known S.L.P.P. candidates, for reasons which were less clear, though chiefly influence may again have come into it. In Kailahun East the current ruling family of Luawa chiefdom, containing the district centre, openly disclosed its intention of trying to organize an unopposed return; but its chances were never good, as there was a militant pretender family plotting its discomfiture at home and at least one other independent-minded chiefdom had a favourite son to place. In the end this constituency attracted more candidates than any other in the Protectorate, and the second highest turn-out of voters there.

It was therefore necessary to emphasize that Government not only approved but positively favoured the participation of even the humblest citizen in the election; that the election was something which concerned all and about which all might reasonably have opinions; and above all that the citizen's vote was secret, and so could not attract the vengeance of chief, political party, secret society, or other interest. This was something that only the public authorities could do. But in suggesting the considerations which should guide the voter in his choice the agencies of Government had to be cautious lest they be suspected of partiality; indeed, this was a task which could be done effectively only by the political parties in controversy with one another.

The district elections had also suggested the necessity for some instruction in the techniques of voting—why it was necessary to remember the name given at the time of registration and to give that name and no other at the polling station, where to put the ballot paper in order that it might be counted as a valid vote, the use of tax receipts as indications of identity and the futility of putting them in ballot boxes in place of ballot papers, what to do with the thumb when it had been inked to prevent revoting, and so on.

These matters concerned also those who had an interest in getting out the vote and avoiding the disqualification of their supporters, but in fact the weakness of party organization obliged the department of the Public Relations Officer to do most of the work. That prodigiously busy department, responsible for the whole of the Government's publicity work, including at that time the day-to-day management of the broadcasting service, was (like all others) assisted and supplemented in the field by the District Commissioner, the Government's general agent within his area. For him too the task of election publicity was a very heavy one; a limited amount of additional funds was made available for this work to district commissioners, but no additional staff.

Apart from the party political broadcasts, talks were given by the Colonial Secretary on the significance of the elections and by the Elections Officer on the successive stages of registration, nomination, and voting; and there were a number of other special programmes and items in regular series in both the English and the vernacular services. Press releases were issued at each stage in the work of preparation and on the successive difficulties as they arose, and most of these were reproduced more or less accurately by most of the press. In addition the department's own weekly bulletin, issued widely without charge, carried a number of articles on the election.

But the principal resource for getting to the people was one publicity van allotted to each of the three provinces of the Protectorate, each manned by a responsible member of the Public Relations Office staff and by a driver who was also a cinema operator. This campaign was not entirely successful. The vans could go only where there were motor roads, and this meant that a large proportion of the population was out of reach. They suffered seriously from mechanical defects, as does almost any vehicle of a certain age under the circumstances of Sierra Leone, and this caused some inconvenience to audiences, which had sometimes to come in from considerable distances to prearranged meeting-places. It also seems to be agreed that their cinema equipment was not always in good order. The films—films of general interest and about the use of similar techiques of election in other territories—were clearly the main attraction; it was virtually impossible to hold an audience without them, and even with them it was hard to secure attention during the political talks, though the officers of the department seem to have been very ingenious in the devising of strategems to this end.

District commissioners and their principal assistants were probably more generally effective, where they could find time for the work, because people had come to believe, through years of familiarity, that any matter over which they took trouble must be important and that their advice was the most direct expression of the wishes of Government. This had been shown in the district council polls. For the present elections the District Commissioner of Bonthe district, who was no doubt representative of many, made at the beginning of March 1957 a protracted progress throughout his largely roadless district, bearing the usual messages of his office about tax payments, abuses in the native courts, excessive felling of palm-trees, smallpox, and the rest, and also bringing with him two ballot boxes duly sealed and bearing fictitious symbols and fictitious but locally possible names; with these he staged demonstration elections with his interpreter as the voter. The work showed results in a poll of 62·4 per cent. in Bonthe North, the highest in the country, though this was probably affected also by the activities of at least one energetic candidate. It was in this instance unfortunate that the education of the simple villagers was not supplemented by a more thorough education of the schoolmasters and other members of the intelligentsia who made up the polling staff, so that on election petition 774 of the 6,239 votes cast were disallowed for technical faults and the energetic candidate lost his seat. In Bonthe South there was a poll of 33·9 per cent. which was not bad by Sierra Leone standards, especially as the only candidate standing against the Chief Minister in the constituency had said that he no longer wished to contest the election and had attempted belatedly to withdraw.

The production of printed election publicity material was also a function of the Public Relations Department. Pamphlets on registration were issued in English, Mende, and Temne, and there were also produced and widely distributed to district centres booklets with coloured illustrations of the process of voting, posters urging people to register and subsequently to check their registration, a multilingual poster seeking to explain what an election is about, and a cartoon poster to the same end. How far the Mende and Temne pamphlets justified their production would be difficult to determine; there can be comparatively few people in the country who are literate in those languages without having some literacy in English. Casual examination of District Commissioners' and native authorities offices certainly suggested that many of the vernacular pamphlets produced for the district council elections had failed to reach the public. The English versions were informative, but there was not much evidence in conversation that they had been widely read. The illustrated election pamphlet used for its illustrations blocks supplied from Nigeria. These had been slightly amended, but still included pictures which did not represent Sierra Leone usage correctly.

The unluckiest item of election publicity was the cartoon poster on the purpose and nature of the election. The authorities set the artist the problem of conveying to illiterates the idea 'secret, no man knows'; they also allowed him to give a suggestion of reality by placing in the background two palm-trees. Mr. Rogers-Wright at his public meetings denounced this as clear evidence of intention to favour the S.L.P.P. After representations to the Governor the offending portion of the poster was in some places covered over with labels giving the date of polling day, in others with blank pieces of paper; but in some places it remained exposed until polling was over. It is clear that there was no such intent as Mr. Rogers-Wright suggested, but it is quite probable that some candidates exploited the coincidence in order to suggest official support.

Staff. All District Commissioners were appointed returning officers for both constituencies in their districts, and the District Commissioners of Bo and Bonthe districts were also charged with the same duty in respect of Bo town and Sherbro respectively. For each of the constituencies in Freetown and the Colony rural area a returning officer was appointed by name from among senior government officers of various departments.

There was greater difficulty in filling other responsible posts. In the district council elections some returning officers had been hard put to it to provide each station with a presiding officer, a polling assistant or sometimes two, and either one or two policemen. The limited supply of persons of suitable capacity had been made to suffice largely by holding polling on several days and moving the staff about, and also in some districts by the good fortune of having several unopposed returns. In the national elections these favourable circumstances were absent for all districts except Bo and Tonkolili, which had unopposed returns in both constituencies—though Bo town had a contest. At best a district had only two polling days, and the decision to take all Freetown's near neighbours on one day meant that all polling was on one day in two districts, Port Loko and Moyamba, which had experienced special difficulties in the local elections. Bonthe and Pujehun also had only one day for polling. The District Commissioner in Koinadugu district urged that by reason of the enormous distances and lack of roads with which he had to contend he must be allowed three weeks between polling days; it was in .practice only possible to give him ten days. Fortunately the unopposed returns in Tonkolili district, which contained the Protectorate's principal teacher training college, eased Koinadugu's difficulty by enabling it to have for its first polling day the services of a bus-load of students. Some districts were comparatively favourably placed. The District Commissioner of Bonthe town had himself proposed, in advance of the government instructions to that effect, to hold all his polling on one day, but he had at his disposal in Bonthe town one of the country's larger reserves of educated retired persons. Even so, the Bonthe North election petition case, which drew from the judge some severe comments upon the competence of the election staff there, suggests that there was not much talent to spare.

Polling stations. The siting of polling stations and the division of constituencies—or electoral districts as they were called in the legislation—into areas to be served by such stations was left to the returning officers, though in Freetown the selection was made and the outcome announced with the help of the Elections Officer. Outside Freetown and the rural area of the Colony the experience of the recent local elections could be drawn upon. In the district council elections each chiefdom had formed at least one ward, some as many as five or six, the arrangement being intended to provide over the district as a whole, and as far as possible by individual wards, one member to about a thousand voters. The largest contested wards, or those with the most imperfect communications, had been divided into two or three polling station areas, though for the majority one was sufficient.

The accommodation most favoured was a court *barri*, especially where this had an enclosed room at one end which could be used as polling room. Where there was no such room a part of the *barri* was screened off with borrowed raffia mats or country cloth or with palm branches. In the absence of a court *barri* a market *barri* of similar construction would serve, or a school with two inter-communicating classrooms, or two rooms—or one room and a veranda—of a private house or of a house in disrepair or under construction, suitably patched up with matting. One station in Kenema South was established in one room of a district council's offices while the rest of the building went about its normal business, and one in Koinadugu South had its polling room in the store room of a village shop; the polling officials sat on the veranda outside and the shop plied its everyday trade behind them. In general the polling stations for the national elections were sited in the same places as those for the local elections, with additions for those which had been uncontested on the previous occasion, and in a few cases for villages which had found it difficult, or even impossible, to get to the stations then provided. A very few polling stations provided for the local elections could not be staffed for the national elections, and their areas were merged with others. The largest number of stations was thirty-two in Kenema South, the smallest eleven in Kambia East, and there was a fairly even spread between these extremes.

Freetown was given five polling stations each in the East and West constituencies, and four in the centre. There the decision had to be taken without the benefit of previous experience. One in the West was established in the court-house of one of the minority communities, and the rest were all in schools or public halls. In most stations screens provided by the Elections Office were used to form the polling room. In the rural area of the Colony schools again generally met the case, together with a few court-houses and private houses. When the headman's house in a village in York constituency had to be ruled out at a late stage because it had recently displayed party symbols an angry crowd gathered and had to be dispersed by the police.

The electoral regulations made no stipulation as the the form of the polling room or booth, but the notes issued to returning officers required that it should have only one entrance and exit, which should be within the view of the presiding officer, and that all windows should be screened so that no one could see inside. At least one breach of this rule was observed, at Wilberforce village in the Colony, which had a polling room with separate entrance and exit, the latter not being within the sight of the presiding officer.

15. Polling and Counting the Votes

The turn-out. It is difficult to give a reliable index of participation in different constituencies. The figures for those casting valid votes differ substantially from those for total votes cast, because large blocks of votes were disallowed in some constituencies for various irregularities: for instance 4,597 out of 12,970 in Freetown East, 774 out of 6,239 in Bonthe North, about 500 out of about 5,600 in Kambia West, 1,264 out of 5,061 in Koinadugu North. It is possible to allow for these discrepancies and also for papers deliberately discarded into the box provided or improperly cast two at a time for one candidate in a two-member constituency. But there can be no figures for those who attempted to vote and then 'spoiled their papers' through ignorance by failing to put them in any box at all; or for those who presented themselves in good faith but were refused papers because something had gone wrong in the procedure for registration and identification of those registered.

Figures comparing valid votes cast with voters on the register may therefore be misleading. For what they are worth, they suggest a rough correlation between the size of the constituency and the percentage voting: subject to some exceptions the larger the constituency, the smaller the percentage voting. Apart from this, one must look for local factors to explain variations: rivalry between chiefly dynasties or between localities within a constituency tended to a high poll, as did party activity in the three Freetown constituencies. On the other hand, the 'disturbed' districts in the north of the Protectorate relapsed from high polls in the district council elections to low polls for the House of Representatives, except in one constituency, Kambia West, where there was the appearance of a chiefly counter-attack. Presumably these areas had had their fill of excitement, and felt that the issues concerning them had been settled fairly decisively for the moment. There were other areas, such as Koinadugu North, where the poll was clearly much lower than in the district council elections, presumably because the novelty of elections had worn off and the idea of a 'national' election was rather beyond the comprehension of the inhabitants of this remote area.

The highest turn-out on this basis was 58·2 per cent., the lowest 20·3 per cent. Most constituencies were in the group between 35 per cent. and 45 per cent. Considering the difficulties, such participation is certainly respectable, though not outstanding.

Identification. Almost all polling stations worked, for a time at least, under very severe pressure. As in the Protectorate district council elections, this was caused principally by the high average time taken to trace voters' names in the registers, which for the reasons already suggested had not improved much in the meantime. Some new errors had in fact appeared owing to poor clerical work and inadequate checking in some places, particularly, it seemed, where the number of polling stations had changed, necessitating a change in the order of villages on the list; and in such cases unawareness of what was happening and what they should do led some villages to present themselves at the wrong polling station. For many villages which had had unopposed returns in the district council elections the whole question of where and how to vote was a new one.

In some cases the causes of imperfections in the registers were readily apparent. Many of the rejected applicants to vote in the village of Gloucester in the Colony constituency of Mountain explained that they had submitted their applications through the same man. But the greater part of the difficulty arose from factors against which organizational efficiency was no remedy, though intensive propaganda might do, and did do, some good. Few voters (apart from a minority in the major towns) had a combination of names of which one was invariably used as the primary means of public identification, after the fashion of a European's surname; and of these few, very few indeed, could offer the polling assistant any suggestion as to how to spell it if he could not work it out for himself. This eventuality was more than probable; in Koinadugu district the clerks, who by reason of the educational backwardness of the district were almost all strangers from the Colony or the south, were often very obviously at a loss to put any spelling to the sounds made to them by voters. Moreover the knowledge that the compiler of the register had been in the same difficulty presented polling assistants and presiding officers with some nice problems, such as whether to believe that Sayu File and Sayu Kule, or Bobo and Boba, were the same persons. All over the Protectorate this difficulty was present in sufficient measure to prevent any reasonably consistent arrangement of names in alphabetical order. Moreover there could be no certainty that the name given by the voter at the polling station was that which he had given when registering, though the necessity of giving this formed the burden of most official messages to voters in preparation for the election. In one station observed in Kenema district a vain search was ended when the polling assistant looked up at the voter, recognized him as a minor traditional local dignitary and found him under another name. At various stations voters were sent aside to think out by themselves other names which they might have given. Names might be repeated in the register several times over; in one typical register page of nineteen names there were two voters called Tamba Yesse—not consecutive in the list—and one called Tamba Yesse Saliu; a Yakar I and Yakar II were at least distinguished by the numbers, but may well have been unaware of them. 'W. Kamara' and 'E. J. Francis' of Kono district were probably literates who would recognize their initials—but some initials may have been set down in despair of the possibility of spelling the name in full. 'Mr. Williams' and 'Little Joe', included in Kenema district registers, were probably adequately identified by those names in the communities in which they lived, but there were obvious dangers.

In view of the repetitiousness and lack of order it was as rash to assume that the voter who called himself—and produced his tax receipt to prove that he was called—Blango was the S. S. Blango set down in the list (in a case observed in Kenema district this was allowed after some discussion), as it was to suppose that 'James' had been the victim of personation because somebody had already voted in that name. In many cases reasonable discretion was used where time allowed, as in one Kenema polling station where the claim of

S. Kemoh Kai to be 'Kemoh Kai'—after it had been decided that not he but someone else was Momo Kemoh Kai—was allowed after some discussion between the presiding officer and candidates' polling agents, which led to a decision that the claimant should be interrogated on his knowledge of the persons registered above and below that name, on the reasonable ground that he might have registered at the same time, and to a satisfactory performance in this test. Fortunately he arrived in the unhurried afternoon.

More precise addresses would have helped. Outside Freetown the lowest division used in the lists was the town or village. Where this had only some thirty voters the problem presented by the names was not too serious; where it had over 900 it was a very different matter. In fact this remedy was not immediately available; further subdivisions did not exist, and even in Freetown Protectorate people were often very vague about their addresses—and this fact had some part in creating the distrust which clouded the election there. Probably most stations in the Protectorate tried at times during the day the roll-call method of identifying voters, which on the basis of experience of the local elections was favoured and counselled by District Commissioners. But this method was very laborious, especially if the crowd was thin or wrongly composed, and presiding officers fell back from time to time, and usually for the greater part of the hours of polling, upon the method of trying to trace voters as they offered themselves.

Congestion. There was for this reason some advantage in the presence of the massed populace in the early hours of voting, but they were often anxious to be as near the scene of action as possible, crowded into the station and round the staff, and added considerably to the atmosphere of strain. In a few places there seemed to be rather more natural discipline. At Giema (Kenema district) the village layout provided a square surrounded by a number of buildings offering shelter from the sun, while the front of the polling station itself, on the very small veranda of the village post office, offered little, and the villages waiting their turn were disposed at a reasonable distance from the point of action. But even there the pressure of work was such as to tempt the presiding officer into seeking to speed the process by tearing all ballot papers out of the book at once instead of individually as they were issued, with the technically serious, though practically unimportant, consequence that he was subsequently unable to find the right counterfoil on which to enter the register number of the voter to whom the paper was issued. In fact he entered them at random.

The duration of the period of intense pressure varied. One small polling station in Koinadugu South district reported at about 2.30 p.m. that it had not recorded a vote since 10.30 a.m.; and probably at most stations in the Protectorate, other than those providing for miners, road workers, and similar employed persons—and apparently many of these failed to vote at all—polling was virtually over by 2 p.m. or earlier. In Freetown, however, the situation was very different. Apart from the effect of the much higher proportion of employed persons arriving late in the day—though government officials and many others were released at mid-day—it was complicated by a complete mis-estimation of the number of polling stations required. The West constituency had five polling stations with an average of 2,056·7 registered voters each, the Centre four with an average of 2,864·5 each, and the East five with an average of 2,575·6. The day's experience suggested that even under reasonably favourable circumstances 1,500 was the absolute maximum for any one polling station, and in fact circumstances were far from favourable. In the atmosphere of distrust surrounding the elections in Freetown the candidates' polling agents, who in the Protectorate were peaceable and often helpful, were there generally obstructive, challenging any device which might seem to threaten their minute control of proceedings. Thus attempts at several stations to divide the register so that two polling assistants might simultaneously pass voters through the most difficult stage of the process were all challenged and frustrated by them, on the ground that they were entitled to have each voter's name called out to them to check on their duplicate copy of the register, and that with two voices calling at once they would be unable to carry out this check. Since by their vigilance there were detected several cases of what the courts were prepared to accept as personation, as well as sufficient malpractice by one candidate to secure her resignation of her seat under threat of election petition, it is hard to say with conviction that they were wrong. An attempt at one station to establish a duplicate set of ballot boxes—though congestion at this stage of voting was less generally a problem—was also frustrated by some of the agents, on the ground that they had no duplicate copies of their candidates' photographs to attach to the boxes. Polling was probably no slower than in most polling stations in the Protectorate, but it was hardly faster—reaching some four a minute for at most two or three minutes at a time, and averaging something over a hundred an hour—despite the advantage of detailed, even if not accurate, addresses.

In consequence, the Governor satisfied himself by personal observation that the polling hours of 8 a.m.–6 p.m. prescribed for the whole of the country were insufficient for Freetown, and issued an order extending them within the city to 10 p.m. This order was not published until the following day, though it was made known to polling staffs in the early afternoon, and by them to the waiting crowds. The Governor's specific authority for so acting was not apparent from the published instruments and was commonly doubted, but the action was obviously necessary at some polling stations in the East and (even more) the Central constituencies. At the end only twenty-five persons were visibly turned away from the hardest-pressed of the Central stations at 10 p.m., and it seems that all the others had cleared their floors of voters by that time. Some in fact could have closed an hour or more earlier. But had public interest been adequate to produce a poll worthy of the importance of the occasion the organization would not have stood it. As it was the stations of the West constituency dealt on average with some 1,100 voters each, and those of the Centre and East with some 1,350. In the rural area of the Colony also too few polling stations had been provided, but with the factor of distance intervening this deficiency expressed itself in another way; it was reported from York constituency that few voters from the many villages situated more than two miles from a polling station came to the polls at all. The same was probably true of other rural areas and many Protectorate constituencies; certainly this obstacle of distance contributed to the low poll of Moyamba district.

The ballot papers. Another serious cause of delay in many polling stations was the requirement that all ballot papers be validated upon issue to the voter with the official mark, a metal stamp bearing a code number differing for each station. The delay would often have been less had it not been necessary, as it was in the smaller stations, to use the same ink pad for inking the left thumbs of voters, on the theory, generally applied by British West African election regulations, that this would prevent their voting twice—a theory probably incorrect unless the ink was very carefully applied. In any case the gain to security resulting from the stamping of papers, which (as the Gold Coast accepted for its 1956 election) might be more effectively achieved by precautions in their printing which would make them impossible to forge, was made at the price of considerable inconvenience; and the attempt made by polling-station staffs (in the case of one Freetown East station apparently on the instruction of an assistant returning officer) to speed the process by omitting this formality was the cause of disallowance of nearly all the large number of voting papers rejected at the count or upon election petition. In Freetown East where the area was compact enough and party discipline strong enough to maintain a close similarity of proportion between the votes cast for any one candidate at the various stations, and in Kambia West where there was a straight fight and a large majority, the error had no material effect on the result, but it was a more serious matter in the typical Protectorate constituencies where the candidates were supported by local followings rather than by constituency-wide sections of opinion. The papers disallowed for lack of a stamp meant the loss of a seat for the candidate originally declared successful at Bonthe North, and the loss of their deposits for two candidates at Koinadugu North, though in the latter case restitution was subsequently made.

In one polling station in Kambia district all votes cast had to be rejected because the presiding officer had written the voters' registration numbers on the ballot papers, allegedly because the people insisted on it, which on the experience of other stations seems improbable. In the circumstances of the Kambia election this may well have been done deliberately to disqualify the votes, but it could have been due to the failure to understand the requirement that such numbers should be written on the counterfoils. This rule, adopted in imitation of British practice, is intended to permit identification of voters who cast ballots found upon petition to be irregular, but it could probably not conveniently be used even in Britain, and given such practices as those of the presiding officer at Giema (above, p. 246) would be quite useless for any purpose. After the election a number of politicians and senior officials expressed concern lest the practice should at some time be used for party advantage in breach of the ballot.

Voting. Some concern was expressed in Sierra Leone, as it has been expressed elsewhere, about the possibilities of irregularity offered by the method of voting by use of separate ballot boxes for the several candidates, which requires that the voter be for a time left alone in an enclosed polling room or booth, but in fact nothing serious seems to have occurred. One leading official of the S.L.P.P. was convinced after the election, probably wrongly, that the box of one of his party's candidates in a Freetown polling station had for a time been hidden under the table and the attached photograph crumpled up. He considered it essential before the next election to introduce a system whereby the symbols could be printed on the ballot papers, so that these could be marked and placed openly in the ballot box as in the British system. There was in fact one conviction in Freetown for smuggling ballot papers out of a polling station, but there was no widespread suspicion that this practice was general and no complaint about the omission from the regulations of provisions for searching suspects, such as had been included in the legislation of other West African territories. Nor was it suggested that any attempt had been made to damage the contents of ballot boxes.

The new regulations about the disposal of papers left outside the boxes worked satisfactorily. Delays often resulted from the inability of the less dexterous voters to get their papers through the slit provided in the lid of the box and the necessity of clearing the resulting jam. In one Freetown Central polling station the sound of a voter beating on a ballot box was heard as early as twenty minutes after the opening of the poll. The regulations required the presiding officer together with an agent for each candidate, to inspect the boxes every hour, but in fact the occurrence of blockages commonly necessitated much more frequent visits. The presiding officer at Giema (Kenema South) made his routine inspection of the boxes at 12.20; at 12.22, when two more voters had passed through, the policeman on duty at the door of the polling room reported that the box was jammed, and another visit was made to shake it; twenty-three voters later, at 12.34, the same happened again. On each occasion there was a hiatus of about a minute for an address by the presiding officer to the assembled crowd explaining the right procedure. Much the same happened at other stations. As far as could be observed presiding officers were always scrupulous in observance of the requirement that when inspecting the boxes they should be accompanied by such polling agents as were available.

Another problem arising from the method of voting was that presented by the voter who having got into the voting booth showed no inclination to come out. This was of general occurrence, but was particularly noticeable in some polling stations in Freetown West, where voters were possibly somewhat bewildered by the array of twelve boxes—eleven for candidates and one for discarded papers—and the gallery of photographs presented for their inspection. No procedure was provided for dealing with this situation; commonly it was remedied by the policeman or other official at the door or entrance to the voting booth looking in and counselling haste. In one or two places the power given to the presiding officer to accompany into the booth and assist persons who by reason of blindness or other physical disability were unable to cast their votes by themselves was improperly extended to accompanying the merely stupid.

The rift of Colony (or Creole) and Protectorate was continually manifested, at least in the understandable form of mutual irritation between polling staff and voters who did not speak one another's language. One harassed polling assistant in a Freetown Central station was heard to say, 'They should have interpreters for you people', and in another station in the same constituency a polling agent protested to the Elections Officer that the presiding officer had refused to seek someone to interpret for one voter.

Public order. The public conducted itself, almost without exception, with the most admirable patience. At one polling station in Freetown East voters casting their votes at about 5.30 p.m. had been in the queue for one hour and twenty-five minutes, and it seems that up to about 3 p.m. it must have taken at least twice as long in that and a number of other Freetown polling stations. Particularly in Freetown East, where there had been some confusion about the number of polling stations to be established and the streets to be allocated to them, numerous voters had first presented themselves at the wrong station and only established that fact when they came to the head of the queue. In some Protectorate areas much the same happened, with the added inconvenience that the walk to the right station was often a long one. Allocation to stations in the Protectorate was announced in terms of sections—subdivisions of the chiefdoms; this was a social unit familiar to the Mendes, but it meant little to the Temnes and some other peoples of the north, who often had little idea to which section they belonged unless they had been taught by contested district council elections. Cases of this sort were reported from Kambia district, and the Fulah headman in Koinadugu district was anxious to persuade the present writer that the register should have been drawn up by 'sections', by which, however, he meant not the geographical units so called in official terminology, but peoples or language groups. Such confusions were often not realized until the election. But such discontent as there was was limited to muttering. Police intervened in small force to form queues at two Freetown polling stations, and to suppress the troubles about the siting of the polling station at Tissana in York constituency, but these matters were soon and easily settled.

Personation. As a political missile the word 'corruption' was a word extensively used in the course of the campaign and of very comprehensive meaning; it was most commonly used to mean personation, the fear of which was very active in Creole minds. Whatever may have been the intentions of some candidates or party workers in the earlier stages of preparation for the election it seems improbable that personation took place on any very large scale. On the day after polling in Freetown thirty-seven persons were brought before the magistrates on that charge, as a result of denunciation by candidates' polling agents, and in subsequent proceedings a large number of these were convicted and sentenced to terms of six months' imprisonment. Probably there were other cases which escaped detection, but the prominence given to this theme during the campaign and the vigilance of the opposition agents on the day were probably sufficient deterrents. A particular cause of opposition complaint was the S.L.P.P.'s practice of issuing to as many of its adherents as it could reach slips of paper bearing their names and register numbers, which they commonly presented at the polling stations. In effect these were merely poll cards, but they could be, and perhaps were, applied to improper ends. In a successful election petition against one S.L.P.P. candidate, who had been declared elected in Freetown West, a witness professed to have distributed such papers to persons whose names were not on the register. His evidence was apparently accepted by the court.

In these Freetown charges of personation the suggestion was generally that the names given were those of fictitious or absent persons, and of this there can be no reliable measure. Tendered ballot papers, which might be cast after the fashion of ordinary ballot papers but which were not to be counted or to have any validity, except presumably as evidence in legal proceedings on this issue, were to be issued to those claiming to be registered voters and giving names under which someone had already voted, and these were issued in considerable numbers, 78 in Freetown East and 122 in Bombali East. But this is not a good measure of even this form of personation, since in some places they were issued irregularly, as a form of meaningless consolation to the more insistent applicants whose names could not be found in the register. Even where there did seem to be a clear case of such personation it could well have been due to faulty registration, for instance to failure to enter on the register enough persons of the same name in a particular place.

In all parts of the country a number of people who were obviously under age presented themselves to vote, and were allowed to do so, since there was no power to refuse them once registered in a duly revised register. In the atmosphere of Freetown this also was frequently imputed to a plot of the S.L.P.P. In fact there was almost certainly no organization behind it even there. In a few cases personation was involved, and even this could be in all innocence. One particularly young-looking voter at Wilberforce, on being questioned as to his age, explained that he was not voting for himself, but for an older relative; he was rejected.

Party activity. Apart from the work of polling agents the activities of the candidates and parties on polling days were largely ornamental. Though in Freetown party cars moved about briskly showing the colours and candidates' election posters and conveying party staff from one point of observation to another, they seemed to be doing little conveying of voters after the fashion familiar in elections in

Britain. Organization was probably not sufficient for any systematic hunting-out of those who had not yet voted. In Kambia West, however, Mr. Ahmed of the U.P.P. who among other activites was a transport contractor, is reported to have had at least eight lorries in action conveying voters in the neighbourhood of Kambia town, and the same may have been done elsewhere. The candidates, who alone had the right of wearing within the polling stations their emblems and colours, commonly availed themselves of this privilege, but with restraint. The present writer observed in this election nothing so spectacular as the candidate in Koidu town (Kono district) in the district council elections, who appeared in a sort of tabard consisting of a painting on cloth of two copies of his election poster with symbol and slogans. The S.L.I.M. candidates were visually most in evidence, since they not only wore party rosettes but also carried flags. One of the two National Council candidates in Freetown East created something of a stir in one of the polling stations by protesting against the production by voters of party polling slips; other candidates joined in, and the incident culminated in something of a shouting match, above which rose from time to time the words, 'It is corruption. I say so.' With the aid of three persuasive policemen peace was soon restored. Mr. Rogers-Wright in the Centre protested at anything on which the drafting of the regulations left him an opening, including the participation of the Elections Officer, since in prescribing powers the regulations overlooked the existence of that officer. Mrs. Cummings-John, the more active of the S.L.P.P. candidates in the Centre, seemed to be occupied throughout the day in seeking to persuade polling officials of the soundness of the claims of a succession of Protectorate people to vote; her party colleague, Mrs. Richards, in the West, seems, according to the evidence offered in the successful election petition against her, to have spent the day at home dispensing hospitality. Other candidates were in constant motion about the city or were churning up the red dust of the Protectorate roads from one remote polling station to another, doubtless bolstering the morale of their followers and quieting their own impatience, but achieving little else.

The count. Counting was done in the Colony rural area constituencies on the night of polling day, in Freetown on the day following polling day, and in the protectorate districts—where it was carried out at district headquarters for both constituencies in the district—up to six days after polling, according to the distances and the state of the communications involved. Nothing was prescribed in the elections regulations about the manner of counting, other than that the work should not begin until all boxes for the constituency had been gathered in, and that candidates and a counting agent appointed by each of them had a right to be present. Attendance of others was left to the discretion of the returning officer, and in Freetown Central the extreme caution of that official, combined with the suspicion and desire for self-assertion of the opposition agents, led to the early exclusion of the press; elsewhere it was admitted, and in the Protectorate counting commonly took place in the open court *barri*. Since, once out of the box, the ballot papers could not be identified as having been cast for one candidate rather than another, returning officers were instructed by circular of the Elections Officer not to open more than one box on one table at any one time. In most places, however, several counting tables were used simultaneously, and the circular, which required all boxes from any one polling station to be counted before another was started, recommended this. Here again, however, Freetown Central was different; the agents vetoed the proposal to use more than one table, with the result that counting there went on from 9 a.m. one day until 1 a.m. the following morning. In the four two-member constituencies the papers had, owing to the prohibition of plumping, to be arranged first in order of serial numbers, so that duplicates might be detected and called to the attention of the returning officer for disallowance; only after that could counting proceed.

Procedure seems in general to have followed regulations closely, though the Bonthe North election petition shows that there unstamped ballot papers had wrongly been counted. Few incidents were reported, though in Freetown Central two agents denounced the European assistant returning officer at a late hour of the night, on the ground that he had put ballot papers into his pocket. He was made to empty his pockets, but nothing was found.

The protests in Freetown about the postponement of the count until the following day were, in part at least, a reflection of a suspicion felt and expressed in many parts of the country that the ballot boxes might be tampered with. There had been widespread rumours of such happenings—both stuffing of boxes and switching of labels—after the district council elections, especially in places where the journey in with the boxes to the counting station took several days and so necessitated their retention overnight in imperfectly secure accommodation. The election regulations for the House elections required presiding officers to seal the symbol allocated to the candidate and his photograph, if any, to the ballot box as well as sealing the box itself. The notes issued for the guidance of returning officers —copied almost verbatim from a Gold Coast original—suggested that the symbol be sealed on before issue to returning officers, and the similar instructions issued to presiding officers required them to ask polling agents to initial the corner of each symbol label. In practice it does not seem that the requirement as to sealing on symbols was commonly observed—though the boxes themselves were always sealed—and observation revealed omission of the initialling also, though not its extent. A practice used by some returning officers in the local, and perhaps in the national, elections was to stick a duplicate symbol inside the box before it was sealed up at the beginning of voting.

Other methods for the security of the poll seem in general to have been adequate; the Bonthe North election petition alleged insufficient care in the custody of ballot boxes on the move, but the court was satisfied by the returning officer's explanations. Once in the town where they were to be counted ballot boxes were always kept in a locked and sealed police cell until required, and candidates' polling agents were entitled to see them lodged there and subsequently removed.

16. The Results

Uncontested seats. Four constituencies, all in the Protectorate, had unopposed returns, and of these three, the two Bo seats and Tonkolili East, had from the first been thought safe beyond all possibility of a serious contest. The other, Tonkolili West, came very near to being contested. It was one of the few seats in the Protectorate in which the central organization of the S.L.P.P. was anxious to place a man of its own, a man who could claim local origin but had been travelling abroad for the past few years. However, a well-connected local resident, possessing in a high degree the qualities thought to win elections in Sierra Leone, was determined to oppose him. The situation was somewhat complicated because the chief of Yoni chiefdom within the constituency had been deposed in February 1957, as a result of one of the inquiries, and the prospective challenger for the seat was elected regent chief in his place. Temne custom, under which the head of a deceased chief plays an essential part in the ceremonies of installation of his successor, prevented his becoming a full paramount chief while his predecessor still lived, but the wording of the election regulations did not make it clear whether as a regent chief he was eligible for election to the seat reserved for a paramount chief from his district. He explained that if so he would gladly renounce the commoner's seat to his party-sponsored rival, since as the only literate chief in the district he could not then fail to be included in the House; if, however, he was not eligible to a chief's seat he would use his full influence as a chief to procure his own election as a commoner. The general informed opinion was that regent chiefs were eligible, and the interested chief must have thought so, for he did not stand, and the party's man got his unopposed return and in due course a portfolio. On the day after the last day for nominations for the popular election, however, an amendment to the regulations ruled that regent chiefs were not eligible to enter the House as paramount chiefs.

Freetown. In Freetown the result was decisive to a degree which few even of the leading officials of the winning party seems to have expected; all six seats fell to the S.L.P.P., and of the twenty-one other candidates sixteen, including the Leader of the Opposition in the outgoing Legislative Council, lost their deposits. In fact the vote of confidence in the S.L.P.P. was neither so wholehearted nor so surprising as it seemed. The U.P.P. also had achieved something, though less than its leaders thought it could reasonably hope. The five saved deposits of unsuccessful candidates were all theirs, and they would not have lost that of their sixth candidate had the regulations allowed for the fact that in a two-member constituency 10 per cent. of the votes cast means the support of some 20 per cent. of the voters; had they had a straight fight against the S.L.P.P. they would probably have won half the seats. There seems to be little doubt that those who voted for the candidates of the three minor parties would have preferred the U.P.P. to the S.L.P.P. had they had to make the choice, and the addition of their votes to those cast for the former would have given it the two seats in the West constituency and one of those in the Centre, though the latter (which would have fallen to Mr. Rogers-Wright) would certainly have been contested by election petition. In the following October the U.P.P. won both of the seats —one in the Centre and one in the West—offered in by-elections resulting from election petitions. These were held as single-member elections and only two parties—S.L.P.P. and U.P.P.—were in the field as such.

The three minor parties together polled some 16 per cent. of the votes cast in the West, where alone they all had two candidates, and between 13 per cent. and 14 per cent. in the other constituencies. This massacre and the fall of the National Council, formerly the party of the official Opposition, can be explained by the restricted public to which they all appealed—those who thought of themselves as Creoles. Dr. Bankole-Bright's 316 votes would have sufficed to give him victory in 1951—when in fact he won with 455—but they were only a ninth of those given to the leading candidate in the constituency in 1957. Possibly many of his supporters had died; certainly he had attracted few in the interval, for many Creoles felt that by the poverty of ideas in his campaign, the recitation of old rights and claims of superiority and of phrases of heroic suggestion but uncertain meaning he had made their cause look ridiculous, and his party colleagues had done little to make good the deficiency. Mr. Rahman, one of the party's candidates in the East, greatly outshone his leader, with 726 votes—918 but for disallowances—but he owed them mainly to personal reputation and the loyalty of his coreligionists. Mr. Blyden who, standing in the Centre, followed him and greatly overtopped Dr. Bankole-Bright, with 536 votes, seemed to have stolen a substantial section of the National Council's younger generation; but some of these were too young to vote and some perhaps had been antagonized before election day. Despite his claims of support in Kono district and his announcement shortly before polling day of the establishment of a Bo branch, he never gave proof of much appeal to the Protectorate people, at home or in Freetown. Nor did the Labour party, despite Mr. Grant's demonstration in 1955 of his power to move them in industrial affairs. Mr. Grant won more votes—270 in Freetown West—than his party's leader or any other of its candidates, except for one in Waterloo constituency who seems also to have rallied a remnant of National Council support.

It seems that many who considered themselves Creoles failed to vote at all. In any case they could do nothing against the Protectorate masses, who in Freetown felt a solidarity quite lacking in their native surroundings, and of this the S.L.P.P. were the principal beneficiaries. Except for Mr. Kande Bureh, the party's candidates in the Colony were all Colony-born, but it was not in their own community that their strength lay. Mrs. Cummings-John, who headed the poll in the Centre, was far from conforming to the pattern of the Creole upper class, and apparently was generally unpopular with them; her running mate, Mr. Paul Wright, was little known. But Mrs. Cummings-John's past works and her brisk bellicosity endeared her to the new mass electorate, and in a two-member constituency she towed in Mr. Wright with a lag of only 180 votes. Probably 143 of these were accounted for by the independent candidate set up against him. Similarly in the West, the party's very able National General Secretary, Mr. H. E. B. John, a Creole intellectual in the Protectorate party who apparently did not enjoy the full confidence of either side, came in seven votes behind, in the wake of Mrs. Richards. In that constituency the Independent probably harmed the leading, rather than the second, S.L.P.P. candidate, though he may have drawn support from young Creoles who otherwise inclined towards the Opposition parties. In Freetown East Mr. Mustapha, generally accounted less popular than Mr. Kande Bureh, was nevertheless returned some 400 votes ahead of him; presumably he had added the whole or greater part of his fellow candidate's disciplined Protectorate following to his own personal following in his own community.

The strength, or potential strength, of the U.P.P. lay in the demonstration that it was not purely a Creole party in the same sense as the others of the Opposition. Apart from its wooing of anti-tax and other discontents in the Protectorate, it had some appeal for the section of Protectorate opinion in the capital which had too naïvely hoped for dramatic change to follow from the establishment of a Government of its 'own' people, for those who were convinced by the allegations of excessive corruption against most of the ministers, and for the otherwise disillusioned. The U.P.P. alone could there meet the S.L.P.P. on something like equal terms.

The two Independents standing in Freetown received the lowest numbers of votes of all: 143 in the Central constituency and 152 in the West. This was a field where the party label mattered.

The Protectorate. In most of the Protectorate the contrary was true. An S.L.P.P. candidate stood in each of the twenty-one contested constituencies; ten of them were successful—though four were unseated on election petition and one resigned for professional reasons without opposing a petition entered against him—and four members of the party were returned unopposed. U.P.P. candidates stood in six constituencies and were successful in two, both of them straight fights, as were two of the contests in which they lost. There were 6 other candidates in Kailahun East, 4 in Koinadugu North and Bonthe North, 3 in Pujehun North and Kenema North, 2 in Kailahun West and 1 each in 11 other constituencies, in 2 of which they stood against both parties. There were only 4 contested seats without independent candidates. All these were independents in that they chose their symbols from among the range made available to candidates not having a party letter of appointment. Nine of them were returned—in two cases upon election petition against the S.L.P.P. candidate who had originally been declared elected; and all were immediately received into the parliamentary group of the S.L.P.P., of which party they had always considered themselves members, as also had most of the unsuccessful independents. One of them was given junior ministerial office.

Thus it does not seem that possession of the S.L.P.P. party symbol gave a candidate any marked advantage in the Protectorate. Opponents treated it as merely one symbol among others; one who had the independent symbol of the matchet explained that he had used incidentally the argument that a palm-tree was useless without a matchet to cut the fruit. Official candidates seem to have attempted to draw from it what advantage they could by presenting it as an indication of approval by Government or by Dr. Margai, but to little purpose.

It seems that the U.P.P. candidates made more use of their party connexions in order to profit by the association of the party with resistance to chiefs and taxes. But for the most part both parties' candidates relied, like all others, on their personal and family merits. Where the details of voting at the several voting stations are available they show wide variations, with the various candidates having their centres of strength in places where they were of the local tribe, or related by birth or marriage to the local chiefly family, or linked by personal friendship to the local chief, or (occasionally) known for their trading or other business activities. For example, in Koinadugu North each of the five candidates had a majority in at least one of the twenty-one polling stations (for three of the candidates these were substantial absolute majorities) and had no votes at all in at least two. Campaigning may have had some effect on the result where there were few candidates, so that some chiefdoms were left without men of their own and presented a field for competition; certainly the candidates thought so, and in three such cases (Kenema South, Koinadugu South, and Kailahun West) the belief seemed to be proved right, in that the more energetic man won, although standing as an independent.

The successful candidate in the first of these cases had the disadvantage of being a native of the neighbouring administrative district, though he resided in his constituency and had practised there for some time as a druggist. In the second case the successful candidate was the son of the deceased chief of a since amalgamated chiefdom, and apparently retained the loyalty of his father's subjects and was of recognized status in the other chiefdoms. On the other hand he was only a village schoolmaster, and had been unsuccessful in the District Council election. His opponent, who was also the son of a man of note, although not a chief, was a District Councillor, and as secretary of the Ex-Servicemen's Association was held in the popular estimation to be equivalent to a senior civil servant, and since he had a car he was able (the schoolmaster complained) to impress the chiefs by conveying them to and from District Council meetings. The schoolmaster declared in the early days of the campaign that he would profit by his local residence to get about more than could his opponent, who lived in Freetown and had to leave much of the campaigning to his brother. He also intended to make much of the claim that he had never cut himself off from the local culture.

The Kailahun West result was similar; the successful candidate was a young man who had just returned, at the end of 1956 after some years' absence as a student in the U.S.A., but apart from his university degree he could rely on the fact that his father had been a much respected chief of a major chiefdom within his constituency. Both his opponents were in advanced middle age. One of them, the official party candidate, was over-confident and also somewhat discredited in popular talk, and the other had been employed in business outside the constituency and at the beginning of the year clearly still had little idea of how to set about campaigning. Despite these disadvantages the latter got 3,158 votes to the successful candidate's 4,165 and the official candidate's 1,654.

In Kenema North, in contrast, the official S.L.P.P. candidate won despite a late choice of constituency; for some time he had cast his eyes upon the possibilities of Kailahun West where he had previously been employed, and when he made his choice he left himself little time for canvassing. Even in this case, however, it is improbable that he owed his seat substantially to his party symbol. He was the provincial education secretary and his headquarters were in Kenema, though not within the northern constituency, and he was well provided with contacts in the area; he was brother-in-law to the Chief Minister and if elected was virtually certain of ministerial office (which he subsequently received). The strongest rival candidate was in government service and was little better placed than himself to canvass. Even so he won only on a plurality vote in a four-cornered fight, with a lead of 318 out of 7,000 votes cast.

As expected, the evidence indicated the favour of chiefs to be the greatest aid to victory in popular election. The people in Kambia East who said they would look to their chief for guidance evidently did so; the results at the polling station in the chiefdom town showed that all votes but one had been cast for the S.L.P.P. candidate.

Bo. The results in Bo town were generally expected. The official S.L.P.P. candidate, a druggist and a long-standing resident in the town, enjoyed general popularity, but he could not as a Creole overcome the gulf of communal division to defeat an opponent who possessed the advantages of local birth and office. On a surprisingly low poll of 36·7 per cent. (1,717 votes) the local man had a majority of 397. There also, as in Kailahun West, the successful candidate immediately received junior ministerial office in the Government formed by the party against which he had nominally stood.

Sherbro. The two-member Colony constituency of Sherbro was the only one in the country in which no party symbols were displayed. Two candidates had been named by the S.L.P.P., one of them being the sitting member and Minister for Commerce and Industry, Mr. A. G. Randle, and one by the National Council, which was also thought to be supported by another of the candidates. At the time of nomination the S.L.P.P. candidates were unable to produce their letters of appointment from the party, without which the returning officer was not authorized to assign to them the party symbol, and whether from consideration for them or from belief that in the intimate little island town voting would in any case be personal, all other candidates decided to take independent symbols. The results indicated that this did not misrepresent the nature of the election; although each voter had two votes no obvious pairs appeared in the score. The two successful candidates, with 679 and 498 votes respectively, were the former chairman of the Urban District Council who had suffered defeat as an S.L.P.P. candidate in the local election some five weeks before, and a man who had stood successfully on that occasion as a Ratepayers Association candidate, which was thought to indicate National Council sympathies. The former had for some time been campaigning to keep the latter out of politics on the ground that he was a stranger to the place, but within a few days of the election they were established as party colleagues within the parliamentary group of the S.L.P.P. The ex-minister received only 380 votes, largely, it seems, because he was thought to be indifferent to the interests of his constituency and possibly too old for politics; his fellow on the S.L.P.P. list was 115 votes behind him. The principal National Council contender, a leading figure of the Ratepayers' Association, came between them with 368 votes. Another who had successfully defended his seat on the Urban District Council as an S.L.P.P. received 322, and two others had under a hundred; one of these had rather individual views, and the other had in the general opinion ruined his political chances some twelve years before by writing a book denouncing the secret societies.

The rural area. The six constituencies of the Colony rural area were intermediate between the Freetown and the Protectorate patterns. The Freetown influence was shown in the general use of party labels, all except that of the S.L.I.M., and by the limited number of independents, one each in Mountain and British Koya, both unsuccessful contenders for the S.L.P.P. nomination. There were also some faint indications that (as in Freetown) the greater part of the Protectorate people were behind the S.L.P.P. This last factor was perhaps most clearly shown in the industrial suburb of Kissy, where a comparatively obscure S.L.P.P. candidate badly upset the calculations of promising U.P.P. and National Council men, and in Wilberforce, where an energetic candidate of no local standing mustered to his own surprise 265 of the 967 votes cast; he came well behind the sitting member, Mr. Wallace-Johnson, but did better than the National Council candidate who had a strong following in some of the villages. These constituences resembled the Protectorate chiefly in the importance of such village connexions, most marked in the smallest constituency, Mountain. The successful candidate there clearly owed his success less to his U.P.P. symbol than to the fact that he lived and worked, in the influential capacity of local schoolmaster, in the largest of the villages; he lost a considerable number of votes to another schoolmaster from the same village who worked in Freetown. Another resident candidate, but from a much smaller village, came second, and one who had the dual disadvantage of a small village and Freetown business preoccupations came at the foot of the poll.

Members elected. By professions the successful candidates were a fairly representative sample of the candidates as a whole. Of 18 Colony and 13 Protectorate candidates who may roughly be described as traders, merchants, contractors or business men 6 and 4 respectively were successful. In the category of retired and independent persons and farmers the Colony produced 15 candidates and the Protectorate 14, of whom 1 and 5 respectively were returned—1 of the latter only on election petition. Four lawyers stood in Freetown, all unsuccessfully, and 5 in the Protectorate, of whom 4 were elected. Three medical practitioners, none practising, stood; 1, in Freetown, was defeated, the others in the Protectorate, were elected, 1 unopposed. A druggist standing in Freetown and another in Bo town were unsuccessful, but of 5 standing in the Protectorate 2 were elected, and 1 successfully petitioned for the annulment of the election in his constituency. Two practising clergymen stood in the Colony constituency of Sherbro, and 3 in the Protectorate; none was properly returned, though one achieved a seat in the House and ministerial office until unseated on petition. Mr. Fitzjohn, the clergyman employed at Fourah Bay College, was elected for Moyamba North in the Protectorate, though he resigned his seat at the beginning of November while an election petition against him was pending. Seven teachers stood in the Colony, of whom 5 were elected—1 of them being subsequently unseated on election petition and 1 resigning under the same threat—and 5 stood in the Protectorate, of whom 1 was elected and 1 sat and spoke in the House until dislodged by election petition. One of the 2 provincial education secretaries and 1 of the 6 local government officers who stood in the Protectorate were elected.

Mr. Stevens, the former trade union secretary and minister of the outgoing government was returned, but was not reappointed to ministerial office and was subsequently unseated for corrupt practices. A clerk of a shipping firm standing in the Colony was successful.

Two women who stood in Freetown were both returned, but soon eliminated from the House (they were the two teachers just mentioned). Two who stood in the Protectorate were unsuccessful, though a woman paramount chief was returned to the House in the indirect chiefly elections.

17. *The Sequel*

The declaration of the result in the last constituency a week after polling by no means ended the contest, which continued into November 1957, in the form of the hearing of election petitions and other legal proceedings. The first step, however, consisted of disruption in both the parties represented in the new House, not unexpected in either case.

In the S.L.P.P. the two sides of the division were represented by the Margai brothers. The elder brother, who had been Chief Minister, attracted those who shared in some measure his extreme caution, apparently also some of the more ambitious, hoping perhaps for an early vacation of the leadership by retirement, and above all the solid numbers of the northern peoples, the basis of the party's strength in Freetown East. The considerably younger brother who had been Minister for Education and Local Government, a much more forceful, if rather erratic, character, seemed to rally the youthful enthusiasts for more positive and conspicuous courses of action. A meeting of the parliamentary group on 19 May, intended to clarify the issue, in part confused it, since apparently the younger brother was elected to the leadership and then, under pressure from the northerners, stood down in favour of his senior and took the new office of Deputy Leader. Subsequently he refused to serve in a ministry in which he was offered only a less important post than before and his followers nothing. Public meetings by both factions followed, with demonstrations of confidence and statements to the press. A conciliation committee of eminent party members was reported on 4 July to have achieved a settlement. The followers of the younger Margai remained out of ministerial office, though some of his supporters had been among the four who were offered and accepted newly created junior ministerial posts. It was understood that portfolios would be offered to the reconciled faction as they became available.

Meanwhile, on 28 May, the U.P.P. expelled one of its four

members in the House, Mr. Wallace-Johnson, who on the basis of seniority of membership of the legislature and prominence in the party had been thought certain to succeed to the leadership of the Opposition. In the event Mr. Ahmed was appointed leader, though with specific reservation of the post to the party leader, Mr. Rogers-Wright, if he should ever be elected to the House, as in October he was, at the by-election in Port Loko East, after removal of the disqualification upon him.

Eight election petitions were entered, all against members who had stood as official S.L.P.P. candidates, two of them in Freetown and six in the Protectorate. One, concerning the result in Moyamba South, was withdrawn; one, concerning Moyamba North, was unopposed by the candidate declared returned who had decided to resign his seat, and no evidence was offered. That for Freetown Central was similarly withdrawn upon the resignation of the member protested against and on payment of costs by her. The other five were all successful.

In Bonthe North unstamped ballot papers were found to have been counted in favour of the member returned, in sufficient quantity to affect the result, and in Bombali East the candidate declared elected was found both to be disqualified, in that his resignation of his post on the staff of a government training college had not taken effect by nomination day, and to be improperly nominated, since one of his nominators was not on the local register of electors. These two seats passed to the petitioners, runners-up in the polls, in the former case very close, in the latter very distant. In Kono South and Port Loko East corrupt practice and undue influence by the Rev. P. L. Dunbar and illegal practices by Mr. S. P. Stevens were found proved, and in accordance with the regulations the whole elections in those constituencies were voided. Almost certainly these men were not alone in resorting to practices which were not in accordance with the regulations—though few perhaps went as far as Mr. Dunbar, or a chief supporting him, in having an agent of the rival candidate kept in chains for several days and beaten. It seems, however, probable that these were extreme cases, and proceeded from a common cause; the sitting member, who felt that politics still had much to offer him, had become aware during the course of the campaign that the tide was running strongly against him in his constituency and that once out he could probably never hope to get back. Mr. Stevens might perhaps legitimately have complained that had there been a legal definition of election expenses, and one which took account of the necessity, in the circumstances of the society, for any candidate to make limited gifts to chiefs and others, he would have kept his seat. The first member elected for Freetown West was found guilty of treating, though undue influence which had been alleged was not proved, and the court found no evidence that unqualified persons had in fact voted. The election was voided in so far as concerned the candidate objected to. The other candidate elected in the constituency kept his seat, as did the second member in Freetown Central, though it might well be claimed that they had innocently profited by whatever irregularities occurred.

18. *Political Attitudes*

Candidates in the Protectorate, the Colony rural area, and Sherbro mostly admitted frankly to an interest in the material rewards to be derived from membership of the House and the possibility of office. It could hardly have been otherwise; they were largely retired persons or farmers or traders in a very small way of business, and observation of the previous legislature suggested that it was possible to do reasonably well in politics, besides acquiring the style Honourable. Experience had not given such service the immaterial prestige value which it acquires in time in most societies, or taught the seekers of office to dissemble motives which politicians in all countries seem to feel. Even in traditional chiefly office the material reward had latterly been accepted as an important attraction and as a legitimate motive resented only when it led to gross extortion. Even local councils were new and men had no means of being sure that they would like such service; but there did seem to be a general feeling that it would be rather fun, and this appreciably reinforced the financial motive. The most ambitious seem also to have had visions of a statue on the Freetown equivalent of the Accra Freedom Arch. Probably most candidates genuinely considered that they could give as good service to their people as anyone else, even if they were not quite sure what form of service they might find themselves called upon to give.

In Freetown, and among the lawyers and the few other men of the city who sought seats elsewhere, there was naturally greater sophistication in speech and probably in thought. Politics and entry by election were more familiar: in the middle-class English world of the Creole it had long been desirable to gain this sort of prestige even at the cost of personal inconvenience, and the possibility that honourable office might in some intangible way further a professional career was familiar. On the whole to be thought to be in politics for the money seemed to be a disadvantage in Freetown. This was not so in the Protectorate, where literates were at a premium, and the price would not be paid locally.

Popular attitudes to the process of election were hard to assess by inspection, and few could put them into words. Polling days were colourful, closely packed, exciting affairs. As ritual gestures of social solidarity they were more impressive and very probably more satisfying than the solitary affairs held in nearly empty schoolrooms in Britain. Probably also in many places the campaign it its latter stages was as exciting as in Britain, though it lacked the build-up in the press which seems to make some impression on even the least literate Britons. For those citizens, noticeable at almost every polling station, who having had their names traced in the register, and sometimes having received their ballot papers, sought to make off, this fact of participation was presumably enough, and possibly many who duly carried through the whole ritual thought just as little about its possible effect on the fate of some politician. But it seemed that most realized that much. The grounds on which they thought it proper to form a preference as between candidates were probably indicated by the arguments used in the campaign. The voter sought the local man, even if in some cases this local status had been overlaid by years at the Freetown bar and needed to be demonstrated by the wearing of a Protectorate gown and assiduous wooing of the chiefs, the man with chiefly connexions (for the chiefs, the only form of leaders known to the people, provided in their minds the best available model for the new type of 'big man'), the man whose actions had shown solicitude for the people, and concern for his own people in preference to other tribes, the man who knew how to get favours from the administration. It was in general an election of delegates, without precise instructions, since there was no precise knowledge of the work to be done, but with a mandate to speak for their peoples, to see, and to report back. In Port Loko West and Kambia West there was some trace of a more general issue—loyalty to chiefs or freedom from excessive exactions. In Freetown, and to some extent elsewhere in the Colony (but not in Sherbro where the whole matter was as personal, or in Mountain where it was as locally sectional as anywhere), there was an issue, that of Creole supremacy, which was a matter of strong feeling, though it had in fact been settled long before by the unplanned processes of population growth and movement. Only there, perhaps, was there any general sense that the composition of the Government—of the Governor's Executive Council—was at stake or was particularly important.

It is pointless to inquire whether the coming of nation-wide popular elections to Sierra Leone is a beneficial development, whether the utility which it produces justifies the almost unassessable cost of producing ballot boxes, ballot papers, symbols, posters and leaflets, official and unofficial, diverting transport from its normal use, diverting administrative and departmental officers, teachers, missionaries, and lawyers from the practice of their usual skills to unfamiliar tasks for periods from a day to several months. Senior officials seemed to agree that they could have made better use of the resources, but they would perhaps have found it difficult to agree with one another about what they preferred. District Commissioners' clerks expressed themselves forcibly on the typing of registers, assembly of materials, and the more tedious aspects of election-making generally. Chiefs and other, less interested, rural inhabitants professed uneasiness about a foreign system based on contest rather than on what they represented as the characteristically African way of compromise; a contest which gives one man the prize of office and leaves the other to bear the cost of his own campaign, and even sometimes of his lost deposit, instead of offering him reasonable compensation, which gives victory to unpopular men on bare plurality votes without a chance for the community to give the matter a second thought, which encourages the un-African vice of personal ambition by enabling all to put themselves forward unasked and to agitate through the villages without seeking the leave of the chiefs. The more extreme Creoles reiterated that the process could mean nothing to illiterates, that the day for a wide suffrage, though coming, had not come yet. Yet in no country perhaps is the minority which follows the ways of the outside world happy without some form of election to office by a wide electorate; however limited the powers of the body which elections produce, they are an essential badge of the nation's political maturity, and this minority can almost always muster public support for its demands. In the British colonies, moreover, imperially appointed officials know that they must shortly surrender the right of final decision on the country's affairs, and they would find it hard to make the surrender into any hands other than those which they can regard as possessing by British standards a legitimate mandate. The elections were necessary; they could have been postponed, but hardly for long; the first attempt, if delayed, would probably not have gone any more easily.

On the whole the attempt was not unsuccessful. The proportion of election petitions to contests was certainly higher than in other comparable territories. This may make it more difficult for simple voters to understand the conventions by which the game is played, and may worry a people whose national vice seems to be a propensity constantly to compare themselves unfavourably to others. But it was perhaps due rather to the greater sharpness of the politicians in employing the means of advancement given to them by the law than to greater dishonesty on the part of candidates or greater incompetence on the part of polling staffs; certainly in all cases those likely to gain by the courts' decisions were among the most sophisticated of the country's politicians. In the circumstances the election could not have been better, and it probably passes most of the tests of the excellence of such a device which it is reasonable to set. It has produced a legislature from which could be formed a Government which most people are likely to accept as having a sufficient command on their loyalties, and if they do not feel themselves made fully responsible by their participation in the election for that Government's acts and omissions they may well come to do so later. It produced an official opposition of four, raised by resultant by-elections to seven, plus at least one adherent for most purposes, perhaps too few to keep the Government in the state of uneasiness which best conduces to the liberty of the citizens, but on the whole responsible. It has familiarized the people with procedures for use on future occasions. It has done this without more violence than a few stones thrown and an agent or two beaten.

APPENDIX

Candidates and Results

In the following account the poll shown is the number of valid votes counted expressed as a percentage of the number of names on the register of voters, the latter multiplied by two in the case of the four constituencies where the voter had two votes. Imperfections of the register and rejection of ballots make this a poor index of public interest in the election, but it is the only basis of comparison for which figures have been available for all constituencies. In Freetown East, Koinadugu North, and Bonthe North, where the number of ballots disallowed is known in detail and is significant, an account including them is given in italic in the inner column. Occupations shown are as ascertained by inquiry, except in a few cases where for lack of other information the occupation shown on the nomination paper is given. Names of candidates elected are printed in black type. Names of candidates who forfeited their deposits are marked with an asterisk.

COLONY TWO-MEMBER CONSTITUENCIES

FREETOWN EAST, polled 3.v.57

M. S. Mustapha	S.L.P.P.	Minister of Works and transport, and trader (family business).	*4,385*	2,934

Kande Bureh	S.L.P.P.	Headman of Temnes in Freetown.	*3,918*	2,585
S. H. Robbin-Coker	U.P.P.	City Councillor and druggist.	*1,720*	942
*Muktar Kallay	U.P.P.	Trader.	*1,172*	675
*A. F. Rahman	N.C.	City Councillor and retired civil servant.	*918*	726
*Metcalfe A. Cole	N.C.	City Councillor (no occupation).	*540*	344
*K. E. E. Omotayo During	S.L.I.M.	Lawyer.	*317*	167

VOTES COUNTED	. . . .	*12,970*	8,373
Possible votes .	. . . .	12,878 × 2	
POLL	. . . .	*50·4%*	32·5%

FREETOWN CENTRAL, polled 3.v.57

Constance A. Cummings-John	S.L.P.P.	City Councillor (nominated) and teacher (private school).	2,823

(resigned the seat while an election petition against her was under consideration)

P. W. H. Wright	S.L.P.P.	Company secretary.	2,642
C. B. Rogers-Wright	U.P.P.	Lawyer, leader U.P.P.	2,048
J. Nelson-Williams	U.P.P.	National Secretary-General (full-time) of U.P.P.	1,550
*E. W. A. Blyden	S.L.I.M.	No occupation, leader S.L.I.M.	536
*H. C. Bankole-Bright	N.C.	Leader of the Opposition in outgoing Legislative Council and of N.C., retired medical practitioner.	316
*A. Alhadi	N.C.	No occupation, former master of the Supreme Court.	300
*R. M. Beoku-Betts	Lab.	Lawyer, leader Labour Party.	236
*A. B. Mansaray	Ind.	Shop-keeper.	143

VOTES COUNTED	. . . .	10,594
Possible votes .	. . . .	11,458 × 2
POLL	. . . .	46·2%

FREETOWN WEST, polled 3.v.57

Patience I. A. Richards	S.L.P.P.	Teacher.	1,903

(unseated on petition for corrupt practices)

H. E. B. John	S.L.P.P.	National General Secretary of S.L.P.P. and schoolmaster (Mission Grammar School).	1,896
J. N. A. Jones	U.P.P.	Retired civil servant.	1,735
J. Barthes Wilson	U.P.P.	Accountant.	1,666
*C. M. A. Thompson	N.C.	Member of outgoing Legislative Council and merchant (produce, &c.).	345

*C. M. Grant	Lab.	General Secretary of a trade union; Joint National Secretary of Labour Party.	270
*S. E. Balogun Palmer	S.L.I.M.	Alderman of City Council and druggist.	267
*E. R. G. Davies	N.C.	Alderman of City Council and merchant.	196
*W. B. Sawyerr	Lab.	Journalist (main occupation unknown), Joint National Secretary of Labour Party.	170
*D. Juxon Smith	S.L.I.M.	Transport contractor, ex-member Labour Party National Executive.	156
*B. Macaulay	Ind.	Lawyer.	152

VOTES COUNTED 8,756
Possible votes . . . . 10,283 × 2
POLL . . . . 42·8%

SHERBRO, polled 3.v.57

W. A. Jackson	Ind.	Latterly President of Urban District Council (defeated at recent election), produce merchant and launch-owner.	679
J. Baimba	Ind.	Newly elected Urban District councillor, produce merchant.	498
A. G. Randle (adopted by S.L.P.P.)	Ind.	Minister of Trade and Commerce, baker and shopkeeper.	380
C. A. B. Kenny (adopted by N.C.)	Ind.	Urban District Councillor, General Secretary of Local Ratepayers' Association, secretary N.C. branch, merchant.	368
O. B. Cummings-Spaine	Ind.	Urban District Councillor, retired civil servant, trader.	322
*M. E. S. Gbundema (adopted by S.L.P.P.)	Ind.	Clergyman (E.U.B.) in Moyamba district.	265
*M. Gorvie	Ind.	Clergyman (American Baptist, formerly E.U.B.), author.	88
*H. B. Williams	Ind.	Retired schoolmaster.	71

VOTES COUNTED 2,671
Possible votes . . . . 3,642 × 2
POLL . . . . 36·6%

COLONY ONE-MEMBER CONSTITUENCIES (RURAL AREA)

BRITISH KOYA, polled 3.v.57

| **R. G. O. King** | S.L.P.P. | President, Rural Area Council (3rd-tier L.A.), Teacher, resigned from Labour Party, August 1956. | 782 |

| S. C. Bull | Ind. | Retired civil servant. | 233 |
| A. E. Johnson-Wright | U.P.P. | Farmer (pig breeder). | 123 |

VOTES COUNTED	. . . .	1,138
Possible votes .	. . . .	3,301
POLL .	. . . .	34·5%

KISSY, polled 3.v.57

T. S. Johnson	S.L.P.P.	Retired railway mechanic.	430
N. G. J. Ballanta	N.C.	Music teacher.	296
G. E. A. Forster-Jones	U.P.P.	Recently retired railway official.	244
*C. S. Harding	Labour	National Vice-President of Labour Party, former trade union official, farmer.	26

VOTES COUNTED	. . . .	996
Possible votes .	. . . .	3,262
POLL .	. . . .	30·5%

MOUNTAIN, polled 3.v.57

G. D. Dickson-Thomas	U.P.P.	Teacher at school in Regent village.	216
H. E. During	Ind.	Retired senior commercial employee (of Leicester village).	119
O. P. A. Macaulay	S.L.P.P.	Schoolmaster (mission grammar school, Freetown, from Regent village).	111
E. J. E. Ashwoode	N.C.	Freetown City Councillor, baker in Freetown, retired police inspector (from Gloucester village).	77

VOTES COUNTED	. . . .	523
Possible votes .	. . . .	898
POLL .	. . . .	58·2%

WATERLOO, polled 3.v.57

J. C. O. Crowther	S.L.P.P.	Member of Legislative Council for Waterloo and British Koya (elected 1951 as N.C.), trader.	584
W. A. K. Williams (also adopted by N.C.)	Lab.	Retired civil servant.	355
J. A. Cole	Ind.	Druggist.	163
*C. S. B. Terry	U.P.P.	Building contractor.	54

VOTES COUNTED	. . . .	1,156
Possible votes	. . . .	3,473
POLL	. . . .	33·3%

WILBERFORCE, polled 3.v.57

I. T. A. Wallace-Johnson	U.P.P.	Member of Legislative Council for Wilberforce and York (elected 1951 as N.C.), merchant (rice, &c.), lorry-owner, trade union organizer, journalist (paper in abeyance).	469
J. Galba-Bright	S.L.P.P.	Auctioneer, merchant, journalist (British press) (resident in Freetown).	265
J. C. Dougan	N.C.	Lawyer's chief clerk (in Freetown, resident in Wilberforce).	233

VOTES COUNTED 967
Possible votes 2,128
POLL . . . . 45·4%

YORK, polled 3.v.57

G. K. Campbell	U.P.P.	Senior clerk of shipping company.	279
J. E. Hanciles	S.L.P.P.	Retired civil servant.	162
J. Akinola Wright	N.C.	Retired civil servant.	149
S. A. Garber	Lab.	Farmer, former carpenter, teacher, trade union worker.	71

VOTES COUNTED 661
Possible votes 2,194
POLL . . . . 30·1%

PROTECTORATE URBAN CONSTITUENCY
(ONE-MEMBER)

BO TOWN, polled 5.v.57

M. J. Kamanda-Bongay	Ind.	Chairman of the Town Council, and trader.	1,057
P. J. Williams	S.L.P.P.	National Vice-President S.L.P.P., town councillor, druggist.	660

VOTES COUNTED 1,717
Possible votes 4,681
POLL . . . . 36·7%

PROTECTORATE DISTRICT CONSTITUENCIES
(ONE-MEMBER)

NORTHERN PROVINCE

BOMBALI EAST, polled 8.v.57

S. F. Koroma	S.L.P.P.	District councillor, teacher (Government training college).	2,225
		(held disqualified upon petition)	

| H. I. Kamara | Ind. | Retired from civil service and from business, failed candidate for chiefly office. | 1,117 |
| S. M. Koroma | U.P.P. | Farmer. | 854 |

VOTES COUNTED	. . . .		4,196
Possible votes .	. . . .		18,855
POLL	. . . .		22·3%

BOMBALI WEST, polled 3.v.57

| Y. D. Sesay | S.L.P.P. | Newly retired vice-principal, Bo Government grammar school, farmer, intending candidate for chiefly office. | 2,279 |
| H. A. Bangura | Ind. | District Councillor, former trader and government clerk, farmer. | 1,545 |

VOTES COUNTED	. . . .		3,824
Possible votes .	. . . . :		13,010
POLL	. . . .		29·4%

KAMBIA EAST, polled 8.v.57

| I. B. Taylor-Kamara | S.L.P.P. | District Councillor (for ward in west half of district where he was born), lawyer. | 3,997 |
| H. Kai | Ind. | District Councillor (for ward in west half of district, newly retired chiefdom clerk in west half of district), trader. | 1,090 |

VOTES COUNTED	. . . .		5,087
Possible votes .	. . . .		10,246
POLL	. . . .		49·6%

KAMBIA WEST, polled 3.v.57

| Mahmoud Ahmed | U.P.P. | Business man (family transport, contracting, and furniture business in Freetown), active U.P.P. worker in Freetown and the north (mainly Port Loko district). | 3,709 |
| A. R. T. Bangura (recently Bai Farima Tass II) | S.L.P.P. | Recently resigned paramount chief in Kambia, Minister without Portfolio and Deputy Leader of government business in Legislative Council, farmer. | 1,396 |

VOTES COUNTED	. . . .		5,105
Possible votes .	. . . .		12,592
POLL	. . . .		40·5%

KOINADUGU NORTH, polled 3.v.57

A. Kande	Ind.	Unsuccessful candidate and co-opted member of District Council, trader. Of Mandingo people, supported by Yalunkas.	*1,671*	1,502
A. S. Mansaray	Ind.	District Councillor Koinadugu, son of a paramount chief in constituency, assistant clerk Makeni District Council. Of Limba people.	*1,313*	1,001
T. F. Kaba	Ind.	Former District Councillor, trader. Of Mandingo people.	*747*	722
*L. Kamara	S.L.P.P.	Member of Legislative Council for Koinadugu district, trader. Of the Temne people.	*656*	329
*S. B. Mansaray	Ind.	District Councillor, central native administration clerk. Of the Limba people.	*674*	243

VOTES COUNTED	*5,061*	3,797
Possible votes		12,620
POLL	40·1%	30·1%

KOINADUGU SOUTH, polled 13.v.57

S. B. Marah	Ind.	Head teacher, village school (District Council), unsuccessful candidate for District Council. Of the Kuranko people.	2,527
A. B. Magba Kamara	S.L.P.P.	District Councillor, General Secretary of Ex-Servicemen's Association (in Freetown). Of Temne people.	2,425

VOTES COUNTED	4,952
Possible votes	13,737
POLL	36·0%

PORT LOKO EAST, polled 3.v.57 (*election voided for illegal practices*)

S. P. Stevens	S.L.P.P.	Minister of Lands, Mines, and Labour, elected to Legislative Council by Protectorate Assembly, former General Secretary of Mineworkers' Union.	2,381

| B. Tejan-Sie | Ind. | National Vice-President of S.L.P.P. until publication of party list of candidates, lawyer. | 2,181 |
| S. D. Koroma | U.P.P. | Retired, U.P.P. organizer. | 1,357 |

VOTES COUNTED	.	.	.	.	.	.	.	.	5,919
Possible votes	.	.	.	.	.	.	.	.	29,181
POLL	.	.	.	.	.	.	.	.	20·3%

PORT LOKO WEST, polled 3.v.57

| **A. B. Kamara** | U.P.P. | Farmer, former transport driver, letter-writer to 'strikers' in troubles of 1955–6, frequent speaker for U.P.P. in Port Loko and Freetown. | 3,022 |
| A. Wurie | S.L.P.P. | Provincial Education Secretary. | 2,406 |

VOTES COUNTED	.	.	.	.	.	.	.	.	5,428
Possible votes	.	.	.	.	.	.	.	.	25,064
POLL	.	.	.	.	.	.	.	.	21·7%

TONKOLILI EAST, unopposed return

| **H. A. Conteh** | S.L.P.P. | President of District Council (elected councillor unopposed) trader, son of a paramount chief. |

TONKOLILI WEST, unopposed return

| **J. A. Karefa-Smart** | S.L.P.P. | Official of international organizations (World Council of Churches and formerly W.H.O.), medical practitioner, early active member of S.L.P.P. |

SOUTH-WESTERN PROVINCE

BO NORTH, unopposed return

| **S. T. Navo** | S.L.P.P. | Lawyer, a central officer of the S.L.P.P. |

BO SOUTH, unopposed return

| **A. J. Demby** | S.L.P.P. | Retired civil servant, part-owner of hotel in Bo. Section chief, member of local executive of S.L.P.P. |

BONTHE NORTH, polled 3.5.57

| **C. F. Massally** | Ind. | District Councillor, 2,308 druggist, brother to member for Pujehun South. | 2,285 |

| S. B. Goba | S.L.P.P. | Chairman District Council, chiefdom speaker (traditional office). | 2,566 | 1,815 |

(originally declared elected, unseated on petition).

*A. M. Tucker	Ind.	District Councillor (returned unopposed), trader in out-lying town.	567	567
*Catherine T. Williams	Ind.	Unsuccessful candidate in district council election (supported by U.P.P.), trader in Bo.	445	445
*J. T. Harvey	Ind.	Clergyman (U.B.A.) serving in Bonthe town (outside district and constituency).	353	353

VOTES COUNTED	. . . .	6,239	5,465
Possible votes .	. . . .		10,003
POLL	. . . .	62·4%	54·6%

BONTHE SOUTH, polled 3.v.57

| M. A. S. Margai | S.L.P.P. | Chief Minister, Leader, and a founder of S.L.P.P., member of Legislative Council for Bonthe district, retired government medical officer (served widely in Protectorate). From Moyamba district. | 3,062 |
| T. N. Chalobah | Ind. | Unsuccessful candidate for re-election, subsequently co-opted, to District Council, teacher (E.U.B. mission) formerly in Bonthe, but latterly posted away. | 597 |

(The second candidate had expressed the wish to withdraw but was out of time.)

VOTES COUNTED	. . . .	3,659
Possible votes .	. . . .	10,792
POLL	. . . .	33·9%

MOYAMBA NORTH, polled 3.v.57

| W. H. Fitzjohn | S.L.P.P. | Member of Legislative Council for Moyamba district, District Councillor, teacher-training lecturer of Fourah Bay College, clergyman (E.U.B.). Half-Creole, born in district. | 4,453 |

(resigned the seat while an election petition against him was under consideration.)

| Ellen C. A. Caulker-Caulker | U.P.P. | Teacher in coastal town in constituency, wife of U.P.P. organizer for district, daughter of a paramount chief. | 1,740 |

VOTES COUNTED 6,193
Possible votes 24,586
POLL . . . . 25·2%

MOYAMBA SOUTH, polled 3.v.57

| **A. M. Margai** | S.L.P.P. | Minister of Local Government, Education and Welfare, member of Legislative Council elected by the Protectorate Assembly, lawyer, brother to the Chief Minister, native of the constituency. | 7,192 |
| *T. M. B. Williams | U.P.P. | Recently retired teacher (E.U.B. mission) in other half of district, unsuccessful candidate for chiefly office, U.P.P. propaganda secretary for district. | 252 |

VOTES COUNTED 7,444
Possible votes 28,008
POLL . . . . 26·6%

PUJEHUN NORTH, polled 3.v.57

A. B. M. Jah	S.L.P.P.	A clerk on staff of Moyamba District Council, former central native administration clerk in Pujehun and, subsequently, Moyamba districts. Of ruling house of a chiefdom in constituency.	2,365
M. J. Kuyateh	Ind.	District Councillor (co-opted after being asked by friends not to stand for election), trader, pensioner from Court Messenger Force (interpreter), member of tribal authority, related by marriage to chiefly family.	1,391
D. Caulker	Ind.	District Councillor, druggist, from Moyamba district, friend of paramount chief in part of constituency where he worked.	1,122
*J. M. Bockari	Ind.	District Councillor, Assistant Headmaster of primary school (R.C. mission).	254

VOTES COUNTED 5,132
Possible votes 11,206
POLL . . . . 45·8%

PUJEHUN SOUTH, polled 3.v.57

| A. J. Massally | S.L.P.P. | President of District Council, lawyer, native of constituency, brother to member for Bonthe North. | 2,773 |
| M. Kpaka | Ind. | Farmer, former government clerk, member of ruling family of a chiefdom in district. | 2,685 |

VOTES COUNTED	. . . .	5,458
Possible votes .	. . :	10,319
POLL	. . . .	52·9%

SOUTH-EASTERN PROVINCE

KAILAHUN EAST, polled 8.v.57

T. Ngobeh	Ind.	District Councillor (co-opted after defeat at election), trader, member of current ruling family in central chiefdom of district.	4,453
M. Keili	Ind.	District Councillor (returned unopposed), clergyman (Anglican), serving, and influential in isolated part of constituency.	2,125
F. E. Allen	Ind.	Unsuccessful candidate for District Council (against member of own family), Bo district council health inspector, member of ruling family in a major chiefdom in constituency.	1,594
A. K. Banya	S.L.P.P.	Unsuccessful candidate for District Council, druggist, member of rival 'ruling family' in central chiefdom of district, nephew of a town chief.	1,538
*K. Tongi	Ind.	Deposed chief of one of minor chiefdoms in constituency, building contractor in Freetown.	1,296
*B. Lahun	Ind.	District Councillor, newly retired central native administration clerk.	1,149
*A. K. Lamin	Ind.	District Councillor (defeated T. Ngobeh in election), shopkeeper and produce buyer. Of stranger (Mandingo) stock.	1,140

VOTES COUNTED	. . . .	13,295
Possible votes .	. . . .	22,994
POLL	. . . .	57·8%

KAILAHUN WEST, polled 3.v.57

M. Kallon	Ind.	Farmer, newly returned from university studies in U.S.A., son of deceased paramount chief of major chiefdom in constituency.	4,165
C. L. Samba	Ind.	District Councillor for ward in constituency, shop manager for trading firm in other half of district.	3,158
J. C. Barnett	S.L.P.P.	District Councillor, farmer, pensioned former agent of trading firm.	1,654

VOTES COUNTED 8,977
Possible votes 18,933
POLL . . . . 47·4%

KENEMA NORTH, polled 3.v.57

D. L. Sumner	S.L.P.P.	Provincial Education Secretary, one of founders of S.L.P.P., brother-in-law to Chief Minister and Minister of Education. From Kailahun district.	2,458
E. B. Gbassa	Ind.	Government agricultural instructor (resigned upon nomination), of chiefly family of a major chiefdom in constituency.	2,140
A. L. Baio	Ind.	District Council agricultural overseer. Of chiefly family of somewhat smaller chiefdom in constituency.	1,502
A. G. Lappia	Ind.	Local education authority supervising teacher. Of same family and chiefdom as Mr. Baio.	907

VOTES COUNTED 7,007
Possible votes 25,497
POLL . . . . 27·5%

KENEMA SOUTH, polled 8.v.57

A. H. Demby	Ind.	District Councillor, druggist, brother of member for Bo South (from which district he comes).	7,967
J. K. Taylor	S.L.P.P.	District Councillor. Local education authority supervising teacher, related to a paramount chief in constituency.	6,322

VOTES COUNTED 14,289
Possible votes 25,819
POLL . . . . 55·3%

KONO NORTH, polled 3.v.57

T. S. Mbriwa	Ind.	District Councillor for ward in other half of district (where he is brother, but also former rival, of chief), and president until January 1957, druggist, formerly member of U.P.P., leader of Kono Progressive Movement.	2,977
A. Kai	S.L.P.P.	District Councillor for ward in constituency, central native administration clerk.	2,572

VOTES COUNTED	5,549
Possible votes	18,047
POLL	30·7%

KONO SOUTH, polled 8.v.57 (*election voided for corrupt practices and undue influence*)

P. L. Dunbar	S.L.P.P.	Member of Legislative Council for Kono district, District Councillor for ward in constituency, clergyman (E.U.B.), of humble birth, but related by marriage to chiefly family in constituency, officer of Sierra Leone National Association (chiefs' pressure group), spokesman for local interests in 1955 diamond-mining concession revision.	3,105
A. A. Mani	Ind.	District Councillor for ward in other half of district (where his father is paramount chief), active in Kono Progressive Movement.	3,061

VOTES COUNTED	6,166
Possible votes	16,754
POLL	36·8%

ACKNOWLEDGEMENTS

My thanks are due to the Colonial Social Science Research Council and Manchester University for financing my observation of the events here described; to the Government of Sierra Leone for sanctioning and facilitating the work; to the Principal and staff of Fourah Bay College for their generosity in the provision of accommodation, care, and counsel; to officers of the Civil Service of Sierra Leone, candidates and prospective candidates for election and their party workers and supporters for their courteous acceptance of the addition to the burdens of their several forms of election campaign; to the United Africa Company at all levels of its organization and to a wide circle of members of the press, the commercial community, and other private citizens for information and for much kindness. To mention only two names to stand for many, I must thank individually the Elections Officer, Mr. A. G. Simpson, and the Director of Information Services, Mr. B. C. Freestone. They, with their assistants, had even more to endure at my hands than most, and did so with imperturbable urbanity.

VI

SENEGAL: THE ELECTIONS TO THE TERRITORIAL ASSEMBLY, MARCH 1957

1. *The Social and Economic Background*

SENEGAL, one of the eight territories which together make up French West Africa, is a country about the size of England and Scotland but with a total population of only 2¼ million.[1] It provided the original base of French expansion throughout West Africa. Its administrative capital, Saint-Louis, was established as a fort and trading post in 1659 and submitted its *cahier* for the States General in 1789. Confined until the middle of the nineteenth century to a few such foot-holds (of which the other most important was the little island of Gorée in the bay now dominated by the great port of Dakar), French authority was for long centred in Saint-Louis, and it was from there that its extension throughout what is now French West Africa was directed. By 1904 that process was complete, a 'government-general' had been created, separated from the administration of Senegal itself, and transferred to Dakar. This establishment within its boundaries of the administrative headquarters of French West Africa, and the development of Dakar as a naval base and an international port, secured for Senegal social and economic advantages which reinforced the results of the successful growth of peasant production of groundnuts, still the most obvious feature of the Senegalese economy. Exporting 8,772 tons in 1870, 140,000 in 1900, over 500,000 in 1930, Senegal produced, in the year of these elections, a record crop of 710,000 tons.[2] Its position as the main base of French activity in French West Africa resulted in the construction of the railway from Dakar to Saint-Louis (opened in 1886), and the groundnut production thereby stimulated was further extended by the construction of the link with the French Sudan begun in 1907, but finished only in 1923. Over a quarter of the railway mileage of French West Africa is within the territory and the railway workshops at Thiès, junction for Saint-Louis, Dakar, and Bamako (capital of the French Soudan) are the largest single industrial

---

[1] Area of Senegal: 78,000 sq. miles; Area of England and Scotland, 80,737 sq. miles. Population (1956) 2,223,000.

[2] Figures for 1870–1930 from A. Villard, *Histoire du Sénégal* (Dakar, 1943), p. 160. Figure for 1956–7 from *Marchés tropicaux*, No. 645, 22 Mar. 1958, p. 783.

establishment in French West Africa.[1] The Second World War gave a great impetus to the local processing of ground nuts, and some 60,000 tons of oil are now produced annually. Other secondary industry, including the manufacture of textiles, footwear, and brewing and cement, has followed since the war, particularly in the region of Dakar and Rufisque.

Some social and economic characteristics of potential political significance derive from these historical facts. Some 43,000 Europeans, more than half those in French West Africa, live in Senegal.[2] About a quarter of its population live in towns, a much higher proportion than elsewhere in French West Africa: of these about two-fifths live in Dakar, two-fifths in seven other towns with populations between 10,000 and 40,000, and most of the remainder in five towns with populations between 2,000 and 10,000.[3] Originally all these towns were trading stations or administrative centres. The proportion of wage earners in the African population was for many years considerably higher than in the rest of French West Africa, though since the war the Ivory Coast has caught up and is now outdistancing Senegal in this respect. In 1955 about a tenth of the adult African population of Senegal were wage earners and the Labour Department estimated that rather more than half of them (55,000) 'followed the instructions' of a trade union.[4] Official wage-rates in the same year ranged from daily rates of 6s. to 10s. for unskilled, 10s. to 30s. for semi-skilled and skilled labour, to monthly salaries rising to £50–£60 for the highest levels of commercial and clerical work.[5] The national income of Senegal (excluding activities in the non-monetary sector) was put at £66 million in 1953 which gave a *per capita* money income of £30. Even allowing for the greater importance of European incomes, this suggests that *per capita* money incomes in the territory may have been somewhat higher than the average for French West Africa as a whole, though lower than in the Ivory Coast.[6] The relatively favoured position of the territory is also exemplified in the proportion of children of school age in school, which was just under 20 per cent. in 1954–5, compared with 10·9

[1] See G. Savonnet, *La Ville de Thiès* (Saint Louis, 1955), p. 145.

[2] European population (1956), Senegal 42,861; French West Africa 82,210. *Annuaire statistique de l'A.O.F.*, vol. v, tome 2 (Paris 1957), pp. 173–5.

[3] Ibid., tome 1 (Paris, 1956), p. 45. See also P. Mercier, 'An Experimental Investigation into Occupational and Social Categories in Dakar' in *Social Implications of Industrialisation and Urbanisation in Africa South of the Sahara* (Paris, Unesco, 1956), p. 511.   [4] *Annuaire statistique de l'A.O.F.*, vol. v, tome 2, pp. 136–7.

[5] Ibid., p. 131.

[6] *Marchés coloniaux*, 23 May 1953, p. 1466. The *per capita* average money income for French West Africa was put at about £10.

per cent. for French West Africa as a whole. In that year the territory had 61,800 children in school (55,000 of them Africans) out of a total of 285,000 in French West Africa. More than one-third of the 12,000 children in secondary schools in French West Africa were in Senegal and even when the 1,600 European children were deducted, the territory still had a considerable lead over any other part of French West Africa.[1]

The European population of Senegal is, as already noted, more than half that of French West Africa and comparable in size with that of Kenya.[2] Since the Second World War, it has grown rapidly and its social composition has changed; the proportion in 'managerial' jobs is smaller than it used to be, while that of artisans, office workers, and people working in small businesses is larger. Between 1946 and 1951, for example, the proportion of workers and artisans in the European population in French West Africa rose from 5 to 11 per cent. There is also a greater range of occupational diversity at the professional and technical level than before the war. But more than half are soldiers and civil servants. The former were 34 per cent. and the latter 24 per cent. of the European employed population of French West Africa in 1951, and in Dakar 36 per cent. and 19 per cent. respectively. Especially, though by no means exclusively, in Dakar, European ways of living have become more metropolitan and less colonial in appearance, e.g. in clothes, houses, and services like cleaning and hair dressing. As the European community has become larger, it has become more self-contained and this is particularly evident in Dakar. Although no legal colour-bar is tolerated, residential separation is more marked, and outside working hours inter-racial contacts are infrequent. Owing to the increase in the proportion of Europeans employed as clerks, artisans, and workers, and in the numbers of Africans whose training and education permit them to aspire to such occupations (and, indeed, to others higher up the social ladder) there is a more evident conflict of interest between some sections of the European and African populations, typified by African criticism of the *petits blancs*, the tendency to extend this category, and to protest against the entry of Europeans judged to belong to it.

The rapid increase in the European population, its changed social composition, and its more self-contained social life, as well as the evident conflict between the presuppositions on which some European employment is based and African demands for better

[1] *Inventaire social et économique des territoires d'outre-mer, 1950 à 1955* (Paris, 1957), pp. 76–77. Figures for European children in Senegal in *Annuaire statistique de l'A.O.F.*, vol. v, tome 1, p. 73.

European population 1956: Senegal 42,861; Kenya 57,700.

paid and less menial employment, combine to give the casual observer an impression rather like that given by a settler community. But in fact the essentially 'colonial' character of the European population has not changed. Its demographic structure shows an immense predominance of males of working age, and of bachelors, and a markedly small proportion of older children (between the ages of ten and twenty) and of people over sixty; and sociological investigation[1] has confirmed that, in spite of appearances, the European population in Dakar (which constituted more than two-thirds of that in Senegal) was not a settler population: of those interviewed, none wished to settle, two-thirds did not wish their children to take up a colonial career, and all over forty were preparing for their return to France. The European population of Dakar as a whole, the investigator recorded, had practically no political life, and their participation in elections appeared extremely limited. 'Among political parties, even the R.P.F., with its typically "European" outlook, had only a limited following. Other parties, even those which were part of a metropolitan party, had an almost exclusively African membership. Most of those interviewed declared themselves nonpolitical and insisted above all on the necessity of "white solidarity".'[2]

The African population is not linguistically or ethnically homogeneous. The figures in Table 1 give a rough impression of the relative size of more important groups.

TABLE I

Ethnic division of African population, 1948

Group	Estimated Number
Wolof	708,500
Fulani	290,000
Serer	273,500
Toucouleur	194,500
Diolas	136,500
Mande	172,000
Lebu	53,000
Others	136,000
Total	1,964,000

SOURCE: *Annuaire statistique de l'A.O.F.*, vol. iv, tome 1, p. 57.

---

[1] P. Mercier, 'Le Groupement européen de Dakar: orientation d'une enquête' (*Cahiers internationaux de sociologie*, vol. xix (1955), pp. 130–46).

[2] Mercier, *ibid.* pp. 143–4.

The largest single group, the Wolof, together with the Serer, who are closely related to them, and the Lebu, concentrated in the region of Dakar, who are thought to be derived from an earlier fusion of Wolof and Serer, may be considered as the people of the western coastal region, extending from the Senegal river to the Gambia. Toucouleur and Fulani people most of the valley of the Senegal, and Fulani are dominant in the 'desert' of Ferlo (south of the Senegal and east of the coastal region) and numerous in northern Casamance. The Mande include the Mandings of the middle Casamance and the related Bambara and Sarakolé, farther north and east on the borders of the French Sudan. The Diolas are concentrated in south-ern Casamance.[1] Although there are thus well-marked areas in which a particular group is dominant, there is much territorial intermingling which has been promoted in recent times by the relatively easy communications and the extension of groundnut cultivation to new areas.

At least four-fifths of the Senegalese are Muslims; and of the major ethnic groups only the Serer have presented a stubborn, if diminish-ing, resistance to the spread of Islam. The great Islamic confra-ternities, the Qadiriyya and the Tidjaniyya, are represented by several important 'houses' in Senegal, each with their *grand marabout* or leader. Much of the influence of the traditional political chiefs seems to have been acquired by them, and although they are criticized by reformers, they undoubtedly command great popular support, and 'represent today the principal force capable of resisting the modernist *élite*, and the one with which the latter and the political movements identified with it, must to some extent come to terms'.[2] The headship of these groups has become hereditary, but there are often succession disputes, and (as in eighteenth-century England) political parties compete not only for the favour of the present *marabouts* but also for that of potential successors or rivals. The four such 'houses' whose heads are established in Senegal

[1] For the ethnic groups generally, see E. Séré de Rivières, *Sénégal-Dakar* (Paris, 1953), pp. 24–33. The *Cartes ethno-démographiques de l'Afrique occidentale* published by the Institut Français d'Afrique Noire (Dakar, 1952) and based on work by J. Richard-Molard show the density and ethnic distribution of the population. There are no comprehensive modern ethnographic studies of any of the major ethnic groups in Senegal: for the Wolof, see P. Gamble, *The Wolof of Senegambia* (London, 1957); for the Serer, see F. Pellissier, 'Les Paysans Sérères' (*Cahiers d'outre-mer*, vol vi (1953), pp. 105–27, and for the Lebu, J. Gallais, 'Les Villages lébous de la presqu'île du Cap-Vert' (ibid., vol. vii (1954), pp. 137–54), and G. Balandier and P. Mercier, *Particularisme et évolution: les pêcheurs lébus du Sénégal* (Saint-Louis du Sénégal, 1952).

[2] P. Mercier, 'Evolution of Senegalese élites', *International Social Science Bulletin*, vol. viii (1956), p. 443.

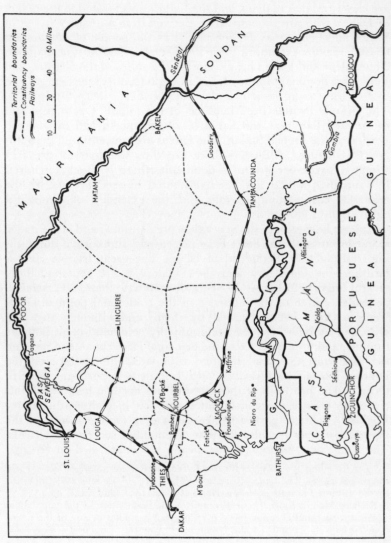

MAP. 6. SENEGAL.

are those of Seydou Nourou Tall, grandson of the legendary El Hadj
Omar, whose Toucouleur followers are mostly concentrated in the
Senegal valley, though he himself lives in Dakar; those of Ibrahima
Nyass of Kaolack, the majority of whose adherents are, however,
outside Senegal, and especially in Northern Nigeria; the followers
of El Hadj Malick Sy, whose headquarters are at Tivaouane in the
district of Thies and whose head, Babacar Sy, died in March 1957;
and, finally, the Mourides, the most specifically Senegalese of the
four, whose headquarters are at Touba, near Diourbel, and whose
present head is Falilou M'Backé. The last is Qadiriyya while the
others are Tidjaniyya.[1]

Christian missions have been long established in Senegal, notably
in Saint-Louis, Dakar, and in Southern Casamance, but the number
of professed Christians is small and is generally put at less than 5 per
cent. of the population. The Catholic weekly, *Afrique nouvelle*, has
considerable influence among the educated intelligentsia whether
Christian or not, fully reports developments in African political and
cultural movements, and supports African nationalism, in its all-out
campaign against communism. The group associated with it is
active in the promotion of study groups on social and economic
subjects,[2] and is in close touch with the younger men in politics
and the trade unions.

It is more than usually difficult, in the absence of so much of the
basic data needed for the purpose, to assess the present vitality of
traditional African social organization in Senegal or the role which
elements derived from that organization play in relation to the
modern Western political system whose development under French
auspices is described in the next section. Here, as elsewhere in
tropical Africa, it must first be emphasized that the extent and
character of the social change which has followed the imposition of
colonial rule and its accompanying economic changes, is by no means
uniform geographically, being a good deal more obvious, for example,
in the western coastal districts than in the valley of the Senegal, and
much less apparent in the remote district of Kédougou, with which
communications are difficult and the peoples of which are affiliated
with their neighbours in Guinea rather than those in Senegal.
Secondly, where larger indigenous political units existed in Senegal
they did not long survive effective French control, and 'chiefs' were
more obviously incorporated as subordinates in the administrative
hierarchy than under systems of 'indirect rule'. Where those so
employed enjoyed some measure of 'traditional' authority and

---

[1] See A. Gouilly, *L'Islam dans l'Afrique occidentale française* (Paris 1952).
[2] See P-H. Siriex, *Une Nouvelle Afrique* (Paris, 1957), pp. 93 et seq.

acceptance, it seems to have been more often at the lower level of village headmen than at that of the *canton* chiefs. The chiefs were, inevitably, closely associated with the administration in the levying of forced labour and in the pre-war system of summary administrative jurisdiction (*indigénat*), while the administration, in turn, was often obliged to acquiesce in the more personal exactions of the chiefs. These two factors seem, here as elsewhere, to have weakened the sanctions on which the position of the chiefs traditionally depended, and they were brusquely deprived of the newer administrative sanctions, on which they had come largely to depend, by the constitutional reforms of 1946 abolishing forced labour and the *indigénat*. Membership of chiefly families is, nevertheless, an important source not merely of prestige but of a political 'interest'. In many interviews with political 'leaders' in the smaller townships and villages, they almost invariably defined their own position, and that of their fellows, in part by reference to their relationship with ruling families, or with the indigenous caste-system. In this respect, the writer's observations led him to similar conclusions to those reached by the French sociologist Mercier, who writes:

> The principal racial groups inhabiting Senegal, [i.e. Wolof, Toucouleur and Serer] whatever their cultural differences and whatever their traditional hostility to one another (which has still by no means completely disappeared) all had the same type of social and political organization. They were strictly graded societies divided into endogamous castes each with its special economic, political, ritual and other functions. In the present context, inter-caste antagonisms and incompatibilities are as a rule more important than racial antagonisms, since several racial groups may have equivalent social gradings or one may have borrowed and adapted another's gradings. This is a fundamental feature; it indicates the framework within which we can explain the problem of relations between the traditional and modernist *élites*. For instance, prestige due to education may be superimposed on prestige based on tradition, in particular prestige due to caste; or else the two may be completely separate. Even today a high standing in the modern context does not often completely redeem a traditional inferiority. The latter obviously does not prevent accession to such rank but it does prevent a man from reaping the full benefit of the prestige which it confers. The old political organizations have either been destroyed or considerably weakened though the prestige of the aristocratic families who hold the *chefferies* or are closely connected with them has not completely disappeared.[1]

In the economic sphere, the subsistence production of traditional society has been largely replaced by ground-nuts grown as a cash-

---

[1] Mercier, op cit., pp. 442–3.

crop, though in contrast to other cash-crops (especially cocoa in the Ivory Coast), Senegalese groundnut production has not given rise to a class of well-to-do planters. The middle-men between the large European firms and the producers are largely Lebanese, and African traders are mostly small shopkeepers. The most significant consequence of the economic impact of colonial rule is to be sought in the growth of towns and the development of a substantial urban wage-earning population, increasingly organized in trade unions, which form the most important and dynamic of the new social groups. There is also a relatively large 'educated' *élite*, many employed in the lower and middle ranks of the administration and commerce and for long assimilationist in ideology. Since the Second World War the numbers of this *élite* have grown with the increased provision of schooling, and its reinforcement by a much higher proportion of Africans educated in France at university or professional levels, and it has become increasingly aware and resentful of 'colonialism'.

The diminished political influence of traditional leaders, the influence of the Muslim groups, the absence of a new rural class of wealthy planters, and the pre-war experience of Western political institutions by the older colonial *élite*, has produced in Senegal a society in which there has been some scope for the development of political parties transcending local or ethnic ties (though these are still strong[1]). To do so, however, parties had to achieve a carefully organized alliance of a wide range of interest-groups, commonly referred to as 'clans', banded together to secure 'place' and 'influence' rather than to seize power, either in the communist or nationalist sense. This type of political organization was still dominant in 1957 but the two important newer groups, the trade union leaders and the newer 'intelligentsia', had stood rather apart from political parties developed on these lines until the last two or three years, which saw a number of developments aimed at incorporating them into a mass party.

2. *The Constitutional Structure*

Under the Third Republic, Senegal enjoyed a special place among French colonies in tropical Africa. It alone elected a Deputy (continuously from 1871); it alone had towns organized as French municipalities with elected councils and mayors (from 1872); it alone had an elected General Council, after the model of those in

---

[1] Evidence of the importance of kinship ties in the towns will be found in Y. Mersadier, *Quelques budgets familiaux du Sénégal* (Saint-Louis, 1957).

metropolitan departments (from 1879). More important still, it alone had African inhabitants who enjoyed the political rights of French citizens while retaining their own private law instead of the French civil code, and who gained this privileged political status merely by virtue of birth in the territory and not as a result of individual qualification. This special position existed, however, only in that portion of Senegal which constituted what was called the 'territory under direct administration'. Essentially, this comprised the 'four communes'—Saint-Louis, Gorée, Rufisque, and Dakar—the *originaires* of which (i.e. those born there) exercised the right to vote on the same conditions as Frenchmen, despite the fact that their civil condition continued to be regulated by native (usually Muslim) and not by French law. Unsuccessful efforts were made from time to time to deprive the *originaires* of their political rights on the ground that they were not French citizens, but their special position was finally confirmed by legislation in 1916. In the latter part of the nineteenth century attempts were made to bring within the territory under direct administration those parts of Senegal in which French rule was then being established but this was found to be administratively inconvenient and in 1890 the territory under direct administration was restrictively defined and the remainder of Senegal was declared a protectorate. The inhabitants of the protectorate, like those of the rest of French tropical Africa, were French subjects, not French citizens, and had none of the political rights of the *originaires*.

In 1920 the two administrative divisions of Senegal were combined and the General Council of the territory formerly under direct administration was replaced by a new Colonial Council whose powers extended to the whole of Senegal. These rested, like those of the old General Council, essentially on control of the territorial budget, though, like all such bodies in France and its empire, they had to make provision for the 'obligatory expenditure'. Like its predecessor, the new Colonial Council had no legislative powers, and its composition was designed to strengthen the position of the territorial administration. In place of a membership wholly elected by the *originaires* under adult male suffrage, it had a membership half of which (twenty members) was elected by the electorate of the old General Council, but half of which consisted of chiefs chosen by the canton and provincial chiefs of the former protectorate, who were in practice nominees of the administration. Their consistent support of the administration and opposition to the representatives of the citizens caused serious difficulty and in 1925 the membership was altered to include twenty-four members elected by the *origi-*

naires and only sixteen chiefs. With modifications in the number of seats allotted to the two groups, these arrangements continued until 1939, when a new group of members elected by French subjects who had completed their military service was added.[1] In 1940, however, both the Colonial Council and the elected municipal councils were suppressed by the Vichy administration.[2]

French colonies were accorded increased representation (compared to that which they had enjoyed in pre-war parliaments) in the Constituent Assemblies of 1945 and 1946, and in the post-war constitutional settlement representation in the National Assembly, the Council of the Republic, and the new consultative Assembly of the French Union, was accorded to all 'Overseas Territories,' a new designation for the former 'colonies'. While French citizenship was granted to all 'subjects', even though they retained their personal status (and were not obliged to accept the French civil code) these new citizens were only given the franchise if they belonged to certain specified categories (e.g. veterans, civil servants, holders of school-leaving certificates, &c.).

At the same time a local representative assembly was set up in each Overseas Territory. These were wholly elected bodies modelled on the General Councils of French departments. Their financial powers were important but they had, strictly speaking, no legislative powers and should not be confused with the Legislative Councils of British territories. A Grand Council was also established for French West Africa composed of five members from each of its eight territories, elected by the Territorial Assemblies. Its powers were analogous, in respect to the 'Federation' as a whole, with those of the Territorial Assemblies in territorial matters.

One of the features of the new arrangements was the establishment of separate electorates (and separate representation) for citizens of metropolitan status (usually almost entirely Europeans) and for those of local status (i.e. the former 'subjects'). In some Overseas Territories these two electorates were separately represented in the National Assembly and in most of them they were separately represented in the Territorial Assemblies. In the French West African territories all elections to the National Assembly were on a common roll, but the system of separate electorates was used for all the Territorial Assemblies except that of Senegal. There also

---

[1] Decree of 8 Apr. 1939 (*J. O. Lois et Décrets*, 9 Apr., p. 4709). See H. Labouret, 'La Représentation des indigènes en Afrique tropicale', *L'Afrique française*, May 1939, pp. 135–9.

[2] The best account in English of the Senegalese régime up to 1925 is in R. L. Buell, *The Native Problem in Africa*, vol. i (New York, 1928), pp. 946–82.

continued to be common-roll elections for the councils of the restored Senegalese *communes*—Dakar, Rufisque, and Saint-Louis—the only towns in French tropical Africa which were full municipalities after the metropolitan pattern.[1] In spite of the fact that the Europeans, whose interests the system of separate electorates and separate representation was designed to safeguard, were so much more numerous in Senegal than in the rest of French West Africa, all elections in Senegal after 1946 were, like those before 1939, on a common roll.

After the constitutional changes of 1946, therefore, Senegal was represented in the National Assembly by two deputies, in the Council of the Republic by three senators, and in the Assembly of the French Union by three members. The members of the Council of the Republic and the Assembly of the French Union were elected by the members of the Territorial Assembly (the deputies joined in the election of the former). Its Territorial Assembly had fifty members until 1957, when the number was increased to sixty, and it elected from its own number five of the forty members of the Grand Council of French West Africa.

The period from 1946 to 1955 was marked by *immobilisme* in the constitutional position of French Overseas Territories perhaps even more than in domestic metropolitan politics. Vocal opinion among Africans was bitterly hostile to the 'second class citizenship' implied by the system of separate electorates but no major changes were secured until 1956, though the franchise was considerably extended in 1951 and 1952. In the elections to the National Assembly in 1951, three new categories of the citizens of local status were given the vote, namely *chefs de ménage* who paid tax, 'mères de deux enfants vivants ou morts pour la France', and pensioners. The first of these categories was susceptible of very varied interpretation and since the law extending the franchise in this way was only finally enacted a few weeks before the election, it was perhaps hardly surprising that the proportion of new voters registered differed greatly from one territory to another. In 1952 the electorate for the Territorial Assemblies was similarly extended, though the requirement that *chefs de ménage* should have paid tax was dropped. The only other change of political significance in this period was the enactment in 1955, after years of frustrated discussion, of a measure of local government reform which provided for the setting up, throughout French tropical

---

[1] For the 1946 constitutional settlement see my papers 'The Public Law of Overseas France since the War' (Oxford: Institute of Colonial Studies Reprint Series No. 1A, 1954), and 'Political Development in French West Africa' in C. Stillman (ed.), *Africa in the Modern World* (Chicago, 1955).

Africa, of 'full municipalities' similar to the three which already existed in Senegal.[1] The law itself established forty-four such municipalities, of which six were in Senegal. These were Gorée (which was now separated again from Dakar, with which it had been amalgamated in 1929), Theis, Diourbel, Kaolack, Ziguinchor, and Louga. Elections to the new municipal councils were to be held on a common roll, though provision was made for the geographical delimitation of wards on an ethnic basis where appropriate, and it was claimed that some European representation could thereby be ensured.[2]

In June 1956, however, the new National Assembly (elected in January) finally passed a major measure of constitutional reform for the Overseas Territories. This *loi-cadre* (outline law) abolished the system of separate electorates, and established universal suffrage on a common roll in all elections in the Overseas Territories. It also laid down the general principles for a revision of the relations between the territories and metropolitan France, the details of which were to be worked out in a series of decrees. The powers of Territorial Assemblies were to be enlarged, and, in particular, they were to be accorded legislative powers in respect of subjects of territorial interest. 'Government councils' were to be established in each territory; the law itself was silent on the subject of their composition, but the Government made it clear in the course of the debates that it contemplated mixed executives, partly composed of officials but containing a majority of members chosen by the Assembly. (In the event, the Councils of Government actually set up contained no officials except the Governor as President.) The powers of the 'governments general' of French West Africa and French Equatorial Africa were to be reduced, to the profit of the constituent territories of each group; and, finally, the public services operating in the territories were to be divided into 'State services' concerned with subjects of interest to the Republic as a whole (i.e. the *ensemble* of metropolitan France and the Overseas Territories), and territorial services, concerned with matters under the control of territorial assemblies and government councils, and organized and operating under their authority.[3] The law provided that the Government's decrees implementing these general principles in detail should be

---

[1] There were, besides the three 'full municipalities' (*communes de plein exercice*) of Senegal, a number of township boards (*communes mixtes*) the essential feature of which was that the mayor was a civil servant appointed by the Governor.

[2] For the background of the municipal reform see my 'Local Government Reform in French Tropical Africa' (*Journal of African Administration*, vol. viii, no. 4 (1956), pp. 179–85).

[3] For the detailed provisions of these reforms, see my 'Constitutional Reform in French Tropical Africa', *Political Studies*, vol. vi, no. 1 (1958), pp. 45–69.

brought before the Assembly of the French Union, the National Assembly, and the Council of the Republic but that if within a specified period the French Parliament had not either approved them or definitely amended them, the decrees would become effective in the form originally proposed by the Government. The decrees were submitted in December 1956, debated by Parliament early in 1957, and finally passed, with not inconsiderable amendments, at the end of March.

Thus, the only part of the new reforms which had come into operation before the elections of the new Territorial Assemblies on 31 March 1957, were the provisions requiring the establishment of a common electoral roll and universal suffrage. The former made no difference in Senegal since separate electorates did not exist there, while the effect of the latter depended, in each territory, on the extent to which the francise provisions of the earlier electoral law had approximated to universal suffrage. In Senegal, at the national assembly elections of January 1956, the electorate was of the order of 36 per cent. of the population, which compared with 38 per cent. in French Guinea, 36 per cent. in the Ivory Coast, and 35 per cent. in Mauretania, but 29 to 30 per cent. in the French Soudan and Niger, and only 24 per cent. in Dahomey, or a general average of 32·8 per cent. Whatever the reasons for these disparities, among which varying degrees of unreliability in the population figures cannot be neglected, it was apparent that the extended franchise might be expected to make a smaller proportionate increase in the size of the electorate in Senegal than in some other territories.[1]

The elections with which this essay is concerned were thus only part of a series which took place on the same day throughout French Tropical Africa, and which concerned the eight territories of French West Africa, with a total of 474 seats, the four in French Equatorial Africa, with a total of 200, and the six provinces of Madagascar, with a total of 240.[2] Senegal, however, constitutes a 'special case' which cannot be regarded as typical of these elections of 31 March in general. This is so not only because of the concentration at least in some parts of Senegal of a relatively higher proportion of 'westernized' Africans than elsewhere in West Africa, but also because of its unique political and constitutional history. This familiarized some of its African *élite* with electoral problems and the use of electoral bodies as a means of securing, if not power, at least the enjoyment of

---

[1] Electoral and population figures are in *Annuaire statistique de l'A.O.F.*, vol. v, tome 1, pp. 13 and 45 respectively.

[2] Law 56–1, 147 of 15 Nov. 1956 relating to the composition of territorial assemblies in French West Africa, &c. (*J. O. Lois et Décrets*, 16 Nov., p. 10975).

spoils; it also created a small privileged class within the African community whose privileges have been largely destroyed by the constitutional changes since the war. This resulted in a relationship between members of this formerly privileged group and the mass of Africans which is in some respects comparable with that between the 'Creoles' of Sierra Leone and the mass of protectorate Africans.

Although the constitutional reforms effected by the *loi-cadre* were not finally settled until just before the election, and discussion of some of the issues involved formed a major part of the background to the election, it may be convenient to set out briefly the constitutional position of the territory as it stood on the morrow of the election. Senegal remained one of the group of eight component territories of French West Africa, constitutionally part of the French Republic, in whose Parliament they were all represented, though not proportionately to their population in comparison with that of metropolitan France. The Government of the Republic was represented in the 'group' by its High Commissioner, 'dépositaire des pouvoirs de la République', and in each territory by a Governor who was the legal head of the administration, and had under his control the officials of the State services, the costs of which were met by the metropolitan budget. These included, besides the District Commissioners (*commandants de cercle*), those responsible for the services concerned with such matters as defence, foreign affairs, external trade, customs, treasury, currency, exchange control, university education, civil aviation, telecommunications, courts of French law, administrative courts, labour inspection, cartography, and geological maps. All other matters were in principle dealt with by territorial services, under the control of the territorial 'government council' and the Territorial Assembly. The government council, over which the Governor presided, consisted of not less than six nor more than twelve members elected by the Territorial Assembly, each of whom could be charged individually with responsibility for a particular territorial service or group of services. They were elected *en bloc* by the Assembly but need not be members of it. The person whose name appeared at the top of the list winning a majority was to be designated as vice-president of the Council and was to preside over it in the absence of the president. The Council might resign 'if it considers that it no longer enjoys the confidence of the assembly'. These rather curious arrangements were intended to go as far as possible towards establishing a form of ministerial government in territorial affairs within the limits set by articles of the 1946 Constitution which provided that the Republic was 'one and indivisible' and that the 'representative of the Government' (i.e. the metropolitan government) was the 'head of the administration in territories'. Some of the features of 'responsible government' in the English sense might, no doubt, develop within these arrangements but there was no provision for dissolving the Territorial Assembly, which was elected for a period of five years.

Finally, although in a unitary territory (like French Somaliland) all revenues locally raised were paid into the territorial budget, the position was more complicated in a group of territories like French West Africa. Before the reforms the basis of revenue allocation had been that all direct taxation went to the territory, all indirect to the group as a whole. One object of the reforms was to increase the relative powers and importance of the component territories as compared with those of the group so the group budget was now assigned only the product of customs duties together with half the revenue from export duties and royalties on mineral and petroleum products. The number of inter-territorial services and the legislative and other functions of the Grand Council were strictly defined, with the object of reducing the activities of the 'group' to a minimum. An important function of the Grand Council continued, however, to be the distribution to the territories in the form of grants-in-aid of part of the revenue accruing to the budget of the group. No provision was made in the decrees of April 1957 for a Government Council at the level of the group as a whole, where executive power remained in the hands of the High Commissioner subject to a certain control by the Grand Council. This attempt to reduce the importance of the group as a whole in relation to individual territories was the subject of much controversy in Senegal during the months immediately preceding the election. It was vigorously attacked by the leaders of the major political party in Senegal and some of the more thoughtful Senegalese were not unmindful of the importance to the territory of the continued existence of French West Africa and of its administrative headquarters in Dakar.

3. The Electoral System

Constituencies and franchise. Elected assemblies for each territory had been instituted by Article 77 of the French Constitution of 1946 which also provided that their composition, powers, and method of election should be determined by statute. The second Constituent delegated this task[1] to the Government which, in ten decrees of 25 October,[2] prescribed what was supposed to be a provisional régime

---

[1] Law 46–2, 152 of 7 Oct. 1946 (*J. O. Lois et Décrets*, p. 8499).
[2] Decrees 46–2, 374–2, 383 of 25 Oct. 1946. That relating to French West Africa is 46–2, 375 (ibid., 27 Oct., p. 9118).

to be replaced by definitive arrangements before July 1947. In the event, however, the 'General Councils' so established remained in existence until 1952 when 'Territorial Assemblies' replaced them.[1] Some changes were then made in the composition and method of election of the new bodies but their powers and other attributions remained as prescribed in the 1946 decrees. The law of 6 February 1952 is the basic document on which the existing Territorial Assemblies depend though it has been amended by the *loi-cadre* of 23 June 1956[2] and by the law of 15 November 1956.[3] The former established universal suffrage and abolished the system of separate electorates (in territories where this existed), the latter increased the number of seats in the various Territorial Assemblies.

The decree of 25 October 1946 establishing General Councils in French West Africa retained the provisions of an earlier decree (25 February 1946) reconstituting that of Senegal,[4] in regard to the number of members and of constituencies and the number of seats allotted to each constituency. The method of election of the General Council of Senegal in 1946–51 thus differed considerably from that in force in the rest of French West Africa, where the constituencies for the African electorate (i.e. that of the new 'citizens of local status') were delimited by the Governor-General, who was also empowered to divide between them the seats assigned to that electorate, provided account was taken of their relative population and none had more than five. In Senegal there was no system of separate electorates, and the fifty seats were divided between four constituencies originally set up in 1939 as follows: (*a*) the River (Bas-Sénégal, Podor, Matam) 15 seats; (*b*) the Railway (Louga, Linguère, Thiès, Dakar) 18; (*c*) Sine-Saloum (Diourbel, Kaolack, Tambacounda and Kédougou) 12, and (*d*), Casamance (Ziguinchor) 5.

Voting was to be by 'scrutin de liste majoritaire à deux tours', in Senegal as elsewhere. This meant that electors voted *en bloc* for the list put up by a party and if no list secured both an absolute majority of the votes cast, and the votes of at least one-quarter of the electorate, a second ballot was needed. In that case, the list securing the most votes won all the seats. In spite of a good deal of criticism on the ground that it denied minorities any chance of representation, the system was retained in the Law of 6 February 1952, except that the second ballot, which had not been utilized in Senegal, was abolished. Changes were, however, made in the method of delimiting

---

[1] Law 52–130 of 6 Feb. 1952 (ibid., 7 Feb., pp. 1587–90).
[2] Law 56–619 of 23 June 1956 (ibid., 24 June, pp. 5782–4).
[3] Law 56–1, 147 of 15 Nov. 1956 (ibid., 16 Nov., p. 10975).
[4] Decree 46–294 of 25 Feb. 1946 (ibid., 26 Feb., pp. 1673–6).

constituencies and distributing seats among them. The administrative districts (*cercles*) were to form the constituencies and seats were to be divided among them in proportion to population. If its population exceeded 450,000 it was to be divided. In single-member constituencies, the simple majority ('first past the post') system was to be used. Elsewhere the 'scrutin de liste majoritaire à un tour' meant that electors must vote for one of several rival lists and for that list as a whole. 'Plumping' and cross voting were prohibited, and so also were incomplete lists. In effect, therefore, electors vote for one of a number of 'collective candidates', and since the one which secures the most votes wins all the seats in that constituency, large parties are encouraged and minority opinion has little prospect of representation except within a large party.

The 1952 law thus brought Senegal into line with the rest of French West Africa so far as concerns the delimitation of constituencies and the allocation of seats among them, but it remained peculiar in not having separate rolls. In this respect the *loi-cadre* of 1956 brought the other territories of French West Africa into line with Senegal. The number of seats, fixed at fifty in 1946, was increased to sixty in 1956. In the meantime the four constituencies of 1946 had risen to twelve under the 1952 law, the creation of a new administrative district (Bakel) in 1954[1] increased their number of thirteen, and the division of the district of Kaolack (whose population exceeded 450,000) into two constituencies, in preparation for the 1957 elections, brought it to fourteen.[2] One of these fourteen consists of the special administrative unit (*Délégation*) at Dakar which the 1952 law specifies should form a single constituency. This includes besides the *commune* of Dakar itself, those of Rufisque and Gorée, together with the subdivision of Rufisque. For the elections of 1957, seats were allocated as shown[3] in Table 2.

Although common roll elections were established throughout Senegal in 1946, the franchise was identical with that elsewhere in French West Africa: all 'citizens with metropolitan status' had the right to vote on the same conditions as Frenchmen in France, but during the decade 1946–56, 'citizens with local status' had the franchise only if they possessed one of the qualifications prescribed in the electoral laws. In Senegal the *originaires* of the four communes had,

---

[1] Arrêté No. 4,426 A. P. of the Governor-General of French West Africa, of 15 June 1954 (*J. O. du Sénégal*, 1 July, pp. 622–3). The new district comprised the subdivision of Bakel, formerly part of Matam, and that of Goudiry, formerly part of Tambacounda.

[2] Arrêté No. 1,731 A.P. 1 of the Governor-General of 18 Feb. 1957 (ibid., 27 Feb. p. 180).

[3] Decree No. 57–258 of 1 Mar. 1957 (ibid., 6 Mar., pp. 209–10).

TABLE 2.—*Constituencies and Seats, 1957*

Number of seats	Constituencies
1	Kédougou, Bakel, Linguère
2	Podor, Tambacounda, Bas-Sénégal
3	Matam
4	Louga
5	Diourbel
6	Kaolack II
7	Kaolack I, Dakar
8	Thies
11	Ziguinchor

as we have seen, enjoyed before the war the right to vote on the same basis as Frenchmen (i.e. adult male suffrage) and they retained it (even if not otherwise eligible under the post-war electoral laws) provided their names were on the register before the enactment of the electoral law of 1946. Their importance in the electorate declined rapidly with the extension of the franchise and even in 1946 they were outnumbered by the new voters. The full effect of the extension of the franchise in 1951 (national assembly elections) and 1952 (territorial assembly elections) was not reflected immediately in the size of the electorate, partly because of the administrative problems involved in adding the new voters to the register. The electorate was, nevertheless, greatly enlarged, and it continued to grow until the elections to the National Assembly in 1956, the last to be held on a restricted franchise, when it was approximately 36 per cent. of the estimated population. The effect of changes in the franchise on the size of the Senegalese electorate is shown[1] in Table 3.

TABLE 3.—*The Electorate in Senegal*

Year	Registered electorate
1946 (N.A.)	192,861
1946 (T.A.)	196,696
1951	655,280
1952	660,931
1956	835,035
1957	1,060,582

[1] Sources of Table 3: National Assembly Electorates 1946, 1951 and 1956, *Annuaire Statistique de l'A.O.F.*, vol. v, tome 1, p. 13; Territorial Assembly Electorate, 1946, *L'A.O.F.*; Territorial Assembly Electorate, 1952 and 1957, Direction des Affaires Politiques, Government General of French West Africa.

Registration. In all essentials, registration is regulated by the same law as in metropolitan France. Those registered must be of French nationality, twenty-one years of age or over, and not legally disqualified.[1] This last means, in general, that they must not be undischarged bankrupts, or within five years of the date of the election have been convicted of a felony. Applicants must also be qualified for registration in the particular municipality or administrative unit concerned: the qualifications are (*a*) being domiciled within it, or (*b*) having resided there for six months (within the period ending on the date on which the registers are legally closed, normally 31 March, but since this would have coincided with polling day, on this occasion 15 March),[2] or (*c*) in full municipalities only, being, for five years in succession, on the register of municipal taxpayers[3] or on that of those liable to *prestations* in kind; or, finally, (*d*) being a civil servant assigned to a post within the area, regardless of the date on which the posting occurred.[4]

Applicants for registration must therefore satisfy the revising commission on these matters. They are not required to prove that they are not legally disqualified, but must prove their French nationality, their age, and their right to be registered in the particular area concerned. Proof of birth in French territory is normally regarded as *prima facie* evidence of nationality but in Africa documentary proof is seldom possible outside the towns and special arrangements have to be made. In the full municipalities the Municipal Reform Law of 1955 made the production of an identity card or one of a number of prescribed documents an essential condition of registration.[5] In the rest of the territory it would at present be impracticable to make the production of such a document essential, and use is made of witnesses (*la preuve testimoniale*) combined with the census books (*carnet de recensement*) held by every compound head (*chef de carré*) in which are inscribed the names and year of birth of each person living in the compound. The latter are often little more than a plausible guess as registration of births is still very incomplete.

As the register is permanent, revision should be concerned only with the addition of the names of those qualified since the last

---

[1] Law 56–619 of 23 June 1956.
[2] Decree 57–168 of 11 Feb. 1957.
[3] Article 14 of Law of 5 Apr. 1884 (*J.O.R.F.*, 6 Apr. 1884, pp. 1857–68).
[4] Law 46–1, 889 of 28 Aug. 1946 (*J. O. Lois et Décrets*, 29 Aug. 1946, pp. 7502–3).
[5] Law 55–1, 489 of 18 Nov. 1955, Art. 14. Governors of territories were empowered to determine the alternative documents which might be accepted, and this was done, in respect of Senegal, in Arrêté No. 7,094 APA.Bc. of 5 Dec. 1955 (*J. O. du Sénégal*, 7 Dec. 1955, p. 1237). They included, besides such documents as labour cards and pension books, university certificates and driving, gun, and shooting licenses.

revision (either by reaching the age of twenty-one, or by reason of the extension of the franchise, or by becoming qualified for registration in a new administrative area) and with deleting the names of those who have died, have become legally disqualified, or have ceased to be qualified for registration within the area concerned. In theory, requests for registration or for deletion from the register may be deposited at any time of the year at the headquarters of the area concerned, and should be handed over to the revising commissions for decision. These bodies are, moreover, fully entitled to make changes in the register on their own initiative, and they may also decide claims made by third parties for the deletion of names from the register, if they consider such claims worth investigation. An applicant previously registered elsewhere must produce a certificate that his name has been removed from the register there and also proof that he is now qualified for registration in the new area. An applicant not previously registered must prove that he is otherwise entitled to registration, and must, in addition, if he comes from another area than that in which he now seeks registration, produce a certificate that he is not registered in the area in which he previously resided or was domiciled.[1]

The revising committees sit annually from 1 December until 10 January of the following year. The list of changes made in the register must be completed by 14 January and deposited at the *mairie* or at the headquarters of the administrative district concerned by the following day. Claims for inclusion or removal may then be lodged until 4 February, and must be decided by the appeal committees (*commissions de jugement*) by 9 February and those concerned informed by 12 February, when the decisions are made public. Appeals may be made to the *juge de paix* until 17 February and his decisions must be arrived at by 27 February, and communicated to the Mayor or District Commissioner and the Governor by 2 March (1 March in leap years). A final appeal to the *Cour de cassation* may be made before 12 March (11 March in leap years) and the registers are formally closed on 31 March. In a number of special cases, names may be added or removed outside the period of the annual revision. Such additions require the authority of a decision by the *juge de paix*, though names may be removed (e.g. of deceased electors) without such authority. Lists of any such additions must be

---

[1] This account of the legal basis of registration is based on several documents prepared by the Government General of French West Africa for administrative use: *Elections à l'assemblée nationale de juin 1951* (Rusfique, 1951); *Mémento sur la révision des listes électorales* (Rusfique, 1952); *Elections municipales (territoire du Sénégal) recueil des textes applicables au 15 octobre, 1956* (Saint-Louis, 1956).

made by the revising committee and published five days before any election.

The revising commissions consist of a representative of the administration (who presides) and representatives of each of the political parties. In the full municipalities[1] there is also either the mayor, one of his assistants, or a municipal councillor. Before the Municipal Reform Law of 1955, this municipal representative presided and the representative of the administration was present merely to see that the law was respected. These arrangements, reproducing those of metropolitan France, led to constant controversy about the alleged manipulation of the registers and the change was strongly supported by African deputies during the debate on the Bill.[2] The *commission de jugement* consists of the revising commission together with two other persons (who must be electors) appointed by the District Commissioner, or in the full municipalities one person elected by the municipal council.

The details included in the register are, besides a number and the elector's name, his age, date and place of birth, his occupation, place of residence, and his *filiation*, i.e. the names of his father and mother. In countries where names are not always expressed in the same order, and people are as likely to be registered under one of their names as under the other, and where there are often, outside the towns, no easy means of proving identity, the inclusion of all these details may help considerably in identifying electors. In particular, although not legally necessary, information about the *filiation* of electors (the electors' cards printed by the Ministry of Overseas France do not include a space for it) is often the easiest means of identifying an elector when he presents himself to claim an elector's card. Electors registered during a revision are given a receipt, containing the number under which they have been registered, and this facilitates the issue of electors' cards.

Before an election, the registers must be copied for use in the distribution of electors' cards and in polling stations and the electors' cards must be prepared. There must be at least one polling station for every 1,500 electors[3] and it is the aim that electors' cards should, so far as possible, be available during the distribution period, at the

---

[1] See above, p. 289, for these in Senegal.

[2] The municipal elections in the three Senegalese municipalities were frequently attacked. Those in Rufisque and in Dakar in 1953 were quashed by the Conseil d'État in 1955 on account of irregularities in electoral administration. See the decisions of the Conseil d'État in *Revue juridique et politique de l'Union française*, vol. x (1956), pp. 189–99.

[3] Law 51–586 of 23 May 1951, Art. 14 (*J. O. Lois et Décrets*, 24 May, p. 8534).

same place as the elector will have to go to vote. In the rural areas, however, this is clearly impracticable and arrangements are made for the distributing committees, to whom the distribution of the cards is entrusted, to travel from hamlet to hamlet for the purpose. These committees follow the general pattern, consisting of a representative of the Administration (who presides) and representatives of each list or (in single member constituencies, of each candidate) to whom is added in full municipalities an assistant to the mayor or a councillor.[1] The law prescribes that the distribution of electors' cards must begin at the latest twelve days before polling day, and end at midnight on the day before polling day in municipalities and three days before polling day elsewhere. This earlier cessation of distribution in the rural areas is to allow the electors' cards which have not been distributed to be brought into the subdivisional headquarters. They may be claimed there during this period, when a special distributing committee sits for the purpose, and those not claimed must be made available in the appropriate polling stations on polling day, where they can still be claimed.[2] In municipalities a distributing committee functions on polling day itself so that those who have not claimed their cards may do so.[3]

Polling. Each polling station has its *bureau*, consisting of a president appointed by the District Commissioner, and at least four assessors; each list (or candidate) must nominate an assessor for each polling station. If there are less than four lists (or candidates) the president appoints the necessary assessors to bring the total to four, from the two oldest electors (and then the two youngest) among those present when the poll opens. They must be able to read and write, and all must be on the electoral register of the constituency. The *bureau* choses its own secretary who must be similarly qualified. He has no vote in the event of disagreement among the members but the President has a casting vote as well as an original vote if the *bureau* is divided. At least three members must be present at all times during the poll.[4]

Electors presenting themselves to vote must first establish their identity and their right to vote: this should normally be done by presenting an identity card and an electors' card. Having done this the voter takes a single envelope from the pile and one or more voting papers. There is a separate voting paper for each list (or

---

[1] Law 52–130 of 6 Feb. 1952, Art. 15.

[2] Government of Senegal, Circular No. 62 APA 1 of 4 Mar. 1957.

[3] Law 55–1, 489 of 18 Nov. 1955, Art. 22 (*J. O. Lois et Décrets*, 19 Nov., pp. 11274–9).

[4] Law 51–586 of 23 May 1951, 16 and 17; Law 52–130 of 6 Feb. 1952, Art. 18.

candidate, in single-member constituencies); they are printed on different coloured paper and may also have printed on them the emblem chosen by the list. (Thus, one list may have chosen green as its colour and a five-pointed star as its emblem; another red and three arrows.) The voter takes his envelope and his voting papers into one of the booths (*isoloirs*) provided, puts the voting paper of the list for which he wishes to vote into the envelope in the privacy of the booth and then emerges and after showing the President that he has only one envelope himself puts it publicly into the ballot-box. His elector's card is then stamped (or part of it torn off) and one of the members of the *bureau* initials the margin of the register against the elector's name to show that he has voted.

The count. Votes are counted separately at each polling station, and if there are less than 300 voters the count may be made by its *bureau*; otherwise, scrutineers whose names must have been given to the President at least an hour before the poll closes, may be nominated by the party assessors. Each counting table must have four scrutineers, so that the reading of the voting papers and the checking of the votes can be supervised simultaneously by one scrutineer from each party. Scrutineers must be literate electors registered in the constituency. The public having been admitted and the scrutineers having taken up their places, the ballot box is emptied and the number of envelopes counted. If the total disagrees with that obtained by counting the marginal initialings (*emargements*) on the registers, the envelopes must be recounted. Any discrepancy must be recorded in the *bureau's* written report (*procès verbal*). (The number of marginal initialings is legally decisive, but many difficulties arise from the failures of the *bureaux* to initial the names of some voters.) The President next divides the envelopes between the counting tables, preferably in lots of a hundred. At each table one scrutineer opens the envelopes and passes the voting papers, unfolded, to another who calls out the votes and puts the papers in separate piles for each party. The votes are recorded by at least two scrutineers by marking count sheets (*feuilles de pointage*). When these have been signed, they are handed, together with any doubtful or contested voting papers, to the *bureau*, which alone is competent to decide whether a voting paper is invalid. If an envelope contains more than one voting paper, the vote is invalid if they are of more than one party; if they are all of the same party, they count as one vote only. All voting papers considered invalid, and their envelopes, must be kept with the *bureau's* report together with a statement of the reasons why they are considered invalid. This report, which must be signed by the *bureau* of the polling station, including the party representatives if any have been appointed, must be completed and signed on the spot, in the presence of the public. After the count, the results must be posted outside the polling station and the President must then take the report, the count sheets, the initialed registers, and any voting papers considered invalid (along with their envelopes, and signed by the members of the *bureau*) to the central polling station of the electoral district. The *bureau* there is only required to add up the totals for each station, and has no authority to revise any decisions taken by their *bureaux*. Before the documents are taken to the central polling station, all valid voting papers are publicly burnt. Once the totals for the district have been arrived at, all the documents must next be taken to the official in charge of the administrative district for transmission by the quickest available means to the Governor, for examination by the territorial commission appointed by the Governor and charged with checking the count for all constituencies.[1]

In British colonial territories electoral arrangements are prescribed by local ordinance; the influence of United Kingdom practice is everywhere apparent but there are marked local variations. In Senegal the electoral system was prescribed in French metropolitan legislation applicable in all French Overseas Territories and much of it applicable in France itself.[2] Moreover, in respect of all elections in Overseas Territories except those to the French Parliament[3] complaints that the law was not properly applied and that the irregularities benefited a particular party could be made in the first instance to the local administrative tribunal, in this case the *Conseil du Contentieux administratif* of French West Africa and, on appeal, to the *Conseil d'État*. If such complaints were held to have been established, the election might be quashed.[4] In the administration of the electoral laws the local authorities had therefore to consider not only the letter of the law but also the decision of the *Conseil d'État* in cases concerning its application in Overseas Territories. Their practical application accordingly presented perhaps even greater administrative problems than those inevitable in the attempt to

---

[1] *Mémento 1957 sur l'organisation matérielle des élections aux assemblées territoriales* (Dakar: Government General of French West Africa). For the personnel of the *Commission du recensement général des votes*, see *J. O. du Sénégal*, 27 Feb. 1957.

[2] As will be clear if it is compared with H. G. Nicholas, 'The French Election of 1956: Electoral Law and Machinery' (*Political Studies*, vol. iv, 1956, pp. 139–50). Even the acceptance of such documents as driving licenses as a means of establishing identity at the poll is a metropolitan practice.

[3] The National Assembly itself examines and validates the election of deputies.

[4] See A. Holleaux, 'Les Élections aux assemblées des territoires d'outre-mer', *Revue juridique et politique de l'Union française*, vol. x (1956), pp. 1–54. The delay and the difficulties of proof in the procedure reduce its value.

hold 'free and fair elections' in countries where the notion is still novel. Some of the practical problems most in evidence in Senegal in 1957 are discussed later.[1]

4. Political History to the National Assembly Elections of January 1956

To understand the contemporary political scene in Senegal, it is necessary to know something of the political history of French West Africa as a whole. Not only do its political leaders have to operate within a wider context than that of Senegal, particularly in their relations with other French West African leaders in the French Parliament and in the Grand Council of French West Africa, but also their supporters, and especially many of the politically conscious middle-rank party officials, are increasingly influenced by, and responsive to, political developments elsewhere in French West Africa. The constitutional evolution of Senegal has, however, as we have seen, been very different from that of other parts of French Africa and its political history has in consequence been much longer. It therefore constitutes in many ways, a 'special case' for the student of African politics. This section seeks to sketch the characteristics of this 'special case' and also to relate it to the wider context of post-war politics in French West Africa.[2]

The first deputy from Senegal was elected to the French Parliament in 1848, but it was not until the early years of the Third Republic that the privilege of parliamentary representation was re-established and those of electing a General Council and municipal councils in the four old *communes* added. There is, so far as the writer is aware, no published study of the early elections, but an impressionistic contemporary account of the political scene at the end of the nineteenth century[3] suggests that the techniques of the pork barrel were soon exploited:

The great Bordeaux firms wanted to control the administrative and customs policy of the Colony from motives of self-interest which often led to mutual rivalry. Everyone tried, therefore, to catch the half-breed and black

---

[1] See below, p. 346.

[2] I am greatly indebted to Dr. Ruth Schachter, sometime Student of Nuffield College, who has kindly allowed me to use her unpublished Oxford D.Phil. thesis on 'Political Parties in French West Africa'. We have had so many discussions on these matters in recent years that I find it difficult to exaggerate how much I owe to her pioneer work in this field. The responsibility for any errors, whether of fact or interpretation, remains, however, exclusively mine.

[3] P. Mille, 'The "Black Vote" in Senegal', *Journal of the African Society*, vol. 1 (1901), pp. 64–79. For a later example, see R. L. Buell, op. cit., vol. i, pp. 956–7.

vote, and to gain the desired end, voters were promised participation in the revenue in the form of appointments, subventions, or even free-gifts. These expenses absorbed in the long run a large portion of the Colony's finances . . . for instance, nearly half the funds credited to education were swallowed up. The most flagrant abuses no longer astonished anybody. . . .

The author then gives examples of petitions to the General Council which he considers to be examples of such practices (demands for financial help, bursaries, in effect 'pensions') and records that in a single sitting of the ordinary session of 1896, he counted twenty-six petitions of this kind. He continues:

When the great French commercial firms in Senegal realised that in five years the revenue from import duties had fallen from 3,317,000 Fcs. to 2,000,000, they understood that in trying to capture the native vote, each for their own personal interest, they had miscalculated things. . . . And so, bearing in mind their previous cut throat competition in the matter of the purchase of the ground-nut, and how they had put an end to such competition by jointly agreeing upon an average-purchase price, they resolved to combine together to 'run the elections'. As soon as the majority of these firms had come to an understanding the game was won. Together they influenced a large number of votes.

Whether as a result of these early lessons, or of the increasing divergence between the possibilities offered by the Senegalese economy, and the expectations and demands encouraged by close proximity, in the old municipalities, to European standards of consumption, there is a long tradition of political manipulation in Senegal which must have been encouraged by the relatively small number of voters, and also by the realization that the possibilities of radical political change were very limited. The first African deputy Blaise Diagne, was elected in 1914 and retained the seat until his death in 1934.[1] During this period, parties were known as *Diagnistes* and *parti de l'opposition*, and in the middle twenties an American scholar noted that 'in Senegal party labels mean little. At present the only division between the native voters is a personal one between the followers of M. Diagne and M. Lamine Gueye.'[2] To this period,

---

[1] Born 1872. His father was a Serer, his mother a Mandingo. He was a Catholic and was married in France. Employed as a customs official, he had, before his election, served in Réunion, French Guiana, and Madagascar, as well as Senegal, and had been a municipal councillor in French Guiana and Madagascar. See the election results in Table 4.

[2] Buell, loc. cit. M. Lamine Gueye was born in 1891 in the French Soudan of a family of Saint-Louisian origin. Doctor of Law, Paris 1921, his thesis being on the legal position of the *originaires* of the four *communes*. Mayor of Saint Louis 1924; subsequently *magistrat* in Réunion and Martinique. Member of the Constituent Assemblies 1945–6 and of the National Assembly 1946–51; Mayor of Dakar since 1945; Senator 1958.

too, should probably be assigned the mastering of the techniques of exploiting the position of an overseas deputy in a multi-party metropolitan assembly. This involved using that position, not as a point of vantage from which to advocate revolutionary changes, but as a basis from which to secure, in exchange for supporting the governmental majority, advantages or concessions that might be expected to consolidate one's hold on one's constituency. M. Diagne early achieved success of this kind when he obtained in 1916 the enactment of a law confirming the special political and juridical position of the Senegalese citizens and accepted the responsibility for securing increased military recruitment in West Africa.[1] During most of his parliamentary career he sat as a Republican Socialist, one of the small centre group of *ministrables* with which M. Briand was associated, and at one time he held the post of Under-Secretary for the Colonies.

TABLE 4

Elections to Chamber of Deputies, 1914–36

Year	Electorate	Valid votes	Diagne	Diouf	Others
1914 (1er Tour)	8,674	4,863	1,910	..	8 candidates with votes varying from 671 to 2
1914 (2e Tour)	8,677	5,155	2,424	..	Heimburger 2,249; Carpot 472
1919	16,013	8,724	7,444	..	Carpot 1,252
1924	..	..	6,118	..	Defferre 1,884
1928	16,553	9,672	5,175	4,396	Others 154, 37
1932	18,797	12,031	7,250	3,785	Others 730, 205, and 61
1934	..	..	..	6,126	Lamine Gueye 4,584
1936	20,746	13,819	..	8,466	Lamine Gueye 5,145; others 122 and 86

At the by-election occasioned by the death of Diagne, the seat was won by Galandou Diouf who had been Diagne's opponent in the elections of 1928 and 1932, in the latter of which he had stood as an S.F.I.O. candidate. Lamine Gueye, at that time absent in the West Indies where he held a post as judge in Martinique, returned to Senegal not long before Diagne died and contested the seat in opposition to Diouf, campaigning for the purpose with the support of many Diagnists, and in association with several Europeans including the

[1] His election in 1914 was contested on the ground that he was not a French citizen and was therefore ineligible (see *J. O. Débats parlementaires, Chambre des Députés*, 7 July 1914, p. 2735).

President of the Chamber of Commerce Charles Graziani, under the title of *Parti Socialiste Sénégalais*.[1] In spite of its name, this seems to have been essentially 'anti-Diouf' though it secured the support of some European socialists and some European trade unions. The impression of Senegalese parties in the inter-war years which we get from scanty evidence is that of a political machine, deriving its strength mainly from the influence it could bring to bear in the metropole on the colonial minister and its ability to exercise, in one way or another, substantial patronage, and organized round a leading personality, almost a political boss, rather than any set of political principles or a specific party programme.[2] These Senegalese parties, so often dismissed by Europeans unfamiliar with the realities of metropolitan parties, as unworthy of the name, seem to have had at least a measure of the characteristics of what Duverger calls '*cadre*-parties': 'Influential persons, in the first place, whose name, prestige, or connexions can provide a backing for the candidate and secure him votes; experts in the second place, who know how to handle the electors and how to organise a campaign; last of all, financiers who can bring the sinews of war.'[3] Much of this way of thinking about politics was carried over into the post-war Senegalese parties: an emphasis on the party as an electoral organization, rather than a movement of those agreed on doctrine, finding its basis in a coalition of leaders of 'connexions', whether of a local, family, or religious kind, and seeking similar 'connexions' among the emerging social groups of a more modern kind, such as traders' associations, cultural societies, and trade unions.

But even before the war there were signs which might presage a more 'ideological' development. The French socialist party (S.F.I.O.) had some supporters in Senegal, most, though not all of them, Europeans. In the early thirties some of them contested the Dakar municipal elections (on an anti-Diagne ticket). They are said to have recommended Lamine Gueye to the S.F.I.O.[4] The setting up of a

---

[1] The party seems to have been formed *c.* 1929 (oral information).
[2] K. E. Robinson, 'Political Development in French West Africa', *Africa in the Modern World*, Chicago, 1955, p. 150. Cf. 'De Blaise Diagne à Lamine Gueye . . . les rassemblements politiques s'effectuent autour de certaines individualités qui elles-mêmes s'incarnent rarement — pour ne pas dire jamais — une idéologie.' Mamadou Dia, *Condition humaine*, 23 Feb. 1948.
[3] M. Duverger, *Political Parties*, London 1954, p. 64.
[4] Oral information from M. Assane N'Doye, first assistant to the Mayor of Dakar. The anti-Diagne list of the Dakar municipal elections in 1933 included Paul Deffere, who had been the opposition candidate at the parliamentary election of 1924 and whose son, Gaston Defferre, was Colonial Minister in the Guy Mollet Government of 1956.

Senegalese S.F.I.O. federation seems to have been occasioned by the creation of the Popular Front Government in France and the visit, in 1936, of the new socialist colonial Minister, Marius Moutet. Lamine Gueye took a prominent part in the minister's reception by the Senegal *Comité du Front Populaire* and this was quickly followed by the formal foundation of the Senegal S.F.I.O. at a Congress held on 2 March 1937. Although Lamine Gueye became political director of the new party, it was not until June 1938 that a majority of the *Parti Socialiste Sénégalais* voted to merge with it. It is difficult to assess how far the initiative for the creation of the Senegal S.F.I.O. came from France, where it must have seemed to offer promising possibilities of a parliamentary seat, or how far, with the slow but steady move to the left in French politics, alliance with the socialists may have seemed to offer local party leaders the best hopes of effective metropolitan assistance, or how far it reflected a response to the somewhat more liberal approach to colonial problems shewn by the Popular Front government. Socialist terminology was certainly used in the party paper, 'sections' were created in Thiès and Kaolack, as well as in the old municipalities, and the federation was represented at S.F.I.O. congresses in France. The new party secured control of the municipality of Saint Louis in 1937 and by the outbreak of the war had obtained some representation in the Colonial Council and in the other municipalities. Further progress was, however, abruptly curtailed by the abolition of these institutions under the Vichy régime which remained in control of French West Africa until 1943.

With the Liberation, there was a great outburst of political activity and a large number of groups emerged, mostly in Dakar, whose mere names give a vivid impression of the atmosphere: *Mouvement Nationaliste Africain, Mouvement Autonomiste Africain, Comité Franco-Africain, Groupe d'Études Communiste, Union des Jeunes Bloc Sénégalais*. Many of them produced 'newspapers': *Communauté, Le Sénégal, Clarté*. What exactly they stood for or represented is doubtful, but by 1945 they had come together in a *Comité d'Entente* and attempted to create a united African party, the *Bloc Africain*. Once again, Lamine Gueye emerged as its leader.[1] This movement (if such it should properly be called, it was perhaps rather an aspiration) was stimulated by the increasing signs of reaction in France against the implications of the First Constitution for the future of the French Empire. Some at least of those in the *Bloc Africain* responded by demanding absolute equality and even independence.

[1] I have drawn heavily on Dr. Schachter's study for this account of the *Bloc Africain*.

TABLE 8

Elections to National Constituent Assembly, 1945–6

Year	Electorate	Valid votes	S.F.I.O.	Others
1945 Citizens	44,292	25,439	21,528 Lamine Gueye	Ousmane Soce Diop 3,633; Maillat 1,278
1945 Non-citizens	25,188	19,126	15,095 Senghor	Ely Manel Fall 1,695; Cros 1,302; Djim Momar Gueye 964; P. Diagne 37; A. Kolte 33
1946 Citizens	46,985	32,213	31,288 Lamine Gueye	..
1946 Non-citizens	28,461	20,718	20,718 Senghor	..

For the elections to the First and Second Constituent Assemblies, Senegal returned two deputies, one elected by the citizens, one by those of the subjects who were now enfranchised. Lamine Gueye, of course, was the obvious candidate for the former seat and he chose as the candidate for the latter, Léopold Sédar Senghor, the son of a prosperous Serer family, educated at the Catholic mission and at the Lycée in Dakar, and later in France, where he had been the first African to obtain his *agrégation* and had become a teacher in a Paris lycée and a poet of distinction. Lamine Gueye presented him to the 'subjects' as their deputy, the deputy of the bush as he was the deputy of the towns, meaning by that the old municipalities. Both took a prominent part in the debates on the Constitution: Senghor, indeed, became 'the grammarian of the Constitution' while Lamine Gueye secured the passage by the First Constituent Assembly of a law extending citizenship to all the former subjects and fought against the system of dual electorates. But the rejection of the April Constitution in the referendum (it had been overwhelmingly accepted by the Senegalese citizens), and the less liberal colonial provisions of the October Constitution, provoked a marked reaction among the new African leaders, of which the communists rapidly sought to take advantage. The *Groupe d'Études Communiste* at Dakar launched the idea of an African popular front which was taken up and recommended by a number of the African members of the Constituent Assembly. A manifesto issued in September 1946, called for a 'rally of all the organisations whose rapid development is the sure sign that they are pursuing the realisation of political and social democracy in Black Africa', and ended by convoking a Congress to be held at Bamako in the French Soudan in October 1946.[1]

These developments placed the Senegalese deputies in a difficult position. They had opposed the 'reactionary' provisions of the new Constitution and, with all the other African deputies, walked out when it was passed by the majority in the Assembly. Lamine Gueye was one of the signatories of the Bamako Congress Manifesto. On the other hand, he and Senghor were members of the S.F.I.O., and the Colonial Minister from January 1946 to October 1947 was the socialist Marius Moutet. At first, it seems, Moutet thought that the socialists would be able to dominate the Congress as they had been able in Senegal to utilize the confused enthusiams of the *Bloc Africain*. But when it became clear that this would not be the case, the African socialist deputies (Lamine Gueye, Senghor, and Yacine Diallo of Guinea) did not attend. The Congress, nevertheless, was held and a new 'movement' was created under the name *Rassemblement Démocratique Africain*. Its strongholds in French West Africa were the Ivory Coast, under the leadership of a wealthy planter and *médecin africain*, Houphouet-Boigny, and certain parts of the French Sudan, where its most prominent personality was Mamadou Konaté. It was not a purely French West African movement but, as its name implies, sought and obtained support elsewhere in Black Africa, notably in the Cameroons and in French Equatorial Africa. At the elections in October 1946 for the new National Assembly, candidates supporting the R.D.A. were elected in the Ivory Coast (3), the Soudan (1) and the Niger (1), while candidates supporting the S.F.I.O. were elected in Senegal (2), the Soudan (2), and in Guinea (1). The remaining three seats were won by purely local parties.

When the elections to the First Constituent Assembly took place, the 'old guard' politicians of the S.F.I.O. in Senegal had a great advantage. The spate of new 'organizations' committees, study groups, &c., mostly in Dakar, did not provide any effective network of communication with the new non-citizen electors. Lamine Gueye and those associated with him were, however, in touch with those old citizens who lived in the bush or the other towns of Senegal, with the chiefs, many of whom they had known in the pre-war Colonial Council, and with the major Muslim religious leaders.[2] For the elections to the Second Constituent, there were no other candidates, and by the end of the constitutional debates, the prestige not only of Lamine Gueye but also of Senghor was securely

---

[1] *Le R.D.A. dans la lutte anti-impérialiste* (Paris, 1948).

[2] Ibrahima Niass, Falilou M'Backé, and Babacar Sy all had personal links with the pre-war political leaders.

established. The R.D.A., which had a nucleus in Senegal in the *groupe d'études communiste*, put up candidates at the elections to the new National Assembly in 1946: they received 1,180 votes, to the socialists' 128,000. In elections for the General Council, all the seats had been won by a single *Bloc d'Union Socialiste et Républicaine*, which included besides the S.F.I.O., representatives of diverse interests and groups—European business men, the old *Métis* families, even R.D.A. sympathizers—a success which not only illustrated the continuance of one characteristic feature of Senegalese politics but also the advantages to the reigning politicians of the retention in Senegal of the system of four large multi-member constituencies.[1] A socialist group was immediately formed in the Council to manage business there but its importance in the party organization was much less than that of the *Bureau Fédéral*, on which the great majority of the fifteen members were Dakarois associates of Lamine Gueye.

There were soon signs of serious dissensions within the party. Their causes were complex. In part, they represented the jealousy of the newly enfranchized citizens of the bush (the former subjects) at the continued dominance, in the party councils and in the distribution of the spoils, of the old citizens' cliques; in part the natural hostility of the countryside to the towns; in part the rivalry of different ethnic groups and local associations, most of which were against the old citizens who had so long enjoyed a privileged position; in part dissatisfaction with the preoccupation with questions of political and juridical status which characterized socialist policy as represented by Lamine Gueye and his friends, and a demand, however vaguely felt, for more emphasis on the immediate social and economic problems of the hitherto less favoured subjects. In terms of party organization, these dissensions represented a conflict between the old conception of a small caucus of close associates around a dominant leader, appropriate to a numerically limited electorate, and a groping towards a more modern type of party organization, appropriate to a wider electorate and looking to an eventual establishment of universal suffrage. The newer outlook was voiced by Senghor at the 1947 Congress of the Senegal S.F.I.O. when he denounced 'clan policies', 'deputies of the first and second degree', and the 'nepotism' of the leadership. The report of the administrative secretary Paul Bonifay, a European lawyer in Dakar and one of the founders of the party, was rejected by a substantial majority. Senghor's support came from the main centres in the newly enfranchised areas, Kaolack, Thiès, and Ziguinchor, but the representatives of the old communes remained

[1] See above, p. 297.

loyal to Lamine Gueye.[1] Senghor's next step was the publication, in February 1948, of his own journal, *Condition humaine*, represented as an unofficial organ alongside the official S.F.I.O. paper, *l'A.O.F.* It would, said a leader in its second issue, 'denounce, with objectivity, errors, deviations, and routines'. While it asserted that 'assimilation is an illusion in a world whose peoples have become aware of their personality' and declared itself partisan of 'a rapidly increasing autonomy for French Black Africa', it would not nourish the myth of independence.[2]

Meanwhile in France there were important changes in the political scene. The socialist Moutet was replaced by the M.R.P. Coste Floret as Minister of Overseas France at the end of 1947, thus inaugurating a period of three years in which that party remained in control of the Ministry. It became more and more obvious that Senghor, who had only joined the S.F.I.O. in 1945,[3] could expect no help from the metropolitan hierarchy in a struggle against the long-established Lamine Gueye, whom many considered as having Black Africa solidly behind him. At the end of 1947 and early in 1948 a strike of the railway workers in West Africa, maintained in Senegal for five months under the direction of the C.G.T. trade union might have suggested that an effective R.D.A. section could be developed there. But such a development had no attraction for the Catholic Senghor at a time when the effects of the communist affiliation of the R.D.A. were every day becoming more obvious, when the struggle with communism in France itself was reaching its height, and when the centre of gravity in metropolitan politics was moving towards the right. In September 1948, with M.R.P. encouragement, a new French parliamentary group of Overseas deputies, the *Indépendants d'outre-mer*, was created, and on 27 September Senghor resigned from the S.F.I.O. The grounds on which he justified his resignation were not doctrinal. He remained faithful, he said, to socialist ideals. It was essentially a protest against the dictatorship of Lamine Gueye in Senegal and the lack of internal party democracy, not only in Senegal but in the metropolitan party hierarchy in its dealings with Overseas Territories. How, he asked, could Africans understand an invitation to fight communist dictatorship if for it there was to be substituted not even a socialist, but a 'Laminist', dictatorship. In Black Africa at any rate, the party was neither democratic in organization nor socialist in action. The S.F.I.O. in the National Assembly, moreover, had voted against equal pensions for Africans and metropolitan veterans; it had abstained on a pro-

[1] Schachter, op. cit.   [2] *Condition humaine*, 11 and 25 Feb. 1948.
[3] *L'A.O.F.*, 4 Nov. 1948.

posal to abolish the system of separate electorates (and but for the Overseas deputies would have opposed it); it had voted against the extension of French social security arrangements to the new Overseas departments. In fact, the party 'in the French Union and often in the *métropole*, sacrifices principles to electoral results, Marxist ethic and socialist action to tactics. The truth is that the party uses the Overseas Territories as means not ends. In Black Africa, these means are very often administrative pressure, corruption, spying and secret accusation'.[1]

Senghor had not acted impulsively. He had consulted his friends in Senegal and especially the leaders in the Sine Saloum constituency, which he claimed had one-third of Senegal's population, and he was assured of their support. It was soon avowed, when Ibrahima Seydou N'Dao, a lifelong associate of Lamine Gueye and the dominant figure in politics in the Kaolack region, joined the new party,[2] and this example was quickly followed by other areas. The new party took the name *Bloc Démocratique Sénégalais*. It was essentially constitutional in outlook and sought electoral success. It aimed at building up an organization reflecting the actual social structure of the country, and representing its ethnic, economic, religious, and social interests and groups. In this it to some extent took over the outlook of the older political leadership while adapting it to the new conditions brought about by the extension of the electorate, but it combined their practical preoccupations with much more attention to ideological needs. Its attempt to reflect within itself the actual structure of Senegalese society—'to work for the unity of the country by the unity of the party'—was accompanied by a new emphasis on African culture and the elaboration of an African socialism emphasizing social and economic needs rather than constitutional niceties. Although it violently attacked the Senegal administration, it was not because it was French but because it was directed by a socialist governor, Wiltord. The autonomy which it declared to be its objective was to be found in a federal relationship between metropolitan France and the Overseas Territories, a 'Republic one and divisible', in a phrase Senghor was later to make famous.

---

[1] Senghor to Guy Mollet, *Condition humaine*, 5 Oct. 1948.

[2] Like Senghor, he was irritated by Lamine Gueye's decision to elect as one of Senegal's three representatives in the Assembly of the French Union, his personal friend, Djim Momar Gueye, who had created a *Parti Travailliste Indépendant* in N'Dao's fief, the Sine-Saloum, polled 7,000 votes against the socialist list in the general council elections, and had only recently joined the S.F.I.O. Senghor's candidate was Mamadou Dia, the exceptionally able Toucouleur schoolmaster from Fatick in the Sine-Saloum, and General Secretary of the new party. Ibid. and 2 Nov. 1948.

Initially this theme, never violently advocated, was little in evidence. The only specific institutional reforms demanded in the policy statement at the first Congress of the new party were municipal reform and the substitution of the administrative districts as constituencies for the four constituencies established for the Senegal General Council in 1946. Both had a direct relation to the struggle with the Senegal S.F.I.O., with the means for waging which the remaining paragraphs of the political section of the party programme were concerned. Its emphasis was strongly on social and economic problems. Pride of place was given to education (village schools, improved conditions for teachers, scholarships, technical education and the inclusion of Arabic and African languages in secondary school curricula) and health (dispensaries and maternity centres in the bush). The programme also included the early enactment of the Labour code for Overseas Territories (long delayed by colonial interests in the metropolitan legislature), the promotion of genuine co-operatives and the reform of agriculture credit, improved groundnut prices, the encouragement of rice and other food-crops, the multiplication of markets, post-offices, wells, and roads.[1] If it could be stigmatized as rather a list of desiderata than a statement of policy, it was nonetheless closely related to the everyday life and grievances of the new electorate. The success of the new party, which secured both Senegal seats in the National Assembly elections of 1951 and forty-one of the fifty seats in those for the Territorial Assembly (as the General Council was rechristened) in 1952, showed that its assessment of the political situation in Senegal was accurate and its organization effective.

TABLE 6

Elections to National and Territorial Assemblies, 1946–57

Year	Electorate	Valid votes	Socialist	B.D.S. B.P.S.	Others
1946 (A.N.)	192,861	130,118	128,284	..	1,180 (R.D.A.) 654 (Front Intercolonial)
1946 (C.G.)	196,696	103,566	87,215	..	16,351 (several lists)
1951 (A.N.)	665,281	314,681	96,101	213,182	..
1952 (T.A.)	660,981	319,385	95,560	223,825	..
1956 (A.N.)	835,035	454,886	101,732	346,266	6,888 (U.D.S.)
1957 (T.A.)	1,068,811	580,839	105,085	454,533	21,221 (18 lists)

But a purely territorial basis was inadequate in French West African politics, not only because of the federal organization of the

[1] *Condition humaine*, 26 Apr. 1949.

group as a whole and the important functions allocated to the Grand Council, but also because of the 'metropolitan axis'[1] which arises from the representation of the Overseas Territories in the French parliament. We have already noticed the formation, just before Senghor's resignation from the S.F.I.O., of the group of *Indépendants d'outre-mer*. In November 1948 he joined it and soon became *its* leader. The I.O.M. was in its origins essentially a parliamentary group whose members had been elected by very diverse local groups and their territorial support outside Senegal was not solidly based on local party organizations comparable with the B.D.S. Its policy statement of 1949 makes no reference to organization in Africa, and under the heading *raisons d'être* is concerned only to explain that the metropolitan parties had been too preoccupied with their own problems to devote themselves seriously to those of the Overseas Territories, while their rigidity had deprived the Overseas deputies of any real chance of effective parliamentary action. It was, however, at pains to deny that it sought to play the role of arbiter in a pre-dominantly metropolitan assembly.[2] In 1950 it showed signs of an approach, albeit somewhat tentative, towards developing a basis outside parliament, and referred to its role of 'parliamentary spokes-man of the overseas groups of which it is the emanation'.[3]

Meanwhile a crisis was approaching in the affairs of the R.D.A. The absence of the socialists at Bamako in 1946 left the communists with a clear field, and the new movement's affiliation to them became more and more pronounced in its propaganda. It retained its radical outlook and emphasis on racial equality in such matters as citizenship rights, discrimination in conditions of employment, and trade unionism, but in addition its publications were full of denuncia-tions of Western imperialism, opposition to the Indo-China war, to the Marshall plan, to the Korean war, and to N.A.T.O. Communist influence in the movement was most marked at its second Congress, held at Abidjan in the Ivory Coast in 1949. But with the steady right-ward trend in French politics, M.R.P. control of the Overseas Ministry, and the recovery of the local administration from its post-war confu-sion and uncertainty, the practical disadvantages of this association with the communists became more and more evident. The strong policy pursued by the Ivory Coast administration in combating the R.D.A. by every means open to it and the evident support of the local administration by the metropolitan government, made some headway in detaching support from the R.D.A. in the Ivory Coast

---

[1] T. L. Hodgkin, 'Political Parties in British and French West Africa', *Africa Bureau Information Digest* (Aug. 1953), p. 14.   [2] *Condition humaine*, 11 Jan. 1949.
[3] *Journées d'études des I.O.M.* (Paris, July 1950).

Assembly, and in 1950 a conciliatory move by the new U.D.S.R. Overseas Minister, Mitterrand, convinced Houphouet-Boigny that it was necessary to break decisively with the communists.[1] Although he was able to avoid a formal split in the party in the Ivory Coast and the Soudan, the small R.D.A. section in Senegal, the *Union Démocratique Sénégalais*, never accepted the new line and remained representative of the old *communisant* R.D.A. until it was formally expelled from the party at its third interterritorial meeting (held at Conakry in June 1955) when a new orthodox Senegalese section of the R.D.A. was established under the title *Mouvement Populaire Sénégalais*. The official R.D.A. policy in 1951 became much more 'collaborationist' in tone. It explained that its alliance with the communists had been made when the communists were members of the French Government and because they seemed most sympathetic to R.D.A. policy, but that when the communists left the Government, the fight against them had been extended to the R.D.A. who were, however, neither communist nor anti-French: the class war was irrelevant to the actual conditions of African society and it was 'impossible to think that France and the Territories could do without each other'.[2]

Thus, by the national assembly elections in June 1951, three major groups, each with pretensions to being something more than merely territorial movements, had emerged in French West Africa, the S.F.I.O., the I.O.M., and the R.D.A. In fact, however, they were not at all comparable. The socialists had been left behind in the post-war development of African politics. Their strength was in the older generation of administration employées, and their appeal was more to their achievement in 1945–6 than to any positive policy for the future. Nevertheless in the Soudan and in Guinée their deputies still commanded substantial support. The R.D.A., in spite of its new look, was still regarded by most of the local administrations as the enemy, and these undoubtedly gave their support to any local personality who appeared to offer an alternative: the *parti de l'administration*, whatever its local name, existed in many territories, and in some it was the party associated with the I.O.M. In Senegal the B.D.S., in the Ivory Coast (and also in parts of the Soudan) the R.D.A. represented by contrast real political machines, carefully organized to include all the major interests and regional groups. The elections of 1951 saw a considerable extension of the franchise but the extent to which it was reflected in the electoral registers differed greatly in different territories, partly because of the electoral preoccupations of the administration.[1] For these reasons, it is difficult to interpret the results, which appeared to show considerable success for the I.O.M. (which won eight of the twenty seats) and a resounding defeat for the R.D.A. (which had only two seats) with the S.F.I.O. still strong with five.

In the following years, the *immobilisme* of metropolitan politics was paralleled by something of a 'pause' in political activity in French West Africa, to the detriment of the political forces which had, with or without administrative support, emerged as the victors in 1951 and 1952. After the long-delayed enactment in 1952 of the Labour Code for Overseas Territories and the Territorial Assembly law (which made no change in the powers of these bodies) no further institutional changes affecting the Overseas Territories were made until the Municipal Reform law was at last pushed through as the National Assembly neared the end of its term in November 1955. Nothing was done about the extension of the franchise, the abolition of separate electorates, the enlargement of the powers of the territorial assemblies, the participation of Africans in the territorial executives, Africanization of the public service, or the revision of the French Union chapter in the 1946 Constitution.[2] There was a pause, too, after the end of the 'plan' for 1949–53, in the tempo of overseas investment financed from F.I.D.E.S., greater emphasis on economic, as opposed to social, development seemed (and could certainly be represented) to mean more emphasis on projects of a traditional colonial type favouring European commercial interests, while the grandiose schemes of mechanized agriculture started in the enthusiasm of the earlier 'plans' were one by one written off as uneconomic.

Such an atmosphere could not fail to be disadvantageous to the politicians elected in 1951, who generally were to be found in the metropolitan government's majority but seemed to get little from it except a minor ministerial post which merely compromised them the more. More and more, after 1953, observers remarked the gulf between the parliamentarians and the younger generation of educated Africans, many of whom were radical in outlook, strongly anti-colonial, hostile to Europeans, preaching the virtues of *négritude*, much influenced by Marxist theory and by communist ideas about political organization.[3] Especially in Guinea and the Soudan, they gravitated

---

[1] See Robinson, op. cit., pp. 163–5.

[2] See the debate on Overseas policy in the National Assembly in Apr. 1954 (*J. O. débats parlementaires, Assemblée Nationale*, 10 Apr. 1954, pp. 2024–8).

[3] Cf. P. Mercier, 'Evolution of Senegalese Elites', *International Social Science Bulletin*, vol. viii (1956), p. 450; *Les Etudiants Noirs parlent* (Paris, 1953); Abdoulaye Ly, *Les Masses africaines etl'actuel le condition humaine* (Paris, 1956).

to an R.D.A. which had retained much of the radical fervour of the pre-1950 movement. Many were active in the youth movement and some in trade unionism, predominantly C.G.T. in West Africa. In Senegal a few were attracted to the small but tough core of the U.D.S., which had never accepted the official post-1950 R.D.A. line. Others remained aloof from specifically political action, or formed small 'discussion groups' and coteries, critical of the local political 'establishment'.[1]

The *Indépendants d'outre-mer* made a further effort at a Congress in Bobo Dioulasso in 1953 to establish themselves as a real inter-territorial movement based on strong territorial organizations,[2] but the B.D.S. remained the only really solidly based and territory-wide West African party within the group. Dr. Conombo's *Parti social d'éducation des masses africaines* in Upper Volta, which came nearest to it in achieving a popular political movement, found itself opposed by another also claiming to be I.O.M.; M. Hubert Maga's *Groupement ethnique du Nord-Dahomey* was frankly an organ of regional (and ethnic) particularism.[3] It was, indeed, a characteristic of this period that much of such feeling, long concealed by the iron grid of the French administration in pre-war years, now emerged. In Senegal the B.D.S. was to some extent founded on it, but it had succeeded in welding the mass of such ethnic and local groups into a territory-wide movement. In this respect it had structurally much in common with Houphouet's Ivory Coast R.D.A.[4] After the internal R.D.A. crisis of 1950, an alliance between them might have seemed in the natural order of things and would have given the Senegalese party a solid beginning in the interterritorial support which it later sought through the I.O.M. In 1950 there were indeed *pourparlers* between the R.D.A., *tendance Houphouet*, and the I.O.M., but they came to nothing, and in the end the R.D.A. chose to ally itself for parliamentary purposes with the U.D.S.R., the small centre group that included M. Mitterrand and M. Pleven. Subsequent tentative discussions between the B.D.S. and the R.D.A. leaders equally led to nothing, nor did more public talk of a *regroupement* of the political parties which continued intermittently after 1953. Thus, when the elections of January 1956 took place, the three major groups confronting each other in West Africa were once again the S.F.I.O., the I.O.M., and the R.D.A.

---

[1] The small group who published the journal *Réalités africaines* from Feb. 1954 to early 1956 and subsequently joined the B.P.S. are one example.

[2] *Congrès des indépendants d'outre-mer de Bobo Dioulasso*, 1953.

[3] See R. Grivot, *Réactions dahoméennes* (Paris, 1954), p. 85.

[4] See M. Vignaud, 'Les Elections du 2 Janvier 1956 en Côte d'Ivoire', *Revue française de science politique*, vol. vi (1957), pp. 570–82.

The most important fact about these elections was that the French administration in West Africa, which in 1951 had thrown all its weight against the R.D.A., remained neutral.[1] The R.D.A. more than recovered from its 1951 losses. It won 2 seats in Guinea, 2 in the Soudan, 2 in the Ivory Coast, and 1 in the Niger, a total of 7 to the 4 of the I.O.M. and 2 of the S.F.I.O. In Senegal, the solid position of the B.D.S. was once more demonstrated (see Table 7). Their two candidates, Senghor and Mamadou Dia, were of course easily elected; while the S.F.I.O. vote remained practically the same as in 1951, that of the B.D.S. showed an increase of about 60 per cent. The U.D.S. polled a mere 6,000 votes. In their electoral campaign, the B.D.S. stressed the theme of 'autonomy', a complete reorganization of relations between France and Africa in the French Union, and a much greater measure of self-government for its constituent territories. This was to be the theme of the following year.

5. *The Background to the Election: Political History, 1956–7*

In their 1956 election campaign, the B.D.S. put more emphasis than previously on the demand for self-government (*autonomie*) within a federal association with France. They had shown that they were aware of the importance of capturing the support of the recently returned students and other uncommitted members of the intelligentsia, most of whom had held aloof from the older political formations in Senegal and whose general outlook was closer to that of the more nationalistic wing of the R.D.A., and particularly to that of its young and dynamic leader in Guinea, M. Sekou Touré. They had also referred sympathetically to the need for a new union of African political parties, intermittently discussed for some years, a proposal which now had a decidedly nationalist undertone. Among the S.F.I.O., too, there were more dynamic elements to whom such a conception was more attractive than to the party stalwarts, in whose essentially conservative and empirical approach to Senegalese politics they found an obstacle to the rejuvenation of their party on more ideological lines. The U.D.S., for its part, could not be unaware of the potential advantages, to a trained and politically conscious group of theoreticians, of capturing the mass support of the B.D.S. by securing an influential place in the leadership of a new, united party. The small orthodox R.D.A. section in Senegal, the M.P.S., flushed with R.D.A. success in the elections elsewhere in West Africa, saw no future for the B.D.S.; if it did not, under cover of the

[1] 'French Africa's New Deputies', *West Africa*, 15 January, 1956; André Blanchet, *Le Monde*, 11 May 1957, p. 4, and much oral information.

call for African unity, merge with the R.D.A., it would, before long, find itself virtually isolated in French West Africa. Even in Senegal the new movement for an autonomous African trade union organization, led in West Africa as a whole by Sekou Touré, might soon afford a basis of organized mass support for the R.D.A.

On the wider West African front, the situation facing the B.D.S. was, indeed, not encouraging. There were bound to be elections for new territorial assemblies early in 1957 and these in turn meant a new Grand Council. Since 1952 the B.D.S. and its allies in the I.O.M. had enjoyed a dominant position in the Grand Council; but if the national assembly elections presaged, as they almost certainly did, comparable R.D.A. successes in the territorial assembly elections in the following year, that dominance would be destroyed and the B.D.S. might be reduced to its few Senegal seats. This could be avoided either by a fusion with the R.D.A. or by a new attempt to develop in some other West African territories parties allied to the B.D.S., which were not mere electoral committees but genuine mass-parties. The latter seemed possible only through greater emphasis on African nationalism, already apparent in the B.D.S. campaign in the National Assembly elections.

It would, however, be misleading to imply that tactical considerations of this kind were the only effective, or even the dominant, factors in the movement for a united front of African parties, though they were assuredly not absent. Among politically conscious West Africans there had undoubtedly been for several years increasing nationalist feeling, a mood more and more outspokenly hostile to colonial rule, less and less interested in the refinements of juridical forms, more impatient of reformist schemes, and more and more determined that Africans must be masters in their own house.[1] Certainly, there was little agreement about the precise nature of the future West African polity, its relation to existing territorial units, or the character of its association with metropolitan France. None of the older and more experienced leaders wished to see an outright breach with France: they hoped to avoid it. But they could not ignore the rising tide of feeling among the newer élite that the time for temporizing was passing, and in fact many of them shared it. At the very least, another instalment of reforms, this time effecting some

---

[1] I am aware of the criticisms that have been made of the use of the word 'nationalism' in African contexts [see J. S. Coleman, 'Nationalism in Africa', *American Political Science Review*, vol. xlviii (1954), pp. 404–26, and Lord Hailey, *An African Survey* (London, 1957), pp. 251–60] but for my present purpose it seems to me less misleading than any other word, and I have tried briefly to indicate its scope and limitations in the context in which I employ it.

real transfer of executive power into African hands, was overdue. If it did not come soon, the growing nationalist surge might burst its banks and sweep them away with it.[1] *Regroupement*, as it was generally termed, was, therefore, much more than a mere matter of political tactics *vis-à-vis* the metropolitan government or metropolitan parties; it was, pre-eminently, an aspiration, as well as an instrument, of nationalism. But it could not free itself from the political history of the last ten years, from the conflicts of personality, of metropolitan alliances, of doctrine and, perhaps most of all, of individual temperament, expressed in that history. It remained a subject for cool tactical appraisal by political operators and theoreticians as well as an expression of the mystique of nationalism.

The established B.D.S. approach to *regroupement* had been outlined in reply to earlier overtures from the U.D.S. Party unification must be interterritorial and based on African needs, not on the interests of metropolitan parties; within Senegal itself any such proposals called for an honest recognition of the efforts and achievements of the B.D.S. if they were to carry conviction as more than a pretext by which those defeated at the polls sought to climb on the backs of the victors.[2] Both parts of this analysis seemed relevant to the fate of their own approach to the R.D.A. immediately after the 1956 elections. Although apparently sympathetic initially, the R.D.A. declined to pursue the B.D.S. suggestion: they were unwilling to abandon their association with the U.D.S.R., with whom they supported the new French Government formed by Guy Mollet, in which their leader, Houphouet-Boigny, was the first African to enjoy full ministerial rank in France. And far from joining in any move towards a union of African political parties, the R.D.A. seemed more disposed, in those territories where they had not yet achieved a dominant position, to work towards detaching parties hitherto associated with the I.O.M. and so to increase the isolation of the B.D.S. The prospects of party unification on an interterritorial basis were, for the present at any rate, evidently bleak. In the meantime, the accession to the B.D.S.

---

[1] A well-informed commentator in 1954 quoted L. S. Senghor as saying, 'Il ne faut pas oublier les aspirations de la génération montante qui s'expriment avec plus de netteté lors du retour de France des étudiants. Si un programme d'évolution politique n'est pas proposé à leur suffrage, il est à craindre qu'elle ne présente un ensemble de revendications beaucoup plus radical', and commented ,'M. Senghor laissait entendre encore qu'il ne pourrait personnellement plus rien faire pour empêcher l'éclosion du nationalisme et qu'alors les hommes qui seraient portés à la tête du mouvement se soucieraient peut-être moins que lui de réaliser l'équilibre harmonieux entre les positions française et africaine . . . cela est vrai.'

[2] L. S. Senghor, 'Les Conditions de l'unité d'action', *Condition humaine*, 10 Sept. 1954.

of some leading personalities[1] among the hitherto uncommitted intelligentsia in Senegal resulted in the emergence within that party of energetic support for an immediate attempt at unification within Senegal, in advance of any interterritorial agreement, for which a new proposal was made in March 1956 by the U.D.S. At the eighth annual congress of the B.D.S. at Kaolack in May, this opinion carried the day, and the newly elected executive bureau, in which the younger, pro-fusion, element was strongly represented, was authorized to organize meetings with the other Senegalese parties with a view to 'clarifying the methods' by which a 'unified workers' and peasants' party' might be created in Senegal—a party in which, of course, the B.D.S. would necessarily be predominant.[2]

Such a territorial approach was of course most likely to mean, in practice, the merging of the U.D.S. in the B.D.S., since neither of the other parties, the S.F.I.O. and the M.P.S., were under the final control of leaders in Senegal, and they would hardly be allowed to join in any local fusion in the absence of an interterritorial one. (The B.D.S. invitations indeed recognized this difficulty in the case of the M.P.S., and referred to a possible agreement for 'unity of action' pending interterritorial agreement for union.) But from the B.D.S. point of view even the elimination of the U.D.S. offered some advantages: the M.P.S. would be precluded from any similar move and so from securing the support of a nucleus of Senegal politicians who, if few in number, were disciplined and politically sophisticated. There would be an end of any immediate possibility of an opposition which could outbid the B.P.S. 'No enemies on the left' is a maxim particularly relevant to an established (and hitherto rather 'reformist') party in a colonial situation. Moreover, such a merger would strengthen those now within the B.D.S. who were anxious to transform it into a more dynamic, not to say revolutionary, party. And if some of the younger and more ebullient members of the S.F.I.O. and the M.P.S. should be detached in the process, that would be all to the good.

At first, however, it looked as if all parties might accept fusion. On 11 June their delegates to the special meeting called by the B.D.S. agreed to recommend it, and to meet again on 30 June to confirm their agreement and to set up a commission to work out the practical details. Still more remarkable, a socialist conference at

---

[1] Notably Dr. Abdoulaye Ly and M. A. M. M'Bow (*Condition humaine*, 26 Jan. 1956). Although uncommitted in Senegalese politics they were avowed Marxists. They later broke with the older Senegalese leaders when the latter decided to campaign for the constitutional proposals of De Gaulle in the referendum of 29 Sept. 1958.   [2] *Condition humaine*, 31 May 1956.

Saint-Louis on 13 June agreed to fusion in principle and decided to break from the metropolitan S.F.I.O. as a necessary preliminary. But on 29 June, Lamine Gueye told the S.F.I.O. congress at Lille that there was no question of the Senegal federation leaving the S.F.I.O.; all that it sought was a certain autonomy.[1] Although the discussions continued (for the Senegal socialist leaders were divided) it was clear that the socialists as a whole would not agree to fusion; and, in the event, only the *Mouvement Autonome Casamançais*, which had had an electoral alliance with the S.F.I.O. at the 1956 elections, joined as a party. The next to withdraw were the M.P.S., who demanded that each of the three remaining parties (i.e. the B.D.S., U.D.S., and M.P.S.) should be equally represented in the proposed commission, a demand obviously unacceptable to the B.D.S. It seemed that when the R.D.A. high command realized that the B.D.S. did not intend to join the R.D.A., they decided to withdraw.[2] Nevertheless, the B.D.S., the U.D.S., the M.A.C., and some individual members of the M.P.S. continued their negotiations and on 12 August they agreed to form a new party, the *Bloc Populaire Sénégalais*. This was to be created after 1 September and to be formally established at a constituent congress in February 1957.

Meanwhile, these developments in Senegal had been followed by others at the interterritorial level. On 30 June 1956 Mamadou Dia launched a new call for party fusion, this time from Paris and in his capacity as Secretary-General of the I.O.M.; he proposed a Congress, aiming at the unification of all autonomous political movements in the overseas territories and departments, to be held in Dakar not later than December. The prospects for any really inclusive fusion, even of West African parties, seemed, however, to be deteriorating. The R.D.A. continued to hold aloof. It was planning its own congress, to be held, it was hoped, at Bamako on the tenth anniversary of its founding there in the autumn of 1946. The African socialist leaders, following Lamine Gueye's pronouncement at the Lille congress of the S.F.I.O., were considering ways and means of turning the African branches of the party into an 'autonomous' African socialist party which would remain formally associated with the S.F.I.O. After discussions in Paris in September and October with the executive of the S.F.I.O., it was decided that a *Mouvement Socialiste Africain* should be established, for which purpose a congress was to be held in Conakry at the end of November. The platform of the new movement,[3] true to the assimilationist tradition of the socialists,

---

[1] *Le Monde*, 30 June 1956.
[2] For the documents relating to fusion, see *Condition humaine*, 11 July, 26 July, and 16 Aug. 1956.   [3] Text in *L'A.O.F.*, 30 Nov. 1956.

emphasized the independence of the individual as the prerequisite of any true independence of peoples. Such individual freedom and political democracy, it pointed out, implied the existence of several parties and the right of opposition. The new movement, its manifesto expressly stated, was, accordingly, opposed to the setting up of any single party.

In the event, all the congresses were postponed: those of the I.O.M. and the socialists until 10–13 January 1957: that of the R.D.A., after several more postponements, was held in September 1957. Party activities in the autumn of 1956 were concentrated on the elections for the newly created full municipalities held in November 1956.[1] Under the Municipal Reform law of 1955 Gorée was to be separated from Dakar, so that elections were also called for in Dakar itself. The results of these elections in Senegal gave the B.P.S. control of the new municipalities in Kaolack, Thiès, Ziguinchor,

TABLE 7

Senegal Municipal Elections, November 1956

Town	Electorate	Valid votes	B.P.S.	Seats	S.F.I.O.	Seats
Dakar	50,371	41,963	17,737	16	24,226	21
Gorée	372	262	Single list elected			..
Thiès	13,150	9,354	6,611	22	2,933	9
Kaolack	11,097	8,278	5,991	25	2,287	8
Diourbel	7,138	5,335	3,281	17	2,054	10
Ziguinchor	4,905	4,131	2,932	21	1,199	6
Louga*	5,609	4,267	1,557	10	930	5
All	129,642	76,170	38,109	111	33,619	59

* The dissident B.P.S. group, with 1,780 votes won 12 seats.

Source: Direction des Affaires Politiques du Haut-Commissariat de L'A.O.F.

and Diourbel. The socialists retained control of Dakar, while at Louga a new party of dissidents from the B.P.S. won twelve seats to the ten of the B.P.S. and, in alliance with the socialists who had secured five, gained control of the municipality.[2] As these elections were the first widespread appeal to the electorate since 1952 and also the first to be held on the new registers drawn up in the summer after the introduction of universal suffrage, the results were of some general interest. In spite of the apparently sweeping success of the B.P.S.,

[1] See above, p. 293.
[2] The new party called itself the *Bloc démocratique du N'Diambour*. The proximate cause of the split within the B.P.S. was disagreement about nominations for the municipal elections; the underlying reasons were acute disagreements between two 'factions'. See below, p. 344.

the difference between the two parties in terms of votes cast was calculated to give the socialists some encouragement for the future. In fact such strength as they had was disproportionately represented in the towns; in the 'bush' the B.P.S. support was much more overwhelming. The socialists, however, contended that their good showing in the larger towns only went to prove their contention that in the bush socialist voters were intimidated and elections were a farce. When proper control was possible and insisted on by the authorities, they were, they could argue, much more nearly a match for the B.P.S. than earlier elections suggested.

One further development in 1956 was of great interest to the politically minded, as well as providing further evidence of the rising tide of nationalist feeling. This was the growth of a movement for the transformation of the various trade unions which had grown up in French West Africa since the war into a single African trade union organization, wholly independent of metropolitian trade unionism and, for the present at least, of the rival international trade union organizations.[1] Trade unionism in French West Africa had developed within the orbit of the French trade union movement with the result that there were unions affiliated to each of the three rival metropolitan organizations, the communist C.G.T., the socialist C.G.T.F.O. (*Force Ouvrière*), and the catholic C.F.T.C. In West Africa, unions were organized both on a territorial and an occupational basis. The union concerned with one occupation, e.g. railwaymen, might in one territory be associated with the Christian trade unions, while in another the railwaymen's union was affiliated to the C.G.T. This had resulted in the establishment of several federations of all unions in French West Africa concerned with a particular occupational group, whatever the metropolitan organization with which the various territorial unions might be associated. The most important of these so-called 'autonomous' trade union federations was that of the railwaymen.

Ever since the R.D.A. break with the communists in 1950, some nominally C.G.T. unions, especially in the Ivory Coast, had been in a somewhat ambivalent position, and the C.G.T. had violently attacked autonomist tendencies as a betrayal of the class struggle, which, indeed, Houphouet-Boigny had specifically declared irrele-

[1] The history of trade union development in French West Africa remains unwritten. This account is based on oral information from Senegal trade unionists and on articles in *Afrique nouvelle*, *L'Unité* (the B.P.S. newspaper) especially 4 Feb. 1957, *La Liberté* (the R.D.A. newspaper in Guinea) especially 11 Dec. 1956, and *L'Afrique force ouvrière*, especially 9 Feb. 1957. See also R. Schachter, 'Trade Unions seek Autonomy', *West Africa*, 19 and 26 Jan. 1957, and P-H. Siriex, *Une Nouvelle Afrique*, pp. 251–61.

vant in African colonial conditions. The I.O.M., for their part, pronounced in 1953 in favour of an autonomous and unified trade union movement, a view which fitted in logically with their general policy. They had, however, little influence with the African leaders of the C.G.T. unions which had the largest following in West Africa, and it was not until the R.D.A. pronounced in favour of an autonomous African trade union movement at its Co-ordinating Committee meeting in Conakry in 1955 that there appeared to be any serious possibility of such a development. Immediately after the National Assembly elections of 1956, Sekou Touré, the R.D.A. leader in Guinea who was also Secretary-General of the C.G.T. unions there, proposed the formation of an independent African trade union movement. He obtained some support from other R.D.A. sympathizers among C.G.T. union leaders, particularly in Senegal, and in April 1956 the *Confédération Générale des Travailleurs d'Afrique* (C.G.T.A.) was formally established. Throughout 1956 there was a prolonged struggle between the new movement and the C.G.T. African leaders, who tried to recover the ground they had lost by calling for a great African trade union conference (at which C.G.T. unions from French territories outside West Africa would redress the balance) with a view to the establishment of an African trade union movement allied to the communist W.F.T.U. Ultimately, however, faced with the support given to the C.G.T.A. idea by the railwaymen's union, they were obliged to acquiesce in the conference being called to establish a movement independent not only of French metropolitan unionism but also, initially at least, of the international organizations. Meanwhile the Christian trade unions had, at their congress in Wagadougou in July 1956, transformed themselves into a *Confédération Africaine des Travailleurs Croyants* (C.A.T.C.), directly linked with the International Federation of Christian Trade Unions. The socialist C.G.T.-F.O. alone refused to abandon the old policy of integration with the metropolitan movement. It was, however, by far the weakest of the three metropolitan movements in French West Africa. By the end of the year the C.G.T., the C.G.T.A., and the C.A.T.C. had joined in summoning a conference, to be held at Cotonou in January 1957, to set up a single African trade union movement, free of any affiliation with French metropolitan or rival international trade union organizations, and wholly independent of any political party.

These developments among trade unionists paralleled those in the political sphere. Trade union fusionism, like political fusionism, was an expression of nationalist feeling. But, like the movement for political *regroupement*, it was also part of the struggle for power between rivals. As such it exemplified the ambivalent role of the R.D.A. and of the newer Marxist intelligentsia as well as the increasing difficulties of orthodox communists in the face of rising nationalism. No doubt the R.D.A. genuinely wished to detach the C.G.T. unions, in which many of its important personalities were leaders, from their affiliation with metropolitan communism, but their campaign for an autonomous trade union federation could also be considered a natural means of increasing R.D.A. strength; for example, in Senegal, it might provide the real foothold the M.P.S. had so far lacked. The small group of Marxist intellectuals in the B.D.S. who had successfully worked for a territorial fusion of political parties had also played an important part in the formation of a C.G.T.A. movement in the Senegal unions. They saw the trade unions as a major instrument in their struggle to bring about a united, disciplined, and revolutionary anti-colonial movement in which by reason of their superior political education they would enjoy a decisive influence. The C.G.T. communists, for their part, hoped to retain control of West African trade unionism, to avoid being swallowed up in an autonomous movement which they could not control, and to keep any such movement within the world communist trade union federation.

The opening weeks of the year 1957 marked a momentary climax in all this political activity. The interterritorial party conference, sponsored originally by the I.O.M., was held in Dakar, 11–13 January.[1] If it was now emphasized that it was not an I.O.M. conference, an attentive student could not fail to notice that although some other parties, notably the R.D.A., were represented by ob- servers, the fully participating parties were all ones which were, or had earlier been, associated with the I.O.M. The conference, which was remarkably harmonious, decided to create a new interterritorial party, the *Convention africaine*. Besides working for a fusion of all African parties and an independent parliamentary group, the new party would seek a revision of the Constitution on federal lines. Territories should be free to accept internal autonomy within a federal French republic or to become Associated States in a con- federal association with it. While each territory was entitled to auto- nomy, those which now made up the federations of French West Africa and French Equatorial Africa must remain associated in these two groups which should be transformed into two states capable of being integrated within the federal republic. If all this sounded much like earlier pronouncements of the B.D.S. and the I.O.M., the

---

[1] See *Convention africaine: Congrès interterritorial du regroupement des partis politiques africains* (Dakar, 1957); also *L'Unité*, 4 Feb. 1957.

atmosphere of the conference, as well as the tone of the lucid report on general policy presented by the indefatigable Mamadou Dia, was very much more obviously revolutionary and nationalist. The impressive R.D.A. delegation,[1] in a declaration which, though non-committal was nevertheless encouraging to the protagonists of fusion, offered the conference a rendezvous at the forthcoming R.D.A. congress at Bamako and remarked that India, Morocco, Tunisia, and Ghana had attained their 'political majority' only after achieving a single, or at least overwhelmingly predominant, party.

Simultaneously, the socialists were launching their new African Socialist Movement at a conference at Conakry in French Guinea.[2] The general policy report, presented by Lamine Gueye, was, after numerous speeches, passed unanimously. It endorsed the themes of the original manifesto of the previous October: a free association between metropolitan France and the Overseas Territories, the immediate creation in those territories of African governments responsible to their elected assemblies, and the liberation of the individual by extensive social, educational, and economic reform. The most heated debate, which some thought threatened the very existence of the conference, occurred on the first day. In the embarrassed presence of the large contingent from the metropolitan S.F.I.O., speaker after speaker denounced subordination to that party and demanded a complete independence for the new movement and its representatives in the metropolitan assemblies. A diplomatic speech by the acting Secretary-General of the S.F.I.O., Pierre Commin, finally persuaded the conference to agree that the parliamentary representatives of the new movement should be 'administratively associated' with the S.F.I.O. parliamentary group,[3] and its rules also made provision for it to be represented at S.F.I.O. conferences by observers with the right to speak but not vote. The net effect of the congress resolutions was to convey the impression that the new M.S.A. was little more than the old S.F.I.O., as the C.A. was linked with the I.O.M. Yet even the report of the conference in the socialist organ L'A.O.F. did not conceal that at Conakry too the currents of African nationalism were flowing strongly. Assimilation was condemned, there was an emphasis on African culture and values,

---

[1] It was led by Ouezzin Coulibaly, R.D.A. Ivory Coast deputy, and included Doudou Gueye, the Senegal R.D.A. leader, who was a Vice-President of the party.

[2] L'A.O.F., 28 Jan. 1957.

[3] Under the rules of the National Assembly at that time a parliamentary group required at least fourteen members. Pierre Commin explained that if the M.S.A. should have fewer deputies, the only alternative to its affiliation to the S.F.I.O. parliamentary group would be its affiliation to a non-socialist group.

the teaching of African languages was demanded, and even Senghor got a sympathetic reference for his *mot* 'assimiler non être assimilés'. The Trade Union Conference at Cotonou in Dahomey was held in the following week. It decided to create a *Union Générale des Travailleurs d'Afrique Noire* (U.G.T.A.N.), but it seemed that this might turn out to be not much more than the re-creation of the old C.G.T. organization on a formally autonomous basis, with the real issues still to be settled. It was not perhaps very serious that the C.G.T.F.O. had held aloof, but it was more disturbing that the C.A.T.C. should accuse the C.G.T. leaders of having rigged the conference in advance, and of having failed to satisfy the essential preliminary of constituting themselves an autonomous African union, and should have refused to join the new organization until the whole question had been submitted to their own congress. Nevertheless, it seemed that the new union might, at the least, bring together in one African trade union movement more than two-thirds of the trade unionists of French West Africa. In this sphere too autonomy and fusion, if not yet triumphant, were undoubtedly rolling along.

Meanwhile on the constitutional front the long-awaited decrees to give effect to the *loi-cadre* had been published at the beginning of December 1956. Under the procedure prescribed by the *loi-cadre*, they had to be finally approved by parliament, after being examined by the Assembly of the French Union, within a period of four months. Criticism of them concentrated on two points: the composition and powers of the territorial councils of government and the absence of any such council for French West Africa as a whole.[1]

In January 1957 the Overseas Territories Committee of the National Assembly proposed that the decrees should be amended so as to bring the new régime in the Overseas Territories into line with that recently established in Togoland. Instead of being presided over by the Governor and containing a minority of officials appointed by him, as well as members elected by the assembly, the new Councils of Government should be chosen by a Prime Minister, wnose appointment would require the approval of a majority of the assembly, and could be ended by a majority vote of censure. The Government maintained that such a system would be unconstitutional (for the Republic of which the territories formed part would not then be 'one and indivisible'), but eventually a compromise was agreed whereby all the members of the Council of Government were to be elected by the assembly on a list system, the candidate

[1] For a full discussion of the *loi-cadre* decrees, see my 'Constitutional Reform in French Tropical Africa', *Political Studies*, vol. vi (1958), pp. 45–69.

at the head of the winning list being Vice-President of the Council and presiding over it in the Governor's absence. The Council could resign if it considered that it no longer enjoyed the Assembly's confidence.

The government scheme also severely limited the competence of the Grand Councils, to the profit on the one hand of the constituent territories, on the other of the metropolitan government, 'interterritorial' services being restricted to the barest minimum. On 13 December the Grand Council of French West Africa ended its session without having passed the budget, on the ground that these arrangements would have the effect of removing certain public services from its control while leaving their cost as a possible charge on the federal budget and, more generally, of 'suppressing French West Africa as a political or administrative entity'.[1] This aspect of the decrees was also bitterly attacked by Senghor and other I.O.M. deputies as designed to 'balkanize' the federation, whose real political existence should, they argued, be recognized by establishing a Council of Government at the federal level and increasing the number and scope of interterritorial services. In the end, some additions were made to the interterritorial services, and the interterritorial conference, which the government proposals set up to resolve difficulties and conflicts over matters of interterritorial concern, was recast so as to include the vice-presidents of the Councils of Government as well as the High Commissioner and the territorial governors.

Since the Government was one in which the S.F.I.O. was the dominant party and the ministers responsible for the decrees were the socialist Gaston Defferre and the R.D.A. leader Houphouet-Boigny, African socialist and R.D.A. leaders could not be openly hostile to its proposals, particularly after their amendment. The R.D.A. was not, however, wholly agreed about the future of the two groups of territories. Some among its leaders, notably Sekou Touré, were in favour of a federal executive and opposed to the weakening of interterritorial ties, but the government scheme reflected the views of Houphouet-Boigny and many of his supporters in the Ivory Coast, who regarded without enthusiasm a system under which the wealthy Ivory Coast saw its revenue used to subsidize the rest of French West Africa. The R.D.A. had been divided about the advantages of participation in the Guy Mollet Government, and the warmth with which Houphouet-Boigny defended his slogan 'a Franco-African community' was not shared by some of his foremost lieutenants. These divisions accounted for the continued postpone-

---

[1] *Afrique nouvelle*, 18 Dec. 1956.

ment of the R.D.A. congress, but all R.D.A. spokesmen were adept at defending the party position in general terms while conveying the impression of sympathizing with much that their critics said. The party was at least united, it seemed, in its determination to avoid a split, particularly before it had secured the full fruits of its victory at the National Assembly elections of 1956 and gained control of the assemblies in the territories where its strength had undoubtedly been growing since then. This uncertainty about the future position of the R.D.A. made the denouement of the drama of fusionism obscure. The R.D.A. was in no hurry to show its hand and it did not seem at all disturbed by the attempt of the *Convention Africaine* to make itself the voice of nationalism.

The major political issues which thus occupied politically conscious people in Senegal, as elsewhere in West Africa, on the eve of the elections were those of self-government and the means of achieving it. This meant not only the constitutional and political problems associated with the new arrangements to be introduced as a result of the *loi-cadre*, and the wider issues of the basis of future relations between West Africa and France, but also the political instruments, which centred round party fusion and trade union unity, by which African purposes, whatever shape these might take, could best be secured. None of these matters could be settled on the territorial or even the West African plane alone, for they were enmeshed in metropolitan politics. In Senegal, in spite of much calculated ambiguity of language, they were not yet being considered in a predominantly revolutionary frame of mind, though the B.P.S. was potentially a more revolutionary party than the B.D.S. had been. The prevailing temper in Senegal politics could still be characterized as reformist, but only on the assumption that France could, without undue delay, be brought to concede both the form and the substance of full internal self-government, a perspective in which the *loi-cadre* reforms were really only a step, soon to be followed by the next step. Few of the political *élite* in Senegal seemed to appreciate the danger to its fragile economy which might be presented by any disruption of French West Africa. More were perhaps conscious of the political isolation that threatened the territory if the B.P.S. were to prove unable either to secure substantial allies elsewhere in French West Africa or to arrange a *modus vivendi* with the R.D.A. that would enable it to play a major part in the remaking of the West African polity and its relations with France. Meanwhile the elections to the territorial assembly could not, in themselves, change the data of political calculation in relation to these problems. They offered the B.P.S. leaders another opportunity for securing a renewed vote of confidence from Senegal and perhaps of wresting Dakar from the socialists. But in the wider context of French African politics they were only an incident.

6. *Party Organization and Nominations*

Thus, in the months immediately before the elections, both the major Senegalese parties were being reorganized. The *Parti Sénégalais d'Action Socialiste* was created at the congress held in Dakar on 2 and 3 February; and the B.P.S. held its *Congrès Constitutif* on 23, 24, and 25 February. In one sense, these were constituent assemblies: new party constitutions emerged from them. The P.S.A.S. was simply a new name for the old S.F.I.O. of Senegal, formally reorganized in conformity with the new 'autonomous' model of a territorial section of the *Mouvement Socialiste Africain*. Even L'A.O.F. advertised the party congress at which it was to be set up as '*Congrès Ordinaire*: Agenda: Constitution of the Senegalese section of the M.S.A.; Re-election of the administrative and directing organs.'[1] The *Rassemblement Démocratique Sénégalais* which joined in the new party was no more than the following of M. Gueye Abbas, who had been the second B.D.S. deputy from 1951 to 1956 and left that party when he failed to secure renomination at the National Assembly Elections of 1956.[2] The B.P.S. had in fact been created in the autumn of 1956, on the basis agreed upon by the fusionists in August, and so was really a going concern (which had fought the municipal elections in November) long before its formal constitution in February, and there was no disguising the fact that it was predominantly the old B.D.S. The two organized parties which had, as such, formally joined with the B.D.S. to create the B.P.S., the ex-R.D.A., U.D.S., and the *Mouvement Autonome Casamançais*, had neither of them any significant mass following in comparison with the B.D.S. At the National Assembly elections of 1956 the total U.D.S. vote was less than 7,000 compared with nearly 350,000 polled by the B.D.S. The M.A.C. was a group of dissidents who had broken away in 1955 from the *Mouvement des Forces Démocratiques Casamançais* (an expression of Casamance regionalism which had long been associated with the B.D.S.), when the B.D.S. successfully insisted that its members should become individual members of the party instead of being collectively associated with it.[3] Even in alliance with the socialists, the M.A.C. candidate at the national assembly elections had polled only 6,335 votes in Casamance compared with over 55,000 for the B.D.S. Although it was essential to the ideo-

---

[1] *L'A.O.F.*, 29 Jan. 1957.   [2] *L'A.O.F.*, 15 Mar. 1957.
[3] *Réalités africaines*, 17 Aug. 1955. See below, p. 336.

PLATE 4

a. Bloc Populaire Sénégalais Congress, February 1957

b. Parti Sénégalais de l'Action Socialiste Congress, February 1957

PARTY CONGRESSES IN SENEGAL

logy of fusion to represent the B.P.S. as something entirely new, in which all the constituent parties had sunk their separate existences (and there was much geniune loyalty to this ideal) there was a real sense in which what had happened was that the others had joined the B.D.S. That they had been offered generous terms on which to do so (e.g. the fusion agreement guaranteed the U.D.S. four out of thirteen places in the party office)[1] showed that the B.D.S. leaders genuinely wanted to bring about fusion but it could not alter the fact that, in the new party, the former B.D.S. was overwhelmingly predominant in terms of numbers and of the all-important middle rank leadership in the districts. What might be changing, as a consequence of fusion, was the character of the party leadership. Fusion might give opportunities to the major figures in the U.D.S. (and some of the other fusionists) that they could never have outside the mass party, while within the B.D.S., as in any other political movement there were differences of outlook, ideology, and political interest which might mean that the addition of the new men would change the balance of power within the party. All this was extremely difficult to assess at a time when the tide of nationalist feeling was steadily rising. The B.D.S. would no doubt have moved towards a less reformist temper irrespective of fusion: its willingness actively to promote fusion was no doubt one indication of the extent to which this was happening. But the prominent part played by some of the ex-U.D.S. leaders in the B.P.S., and their constant articles in the B.P.S. newspaper, suggested that they were working hard, as was indeed quite legitimate, to transform the party into something more like the disciplined revolutionary army their ideology demanded that it should be.

It is thus extremely difficult to characterize the nature of the party organizations at the onset of the elections. It is always difficult to move from discussing the formal constitution of a political party to a realistic account of how it works; this difficulty is increased in countries (like those of Africa) in which the formal constitution of the party is derived from foreign models and is silent about vital factors in party formation and activity which are on the contrary derived from the social and cultural environment of Africa. But in this case there is the further difficulty that party organization was in a particularly fluid state and the relation between formal constitution and the realities of party organization was all the more uncertain.

The formal organization of the two major political parties in Senegal owed much to the model of the S.F.I.O., of which the

[1] *Condition humaine*, 16 Aug. 1956.

Senegal socialist party (unlike socialist parties in other French West African territories) had been a constituent federation until the creation of the P.S.A.S. The B.D.S., as we have seen, was in origin the outcome of a split in that federation. It was therefore to be expected that the B.D.S. should, in its formal constitution, follow closely the general structure of the S.F.I.O. and should lay down rather precisely the rules deemed to be necessary to ensure that the Constitution was observed. But it also followed from the political history of Senegal that the S.F.I.O. federation should embody some of the habits and outlook appropriate to a party which had grown up at a time when the electorate was limited in numbers and largely concentrated in one or two towns, and that it was hardly a mass party. Equally, the B.D.S. had not been able easily to shake off some characteristics which perhaps owed some of their persistence in the B.D.S. and its successor to the circumstances of the party's origin. It was a sound political instinct as well as the deeply held conviction that an African political movement should reflect in itself the actual structure of African society which led Senghor and his supporters in the B.D.S. to seek to incorporate in the new party the various groups, associations, and movements which were growing up in different parts of the country and in different social and ethnic groups. Accordingly, the rules of the B.D.S. not only provided for individual membership and geographical organization as in a European socialist party, but also empowered the party to enter into a federal relationship (*organisation fédérative*) with 'local parties' defending the same objects as the B.D.S. This was, from the point of view of party organization, the origin of the problem, constantly discussed at B.D.S. party congresses throughout its history, of 'ethnic and regional particularism'.[1] The most important of these organized local groups were the *Mouvement des Forces Démocratiques Casamançais*, the *Union Générale des Originaires de la Vallée du Fleuve*, *La Collectivité Lébou*, and *l'Union Générale des Peulhs*. But such local and ethnic factors were not only exemplified within the B.D.S. in federated groups of this kind but also in the main party organization, in such bodies as the *sous-section des Bijoutiers Guinéens de Dakar*, and in many less formalized followings of particular individuals within a section. It was not until the party congress at Ziguinchor in 1954 that it was finally decided to 'integrate' the organized ethnic and regional groups by abolishing the federal aspects of the party structure and insisting on individual membership. This caused considerable difficulty: we have already,

---

[1] See especially the *Rapport Moral* presented to the Annual B.D.S. Congresses by Mamadou Dia at Kaolack (*Condition humaine*, 16 Apr. 1951), Ziguinchor (ibid. 28 Apr. 1954) and Diourbel (ibid. 22 Apr. 1955).

for example, seen that it led to the creation of the *Mouvement Autonome Casamançais*.

Careful research into the history and dynamics of these regional associations would be of great interest. In one of his reports, Mamadou Dia commented that they were 'more regional than ethnic in character' and, in Senegal at any rate, ethnic differences, regional interests, and personal conflicts of local leaders, all seem to play a part in these groups and their inter-relation with political parties. Politics interacts with other factors and helps to shape the form which traditional and local conflicts take, as well as being influenced by them, and it seems a great over-simplification to contend that, even at the local level, it is *merely* the expression of 'tribal feeling' But it is doubtful whether the abolition of the federal aspect of party organization and the attempt to integrate these movements into the ordinary membership of the party did much more than bring such conflicts more fully within the party.

No more than in parties elsewhere in the world, therefore, did the formal constitution of the parties give a complete picture of their actual organization. In spite of such reservations it is essential first to summarize the organization of the two major parties as set out in the rules made by their constituent congresses in February 1957. That of the P.S.A.S. was based on sections to be established in each village. Sections were grouped in regional unions for each constituency. In the larger towns there was to be a sub-section in each of the wards into which they were legally divided. Every member must have a party card and pay an annual subscription through his section (or sub-section) 'au profit de l'organisme central'. In each section, members must be grouped in 'committees'. The committee, said the rules, was to be the 'basic unit' of the party. There was a youth movement, organized in exactly the same way as the party; supporters between eighteen and twenty-five must belong to it and those up to the age of thirty-five could do so. No one could belong to both the youth movement and to the party. The supreme authority in the party was the Annual Congress, in which each section was represented by delegates in proportion to their membership. Voting was by mandates, one mandate for every twenty-five members who had paid their subscription. Each annual congress would determine the place where the next was to be held. There was to be an Executive Committee elected annually by the party congress (its size was not mentioned) which was to 'administer the party', and to elect from its own members the party office composed of fifteen officials and two youth delegates, two delegates for labour problems and two for peasant problems. In addition, 'for the

administrative attachment of the party's representatives in the
M.S.A.' there were to be posts for a Political Director and two
assistants (in fact, three of the latter were appointed). The rules also
provided for the election by the congress of a central disciplinary
committee of twenty-one members and for similar bodies in each
section, from whose decisions appeals could be taken to the central
committee. The appropriate officials were required to present, at
each annual conference, a financial, an administrative, a propaganda, and a policy report.[1]

Although they contained considerably more precise details on
many points, the rules of the B.P.S. clearly followed the same model.
The essential unit was still the section, though much more attention
was given to the smaller units below it in the party hierarchy. The
basic unit was, in this case, said to be the 'group' of twenty members
living in the same quarter, each of which was to elect a *responsable*.
Groups in one electoral area were to be combined into sub-sections,
which should have at least a hundred members who were to elect
annually, before the party congress, their office of seven officials.
These sub-sections in turn were to be combined into sections for
each locality or group of villages. Each of these had an administrative committee, composed of delegates from each sub-section, one
for each fifty members. The nine section officials were elected by
this committee. The sections in each constituency were to form a
regional union, directed by a *responsable* elected by the assembly
of the union, made up of three office-holders from each section. The
youth movement, like that of the P.S.A.S., was to be similar in
organization to that of the party itself and party supporters between
the ages of twenty-five and thirty-five could be members of either
but not both. Each sub-section should have a women's committee
and each section a women's council of one member from each
sub-section. Women were, however, full members of the party.
Party groups should also be established in every enterprise or public
service and should each have their *responsable* in close touch with
the appropriate section. Members must have party cards and voting
at the party congress should be by mandate, one for every twenty-five
paid-up cards. The executive committee was to consist of the party *élus*
(not only members of the metropolitan or Territorial Assemblies but
also mayors who were party members), nine youth movement officials,
together with constituency members numbering at least one more
than the total number of *élus*, the quota for each constituency being
determined in proportion to population. Where a constituency was
not held by the B.P.S. in the territorial assembly, it would be

[1] P.S.A.S. *Statuts* (*L'A.O.F.* 15 Mar. 1957).

allowed besides its quota of constituency members extra members equal to the number of seats in the constituency. At the congress Kaolack, which had a paid-up membership of 55,000, demanded that the quota should be fixed in proportion to party membership in each constituency, a proposal which, as Senghor said, would, if adopted, break up the party. He proposed that an additional ten members of the executive committee should be divided between the constituencies, in proportion to their party membership, and this was adopted. The representatives selected by each constituency must be confirmed by the party congress. The party *bureau* (numbering eighteen) was elected by the executive committee from its own members. Besides the director of the parliamentary group (*ex officio*) it consisted of a secretary-general and four assistants, three secretaries for organization and propaganda and three assistants, an administrative secretary and two assistants, and a treasurer and two assistants.

What relation was there between these party constitutions and the facts of party life at the time of the elections? To begin with membership, at the time of the B.P.S. Congress in February 1957, the report on the party organization gave its membership as 165,000 while that on which representation at the congress was based was 180,000. Although the figure in the report was probably a slightly earlier one, there is undoubtedly a good deal of buying of cards in order to ensure voting power at the congress.[1] It is difficult to see how this can be controlled. In some instances, the writer was informed, the local organizations had been required to produce their membership lists for inspection by representatives of the executive committee of the party, but it was only possible to see that actual names were duly recorded for each card issued. It was quite impracticable to determine whether they were genuine, or, if so, whether those concerned had themselves paid for the card (a local politician of substance may 'lend' some of his supporters the price of their cards, and if challenged he will naturally assert that he has subsequently been repaid).[2] It is accordingly difficult to guess how many of the cards actually sold represent genuine members. No figures of membership were obtained for the P.S.A.S. There was a consensus of opinion that in many parts of the territory outside the largest towns the socialists did not seriously attempt to sell cards though some held that more might be done in future in view of the creation of the P.S.A.S. and the reduction in the price of the card.[3]

---

[1] This, of course, is a common practice in French metropolitan party congresses. Cf. P. Williams, *Politics in Post-War France* (London 1954), p. 64 which expressly mentions the Senegal federation in discussing its prevalence at S.F.I.O. congresses.

[2] Oral information from several sources.   [3] See p. 341.

The conception of 'groups' as the basis of party organization was one of the new features of the B.P.S., in comparison with the B.D.S., and it was frankly admitted at the party congress that not even a beginning had been made in establishing them. It seemed likely that the 'committees' for which the P.S.A.S. rules provided were equally non-existent, at least in most parts of Senegal. Sub-sections and sections of both parties, on the other hand, were to be found even in fairly remote areas and quite small villages, though it would be fair to say that the B:P.S. network was much more nearly universal. In the large towns both parties were represented by such an organization (the fact that elections in the new full municipalities were by proportional representation ensured the socialists some seats in councils elected in November and may well have stimulated party activity). Socialist sections were also to be found in smaller townships and trading posts and at least in some villages. But taking Senegal as a whole, it seemed evident that the B.P.S. was not only far more widely but far more solidly established. Socialist organization was often sketchy, if not non-existent, and displayed, especially in the rural areas, much more the character of an *ad hoc* electoral committee than of the kind of organization suggested by the P.S.A.S. rules.

How far the elaborate organization prescribed in the B.P.S. rules actually ensured any measure of control over the leading personalities by the membership at the local level it is impossible to guess. Much, even in the party literature of the B.D.S., supports the hypothesis that it provided the basis on which individuals consolidated their personal followings, the *clans* and *tendances* within the party, whose manœuvres, particularly in connexion with the nomination of candidates, have been so constantly denounced at congresses as endangering party unity and the resolution of which is an important task of members of the central committee. Such personal followings were no doubt also significant among the socialists, though they were less openly discussed. Since the model of party organization to which politicians appealed (and which European critics of African political life also employed) was that of individual members electing officers and deciding policy by majority voting, there was much denunciation of these features of political life, especially in the B.D.S. and its successor. A detached observer, particularly an Englishman, is more inclined to consider such activities as evidence that the parties are in large measure genuine political organizations resembling in many respects those familiar in Western countries and struggling to conciliate the diverse interests of real life within a single movement. Seen from this point of view, the P.S.A.S. offered something more than the mere boss politics of which the Senegal socialists had often been accused, while the B.P.S. had not yet been reduced to the monolithic totalitarianism for which a few of its prominent (if recent) adherents hardly concealed their preference. Other issues familiar in Western party organization were clearly evident: for instance the tension between a parliamentary party (the *élus*) and the party as a whole, and the anxieties about the proper role of a party Youth movement well known both to the French S.F.I.O. and the British Labour Party. The rules of both parties formally subordinated the *élus* to the party but those of the B.P.S. made their real importance in the party hierarchy more evident, just as they accorded the still unformed youth movement[1] a substantial representation in the central committee.

Although the rules of both parties provide for annual subscriptions and imply that these are distinct from the purchase of the party card, it seemed that in practice the annual sale of the cards was the equivalent of a subscription. The old S.F.I.O. cards were more expensive but those of the P.S.A.S., like those of the B.P.S. (and the M.P.S.), cost 100 Fr. (about 4*s.*). Of this, B.P.S. sections retained 25 Fr. and 75 Fr. went to central party funds. Income from this source was put at 14 million Fr. (about £29,000) in the treasurer's report to the February congress. This would be equivalent to a membership of between 180,000 and 185,000 which was that represented by mandates at the congress. Such receipts could be supplemented by special subscriptions levied on *élus*, the proceeds of party fêtes and similar gatherings, and donations from wealthy supporters. Unfortunately the writer can give no estimate of such receipts for any of the parties. The B.P.S. was the only party to maintain a permanent headquarters in Dakar (as the B.D.S. had done before it). This was a modest establishment, sparely furnished with essential equipment but it provided the necessary base for the party administration.

To summarize, in spite of the formal creation of the two major parties immediately before the election, both were substantially well-established parties, and some of their characteristics were the outcome of a considerable historical experience of political activity. Both had claims to territory-wide organization which in many of its formal aspects owed much to the example of the metropolitan S.F.I.O. But the socialist organization in the rural areas was often sketchy, and in many areas non-existent, it had many of the

---

[1] The B.D.S. had created a youth movement in 1956 but the formal creation of a B.P.S. 'united' youth movement took place only in Mar. 1958 (*Afrique nouvelle*, 28 Mar. 1958).

characteristics of a local electoral committee rather than those of a continuously engaged mass-party, the personality and outlook of many of its *responsables* or *militants* in the rural areas was markedly conservative, and its leadership very remote in comparison with that of the B.P.S. The B.P.S., though still engaged in the task of absorbing its constituent parties, was substantially the B.D.S., especially in the rural areas. It put more emphasis on organization, and its sub-sections and sections were more numerous, but in many rural areas they had a somewhat formal existence (as it was put by a B.P.S. politician they 'did not live like the sections' in the country towns, let alone those of the major towns). Socialists, even those in small trading posts, were contemptuous of the rural masses; 'they don't know why they are voting' as one of them remarked. While the B.P.S. emphasized much more strongly the importance of party organization, party discipline, and the social solidarity appeal of a mass party, it had, in its origins, leant heavily on local feeling, on the hostility of the remoter and poorer, as well as the richer, rural areas to the *citadins*, particularly those of the old municipalities. Its leaders were constantly aware of the dangerous pressures which these varying kinds of organized sectional feeling could exert on party unity, especially when elections were impending. The B.P.S. was more obviously vulnerable to such pressures, since it was the party in power in most of the territory and in all the rural constituencies. To the normal difficulties to be expected from regional and ethnic groups and the *clans* and *tendances* within the party, there were added on this occasion the special problems caused by the need to find some places for candidates from the groups which had joined the B.D.S. to form the new party.[1]

These difficulties would have been greater if the single-member constituency had been the rule. In two of the three single-member seats, and in two of the three double-member seats, there were party splits of this kind. On the other hand, there were splits also in larger constituencies and much friction over nominations in the largest of all, Ziguinchor (i.e. Casamance) with eleven members.[2] Multi-member seats may facilitate, on occasion, the conciliation within one list of the claims of different groups within a party but in Senegal room for manœuvre was limited by conventions according to which particular members were considered to represent each of the administrative subdivisions of a large constituency, correspond-

---

[1] If one includes two of those who had joined the B.D.S. only after the 1956 elections, and had worked hard to promote fusion, at least nine of the sixty B.P.S. candidates could be so regarded.

[2] Reported at length but not illuminatingly in *Paris-Dakar*, 29 Mar. 1957.

ing to distinct territorial 'sections' within each party. It was, for example, customary within the Kaolack constituency to speak of the 'member for Fatick' and within Casamance it was claimed that the subdivision of Kolda, in virtue of its population, was entitled to two of the eleven seats. Difficulties of this kind seemed less serious among the socialists, probably because central control was much less effective and prospects of success were more remote. The one P.S.A.S. split occurred in the only really safe socialist seat, Saint-Louis itself, where one of the retiring members, M. Fall Mafall, was not renominated and stood as an Independent, claiming that he had been chosen by the constituency party but that the party secretary had substituted a candidate of his own choice.

A further factor made the B.P.S. particularly susceptible to conflicts about nominations. It did not hold either of the two 'capitals' of Senegal, Saint-Louis and Dakar. On the other hand, some of its leading personalities lived in these towns, and indeed, for practical purposes, it was essential that the party should have available for various political posts (e.g. president of the permanent committee of the territorial assembly, or member of the permanent committee of the grand council) members who did. Such leaders must therefore be found a place in a rural constituency. This 'parachuting' of party leaders is, in Senegal as in other countries, a potential source of local grievance which opponents seek to exploit. In the nominations battles of 1957 it was difficult—indeed, for an outsider, impossible—always to distinguish difficulties arising from this problem from those which arose from the necessity to find seats for some of the leaders among those who had joined the B.P.S. from parties other than the B.D.S. In principle, the constituency party chooses its list, but it had been agreed that the ten additional seats created in 1956[1] should be filled by candidates chosen from nominees put forward by the executive committee. But in practice there were frequent appeals to that body from those whose hopes of nomination had been disappointed. Such appeals were followed by visits by special representatives to the party executive during the hectic days before nominations closed. Their efforts to smooth out such difficulties were, however, sometimes only ended by the necessity of depositing the list with the District Commissioner.

One final factor which played its part in B.P.S. difficulties over nominations was more closely related to the immediate political scene. Preoccupation with the formation of the new party and with the holding of the party congress left very little time to sort out conflicts where there was disagreement about the degree of local

[1] See above, p. 298.

support enjoyed by particular individuals. The clearest example of this was the split in Kédougou, where the party renominated the out-going member, a decision challenged on the ground that the representative of the executive committee who had been sent to settle the conflict had been biased and had ignored the results of voting by the section of Kédougou. The rejected candidate for B.P.S. nomination, protesting continued loyalty to the party and expressing the hope that it would be reunited after the election, stood as an Independent and, in spite of his expulsion from the B.P.S., won the seat,[1] securing fifty-four votes more than his B.P.S. opponent. Many such conflicts had their roots in complex personal differences between leading members of the party. It was such differences which led to a split in the B.P.S. in Matam, a three-member constituency, in which the two retiring members were disagreed about the succession to a *chef de province*. One was renominated, the other formed an independent list, split the B.P.S. vote and allowed the P.S.A.S. to win the constituency on a minority vote. Many of these differences were deep-seated. In Linguère, for instance, a single-member constituency, the population was divided between Fulani and Wolof approximately in the proportion of 3 : 2. A Djoloff 'regional' movement had been developing for some years. The renomination of the sitting member, a Fulani, was accompanied by the creation of a *Bloc Démocratique du Djoloff* whose candidate polled 6,000 votes to the 8,000 of the sitting member. In Louga, the *Bloc Démocratique du N'Diambour* originated in a split within the B.P.S. over the nominations for the municipal elections of 1956. Two of the constituency's three B.P.S. members in the Territorial Assembly, M. Moustapha Cissé and M. Alioune Tall were personally opposed. Each had his own *clientèle* or (in the word generally used in Senegal) *clan*. The third B.P.S. member for Louga, Maître Guillabert, was a Saint-Louis lawyer of a distinguished political family and first Vice-president of the Territorial Assembly. As the President, M. Seydou N'Dao, lived at Kaolack and was badly crippled as a result of a motor accident in 1949, M. Guillabert was the effective President of the Assembly. Had the B.P.S. won the municipal elections M. Guillabert would almost certainly have been mayor, but since he would normally have been in Saint-Louis the effective mayor would have been the mayor's first assistant, most probably M. Cissé. All this exacerbated feeling about the allocation of places in the party lists between the two *clans*, and difficulties were increased by the need to give some representation to the ex-U.D.S. and socialists who had joined the B.P.S., notwithstanding that they had only a derisory following in the town. The dispute turned on

[1] *Paris-Dakar*, 19 Mar. 1957.

whether M. Tall's group should be allowed twelve or eleven of the twenty-seven places in the lists, as compared with nine or ten for that of M. Cissé, six being assigned to the former U.D.S. and the *socialistes únitaires*. Although M. Tall accepted the decision of the party in the sense that he did not personally contest the municipal elections, his followers did and subsequently joined with the socialists to outvote the orthodox B.P.S., and secure for themselves the mayoralty. (It is interesting that this group did, in fact, secure twelve of the twenty-seven seats!) M. Tall clearly hoped for a reconciliation with the party and at one stage before nominations closed withdrew his resignation, which he had offered a few days before after the party congress. In the event he stood as an opposition candidate but was easily defeated in the constituency as a whole, although his list had a majority in the town of Louga itself. This dispute well illustrates the problems of *clans*.[1]

Apart from the political difficulties of arranging a list, there are, of course, legal rules about eligibility. Essentially, candidates must be at least twenty-three years of age, registered (or eligible for registration) as electors in the territory, domiciled in French West Africa for at least two years, and able to speak French. The holders of a large number of government posts, or persons who have held such posts within six months of the election, are ineligible. The basic idea is that all who exercise functions of authority (e.g. governors, their private secretaries, administrators, judges, heads of technical departments, labour and school inspectors and so on) are ineligible.[2] In addition, persons who have been employed within six months of the date of the election in the *cabinet* (private office) of the President of the French Union, of the Presidents of the metropolitan assemblies, or of a minister or state secretary, are ineligible. This latter disqualification was the only one mentioned in connexion with the nominations; M. Diop Obeye, the former general secretary of the S.F.I.O., who had been their representative at the fusion discussions but had joined the B.P.S. only in February,[3] explained that he could not be one of the B.P.S. candidates for Dakar because he was so disqualified. He had been a member of the private office of M. Hammadoun Dicko, the Soudan socialist deputy who was an Under Secretary of State in the Guy Mollet Government.[4]

---

[1] Oral information from a number of sources in Louga and elsewhere.
[2] Law 52–130 of 11 Feb. 1952. See also Holleaux, op cit., pp. 14–20.
[3] *Paris-Dakar*, 26 Feb. 1957.
[4] Ibid., 11 Mar. 1957.

7. *Electoral Administration: Practical Problems*

Between 1945 and 1957 there were eight 'territory-wide' elections in French tropical Africa, and at least since 1951 the electorates were large enough for the administrative problems involved in holding them to be much the same as those of elections held on universal suffrage. In Senegal, moreover, there have been elections in the old communes for three-quarters of a century, and political parties have been described as 'an almost traditional part of the social system'.[1] Direct elections are thus much less novel in Senegal than in most parts of British Africa. Before the Second World War, however, the electorate was small and largely illiterate and Senegalese elections became notorious for irregularities. In more recent elections elsewhere in French West Africa (notably those of 1951 and 1952) the administration did not always maintain impartiality but, as an experienced French journalist put it, 'on their own authority or on orders from above, obstructed by every means certain movements or certain men declared dangerous'.[2] Inevitably there were serious practical problems about the application of the electoral laws (particularly, perhaps, ones so largely designed for metropolitan France). And the suspicion that administrative decisions on such matters were intended to benefit one party or injure another, which is widespread, was itself sometimes an independent source of such problems. The three major problems were the establishment of the registers, the distribution of the electors' cards, and actual voting. At the root of each was the difficulty of establishing the identity of the elector. Not only was it difficult to establish age, but many names are identical and the same man may be indifferently known under one or another of his names. Few people outside the towns have identity cards or other similar means of establishing their identity.

The registers. Registration is not in fact the result, for the most part, of individual application but is based on the census registers.[3] Moreover, there is much migration, some of it temporary, and the procedure for transfer on the register involves the production of documents with which Africans seldom provide themselves. In these circumstances, it is not surprising that names are frequently

---

[1] P. Mercier, 'Evolution of Senegalese Elites', *International Social Science Bulletin*, vol. viii (1956), p. 450.

[2] André Blanchet, 'Des Elections à la Désignation des Conseils de Gouvernement', II. *Le Monde*, 11 May 1957.

[3] André Blanchet, 'Des Elections à la Désignation des Conseils de Gouvernement', I. *Le Monde*, 10 May 1957. In small communes in France, similarly, registration is based on the conscription registers, but these are no doubt more accurate (Nicholas, op. cit., p. 140).

included twice on the register, or that those who have left or died may not be removed. Since the register is permanent, revision is particularly important and the time allowed for it is, in fact, longer than in France. The extension of the franchise involved in the institution of universal suffrage by the *loi-cadre* of 1956 obviously necessitated a major revision of the register, and a special revision for this purpose took place in the late summer of 1956.[1] The time-table followed the usual plan for the annual revisions. Revision began on 9 July and the register was finally closed on 30 September. The new registers were then in force until 31 March 1957 but were subject to the usual annual revision, beginning in December. Owing to the decision to hold the territorial assembly elections on 31 March 1957, however, the revision was completed on this occasion by 15 March. Since the writer was not in Senegal during the special revision of 1956 and was only able to see a little of the normal annual revision towards its end, he can offer no judgement on the way in which this revision was effected.

The new registers showed an increase of some 27 per cent. on the electorate registered at the National Assembly elections in 1956 and constituted 46·6 per cent. of the territory's estimated population in contrast to an electorate of 36·4 per cent. in January 1956. There were, of course, considerable variations from district to district, and it is difficult, and perhaps not very useful, to account for these. The population figures themselves are only estimates, and extensive seasonal migration within the territory may affect registration differently in different areas at different times of the year. The considerable differences in the extent to which the electorate was increased in one district as compared with another by the introduction of universal suffrage—if we assume that the major part of the increase in 1957 as compared with 1956 may be accounted for by the extension of the franchise—seems as likely to be due to variations in the application of the earlier franchise as to variations in the efficiency of registration in 1956–7. Table 8 assembles the figures for registration from 1951–7 and shows that there were two divergences from the general pattern sufficiently striking to merit comment. Only two districts showed a percentage below 40; these were Dakar and Kédougou, at opposite ends of the scale of 'modernity', which both had no more than 26 per cent. Two districts actually showed a reduction, as compared with January 1956: Dakar fell from nearly 120,000 to just under 75,000, while Bas-Sénégal, which includes Saint-Louis, fell from 38,000 to 32,000.

The density of Kédougou's population is very low (2·3 per square

[1] Decree 56–669 of 7 July 1956 (*J. O. Lois et Décrets*, 8 July, p. 6364).

kilometre) but not so low as that of Bakel (1·8), and about the same as Linguère and Tambacounda, all three of which had percentages above 50. Communications are poor as well as difficult and the district is largely cut off, in many parts, from the influences which play, in varying degree, on the rest of Senegal. Administrative difficulties are probably the major cause of the low registration, in particular the absence of sufficient qualified persons to man the revising committees and the difficulty of moving about in the district.

TABLE 8

Electoral Registration in Senegal by Districts, 1951–7

Constituency	Estimated population 1956	Electorate 1951	Electorate 1952	Electorate 1956	% of pop.	Electorate 1957	% of pop.
Dakar	283,000	97,230	97,208	117,206	41·4	74,744	26·4
Bas-Sénégal	77,000	28,160	31,548	38,524	50	32,480	42
Bakel*	41,000	..	..	12,088	29·4	24,240	59·1
Diourbel	192,000	64,526	61,822	79,758	41·5	101,310	53
Kaolack	479,000	135,489	128,542	194,120	40·5	222,147	46·5
Kédougou	41,000	6,391	6,181	9,016	21·9	11,544	26·5
Linguère	44,000	10,962	11,584	12,709	28·8	29,797	68·9
Louga	145,000	23,114	35,379	52,932	36·5	61,955	42·5
Matam*	99,000	42,761	40,709	35,058	35·4	59,489	59·4
Podor	86,000	32,254	32,056	38,834	45·1	56,998	65·9
Tambacounda*	51,000	16,082	15,257	13,792	27	27,919	54·1
Thiès	312,000	104,731	104,871	125,744	40·3	168,968	50·9
Ziguinchor	372,000	95,581	95,790	113,016	30·3	199,834	53·8

* The cercle of Bakel, created in 1954, comprised parts of the cercles of Matam and Tambacounda.

The fall in the electorate in Dakar, as compared with 1956 is, however, susceptible of explanation, at least in part. The Municipal Reform Law of 1955 declared the existing registers invalid and required the production of an identity card, or of one of a number of specified alternatives, as well as a certificate of residence in claims for inclusion in the new one. The new registers were therefore compiled on a much more restrictive basis than the old, and almost everywhere in Senegal the electorate in the municipalities, whether the old communes like Rufisque, or the new ones like Thiès, Diourbel, Kaolack, was considerably smaller than it had been in 1956. In Dakar municipality,[1] the figures are indeed striking: for a population of 230,000 an electorate of 55,387 compared with one of 90,827 in January 1956. It is universally agreed that the registration

[1] For the following discussion of the Dakar municipality, I am indebted to an unpublished paper by M. Raymond Lecques, of the Institut Français d'Afrique Noire, Dakar, analysing the reasons for the smallness of the electorate in Dakar at the municipal elections of Nov. 1956.

of Europeans was small,[1] but it may have been higher than at the municipal elections in November 1956, when the Dakar electorate was only 50,371 and the 30,000 non-Africans in Dakar are said to have produced no more than a few hundred electors. But even if we assume that virtually only Africans were included in the electorate of 55,387, the proportion in comparison with a census population (in 1955) of 200,000 remains very low. Of the African population, however, only 179,000 were considered as habitual residents by the census. These included some non-French Africans (Gambians, Cape Verde islanders, &c.) and also were divided among over thirty ethnic groups, of which Wolofs and Lebus, the latter of whom are the original inhabitants of the Dakar peninsula, numbered 103,460, including 53,773 over the age of twenty-one. It had been shown by analysis of the administrative archives and by sample investigations in the African areas of Dakar that over four-fifths of the settled population are Wolofs and Lebus, while a further investigation of the electoral cards in the municipal election in Dakar, made in forty-two of the fifty-four bureaux from which they were distributed, showed an average of 90 per cent. Wolof and Lebu names. It thus seems probable that the register includes the great majority of those who are really established residents in the town and that it is the less settled migrants from other areas who are not registered, though it is impossible to say how far this is due to their not being able to satisfy the requirement to produce proof of their age and nationality in documentary form, their absence from Dakar at the relevant time, their inability to prove habitual residence, or to show that they were not registered elsewhere, or simply to their failure to seek registration.

Electoral cards. But great as are the problems of registration, in Senegal, as elsewhere in French tropical Africa, it would be generally agreed that the worst practical, as well as the most politically sensitive, problems arise in connexion with the distribution of electors' cards.[2] Given the difficulty of establishing identity, it is obvious that if supplies of electoral cards can be improperly obtained, the possibilities both of depriving hostile electors of their votes and of personation are considerable. The stricter provisions of the Municipal Reform Law of 1955 may have reduced the electorate, but at least they simplify the practical problems of distributing the

---

[1] One of them alleged that the cumbrous administrative procedure made it hard work to secure registration and took too much time (*Afrique nouvelle*, 5 Mar. 1957).

[2] Cf. Holleaux, op. cit., p. 23, who writes 'the distribution of electors' cards is of all the stages in electoral procedure overseas, the most difficult to organize and the one in which abuses are most likely'. Copies of M. Holleaux's article were sent to District Commissioners in Senegal by the territorial administration, but few can have had time to study it, as they were sent at the beginning of Mar. 1957.

electors' cards in towns. In the rural areas these problems remain acute. It is impossible to follow metropolitan practice and send the cards to individuals at their homes. That would present difficulties even in the towns, and is quite out of the question in the bush. Even setting up a distribution point in each of the main villages would leave many people with a long journey to collect their cards, as well as a subsequent journey to the polling station on election day. If very large numbers of cards were left undistributed, to be claimed, as the law allows, at the polling stations on election day, the whole machine would break down and the danger of violence would be very great. At the elections in 1952, therefore, the distribution committees were allowed to distribute bundles of cards to the village headmen (*chefs de village*) for them to give out to the electors in their villages. This practice, although accepted by the *Conseil d'Etat*,[1] is unsatisfactory. Even when the headmen are not themselves active in party politics, or even candidates, experience shows that after distributing some of the cards to the electors concerned, they have not infrequently handed over the cards which remained undistributed to some third party. In Senegal, distribution of the electors' cards through *chefs de village*, or even *chefs de carré*, the compound heads, was a source of bitter controversy. The administration hoped to avoid any such distribution on this occasion and to insist that the cards were given individually to the elector concerned after he had satisfied the distribution commission of his identity by producing the two witnesses legally necessary in the absence of documentary proof (the witnesses must themselves be electors registered in the district and able to prove their own identity).

It was accordingly decided that, to ensure the maximum distribution of electoral cards, the period of distribution should begin fifteen days before polling, instead of the minimum of twelve days legally required (i.e. on 16 March, instead of 19 March);[2] further, in addition to establishing distribution committees in the townships, major villages, and trading points, there should be as many travelling committees as possible having regard to the personnel available to act as presidents, and if necessary vehicles should be hired for their use. Ideally, there should be one distribution committee for every polling station, but this was evidently unattainable, and there would once again be the problem that either the travelling committees should attempt themselves to distribute the cards individually (with the result that many would remain undistributed and have to

---

[1] Conseil d'Etat, 18 Dec. 1953, elections to Togoland Territorial Assembly, 1953, Anecho district (*Recueil*, p. 563).

[2] Government of Senegal Circular, 62 APA/1 of 3 Mar. 1957.

be sent to the polling stations on election day, which would produce bottlenecks in the polling stations) or, alternatively, having done what they could themselves, the distribution committees might hand the remainder over to the village headman. This could be justified by analogy with metropolitan practice in rural areas, where the cards of electors in isolated farms and homesteads are delivered by the rural constables. But, the Senegal administration observed, 'previous local experience, especially on the occasion of the 1952 elections, showed that in practice handing over the cards to individual village headmen gave rise to too much criticism and recrimination to be envisaged again'. The administration therefore recommended careful programming of the operations of the travelling committees, and wherever possible two visits to all the more important centres in the area assigned to a committee. If it was nevertheless impossible to distribute all the cards, a distribution committee might itself appoint a sub-committee, consisting of someone chosen by the President as representing the administration (who might be the village headman) and representatives chosen by each of the party representatives on the committee from their local supporters; such sub-committees would function in a particular centre, and their establishment and the number of cards given to them were to be recorded in the *procès-verbal* in which the distribution committees are required to record their operations. How far this ingenious, though perhaps rather theoretical, device was adopted, the writer cannot say. In the course of his own investigations of the activities of the travelling distribution committees, which were necessarily limited to some three or four districts and to one or two committees in each, he came across no admitted cases of the use of sub-committees, but these investigations were made rather early in the period of distributing the cards.

The attempt to ensure individual distribution of the cards, and to avoid distribution through *chefs de carré*, let alone *chefs de village*, was inevitably a source of party-political controversy. The socialists, who considered themselves stronger in the towns, especially some of the smaller towns or *'escales'*, and who argued that identity cards were insisted upon there (though this was only strictly true in the full municipalities, in most of which they had been decisively beaten in the November elections), strongly opposed any distribution to village or compound heads; on the other hand, the B.P.S. felt that this was an attempt to reduce the effective electorate in the bush, where they were particularly strong, and claimed that it would deprive many electors of their votes. The administration, whose circular implied that there was to be no distribution through village headmen and was silent about compound heads, but did not in forthright terms forbid either, attempted to leave the decision to the distribution committees, which, in practice, would mean their presidents, since the socialists declined to agree to any such arrangement and the B.P.S. demanded it. For a day or so, it was understood that the administration had authorized distribution to *chefs de carré*, but this was followed by further instructions which insisted that this was merely a possibility which was open to distribution committees if they chose to use it. It seemed unfortunate that on such a matter a more definite line could not be taken. Yet, in view of the precedent of the use of the rural constables in France itself, and of the *Conseil d'Etat*'s acquiescence in distribution through the village headmen, it is difficult to see how the territorial administration, which was, for other reasons,[1] being accused of favouring the socialists, could have ventured further, especially bearing in mind the possibility of a subsequent recourse to the *Conseil d'Etat*.

At the polls. A polling station must be provided for every 1,500 electors,[2] but the Administration decided that the aim should be to have one for every thousand. In fact there were 1,066 in Senegal (for an electorate of 1,060,582).[3] Each of course required its *bureau*, and if it was not, on the whole, unduly difficult in Senegal to find the 1,066 presiding officers with the educational level required (as it certainly was in some other parts of French Africa) it was by no means always possible to find for these important functions men devoid of political partisanship. The most one could do, a number of District Commissioners told the writer independently, was to try to choose them from those whose political sympathies, though no secret, were less violent. The parties not infrequently agreed among themselves about which polling stations should have a B.P.S., and which a socialist, President. It is this fact which accounted for socialist hostility to the multiplication of the number of polling stations, since they could not find enough local party representatives either as presidents or as members of the *bureaux*. After this election, they complained of 'la multiplication des bureaux de vote créés arbitrairement dans les conditions qui rendaient impossible tout contrôle des opérations'.[4] Nevertheless, it should be emphasized that, in Senegal at least, the administrative machinery needed for setting up the elections was almost entirely in the hands of Africans. Not only were

---

[1] Below, p. 383.   [2] Law of 11 Feb. 1952, Art. 16.
[3] Government of Senegal, Arrêté No. 1,840, APAI of 16 Mar. 1957 (*J. O. du Sénégal*, 16 Mar. 1957).
[4] *Paris-Dakar*, 17 Apr. 1957. The difficulty of the socialists in finding people for the *bureaux* (and for the distribution committees) was mentioned to me in the rural constituencies frequently, both by B.P.S. and socialist party men, and by chiefs and others.

the personnel of the *bureaux* almost all African (the writer came across none who were not) but this was also true of that of the revising and distributing committees. It was with the latter that he was able to talk most; revising committees had practically finished their jobs before his investigations began, while polling-station *bureaux* were too preoccupied as a rule, unless, as happened on several occasions they were identical with the personnel of a distributing committee whose activities had been earlier observed. There were evident signs of a kind of team-spirit: members—particularly but by no means exclusively those working in the travelling distributing committees— seemed to have something of a 'professional spirit'; they had some-times acted in a similar capacity before and some of the members were familiar with the practical difficulties most likely to arise. In the towns, at any rate, the atmosphere was, so far as a foreign observer could judge, genial rather than strained. Although the administra-tive machinery at the executive level was thus remarkably completely 'Africanized' its direction and supervision was entirely in the hands of the district administration and the political branch in the terri-torial secretariat. In Senegal in March 1957 this was still almost wholly European.

The administration has not, it seems, considered it part of its duty to conduct propaganda campaigns to explain the procedure of registering, getting electors' cards, or voting, similar to those carried out in British territories in West Africa, and, given the French suspicion, by no means always unfounded, of administrative inter-ference in politics, this is not surprising. In the circumstances, the parties, especially the *Bloc Démocratique Sénégalais*, have had themselves to spend much of their energies in the bush in making sure that their supporters could recognize the ballot paper and knew how to vote. From this point of view, the most important consideration is that voters should make no mistakes about the party colours. In Senegal symbols do not appear on the ballot papers and although symbols are used by the parties as a means of propaganda (e.g. the B.D.S. used to use the lion as its symbol) printed propaganda plays a very limited part and the recognition of the party colour on the ballot paper is of crucial importance.

The use of polling booths is legally necessary and any votes cast without using the booth may be discounted and if their number cannot be determined, the election may be quashed.[1] At least one booth must be provided for every 300 electors (which meant some 4,000 in Senegal). This requirement is often quoted as an example of the irrelevance of metropolitan legislation, since in Senegal many of

[1] Cf. Holleaux, op. cit., p. 45 n.

the voters will wear hats, dresses, or shirts of the party colour; moreover many pick up only the ballot paper of the party for which they wish to vote before they enter the booth and thus show how they intend to vote. All this is true enough; but even in a relatively 'unsophisticated' area, one man was seen to cast his vote in a way which showed that he was fully aware of, and determined to profit by, the opportunity of the secret ballot. It is, too, a mistake to underestimate African subtlety: in quite a different context some time before the election, talking about the fact that many canton chiefs were (and still are) socialist, an experienced politician in a small country town remarked that at the election in 1952 some new voters in a particular area, afraid of incurring its socialist chief's displeasure, wore the socialist colours—but had nevertheless voted B.D.S.

It would be wrong to omit any reference to the problem of maintaining order. It was not always, the writer was told, possible to have even a *garde de cercle* at each polling station. In fact, on polling day, all the polling stations visited (in Dakar, Thiès, and Kaolack districts) had a policeman or a gendarme. In many parts of Senegal there were considerable military moves: troops were ostentatiously transferred to potentially troublesome areas, or where they were already available, equally ostentatiously displayed. The major anxiety of every District Commissioner or District Officer with whom the administrative problems of the election were discussed was to avoid *la bagarre*, and great attention was undoubtedly paid to the problem of public order. The socialists based their objection to the increased number of polling stations on the contention that they could not be properly supervised and that the absence of sufficient police encouraged almost everywhere the creation of veritable B.P.S. commandos said to have exercised all kinds of pressure, often accompanied by threats, both on voters and on the non-B.P.S. members of the *bureaux*.[1] Such lorry loads of B.P.S. *militants* were certainly to be seen on polling day, but in the village where the writer encountered one, the atmosphere was not tense, the polling station seemed to be functioning quite normally though business was no longer brisk and no suggestions of intimidation were made after the departure of the lorry. The possible abuses arising from this kind of action are real enough though the extent to which they actually occurred on 31 March 1957 could easily be exaggerated.

At all stages the electoral system in French Tropical African territories relies on the supervision of electoral administration by party representatives and the recording in the reports of their operations by registration and revising committees, distribution com-

[1] *Paris-Dakar*, 17 Apr. 1957.

mittees, and polling station *bureaux* of all matters on which disputes may arise and of any complaints or claims lodged with them. These documents are the essential material for the decisions of the administrative courts (the *Conseil du Contentieux Administratif* in West Africa and the *Conseil d'Etat* in Paris) in the event of claims for the quashing of the elections. In practice, of course, this system is imperfect because of the long delays which usually occur before a final decision is obtained, if the results are contested before these courts, and because it is often impossible to obtain from the written reports the details actually needed. The evidence is frequently inconclusive. Moreover, so elaborate a system of recording is very difficult to carry out in practice, perhaps more so in West Africa than in metropolitan France. For example, the reports are not always signed by all the party representatives (or the deputies for whom the law provides) on every day on which the committee operates, for the sufficient reason that they were, as the report records, not present. The writer has seen, for instance, reports of distribution committees of which the full membership signed only on the first and last day. It is impossible, without a large-scale examination of such documents, to assess the extent to which the system provides a measure of effective control of the impartiality of the operations concerned.

So far as the actual polling was concerned, the report of the central counting committee is of interest.[1] Having examined reports from the 1,066 polling stations in Senegal, the committee commented on deficiencies or discrepancies in 144. Some of these comments are concerned with formal points—e.g. cases in which the statutory maximum of 1,500 registered electors per polling station was exceeded. Most draw attention to such deficiencies as failure to indicate the reasons for considering voting papers invalid, or to attach them to the reports, absence of some (or all) of the required signatures on some of the documents, failure to state the names of scrutineers or substitute party representatives, or to sign the count sheets. There were numerous cases in which only a single count sheet was attached, instead of all those required, while some lacked the single marks for each vote (written down as the votes were called out) and contained only a total figure. There were blank spaces in the reports—sometimes whole pages were left blank. Many of these deficiencies appeared to be of no great importance and for the most part the result of lack of experience or understanding of the procedure rather than obvious attempts at electoral frauds. Nor should it be thought that in all the cases commented on by the committee any significant number of votes were involved: frequently the discrepancy was a matter of one

---

[1] I owe to the kindness of M. Senghor the opportunity of studying this document.

or two votes, though there was at least one instance where it was a thousand. The committee is not concerned with complaints or appeals for the setting aside of votes at a particular polling station on the ground of misconduct or mal-administration, which are a matter for the appropriate tribunal. It drew attention to only two cases in which the polling station's report itself referred to interference in the conduct of the election. One of those in the Thiès constituency recorded a comment by its president that voting had not been free because a B.P.S. gang from M'Bour (a small coastal township) had prevented voting for one hour and had 'not wanted' the booths to be used. The socialist representatives at another polling station in the same area complained that voting had not been secret because voters had taken only one voting paper before going into the booth. B.P.S. candidates in the Bas-Sénégal (Saint-Louis) constituency claimed that in five polling stations more people had voted than there were names on the register or that had been issued with electoral cards.

There can be little doubt that such things happened, if not in the instances referred to, then elsewhere. But the writer's general impression was that the election was reasonably free from gross pressure or fraudulent manipulation.

8. *The Candidates*

The B.P.S. was the only party which put up sixty candidates, i.e. one for every seat. Their candidates were truly their own. The P.S.A.S. contested every constituency but in four of them (Diourbel, Thiès, and the two Kaolack constituencies) its candidates ran on joint lists with others supported by the M.P.S., while in a fifth (Louga) the P.S.A.S. ran on a joint list under the label *Bloc Démocratique du N'Diambour*,[1] which the M.P.S. also supported. It is difficult to know what significance to attach to these alleged M.P.S. candidates on joint lists with the P.S.A.S. Indeed it was not always easy to identify them. Several were in fact men who had only left the B.P.S. when it was evident that they would not be nominated by that party.[2] Another, expelled from the B.P.S. in 1956, had been elected as a socialist in the municipal elections of that year. Neither the M.P.S. leader, Doudou Gueye, nor Gabriel d'Arboussier,[3] one of

---

[1] The Table in the report of the central counting committee treats the *Bloc Démocratique du N'Diambour* as wholly independent and shows no P.S.A.S. list in Louga. The total 'P.S.A.S.' candidates are accordingly reduced to fifty-six. I have treated it as comparable with other mixed P.S.A.S. and 'dissident B.P.S.' lists.

[2] M. Oumar Sy at Fatick; M. Alioune Tall at Louga, both expelled from the B.P.S. on 24 Mar. (*Paris-Dakar*, 25 Mar. 1957).

[3] M. d'Arboussier had been Secretary-General of the R.D.A. until the decision

its best-known personalities resident in Senegal, contested the election there. Both stood (and were elected) in other territories, the former in Guinée, the latter in Niger. The official R.D.A. position in Senegal was that the joint lists were those of 'men of goodwill' who had come together in opposition to the B.P.S., and not an electoral alliance with the P.S.A.S. as such.[1] The great majority of the candidates fighting on the lists supported by the P.S.A.S. were men of that party, and most of the rest were ex-members of the B.P.S. In these circumstances no attempt has been made in this section to present separate information about alleged 'M.P.S.' candidates: where such candidates stood on joint lists with those of the P.S.A.S. they are included under that heading.

In nine of the fourteen constituencies there were others besides these two major lists, and the number of candidates was thereby increased to 179. But thirteen of these eighteen other lists, representing fifty of the fifty-nine 'independent' candidates, polled no more than 2,342 out of the 21,221 votes cast for lists other than the two major ones. (Two of them, indeed, received no votes at all and another only one[2].) The remaining five lists,[3] representing nine candidates, were in fact those of men who had failed to secure the nomination of one or other of the major parties, of which they sometimes claimed to remain loyal members, victims of 'undemocratic' procedure at the nominations.[4] Only one of these five polled less than 2,000 votes. Some information about candidates not campaigning on one of the two major lists has been presented in the tables under the heading 'Independents', and relates only to these five lists, since they are considered to have been of some political significance. Occasionally information about the remaining fifty 'Independents' has been included under the heading 'Others'.

in 1950 to break with the communists. He had been reintegrated in the R.D.A. in 1955.   [1] *Paris-Dakar*, 9 Mar. 1957.

[2] Some of these other lists were said to be devices to secure extra representation in polling stations. This may have been true of the three Bas-Sénégal lists which received a single vote between them, but most of them seem to have been vestigial relics of earlier local parties subsequently incorporated in one or other of the major parties.

[3] These were: (a) *Liste d'Union pour la défense des intérêts du Bas-Sénégal* (Saint-Louis) (2)—dissident socialists; (b) *Bloc Démocratique du Fouta Toro* (Podor) (2); (c) *Bloc Démocratique de Kédougou* (Kédougou) (1); (d) *Bloc Démocratique du Djoloff* (Linguère) (1); and (e) *Bloc Progressiste du Cercle de Matam* (Matam) (3)—all dissident B.P.S.

[4] See e.g. letter from Cissokho Mady (Dissident B.P.S. candidate in Kedougou), *Paris-Dakar*, 19 Mar. 1957, and reports on resignation of Alioune Tall from B.P.S., ibid., 2 and 5 Mar. 1957; of Fall Mafall from the P.S.A.S., ibid., 11 Mar. 1957, and letter from Senghor expelling five members of B.P.S. who had stood as independents after failure to secure nomination by that party, ibid., 25 Mar. 1957.

Table 9 assembles some data about candidates' ages. Although the socialists had the youngest candidate in the two major parties (M. Dansy Danara at Tambacounda who was twenty-five) they had, as was to be expected in view of the political history of Senegal, a larger number of older men than their rivals, and almost half of all the over-fifties competing (nineteen out of forty-one). If the average age of socialist candidates (forty-five and a half) was nevertheless not markedly higher than that of the B.P.S. (forty-three) the subtraction of the four candidates who could readily be identified as recent members of the B.P.S. and of one other definitely M.P.S. candidate raised their average age to forty-seven. By contrast, that of the 'Others' was noticeably lower (thirty-eight and three-quarters) than that of either of the major parties.

TABLE 9

Age of Candidates

Age Group	B.P.S.	P.S.A.S.	Independents	Others	All
Over 60 . .	3	6	..	2	11
50–59 . . .	9	13	2	6	30
40–49 . . .	28	26	..	21	75
30–39 . . .	20	13	5	13	51
Under 30 . .	..	2	1	8	11
Unknown . .	..	..	1	..	1
All candidates .	60	60	9	50	179

The absence of any women candidates is the more remarkable, even in a predominantly Muslim country, in view of the importance commonly attached to the 'women's vote' in any discussion of politics in Dakar, the large attendance of women in all political meetings, and the existence of 'women's sections' in both the major parties.

Table 10 shows the ethnic origins of candidates of the two major parties, arranged in the major groups discussed in the first section of this chapter; the estimated number in each group in relation to the total population is also shown, but should not be regarded as giving anything more than a very rough guide to their relative numerical importance. Candidates of mixed European and African origin (*Métis*) have been shown separately because members of this group were important in the earlier political history of the territory.[1]

[1] One of them, Maître Guillabert, Vice-President of the Territorial Assembly, is, for example, a descendant of the first Senegal deputy (Valentin, elected in 1848). His father was President of the *Conseil Général* for twenty-one years, and his grandfather also held that office, besides being Mayor of Saint-Louis.

The category called 'rest' is residual and includes some candidates about whom information is unsatisfactory and others who are the offspring of mixed marriages between members of different African ethnic groups, e.g. Lebou and Serer, Wolof and Toucouleur. Any general assessment of the importance of membership of a particular ethnic group in the selection of candidates is very difficult. Its importance, though real, should not be exaggerated, and in much of Senegal it is only one among a number of factors. It is also difficult to assess the importance of being a 'local man', and to distinguish between the weight given to ethnic considerations and to residence in the constituency. Information about the place of residence of candidates is, unfortunately, very incomplete.

TABLE 10

Ethnic Origins of Candidates of Major Parties

Ethnic group	Total number	% of popn.	B.P.S. (60)	% of cand.	P.S.A.S. (60)	% of cand.
Woloff . .	750,000	35·7	21	35	30	50
Serer . . .	265,000	12·6	5	8·5	3	5
Lebou. .	55,000	2·1	4	6·6	3	5
Toucouleur . .	203,000	9·6	7	11·4	9	15
Fulani. . .	288,000	13·7	2	3·3	1	1·6
Diola . . .	127,000	6·0	7	11·4	3	5
Mande . .	137,000	6·5	1	1·5	4	6·6
Europeans . .	33,000	1·5	3	5	2	3·3
Métis . . .	..	..	2	3·3	1	1·6
Rest . . .	334,000	13·3	8	13·2	4	6·6

Place of birth, which is the subject of Table 11, is, obviously, a somewhat different criterion. In Senegal, as elsewhere, all three considerations, ethnic origin, residence, and place of birth, are mixed up in political arguments. A man who admittedly lives in the constituency may be objected to because he was born elsewhere: another may be of a different ethnic group but the complaint voiced (at least to strangers) may be that he doesn't live in the constituency. It is commonly said that the socialists seldom 'belong to' the area outside Dakar, Rufisque, and Saint-Louis. Table 11 shows, however, that, judged by place of birth, their candidates were no less 'local' than those of their rivals. It also shows that a markedly higher proportion of the fifty-nine candidates not on either of the major lists (i.e. 'Independents' and 'Others') were born in their constituencies.

Candidates born outside Senegal include the five Europeans, the socialist leader and his brother, both born in the Soudan (a link with the heroic epoch when Senegalese accompanied French forces or the French Administration as it extended from the historic base in Senegal), Maître Boissier-Palun, (B.P.S.) President of the Grand Council of French West Africa 1952–7, who was born in Dahomey, and several Guineans.

TABLE 11

Place of Birth of Candidates

Born	B.P.S. (60)	P.S.A.S. (60)	Indepen- dents (9)	Others (50)	All (179)
1. Within constituency . .	34	35	8	36	113
2. Outside constituency, in Dakar, Rufisque, Gorée, or Saint-Louis . . .	15	12	..	8	35
3. Outside constituency, else-where in Senegal . .	5	7	..	5	17
4. Outside Senegal . .	6	5	..	1	12
5. Unknown. . . .	..	1	1	..	2

The most striking fact about candidates' occupations was that 60 per cent. of those of the two major parties worked in the public sector, as shown in Table 12. In compiling that table, a candidate's earlier occupation has been regarded as his occupation in the one or two cases in which his major activity in recent years has been in politics or trade union organization: thus Senghor is included under 'higher education'. It has also been assumed that all school teachers worked in government schools: this was so in all cases investigated individually, but it is possible though unlikely that a few of the remainder worked in mission schools. In some cases not individually investigated it has not been possible from the mere description of the occupation to assign it to the public or the private sector and these are shown as 'doubtful'. Table 12 shows the important part played in political life by school teachers, especially in the B.P.S., and also the support given to that party by some of the small number of Africans who have made their way into higher education. Besides the party leader, there were in this category three younger men, two actively engaged in education work (one as head of the 'mass education' service in Senegal) and one able young historian, Deputy Director of the Institut Français d'Afrique Noire. The table also suggests the greater support given to the P.S.A.S. by 'business men'. Each party had two European business men among its candidates and if these are deducted the much greater number of African 'traders' among the P.S.A.S. candidates is even more apparent (eleven as against four B.P.S.). The 'civil servants' are divided into three groups: (a) are men employed by the Administration who are not professional or technical men, e.g. produce inspectors, postal workers, and clerks. In category (b) are the 'professional civil servants', in this case veterinary surgeons and 'African doctors'. These two occupations were at one time the highest to which Africans might aspire: the former was one of the first full professional qualifications effectively open to them, the latter were the graduates

TABLE 12

Candidates' Occupations

	B.P.S.		P.S.A.S.		Others		
	Candidates	Successful	Candidates	Successful	Candidates	Successful	All members of Assembly
Teachers . . .	21	17	8	2	1	..	19
Higher education . .	4	3	..	..	..	..	3
Civil servants (a) . .	8	7	13	2	4	..	..
,, ,, (b) .	1 }11	0 }8	5 }21	2 }4	..	..	12
,, ,, (c) .	2	1	3	0	..	..	..
Railway	4	4	2	..	..	..	4
Municipal employees .	..	..	1	..	..	..	..
Total public sector . .	40	32	32	6	5	..	38
Business men . . .	6	5	13	3	..	..	8
Lawyers	5	4	4	3	..	..	7
Others	3	3	4	..	..	..	6
Total private sector . .	14	12	21	6	..	..	18
Doubtful	4	1	4	..	3	1	2
Retired	..	..	2	..	..	..	..
Unknown . . .	2	2	1	..	1	..	2
Total	60	47	60	12	9	1	60

of the Dakar medical school, designed to supplement the meagre numbers of fully qualified medical men.[1] Both therefore tended to represent the older 'intelligentsia' and it was characteristic of the social composition of the P.S.A.S. that there should have been two of the former and three of the latter among its sixty candidates. Category (c) civil servants are the minor professional class, e.g. nurses, veterinary assistants. The larger number of 'civil servants' among P.S.A.S. candidates also exemplifies the extent to which it derived its support from those who had 'arrived', and perhaps also the extent to which it was once, in Senegal, the parti de l'administration.

[1] Cf. the similar arrangements in Nigeria (Yaba Medical School) and Uganda (Mulago Medical School). In all three cases these have now given place to a medical school attached to the new local universities.

Its civil servants were, on the average, slightly older than those of the B.P.S. (forty-five as against forty-three and a half) but its youngest candidate belonged to this group which contained five candidates under thirty-five, so the point must not be exaggerated.

Table 13 shows the extent to which candidates were chosen from those with previous political experience, interpreted, for this purpose, as membership of a metropolitan assembly since 1946 (i.e. National Assembly, Council of the Republic, or Assembly of the French Union) or of the two previous territorial assemblies. Where a candidate sat at different times in more than one of the metropolitan assemblies, account has been taken of his most recent office only. Thus Mamadou Dia figures in Table 13 under National Assembly (to which he was elected in 1956) and not under Council of the Republic (in which he sat before). On the other hand, members of metropolitan assemblies who have also been members of the Territorial Assembly are included both under the appropriate metropolitan assembly and in the territorial assembly figures.

TABLE 13

Political Experience of Candidates

	B.P.S.	P.S.A.S.	Independents
National Assembly	2	2	..
Council of the Republic	1	1	..
Assembly of French Union . . .	3	..	..
Territorial Assembly 1947–57 . . .	5	4	..
Territorial Assembly 1947–52 . . .	1	6	..
Territorial Assembly 1952–7 . . .	24	4	4

The Assembly elected in 1952 had nine socialist and forty-one B.D.S. members. Of the nine socialists, two had joined the B.P.S. before the end of the assembly's term, one did not seek re-election, one stood as an Independent, and five stood again as socialists. Of the forty-three B.P.S. members of the old Assembly, one had joined the Opposition, and stood on a joint P.S.A.S.–M.P.S. list, one had been sentenced to a term of imprisonment, and one did not seek re-election. Twenty-nine were renominated. Of the eleven not renominated by the B.P.S., three stood as Independents and two on joint lists with the P.S.A.S. Of the 129 'serious' candidates (i.e. B.P.S., P.S.A.S., and the 'Independents') forty-eight had previous experience as members of the Territorial Assembly. It is unfortunate that insufficient data were obtained to make it possible to show completely the extent of the candidates' experience as municipal councillors.

At least forty-five of the 120 candidates of the two major parties (twenty-six B.P.S. and nineteen P.S.A.S.) were members of the councils of the nine full municipalities.

Nor are there adequate data about the religions professed by candidates. The religious factor has not been prominent in the politics of Senegal elections, though on occasion attempts have been made to represent Lamine Gueye as a Muslim, in contrast to the Catholic Senghor, and references were made in this election to the fact that the latter and his party have always supported the continuation of government grants to mission schools, but had not, it was alleged, pressed for similar assistance to Muslim schools. It is safe to assume that the great majority of the candidates were professing Muslims, and that in some areas at any rate it would be unlikely that a non-Muslim would be elected if he stood. But one of the two leaders of the P.S.A.S. was a European Frenchman, and the Catholic Senghor was the undisputed leader of the B.P.S., working side by side with the Muslim Dia. Of the 120 candidates on the two major lists, at least nine were not Muslims.

9. *The Electoral Campaign*

The opening of the campaign. The date of polling day was fixed by metropolitan decree signed on 22.February.[1] Until the official announcement, there had been some uncertainty about the date, particularly in administrative circles, where it was rumoured that the authorities in some of the less developed territories, faced with the increased administrative problems of universal suffrage and a shortage of suitable personnel to man the larger number of polling stations that would be needed, had proposed that the elections be spread over a longer period. Even in political circles the approaching elections were scarcely mentioned in public and attention was concentrated on the problems of party fusion and on disagreements and uncertainties about the new constitutional arrangements. It was not, therefore, until the end of February that the elections began to move towards the foreground of the political scene. The B.P.S. Congress was from this point of view well timed, since it provided the opportunity for a political rally of the rank and file local leaders, at which the party programme could be explicitly related to the new responsibilities which the party would be called upon to undertake if successful at the elections, as it could be quite confident of being. It also provided a useful piece of electoral publicity, since it was well reported in the solitary local daily and even in the French metropolitan press (which

[1] Decree 57–204 of 22 Feb. 1957 (*J. O. du Sénégal*, 27 Feb. 1957).

is on sale in Dakar). As soon as it was over, the B.P.S. was faced with the problems of nomination, greater and more widespread in its case than in that of its rival, since it had to find room for the new groups now joined with the old B.D.S. Both parties were in any case fully occupied with the problem of nominations until they closed on 10 March. The elaborate time-table of the various operations prescribed by the electoral laws laid down that the campaign, from the official point of view, began on the following day.

Party posters and printed propaganda. French electoral law does not seek to control the expenditure of candidates or parties during the electoral campaign but merely to secure equal access to certain forms of publicity. It requires the Administration to provide sites for posters in each constituency in proportion to the number of electors, equal space being allotted to each party. Posters relating to the election may only be put up on the prescribed sites. Candidates, or in multi-member constituencies lists, may make a deposit of 5,000 francs C.F.A. (about ten guineas) within forty-eight hours of nomination and if they do so, the cost of printing posters, voting papers, and circulars and of putting up the posters will be met by public funds.[1] The deposit is returned to any candidate or list securing at least 5 per cent. of the votes cast. The costs allowed under these arrangements are fixed by a commission appointed for the purpose by the Governor. Only the various official texts which have to be posted at polling stations and certain other public offices may be printed on white paper, and no posters, circulars, or voting papers may use any combination of red, white, and blue (the colours of the French flag). There is no limit to the additional propaganda material which the parties, or any of their supporters, may publish, except that any further posters will not be exempted from the stamp duty and may only be put up on the prescribed sites allotted to the party concerned.

The effect of these provisions seemed to be that posters simply reproduced the party manifestos (*professions de foi*), as did the circulars, and these were in practice the only electoral publicity issued by the parties. The most important practical consideration is that the electors should be in no doubt of the party colours; posters, manifestos, and voting papers were accordingly all printed on paper of the party colour. But these rather drab looking documents were little in evidence. Even in towns there was little sign either of posters or manifestos, and many of the officially designated poster sites remained unused. In Dakar itself, it was only about half-way through the campaign that party manifestos suddenly made their appearance, contrary to these rules, on walls, trees, and other odd spaces, though

[1] Law 52-130 of 6 Feb. 1952, Article 14.

the larger posters were to be seen near the town hall. No posters advertising meetings were seen, nor were people reading or distributing manifestos. It was not possible to visit more than a few constituencies during the campaign and conditions may have been different elsewhere or later in the campaign but the general impression was that printed material of this kind was the only propaganda material used by the parties and that it played a relatively small part in the campaign except in popularizing the party colours and familiarizing new electors with voting papers. At major meetings copies of the respective party newspapers were sold and, on occasion, photographs of the party leader, with a short biography or made up in the form of a calendar.

Much the most obvious sign that an electoral campaign was in progress was the gradual appearance, not only in the African areas of the larger towns but in villages in the bush, of small flags in the party colours (green for B.P.S., red for P.S.A.S., yellow for M.P.S.) and the increasing number of people, especially though by no means exclusively, women, dressed in the party colours. Senegalese women are on most occasions elaborately and beautifully dressed, and kerchiefs and other head-dresses of red or green, always worn at party gatherings, became more and more widespread during the campaign. Many wore dresses or *boubous* of red or green in various shades. Occasionally the yellow of the M.P.S. was to be seen, and in the Thiès constituency, where the P.S.A.S. and the M.P.S. had a joint list, many attractive combinations of red and yellow were sported. Men, especially youths, also wore shirts or peaked hats in the party colours. French residents often criticized this publication of one's political opinions, and pointed out its incompatibility with the secrecy of the ballot but an Englishman, accustomed to rosettes and similar devices, was more at home in such an atmosphere.

The press. But if the legal provisions encourage parties to limit themselves to the publicity provided at public expense, the lack of resources and the limited audience for printed matter, even in Senegal with its greater proportion of literates, do more. There is no contrast between the French and the British territories in West Africa which is more marked than the limited development of an African press in the former as compared with the latter. In spite of its 40,000 Europeans, Senegal has only one daily newspaper, *Paris-Dakar*, and this is European-owned and managed. Its circulation has been estimated at about 15,000. It is quite well produced and has six (or on occasion eight) pages. One is devoted wholly to a selection from the more popular metropolitan dailies, another to advertisements, a third to sport, and a fourth largely to advertisements of cinemas and other amusements and to social news. The two pages devoted to news include, naturally, some of international or metropolitan origin and, since the paper is not produced exclusively for sale in Senegal, some relating to the rest of West Africa. The paper contains a good deal of local news from the smaller towns and townships in Senegal, rather reminiscent of the similar pages of news from the villages in an English country town weekly. There is no editorial and the policy of the paper seems to be to eschew comment. (This does not, of course, spare it from accusations of bias in the selection of news items, the space given to them, or in the speeches (or points in speeches) reported, unfounded though these seemed to the writer.)

Within the narrow limits thus available, *Paris-Dakar* gives a good deal of space to Senegal politics, and it reported the electoral campaign objectively in so far as this was represented by the major meetings in Dakar. Full lists of the candidates of the two major parties appeared on 11 March, as well as a page of pictures of earlier elections in Dakar. A great deal of other factual information was published: the numbers on the new registers,[1] arrangements for distribution of electors' cards in Dakar and Thiès,[2] an account of 'how voting works',[3] the Governor's broadcast,[4] and the High Commissioner's instructions to the administration on impartiality,[5] the full texts of the party manifestos,[6] and the information that the opening and closing of the poll in Dakar and Saint-Louis would be announced by *un coup de canon*.[7] Of more partisan interest were announcements of the defection of prominent members (or whole groups of less prominent people) from one party to the other and personal explanations of their motives. Such moves are traditional in Senegal but may possibly have been greater this year because of the prominence given to the issue of party fusion during the year preceding the election. In any event more space was given to them than to any other single aspect of election news.

The only occasions on which anything resembling editorial comment appeared in *Paris-Dakar* were a week before polling day, when an article discussed election prospects in certain constituencies where the issue might be in doubt, and the day before the poll, when under a banner headline, 'Tomorrow: Territorial Elections: The most important in the history of Black Africa' the significance of the elections was discussed. In the appreciation of electoral prospects, the con-

---

[1] *Paris-Dakar*, 15 Mar. 1957.
[2] Ibid., 18, 22, and 27 Mar. 1957.   [3] Ibid., 20 Mar. 1957.
[4] Ibid., 25 Mar. 1957.   [5] Ibid., 26 Mar. 1957.
[6] Ibid., 30 Mar. 1957.   [7] Ibid., 29 Mar. 1957.

stituencies considered were Dakar and Saint-Louis, the only ones held by the P.S.A.S., and some of those in which there had been a split in the B.P.S. Readers were left to judge for themselves whether the B.P.S. might capture Dakar, while an analysis of past voting in Matem suggested that the outcome was pretty doubtful; in Louga the B.P.S. appeared the most likely winner, as also in Podor and Linguère; in Saint-Louis the P.S.A.S. split would not, the paper thought, lead to its defeat.[1] The front-page article the day before the poll asserted that all political leaders were agreed that these were the most important elections yet held in Africa, in view of the increased powers of the Territorial Assemblies to be elected. It drew attention to the fact that they were to be held on universal suffrage and on a common roll and that for West Africa as a whole 53 per cent. of the population were on the register. They would also be as 'free and sincere' as in France; no administrative pressure or interference would occur. After all it was surely in France's own interest for this to be so. The article expressed satisfaction at the inclusion of Europeans in the various party lists, the calm in which the campaign had been conducted ('it was not always thus'), and the absence of any whisper of secession.[2]

Besides *Paris-Dakar*, two weeklies were published regularly in Dakar. One of them, *Échos d'Afrique noire*, proclaimed itself the 'weekly of Franco-African fraternity'; in fact it specialized in the defence of *la présence française* and the publication of 'inside stories' and 'scandals' implicating those it disliked. Besides African nationalists —and especially Senghor—these included the French administration, America, Nehru's India, *perfide Albion* (when space permitted), the left-wing Catholic group which produced *Afrique nouvelle*, and even the M.R.P. (for supporting the revised text of the *loi-cadre* decrees). It was the authentic voice of *petit-bourgeois* French colonial xenophobia. Its circulation has been estimated at 8,000–12,000. During the five weeks before polling day, it made no direct reference to the elections, though it attacked the new Governor of Senegal far more violently than Senghor had attacked the French Government for making such an appointment immediately before the elections. Its reasons for doing so, however, was that the new Governor would, it claimed, support the B.P.S.[3] because it was the stronger party. Earlier in February, its readers had been urged to support the M.S.A. but the demand, made in the report on general policy approved by the P.S.A.S. at its congress, for French recognition of the right to independence, as the basis on which a great French African

[1] Ibid., 23 Feb. 1957.   [2] Ibid., 30 Mar. 1957.
[3] *Échos d'Afrique noire*, 291 (18–24 Mar. 1957).

community could be freely entered, led to a fresh outburst and a demand that this should be disavowed by the Socialist leader Lamine Gueye.[1]

The other weekly, *Afrique nouvelle* (circulation about 5,000–7,000) was published under the auspices of the Catholic mission in Dakar, and sold throughout West Africa. It had taken up a position sympathetic to African aspirations, and its well-informed reports of political and trade union news in French West Africa gave it considerable influence among Africans far beyond merely mission circles. Printed at the mission press, it was technically the best produced newspaper in French West Africa. Besides a page of local news, sports features, a religious page, and a page of metropolitan and international news, it normally carried two or more pages of articles and editorials on French West African topics and also frequent articles and reports on ideas and events in British and Belgian Africa. Although edited by a European priest and employing two European journalists, its staff included a Togolander, and much of it was written by African contributors.

During the five weeks before polling day, it gave some space to the elections but not so as to concentrate attention on them to the exclusion of other political issues, especially that of independence. The B.P.S. Congress was fully reported in its issue of 26 February, which also reproduced extracts from the report on general policy adopted on that occasion. In these, its author Mamadou Dia called for a régime of austerity: an African administration must be one of work, order, discipline, and financial rigour. An interview with Senghor reported that the forthcoming elections were, in his view, of the greatest importance since the assemblies would be called upon to elect senators and members of the Assembly of the French Union, and above all the new Councils of Government. True, Senghor had described their powers as 'toys and dummies' but 'our business is to make them an effective means of self-government'. Did Senghor think the elections would be free? He did, both because he did that much justice to the local administrations and because Senegal electors were not to be intimidated. But the socialist government in Paris did not want free elections, otherwise it would not have resorted to changing governors or sending two of its ministers to Africa on electoral tours. The greatest difficulty confronting the new Councils of Government would be the need to take measures of financial austerity while having no means of arousing popular enthusiasm, for which internal self-government was essential. Europeans were ready to co-operate with Africans, especially industrialists and

---

[1] *Échos d'Afrique noire*, 285 (4–10 Feb.) and 288 (25 Feb.–3 Mar. 1957).

even traders, but civil servants spoke wildly of packing their bags. African and European would live side by side though different.

The following week a French resident,[1] under the title 'Europeans must vote' criticized strongly the apathy of his compatriots in local politics. Less than 5 per cent. of those living in Dakar had voted in the recent municipal elections. Admittedly, the administration did not make it easy either to register or to vote, but European indifference was the real obstacle to that co-operation for which African leaders appealed. One page reproduced a radio debate on French West Africa and the common market in which the B.P.S. leader, Boissier-Palun, was one of three speakers. The others were the Director of Economic Affairs in French West Africa and the chairman of the Dakar Chamber of Commerce. M. Boissier-Palun took part as President of the Grand Council, and not as a political partisan. The next issue, that of 12 March, was a special number on Ghana independence, with a first-hand report of the celebrations in Accra from the editor. It also contained the first of two factual surveys of candidates and parties contesting the elections throughout French West Africa and an interview with the nationalist mayor of Tananarive, the capital of Madagascar, emphasizing that the forthcoming elections must be 'free and sincere'. The following week a long article from a reader in the Soudan called for a halt to electoral lies and corruption, while in the paper's 'Open Forum' Senghor set out the case for a Federal State of French West Africa and attacked the decrees giving effect to the *loi-cadre* as designed to 'balkanize' Africa, to divide and rule, using the same arguments as he had developed in the National Assembly. Doudou Gueye, in an interview on the same page, defended the decrees, 'with their inadequacies', as nevertheless setting up territorial self-government, denied that they would lead to 'balkanization', and contended that they would promote a federal association of the territories in the future. He was diplomatic about party unification. What mattered was African unity, which must respect diversity. But however much they might differ on ways and means, African parties and leaders had, he thought, no radical disagreement about ends. Even those who talked of immediate independence had no other object than the freedom and happiness of Africans. An editorial note emphasized that *Afrique nouvelle* had no intention of taking sides in the election but only of providing the material for reflection and judgement. *Afrique nouvelle* also issued a small leaflet 'How to Vote on March 31st' which explained the

---

[1] M. André Peytavin, in *Afrique nouvelle*, 5 Mar. 1957. After the elections, he was elected by the B.P.S. majority a member of the Senegal Council of Government (though he was not a member of the Assembly) and became Minister of Finance.

organization of polling stations, what to do to vote, and how the votes were counted.[1] Finally, in its issue of 26 March, a page of articles appeared under the title 'Before the elections'. This included a manifesto addressed to all candidates by the C.A.T.C. unions of Senegal setting out 'the wishes of the workers', in respect of social, economic, and education matters. These dealt with industrial accidents legislation, the administration of the Labour Code, Africanization of the private as well as the public sector, housing, workers' education, the creation of an African regional office of the I.L.O., and various aspects of agricultural and mining activities. Another contributed article attacked the cupidity of politicians who sought to collect all jobs—to be deputies, ministers, and mayors, and so prevented the young from getting any office. An 'Appeal to the Electors', also contributed, urged them to vote for those really devoted to the ideal of public service and not those, much more numerous, actuated by greed and ambition, who sought only a villa for themselves, a better standard of living, and jobs for their close relations.

Both the major Senegalese parties have their newspapers, published somewhat irregularly but nevertheless continuously, the socialist *L'A.O.F.* and the B.P.S. *L'Unité*. The former has a long history; its first number appeared in 1907, and it first called itself 'journal socialiste' in 1937. Its publication, interrupted during the war, was resumed in 1945, when it became 'organe de la fédération socialiste S.F.I.O.' On the formation of the P.S.A.S. in 1957, its sub-title was once more changed, this time to 'organe officiel du P.S.A.S., section sénégalaise du M.S.A.' Its circulation has been estimated at 2,000. The first issue of the latter appeared on 2 October 1956 on the formation of the B.P.S. It was, in fact, though the ideology of fusionism precluded admitting this, the successor of *Condition humaine*, which had appeared under Senghor's direction since 1948. Six numbers of *L'A.O.F.* were published between 30 November 1956 and 27 March 1957 and three of them appeared during the campaign period. Each consisted of a single unfolded sheet. *L'Unité* did not appear during the campaign; its seventh issue was published on 5 March, just before the official campaign period began. This was of four pages, equivalent to two sheets of *L'A.O.F.* in size. The circulation of *L'Unité* was probably about 4,000.

L'A.O.F. of 12 March printed the constitution of the P.S.A.S., the membership of its central committee, and a list of 'our candidates' which nevertheless included the names of those of the M.P.S. in constituencies in which there was a joint M.P.S.-P.S.A.S. list. Three

---

[1] This was the text printed in *Paris-Dakar* under the title 'How voting works'. See p. 366.

articles attacked the B.P.S.: its adoption of a European contributor to *Paris-Dakar* as one of its candidates in Diourbel was hailed as explaining the long-evident B.P.S. bias of that newspaper, which had obviously been promoting his candidature. The association of such a man, 'devoured by political ambition as he was'; with the communists surrounding Senghor was indeed surprising. The B.P.S., of course, for all their 'outrageous demagogy', were making a deal with the very business circles they so readily stigmatized as colonialist enemies of African progress. Another article admitted that the P.S.A.S. must find its way to the furthest depths of the bush in spite of the grave obstacles presented by B.P.S. use of the Provident Societies, and of compound heads and other officials as a means of intimidation. The third consisted of a letter from a socialist councillor in Thies, addressed to the mayor (Senghor) accusing the B.P.S. of electoral manœuvres in connexion with the dismissal of some municipal employee and the return of certain central administration officials previously seconded to the municipality. These 'fascist methods' would only strengthen socialist resistance.

The main feature of the two following issues was a lengthy survey of P.S.A.S. policy, by Maître Bonifay, the French lawyer long associated with Lamine Gueye in the Senegal S.F.I.O. The first of these 'For Safeguarding Peasant Incomes and the Expansion of the Rural World' was mainly concerned with groundnut marketing, village co-operatives, and the production of foodstuffs. It advocated a single price for groundnuts, transport costs being averaged over the territory by an equalization fund, a differential price for decorticated groundnuts to encourage the producers to decorticate the nuts themselves, as was done in the Niger territory, the creation of village co-operatives and their grouping in a territorial association, and the promotion of food production by encouraging the rotation of food crops with groundnuts and controlling the price of rice and millet, the two major crops. These topics were taken up again in the second of the two articles, 'Senegal Electors, here is our programme', which was accompanied by photographs of the author and Lamine Gueye, together with those of four other P.S.A.S. candidates, all standing for Dakar. The second article added some more details in the field of industry and urban areas. This criticized B.P.S. advocacy of fiscal encouragement for investment on the ground that such encouragement should be selective and should be directed in particular to processing industries and transport, while mining, as the exploitation of wasting assets, should pay both royalties and other taxes. Interterritorial trade should be encouraged, especially by the joining up of the Dakar–Niger railway with that from Conakry to Kankan in

French Guinea. Senegal and West Africa should have 'economic representation' in France, other European countries, and America. Scientific and technical research, particularly in nutrition and the food value of local products should be developed, technical and vocational education directed towards Africanization must be greatly increased; equal pay for equal work, the encouragement of African enterprise, control of rents and public housing programmes and the establishment of a pilot project for public transport in the bush were other points in a programme of 'progressive socialization'.

Other articles were more specifically political. 'Towards a fighting front for the democratization of dependent peoples' admitted that since their defeat in 1951 'by prefabricated elections' the socialists had suffered a severe crisis both in recruitment and slogans, and that besides the collaboration of the colonialist administration in electoral manipulation the party's successive defeats had been due to its adoption of a metropolitan programme which needed some adaptation to local peculiarities. Claiming that proposals for an autonomous African socialist movement had been made by M. Pineau at the S.F.I.O. Congress in 1953, and discussed at the Senegal party's Kaolack Congress in 1954, it denied that the M.S.A. was, as its opponents alleged, the creation of the socialist government then in office. Another article depreciated some recent resignations from the P.S.A.S. Those concerned had merely exemplified 'the politics of personalities'. 'A Warning to Electors' asserted that the B.P.S. was about to launch a new campaign of intimidation. People were, however, beginning to see through Senghor's attempt to take credit for the reforms of 1946. Everyone knew that it was Houphouet-Boigny who had secured the abolition of forced labour and Lamine Gueye who had brought about the extension of citizenship to the people in the bush. Senghor's attacks on the *loi-cadre* reforms were 'really extravagant' and heedless of the bad impression made on those in France and Africa willing to help Africans. When he was Secretary of State he hadn't bothered about self-government or independence but only his own position. Senegal under his control couldn't get the advantages that were secured for their territories by Houphouet-Boigny and Fily Dabo Sissoko (socialist leader in the Soudan), both 'faithful defenders of the canton chiefs'. He was only waiting to replace experienced chiefs enjoying their people's confidence by policemen under his own orders. The electors should choose members belonging to serious parties like those of the M.S.A. In heavy type 'Electors Demand' told the *camarades de brousse* they must insist that an identity card with a photograph must be produced personally by the claimant before electoral cards were issued or voting allowed, and each voter must vote in the booths provided. These conditions obtained in the four communes and should be insisted on everywhere in the country. Yet another short note claimed that although, as usual, the administration had issued formal instructions that officials must preserve neutrality in the elections, everyone knew they were immediately flouted outside the four communes and that everywhere in the bush the nepotism and dictatorship of the B.P.S. bosses, for the most part canton chiefs, produce inspectors, and provident society officials, prevailed.[1]

The issue of 26 March was almost wholly taken up with Bonifay's article on the party programme, but included also an appeal to the Senegal voters which contrasted 'the *autonomistes* of the *Convention Africaine*', whose policy of federalism remained for most Africans indefinite and hazardous, with the ripe wisdom of African socialists who, on the contrary, demanded a closer association of Senegal and France. The complete silence of the B.P.S. in the economic sphere, which was the real key to all other problems, showed that they put the cart before the horse. On the social plane, town workers must have better conditions, especially housing. The total inadequacy of the B.P.S., and its predecessor the B.D.S., was illustrated by the construction of the new *Palais du Grand Conseil* when Dakar lacked an up-to-date hospital.

The single issue of *L'Unité* which appeared in March was entirely devoted to the B.P.S. Congress held at the end of February. It reprinted all the resolutions, the report on general policy, part of that on economic policy, the opening speech of welcome (by the secretary of the Dakar branch), and the composition of the new executive committee of the party. There were two articles, one on the *loi-cadre* decrees by Senghor and one on the significance of the Congress by Abdoulaye Ly. Senghor's article was a detailed exposition of the position he and other African deputies and parties had adopted in the National Assembly debates on the decrees.[2] Its sub-title was 'Donner et Retirer ne vaut', a phrase much used in the debates themselves, and it was a measured defence of his conclusion that although the decrees as amended by the National Assembly marked some advance it had been attained at the cost of increased concentration of metropolitan control over the major services and the 'balkanization' of the two federations and Madagascar. The central point in Abdoulaye Ly's article was that the B.P.S. would be called upon to be both a

<hr />

[1] All in *L'A.O.F.*, 19 Mar. 1957.
[2] For the main points made in the National Assembly debates see my 'Constitutional Reform in French Tropical Africa', *Political Studies*, vol. vi, 1958, pp. 56–61.

party of opposition and a party of government. It would be in the same position as that of the C.P.P. in Ghana when it took office under the 'bastard Coussey constitution' of 1951.

It is not easy to assess the importance of the press in the electoral campaign. The account just given makes it clear that it was limited. Perhaps the most striking indication of this is the fact that the B.P.S. did not attempt to produce anything like an election number of *L'Unité*. They were too busy with their party Congress, with nominations, and the inevitable dissensions they produced, to devote their energies to such a task before the campaign began, and once it had begun they were too busy campaigning. But the party newspapers (and also *Afrique nouvelle*) were of great importance in a more long-term view of political activity. They helped to build up some coherent political opinion among the politically conscious and especially among the active party members, which played its part in the electoral campaign. This was probably more important for the B.P.S. than the P.S.A.S. which still appeared to retain more of the characteristics of an electoral organization than of a mass political movement. Although the party papers normally contained a reasonable amount of political mud-slinging, the solidity and seriousness of their major articles deserve emphasis: they were far removed from the incoherent repetition of slogans which sometimes does duty for statements of party policy elsewhere. The single issue of *L'Unité* which appeared in March had, indeed, no mud-slinging at all. *Afrique nouvelle* also performed a considerable service in the definition of political issues and in providing a forum for serious debate. In spite of constant criticism from all sides, in the writer's opinion *Paris-Dakar* compared quite favourably with popular newspapers in other countries in its political coverage and provided fairly adequate knowledge of current political happenings for anyone actively engaged in politics. What it did not do, was to give its ordinary European readers sufficient material to form a balanced and knowledgeable appraisal of African politics or of African political leaders. Perhaps it would be unreasonable to expect it to do so, especially in face of the well-attested apathy of most Europeans. But the absence of any journal which carries out this function is a serious impediment to Franco-African understanding in French West Africa.

Radio. Although there is a federal broadcasting service the role this played in the elections was extremely small. There were no party political broadcasts, and election and local political news was, so far as the writer's observation went, hardly ever mentioned in the news broadcast, and then reduced to the minimum of factual reporting.

The party manifestos. The manifestos issued by the two major parties differed in many respects but were alike in having no reference to specific issues relevant to the activities of the Territorial Assembly. That of the B.P.S. consisted simply of the general policy resolution of its February Congress. This began by asserting that the most urgent task was to contribute actively to a true *regroupement* of parties on an interterritorial basis within an organization whose activities extended throughout Black Africa. To this end, the B.P.S. gave its definite agreement to the programme of the Convention Africaine. To realize that policy at the territorial level, the party must set an example of cohesion, austerity, and African consciousness. The administration of indigenous peoples by themselves, the principle of which was no longer contested, must not be an administration of convenience and *laisser-aller* but one of work, order, hierarchic discipline, and financial rigour. The organs of the party at all levels must ensure that party discipline and ideals were rigorously respected. It undertook to practice a policy of strict austerity both in the municipalities and in the territorial assembly and to 'help to show the world that, deserving something better than the semi-autonomy granted by the *loi-cadre*, our people are firmly resolved to liquidate any kind of survival of the colonial system'. 'Having regard to the final manœuvres of colonialist reaction against the rights now irrevocably considered sacred by all peoples hitherto oppressed—the right to the fullest self-government, to self-determination, progress in dignity, freedom, and equality between individuals and between human communities'—the B.P.S. was solemnly declared 'in a state of emergency'. It called upon the people of Senegal in its entirety—peasants, workers, intellectuals, and all mass organizations—to mobilize in the B.P.S. to safeguard their vital interests and secure all their rights. It solemnly appealed to the French people to demand from their Government scrupulous respect for the rights of the peoples of Black Africa which alone could guarantee the maintenance of the ties of friendship between the peoples of Africa and the French people.

In comparison with this stirring call to African nationalism—for there could surely be no doubt that that was what the B.P.S. manifesto was—that of the P.S.A.S. was a party appeal within the régime rather than a call for radical change in the régime itself. Addressed to 'Dear Fellow Citizens', it began by emphasizing the importance of the elections since the new assemblies 'would have the responsibility of taking part in the direct management of our own affairs' through ministers responsible to them. This peaceful revolution had been realized by the *loi-cadre* and the immense progress this constituted for an Africa which had become conscious of herself and her role in the evolution of the world' was due to the courageous initiative of a socialist minister, Gaston Defferre. 'Confronted by the new perspectives thus opened to Africa in general and Senegal in particular, we must face the issue of the choice of the men who will have to ensure the progress of the territory.' Since 1952 the B.D.S., recently become the B.P.S., had been in control, with the results of which everyone was aware and which enable everyone to have an idea of the *régime* to which he would be submitted if the fate of the country were to be entrusted to them for a further five years. 'The Senegalese are not, however, the kind of men to be taken in indefinitely. That is why they will vote *en masse* for the P.S.A.S. candidates and its programme of political economic and social emancipation.'

The remainder of the circular reproduced the sections of the manifesto of the M.S.A. under its three headings of Political, Cultural, and Economic and Social Democracy, and concluded with the assurance that the party had the will to carry out this programme as rapidly as possible; the best guarantee it offered was 'its action in the past as in the present directed towards a single end: always more freedom, justice, and progress in every field for "nos vaillantes populations" '.

Other *professions de foi* were no doubt issued by the dissentient groups in such constituencies as Louga, Podor, Matam, and Kédougou, but in spite of various attempts the writer was unable to get copies of these.

An impression of the campaign. The limitations of this account of the campaign must be made clear. What can be seen by a single observer of an electoral campaign lasting a little more than two weeks[1] and taking place throughout a country as large as England and Scotland combined, in which means of communication, though good by comparison with many parts of Africa, are nevertheless patchy, can only be a very small part even of public activity. An attempt to recruit African observers in some other constituencies than those actually visited by the writer during the campaign was unfortunately unsuccessful. Nor could the deficiencies of personal observation be supplemented from radio or press reports since these were, in general, only available for major meetings in Dakar itself. Outside the major towns, almost all speeches were made in one of the African languages spoken in Senegal, of none of which had the writer any knowledge: it was not always possible for him to secure even an extempore trans-

---

[1] The campaign opened officially on 11 Mar. but it was not really under way much before the end of that week.

lation, though on some occasions he was fortunate enough to have the help of a skilled African journalist, and usually had some help from African friends.[1]

Some time was spent in five constituencies during the campaign, not all of it in following the activities of political parties since it was also necessary to see something of the procedure for the distribution of electoral cards and other aspects of electoral administration. The five constituencies chosen were Bas-Sénégal, Louga, Thiès, Kaolack II, and Dakar. They included the constituencies of the leaders of the two major parties, Thiès (Senghor), and Dakar (Lamine Gueye); the administrative capital of the territory, Saint-Louis, a socialist stronghold in which a dissentient socialist list stood against the P.S.A.S. candidates; a constituency in which both major parties were strong and a change of party possible though unlikely (Dakar); two constituencies in which former B.P.S. members had not been renominated and were standing on joint lists with the P.S.A.S. and in some kind of association with the M.P.S. (Louga and Kaolack II). They also included constituencies which were predominantly rural (Louga, Thiès, and Kaolack II) as well as four of the five largest towns in Senegal (Dakar, Rufisque, Thiès, and Saint-Louis).[2] Apart from the larger meetings that he attended, the writer was able to accompany the B.P.S. leader (M. Senghor) during part of his campaign in the rural areas in the Bas-Sénégal constituency, the P.S.A.S. candidates in Thiès in part of their campaign in the rural areas of that constituency, and also the M.P.S. leader (Dr. Doudou Gueye) in some village meetings.

The most striking feature of the campaign as a whole, from the point of view of methods, was its concentration on oral propaganda and meetings. The limited role of the press and of printed party propaganda, including posters, has already been indicated. One practical difficulty in following the campaign was that of finding out in advance what meetings and *tournées electorales* were planned. It was fatally easy to arrive in the headquarters town of a rural constituency only to discover that all parties were out campaigning in different parts of the constituency and that an attempt to reach either involved not only a complete rearrangement of plans but a very real risk that contact with the quarry would not be made. Although the campaign was so essentially a question of meetings and rallies, no use was made, so far as the writer was able to discover, of loudspeaker vans though

---

[1] Some speeches were recorded by the writer on a wire recorder and subsequently translated for him. With proper arrangements with party leaders this technique could be used on a much more systematic basis.

[2] The fifth was Kaolack; all had a population of more than 30,000.

public address equipment was invariably used at major meeting (and not infrequently gave trouble).

Political meetings, large or small, and of all parties, follow a broadly similar pattern. Those in the bush are held in a patch of cleared ground under an outsize baobab[1] or under an awning in the village 'square' (so as to give some shade to the speakers and prominent personalities); those in towns in some public square, a sports stadium, or an open-air cinema; there will be a few chairs and a table, or perhaps, at a bigger meeting in an important township, a rough platform of planks supported on sandbags, on which the notables will be given chairs or a share of a form; high up on top of the tree someone has tied the party flag, or there may be a rough flagstaff set in the ground; drummers beat out intermittent messages and to while away the time before the speakers arrive some of the women, who are sitting together in a solid phalanx, wearing head-scarves or dresses in the party colours, may advance in ones or twos into the open space in the centre and execute a dance; there will perhaps be a long succession of speeches by local worthies, expounding their loyalty to the party (on the whole this was a more marked feature of socialist meetings); when the speakers arrive and have been introduced, if not before, the bureau of the meeting will be announced amid applause (they have certain legal responsibilities for the orderly conduct of the meeting under the law about street meetings); then may follow a song by the griot[2] in praise of the party and its leaders; and, finally, the main speeches. In election meetings, the candidates (or some of them) will speak first, and then the leader, if it is a meeting in his tournée électorale; if not, there may be speeches by local leaders and then by the candidate. Meetings held at certain times of the day (e.g. before sundown) must end with fair promptitude, for Senegal is a Muslim country and they must be over in time for the prescribed prayers. During a tournée électorale, this general pattern may be considerably shortened; or much of it will have taken place before the arrival of the principal speakers. But in spite of such efforts, keeping to a time-table except in a fairly rough and ready way is difficult, so that major meetings, particularly those at the end of a day's campaigning, may not effectively begin until some hours after the advertised time. Punctuality is not an African virtue, as Mamadou Dia seldom failed to point out, as meetings at the party congresses got later and later (he might have added that it isn't a French

---

[1] The characteristic tree of Senegal.
[2] A traditional caste in many ethnic groups in Senegal whose function is to sing the praises of a great notable. On political occasions, they do not necessarily perform it in an African language.

one either). But quite apart from this, it is in fact almost impossible to keep to a time-table in a Senegalese electoral campaign; if important people are late at the original assembly point, they must within reason be awaited since they will not be able to come unless they are taken in one of the two or three cars; one or other of the cars may all too easily, in spite of often very skilful driving, become sand-bound on the hardly visible tracks through the sandy scrub which do duty for roads once the main road has been left; and it may take a good quarter of an hour to get going again; apart from more serious breakdowns, it is often necessary to stop and greet prominent men or parties of sympathizers. All this is cumulative, and it requires constant effort to be as nearly on time as Senghor generally was.

Superficial appearances apart, the atmosphere at these meetings did not seem markedly different from that of political meetings in Britain. Perhaps it was an illusion that B.P.S. meetings had an atmosphere of fervour, an indefinable impression of a 'movement' such as used to characterize meetings of the Labour Party, while those of the P.S.A.S. often seemed more reminiscent of Conservative Party *fêtes* in rural districts. But one important difference between election meetings in Senegal and those in Britain is the entire absence of heckling or of questions from the audience. This was equally true of all parties and all types of meeting. Nor were there *réunions contradictoires*, as the French call them, at which speakers from several parties address the meeting, because, it was stated, they had been found too great a strain on partisan feelings. Interjections from members of the audience were not unknown, but they came from supporters, not opponents.

Generally, the atmosphere at meetings was good tempered though on occasion a little excitable. This was mainly due to the practical problems involved in controlling large crowds, and was often the result of the activities of young party stewards. On one occasion in Fatick where there was strong feeling owing to the fact that the former B.P.S. member, who resided there, was standing on the joint P.S.A.S.-M.P.S. list, a small meeting of his supporters was being held not far away from a major B.P.S. meeting, at which Senghor himself was to speak. There was, however, no sign of any disturbance, and the P.S.A.S.-M.P.S. meeting apparently petered out long before the belated arrival of the main B.P.S. spokesmen.[1] Yet Senegal has a bad reputation for political violence. As recently as 1955 the arrival of Lamine Gueye in a small town in Casamance led to serious disturbances in which five people were killed.[2] There is no question

---

[1] For an account of this B.P.S. meeting see 'Senghor of Senegal', *West Africa*, 6 Apr. 1957, p. 315.   [2] See, e.g., *Condition humaine*, 27 Jan. and 10 Feb. 1955.

that the responsible party leaders are wholly opposed to violence, but they cannot always control their followers. They have, however, apparently succeeded in reducing serious incidents, and in this particular election it was generally agreed that calm had prevailed. Parties did not, of course, carry out electioneering simultaneously in the same parts of a constituency.

The writer was informed by experienced politicians in some of the more remote and 'undeveloped' areas that much of their time during the campaign was spent in explaining voting. On occasions at meetings he attended, even in Dakar itself, some of the preliminary speeches were concerned with such matters. But he saw no actual demonstrations of how to put the ballot paper in the envelope and how to put the envelope in the box, and at least in the relatively central areas in which he followed the campaign there were no obvious signs that this was an important problem, even though a proportion of the electorate was presumably voting for the first time. One great advantage of the system of voting would seem to be that voters are perhaps more easily made aware of party colours than of often poorly reproduced symbols. Flags and coloured head-dresses may be more effective propaganda devices than symbols and lapel buttons.

One interesting event of the campaign period was the suspension of party meetings, in Dakar, Thiès, and probably also in other constituencies in the 'central core' of the territory, which followed the death, on 25 March, of El Hadj Babacar Sy, the *grand marabout* or head of the Tidjaniyya confraternity centred on Tivaouane, a small township near Thies, and about fifty miles from Dakar. Immediately the news of his death became known (his serious illness had not become public), immense numbers of people began to make their way to Tivaouane to pay their last respects to the dead Khalifa. It was estimated that as many as 100,000 people made the journey to Tivaouane, in lorries, buses, and cars, as well as on foot from the nearer countryside. Both Senghor and Boissier-Palun, the B.P.S. leader in Dakar, were among them. Babacar Sy had been a supporter of the B.D.S. and his influence was undoubtedly very great. One can only speculate on the result which his death would have had on the poll if it had occurred immediately before the day of the election.

His brother, El Hadj Mansour Sy, who had supported the socialists, survived him by only a few days, dying on 29 March. Socialist meetings were suspended, at least in Dakar, on that occasion, but by the next day political activity was again in full swing. Both parties held monster meetings in Dakar on the last afternoon of the campaign, at which their respective leaders spoke.

The themes. In Senegal, as in other colonies today, politics are dominated by the fact of dependent status. All parties from this point of view must be parties of change, and there is undoubtedly a sense in which the criterion of party differences is the attitude which their spokesmen adopt with regard to the speed and manner in which colonial rule is to be transformed. But for this very reason the language of party pronouncements on this subject often obscures the nature of division. On the basis of such pronouncements, no real differences of policy might appear to divide the parties. In section 5 of this chapter, it has been shown how the party 'platforms' in Senegal differed on such matters as self-government and the future relations of Senegal and of French West Africa with France. But these were differences which had to be detected in the implications of phraseology, which were subtle and relatively complex rather than easily reduced to slogans. It cannot be supposed—at least without much detailed investigation—that such differences were clearly apprehended by many of the party militants, let alone by ordinary voters. But the difference between the essentially conservative temperament of many of the P.S.A.S. militants and the more radical disposition of their opposite numbers in the B.P.S. was, on the basis of the writer's investigations, easily apparent though difficult to prove.

Even in electoral meetings P.S.A.S. spokesmen provided evidence of this. They invariably emphasized the French connexion. In a small town in the Thiès constituency, for example, a socialist candidate began by referring to the historic ties of France and Senegal. He mentioned the *cahier* that Saint-Louis had presented in 1789. Separation was not an issue. Independence was the demand of demagogues and *communisants*. But, he continued, all they wanted was the right, guaranteed by the Constitution, of managing democratically their own affairs. Even in a family, children grow up. The *loi-cadre* provided for this: the election was of historic significance because the new assembly would have to choose a 'council of government' with ministers responsible for the administration of territorial matters. B.P.S. spokesmen, on the other hand, especially Senghor himself, always devoted some time to protesting that, because the B.P.S. demanded genuine internal self-government, they were denounced as separatists and anti-French, and accused of being anti-white. Such accusations were false. They believed in a Franco-African community, but it must be a community based on equality not on exploitation. And there could be no such community unless the African community was first achieved. This meant full internal self-government, the necessary precondition of any adequate social and economic policy. It was a monstrous travesty for Europeans to say that the B.P.S. wanted to 'show them the door'. All they wanted was the right to manage democratically their own affairs, as provided in the Constitution. In French West Africa, however, this could not be secured by each territory alone. At a time when great countries like France and Germany could not stand alone and had just agreed to set up the Common Market, how could Senegal, with only 2 million people, or the Soudan with three? French West Africa must be preserved from 'Balkanization'. A community of 20 million people would count for something in a Franco-African association. That association was like a wrestling match: it couldn't take place if there was only one wrestler. And the essential basis of any African community which could form, with France, a Franco-African community, was full internal self-government, political, administrative, social, economic, and cultural. The old notion of a unitary and centralized Republic must give way to a federal republic in which only the essential federal powers, foreign affairs, defence, and currency were retained by the federal government.

The difference of emphasis is apparent. If both parties expressed concern to maintain some kind of association with France, the B.P.S. was much more critical of the past and present character of that association and much more insistent on full internal self-government, while the P.S.A.S. still tended to emphasize the prior importance of the emancipation of the individual. The B.P.S. appealed much more to nationalist feeling and even used highly charged words like self-determination, besides underlining the essential requirements of real self-government such as genuine control of the civil service and of the interterritorial administration. For them the new reforms were phony ('toys and dummies' as Senghor had called them in the National Assembly) while by the P.S.A.S. spokesmen they were represented as another great step forward, and one moreover that had been carried through by a socialist minister, like the beginnings of trade union rights in 1936 and the grant of citizenship in 1946. Here could be seen at work the 'metropolitan axis' of party politics in French Africa. The socialists and the R.D.A., their rather distant electoral allies in some Senegalese constituencies, were part of the Government, while the B.P.S. deputies were two of its most vehement parliamentary critics. The socialists variously accused Senghor of having been in 1955 a minister in the Faure Government, which had failed to carry through the long projected overseas reforms, and of now taking credit with the gullible electorate in the bush for the very reforms he had opposed in Parliament. They assured the electors that this time, the socialist Government in power had promised to put a stop to the use of all kinds of improper pressures, on which the B.P.S. had, with the connivance of the local French Administration, risen to power.

The B.P.S., for their part, and especially Senghor himself, bitterly attacked the Guy Mollet Government on every occasion. In the latter half of February, the Governor of Senegal had been abruptly replaced by the Governor of the Ivory Coast. It was the news of this appointment which really marked the beginning of the electoral campaign. Immediately on his arrival in Senegal to attend the B.P.S. Congress, Senghor strongly criticized this appointment made 'a few days before the elections', and asked whether in the light of it the minister's proclaimed determination that the administration should be scrupulously impartial and refrain from any interference in the elections could be regarded as anything more than another astute move directed to the United Nations. He deplored such moves, which could only compromise in African eyes the credit that he and his friends had never ceased to accord to metropolitan France. They were determined to defend, by all legal means, their dignity and their personality. Truth would prevail in the end. They remained attached to France. But for them the French genius did not consist of such deals between party bosses. At the congress, which opened next day, he seized the opportunity to whip up party fervour. All these goings on would not impress people. The change of governors would only strengthen the B.P.S. in the elections. It had been demanded by Lamine Gueye to show the power of the Senegal socialists.[1] But from now on the B.P.S. would be in a state of 'legal resistance'. Although, as always, Senghor spoke warmly of the people of France (un peuple ami) this speech, with its reiterated warnings to 'the government of Guy Mollet', its demand for peace in Algeria, its declaration of non-violent resistance, even if it led to imprisonment or death, and its final peroration declaring that Africans would never recognize anyone's right to decide their destiny and that force would not prevail against the people of Senegal who would show on polling day that they were a free people, was the most outspoken appeal to African nationalism that he made during what was in effect the election campaign.

Throughout the campaign the B.P.S. leaders continued to attack the Guy Mollet Government on the basis that it was a partisan administration trying to help its friends by every kind of interference in the elections in West Africa, and alleging that the Senegalese socialists enjoyed extensive financial as well as other forms of support

[1] In addition to the change of governor, the commandant of the cercle of Kaolack, a great B.D.S. (and B.P.S.) stronghold, was also abruptly replaced by an officer transferred from another territory.

from this source. This use of the metropolitan aspects of French African politics as a basis on which to attack the Senegal socialists found its counterpart on their side at a more local level. If the B.P.S. attacked them as engaged in discreditable and underhand efforts to influence the electors by making use of their connexion with the socialists now in power in the French Government, the socialists as constantly claimed that B.P.S., like its predecessor, brought political pressure to bear on the illiterate voter in the bush through the supporters they had carefully placed in such key posts as those of canton chiefs or secretaries of groundnut stores and, above all, in the administration of the 'provident societies' (*sociétés de prévoyance*).[1] To understand the point of such allegations a brief explanation of the functions of the provident societies is necessary.

In every *cercle* a provident society exists of which all cultivators are compulsorily 'members'. They pay a 'subscription' which is in effect a special tax, and in return are entitled to such benefits as loans of seed at planting time, loans and other forms of assistance in the purchase of tools and equipment, and loans to finance the sale of produce during the buying season. The provident societies thus play a vital part in the life of an ordinary peasant, especially in the ground-nut areas where they are rich and substantial enterprises. It is alleged that their secretaries and other officials utilize their positions in order to ensure that those who benefit from loans and other advantages of the societies support the 'right' party. Whatever the truth of these allegations, they were in some sense the counterpart to the B.P.S. contention that the socialists sought to make use of their friends in the metropolitan government and to bring about improper interference in the conduct of the elections. Just as the socialists were in fact the dominant party in the metropolitan government, so the B.P.S. were in fact overwhelmingly in control of politics in the rural areas. It was not possible for the B.P.S. to make use of the metropolitan government at that time and in most rural areas it would not have been possible for the socialists to make use of the methods of which they accused their opponents.[2]

---

[1] For 'sociétés de prévoyance' and their functions, see my 'The Sociétés de Prévoyance in French West Africa', *Journal of African Administration*, vol. ii (1950), pp. 29–34.

[2] The High Commissioner of French West Africa, an appointee of the socialist Government, issued some instructions on the necessity for administrative impartiality in the elections, which were published on 26 Mar. In these he drew special attention to the importance of ensuring that the provident societies were not utilized for political purposes. All recommendations about loans and all grants of a financial kind should be suspended during the 'present period', and special attention paid to ensuring that their vehicles and other equipment were used only

Alongside these three themes, the character of the future African polity, the metropolitan connexions of the parties, and accusations of 'dirty politics', there was, particularly in the rural areas, the more familiar stock-in-trade of politicians everywhere: B.P.S. spokesmen naturally assumed to themselves credit for any local improvements which had been brought about in the past, such as the provision of telephones, maternity centres, improved roads, schools and the like, or else they promised that when they were in power more of this kind would be done in future in the particular area in question; the socialists, on the other hand, seldom seemed to devote much attention to attacking the B.P.S. on the ground that they had in fact achieved very little of this practical kind or that it was really the French administration and French financial assistance which had made possible the improvements for which Senghor and his friends took credit. Both these points were of course made but (particularly in the rural areas and even on occasion in Dakar itself) much time at socialist meetings was taken up with declarations on the part of the speakers of their undying loyalty to their leader Lamine Gueye. Speaker after speaker would expound this point and expatiate on the fact that 'Senegal does not love traitors', an allusion to Senghor's break with the socialists in 1948.

So far as the militants of the party were concerned, the themes which made the most appeal were those in B.P.S. policy which emphasized African determination to run their own affairs, but the writer was invariably informed by experienced candidates that in the bush the elaborate discussion of such topics was pointless, and that emphasis was always placed on the concrete achievements in the way of improved local amenities for which the party took credit. When Senghor himself spoke in small meetings in the rural areas, his speeches covered essentially, though in simplified form, the same points that he had made at large meetings in major towns. The speeches of socialist spokesmen devoted noticeably less time to 'ideological' points and, indeed, to questions of general policy, and concentrated largely on the well-worn themes of loyalty to the French connexion and to the party leader, and on the conviction that the empty promises of Senghor and his friends had now been exposed by their total failure to redeem them during the years in which they had been in office.

Polling day. Polling day was something of an anti-climax after so

for economic and agricultural purposes. He also discussed the role of canton chiefs, if it were unavoidable to employ them, as subordinate officials in electoral administration. The houses of chiefs must on no account be used as polling stations—neither, of course, must those of 'religious chiefs': *Paris-Dakar*, 26 Mar. 1957.

C C

much concentrated political activity. This was particularly likely to be the impression of a visitor to Dakar. As it was a Sunday, there would in any case have been less bustle than usual. But on polling day no motor vehicles (including motor-bicycles) are allowed on the roads without special authorization. This regulation is strictly observed, and in the course of a tour of the constituency (which includes, of course, the town and rural district of Rufisque as well as Dakar itself) and of the constituency of Thiès, the writer saw very few motor-cars on the roads anywhere before the close of the poll. This absence of the usual traffic, which is very dense in many parts of this area, gave a curious impression of a public holiday. Although the streets were crowded, the absence of motor traffic made this much less obvious. Quite early in the morning, before the poll began at 8 a.m., there were long queues at some of the polling stations; some of these were for women voters only, and the long line of brightly dressed *électrices* with their green or red head-dresses and frocks added to the holiday atmosphere, though substantial numbers of police were a reminder of grimmer possibilities. In one of the suburban areas where the B.P.S. were strong, the appearance of Lamine Gueye (who had gone to vote and to be photographed while doing so by the French news camera men who had arrived to film the election) was followed by some scuffling in the large crowd waiting to vote, which was firmly suppressed by another substantial force of police, or, as the French commentators usually call it, *un impressionnant service d'ordre.*

Most people seemed to vote in the morning. There were large crowds outside all polling stations seen by the writer in the course of the morning. But by the early afternoon, as might be expected in a tropical country, business was so slack at one Thiès polling station that it was necessary to wait for some minutes before anyone arrived to vote. In the villages in the Thiès constituency, too, the afternoon, even the later afternoon, seemed to produce many fewer voters. In some visited then, it was not easy at once to identify the polling station, until the *garde de cercle* on duty outside was seen. Later, at least where the writer was, business was more brisk at the close of the poll. One of the consequences of the French system of counting the votes at each polling station is that it is not possible for a single observer to see very much of it, for while he has watched it in one, many others too will have completed their count. The count is, however, obviously one of the danger periods from the point of view of possible disorder, and there were several instances of trouble, of a relatively minor kind but sufficiently serious to call for the intervention of the authorities. On the whole, however, it was a quiet election which reflected credit on all concerned, not least on the hard-pressed French administrative and police officials, whose arrangements for ensuring order must be adjudged remarkably effective.

The Political Affairs Department of the Government General of French West Africa, who were concerned with all the eight territories, had made arrangements for the results to be posted up on blackboards in the entrance hall of the Secretariat in Dakar (to give it the name of its British equivalent). Here gathered a large number of officials, and the leading Dakar journalists. Most of the Senegal results were available by the early morning, as were a surprisingly high proportion of the 474 results in French West Africa. Results for Senegal were also received and published at the offices of the *Délégation* of Dakar outside which a large crowd gathered. But by two o'clock in the morning all was quiet in the centre of the town—the provincial Sunday atmosphere of the earlier part of the day had once more returned. The election was over.

10. *The Results*

A little more than half (54 per cent.) of the electorate went to the polls. This was, in fact, the same proportion as had voted in the National Assembly elections of 1956, though as a result of the introduction of universal suffrage, the electorate on the registers had increased from a little more than a third to nearly half the territory's estimated population. The proportion of spoilt votes was somewhat higher than it had been in 1956, as was perhaps to be expected in view of the numbers who may have been voting for the first time. It was 6·5 per thousand as against 4·6 per thousand in 1956. Of course, the territorial average of 54 per cent. concealed very considerable variations in the turn-out in different parts of the territory, ranging from 81 per cent. in the constituency of Dakar to 33 per cent. in that of Tambacounda. In each of the three 'old communes' of Dakar, Rufisque, and Saint Louis, over 80 per cent. voted, and similar turn-outs were achieved in some of the small townships in the second Kaolack (Fatick) constituency. In the town of Fatick itself it was 78 per cent., and in the first Kaolack constituency the municipality achieved 69 per cent. But in other towns and townships it was generally lower, and in most of the rural districts considerably so. Four constituencies had polls of 41 per cent. or lower (Tambacounda 33 per cent., Podor 36 per cent., Matam 39 per cent., and Kédougou 41 per cent.). While these were all relatively poor areas somewhat remote from the main centres of Senegalese life, they did not appear to be noticeably more so than Bakel which achieved 46 per cent. or

Linguère with 51 per cent. By contrast, in each of the six richer, more populous, and more urban constituencies of Dakar, Thiès, Diourbel, the two Kaolacks, and Bas-Sénégal, which together contained about three-fifths of the electorate, the turn-out was above 55 per cent., and averaged over 62 per cent.

With over 78 per cent. of the poll (454,533), the B.P.S. won 47 seats (78 per cent.). Candidates supported by the P.S.A.S., with 19 per cent. (105,085) won 12 seats (20 per cent.) The one successful candidate not supported by either major party—the dissident B.P.S. candidate in Kédougou—won by a majority of only 54. The 59 'independents' together polled only 21,221 votes (3½ per cent. of the poll) and 16,326 of these were cast for the seven B.P.S. dissidents who stood on independent lists and not in alliance with P.S.A.S. candidates.

Candidates supported by the P.S.A.S. polled nearly 4,000 more votes than the S.F.I.O.-M.A.C. list in 1956 and 10,000 more than the S.F.I.O. had done in 1952. Indeed, they won three seats more than the S.F.I.O. in 1952, but the elections nevertheless seemed to mark a further decline in socialist fortunes in Senegal. Not only had they failed to keep pace with the increase in the size of the electorate, but also it seemed that their absolute vote had fallen. For in three of the four constituencies where (apart from their strongholds of Saint-Louis and Dakar) their vote had risen by comparison with 1956, they had fought in alliance with former B.P.S. members of the Assembly who had not been renominated, and some part of the increased vote must be credited to the clientele of the latter. It was difficult to assess the results in the two Kaolack constituencies from this point of view, owing to the division of the constituency in this election, but in the second Kaolack constituency (Fatick) 10,467 of their 12,262 votes were obtained in the subdivision of Fatick and the town itself, where the former B.P.S. member resided. In the first Kaolack constituency, the socialist vote in the municipality was actually slightly lower (2,241 as against 2,566 in 1956) while the rise in the P.S.A.S. vote in Thiès constituency (from 10,721 in 1956 to 12,138) was hardly sensational. In Matam, where the socialists fought alone, it was true that their vote increased by some 4,000 votes—but this was not much more than half the increase in the combined B.P.S. and rebel B.P.S. votes. In Saint-Louis and Dakar, the socialist share of the vote fell from 76 per cent. and 65 per cent. of the poll in 1956 to 50 per cent. and 51 per cent. respectively. In Podor it was stationary, as it was in Tambacounda (where, moreover, it was derisory at 596). Everywhere else it had actually fallen, and in Kédougou and Linguère was less than 300.

The B.P.S. could congratulate themselves on their solidity through-out the territory, and on the narrowness of their defeat in Dakar and even in Saint-Louis. Although their divisions in Kédougou and Matam had lost them four seats, elsewhere their majorities were

TABLE 14

Results of the Elections to the Territorial Assembly of 31 March 1957

Constituency	Valid votes	B.P.S.	P.S.A.S.	Others
Bakel	11,262	9,905	1,357	..
Bas-Sénégal	19,284	8,566	9,771	946 Liste d'Union pour la Défense des Intérêts du Bas-Sénégal
				1 Others
Dakar	61,974	29,926	32,048	..
Diourbel	58,425	55,689	2,736	..
Kaolack	74,935	67,791	6,558	586
Fatick	65,283	52,690	12,262	331
Kédougou	4,519	2,173	119	2,227 Bloc Démocratique Kédougou
Linguère	14,834	8,392	283	6,159 Bloc Démocratique Djoloff
Louga	29,624	21,807	7,607*	* Bloc Démocratique Diambour
				210 Others
Matam	23,256	8,140	9,289	5,827 Bloc Progressiste Cercle Matam
Podor	20,568	11,689	4,776	3,720 Bloc Démocratique Fouta Toro
				383 Union pour la Défense des Intérêts du Cercle du Podor
Tambacounda	9,180	7,753	596	791 Bloc Ouvriers et Paysans
				40 Parti Radical
Thiès	92,646	80,508	12,138†	† Union pour la Défense des Intérêts du Cercle de Thiès
Ziguinchor	95,049	89,504	5,545	..
TOTAL	580,839	454,533	105,085	23,933

comfortable, even where B.P.S. rebels had stood on joint lists. More-over, they had greatly increased their total vote—from 346,266 B.D.S. (and 6,888 U.D.S.) in 1956 to 454,533 in 1957, and it seemed clear that the majority of the new voters must have voted for them. They had once more shown that the B.P.S., successor in this to the B.D.S., was a real mass party which enjoyed overwhelming support in Senegal. They could justifiably take pride in the vote of renewed confidence which they had obtained from the people, and regard it as manifesting popular enthusiasm for their leaders, and perhaps even as indicating in some degree support for their general policy of securing real self-government within as friendly an association with France as French policy could be induced to permit.

ACKNOWLEDGEMENTS

THE author wishes to thank the Warden and Fellows of Nuffield College, Oxford, and the Rockefeller Foundation for their generous support; the members of the *Bloc Populaire Sénégalais* and especially M. L. S. Senghor, M. Mamadou Dia, and M. Alioune M'Bengue; the members of the *Parti Sénégalais de l'Action Socialiste* and especially Maître Lamine Gueye, Mayor of Dakar; and the members of the *Mouvement Populaire Sénégalais* and especially M. Doudou Gueye. Without their collaboration the research would have been impossible. The good offices of his old friend, M. le Haut Commissaire Torré, at that time Secretary General of French West Africa, greatly facilitated all his work and more especially his study of the problems of electoral administration; Professor Théodore Monod, Dr. Abdoulaye Ly, and many members of the staff of the Institut Français d'Afrique Noire at Dakar, and Professor Pellissier of the Institut des Hautes Études (now the University of Dakar) generously gave him the benefit of their specialized knowledge of various aspects of Senegalese life. He much regrets that it is impossible for him to thank individually all those members of the political parties and the public service in Senegal who afforded him such generous hospitality and gave so freely of their time and expert knowledge in answering his questions. M. Senghor, Mr. Philip Williams, Mr. F. J. Pedler, and the Hon. Nigel Bruce very kindly read the typescript and the author is most grateful to them for valuable comments and corrections. The responsibility for what remains is, however, entirely his.

VII

AFRICAN ELECTIONS IN KENYA
MARCH 1957

1. *Political and Constitutional Background*

THE events here described may take a place of some importance in the constitutional history of East Africa because this was the first occasion on which Africans in any British territory there voted in a direct election to choose members of a legislative assembly.[1] They are also important because they mark the first step in the reconstruction of African political life in Kenya after the tragic events which led through the development of the Kikuyu Central Association to the creation of the Kenya Africa Union in 1946 and the Mau Mau outbreaks in August 1952. The state of emergency declared on 20 October 1952 still existed at the time of the election, but the crisis of Mau Mau was past, and Kenya was economically prosperous and full of projects for industrial and agricultural development.

We must here assume familiarity with the geographical and social structure of Kenya,[2] but it may be of use to insert some simple data for reference. The most recent figures for the population of Kenya are as shown in Table 1.

TABLE I

Population of Kenya, 1956

European	57,700
African	5,902,000
Indian and Goan	151,900
Arab	33,000
Others	5,300
	6,149,900

SOURCE: *East African Statistical Dept. Quarterly Bulletin*, No. 35, Mar. 1957, Tables A. 2. and A. 3.

[1] The closest parallel is that of the direct elections which were held in some parts of the Southern Sudan in Dec. 1953, after the attainment of independence. See the report of the Electoral Commission (Cmd. 9058 of 1954).

[2] Some sources of information are: *African Land Development in Kenya, 1946–55* (Ministry of Agric., &c., Nairobi, 1956); *Report* of the East African Royal Commission, 1953–5 (Cmd. 9475 of 1955); Elspeth Huxley and Margery Perham, *Race and Politics in Kenya* (2nd ed., London, 1956). For monographs on particular tribes see *Annual Reports* of the Colony and Protectorate of Kenya (H.M.S.O., London).

The African population is becoming increasingly mobile; there are substantial African urban communities of mixed origin in Nairobi (about 140,000) and Mombasa (about 100,000), and in addition there are about 235,000 Africans[1] engaged in agricultural work on European and a few Asian estates. But the old African ways of life are still strong, and tribal divisions are very important. The main tribal groups are shown in Table 2.

TABLE 2

African Population of Kenya by Tribes, Mid-1956

Kikuyu	1,155,000
Luo	852,000
Baluhya	736,000
Kamba	689,000
Meru	366,000
Nyika	333,000
Kisii	287,000
Embu	230,000
Kipiigis	180,000
Nandi	132,000
Other tribes	940,000
	5,900,000

SOURCE: The 1948 Census figures, Table A. 10 (p. 10) 'Main Tribes of Kenya'. A 1½ per cent. annual increase has been allowed for, which is the official formula. The slight discrepancy between the figure given above and the official figure of 5,902,000 arises from the fact that the tribal figures were taken to the nearest thousand.

The age structure of the African population in Kenya differs markedly from that prevailing in European countries, as is shown in Table 3. It will be seen that nearly half the total population is under sixteen.

TABLE 3

Age Distribution of African Population, 1948

	Under 1 year	1–5 years	6–15 years*	16–45 years†	Over 46 years
Per cent. of total population	4·5	19·0	24·6	43·2	8·8

* 6–13 years for females.   † 14–45 years for females.

SOURCE: *Annual Report* on the Colony and Protectorate of Kenya for 1956, p. 8 (London, 1957).

[1] *E. A. Stat. Dept. Quarterly Bulletin*, Table E. 4.

The area of the Territory is 225,000 square miles, but much of this is semi-desert, so sparsely populated that it is of no electoral importance at present. About 16,200 square miles constitute the 'White Highlands', the area of European agriculture; about 52,141 square

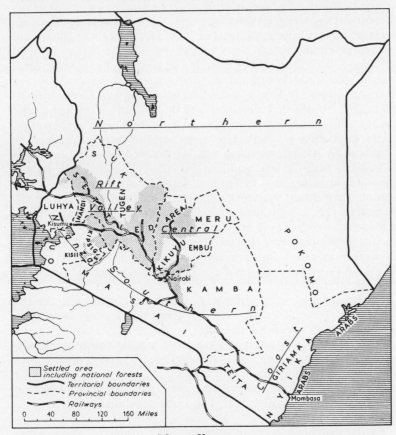

MAP 7. KENYA

miles are given over to 'Native Areas' (including native settlement areas) with relatively dense populations at various stages of agricultural development.[1] The future of African politics is likely to depend on interaction between the new urban population and the settled but not unchanging population of the countryside.

Elections were first introduced in Kenya in 1920, when the whole

[1] *Annual Report* for 1956, p. 53.

of the old East African Protectorate was annexed and became Kenya Colony, except for a coastal strip (administered as part of the Colony) which remains in law part of the dominions of the Sultan of Zanzibar. There had been nominated unofficial European representatives in the Legislative Council from its first meeting in 1907 and in the Executive Council since 1910 (the Legislative and Executive Councils were set up by Order in Council in 1906, first meeting in 1907), and an Indian unofficial member was added to the Legislative Council in 1909. The decisive step of introducing elections on separate communal rolls was taken in 1919, when provision was made for 11 Europeans and 2 Indians to be elected on a wide franchise in 13 constituencies.[1] Since that time the logic of the system has led to the creation of further communal electorates in step with the expansion of the Legislative Council. The stages are summarized in Table 4.

When an African member was first added to the Legislative Council in 1944, he was nominated by the Governor in the latter's absolute discretion, but in 1948 an element of election was introduced. Each Local Native Council (as African District Councils were then called) sent three councillors, including its African Vice-President, to one of four area meetings, over each of which a Provincial Commissioner presided. The areas were Central Province, Nyanza Province, Coast Province, and the Rift Valley Province, Northern Province, and Masai District taken together. The purpose of these meetings was to choose from three to five people whom the members thought were suitable to represent the Province in the Legislative Council. Finally, the Governor selected one name from each of the lists submitted to him.

A further step was taken in 1952, some months before the Emergency. In many ways the system adopted bears a striking resemblance to that employed in March 1957, which might in some respects be regarded as a logical development from it. It should be borne in mind that the procedure varied in certain details in the six constituencies.[2]

In the first place six constituencies were declared. These were: Nairobi City, Central Province, Coast Province, Rift Valley Pro-

---

[1] This resulted in a prolonged controversy. Indians in Kenya demanded, among other things, a common electoral roll and freedom of immigration. For details of events see: *Indians in Kenya* (Cmd. 1922 of 1923); A. B. Keith, *The Constitution, Administration and Laws of the Empire* (Edinburgh, 1924), pp. 114–17; W. K. Hancock, *Survey of British Commonwealth Affairs*, vol. i, *Problems of Nationality*, 1918–36 (Oxford, 1934), pp. 209–27; Elspeth Huxley, *White Man's Country. Lord Delamere and the Making of Kenya* (London, 1953), ch. xviii, pp. 110–39.

[2] The full regulations and procedure may be found in Government Notice No. 421 (*Kenya Official Gazette*, vol. liv, 22 Apr. 1952, pp. 441–4).

vince, including the Masai Extra Provincial District, South Nyanza
(i.e. Nyanza Province less the North Nyanza District), and North
Nyanza. Any African could stand provided that he was resident in
the constituency and was a Kenya African. There were no restrictions based on age, income, or property. However, candidates, unless
exempted by the Provincial Commissioner, were obliged to pass a
test in English, which was conducted by a committee of three presided over by the Provincial Education Officer, who nominated the
two other members, also officers in the Education Service. A candidate could not be nominated for election if he had been convicted of
a criminal offence and had been sentenced to imprisonment for six
months or more and had not received a pardon. The Governor was
empowered to remove this disqualification.

Nomination papers were to be signed by a proposer, seconder, and
seven supporters who would be disqualified if they had been imprisoned for twelve months or more, and were completed on oath.
District Commissioners forwarded nomination papers to their Provincial Commissioners, who made arrangements for the English test.
On nomination day the names of the qualified candidates were published at provincial and all district headquarters.

When the regulations were published on 22 April 1952, the
District Commissioners called in the Chiefs and explained to them
the procedure for nominating candidates and for selecting the names
of candidates for submission to the Governor. Chiefs had then to
return to their locations and hold explanatory *barazas*. (In Mombasa
and Nairobi, District Commissioners were to arrange publicity
through the African Advisory Councils of the municipalities.) Nomination day was fourteen days after the publication of the regulations
in Nairobi and twenty-one days later elsewhere. Government or
local authority employees were only required to resign if actually
elected; and leave with pay was granted them from nomination day
to the date when appointments were announced. Candidates were
not permitted to sit on the District Advisory Nomination Committees
or colleges described below and a candidate could only stand in one
constituency. All questions concerning the qualifications of candidates or their nomination were decided by the Provincial Commissioners without right of appeal.

The procedure for the selection of candidates in all constituencies
except Nairobi City was as follows. Each locational Council[1] sent
delegates (the exact number was decided by the Provincial Commissioner), to sit as members of a District Advisory Nomination

---

[1] Where there were no locational councils, similar bodies acted, e.g. Section
Councils in Masai Province, Chiefs' *barazas* on the Coast.

TABLE 4

The Main Changes in the Composition of the Legislative Council in Kenya since 1920

		Government or official side				Non-government or unofficial side				
		Members of the public service		From outside the public service						
Year	H.E. as President	Ex-officio	Nominated Officials		Total	European	African	Indian	Arab	Total
1920	1	10	7	Nil	18	11 E	Nil	2 E (or N)	1 N	14
1924	1	10	9 (including one Arab, Liwali for the Coast)	Nil	20	11 E: 1 N to rep. African interests	Nil	5 E (or N)	1 E	18
1927	1	11	9 (ditto)	Nil	21	11 E: 1 N to rep. African interests	Nil	5 E (or N)	1 E	18
1934	1	11	9 (ditto)	Nil	21	11 E: 2 N to rep. African interests	Nil	5 E (or N)	1 E	19
1944	1	11	9 (ditto)	Nil	21	11 E: 1 N to rep. African interests	1 N	5 E	1 E	19
1947	1	11	9 (ditto)	Nil	21	11 E	2 N	5 E	1 E	19

			Nil	16	11 E	4 N	Asian 5 E	1 E: 1 N	22
1948. First unofficial majority	H.E. as President/Vice-P. as speaker	7	9 (ditto)	Nil	16	11 E	4 N	Asian 5 E	1 E: 1 N	22
1952. Griffiths Constitution	Speaker	8	10 (including 2 Africans and 1 Arab)	Nominated 8	26	14 E (2 in Ex. Co.)	6 Rep. (1 in Ex. Co.)	6 E: 2 M: 4 non M. (1 in Ex.Co.)	1 E: 1 Rep.	28
1954. Lyttelton Constitution. Council of Ministers set up	Speaker	8	10 (ditto)	8	26 (34)	14 E (3 in C. of M.)	6 Rep. (1 in C. of M. and 1 P.S.)	6 E (2 in C. of M.)	1 E: 1 Rep. (1 P.S.)	28 (20)
1956. Negotiations following Sept. 1956 elections	Speaker	8	10 (ditto)	8 (one Afr. P.S.)	26 (34)	14 E (3 C. of M.)	8 Rep. (1 in C. of M+ 1 P.S.)	6 E (2 in C. of M.)	1 E: 1 Rep. 1 P.S.	30 (22)
1957. Following Mar. 1957 African elections	Speaker	8	10 (ditto)	10 (two more Europeans 1 Afr. P.S. as before)	28 (34)	14 E: 2 C (3 C. of M.)	8 E	6 E (2 in C. of M.)	1 E: 1 Rep. (1 P.S.)	32 (26)

Note: E = Elected
N = Nominated
Rep. = Representative Member
C. of M. = Council of Ministers
P.S. = Parliamentary Secretary
C = Corporate Member

The figures in brackets show the voting, as opposed to the 'paper', strength of the two sides of the Council.

Committee (in Mombasa, the African Advisory Council itself became the District Advisory Nomination Committee). All the candidates' names in that constituency were then presented to the committee, who were free to discuss them but did not vote (except in Central Province). The real business of the District Advisory Nomination Committee was to send delegates to the Constituency Advisory Nomination College. As there was only one district in North Nyanza the District Advisory Nomination Committee became the Constituency Advisory Nomination College. Nyanza South sent five delegates from each District, Rift Valley three from each District, and Coast nine from Mombasa and three from each of the other Districts. In Central Province there was no Constituency Advisory Nomination College; instead, each District Advisory Nomination Committee voted for the candidates, in the manner described below. In Nairobi City the twelve inter-tribal village committees voted on the candidates.

In all cases the method of voting was by secret ballot, the members of the college or committee casting three votes for the candidate of their first choice, two votes for their second choice and one for their third choice.

Lastly, the Provincial Commissioner forwarded to the Governor the names of the three candidates who got most votes or points in each constituency, and included his recommendations with the submitted list. The Governor then nominated one candidate from each constituency for membership of the Legislative Council; he was under no obligation to select the candidate with most points. The list of names submitted to the Governor was to be published in each constituency, but not in order of preference.

There is evidence that the candidates themselves were anxious to find out how the voting went, and Mr. Mathu, one of the successful candidates, asked the following question in the Legislative Council:

As it is imperative that the African Community should have confidence in the African Members of the Legislative Council, and as this confidence would be enhanced by the knowledge of the votes polled by each candidate, will Government please state the number of votes polled by each candidate in each of the six constituencies in May last?

The Member for African Affairs replied:

In view of the fact that the African Representative Members to the Legislative Council were nominated by the Governor on the advice of the Electoral Colleges set up in varying form in each of the constituencies, it is not considered that any useful purpose would be served by declaring the number of votes polled by each of the candidates in each of these constituencies in

May last. All those African Representative Members can, however, rest assured that each of them headed the list submitted by the Electoral College of his constituency.[1]

This system produced African Legislative Council members of some competence, but the only man of distinction among them was Mr. Eliud Mathu, a Kikuyu, then about fifty, who represented Central Province. At the beginning of 1956, the six African Representatives were:

North Nyanza:	W. W. W. Awori (Jaluo)
Nairobi City:	M. Gikonyo (Kikuyu)
Coast:	J. Jeremiah (Taveta)
Central Province:	E. W. Mathu (Kikuyu)
Rift Valley and Masai:	D. T. arap Moi (Tugan)
Nyanza South:	B. A. Changa (Jaluo)

The system was certainly not unsuccessful: it did, however, operate (as it was intended to do) to discourage the emergence of any African electoral organization, so that there was a sharp distinction between the process of choosing African members of the Legislative Council and the beginnings of African party organization. This was not altogether healthy for the development of African politics: and it was in any case resented by Africans as implying inferiority to the other 'races'. One of the demands generally expressed by Africans at the time of Mr. Lyttelton's visit to Kenya in February 1954 was, therefore, that the system should be replaced by direct African elections as soon as possible.

2. The Lyttelton Plan

Mr. Lyttelton's visit was concerned partly with operational questions relating to the campaign against Mau Mau, partly with the problem of constitutional development. Some of the most important decisions taken concerned the organization of the executive: these do not directly concern us here, but some brief explanation is necessary.

Since 1910 there had been unofficial members on the Executive Council, who had access to the confidential business of government but were not restrained by any principle of collective responsibility from criticizing the administration in the Legislative Council or

[1] *Kenya Legislative Council Debates*, 1st Session, June 1952, Question II, vol. xlviii, col. 5.

outside it. It was, however, possible for the administration to by-pass the Executive Council and to present business directly to the Legislative Council, and to act in some matters on the authority of the Governor alone. The Executive Council did not therefore serve well as a link between the administration and the representatives of the public, even though it included (from 1952) two 'unofficial' European elected members of the Legislative Council, one Indian (a non-Muslim elected member) and one African, Mr. Eliud Mathu. The essence of Mr. Lyttelton's plan was to move towards a system of Cabinet responsibility. The Executive Council remained in existence, for limited puposes. There was added to it a Council of Ministers, consisting of the Governor and his Deputy, six officials and eight 'unofficial' ministers. These ministers consisted of two nominated European members of the Legislative Council, three elected European members of the Legislative Council, two elected Indian members (one Muslim, one non-Muslim), and one African representative member, Mr. Ohanga. The unofficial members of the Council were to take an oath of allegiance to the Queen, to accept the principle of collective responsibility, and to agree that no controversial issues concerning the tenure of land (i.e. about the 'White Highlands') would be raised by the Government before 1960. There was thus created a 'quasi-Cabinet', with a balance between official and unofficial members and a reservation of seats for different 'races' on the unofficial side: at the same time a 'Cabinet' majority was created in the Legislative Council, as six 'unofficials' 'crossed the floor', and there were now thirty-two on the government benches, twenty-two on the unofficial side. The gap was widened by the eventual appointment of Parliamentary Secretaries: two of these were from the unofficial side, an African (Mr. James Jeremiah) and an Arab.[1] The third, Mr. Wanyutu Waweru, was an African nominated member from the official side. The balance in 1956 was therefore thirty-four to twenty on the side of the Council of Ministers, in spite of the existence of an unofficial majority in the Legislative Council.

These arrangements represented some advance, but were still constitutionally odd, as the 'quasi-Cabinet' was faced by a minority of elected and appointed members of all 'races', an opposition without the sense of responsibility created by the possibility of forming an alternative Government. In addition the Council of Ministers was too large to be an effective instrument of emergency government: and many day to day decisions were transferred to a War Council,

[1] Under the Lyttelton Constitution provision was made for the appointment of not more than five Parliamentary Secretaries nor less than three, of whom one was to be an Arab, and two to be Africans.

consisting of the Governor, the Deputy-Governor, the Commander-in-Chief, and one European unofficial elected member, Mr. Michael Blundell.

The Lyttelton plan necessarily included some reference to the development of the system of representation, which was in everyone's mind. This is best summarized in the words of the official report. It was agreed that:

(9) The above arrangements will be regarded as experimental until the next general election, which will be held in six months after the Governor has proclaimed that the State of Emergency at present existing in the Colony has come to an end, or on 30th June 1955, whichever is the earlier.

(10) If at that election the electorate return members who are willing to serve as Members of the Government formed in accordance with these proposals, there will be no further changes in the proportion of members of either the Legislative Council or the Council of Ministers, either as between the main racial groups or as between officials and unofficials, before 1960. Changes in the nature of portfolios held by various members of the Council of Ministers after the next election are not precluded provided that the conditions set out at the beginning of this paragraph are met, but H.M. Government similarly will not initiate any changes in the communal basis of franchise to become effective before the election of 1960.[1]

It was further provided that if the proposed arrangements proved unworkable either before the elections mentioned above or as a result of them,

(11) the position will revert to what it was before the Emergency and H.M. Government will be free to take such action as they think fit.

All ministers joining the Council of Ministers were to subscribe to a joint statement of policy which laid down five broad objectives. These were: to pursue the fight against the Mau Mau terrorists, to build a strong and prosperous Kenya within the British Commonwealth, to promote racial harmony, to ensure that individual rights of private property are respected, and lastly,

(v) It is agreed that during the period up to 1956 the Government will initiate a study, in which Africans will play a prominent part, of the best method of choosing African Members of the Legislative Council.[2]

[1] Annexure to Colonial Office Despatch, pp. 228–9 Special Issue *Kenya Official Gazette Supplement No. 18*, 17 Apr. 1954.
[2] Ibid., p. 229.

3. *The African Franchise*

The Coutts Report. Mr. W. F. Coutts, C.M.G., M.B.E.,[1] was accordingly appointed by the Governor in February 1955, to conduct an inquiry with the following terms of reference:

to investigate and advise on the best system or systems to be adopted in choosing African Representative Members for the Legislative Council, bearing in mind the differences that may exist between areas, and also to draw up any draft rules that may be necessary to authorise the suggested procedure.

Two questions were specifically excluded from the inquiry:

(i) The numbers of African representatives on the Legislative Council;

(ii) The demarcation of constituencies.

Mr. Coutts travelled over 7,000 miles in the Colony and Protectorate to hear witnesses: received 120 memoranda and heard oral evidence from 1540 witnesses of all 'races': and reported in August 1955. His report[2] was laid on the table of the House in January 1956, with a Government Sessional Paper embodying certain modifications.[3]

The main proposals of his original plan were as follows:

(i) Direct voting by secret ballot should be adopted for all African elections. (The overwhelming majority of Africans who gave evidence proposed this method.)

(ii) There should not be universal adult suffrage. (Opinions differed widely over this question. The Commissioner wrote: 'Africans had misgivings about whether the system of universal adult franchise would return candidates who, in calibre and character, would most usefully represent their constituents.')

Appendix 4 of the report contains an analysis of views of people appearing before the Commissioner. This is reproduced below. It should be borne in mind that a 'unit' might represent one person or as many as fifty.

The following units gave evidence for the systems mentioned.

(1) Universal male franchise 42
(2) Males and females voting but with a strict limitation of candidates.   56

---

[1] District Officer, Kenya, 1936–49. Administrator, St. Vincent, B.W.I. 1949–54. Special Commissioner, Kenya, 1955. Minister for Education, Labour, and Lands, in Kenya, Sept. 1955–8. Chief Secretary, Kenya, since 1958.

[2] *Report of the Commissioner appointed to Enquire into Methods for the Selection of African Representatives to the Legislative Council* (Nairobi, Govt. Printer, 1955).

[3] Sessional Paper No. 39: 1955/6.

(3) Males and some females voting and a strict limitation of candidates 17
(4) Some males and some females voting and a strict limitation of candidates 26
(5) Males and literate females 7
(6) Males only 30
(7) Literates only 3
(8) Indirect elections 17

This shows a real division of African opinion. On the other hand there is evidence that many Africans resented the idea that Asians and Europeans had virtually universal suffrage, and some pointed to the methods of election in operation in the Gold Coast (as it then was), India, and Ceylon. The Commissioner's own remarks on the English franchise are worth quoting. Britain, he said, had only had twenty-seven years' experience of universal adult franchise, and he went on . . . 'I think it would be wise to see the effects of this method of election working, both in the United Kingdom and elsewhere where it has been introduced, for a further period of about 15 to 20 years, before considering its introduction into the society which now comprises the various races of Kenya.'[1]

(iii) The report set out a list of ten qualifications, for each of which a point was to be earned. These were the age of twenty-one years or more; completion of Form II of a Secondary school; a university degree; proved income of £120 per annum or property worth £500; having reached the grade of elder in a tribe or equivalent women's rank or aged forty-five; five years' service on a local government council; five years' service in the armed forces, police, or tribal police; a civil or military decoration including badge of honour or Chief's Medal; ten years' service in a position of responsibility on a farm, in commerce, Government or Local Government, in private service or having a medal or certificate for more than twenty years' faithful and continuous service. The tenth qualification was that of holding a membership badge in a woman's club, a provision which reflected the difficulty of finding categories under which women could qualify. Three points qualified for one vote, and each additional point above three was to qualify an individual for one extra vote, up to a maximum of six votes (in practice it was unlikely that an individual would obtain more than four or five votes). The only unusual disqualifications proposed were for refusal to take an oath of allegiance to the Queen, imprisonment for offences committed under the Emergency Regulations, and detention without trial.

[1] Coutts Report, para. 20, p. 7.

(iv) Special provisions were recommended for those living in Central Province, the area including the Kikuyu, Embu, and Meru tribes, which was the centre of Mau Mau activity. It was suggested that only those Africans who had not taken any Mau Mau oath should be permitted to vote or to stand as candidates, and that voters in this Province should only be allowed one vote. Also, '. . . males only should be registered except where a woman, who has not taken the Mau Mau oath, has shown exceptional powers of active fighting against Mau Mau and is recommended for inclusion by the district commissioner concerned'.[1]

(v) Candidates were to be qualified as voters and to have either five years' service on a local government council or African court, or ten years' service in a position of responsibility in central or local government, commerce, farming, or private service, or twenty years' faithful and continual service leading to a certificate or medal. There was a language test for those who had not already been members of the Council, or had not obtained a university degree or a Makerere professional diploma; an income of not less than £240 a year or property to a value of £700 was required; the candidate should never have been imprisoned or even detained without a conviction; and there was to be a residential qualification. Civil servants or local government employees were to be given permission to stand, but would be required to resign their posts if elected. There were no unusual disqualifications.

(vi) The new system of election was not to apply to the Northern Frontier Province, the inhabitants of which would continue, at their own request, to have their interests attended to by the Provincial Commissioner.

(vii) Miscellaneous recommendations at the end of the report included suggestions that the Department of Information should explain the report to the African population, that a Supervisor of Elections be appointed, that candidates be allowed to hold meetings, and that Registration Officers be appointed for each District.

Mr. Coutts expressed his own major premise as follows:

The recommendations which follow in this report are based on the assumption that there are three races in Kenya which together will have to work out their *modus vivendi*. Any thesis that one of those races must be entirely dominant or that the future of East Africa lies in Apartheid would render my proposals futile since they are based on the concept of partnership.

In addition, he accepted the doctrine that the vote is a public

---
[1] Coutts Report, para. 38, section (i), p. 37.

privilege or duty, not a universal human right, and that some people are better qualified than others by talents, status, and experience to use their votes rationally with public consideration in mind. The Electoral research in Western countries does not suggest that there is much difference in this respect between voters of different kinds, and this is to some extent borne out by the experience of this election in Kenya. But even though the traditional doctrine lacks empirical confirmation, a multiple-vote system may nevertheless be of tactical value in East and Central Africa, since it introduces a flexible method of 'weighting' votes by criteria other than that of race, and might therefore serve as a bridge between the system of separate racial electorates and that of a common roll. This is one reason for its adoption by the Capricorn Africa Society as a main plank in its platform in all the territories from Kenya to Southern Rhodesia: and it was thought at the time that Mr. Coutts's proposals, with their wide differentiation between the highest and lowest levels of suffrage, might serve as a first step towards some kind of common roll elections in Kenya.

The Government's proposals. This line of advance was made less probable by the Government's decision on the report, which accepted its principles of secret ballot and qualitative franchise but narrowed the differential between the highest and lowest levels, and perhaps somewhat widened the basic franchise. It also made considerable changes in the Commissioner's proposals for dealing with the Kikuyu, Embu, and Meru tribes. The Government's proposals were 'laid on the Table' along with the report early in January 1956, so that public discussion was mainly about the Government's proposals, not about those of the report.

It might be said that the Government adopted Mr. Coutts's arguments but faltered in their application. There is no doubt that their main object was to simplify administration and to reduce the anomalies which always arise in the process of 'ranking' voters according to qualifications. As it was put in the Sessional Paper,

. . . the Government has formed the view that the assessment and checking of the qualifications needed to secure the three points required for registration as a voter would present so great a task that serious delays in the compilation of voters' rolls would be inevitable. From the point of view both of the returning officer and of the would-be voter it is essential that the system should be as little complicated and as easily understood as possible, indeed, the success of the system will depend upon the number of Africans able to grasp both its principles and the procedure to be followed.

The Legislative Council (African Representation) Bill, introduced on 24 February 1956, was based on the new proposals, which may be summarized as follows:

(*a*) Instead of Mr. Coutts's points system, a voter to secure one vote must produce evidence that he (or she) had reached the age of twenty-one and was qualified in at least one of seven specified categories. A voter could secure additional votes for qualification in further categories, up to a maximum of three votes. The categories were:

(i) *Education.* Having completed intermediate school, i.e. Form II of the secondary course or a prescribed equivalent. (Same for women.)

(ii) *Property.* Proved income from all sources of £120 during the 12 months preceding application for registration or property worth £500. (Same for women.)

(iii) *Long service.* Five years' service in Armed Forces of the Crown, prisons or tribal police, excluding those dismissed for misconduct; seven years' continuous service in any form of Government, local government, or High Commission employment. Also, seven years' employment in commerce, industry, or agriculture. (Same for women, excluding H.M. Armed Forces and tribal police.)

(iv) *Seniority.* Having reached the grade of elder or the age of 45 years. (Men only.)

(v) *Higher education.* A degree or diploma of an approved institution of university or university college standing or an approved professional qualification. (Same for women.)[1]

(vi) *Legislative experience.* Membership, past or present, of the Legislative Council or the East African Central Legislative Assembly; or three years' continuous membership of a local government authority or an African advisory council or an African court. (Same for women.)

(vii) *Meritorious service.* A civil or military decoration, including Badge of Honour or Chief's Medal. (Women: Outstanding service to the community as certified by the Provincial Commissioner concerned.)

It was at first thought that under the Government's proposals the number entitled to at least one vote would be about 400,000 to 450,000 out of about 1,876,000 adults. The figure for potential voters was later revised to 386,000 as shown in Table 5. There is no comparable estimate for voters under the Coutts scheme. They would perhaps have been rather fewer, but there was no radical change in

[1] Later modified by an amending Ordinance; see p. 410 below.

this respect. The gradation of votes would certainly have been steeper, but it would have been very difficult to make an estimate and none is available.

TABLE 5

Estimated number of voters entitled to at least one vote under Government's scheme

Constituency	Male	Female	Total
Nyanza North	43,000	5,000	48,000
Nyanza Central	30,000	4,000	34,000
Nyanza South	53,000	5,000	58,000
Rift Valley and Masai . . .	68,000	3,000	71,000
Akemba	60,000	5,000	65,000
Central Province	35,000	1,000	36,000
Coast Province	40,000	3,000	43,000
Nairobi	30,000	1,000	31,000
	359,000	27,000	386,000

SOURCE: Private paper circulated in Ministry of African Affairs by the Supervisor of Elections. The figures are a very approximate estimate.

(*b*) The idea of a loyalty oath was dropped, on the ground that it would be administratively impossible to manage this in a dignified way: and for Mr. Coutts's proposal to admit all members of the Kikuyu, Embu, and Meru tribes certified by a tribunal of African loyalists not to have taken any Mau Mau oath there was substituted the requirement of positive evidence of loyalty, because the other scheme would have exposed loyalists to great pressure and risk and would have been unfair to those who took the Mau Mau oath under duress. Members of these tribes wishing to register were to satisfy the District Commissioner that they had given active support to the Crown during the Emergency. Those holding such a certificate could, like people of other tribes, qualify for extra votes not merely for one.

(*c*) Mr. Coutts's proposals about candidature were considerably widened. The Government agreed that it was desirable to exclude the inexperienced and irresponsible, but Mr. Coutts's proposals would have eliminated everyone who had not served on a local government or African Court or spent ten years in employment, either with Government or in local government, agriculture, or industry. This, it was felt, was too restrictive, and the following simplified criteria were substituted:

(i) Registered as a voter in any constituency;
and (ii) twenty-five years of age;

and (iii) Holding at least the Kenya African Preliminary Certificate, issued on successful completion of the Junior Secondary School course;

and (iv) Proved income of £240 a year: or proved income of £120 a year *and* one of the other five qualifications as a voter.

Those not possessing the higher-education qualification set out for voters and not previously members of the Legislative Council must take a test of proficiency in English.

The position about the candidature of African civil servants was thus expressed in debate by the chief secretary:

> Briefly, the Government proposes that the following persons should not be allowed to stand as candidates, without first resigning from the Government service. Those who are members of Her Majesty's Overseas Civil Service; that is to say those who have been appointed with the authority of the Secretary of State. Members of one of the uniformed disciplined forces of the Colony. Officers who are concerned with the direction of policy to an extent which, in the opinion of the Government, would make it undesirable for them to take part in active politics.

The Government has added a rider that this qualified recommendation should be applicable to the forthcoming election only, and that the whole question of civil servants standing as candidates should be re-examined in time for the election after next.[1]

The Bill contained also various important administrative provisions, which will be referred to later, but debate in the Legislative Council concentrated almost entirely on the qualifications of voters and candidates. The chief secretary (Mr. R. G. Turnbull) introduced the Bill in a speech in which he explicitly accepted on behalf of the government the view that the vote should, in Kenya as it then was, be for Africans not a right but a privilege to be earned by qualifications:

> Does the Government think that one African can be better qualified than another to decide who should be returned as a Representative Member? The answer is yes. At the present diverse stages of development of the African Communities, this is precisely what the Government does think. The Government is firmly of the opinion that those who have contributed a greater share to the welfare of the state or are particularly well qualified to play a part in public affairs, should have a greater say than those who can command nothing more than the minimum qualifications.[2]

In the debate which followed nine unofficial members spoke, four Europeans, three Africans,[3] two Asians, no Arab. The African mem-

---

[1] *Kenya Legislative Council Debates*, vol. lxviii, col. 206.
[2] Ibid., 201.
[3] One other African spoke, the Hon. Wanyutu Waweru, Parliamentary Secretary to the Minister for Education, Labour and Lands, a nominated member.

bers, led by Mr. Mathu, all spoke with moderation, but challenged the principle of qualitative suffrage, and also asked for liberalization of the Bill on a number of minor points. Mr. Mathu in particular emphasized that six members were too few to represent effectively a population of nearly 6 million and asked for an immediate increase to ten. The European speeches, necessarily representative mainly of vocal discontent, were uniformly hostile, in tones ranging from competent criticism of details to Lt.-Col. Grogan's characteristic (and not perhaps wholly serious) denunciations of democracy in general and of British trade unions in particular.

The Bill, introduced on 24 February, was given a third reading without substantial amendment on 29 February, and received the Governor's assent on 21 March, as Ordinance No. 10 of 1956.

(c) *Supplementary Legislation*. A good deal of regulation was required in addition to the provisions of Ordinance No. 10.

In the first place, it was necessary to construe the law about African elections in relation to the existing electoral law of Kenya, contained in the Ordinances relating to the nomination and election of European, Asian, and Arab members of the Legislative Council.[1] These gave the officials concerned some general precedents about regulations and forms of procedure. In addition, a set of rules about the registration of African voters was published on 11 August 1956,[2] under powers given by the principal Ordinance. The effect of these is explained in some detail in Section 4 below. Rules governing other matters of procedure (also explained later) were published on 20 December.[3]

Secondly, there was a matter of constitutional formality to put right. It turned out that the making of Ordinance No. 10 was outside the powers of the Governor of Kenya in Council, because it purported to alter the composition of the Legislative Council without authority under Royal Instructions. This applied also to Ordinance No. 30 of 1956, the Legislative Council (African Representation) (Amendment) Ordinance, 1956, passed on 24 July and given the Governor's assent on 11 August, which amended the principal Ordinance in some purely formal ways. This flaw was put right by additional Royal Instructions dated 20 July 1956 (also published in Kenya on 11 August), which permitted (*inter alia*) the replacement of six 'representative' by six 'elected' African members, and defined the conditions under which temporary members might be appointed by the Governor, the circumstances under which seats might become

---

[1] *Laws of Kenya*, 1948 ed. as amended, ch. 38.
[2] *Kenya Official Gazette*, Supplement No. 48, 11 Aug. 1956.
[3] Legal Notice No. 573 of 1956, *Kenya Official Gazette*, Supplement No. 78.

vacant, and the persons eligible to preside over sittings of the Legislative Council.[1] Past action was validated by the Kenya (Validation)
Order in Council.[2]

Thirdly, there were a number of changes of substance. The most
important of these was an increase in the number of African constituencies from six to eight. It had been known for some time that the
Government favoured this, but it was not possible for it to take action
on such a proposal under the Lyttelton Plan until the European and
Asian elections of September 1956 returned members with adequate
authority to discuss it. The agreement of the unofficial members was
secured, on the basis explained in Section 7 below; and the change
was embodied in an Ordinance gazetted on 18 December.[3] The
eight constituencies were defined by a Proclamation issued on 20
December:[4] Nyanza Province was split into three constituencies,
Nyanza North, Nyanza Central, and Nyanza South; Rift Valley
Province had two administrative districts added to it from Southern
Province, to make up the Rift Valley constituency. The remainder
of Southern Province, consisting of the Machakos and Kitui Districts
formed the Akamba constituency. Nairobi Extra-Provincial District
remained unchanged and formed the Nairobi constituency; the
sixth Province (the Northern Frontier Province) was—as agreed—
left unrepresented at this stage.

At the same time, the higher education qualification for African
voters was somewhat extended. What was now required, instead of
a university degree or diploma or a recognized professional qualification, was that the applicant should at some stage in his career have
been awarded a scholarship, 'approved for the purposes of this
Ordinance by the Director of Education, at an institution for post-
secondary education and should have successfully completed the

[1] This clause merely names people in order of precedence: 1. The President of
the Council; 2. Vice-President (who is the Speaker and who normally presides);
3. If (1) and (2) are absent, then Government may appoint another member;
4. Failing 1–3, the senior minister present appoints to chair.

[2] S.I. No. 1207 (East Africa) of 1956, made 3 Aug., laid before Parliament
10 Aug. coming into operation 11 Aug. Formalities were completed by Legal
Notices Nos. 570 and 571, published in a special issue of the *Official Gazette
Supplement* on 20 Dec.; L.N. 570 stated that the Additional Instructions came
into effect on 20 Dec.; L.N. 571 that Sections II and V of the principal Ordinance (conditions of election and candidature) came into effect on the same
day.

[3] African Representation (Amendment) Ordinance No. 2, passed by the
Legislative Council, 13 Dec. 1956, Governor's assent 17 Dec., made by virtue of
power conferred by Section 3 of the Legislative Council (African Representation)
Ordinance 1956 (No. 10).

[4] Legal Notice No. 572 of 1956, *Official Gazette Supplement* No. 78.

course of studies in respect of which the scholarship was awarded'.[1] Those who had already registered were given up to 31 December to claim a further vote if they thought themselves entitled under the new clause.

The effect of this amendment on the number of voters was trifling, but it became known in the course of the election as the 'Mboya Amendment' because it enabled Mr. Tom Mboya to become a candidate. Mr. Mboya, a Jaluo from South Nyanza, born on Rusinga Island in Lake Victoria and about twenty-eight at the time of the election, had been successively a sanitary inspector with Nairobi City Council, full-time secretary of the Kenya Local Government Workers' Union, and (since 1953) secretary of the Kenya Federation of Labour. He went to Ruskin College, Oxford, with a scholarship awarded by the Workers' Travel Association, subsequently visited first Belgium (to spend some weeks at the H.Q. of the I.C.F.T.U.) and later the U.S.A., and returned to Kenya at the end of October 1956. As will be seen later, his return and candidature were important in the election: but only the new amendment enabled him to qualify as a candidate, because candidates (besides being twenty-five must have intermediate education, and *either* £240 a year *or* £120 a year plus one other qualification selected from items iii–vii in the Schedule to Ordinance No. 10—Long Service, Seniority, Higher Education, Legislative Experience, and Meritorious Service. Mr. Mboya was originally unable to demonstrate that he qualified under any of this last group of headings.

Finally, an announcement was made[2] easing the restrictions on public meetings which had been in force since the Emergency period began in 1952. In future licences would be issued for public meetings to be held in halls or other buildings, provided they were considered to be for 'legitimate purposes'. Outdoor meetings would not be permitted (except in remote areas where no halls were available) lest they attract unmanageable crowds; nor might the proceedings of indoor meetings be relayed by loudspeakers outside. It was originally intended that in Central Province only members of the Kikuyu, Embu, and Meru tribes actually registered as voters should be permitted to attend meetings: in practice this was extended to all who held loyalty certificates.

No change was made in existing practice under the Registration

---

[1] African Representation (Amendment) Ordinance No. 2, passed by the Legislative Council, 13 Dec. 1956, Governor's assent 17 Dec., made by virtue of power conferred by Section 3 of the Legislative Council (African Representation) Ordinance 1956 (No. 10).

[2] Official statement on 21 Dec. 1956, with effect from 1 Jan. 1957.

of Societies Ordinance,[1] which had been passed in 1952 shortly before the declaration of an Emergency and came into effect shortly after it. The object of the Ordinance (as explained in the Legislative Council by the Member for Law and Order) was to give the Government power to regulate and control the formation of societies, 'especially those which collect money without properly accounting for it and those also whose activities are prejudicial to peace, order and good government in this state. That is to say, those societies which are subversive in character'.[2]

So far as political societies were concerned, its chief aim was to uncover the sources from which they were obtaining money, and in particular whether there was a connexion with '. . . any organization or group of a political nature established outside the Colony . . .'.[3]

The Ordinance did not therefore ban the Kenya African Union (K.A.U.), the leading African political organization in the Colony, but was designed to elicit further information concerning the operation of this and other African political bodies. K.A.U. was banned several months afterwards (8 June 1953), under the provisions of the Penal Code,[4] on the ground that it was implicated in Mau Mau activities. Its connexion with Mau Mau seems probable beyond reasonable doubt, but as Mr. Tom Mboya wrote in his Fabian pamphlet, *The Kenya Question*,[5] 'One thing is certain however; the KAU was the only African political organisation in Kenya and its banning has left a vacuum.'

This ban applied to all African political organizations and continued until 21 June 1955, when a Government announcement stated that African political associations would be permitted on the District level, except in Central Province. Such District political associations must register themselves under the terms of the 1952 Ordinance (as amended in 1956). Societies registering are required to furnish the Registrar with a copy of their constitution, a list of office-bearers, a true return of any meetings held for a period of six months preceding the receipt of an order to submit such a return, and 'such accounts, returns and other information as may be prescribed'.[6]

When the election took place in March 1957 there were about ten political associations either registered or pending registration in Kenya. Of these, the Nairobi District African Congress (N.D.A.C.)

---

[1] Ordinance No. 52 of 1952.
[2] *Kenya Legislative Council Debates*, 27 and 30 Sept. 1952 (vol. l, cols. 174–80, 183–218).   [3] *Societies Ordinance, 1952*, section 5 (3).
[4] *Laws of Kenya*, 1948, ed., ch. 24.   [5] At p. 23.
[6] *Societies Ordinance, 1952*, section 7 (I) (d).

headed by Mr. Argwings-Kodhek, was the best known and probably the best organized. Even so, the N.D.A.C. had a paid up membership of only 367 on 14 April 1957. Many of the other associations were rudimentary, and two which had written to the Registrar announcing their intention of registering failed to complete the necessary form giving particulars and to pay the 20s. registration fee. With one or two exceptions the political associations which were registered do not appear to have made any appreciable difference either to the registration of voters or to the outcome oi the election. In fact, no candidate who was supported by a political association was elected.

The term 'association' is used rather than 'party' to emphasize the essentially local character of the groups which were free to form themselves from mid-1955 onwards. To discuss national issues at the local level with even minimum efficiency requires conditions of environment and organization at present lacking in Kenya. There must be newspapers and other media of information, as well as a two-way stream of views flowing between local branches and head-quarters. These elementary marks of political organization had yet to reappear in Kenya, and the upshot was, for the time being at least, local inbreeding reinforced by strong tribal sentiments. The emergence of the three groups 'United Front', 'Capricorn' and 'A–K Plan' (referred to later) represented a more advanced stage of politics than did the local associations; but these groups too lacked local roots, and there was at all times a gap between the centre and the periphery. This situation is likely to continue until the Societies Ordinance is further amended.

4. Registration

The various enactments discussed in Section 3 together constituted the legal framework within which the election was held. The first administrative stage was that of registration, with which we deal next: but of course the process of registration overlapped with the emergence of candidates (described in Section 5) and with the early stages of the electoral campaign. In one respect registration was of unusual political significance, because many observers were ready to take low registration figures as an indication of African 'apathy' or 'conservatism', and of the 'failure' of the introduction of direct election by Africans. Yet it is peculiarly difficult in this instance to assess objectively what the figures for registration mean, because the administrative problems were new and difficult, the public had no experience of electoral procedure, and political organizations were too rudimentary to be of any help.

Procedure. The African Representation Ordinance provided that 'The Governor shall appoint a Supervisor of Elections . . .'[1] for the general direction and supervision of the election, with power to issue orders to Registering and returning officers and to administer any oaths required under the Ordinances and rules. The Supervisor, who had been Officer-in-Charge, Nairobi Extra-Provincial District (i.e. a senior officer in the Provincial Administration) was seconded to the Ministry of African Affairs from 1 November 1955.[2] He acted as an official in that Ministry, without special independence or judicial status. In the elections for other 'races' returning and Registering Officers had been responsible to the Chief Secretary.

The Ordinance also required the appointment of a Registering Officer and a returning officer in each constituency, and made provision for the appointment of Assistant Registering and returning officers. The District Commissioner was in each case appointed Registering Officer for his District: and other members of the District staffs acted as Assistant Registering Officers. In some areas, African staff drawn from the District Administration were specially trained to assist applicants, but in the larger and busier centres, chiefs' clerks, schoolmasters, and others helped in the process of registration. The estimated cost of the whole operation (excluding salaries of permanent officials) was:

	£
Personal emoluments	24,000
Travelling and subsistence	17,000
Vehicles, camp equipment, cost of accommodation . .	9,000
	£50,000

The actual cost was probably about £45,000, including about £4,600 for paper and printing.[3]

The officials organizing registration were to some extent guided by experience in other territories, to some extent by their own experience

---

[1] Ordinance No. 10, 1956, p. 3, section 6.
[2] Mr. R. D. F. Ryland, *Kenya Staff List*, p. 2.
[3] The figures for printing costs were:

	£	s.	cents.
Outside Printing Costs (Voters Rolls) . . .	3,108	17	40
Printing supplied by Government Press. . .	1,496	18	00
	£4,605	15	40

The Government Press supplied 190,000 ballot papers and 720,000 voters' cards, and used 6½ tons of paper.

of elections for other 'races' in Kenya. But the situation and the system of qualifications both presented many new features.

In accordance with the usual British practice, the registers of voters, when duly completed and published, were to be taken as conclusive evidence in determining whether a person was entitled to vote in any electoral area. The register was to be a 'permanent' one: that is to say, names would remain on it until deleted. There would, however, be a revision on 1 March 1958, and annually thereafter.

The most peculiar feature of the registration system, which also affected the electoral campaign, was that Africans temporarily resident in one area, normally resident in another, might apply in their place of temporary residence to be registered as voters in their place of normal residence.[1] An African living temporarily in Nairobi, for example, but normally resident in a rural area, could apply to the Registering Officer in Nairobi, who would send his papers to the Registering Officer in the rural area concerned. If satisfied, the latter would enter the name on the electoral roll there, as an 'absent voter' or 'expatriate'. Such persons could vote on polling day at their place of temporary residence for candidates in their constituency of permanent residence, and their votes would be sent there for counting. Members of the Kikuyu, Embu, and Meru tribes were excluded from this privilege, except that they could register in the Nairobi Extra-Provincial District to vote in Central Province: the reason was that the arrangements about loyalty certificates could not be administered conveniently except in Central Province and Nairobi. It is unlikely that this exclusion disfranchised many people.

Apart from this, the special problems of registration arose mainly from the system of qualifications. The procedure was as follows.

First, the potential voter had to secure Form 1, which was available either in English or in Swahili, the *lingua franca*. After completion, the form had to be returned to the Registering Officer concerned, accompanied if necessary by the relevant supporting documents. There were fifteen headings on the form, the purpose of which was to ascertain how many votes, up to a total of three, the applicant should have. A member of the Kikuyu, Embu, and Meru tribes had to obtain a loyalty certificate from a District Commissioner, and to attach it to his application. At the top of his form each person had to show the District in which he wished to register, and this indicated those who would be 'expatriate' voters. On the back of Form 1 was a list of disqualifications for voting. Any person who was

---

[1] There was a parallel arrangement whereby members of other races might vote by post. A detailed account of the rules is to be found in *Laws of Kenya*, ch. 38, schedule iv (as amended by Government Notice 367 of 1948).

uncertain of his or her position when applying for a vote could raise queries with the Registering Officer and his assistants, who were in addition authorized to help non-literate voters to complete their forms.

Secondly, the names of those who had successfully registered in each constituency were placed in order, taking the first letter only of the name deemed to be the surname; i.e. no attempt was made to draw up a fully alphabetical list. The normal address was added after the name. Against each name a serial number was placed, indicating an abbreviation for the District, the number of the subdivision within the District, the serial number of the voter, and the initial letter of the alphabetical division in which a voter's name was registered. Thus the first name on the register for the Rift Valley constituency was:

'BGO/1/1/C   1   Cheptoo Cheptim, Kabarnet—1

The symbols indicated Baringo District Subdivision 1, serial number of voter, initial letter of voter, first entry under C in that subdivision; 1 after the name and residence indicates 'entitled to "one vote" '.

Thirdly, each voter whose name was entered on the register received at the office (at the time of registration or by calling back later) a card coloured either buff (one vote), yellow (two votes), or blue (three votes). This voter's card had written on it the registration number and name and address of the voter. It had to be signed, or a thumb-print made if the holder was unable to write. This card was to be kept carefully until the election. 'Expatriates' could obtain their cards only at the office where they handed in their forms.

Fourthly, when the register was completed, the Registering Officer certified it in appropriate form, and it then came into operation. Copies were to be posted up outside the offices of the Registering Officer and of the Provincial Commissioner. Information about this display had to be published in the *Official Gazette*, and it was also to be publicized at Divisional and District Headquarters and at *barazas*. Any individual whose claim to be registered was rejected by the Registering Officer, or who felt that he was entitled to a greater number of votes than that entered in the register, could appeal to a magistrate empowered to hold a subordinate court of the first class within two weeks of being notified of the Registering Officer's decision that the first round of his appeal had failed. This decision was made out on Form 2, which ran as follows:

To . . ., Your Claim to be registered as a voter with . . . . vote(s) under item(s) . . . . . . of the Schedule to Ordinance No. 10 of 1956 is rejected/ allowed as to . . . . . . vote(s) under item(s) . . . . . .

In the case of expatriate voters, Form 2 had to be countersigned by the District Commissioner to whom the application was originally presented.

Finally, any individual objecting to the name of another individual on the register, could, within a fortnight of its publication, apply to have the name expunged, accompanying the objection with the sum of two shillings and fifty cents, which might be forfeited if the application proved to be frivolous or vexatious. Once again, appeal could be made to a magistrate: under no circumstances would the result of an election be affected by pending applications or appeals.

Propaganda. As was said earlier, estimates of the number of individuals who might eventually be registered were extremely vague. The Ministry of African Affairs decided to work on a figure of between 400,000 and 450,000, then revised this to 385,000 (Table 5). To be on the safe side, 750,000 copies of Form 1 were printed and distributed. How far these figures (supposing them to be correct) would be realized depended on explanation, encouragement, and incentives, and most of the responsibility for this of necessity fell on the administration. Registration began on 14 August, and the closing date was 31 December; the constituencies were not announced until 20 December, nomination day (22 January 1957) was not announced until 27 December, and it was therefore almost impossible for prospective candidates to declare themselves early and to encourage their supporters to register, even if they had wished to do so. The administration, of course, were not to blame for this, since it was not possible to go ahead with such announcements until after the negotiations which took place between members of all racial groups following the September 1956 elections.

The first phase of the registration campaign lasted from March to August 1956 before registration began, and was directed primarily by the Department of Information. Publicity material was inserted in vernacular newspapers and magazines distributed throughout the Colony. Full reports of the Legislative Council debates were carried in issues of 150,000 copies, and 300,000 copies of a booklet were published in six of the leading vernaculars, tabulating qualifications for the franchise under the heading *The Elections—Your Questions Answered.* The following extract will serve as an example of the method adopted:

'Wambua is one of the most respected men in his location and has been an elder for several years. He was a soldier of the Queen in the K.A.R. for nearly six years and now has a small shop which brings him in a steady income of about 3,500/- per year. How many votes will he get?

ANSWER.

Wambua will get three votes. One because he is an elder, one because he has five years' service in the Armed Forces of the Crown, and one because he has the required minimum income.

How can a man prove that his income during the previous year amounted to 2,400/– and who will decide whether property is worth 10,000/– or more?

ANSWER.

Income can be proved by the production of employment cards. The value of property will be decided on a local basis by a suitable qualified officer and a committee of elders who know the values of land, cattle, and other property in the area.

Can women stand as candidates?

ANSWER.

Yes.'

In addition to printed material, the Department sent twelve cinema vans on tour, to show an explanatory film dealing with electoral matters. At the centre in Nairobi numerous radio talks were given, particularly later in the year; the speakers included Mr. R. G. Turnbull, the chief secretary, Mr. B. A. Ohanga, the African Minister for Community Development, and Mr. Wanyutu Waweru, the Parliamentary Secretary to the Ministry of Education, Labour, and Lands.

District Commissioners and other administrative officers also played an important part on the information side. One of the principal means of informing the public about what they had to do in order to register was the *baraza* or meeting, the normal means by which administrative officers on tour give information and sound public opinion. In addition, posters were used where it was judged that they would have some effect in a largely illiterate society.

At first registration went very slowly. In the first eighteen days only 1,100 voters registered in the Central Nyanza constituency (which eventually had nearly 12,000), and this was typical of the whole territory. By early November North Nyanza and Elgon Nyanza Districts (constituting the Nyanza North constituency) led the field with over 12,000 registrations, and at the other end of the scale only 210 had registered in Mombasa. The response was equally poor in Nairobi (only eighty-three names had come in there by the end of September), and it was decided to hand out forms at explanatory *barazas*, instead of only at the three offices at which they were to be handed in, and also to keep the offices open from 9 a.m. to noon on Sundays. In general, urban areas lagged behind the countryside, but there was a noticeable lag in the European farming area, and employers there and elsewhere were asked to give leave of absence if necessary to help registration. In the last days of registration some prospective candidates began to take an interest in it, but probably with little effect.

A fortnight before registration closed just over 92,000 had registered, and in the last days the figure rose by about a third, mainly through late registration in the towns. The final figure after revision was 126,811, perhaps a third of those entitled. Details are given in Table 6.

TABLE 6
Results of Registration

Constituency (1)	Approximate total adults* (2)	Individual voters registered in the constituency		With 1 vote (4)	With 2 votes (5)	With 3 votes (6)	'Expatriates' registered to vote in each constituency (7)
		Men and women (3)	women†				
Nyanza: North . .	228,200	19,869	91†	12,499	5,554	1,816	771
Central . .	171,000	11,768	37	5,880	4,000	1,888	1,084
South . .	253,000	26,177	313	11,508	11,508	3,161	478
Rift Valley and Masai .	253,000	5,030	4†	1,996	2,161	873	261
Central . . .	480,000	35,893	385†	24,229	8,609	3,055	862
Coast	169,000	7,912	28	4,491	2,425	996	48
Akamba . . .	235,000	17,778	20†	11,439	4,633	1,706	1,446
Nairobi . . .	87,500	2,384	35	655	1,066	663	16
TOTALS . . .	1,876,700	126,811	913	72,697	39,956	14,158	4,966

* SOURCE: *Parliamentary Debates: House of Commons*, vol. dlxv, col. 25, 18 Feb. 1957.

† There are no detailed figures for women voters as some of the supervisors were overwhelmed with work at the end of the registration period. Thus, the figures for Rift Valley in this column are for the end of October, and those for Nyanza North, Central and Akamba for the end of November. The remainder are as at the end of the registration period.

There was much comment in the press on the course of registration. Some European letter-writers took the view that Western electoral methods were meaningless to Africans, who 'haven't a clue and couldn't care less'.[1] The Government (it was said) had given in to a few vocal individuals who 'have been sent to British Universities instead of being educated'.[2] African correspondents wrote also deploring the slowness of registration and urging on laggards: one (from Akamba District) went out of his way to pay tribute to those running the Registration Centres there.[3]

The author of this report was not in Kenya during the registration period, and is not qualified to explain fully what happened. But there is general agreement about the factors involved. These might be listed as ignorance and apathy, rumours, and varying degrees of

[1] *East African Standard*, 17 Nov. 1956; letter signed A. W. Sutcliffe.
[2] Ibid.   [3] Ibid.; letter signed P. Kilonzo.

administrative energy and efficiency. Doubtless all these played some part everywhere, but the natural habitat of rumours is in the towns. They were not absent in the country, but registration went on more steadily there, names gradually came in, and there was an obvious response to extra administrative effort.

Most of the rumours were to the effect that the alleged reasons for registration were not the real ones. In the rural areas (this is reported from Nyanza North and Central and from Rift Valley) there was a dislike, especially among the elders, of giving details about income, property, and stock, because of suspicions about taxation or about a new programme for culling stock in excess of the carrying capacity of the land. In the towns, particularly Nairobi, the most striking rumour was one associated with the Suez crisis (which coincided with the period of registration), to the effect that the Government was collecting names with a view to conscription for service in Egypt. Other rumours in the towns were of a more political kind: that the Government would allow only 'stooge' candidates to stand, that Registration Officers discouraged voters favourable to particular candidates, that they encouraged elders to register and discouraged young men.

There were undoubtedly variations in administrative efficiency. Administrative officers and chiefs (in Kenya chiefs are not hereditary but appointed) seem on the whole to have carried their share of the business through conscientiously. But it should be realized that for the administration this was one job more, superimposed on a heavy load which was not lightened: and that for most chiefs it was a sudden change of front that after being told for years to keep out of politics they should be asked to interest themselves directly in the encouragement of political activity. There are, however, stories of special activity by some chiefs, for instance of one in South Nyanza who induced 300 women to come forward for registration; and there is one case of administrative activity which probably influenced the election results indirectly. This was in the Meru District of Central Province, where 18,000 were registered out of a total population of 366,000, which would include at most about 80,000 adult males. This represented a great administrative effort, as each person registering in Central Province was issued with a loyalty certificate. The issue of these certificates was perhaps for some an inducement to register, since evidence of 'loyal and active support of the Government in the Emergency'[1] might be valuable for other purposes; on the other hand, others who might have qualified may have been held back from applying by bad consciences or by social pressure.

---

[1] Ordinance No. 10 of 1956, part vi, section 19 (1).

Registration in the Meru District (the Meru were less deeply implicated in Mau Mau) was in fact relatively much higher than in the Kikuyu Districts: as will be seen later, this was important in the defeat of Mr. Eliud Mathu.

There was a general absence of specific complaints either about the regulations or about the work of registration centres. There were no successful appeals against the Registration Officers' decisions, and few complaints about the regulations except in Central Province. A small group there, belonging to the educated minority, claimed that the nature of their work had precluded them from giving active assistance to the forces of law and order during the Mau Mau disorders—this group is said to have included schoolmasters.[1] Another more numerous group included those who had been detained for screening under the Emergency Regulations but who had been released as being 'white' (i.e. nothing had been proved against them). Of course, to obtain a loyalty certificate, it was not enough for an African to show that he had not been directly implicated in Mau Mau; what was required was positive evidence of assistance to the forces of law and order. It is clear that some persons in these two groups were particularly resentful against those Africans who had either actively or passively assisted Mau Mau but had then surrendered and joined one of the Kenya forces. There were also more complaints in Central Province than elsewhere about the exclusion of anyone who had been detained under the Emergency Regulations, even though released without a conviction. The numbers involved were, however, relatively small. During an adjournment debate, it was stated on behalf of the Government that in Central Province the proportion of registered voters to the total adult population was 7·4 per cent. 'It seems reasonable to assume that no larger a proportion of the detainees would, if allowed to do so, have qualified for registration or have wished to register, and on this basis it is fair to say that no more than 5,000 or 6,000 people are disqualified because they have been detainees.'[2]

Clearly the registration period was of great importance both in determining the result of the election and as a step in African political development in Kenya. It is perhaps safe to say that (in spite of criticisms) registration went as well as could be expected in the circumstances, and that it will go more actively in future, because public opinion is being shaped fast, as a result of the activity of Mr. Tom Mboya and his group. On the other hand, the fact that a

[1] See Mr. E. Mathu's speech on the Motion of Thanks for the Speech from the Chair; *Kenya Legislative Council Debates*, vol. lxxi, cols. 101–12, 15 Nov. 1956.
[2] *Parliamentary Debates, House of Commons*, vol. dlxiii, cols. 1130–8, 30 Jan. 1957.

complicated system of qualifications worked smoothly on its first trial does not mean that all difficulties have been overcome; the machinery would be under more severe pressure at a time of vigorous campaigning by organizations anxious to get their supporters on the register.

5. Nominations

It was announced on 27 December that nomination day would be 22 January 1957. The announcement was accompanied by a reminder that all candidates would have to prove that they were proficient in reading, writing, and speaking English, and that persons would be exempted from this requirement if they possessed a university degree, a Makerere Diploma, or had already been members of the Legislative Council. Failing these requirements, a candidate would have to make arrangements with the Provincial Commissioner of the area in which he resided to appear before a languages board, which if it were satisfied with his performance would issue him with a certificate to that effect.

Each prospective candidate was required to fill in a nomination paper setting out his qualifications, which was to be signed by a proposer, seconder, and not less than seven supporters, all of whom had to be registered voters of the electoral area for which the candidate was being nominated. All these signatures had to be witnessed by a magistrate, justice of the peace, commissioner for oaths, or a public notary, and the paper was in addition to be stamped with a 2s. revenue stamp in respect of each signature witnessed. On 22 January between 9 a.m. and noon each candidate had to deliver his paper in person to the returning officer of his constituency, along with a deposit of 500s. (£25), which was liable to forfeiture should he fail to obtain one-eighth of the total votes cast in the constituency. Candidates were then required to take an oath of allegiance to Her Majesty and also to make a statutory declaration. After 12 noon, and providing that two or more candidates had been nominated, the Returning Officer would allocate a symbol to each candidate, and the names of the candidates would then be reported to the Governor, who would in due course appoint a day or days on which the election would take place.

Certificates of proficiency in English were to be given by language boards, one for each Province, consisting of two members of the Education Department and two African assessors, all appointed by the Provincial Commissioner. No systematic record of language board proceedings is available, but it is known that eight would-be candidates were unsuccessful; three schoolmasters were among those who failed. It is clear that the main emphasis was on tests of English comprehension of a practical kind. At one Board, a few passages from the Kenya Legislative Council Hansard were read out; those present were allowed to take notes, and were then asked to outline the main points in the excerpts. At one interview a candidate was asked to explain what was meant by the phrase 'ploughing back profits into agriculture'; he was unable to supply an answer. Another candidate was asked his opinion of the acoustics of the MacMillan Memorial Hall—formerly used for Legislative Council meetings—which is notorious for difficulties about audibility. He looked puzzled and then said 'sparkling'. The evidence available indicates that the interviews were carried out honestly, and that no attempt was made to eliminate anyone for extrinsic reasons, such as alleged unpopularity either with the administration or among his fellow Africans.

There were thirty-seven successful nominations for the eight constituencies. Eight of these had been Representative Members of the former Legislative Council.[1] The smallest number of candidates in any constituency was three, the highest (in Nyanza South and Nyanza North) was six.

The average age of the candidates was thirty-eight, the oldest (Mr. Eliud Mathu) being about fifty, the youngest (Mr. Tom Mboya) twenty-eight.

As has been said, eight had Legislative Council experience; nineteen had local government experience, and eight were employed by Government in various capacities, such as Social Welfare Officer, Assistant District Officer, and Community Development Officer. Only three described themselves as farmers, three as business men. There was one trade union organizer (Mr. Mboya) and one well-known Nairobi African (Mr. Kasyoka) who is employed as dispenser in a firm of chemists. A number of candidates did not make any statement about their work, and one or two (such as Mr. Ohanga, the Minister for Community Development) might perhaps be described as full-time politicians.

The educational qualification meant that (as a result of the existing educational organization) a good many candidates were qualified as teachers and had some teaching experience: twelve stated that they were currently employed as teachers. Thirteen candidates had been to Makerere, all of them before it became in 1950 the University College of East Africa, in association with the

[1] Those mentioned on p. 399 with two others added as a result of the changes made late in 1956: Nyanza South: F. F. arap Chumah (Kipsigi); J. Nzau Muimi (Akamba).

University of London: six had British university degrees, and there was one barrister (Mr. Argwings-Kodhek).

The candidates possessed a wide range of experience, and were together a fair sample of the political talent available among Africans in Kenya. They lacked experience of political organization, but did not on the whole lack ability, and a number of them were men of some note. It is impossible to say that the legal provisions about the qualification of candidates made much difference to selection; those who came forward would probably have done so in any case. It is possible, however, that in the absence of effective party organization the rules served as some check on the number of candidates, which was in any case inconveniently large, given a simple plurality system of voting. Only four successful candidates secured 50 per cent. of the votes cast, and two successful candidates had less than 40 per cent.

Candidates whose nomination was accepted were asked by the returning officer to select a symbol[1] which would be used on the ballot box, on the ballot paper, and during the campaign as a means of identification by non-literate voters. Candidates were free to choose from a long list of symbols, and there was no difficulty over choice except in one case when both candidates wanted to use the same symbol, but settled the dispute amicably by spinning a coin. The most popular symbol was a cow, chosen by seven candidates; six chose the lion, six the cock, four an elephant, and four a key. Other symbols used were a motor-car, a clock, a bicycle, an aeroplane, an eagle, and a tree.

It must be remembered that these were the symbols of individuals, not of parties. No parties existed, unless the district associations are to be described as parties. Even when groups of candidates emerged, as described in the next section, their members as often as not chose different symbols.

6. The Emergence of Groups

Though Kenya-wide parties were forbidden, nothing prevented individual candidates in different constituencies from associating in a group for the promotion of a common policy. Three of these groups can be distinguished, covering sixteen candidates out of thirty-seven: of these sixteen, three were successful.

The first group to emerge was that of the eight members of the Legislative Council seeking re-election, who came forward as the

---

[1] Symbols had been used previously in Kenya for Indian elections, both Muslim and non-Muslim.

United Front Group some time before nomination day. On 6 December they issued a nine-point statement of policy, accompanied by some specific recommendations on points of detail. The statement of policy set out the following points:

(a) That the loyalty of the 'United Front' lies to the British Crown and Kenya.

(b) That equality of opportunity be secured for Africans in economical, social and political fields.

(c) That Africans of quality and requisite qualifications should hold responsible positions in the Public Service of Kenya.

(d) That the 'United Front' supports men of long and mature experience in the Legislative Council and in other public affairs.

(e) That the future of the African people can be secured by the united voice on the part of all.

(f) That a majority of seats on the unofficial side of the Legislative Council be occupied by Africans.

(g) That Communal Rolls continue for the present until Africans are on an equality with other races on the subject of the franchise. Until Africans attain full adult franchise we shall not support the principle of the Common Roll.

(h) That we believe that the freedom of assembly, speech, press and association are essential for our people.

(i) The 'United Front' can offer to Kenya an honest, courageous selfless, determined and confident approach to our problems.

It then went on to review the record of African members in the Legislative Council during the twelve years from 1944 to 1956, combining this with specific recommendations for the future.

It is only fair to say that any achievement that the African Members can claim can also be claimed by the Members of other races on both sides of the Legislative Council, in that all must support certain lines of actions to bring about some benefit to the country. It is therefore, as it should be, a joint effort.

During the 1944–56 period, the statement went on, there had been a significant increase from two to eight African representative members in Legislative Council, and of these, two were ministers and three parliamentary secretaries.[1] The same tendency was discernible in urban and rural local government. Colonial Office remote control must continue for the time being, but the first step must be to

[1] In fact only two African Parliamentary Secretaries had been named, but there was provision for three under the Lyttelton Constitution.

achieve an African majority on the unofficial side. In the *Public Service*, more Africans must be given a larger number of responsible posts. In the *Judicial* field the jury system should be extended to Africans. (At present this applies only to Europeans—its extension is being considered for Asians.) In *Education*, a considerable extension of services had already taken place, but the aim should be to instal compulsory primary education, and each African child should receive eight years' teaching without interruption. *Health services* should be extended with particular emphasis on Maternity Welfare and the setting up of a school medical service. *Trade union* activities should be encouraged, and trade unionists ought to play a prominent part on statutory boards and committees. *Labour* should be stabilized and the family taken as the unit when this was brought about. In the towns, there should be more and better *Housing* for Africans, and no racial discrimination. In *Agriculture*, there should be financial assistance for farmers, more land for Africans, and equal marketing facilities. *Water-supplies* in arid places should be arranged. In *Commerce* and *Industry* the African trader must be encouraged. In the *Communications* field, all-weather roads should be built in African areas, and the railway system extended to them. The fight against *Racial discrimination* (here the United Front candidates drew attention to certain restrictions which have been removed, i.e. the prohibition of consumption, possession, and sale of liquor, the derogatory use of the word 'native', and the abolition of the *kipandi* system) would be continued with vigour. Unrestricted *immigration* would be fought against. '*Conclusion*: as we have indicated above, we have not been successful in every case. If returned, we shall continue to urge the Government to effect reforms in matters that are still pending.'

Two of this group were successful in relatively quiet constituencies, Mr. arap Moi in Rift Valley, Mr. Muimi in Akamba.

A second group of candidates signified their general approval of the *Capricorn Contract*, which is, in broad terms, an attempt to find some basis on which a genuine multi-racial society may be built. Four candidates joined this group (Mr. Kasyoka in Nairobi, Mr. Tipis in Rift Valley, Mr. Khamisi in Coast, and Mr. Otiende in Nyanza North); at one time it was thought that Mr. Mathu and Mr. Ohanga would also back it, but they did not do so. These four declared their support for the aims of the Capricorn Contract in a letter published in the *Kenya Weekly News* on 2 February 1957, which went on to associate the name of Mr. T. arap Towett of Nyanza South with their statement. But Mr. Towett vigorously disassociated himself in a letter published in the same paper on 15 February, which said, *inter alia*:

When I went down to Nairobi on electioneering I was amazed and really dismayed to see some of my friends coming to me and accusing me of aligning myself with the Capricornists. Some of them even tried to avoid me as they thought I had done them a lot of harm by being one of the Capricornists.

Moreover, Mr. Khamisi (Coast) who is a nominated member of the East African High Commission Legislative Assembly, was later expelled from the Capricorn Africa Society on the grounds of not favouring multi-racialism.[1] The candidates who did adopt the doctrine were not very vocal in support of it. They did not issue any leaflets or other propaganda centrally; all canvassing was personal and without outside help. Certainly no Europeans assisted. The general impression is that those who had indicated varying degrees of luke-warm approval for Capricorn did not stress this at election meetings, and indeed found the whole thing rather embarrassing. The one exception was Mr. Kasyoka, who stood for Nairobi. His election manifesto (three cyclostyled sheets) began with the words:

Kenya needs a policy of true racial co-operation. Without this our future is doomed. To steer ourselves away from disaster, we must support the principles of equality among human beings as laid down in the Capricorn Contract.

Mr. Kasyoka's manifesto will be examined in detail when the Nairobi election is described.[2]

The third group was more nationalist in tone than either of the two groups just described. Four candidates declared themselves supporters of Mr. Argwings-Kodhek's 'A–K' Plan; Mr. Arwings-Kodhek, who was standing for Nairobi, was then the only African barrister practising in Kenya and was one of the outstanding personalities of the election. Like the Capricorn group, supporters of the 'A–K' Plan produced no written propaganda issued centrally, but as founder and chairman of the Nairobi District African Congress (organized, of course, on a District basis only) Mr. Kodhek seemed to have at hand an organization which would assure him victory, particularly if his more radical views be taken into account.

The main points of the 'A–K' Plan were:

(a) Accelerated Africanization of the Public Service.

(b) Africans to have a common franchise with the other races with universal adult suffrage.

---

[1] E.A.S., 24/7/57.
[2] It is typical of the uncertainty of the situation that the Capricorn Africa Society in a leaflet circulated in England claimed that Capricorn had six candidates, of whom one (Mr. Ngala in Coast) was successful. I have no evidence that Mr. Ngala appeared as a Capricornist during the election period.

(c) Greater control by Africans of African affairs.

(d) African economic and social development to be assisted by a special 'self-help' scheme.

(e) Compulsory education for African children.

(f) No Federation for East Africa except when Africans were in charge in each of the three territories.

(g) Further points included Government 'by the people', improved health services, immigration to be based on the principle of usefulness to the indigenous people, justice for all, including freedom of speech, press and meetings.

Mr. Argwings-Kodhek finished his manifesto with the following words: 'To those who find the Plan unpalatable I recommend The Book of Daniel, Chapter 5, Verse 25.'[1]

Only one out of four 'A–K' candidates was successful; Mr. Argwings-Kodhek failed in Nairobi, Mr. arap Towett in South Nyanza, and Mr. J. Ole Tamero lost his deposit in Rift Valley; Mr. Odinga was successful in Nyanza Central. This must not, however, be construed as the 'failure' of a 'party'. The link between these candidates was nebulous, did not lead to any organized and concerted effort, and gave no guarantee of later co-operation.

7. The Issues

The programmes of these three groups were clearly more marked by similarities than differences, though certain differences became plainer during the course of the campaign. What then were the 'issues' of the election? In a sense there were and could be no 'issues', if 'issues' are defined as questions put before an electorate in a contest between centrally organized parties. But there is plenty of evidence about what was in the minds of candidates and what they thought worth putting before the electorate, and it is possible to generalize with some confidence.

Perhaps the best single source is the *East African Standard*, Kenya's leading newspaper, published in English, which wrote to the candidates and requested them to publish their views on the political issues at stake. All the candidates took advantage of this offer, and the *Standard* published their views, taking each constituency in turn. These individual statements perhaps give a clearer picture of the

---

[1] Dan. v. 25 is 'the writing on the wall'. 'This is an interpretation of the thing: MENE; God hath numbered thy kingdom and finished it. TEKEL; Thou art weighed in the balances, and art found wanting. PHERES; Thy kingdom is divided, and given to the Medes and Persians.'

state of literate African opinion than do the amorphous groups mentioned above.

Measured in terms of space and time devoted to it, in pamphlets and leaflets as well as at meetings, the issue which weighed most heavily on the candidates was education. All the candidates urged the need for greater educational facilities for African children, nearly all of them demanded an eight-year compulsory education scheme for children between seven and fifteen years. The link between education and eventual power was clearly seen; what was not mentioned was that such a scheme is at present beyond the financial resources of the Colony, and raises also the difficult problem of recruiting a sufficient number of trained teachers. Three other issues featured prominently. The first was that of increased African representation in the Legislative Council (sometimes linked with the longer-term view that Kenya should be developed as an African State). The second was a demand that only those immigrants should be allowed in Kenya whose purpose was to help the African in his development. And lastly, there were many suggestions about helping the African farmer by some sort of loan scheme[1] (the most elaborate of these proposals took the form of urging the setting up of Overseas Trade Development Councils in African Districts to explore and develop the sale of African produce abroad).

Featuring less prominently in the manifestos was the demand for equal pay for equal work, which was closely associated with the idea of equality of opportunity. Financial and other forms of aid for Africans in trade were also mentioned by some candidates. Miscellaneous items included the introduction of the jury system for Africans, free medical treatment or (in some cases) improved medical services, and protests against the restrictions on political parties. Better urban housing, the need to develop trade unions, and the need to have freedom of speech, assembly, association, and press were also mentioned. Only two candidates suggested that Africans should pay higher taxes to pay for the increase in services suggested.

The perennial theme of more land for Africans, particularly in the White Highlands, was not so prominent as might have been expected, but could always be relied on to evoke a considerable response from election audiences.

Certain candidates, notably in the Capricorn and United Front groups, took a moderate line on such issues as the readiness of the African for self-government, the need for the three races to pull together, and allegiance to the Crown. One candidate in print, and

[1] About £300,000 p.a. is at present being lent to individuals and co-operatives under various schemes.

several orally, warned their audiences against political agitators, and some went on to urge good behaviour, on the grounds that the world was watching how the election was taking shape. One pamphlet referred to the need to remain 'under' the Colonial Office. There was a plea by one candidate to replace pagan beliefs by Christian doctrines.

Although the election described here was a communal one, it took place in a society in which various 'races' are interlocked, and their representatives have no choice but to work closely together at the centre, unless they are to leave the initiative entirely to the Colonial Office and the 'expatriate' British administration. The stage for the African election was therefore set by the European and Asian elections, which took place in September 1956, during the registration period, after postponement from 1955. In particular, the fate of Mr. Michael Blundell and his fellows, who were pledged to a multi-racial future, was watched with keen interest by African politicians.

Among the Europeans four groups were contending for the fourteen elective seats in Legislative Council. Moving from the extreme right, as it were, leftwards, there was first, the Federal Independence party, which opposed the Lyttelton Plan and proposed the division of Kenya roughly along racial *apartheid* lines. Next, there was Group-Captain Briggs's 'Independent Group', who objected to ministerial posts being reserved for particular races, and also opposed the Lyttelton Plan. Thirdly, there were the 'Independents' led by Mr. Michael Blundell, remnants of the moribund United Country party, whose general policy was to support the Lyttelton Plan. Lastly, there were two Capricorn candidates. As a result of the election, eight Briggsites were returned and six Blundellites. No F.I.P. or Capricorn member was successful. The result was interpreted as a slight move to the right, and it might be supposed that in consequence ministerial offices would have been offered to the largest party, the Briggs Independent Group. But this party had expressed its displeasure with the Lyttelton Plan, and for a time no one felt sure what would happen. In fact, Group-Captain Briggs accepted a ministerial post alongside Mr. Blundell, his erstwhile opponent. Kenya politics were following their usual pattern; the vital issues of one month are overlooked or forgotten a few months later. The Independent Group is no more, the United Country Party has dissolved itself, and the Federal Independence party has split into two, the less Right-wing portion calling itself the Reform party and apparently abandoning the policy of 'provincial autonomy', that is, of racial segregation.

The Asian election, which took place at the same time as the European, is even more difficult to interpret. The leading Asian (non-Muslim) personality to be elected was Mr. N. S. Mangat, a Nairobi advocate and a man of considerable intelligence, who has since startled his followers by declaring his conversion to the Capricorn Contract.[1] It is significant that the Asian bloc have supported the African Elected Members' demand for fifteen additional seats[2] after a honeymoon period during which the Asians appeared to back the Europeans in maintaining the *status quo*.

These elections were followed by discussion between the Governor and all 'racial' groups in the Legislative Council, and agreement was reached on certain constitutional changes. The general tendency of these was to strengthen the non-government side of the Council, and we have already mentioned the provision of two extra seats (and two extra constituencies) for Africans, balanced by two members of unspecified 'races', to be nominated from names submitted to the Governor by the Board of Agriculture and the Board of Commerce and Industry, bodies likely under their present constitutions to produce two European members.[3] The unofficial side of the Council of Ministers would include an additional African and Asian minister—four European, two African, two Asian—and an Arab would be invited to join it with the status of minister, but not as head of a Department. An additional Arab seat was to be created in the Legislative Council after the forthcoming Arab election,[4] and there would also be an examination of the possibility of increasing the total number of unofficial seats further and of the best method of selection. These and other minor proposals, which were all accepted by the Secretary of State for the Colonies, represented together a step forward in restoring the influence of the unofficial side of the Legislative Council without disturbing the delicate balance of the Lyttelton Plan. They held out no prospect of the rapid increase in African representation demanded by almost all African candidates, but they did not close the door to further change, and both

[1] Here, too, there is much uncertainty about the 'Capricorn' position. The Society in England claims four candidates, all elected: this is certainly not realistic.

[2] This was to make twenty-three African representative members against twenty-two for all other 'races'.

[3] That these two seats were commonly held to be non-political appointments is indicated by the resignation (in early Aug. 1957) of Mr. S. V. Cooke, European elected member for the Coast, from the European Elected Members' Association, when Sir Alfred Vincent, the Corporate Member put forward by the Board of Commerce and Industry, accepted the chairmanship of the E.E.M.A.

[4] This was to take place in Mar. 1957, but was postponed. No additional Arab seat had been created at time of writing (Oct. 1957).

Europeans and Asians later agreed (in principle only) to some uni-
lateral increase in African representation.[1]

8. *The Press*

The limited scope for territory-wide manifestos has been explained:
and few candidates campaigned outside their own constituencies;
the most notable exceptions being Mr. Mathu and Mr. Kebaso
from South Nyanza, who came to seek 'expatriate' votes in Nairobi.
Programmes designed specifically for Africans are broadcast daily
from Nairobi, Mombasa, Kisumu, and Nyeri (Mount Kenya); and
the distribution of radio sets is increasing. But it was not the Government's policy to encourage territory-wide campaigning, and no
time was made available for political broadcasts, apart from official
broadcasts encouraging registration. In consequence, there was to all

[1] The refusal of the 8 African elected members to work within the framework of
the Lyttelton Constitution resulted in a period of constitutional uncertainty which
lasted until November 1957, when Mr. Lennox-Boyd announced his proposals for
a new constitution. (Cmnd. 309: KENYA: Proposals for New Constitutional Arrangements.) Three points are of particular interest: (*a*) the creation of 6 additional
African elected seats without any corresponding increase in European or Asian
elected representation. (*b*) the creation of 12 new non-Government seats for
Specially Elected Members who would be elected by the Legislative Council
sitting as an electoral college, the intention being to draw non-official or 'elected'
Ministers from a group which had received support from more than one community;
those not selected as Ministers or Assistant Ministers (as Parliamentary Secretaries
were renamed) would swell the numbers on the 'opposition' side of the House. Of
the 12 seats, 4 were reserved for Europeans, 4 for Africans, and 4 for Asians (one
Muslim, one Arab and two non-Muslims). Election is by secret ballot. After the
first election, which was held in April 1958, a Council of Ministers of 15 was created,
composed of 6 officials, 2 nominated members and 7 elected members, 5 of whom
were Specially Elected Members (2 Europeans, 2 Asians, and 1 African). As the
(now) 14 African elected members boycotted the election on the grounds that the
4 Specially Elected African seats would merely be 'nothing but a rubber stamp for
European selections' much of the purpose of this constitutional device was lost.
(*c*) the creation of a Council of State, designed to protect any one community
against discriminatory legislation harmful to its interests. The Council, which is in
no sense a second chamber, has certain defined powers of delay, revision and
reference, and possesses a multi-racial membership. Insufficient time has lapsed to
guage the usefulness of this body. (Further details on these constitutional changes
may be found in Cmnd. 369: KENYA: Despatch on the New Constitutional
Arrangements.)

The Lennox-Boyd Constitution has, in addition to the above features, a proviso
that no additional seats based on elections by purely communal electorates will be
created. Any further expansion of the membership of the Legislative Council will
have to be on the basis of some form of non-communal representation. Since the
African elected members are pressing for increased representation and refuse to
co-operate in the working of the Lennox-Boyd Constitution, at least on the ministerial level, once again a period of constitutional uncertainty lies ahead.

intents and purposes no 'national' campaign' except for that carried on in the press.

The independent vernacular press in Kenya is limited to a handful of newspapers with small circulations and little influence. The publication of such newspapers came to a stop with the outbreak of the Emergency, and since then a situation had developed which made it difficult for a purely African press to revive. Most of the papers which ceased publication were shoddy cyclostyled productions, and only a few achieved a respectable level of technical competence.[1] Many of the editors were detained. The vacuum thus left was partly met by an expansion of the activities of the Government Information Department, which turned out papers in Swahili as well as in numerous vernaculars. In addition, there are some papers owned by Asian proprietors which cater to a limited extent, in English, for an African audience. Chief among the latter group is the *Colonial Times*, which published a valuable series of manifestos which it received from some of the more prominent candidates. *Jicho* is owned by the same management and has an African editor, and it frequently adopts a more radical line than some of its contemporaries.

The facts are difficult to establish, but there seem to have been three independent African newspapers operating at the time of the election. The *Nyanza Times* is perhaps the most interesting paper in this group. Revived in December 1956, it is the vehicle of Mr. Oginga Odinga, and Mr. Argwings-Kodhek is also on its board of directors. Its circulation figures are not known but are likely to be small. A trade union paper called *Mzangi Kazi* (lit. 'I am a Worker') closely associated with Mr. Tom Mboya, had an initial issue of 5,000. Nothing is known about *Asere* (The Arrow) published in Nyanza Province, with an average circulation of between 500 and 1,000; it may have stopped publication in December 1956.

All newspapers in Kenya must register with the Registrar of Societies, giving fourteen days' notice of intention to publish. In addition, the law of sedition contained in the Penal Code[2] was strengthened by the Printing Presses (Temporary Provisions) Ordinance of 1952,[3] and later legislation. The Kenya Government

---

[1] The Member for African Affairs, when introducing the Printing Presses (Temporary Provisions) Bill for its second reading, stated that there were 34 or 35 African newspapers in Kenya (just about three weeks before the Emergency was declared) and that 11 or 12 of them had started within the last six or seven months (*Kenya Legislative Council Debates*, 30 Sept. 1952, vol. 1, col. 220).

[2] Laws of Kenya, 1948 ed., cap. 24.

[3] For debate on the second reading see *Kenya Legislative Council Debates*, 30 Sept., cols. 218–41, and 1 Oct., cols. 245–60, vol. 1, 1952.

felt that the existing law left too much scope for unscrupulous editors of all racial groups, and the Printing Presses (Temporary Provisions) Bill was intended *inter alia* to prevent the publication of 'matters of near seditious character',[1] designed to stir up hatred among the different races. A licence to print can be refused or cancelled by the Registrar of Printing Presses after consultation with the Member for Law and Order, but provision is made for appeals to the Governor in Council within twenty-one days. Every printed 'document' is required to have the name and address of the printer and publisher on the first and last printed leaf, and a copy is to be kept by the printer for six months in case it has to be produced before a magistrate. Search powers were given to administrative officers or police officers not below the rank of assistant inspector, to be used 'where offences under the Ordinance are deemed likely to have occurred'.[2] The Ordinance was to run for one year only; but in fact it was re-enacted as an Emergency Regulation at the end of this period.[3] It is not possible here to enter into a detailed description of the effect of the Emergency Regulations on publication of all kinds, but reference may perhaps be made to the Emergency (Publications) Regulations 1953,[4] which imposed severe penalties on anyone operating a duplicating machine with the intention of publishing a newspaper in the Kikuyu, Embu, or Meru languages, unless exempted from the provisions of the regulation by special permit issued by the chief secretary.[5]

In addition to the commercial press, there are two series of monthly or fortnightly papers. The first are known as 'District News Sheets', and are printed at the larger centres such as Eldoret, Nakuru, Mombasa, and Kisumu and distributed by the African District Councils These have a circulation of 2,000–5,000 and are mainly devoted to matters of local interest. Also, the Department of Information turns out monthly regional magazines in four vernaculars, that in Swahili having a circulation of 54,000, the Kikuyu issue 30,000, the Kamba issue 15,000, and the Luo issue 30,000. The

---

[1] The Member for Law and Order at col. 248.
[2] Ibid. col. 222.
[3] Government Notice No. 1615 of 1953. *The Emergency (Amendment of Laws) (No. 33) Regulations*, 1953.
[4] G.N. No. 222 of 1953.
[5] Section 7A of the *Emergency Regulations* (which were published on 20 Oct. 1952, when a state of emergency was proclaimed) was entitled 'Subversive Publications' and gave powers to any administrative officer to seize any publications which he was satisfied were subversive or prejudicial to the maintenance of public order. A mass of rules filled out the detail of E.R. 7A.

total circulation from all these official sources is in the region of 180,000.

A list of the leading newspapers is given below, together with circulation figures where available.

DAILY

East African Standard	(English)	20,000
		(33,500 weekly ed.)
Mombasa Times	(English)	4,600
Kenya Daily Mail	(English and Gujerati)	2,000
		(5,000 weekly ed.)
Daily Chronicle	(English and Gujerati)	4,225
		(5,200 weekly ed.)

WEEKLY

Sunday Post	(English)		10,000
Kenya Weekly News	(English)		7,500
Colonial Times	(English and	English	3,700
	Gujerati)	Gujerati	4,300
Baraza	(Swahili)		31,700
Jicho	(Swahili)		7,750
Ramogi	(Luo)		5,000
Tazama	(Swahili)		19,500'
Thome	(Kikamba)		1,000
Omwoyo Kwomuluyia	(Luluhya)		2,000
Ngao	(Swahili)		2,000
Kihoto	(Gikuyu)		2,000

Several points are to be noted about this list. In the first place, there is no daily newspaper in any African language. Secondly, the English press always devotes some of its space to printing letters from Africans, some of which are by no means uncritical of the Government, and it prints news items of general interest to the African community. Thirdly, circulation figures do not give a proper picture of the extent to which the various publications are read. Many of the papers are passed round from hand to hand, and the fact that they are out of date counts for little. *Baraza*, which circulates widely in this way, is a subsidiary of the *East African Standard*, and hence enjoys the same distribution advantages as the parent paper. Fourthly, any group of Africans wishing to start a newspaper comes up against the difficulty of producing something which will bear comparison in technical terms and in cost with the already established newspapers. An extreme nationalist newspaper would probably overcome these difficulties. Lastly, to apply this to the election, there were only two politicians (Mr. Odinga and Mr.

Mboya) who owned or influenced any press outlet which could be used to convey a political message. The other thirty-five candidates relied in varying degrees on the generosity of owners and editors to obtain space.

It may perhaps be added that one of the major difficulties encountered by all newspapers in East Africa is one of distribution over long distances, to which must be coupled the further handicap of extracting the money obtained through sales from the numerous sellers. Of course, these remarks do not apply to well-established shops, and the larger *dukas* (multi-purpose stores, usually Asian owned) but rather to the remoter regions. The English practice of 'sale or return' is subject to some strange metamorphoses in the tropics.

9. The Election in the Constituencies

1. Nairobi

The Nairobi constituency played a curious part in the election. It has an African population of about 140,000 and undoubtedly the proportion of those eligible for registration was fairly large. But only 2,349 men and 35 women registered as voters in Nairobi, and in addition about 1,200 men and women registered there as 'expatriates' entitled to vote in other constituencies. One reason for giving much more space here to Nairobi than to other constituencies is that the campaign there was relatively easy to document and to observe; but this is also justified by its importance, in spite of the small size of the electorate. The campaign was, as it turned out, a highly personal one; yet the conditions gave candidates in Nairobi a better platform than was available anywhere else, the mixed population meant that more attention was paid to territorial than to local politics, and through expatriate voters and many other expatriates events and ideas in Nairobi had a certain influence throughout the territory. In fact, Nairobi's position as a capital city and a 'metropolitan' area was important even in this election: it will be even more important if the size of its electorate increases.

Social and administrative background. Nairobi is the largest city between Cairo and Johannesburg, with a population which exceeds 200,000—about 16,000 Europeans, 56,000 Asians, 140,000 Africans. Its site was chosen originally almost by accident, at the spot where the railway line from Mombasa leaves the plains and begins to skirt the broken ground of the Kenya Highlands. The city has no special natural advantages except a temperate climate and adequate rainfall, but it began to grow as a commercial centre and entrepôt for the 'White Highlands', and industrial development has followed population. It is said that there are now over 1,000 premises registered as factories in the industrial area. Many of them of course are very small, but they employ many people and produce a large range of consumer goods which find markets throughout East Africa. Till recently the city centre, though well planned, retained a 'small town' atmosphere: but a building boom accompanied the Emergency, and about £6 million a year is now being spent on constructional work of all kinds, employing many Africans.

The city is laid out in a way which encourages racial segregation in practice, though this is not erected into a principle and there is a good deal of overlapping between European and Asian, Asian and African areas. The main African 'estates' lie in the Eastern part of the city, away from the higher ground and near the industrial area. They are organized into eighteen villages, each of which has an elected village committee, electing its own chairman; six villages make up a ward, and each village committee elects a member of the appropriate Ward Council. Each of these Councils meets under the chairmanship of one of the three African City Councillors; and in addition there is an African Advisory Council for the whole area, with a complex constitution.[1] Responsibility for African affairs in Nairobi is divided somewhat uneasily between the City Council and the central government. African 'locations' are not (as in some countries) excluded from the city altogether, and there is an African Affairs Committee of the City Council. But the Council includes only three Africans (all nominated) among its thirty-one members, and the political and social problems of Africans in Nairobi during the Mau Mau period have been so far beyond the resources of the city as to require continual central supervision and financial aid. Careful control of movement and attempts to improve housing and social services have gone along with closer administration: in 1955 twenty-three 'chiefs' were appointed to work closely with the police in allotted areas.

Some idea of the tribal composition of the town is given by the poll-tax figures in Table 7. These are not complete, since there are certainly some Africans living in Nairobi illegally, and there are

---

[1] The President is the Officer-in-Charge, Nairobi Extra-Provincial District, and the Vice-President is the City African Affairs Officer. These two are termed *officials* under the Constitution. '*Members*' are made up of three groups. (i) *Ex Officio*, the chairman of the African Affairs Committee of the City Council, all African City Councillors (3 nominated), and the Assistant City African Affairs Officer. (ii) *Elected*, the chairman of each village committee. (iii) *Nominated*, 3 to be nominated by Officer-in-Charge, Nairobi Extra-Provincial District.

others who pay poll-tax in their own Districts: but the proportions
are roughly correct.

TABLE 7

Poll-tax Payers in Nairobi, 1955 and 1956

	1955		1956	
	No.	%	No.	%
Nyanza taxpayers . . .	34,171	48	36,466	48
Kamba taxpayers . . .	17,971	25	17,311	23
Kikuyu, Embu, Meru taxpayers	14,425	21	15,896	21
Other areas	3,262	6	5,730	8
TOTALS	69,829	100	75,403	100

SOURCES: 1955—African Affairs Department, *Annual Report for 1955*. Govt. Printer
Nairobi, 1956, p. 160. 1956—Figures supplied by African Poll Tax Office, Nairobi.

In spite of all the efforts made to establish a stable urban population,
these figures include a high but uncertain proportion of temporary
workers. In addition, there have been a number of shifts in tribal
composition. In 1954 24,000 members of the Kikuyu, Embu, and
Meru tribes were moved out of the city and back to the rural areas during 'Operation Anvil'. In 1955 there was a scare about the spread
of Mau Mau to the Luo and Akamba tribes. The numbers involved
were small, and 'confessional *Barazas*' were successfully held in the
earlier part of the year. But in July the rumour spread that reprisals
were to be taken against those who had not confessed, and this led
to an exodus of Nyanza and Akamba tribesmen from Nairobi. In
1956 political conditions improved, the industrial and constructional 'boom' continued, and Africans began to flood back into
the city, legally and illegally. In consequence, administrative attention shifted again from political security to almost unmanageable
social problems.

The emergence of the Nairobi District African Congress. Towards the
end of 1955 leading African politicians in Kenya reacted to the
relaxation of extreme tension, the discussions of the African franchise,
and the inquiries of the Dow Commission on economic problems in
East Africa[1] by discussing the formation of a Nairobi African political
association, with the ultimate object of making it a colony-wide
organization.

To assist this process there were at hand various tribal associations,
such as the Luo Union, the Abaluha Association, and the Akamba

[1] The East Africa Royal Commission, 1953–5; *Report*, Cmd. 9475 of 1955.

Association. These bodies are not primarily political in character, but perform certain welfare functions for the members of the respective tribes and help to foster a sense of cohesion. Among their most popular functions is that of arranging dances at the weekend. There are links between these associations and the parent bodies in the different Provinces. Hence there is a tendency for them to interest themselves in political matters, but under the provisions of the Societies Ordinance this falls outside their authorized sphere of action, and they were not much in evidence during the election.

The only other organization which should be mentioned is the Kenya Federation of Labour, a society registered under the Societies Ordinance, whose secretary, Mr. Tom Mboya, became a candidate in the constituency. Some nine trade unions of African employees are affiliated to the Federation, which is not itself a trade union and has no power to organize strikes among its member unions. The Federation is affiliated to the International Confederation of Free Trade Unions (I.C.F.T.U.). The Trade Unions Ordinance of 1952 requires all trade unions to register with the Registrar of Trade Unions. At 31 December 1956 twenty-nine trade unions were registered; twenty-one of employees and eight of employers. Among these were ten trade unions of African employees (including one of mixed African and Asian membership). Paid up members of the trade unions affiliated to the Kenya Federation of Labour number about 13,500; about 4,000 more are on the books, but in arrears with dues.[1]

The ban on African political organizations was lifted in June 1955, and a meeting was held in Nairobi on 18 December 1955, chaired by Mr. C. M. Argwings-Kodhek, at which it was proposed to set up a political party called the 'Kenya African National Congress', with Mr. Argwings-Kodhek as President. Its policy was to be slightly left of centre, and it would endeavour to cut across tribal affiliations. One of its functions would be to promote the formation of political organizations elsewhere in the Colony, as well as to open cordial relations with those already existing or proposing to form themselves. Three days later, the Minister for African Affairs announced that the new body would not be allowed to register, since it had as one of its objectives the creation of a colony-wide political party, and this cut across declared government policy. While the Emergency continued, the Government could not permit the formation of an organization, which, previous experience showed,

---

[1] *Commerce and Industry in Kenya 1956–57* (Govt. Printer, Nairobi, 1957), Appendix 16, pp. 85–86, and Labour Dept. *Annual Report for 1956* (Govt. Printer, Nairobi, 1957).

might be used to further the aims of the terrorists. Furthermore, the Government could not allow members of the K.E.M. tribes to join a political party. The minister concluded with the statement that the name of the party was also unacceptable to the Government.

After this set-back, doubtless anticipated, Mr. Kodhek formed the Nairobi District African Congress (N.D.A.C.), which was in due course accepted as a legitimate association. As mentioned earlier, the paid-up membership of the Congress amounted only to 367 in April 1957, and its organization was not strong. But an organization did exist, and represented a considerable floating body of adherents in addition to those who paid dues. Mr. Kodhek therefore appeared to have a good deal in his favour when he let it be known early in November 1956 that he proposed to be a candidate in the Nairobi constituency. His candidature was (as explained earlier) loosely associated with those of other members of the 'A–K' group in Nyanza Central, Nyanza South, and Rift Valley.

Mr. Mboya's candidature and the split in the N.D.A.C. Events then took a new turn, still somewhat obscure, of which we record only what can be adequately documented.

Mr. Tom Mboya arrived back in Nairobi on the last day of October, after thirteen months' absence from the Colony. When he was questioned at the airport, he said that it was premature to make any statement about the possibility of his standing at the election. He added, 'I was merely considering putting my name forward.' He went on to say that it would be necessary to consult friends and colleagues before making a decision.

Just over a month later Mr. Mboya decided to stand,[1] but at the same time made it clear that he did not condone the Government's method of elections.

In the meantime, the N.D.A.C. was being accused of having no policy, and steps were taken to correct this impression. A letter published in the *East African Standard* on 3 November, set out five major points in the Congress's attitude. These were:

  (i) opposition to the idea of multi-racial government and the intention to 'smash the Lyttelton Plan';
 (ii) the intention to throw open the White Highlands to African occupation;
(iii) opposition to the Coutts method of elections;
 (iv) a demand that 50 per cent. of the unofficial seats in Legislative Council should be filled by Africans; and
  (v) the abolition of the colour bar.

---

[1] *East African Standard*, 7 Dec. 1956.

The N.D.A.C. were also finding difficulties over holding meetings. In mid-December, for example, a meeting was cancelled because it did not conform to the official requirement that only certain halls might be used for political meetings. In practice this ruling effectively limited meetings to about 600. There was also a difficulty because of the rule that members of the K.E.M. tribes were not to attend meetings unless in possession of a 'loyalty certificate', and separate entrances had to be used for them so as to enforce this. The administration later lifted these restrictions (pointing out that this was not due to pressure from the N.D.A.C.), but insisted that of the K.E.M. tribes 'only those who have "loyalty certificates" will be allowed to make speeches'. The strong impression of the writer was that no restrictions were placed on anyone who wished to contribute during question time.

On Monday, 14 January 1957, the news broke that a serious split in the ranks of the N.D.A.C. had occurred at the weekend. Six members of the Executive Committee 'suspended' Mr. Argwings-Kodhek, the President, and Mr. J. H. Gaya, the secretary, for alleged mis-management of the Congress. It was announced that six provisional office-bearers would take office until the next meeting of the Committee. Seven allegations were made, of which the following were the most important:

(i) Argwings-Kodhek and Gaya had failed to form a proper Executive Committee and by this failure had managed the Congress 'without the people's mandate'.

(ii) Meetings were conducted without an agenda, and officials had deliberately avoided the question of the election of officers.

(iii) Elections for office bearers were overdue since last November.

(iv) The membership register was not up to date.

The junta which took this step announced that their Committee would run the Congress until they arranged a meeting at which 'the people will elect their leaders'. In overhauling the machinery of the new Congress it was regretted that 'we shall have to dispense with the services of the Founder, Mr. Gaya'.

Argwings-Kodhek was not slow to counter this bombshell. He denied all allegations. The people who signed the statement were, he said, 'self-appointed self-seekers'. He added that 'the so-called executive officer and secretary-general have for selfish, non-African and un-African reasons deviated from the spirit of the voice of the Congress'. Mr. Kodhek maintained that the meeting at which the decision was taken began merely as an invitation to drinks, and that the whole matter of 'suspension' was brought up later during the evening in the beer hall. His own explanation of events was that certain members of the 'irresponsible' group were annoyed when he was nominated as the Congress candidate for the African elections to Legislative Council, and had allied themselves with Mr. Tom Mboya. He ended: 'I am still President. These people have no right or power to suspend either myself or Mr. Gaya. I appointed Mr. Bhengo and Mr. Akuma [the new Secretary-General and executive officer] to the Committee and I can put them off or allow them to stay if they apologise.'

On the following day two denials were published, one from Mr. Chege, whose name had been included among the list of the dissident group—he could not subscribe to their 'degrading views'— and the other from Mr. Mboya. The latter's statement is of special interest since the natural inference about the Congress split was that either he or his lieutenants had engineered it, in order to capture the only effective electoral organization and undermine his main political opponent. Mr. Mboya denied that he had ever been consulted by the group making the allegations against Mr. Argwings-Kodhek, and said that he hoped to fight the election on principles rather than on personalities. If this is so, it is extraordinary that the only organized political party in Nairobi should have committed hara-kiri a few weeks before the election.

The damage had been done. On 17 January Mr. J. D. Howard, Registrar of Societies, announced that he had been obliged in the public interest to initiate an inquiry into the affairs of the N.D.A.C. He stated that 'the inquiry will relate to the production of books, including account books, and papers, the register of members, and in general a disclosure of the present state of the Congress'. Faced with this information, the two factions of the Congress resolved to hold a meeting at the following weekend to paper over the difficulties and to elect officers. However, the District Commissioner, Nairobi, banned the meeting on the grounds that information had reached him that a breach of the peace was likely to occur. His advice to Mr. Argwings-Kodhek was to let the fracas subside and hold the meeting in a fortnight's time. The dissident group welcomed the Registrar's inquiry and appealed to Congress members to assist in the investigation. The opportunity was also taken by the same group to point out that the 'suspension' of former officials had nothing to do with the March elections, and that Mr. Argwings-Kodhek was still regarded as the Congress candidate. It was regretted that he had 'confused the issue' by bringing the name of Mr. Tom Mboya into the internal affairs of the Congress. A few days later Mr. George Bhengo, a member of the splinter group who 'suspended' Argwings-Kodhek, announced that he and others were being victimized in Nairobi. 'Employers have been threatened that unless they discharge members involved, their products may be boycotted.' No such dismissal is known to have taken place.

The Administration discreetly deferred publication of its findings about Congress affairs until after the elections, and the report was not available until the end of March. It revealed certain irregularities, and the Registrar recommended (*inter alia*) that:

(i) books of account were to be audited by an approved auditor;
(ii) the membership register was to be rewritten;
(iii) a General Meeting of members was to be called at an early date, and to be attended only by paid-up members;
(iv) the business was to include the election of new office-bearers;
(v) a bank account should be opened.

The campaign. These events concentrated the limelight on Mr. Argwings-Kodhek and Mr. Mboya, who had in any case the electoral advantages that both had some organized backing and both belonged to the Luo tribe—as we have seen, Nyanza tribesmen are at present the largest element in Nairobi. But there were two other candidates, both substantial people.

Mr. Muchohi Gikonyo, a Kikuyu, of about forty, had been a civil servant at clerical level, then served on the Nairobi African Advisory Council, the Nairobi Municipal Council (as it then was), and (since 1952) on the Legislative Council and the Advisory Council on African Education. He is in business on his own as a bar and restaurant proprietor, and is vice-president of the Nairobi African Chamber of Commerce. For a short time in 1947/8 he had been general secretary of the Kenya African Union. He was now the only member of the Kikuyu, Embu, and Meru tribes in the field, and he stood as a member of the 'United Front' group.

Mr. Mackenzie Kasyoka is a member of the Akamba tribe, the third large group in Nairobi, and works as a dispenser in a firm of chemists. He was a member of Nairobi City Council and of various official and semi-official bodies in the Nairobi District: and stood now as a member of the 'Capricorn' group.

The only effective campaigning was by public meeting. Canvassing was out of the question for technical reasons. There is no direct postal delivery in East Africa, and all mail is collected from 'boxes' at post offices. In consequence, the register of electors gave electors' addresses only by post office box number, generally that of their place of work, and contained no indication of place of residence. It was thus almost impracticable to seek out 2,000 voters in a population of 140,000: and in any case the printed register was not available until ten days before the first phase of voting, that of 'expatriate' voters on 2 and 3 March.

Posters were not common in Nairobi, and those seen included some put up by candidates in other constituencies seeking 'expatriate' votes. Some supporters of candidates put up posters on their doors, and there were occasional brawls when a supporter of candidate X found a poster of candidate Y stuck to his door. A few more posters were seen on cars and lorries.

Meetings took place for the most part in halls situated in the locations or estates. There was also a medium-sized hall at the George VI Memorial Hospital, a training centre for African medical personnel at the other end of the city, and in the central area was the Desai Memorial Hall, capable of holding many hundreds. Except at weekends, meetings were held in the late afternoon or evening, and for the most part candidates carried on with their normal day-time activities—Mr. Argwings-Kodhek in his law chambers, Mr. Mboya in his trade union office, Mr. Kasyoka at the chemist's shop, and Mr. Gikonyo at his bar and restaurant. It was important that arrangements for booking halls should be made efficiently, since the District Commissioner required advance notice of all such gatherings and last-minute alterations were impossible. One candidate, at least, suffered from poor organization, and complained with some heat about the unreliability of his lieutenants, who sometimes booked the wrong hall, or even made arrangements for a meeting of which he had heard nothing.

Attendance at the meetings varied from about 100 to 600–700, partly depending on who was going to speak, partly on the size of the hall. Few women and few members of other races attended. Meetings at the George VI Hall were usually small, but on the other hand the audiences were something of an *élite* in terms of education, and they were always addressed in English, at their own request. Elsewhere Swahili was always used, although this did not rule out occasional remarks or questions in English. One of the most striking characteristics of nearly all the meetings was the very attentive and quiet manner in which the speakers were received. Heckling was never tried, and one gained the impression that at the present stage of *moeurs politiques* heckling verges on bad manners.

The quietness of the meetings was partly due to the technique followed by candidates. A chairman would introduce a speaker, frequently with a long and rambling address, the crowd remaining passive and giving the impression that they were not going to give anything away until they had heard the candidate himself. When the candidate himself started to address the meeting, about twenty minutes or so would pass without any reaction from the audience. Mr. Mboya was the one who generated enthusiasm most quickly, and he was a much better orator than the three other competitors. Mr. Argwings-Kodhek did not enjoy public speaking and left much to his lieutenants. His eve of poll meeting was a good instance; it went on for over three hours, but Mr. Argwings-Kodhek only spoke for thirty-five minutes. After the speeches, many of the members in the audience did not confine themselves to short questions but insisted on rambling on for up to ten minutes. These long-winded questioners were listened to with a remarkable, even incomprehensible, degree of patience. There was one old man dressed in a long khaki jacket, who turned up regularly at meetings held at the Desai Memorial Hall and seldom asked his 'question' in less than ten minutes. Not more than about ten to twenty questions were asked at each meeting. These followed a standard pattern regardless of who was speaking. The most popular were: Do you support the Lyttelton Plan? Are you in favour of an eight years' compulsory education scheme? (There were many variations on the educational question. Audiences made it clear that they were opposed to the Beecher Report,[1] the basis of the Government's African educational system). Would you accept a post as a minister? How can only eight Africans make any difference to the laws passed in Legislative Council? Why is there a Ministry of African Affairs and not ministries for the other races? How do the European and Asian get rich? What should the African do to prevent being discriminated against? Can you not help your people best by remaining poor? (Candidates did not like dealing with this question.)

Candidates varied in their approach to their subject matter. Mr. Kasyoka, for example, used the four slogans adorning his poster—Peace, Wealth, Progress (or prosperity) and Equality—as pegs on which to hang his address. His audience did not respond with any enthusiasm to remarks about the Capricorn Contract, and it was noticeable that he caused most excitement when he left the theme of multi-racial harmony. All candidates could be sure of some sort of response when they referred to the alleged misdemeanours of Asian shopkeepers, and the White Highlands were a universal focus of attack. Mr. Kasyoka pointed out that he had chosen the cow as his election symbol because (formerly) 'the wealth of the Akamba resided in the animal'. 'Give us the White Highlands and my Cow will yield many gallons' proved a very popular line.

[1] *African Education in Kenya* (Report of a Committee under the chairmanship of Archdeacon Beecher) (Nairobi, Govt. Printer, 1949).

Cutting across the general issues of the election was the personal feud between Mr. Argwings-Kodhek and Mr. Mboya. It was alleged that Mr. Mboya referred to Mr. Argwings-Kodhek's European wife, asking the question, 'Will our secrets be safe from the Europeans if Kodhek is elected?' The question was also asked why, if Kodhek was such a good lawyer, he hadn't defended Jomo Kenyatta? Mr. Kodhek replied by drawing attention to Mr. Mboya's youth, and asserted that he had not been particularly successful in organizing the trade union movement and would probably make a mess of organizing political matters. There were clearly limits to the dividends that personal recrimination could yield, and an uneasy truce prevailed in the latter part of the campaign.

These two always attracted the largest audiences, and this itself was some indication of the way in which votes were to be given. Mr. Gikonyo, the sitting member, (so many said) was not putting his full effort into the campaign and intended to retire from politics. At one meeting which he was to address, the only people present were three Africans playing draughts in a corner, who were some-what startled at being disturbed. Mr. Gikonyo put this down to poor liaison work by his organizers. Mr. Mathu, who was almost the only 'outside' politician to come to Nairobi, appeared just before the 'ab-sent voters' polled and held some successful meetings. He emanated the professional confidence usual among full-time politicians, and felt no doubt about his forthcoming success in Central Province. He stated, and insisted on, the view that voting along tribal lines was a thing of the past and had become a sort of *idée fixe* with Europeans.

'*Expatriate*' *voting*. For the expatriate voters there were set out at each polling station seven ballot-boxes (in Northern Province eight boxes, as it was not a constituency in its own right) corresponding to the seven 'home' constituencies. There were ninety-one such polling stations in the whole country, situated for the most part at District Commissioners' or District Officers' offices. In Nairobi there was one absent voters' polling station, in the building of the officer in charge, Nairobi Extra-Provincial District, near the centre of the city. The resident Nairobi voters, the following week, also had only one polling station, at the District Commissioner's office situated near the Southern Estates, but elsewhere throughout the country there were many more polling stations (302 in all) for the main body of voters than for the 'expatriates'.

Upon arriving at the polling station, the expatriate voter presented the voting card which he had obtained at the time of registration. No provision was made for those who had lost their voting cards. The card was checked againt the voters' roll, the larger part of the card was torn off (it had six perforations), and the smaller portion was returned to the voter. The voter's name and the number of votes to which he was entitled was then called out by the presiding officer or the clerk in charge of the roll, and a ballot paper of the same colour as the voting card was handed to him. The ballot form was stamped and the voter's serial number was then entered on the counterfoil. A mark against the voter's name in the register served as a check against personation.

All this applied also to the main voting a week later. There was, however, one important difference between the ballot paper of an absent voter and that used by ordinary voters. The absent voter was to mark a cross against the name of the candidate of his choice; the ordinary voter was only required to take his paper and place it in the box marked with that candidate's symbol. The absent voter, having made his cross, put the ballot paper in the appropriate constituency box. To have had separate boxes for each candidate in each of the 91 polling stations would have created grave administrative problems, for instead of having 638 boxes (90 × 7, plus 8 for Northern Province) over 3,000 boxes would have been required; hence the need to proceed by marking ballot papers.

There was no evidence of a 'trade' in voting cards either during the expatriate voting or on the main polling day. On the basis of the very slender evidence available when the count took place at Nairobi (only about thirty votes were cast for the Nairobi candidates by expatriate voters),[1] it did not seem as if marking a cross raised any difficulties. There were no spoilt papers from this source. No data are available from the rest of the country.

Nairobi had more expatriate voters—about 1,200—than any other constituency, and the behaviour of voters there was watched with interest by politicians all over the colony as an indication of what was likely to happen a week later. The turn-out in Nairobi was just under 50 per cent. and some areas did much better—Nakuru, for instance, had 75 per cent. But on the whole the percentage polling was low, and certainly no one expected the high returns of the following week. Some ordinary voters came to the polls a week early and had to be turned away: some 'expatriates' returned to their home constituencies and tried to vote there, but found that this was not permitted. But on the whole the complicated arrangements were got through smoothly and in good humour.

After the voting was finished 372 sealed boxes from various constituencies, were sent to Nairobi for redistribution; the remainder followed the shortest geographical route. This was done by means of

[1] And these (see Table 6) numbered only sixteen.

road and air transport, the boxes remaining in charge of authorized officers during travel. Many boxes travelled hundreds of miles to the central store where they were placed under a day and night guard. A substantial proportion of all boxes received appeared to be empty. When all had been collected they were sorted into groups corresponding to the constituencies, and were sent off again on their journey to the appropriate constituency, where they were opened and counted at the same time as the local votes. There is no evidence that expatriate votes affected the result in any constituency.

The scheme proved cumbrous but workable as a substitute for postal voting in a country where the working population is mobile, but postal communication is poor and the level of literacy is low. Even where the number of constituencies involved is small, the system requires voting by marked ballot papers dropped in a single box: with eight constituencies only, the number of boxes to be set out in each polling station was inconveniently large, and with more constituencies it would become prohibitive. The alternatives will be to move either to ordinary postal voting or (if this is felt to discriminate unfairly against illiterates) to a system by which each voter is given in the polling station an addressed envelope as well as his ballot paper, marks the paper, seals it in the envelope, and hands both to the presiding officer for transmission.

Final stages of campaign, voting, result. During the last week before the main voting, Mr. Mboya decided to send by post an appeal to all those whose names appeared on the register. No other candidate followed his example. Written in English on one side and Swahili on the other, the sheet was headed by the words 'Elect Tom Mboya the Workers' Candidate. Place your ballot paper in the box with my name and symbol of a cock.'

The main part of Mr. Mboya's appeal is reproduced below; it was in heavy black print.

I shall fight for our political freedom; human dignity; economic opportunities; higher wages and standards of living; security in old age; greater loan facilities and abolition of any unnecessary restrictions on our farmers, traders and businessmen; greater educational facilities for our children, and literacy for all; opportunity for Africans to advance in the Civil Service, Police Force and the Army, the elimination of colour-bar and race discrimination; the White Highlands and the altering of the present constitution of the Government of Kenya; judicial enquiry into the administration of justice and detention camps. I will aim at the creation of democracy on the principle of one man—one vote, and majority rule.

About two days before voting took place both Mr. Argwings-Kodhek and Mr. Mboya presented their followers with lapel labels. Mr. Kodhek's bore the initials A–K and the lion symbol, while Mr. Mboya's read 'Vote Tom Mboya' with the cock symbol.

Mr. Argwings-Kodhek appeared to be rather put out by Mr. Mboya's last-minute appeal, and at one of his meetings a supporter on the platform produced the sheet and proceeded to tear it up, urging those in the audience to do likewise. This manœuvre proved something of a failure, for during question time an African asked why Kodhek had not read the appeal through quietly at home and torn it up there if he did not like it. To do this at a public meeting was very bad manners. The African was not convinced by the explanation given. Another of Mr. Argwings-Kodhek's platform surprises also failed. This was when he dramatically produced a copy of a telegram sent that day to Mr. Nkrumah, congratulating him on Ghana's attainment of self-government. As there was no response from the audience he announced that there would be a minute's silence in appreciation of the great event. On another occasion, Mr. Kodhek drew attention to a passage in his manifesto 'The A–K Plan', in which he had written:

In Kenya at present there are over 6,000,000 Africans. If each of these were to contribute a small sum of 10/– only to a common fund, we could raise sixty million shillings. From the interest accruing from this amount we could build at least two schools and one hospital each year in the districts without begging anybody for help.

He went on to say that if the money were invested and only got a 2 per cent. return that would come to——here there was a pause while he turned to his platform supporters to give him the figure, but despite vigorous work with pencil and paper no one appeared to be able to work the sum out, and Kodhek finished lamely by saying: 'Anyway, it's a large sum of money.'

Mr. Mboya had one anecdote which never failed to raise considerable laughter. He said, 'I can buy a cup of tea in New York, Paris, and London, but they won't serve me in Government Road' (a main thoroughfare in Nairobi). Another very effective oratorical device which he used when speaking Swahili was suddenly to break into 'upcountry' when he wished to stress some point. (Upcountry Swahili is the pidgin Swahili spoken by some Asians and Europeans.) What was said was usually the sort of phrase used by an employer to his servants, and these remarks brought the speaker very close to his audience.

The main polling took place in Nairobi on Saturday and Sunday, 9 and 10 March 1957.[1] The writer observed proceedings at the only

[1] Nyanza North polled on the same days. The days in Rift Valley were 9th and 11th; Akamba and Central, 10th and 11th; Nyanza Central and South, 9th, 10th, and 11th. Coast polled on the 9th only.

polling station, which was close to the southern estate. Polling was brisk and during the first day averaged about 187 votes an hour. No administrative difficulties were encountered, the crowd which gathered to watch the proceedings was orderly, and there were no attempts to gatecrash. Only in one or two cases did the voter fail to put his ballot form properly into one of the four boxes—experience elsewhere was sometimes different. Strict supervision ensured that only one voter at a time was inside the voting room. Candidates had not been allowed to place their posters behind the relevant boxes, and so the voters were guided only by the symbols and names of the candidates on the boxes. On the Sunday the rate of flow of voters was much slower, as most of them (1,496 out of 2,078) had voted on the previous day. As the time grew near 6 p.m. when voting was to finish, the voters were reduced to a thin trickle. With ten minutes to go cheering and cat-calls were heard from the crowd of 2,000 or so gathered outside, and eventually there emerged a woman voter—who can only be described as an African 'Marilyn Monroe', dressed in black jeans and a yellow and black checked shirt.

The count took place with all the candidates present; all declared their complete confidence in success, and the excitement was heightened by the shouts and yells of supporters gathered outside. Many of these were wearing sandwich boards or lapel labels. There was much cock-crowing and lion-roaring in sympathy with Mr. Mboya and Mr. Argwings-Kodhek, but no similar shouts for Mr. Gikonyo and Mr. Kasyoka. The boxes were opened and counted in the alphabetical order of the candidates' names; this meant that Mr. Mboya's was opened last, and this increased the tension in the counting-room. It soon became clear that the expatriate vote was negligible, Mr. Argwings-Kodhek, for example, obtaining 25 votes, Mr. Gikonyo only 3. Mr. Kodhek's total vote was known first: then it was known that Mr. Gikonyo had obtained a mere 238 votes and Mr. Kasyoka only 133; it was obviously to be a straight struggle between Mr. Kodhek and Mr. Mboya.

The result was as follows:

Tom Mboya	2,138
C. M. G. Argwings-Kodhek . .	1,746
M. Gikonyo	238*
J. M. Kasyoka	133*
Majority	392

* Forfeited deposit.

Mr. Mboya's victory was greeted with great yells of triumph by his supporters and it became impossible for the District Commissioner to make his voice heard over the loudspeaker system. He had intended to thank everyone for the orderly manner in which the election had taken place. A large number of police kept the crowd from swamping the polling station.

2. *Other constituencies*

Outside Nairobi candidates were faced by extremely large areas in which it was next to impossible to campaign comprehensively. 'Whistle-stop' electioneering was ruled out by poor communications, and in any case many of the politicians would have found the method too costly. The Akamba constituency, for example, covered some 19,000 square miles. In these circumstances, candidates tended to limit their activities to market days and to speeches at the larger centres.

Two constituencies were of special interest; the first because of the light it throws on the evolution of African politics in Kenya, and the second because of the manner in which it illustrates the power of tribalism. These were Nyanza Central and Central Province.

The *Nyanza Central* constituency, which is predominantly a Luo area, was contested by Mr. Ohanga, the Minister for Community Development and the only African minister in the Colony. Among his four opponents was Mr. Oginga Odinga, President of the Luo Union, a tribal and welfare organization, and founder and President of the Luo Thrift and Trading Corporation, a body which has assisted Africans to set up in trade and business. The three other candidates were 'locational' in the sense of being well known only in a small part of the constituency (possibly Mr. Oranga, an ex-agricultural officer and a member of the Central Nyanza African District Council, was more widely known than the other two). It soon became clear that the real battle was between Mr. Ohanga and Mr. Odinga, and that it turned on their positions in relation to Mr. Odede, a former Nominated Member of Legislative Council, who had been detained in the early days of the Emergency on the grounds that he was attempting to drag the Luo into Mau Mau. It was not difficult in certain quarters to build Mr. Odede up as a martyr and a victim of oppression.

Mr. Ohanga was nominated in Mr. Odede's place, and was appointed a minister. The story which gained popular currency was that Mr. Ohanga was asked whether he regarded himself as simply a 'night-watchman' for Odede, and whether he would step down in his favour when Odede returned. To this, Mr. Ohanga is reported to have given a most emphatic negative.[1] This story has been enough

---

[1] Mr. Odede has been released, but is exiled from Nyanza.

to destroy a great deal of Mr. Ohanga's popularity. To make matters worse, it was asserted, Mr. Ohanga had not toured his constituency since his Legislative Council appointment. There were bitter complaints that when he was in Nyanza he spent the time when he was not in his office attending to business either at home or in an Asian bar adjoining his office. (In fact, Mr. Ohanga not only toured Nyanza but other areas in the Colony in his capacity as minister, a post which, in any case, demanded a fair amount of time in Nairobi.) Invidious comparisons were drawn between his activities and those of Mr. Michael Blundell, who was reported to have genuinely attempted to meet the people and learn about their problems while on tour in the area. It was also alleged, in fact unfairly, that while a minister Mr. Ohanga has done nothing to improve the lot of Africans, especially in his home area. These beliefs, however spread, were important factors in his defeat. When he was questioned, his activities as a minister appeared to loom large; his replies did not seem to give satisfaction.

Mr. Oginga Odinga was at pains to state his position on the Odede question, and to let it be known that he would step down in the latter's favour at the earliest possible moment. Being an office bearer in the two organizations mentioned above has enabled him to build up a special status in the eyes of many of his people, and this has undoubtedly helped him a great deal in the political field. Reports of his campaign speeches suggest that he mainly discussed local problems. On occasion he complained of African under-representation. During the campaign, he does not appear to have committed himself on the question of whether or not he would take a ministerial post. His whole approach was flamboyant compared with that of the other candidates. During the polling, and apparently during the campaign, he wore his own version of the Luo national costume; a photograph of himself in this garb appeared on his campaign poster. On the last day of polling, this costume had added adornments, and his driver was dressed in clothes reminiscent of a Red Indian's.

Neither of these candidates could be said to have a 'platform'; probably Mr. Ohanga came nearer, with his statement that he wished to advance African farmers by means of state loans and the like.

There are clear signs that 'nationalism' (or 'Africanism', to use Lord Hailey's word) as distinct from 'tribal feeling' now has strong roots amongst the Luo. There can be no doubt that their connexion with Government was a considerable political disadvantage to both Mr. Ohanga and Mr. Oranga. How great this was can only be a matter of conjecture, but it was certainly significant.

In *Nyanza South* the Kisii are predominant—21,477 out of 25,177 electors—but the winner was a Jaluo, Mr. L. G. Oguda, a teacher and farmer.

In *Nyanza North*, Mr. W. W. W. Awori, who is a Jaluo and was the sitting member of Legislative Council, was opposed by five other candidates. The ethnic composition of this area is by no means homogeneous, the Luo being only one tribe among many. An analysis of votes cast for the winning candidate Mr. M. Muliro (who obtained only about 30 per cent. of the votes cast), shows that he secured 6,169 votes in Elgon-Nyanza District, his home district, and only 518 votes (the smallest number of any candidate) in North Nyanza District—North Nyanza forms part, the larger part, of Nyanza North constituency. Furthermore, a factor which was to prove decisive in Central Province also played its part in this constituency. About 11,000 voters registered in Elgon-Nyanza, only 8,000 registered in the more populous district of North Nyanza. This was due to greater publicity and greater efforts by the District administration and the chiefs. Also, the Registering Officers visited sub-locational headquarters to a greater extent than in North Nyanza. Another factor which may have been of importance was that land consolidation was further advanced (i.e. was partially accepted) in Elgon-Nyanza than in the neighbouring District. Mr. Muliro succeeded in capturing the lion's share of the votes in the three locations (5,697 out of a total of 6,728 cast for him in the whole constituency) which are predominantly inhabited by his tribesmen, the Babukusu. It is also probable that he secured a certain amount of support from the Roman Catholics. (Another candidate openly attempted to use religion for political purposes, but this completely misfired.) Mr. Awori, who was strongly tipped to win, succeeded in getting the most evenly distributed votes of all candidates in both districts. His election poster was the most ambitious effort of the whole election here; part of it consisted of a photograph of himself seated on his election symbol, an elephant.

In *Rift Valley* Mr. Daniel arap Moi, a Tugan schoolteacher, the sitting member, was opposed by two Masai candidates. There were 5,030 voters and 1,684 of these were in the Nandi District. Mr. arap Moi's home district registered 968 votes. This was regarded as a safe seat for the sitting Legislative Council Member, and indeed it turned out to be so. One of Mr. arap Moi's opponents had previously left the district under unfortunate circumstances, the other was a Capricorn candidate who could hardly be expected to gain many votes in a constituency contiguous to and partly within the White Highlands. Only a dozen or so women registered in the area.

The pastoral tribes in the region, the Masai, the Suk, and the Baringo are essentially moving populations, their cattle following the grazing over wide areas, and the chief administrative problem was the setting up of polling stations in such a way that all who wished to register and vote might do so. Even so, some voters must have spent two or three days in journeying to vote and then returning home. The Registration Officer is reported to have said, 'In my opinion the registration reflects the efforts of the administration far more than the interest of the population.'

In *Central Province* the main battle was between Mr. Eliud Mathu, a Kikuyu, who had been a member of Legislative Council for thirteen years, and Mr. Bernard Mate, a graduate of the University of Wales, the Meru candidate. Mathu was the most outstanding African leader to emerge in Kenya during the last dozen years (apart from the imprisoned Kenyatta), and he had shown himself capable of standing on his own feet in Legislative Council and making a useful contribution. He was also too astute a politician to be indentified too closely with the Kenya administration, unlike some of the less active nominated members, and was thus able to keep himself in a position of 'availability' in the post-Mau Mau period.

On the other hand, he was working against the handicap of the Meru electorate. As has been explained, this was relatively large— 21,145 out of 35,644 registered electors, although the Meru constitute only about 20 per cent. of the population of the constituency. This was due partly to the energy of the Meru District Commissioner during registration,[1] partly to the fact that the Meru were less deeply involved than the Kikuyu in Mau Mau and gained proportionately more loyalty certificates. In addition to Mr. Mathu and Mr. Mate, there was an Embu candidate, Mr. J. Nyagah, who would also attract tribal votes, and two other Kikuyu candidates of only local importance. The result was that Mr. Mate was returned with a majority of 10,000 over Mr. Mathu.

A visitor to the *Akamba* constituency (it is reported) would have seen few signs of electioneering. The remoteness of the outlying parts of the constituency is illustrated by the fact that one returning officer had to travel 300 miles to open his polling station. There

[1] A more elaborate explanation is given in a press report. Mr. Mate (it was reported) '. . . owed his election to the great influence of the Njure Elders, the oldest indigenous native authority which still retains power and influence. The District Commissioner at Meru advised the Njure Elders that the Meru should register for the vote. The Njure Elders told the Meru to register and they did so. They then told them to vote for Mr. Mate and they did so; and that was the end of Mr. Mathu's chance of election' (African World Correspondent, *African World*, May 1957, p. 21). The writer has no other evidence on this.

were three candidates, all teachers. There is no evidence that any of them took positive steps to encourage registration: and their campaigns were limited to open-air meetings on market days. No candidates from other districts visited Akamba during the campaign, there was no candidate from the A–K or Capricorn groups, and one faded poster on a lorry was the only token seen to show that an election was in progress. The constituency is somewhat remote from the issues which generate heat elsewhere in Kenya, and this helps to explain the return by a small majority of Mr. James Nzau Muimi, the sitting member.

The *Coast* constituency presents special problems of interpretation. Mombasa, the chief town and the main port of both Kenya and Uganda, is reputed to have 100,000 Africans living in it, drawn from sixty-seven tribes. The largest group is the Akamba with 12,000, followed by the Luo with about 10,000. Thus the bulk of Africans living there are 'foreigners' from other districts, who come to provide the manual labour required at the port and elsewhere. Standing for the constituency was Mr. J. Jeremiah, who had been a representative member for eight years and had been a Parliamentary Secretary under the Lyttelton arrangements. He was sometimes referred to as 'the non-speaking secretary'. There were four other candidates, one of whom, Mr. F. J. Khamisi, was associated with the Mombasa Democratic Union, a district political party, the paid-up membership of which is believed to be less than 100. Mr. Khamisi was also a Roman Catholic and a Nominated Member of the Mombasa Municipal Board; in addition, he supported the Capricorn Contract.[1] Only 870 voters registered in Mombasa itself, out of 7,912 in the constituency, in spite of the size of the town; there were also 541 'expatriates' there. The largest number registering came from Kwale District (2,326) followed by the Teita District with some 2,262 voters. Mr. Jeremiah was a Wateita, as also was Mr. D. Mwanyumba, another candidate. The smallness of the electorate and the large number of tribes involved cut across tribal considerations to some extent, and Mr. R. G. Ngala's victory with 3,406 votes was clearly an 'extra-tribal' one, since he is a Giriama from Kilifi, which had only 733 registered voters. The campaign was conducted in a friendly way and there were no 'smear' attacks. On one occasion all five candidates appeared on the platform together.

10. *Conclusions*

This study of the election was of necessity made from the centre, and the account given portrays inadequately the complexity of the

---

[1] But see p. 426 and footnote (2) on p. 427.

situation in the constituencies. Many interesting problems about the emergence of local organizations and personalities and about the impact of an election on the ordinary voter can only be explored by detailed studies at the constituency level. We have attempted only to illustrate the inter-play of various factors involved in a fluid political situation; territorial issues, 'race relations', personalities, political and other organizations, tribal and local interests, economic and social change. These factors inter-acted differently in different constituencies, and in the absence of territory-wide parties little was done to prepare voters to look at the election as something affecting Kenya and East Africa as a whole.

We offer four comments only. First, the administration are to be congratulated on the way the election was conducted. The low level of registration was disappointing, and might have been improved if it had been possible to devote more administrative resources to a special effort; in addition, the production of publicity material such as posters and leaflets fell short of the highest technical standards, and might have been designed so to make a greater visual impact. For instance, it could probably have been more effective to have one series of posters and leaflets to catch the eye with a simple general appeal, another to provide information about the complexities of the system. Nevertheless, a start has been made, and the level of registration is bound to improve from year to year. The mechanism of registration worked well and without controversy, as did that of polling. In the end 79·86 per cent. of the electorate voted, using 81·067 per cent. of the available votes: this was an excellent record, and some of the local polls were very high indeed. There were only 610 rejected papers among over 100,000 voters, a trivial percentage and much smaller than is usual in European elections.

Secondly, from the point of view of candidates the position about organization was not so satisfactory. District political associations proved a poor failure, and the election has not served to invigorate them. It seems that the demand for posts of leadership in small organizations is far more disruptive of smooth personal relationships than it would be in a larger body. The tendency is to hive off and form a fresh organization, thus diluting the already small membership. District political associations seem especially prone to this form of disease. When the ban is lifted on Kenya-wide parties it seems likely that these tendencies will be reversed, and that something more like the 'law of oligarchy' will prevail.

Candidates approached a difficult problem of campaigning with limited resources of money and organization, and their troubles were increased by restrictions on meetings, the absence of radio-broadcasting facilities, the virtual absence of an effective vernacular press, the large size of constituencies, the form of the register, the multiple vote and the inexperience of the electorate. It is remarkable that so primitive a form of campaigning was successful in bringing a high proportion of the electorate to the poll. Undoubtedly, those who had registered felt a strong obligation to vote. There is some slight evidence to show that pressure was brought to bear on those who had already registered by those who had missed their opportunity—doubtless as a result of seeing that the election was 'genuine'.

The position in Nairobi was unlike that in any other constituency. A small urban electorate is an ideal field for corrupt practices in a hotly contested election, suspicion and allegations of corruption were widespread, but no case was proved. Mr. Argwings-Kodhek was in July 1957 struck off the Roll of Advocates, on the ground that he had collected rents on behalf of a woman who was in detention and had failed to put the money into his client's account. Fraud was not alleged and the case was not directly related to the election. A petition against the result of the election was, however, made by a group of voters, who alleged undue influence and the sale and purchase of ballot forms. The procedure under the Ordinance is not in open court but it is reported that an inquiry was made on the instructions of the Governor, who decided after receiving a report that such irregularities as had occurred had not affected the result of the election, and therefore dismissed the petition.

Thirdly, there is the question of the franchise, which has two aspects: qualitative suffrage and multiple vote. It is clear that, whatever one's theory of the franchise, qualitative suffrage had in this situation some advantages. The 'quality' of the voters may not have affected—probably did not affect—the results, but the limitation on the number of votes kept the administrative problem within bounds. The result was in at least one case virtually decided by differences in registration: with a wider franchise such divergences might have been more numerous and larger. The 'first past the post' system of voting was adopted without much thought, as being the ordinary practice in Britain and in Kenya: but probably there was no alternative in the circumstances, as the electorate was hardly sophisticated enough for proportional representation by single transferable votes, and the use of a list system with or without proportional representation was impossible in the absence of territory-wide parties. The 'first past the post' system can, however, have odd results in the absence of effectively competing parties, as for instance in the British Guiana election of 1953; in the present case, although only four candidates secured half the votes cast, there were no really startling examples of minority successes, and this may have been in part because the number of candidates was kept within bounds by limitations on the size of the electorate and by the relative difficulty of qualifying as a candidate.

The basic figures about the use of the multiple vote are given in an appendix to this chapter, and can be analysed in various ways. The only point which emerges with certainty is that in all constituencies except one, 3-voters polled a higher percentage than 2-voters, 2-voters than 1-voters. There are unexplained differences between the percentage of voters in different categories in different constituencies: and there are also curious differences in the distribution between candidates of the votes of the three classes of voters. But the results would have been exactly the same if each voter had had one vote only; candidates certainly did not attempt to appeal to one category of elector more strongly than to others, and it is difficult to see any single explanation of the differences in voting between different categories. In fact, the experiment does not strengthen the case for the multiple vote as a means of improving the standard of political debate: on the other hand, it need not tell against it as a device for giving additional 'weight' to special categories of voters in a diverse electorate, because the electorate was in this case relatively uniform in each constituency, apart from tribal differences, and the issue of 'weighting' did not really arise.

Finally, had the election a result? Discounting the intemperance of speech usual among politicians of all 'races' in Kenya, it may be said that African nationalism (of not too virulent a brand) proved the most popular line with voters; it may also be said that the rejection of most of the sitting members was in some sense a censure on them for too close association with government. On the tribal level, pre-eminence has, at least for the present, passed from the Kikuyu of Central Province to the Luo of Nyanza. The grouping of the elected members in the Legislative Council is uncertain; it is natural to expect a certain rivalry for leadership, and this can only be conducted by bidding for popular support on the basis of exploitation of grievances, pressure for African advancement, and dissociation from responsibility for government, many of whose actions are bound to be unpopular. At the time of writing,[1] elected African members had agreed to refuse ministerial office under the Lyttelton Plan, and were pressing for an increase in elected African members to twenty-three. Government on its side shows no inclination to permit violent popular agitation, and African leaders are

[1] October, 1957.

themselves aware of the lesson of Mau Mau about the futility of violent and destructive action. There is no doubt that the election has altered in many ways the conditions of politics in Kenya and that a new phase has begun.

APPENDIX

African Election Results, March 1957

(Sitting members are marked by an asterisk)

SOURCE: *Parliamentary Debates, House of Commons*, 5th Ser., vol. dlxviii, Written Answers, p. 42.

	1 Vote	2 Votes	3 Votes	Total voters	Total votes
(1) NYANZA NORTH					
M. Muliro .	2,656	1,571	310	4,537	6,728
W. W. W. Awori* .	2,744	1,071	395	4,210	6,071
C. N. W. Siganga .	2,095	785	258	3,138	4,439†
J. D. Otiende . .	984	224	107	1,315	1,753
W. B. Akatsa . .	714	259	138	1,111	1,646
J. G. W. Kadima .	700	215	72	987	1,346†
	9,893	4,125	1,280	15,298	21,983†
Rejected papers . .	(73)	(24)	(6)	(103)	(139)
Percentage voting .	79·2	74·3	70·5	77	..
(2) NYANZA CENTRAL					
A. O. Odinga . .	2,266	1,830	1,130	5,226	9,316
B. A. Ohanga* . .	935	644	379	1,958	3,360
H. D. Odaba . .	175	236	75	486	872
G. N. Onyolo . .	230	128	52	410	642
E. P. Oranga . .	180	75	24	279	402
	3,786	2,913	1,660	8,359	14,592
Rejected papers . .	(22)	(30)	(12)	(64)	(118)
Percentage voting .	64·4	72·8	87·9	71	..

	1 Vote	2 Votes	3 Votes	Total voters	Total votes
(3) NYANZA SOUTH					
L. G. Oguda . .	3,802	3,990	700	8,492	13,882
J. K. Kebaso . .	1,684	1,734	1,016	4,434	8,200
T. arap Towett . .	1,487	1,719	461	3,667	6,308
J. J. Bonga . .	745	798	298	1,841	3,235
G. Orinda Okun .	242	347	121	710	1,299
F. K. arap Chumah* .	156	182	67	405	721
	8,116	8,770	2,663	19,549	33,645
Rejected papers . .	(78)	(155)	(35)	(268)	(493)
Percentage voting .	70·5	77·1	84·2	74·7	..
(4) RIFT VALLEY					
D. T. arap Moi* .	1,145	1,013	534	2,692	4,773
J. K. Tipis . .	209	372	129	710	1,340
J. M. ole Tameno .	78	133	61	272	527
	1,432	1,518	724	3,674	6,640
Rejected papers . .				(29)	(70)
Percentage voting .	71·7	70·2	82·9	73·0	..
(5) CENTRAL					
B. Mate . . .	16,052	3,165	792	20,009	24,758
E. Mathu* . .	3,907	3,134	1,533	8,574	14,774
J. Nyagah . . .	1,800	1,279	442	3,521	5,684
D. Waruhiu . .	621	458	163	1,242	2,026
S. Kioni . . .	395	269	144	808	1,365
	22,775	8,305	3,074	34,154	48,607
Rejected papers . .				(13)	
Percentage voting .	94	96·5	99·4	95·2	..
(6) AKAMBA					
J. N. Muimi* . .	3,812	1,732	525	6,069	8,851†
D. N. Mumu . .	1,811	1,522	724	4,057	7,027
M. J. Makilya . .	1,310	612	195	2,117	3,119
	6,933	3,866	1,444	12,243	18,997†
Rejected papers . .	(50)	(28)	(5)	(83)	(121)
Percentage voting .	60·6	83·4	84·6	68·9	..

	1 Vote	2 Votes	3 Votes	Total voters	Total votes
(7) COAST					
R. G. Ngala . .	1,235	613	315	2,163	3,406
D. Mwanyumba .	781	579	200	1,560	2,539
F. J. Khamisi . .	766	434	211	1,411	2,267
C. M. Mwashumbe .	260	124	68	452	712
J. Jeremiah* . .	204	79	42	325	488
	3,246	1,829	836	5,911	9,412
Rejected papers . .	(12)	(27)	(11)	(50)	(99)
Percentage voting .	72·3	74·4	83·9	74·7	..
(8) NAIROBI . .					
T. J. Mboya . .	280	485	296	1,061	2,138
C. M. G. Argwings-Kodhek . . .	187	391	258	836	1,743
M. Gikonyo* . .	19	42	45	106	238
J. M. Kasyoka . .	30	32	13	75	133
	516	950	612	2,078	4,252
Rejected papers . .	(0)	(0)	(0)	(0)	..
Percentage voting .	78·8	89·1	92·3	87·2	..
Percentage voting in all constituencies together	78·0	80·8	86·8	79·86	..

† These figures have been amended since the Hansard figure is clearly an incorrect total of the votes as separately recorded in the first three columns.

ACKNOWLEDGEMENTS

THE author's thanks are due to the Colonial Social Science Research Council and to the Makerere College Central Research Grants Committee for financial assistance; to Mr. R. D. F. Ryland, the Supervisor of Elections, Mr. L. F. G. Pritchard, M.B.E., Secretary for African Affairs, Mr. A. B. Tannahill, M.C., District Commissioner, Nairobi; to Mr. E. P. Wilkinson, Deputy African Affairs Officer, Nairobi City, and to members of the Kenya Department of Information, for much help and encouragement; and to the four candidates in the Nairobi constituency who spared time for discussion in spite of the pressure of work during their campaigns.

VIII

SOME CONCLUSIONS

1. *Introductory*

THE elections described in this book are doubly alien in Africa. In the first place, the idea of government based on an electoral system is characteristically Western. There are other societies in which rulers owe their authority to consent and choice, but it is only in the West that this conception is expressed through the system of large-scale elections. A working electoral system is a curious mixture of legal and administrative ingenuity with imprecise and unspoken understandings about the rules of the game. The mixture is an extremely complex one, and it is rather different in each country where elections have been established, but everywhere a continuous thread of tradition links the notion of elections with the rest of Western politics. In the West elections in a sense *mean* the tradition which leads from the practice of democracy in the ancient world through the medieval estates, the medieval church, and the English House of Commons, to the stabilization of representative government in the nineteenth century. A mass electorate can only choose its Government through a mechanism which is in many ways legalistic, artificial, arbitrary: but in the West such a mechanism is accepted, in spite of its imperfections, because it is securely established in the political habits of the community.

It may be possible for a similar process to take place in non-Western countries; indeed this is one of the things we mean when we express the hope that in the end democracy will triumph over dictatorship throughout the world. But if elections are stabilized outside the West they will in the process change their character. The English[1] device of an elected parliament has been quite securely established in some other countries of Western Europe, but naturalization has in each country created something new. There is perhaps no Eastern or African country in which the process has yet gone so far: it may take a generation, perhaps longer, to 'domesticate' an alien device in a new setting. But in some countries the process seems to have begun: above all in India, perhaps also in some other

[1] Only Sweden and Iceland have also a continuous and independent parliamentary history.

Asiatic countries. Elsewhere, it has come to a standstill, either because elections have been tried and then abandoned, or because they have become a mere façade, used to give a 'democratic' appearance to institutions of quite a different character.

Once the colonial power has withdrawn, the success or failure of elections depends almost wholly on forces within the country concerned. Of course in the modern world all domestic institutions respond in some degree to changes in world-wide fashions: manœuvring in external policy, the search for economic aid, changes in the balance of prestige, even mere chaffering for the best offer, all modify institutions through adaptation to trends of world politics. In this sense world politics already exist, though world government does not. This sort of interaction affects Western countries as much as it does those states in which elections are a new thing: it is very different from the colonial situation, in which elections are still an alien system managed by aliens.

It is this latter case with which we are concerned here. In each of the five elections described an electoral system for Africans has been created by Europeans and is still managed by Europeans, though Africans fill most of the subordinate positions in the administration. This stage in development is not confined to Africa. It has been passed by India, Burma, Pakistan, and Ceylon: Malaya, and in Africa, Ghana are just emerging from it; it is present in other British and French colonies, for instance in the British West Indies, Mauritius, Fiji, and Singapore. But the fact that our studies are all concerned with African territories gives them a certain additional unity, because in Africa electoral organization is superimposed on tribal organization, which has certain common features whether in Sierra Leone, Nigeria, or Kenya. In some African territories, notably those of East and Central Africa, there are both tribal divisions and communal divisions; one must look outside Africa, for instance to British Guiana, Trinidad, Fiji, or Mauritius, for examples of the effects of introducing elections in countries where the main divisions are racial or communal, not tribal.

The effect of this alien management of an alien institution is that each of our studies deals with two separate problems. First, how does the governing power manage elections? Does it succeed or fail in what it is trying to do? Secondly, how do these elections fit into the indigenous political system? How do they modify it, how does it modify them?

This division between alien administration and local politics is paradoxical, because in a developed electoral system administration and politics interlock. The political contest fought out within the system is a contest for the control of executive power. Unlimited executive power would include power to modify the system in favour of the victor, and so to destroy the system and prevent any future contest. Where elections are securely established this does not happen. That is to say, the power which they confer is used subject to certain limits. No politician escapes the temptation to modify the system in favour of his own side: modification of the system so as to support the régime against its enemies is familiar in France and Italy, exists (in a more stable and therefore less suspect form) in the countries of the Anglo-American tradition. But in spite of human failings, there do exist in Western countries unformulated rules about the sanctity of the rules themselves; and there are also formal devices designed to protect the rules of the game from manipulation by the players. No devices can make elections honest unless supported by political opinion; but much ingenuity has been spent upon arrangements tending to bias conduct in the right direction—provisions for non-political administration, for appeal to the courts, for the independent 'policing' of any attempts to use force, bribery, or fraud.

In Africa these devices for the separation of 'administration' from 'politics' are in the first instance brought in from outside. They represent European standards, not African standards; the European administrators are of necessity trying to arrange an election which will satisfy *them*, not one that will satisfy Africans. The administration is (as it were) part of a European political system *in partibus infidelium*: the administrators answer for their success to the House of Commons or to the *Conseil d'Etat*, not to local political opinion.

This division, which we are bound to follow in exposition, gives a certain air of artificiality, even of unreality, to this stage of politics: the air is more bracing when this stage has been passed, as in the Sudan, Malaya, Ghana, and in effect in the Central African Federation. Politics may then become dirtier, the interests at stake more open and vigorous in their tactics: but there is less risk of illusion and double-talk. An indigenous system must be found and made to work, the colonial power is no longer a screen and scapegoat: elections may become farcical, but it is also possible that their real advantages may at last be appreciated in a vivid, homely, and simple sense.

But to say that this last stage of colonial government seems artificial is not to condemn it. It exists because there is no choice. The introduction of elections (even, for instance, in Kenya, where the African population is less advanced politically than in the other countries described here) is enforced by a combination of circumstances: a balance of military and economic power which makes direct colonial government impracticable, a demand from new strata of African society for Western institutions from which they hope to gain power and prestige, a sentiment among Europeans that if they are to go it must be with honour, honour defined by European standards of good government and democracy.. The withdrawing powers and their administrators wish to leave behind democratic government and decent administration. Perhaps the administrators on the spot care most for the latter, and are not much impressed by the value of party politics, either at home or in Africa. But political opinion at home demands democracy. It would be hard for a British Government to withdraw from any territory except in favour of a régime which in some sense owed its power to elections held on a wide franchise. French opinion likewise has been committed to the export of French institutions. It has not (on the whole) favoured the creation of independent states copying the French model, but the National Assembly of the Fourth Republic contained about eighty overseas deputies in a total of about 625 members, and the French colonies in this sense are more closely integrated in French politics than are British colonies in British politics. A bloc of black *Deputés* with votes in Paris counts for more than the same number of leftish M.P.s wandering abroad. Besides, the writ of the *Conseil d'Etat* runs throughout the French colonial empire for all elections except those of the French National Assembly itself, and it sets standards of elegance in drafting and consistency in administrative practice to which the Colonial Office does not aspire.

2. Administration

Little need be said here about differences between the two models, French and English, from which African elections are derived, since the common elements in the problem are much more important. There is, however, one point of difference between French and British attitudes to elections which is perhaps seen in Africa in a simplified and exaggerated form. In both countries the party system forms in practice an integral part of the electoral system, so that the legal provisions and the practical working of the system are unintelligible without reference to the context of party organization. In some countries, notably the U.S.A. and Germany, this situation has led to the formal recognition of parties and the regulation of procedure within parties: this has not happened in France and Britain, which both avoid the legal regulation of parties. Nevertheless, France goes further than Britain in admitting the necessity of party organization. In the single-member constituencies of the British system the ballot papers bear only the names of candidates, not those of parties; under the French list system the lists between which voters choose almost always have a party name at their head, and most voters are voting explicitly for a party, not for individual candidates.

There are of course real difficulties in accepting fully the role of parties in elections in a country where elections are a new thing. Parties tend towards oligarchy, even in countries where political education is widespread; in less developed countries, to recognize parties officially may be in effect to hand over control of candidatures to very small cliques of politicians who are in a position to give or refuse party endorsement. The British are so conscious of these dangers that they try sometimes (as for instance in Kenya) to run elections and yet discourage parties. It is not likely that the French would ever seek a compromise in this way; elections to them mean of necessity parties, parties recognized in practice though not by law, and the representatives of the parties play a substantial part in each stage of electoral administration.

This is perhaps the only difference of principle which has much political importance: solutions to administrative difficulties also differ, but the differences are not much greater than those between different modifications of the British system, elastically applied in different situations.

It is striking that the worst administrative difficulties have not arisen where everyone expected them, in the process of polling. Sceptics about mass democracy in semi-literate countries used to express doubt about the possibility of getting illiterates to come forward and vote in an orderly and legal manner; they expected the system to break down as a result of low polls, spoilt papers, and open violence and corruption. The earliest indication that this was the wrong line of thought came in the first Indian election after independence, the election under universal suffrage in 1951. In that instance over 100 million people recorded their votes in perfect good temper and without the slightest threat to public order. The Indian public behaved as well as the public in Europe and America; and the same has happened elsewhere. There is of course always some risk of local disorder and confusion; this is inevitable in a time of public excitement, and an election would be a failure if it did not arouse excitement. If such excitement expressed itself in violence the situation would be beyond the power of the police or even the military to control: in practice, it seems that the public has everywhere controlled itself. Just how the purpose and the issues of the election appear to the public is not clear; but it is certain that election day has become something of a solemn national occasion everywhere.

This sentiment has in part been created by the administrators, but it seems to be stronger than anything normally generated by government information services. Orderly elections have in some sense become the badge of national consciousness, maturity, and independence: it is a mystery how this has happened and what there is in African life to which the sentiment attaches itself.[1] Whatever the explanation, the attachment is real and has greatly simplified what seemed to be the most difficult part of the job. Much is left for the administrator to do on polling day, but it is now clear that the real burden of his work comes earlier, when he has to toil through a series of intricate and tedious tasks which are quite beyond the comprehension of the public, even in Europe, and which therefore gain little public support. The most important of these[2] are the registration of voters, the recruitment, training, and management of staff for registration and polling, publicity for procedure at each stage, the organization of polling stations, their equipment and necessary transport, and (finally) the clearing up of contested issues after registration and after the election. That is not to say that methods of voting and control of public order on polling day are unimportant, and they are mentioned in their place later; but they are matters on which the administrator is working with the parties and the public, and he can make this part of his task relatively easy by simple, patient, and repeated explanation.

(a) *Registration.* Polling is impossible without some sort of register of electors. Even under complete universal suffrage there are limits on the eligibility of persons to vote, such as age, nationality, and freedom from positive disqualification (for instance through conviction for electoral offences); in addition, it is essential for orderly contests that each elector should be assigned to one constituency and one only, so that he can vote only in his proper place. These matters cannot be decided by adjudication within the polling station, and must be settled well in advance. Furthermore, under any system there must be a check to ensure that no voter votes twice. There are different devices which help to meet these difficulties separately, for instance the previous issue of voting cards to those entitled to vote, and the marking with indelible ink of the person of each voter as he

---

[1] This was written before the experience of resistance to elections in Buganda in 1958, an isolated example of 'traditionalism', looking backwards to a tribal kingdom, not forwards to a nation state.

[2] A more detailed study of these administrative problems as experienced in British colonies has been made by Mr. T. E. Smith, formerly of the Malayan Civil Service, under the auspices of Nuffield College, Oxford.

casts his vote: but the register is a compendious device to meet all of them together.

A register is in principle no more than a list of qualified voters established in advance of the election. It is convenient that it should be divided into separate sections for each constituency, and further sub-divided for each polling station. A voter is to vote only at 'his own' polling station, where the official in charge has before him the section of the list including the voter's name; the voter must identify himself as the person named, that name is then marked off, and he is given his ballot paper and admitted to vote. This system, once established, is simple, though not foolproof. The problem is to introduce it in countries where no *état civil* exists, where most people are illiterate and cannot spell their own names, where addresses are vague and the system of personal names has not adapted itself to the needs of a 'great society', so that there are large numbers of people whose names are indistinguishable; and to do all this with a very inadequate staff of clerks.

These problems are so great that on the whole they blot out the problem of adjudication about electoral qualifications, where these fall short of universal suffrage; but this can also prove difficult and is referred to separately below.

In Sierra Leone and in Senegal the register was based in part on existing records; in the former on the tax register for men in the Protectorate, in the latter on the census books held by each compound head for all members of the extended family belonging to his compound. But there was a substantial difference in practice, in that this was the first use of direct voting in territorial elections in Sierra Leone, whereas Senegal had had eight such elections since 1945, and there existed an electoral register which included almost as many names as that used for the 1957 election. In Nigeria tax registers had hitherto been used as electoral registers, but certain changes in the law made independent electoral registers essential from 1954 onwards; in Kenya the peculiarities of the franchise were such that it was necessary to have a separate electoral register from the first. It does not seem that use of an existing register simplified work very much. It did make unnecessary the intense drive for registration which is needed (as in Kenya) where registration depends wholly on the initiative of the voter, and no party organization exists which has sufficient interest and resources to act for him: the absence of such a drive was one reason why the provision for limited female suffrage virtually broke down in the Sierra Leone Protectorate. Use of an existing register may secure a higher *apparent* registration: but it probably produces no better *effective* registration, firstly, because where registration is automatic many of those registered do not realize at first that they are entitled to vote, and, secondly, because individual application by voters increases somewhat the chances that names will be entered on the register in a form that can be recognized and used on election day.

All who refer to this point agree about the difficulties presented by long lists of similar names, by variants in spelling dependent on the whims of clerks, by the labour required to see a list of names correctly through the processes of duplication and printing. Most of the territories seem to have secured a reasonably full and correct register; these registers are in principle 'permanent', that is to say, they remain in being from year to year, and corrections and changes are embodied annually; and there is therefore a chance that standards of registration will gradually improve. But this depends on the ability of political parties to see to it that their supporters register alterations and new claims accurately and promptly; and perhaps it is optimistic to expect this. It is in any event unlikely that the Administration can afford each year to spend time on the sort of publicity drive organized for the first register.

But even improved registers will not solve the problem of identification. In each of the elections described an attempt was made to give the voter some sort of card or ticket bearing the same particulars as his entry in the register; this was the best hope of establishing identity quickly and accurately on polling day, but it had difficulties of its own. Practice ranged from that in Kenya, where a voter could vote only on production of his electoral card (and could obtain a new card on polling day if he had lost it) to that in Sierra Leone, where slips recording entries in the register were produced only by the parties and only in some constituencies. But everywhere there was alarm lest electoral cards should become the object of traffic and an aid to personation; and in the Western Region of Nigeria there was further trouble about the issue by one party of cards marked with its symbol. There is not much doubt that the use of electoral cards or polling cards can be used by ingenious parties to strengthen their hold over their own supporters: but perhaps the risks of actual personation are not serious except in large towns. In the countryside distances are so great that a personator cannot move from one polling station to another, 'repeating'; in any case people are known by sight within a small community, and devices such as clipping a finger nail or marking the hand with gentian violet may be of some value. In larger towns it is difficult to imagine any effective remedy except the emergence of parties well enough organized to check one another's malpractices: under universal (or almost universal) suffrage the gain by personation is rarely so great as to outweigh a serious risk of detection and the consequent invalidation of the election.

(b) *Staff.* None of our authors was able to obtain precise data about the number and educational levels of the staff required to run an election of this kind, and about the time diverted to it from other administrative business. This was because none of the Governments concerned was in a position to produce any central administrative 'budget' in these terms; arrangements were for the most part extemporized by the man in charge in each district, using his regular staff and such auxiliaries as he could recruit locally. The scale of operation is indicated by the general rules that one polling station is needed for about 1,000 voters in the towns,[1] for a smaller number in the countryside; that each station needs a presiding officer, two literate clerks, and a policeman; and that Registration Officers are needed on a similar scale for less intense work spread over a longer period.

The answer everywhere seems to be that staff can be found from existing resources if the priority given is high enough, so that all other office work comes to a standstill and literates are drawn in from posts outside the ordinary administration—ministers of religion, school-teachers, agricultural officers, and so on. Mr. Price even records the use of secondary school boys as auxiliaries in the Eastern Region. Such an army is of necessity an 'awkward squad', inexperienced in this sort of work: no very elaborate arrangements can be made for training without further expenditure of scarce time. What was done was (with all its faults) much better than a stranger to Africa would expect of Administration under such conditions; and standards improve with familiarity, provided that adequate supervision can be maintained.

(c) *Publicity.* Perhaps the main virtue of elections as a political device is that they hold out an inducement to all and sundry to take *some* initiative—a tiny one perhaps, but their own—in a matter of government. Elections cannot *begin* to work unless there is some small public initiative, both in registration and in voting; and initiative is not possible without some knowledge and some incentive. An election is not an affair that can be fixed up quietly by civil servants; it must be advertised.

This is a matter in which expatriate administration and local politics walk in the same direction, on parallel but separate paths. A territorial election is scarcely possible unless the territory possesses

---

[1] French law requires a polling station for every 1,500, the Senegal Administration aimed at a station for every 1,000, in town and country alike. See p. 352 above.

some means of mass communication, by press and radio. Straight news given out through these channels advertises both the stages of electoral administration and the ambitions of the contending parties: generally, the administrators and the politicians also have special programmes of electoral publicity. Administrative and political publicity are of very different kinds, but both help to emphasize the elementary theme: 'Register, register, register: vote, vote, vote. Why? Because you are a full citizen of this country.' Something might be done to measure the range and depth now attained by mass communications of this sort in different territories; but it is easy to guess that they are by modern Western standards rather slight, and that much depends on more direct and even archaic methods.

In these too the administration and the parties work in parallel but apart. The administration has everywhere two methods at its disposal; first, special publicity teams, with loudspeaker cars, film shows, and leaflets; secondly, the district administrator going about his ordinary business. There is general agreement that the former (not used at all in Senegal) are quite effective within their range, but road-bound; and that the enterprise, initiative, and dramatic sense of the individual administrator count for more than anything else in bringing the villages into politics. In the more developed territories the parties too have travelling 'circuses' and the gospel is carried out from the centre by political caravans; but there is in this a sharp contrast, referred to again later, between the two Regions of Nigeria and Senegal on the one hand, Sierra Leone and Kenya on the other.

(d) *Electoral qualifications.* The qualifications for electors (and also those for candidates) have both political and administrative significance. In Sierra Leone the Keith-Lucas franchise was based on the compromise report of a committee representing various political interests; in the two Nigerian Regions there was a good deal of controversy over the effects of the 'native' qualification, under which people might choose to vote in their constituency of origin rather than in that of residence; in Kenya the Coutts franchise held the centre of the stage: even in Senegal (though to a less extent than elsewhere in French West Africa) the move from limited to universal suffrage was thought to be of political importance. In practice, however, none of these political arrangements came to much, and it is unlikely that any of the elections was affected by manipulation of the franchise. Everywhere except in Kenya this was universal or nearly universal, and as universal suffrage is approached the addition of extra voters has very little political effect, unless manipulation is actually connived at or contrived by the expatriate administration. In Kenya a narrow franchise might have biased the result if there had been any issues before the electorate which could conceivably divide the unenfranchized from the rest. But there were no such issues; if there was any issue at all at the territorial level, it was the elementary one of Africans against Indians and Europeans, on which Africans could not be seriously divided, whatever their social and economic status.

In practice therefore the franchise seems to have been more important to the administrators than to the politicians, and there is no doubt what the former would wish for—a franchise as simple as possible, preferably one related to some existing register of names. The French seem to have come closer to this ideal than do the British.

(e) *Constituencies and methods of voting.* The politicians seem to have been more sensitive about the effects of qualifications for the vote than about those of arrangements for its use. This was perhaps not true of Senegal, where the party leaders are involved in the politics of metropolitan France and are thoroughly familiar with the intricate process of 'cooking' the French voting system by bargaining between parties. The form of constituencies and voting described by Professor Robinson certainly affected the results, but this was perhaps not brought about innocently. In the four British territories the systems adopted had even more drastic effects, but these do not seem to have been planned, except in Sierra Leone, and do not seem to have led to great demands for change.

There were in all the British territories great variations in the size and population of constituencies, in relation to seats allocated. In Sierra Leone this was in part deliberate; the rural area of the Colony was over-represented, in order to give a political base to the Creoles, who are no longer the most important force in Sierra Leone politics, yet are so placed that they cannot be neglected or casually deserted. But in the Protectorate, as in the other British territories (and in Senegal too), constituencies were derived from administrative divisions, subject only to some very simple rules which did little to balance the inevitable inequalities of population. In terms of registered voters the ratio between largest and smallest constituency, taking extreme cases, was 6 to 1 in the Protectorate, 8 to 1 in the Western Region, 5 to 1 in the Eastern Region, and 14 to 1 in Kenya.[1]

This shocked no one very much, because administrative divisions were on the whole chosen to match tribal and other indigenous

[1] Six new African seats were created in 1958 by division of the largest constituencies in Kenya.

divisions, and they had besides acquired a certain traditional sanctity of their own. It would not be popular to break up administrative districts and tribal areas in order to secure more equal constituencies. With the present number of members greater equality could only be secured by a system of constituencies which would be socially arbitrary, and also administratively inconvenient; it makes matters immensely easier for the administrator if his ordinary boundaries serve also for registration and polling.

Unequal constituencies coupled with the British system of simple plurality voting can produce very odd results in the relation between votes cast and seats gained. A well-spread majority among the electorate will do better than a concentrated one of the same size; a majority reasonably well spread will always obtain a bonus of seats as against minorities, and this bonus will be relatively larger the smaller the minorities. These results are further exaggerated if (as in the Eastern Region) all the seats in multi-number constituencies are awarded on a bare plurality of voters.

In practice these effects mattered only in the two Nigerian Regions. In Kenya there were no territorial parties at all; in the Sierra Leone Protectorate there was on the whole no real opposition to the S.L.P.P., and most of the contests were no more party contests than in Kenya. But in the Western Region the Action Group secured 60 per cent. of the seats for 48 per cent. of the votes cast; in the Eastern Region the N.C.N.C. secured 77 per cent. of the seats, 63 per cent. of the votes. In both Regions a substantial opposition now exists, and British opinion may hold that parliamentary government works well enough if there is a majority large enough to govern, an opposition large enough to talk. But this will not do, even in theory, if the opposition is a permanent one without hope of office, dependent primarily on outside support: and the system is in Nigeria particularly awkward because it tends to exaggerate the dominance of Yorubas and Ibos in their own Regions and to make it more difficult to organize Nigerian parties cutting across tribal lines. There is a case here for the introduction of multi-member constituencies with some sort of proportional representation by voting for party lists; but this has no roots in British tradition, and would be unpopular with each party in its own Region, though it might welcome it in the other. The only probable improvement is a division of the Eastern Region into single-member constituencies; this would strengthen the moral position of the N.C.N.C., which is very vulnerable to criticism at present because of the effect of the present system on minorities, and it would not weaken its representation very substantially.

Not much more need be said here about the mechanics of voting, the layout of polling stations, the distribution of party symbols, and so on. All the systems adopted worked pretty well, all met with difficulties in detail. Perhaps our most general impression is that there is a good deal to be said for the French system of voting envelopes. Under this method there is a separate voting paper for each list or candidate, distinguished by colour and printed description, sometimes also by symbol. The voter selects from all these papers the one that he prefers; he can do this privately before he comes to the poll, or he can pick up from a table in the polling station a copy of each of the papers, and can reject in the privacy of the voting-booth those which he does not want to use. When he is accepted as a voter by the presiding officer, he is given an official envelope, indistinguishable from others and not transparent. In this he privately puts his chosen paper, and he shows the closed envelope for inspection before it is dropped in the ballot box. The system requires more paper than any of the British methods, under which there are no envelopes and only one voting paper, and the voter chooses between a number of labelled boxes: but practically all the difficulties met with in polling in British Africa spring from this multiplicity of boxes—from the difficulty of labelling them satisfactorily, or arranging them so as not to bias choice, of seeing that ballot papers are properly inserted, of keeping voters moving through the private room in which the boxes are set out, of preserving and transporting a large number of boxes for the count. The French avoid most of these difficulties and do not seem to meet many others in their place; so an experiment in imitation might be worth trying.

There is also some doubt whether much is gained in Africa by introducing the British devices of the numbered ballot-paper with counterfoil, and the official stamp impressed on each paper as it is handed to the voter. These are ingenious methods of control introduced in Britain in the latter part of the nineteenth century to make the use of forged ballot papers impossible, and to give a means of identifying misused papers in the event of legal proceedings, without at the same time endangering the secrecy of the ballot. In fact, these forms of control are not of the slightest practical importance in British elections today: but they are retained (reasonably enough) as routine precautions, and they do no harm because polling station staff know exactly how to work them. But if they are worked wrongly they may be the means of disallowing perfectly honest votes, as a result of carelessness (or even deliberate malpractice) on the part of clerks. This evil was quite serious in Sierra Leone, and instances of it have cropped up elsewhere. Both devices could probably be abandoned without loss, even though the present system were otherwise retained.

(*f*) *Adjudication.* A hotly contested election is bound to give rise to disputes about justiciable issues of law and fact, and these may be very numerous when the system is new, individuals are uncertain of their rights, and clerks are inexperienced. Sometimes these disputes become so numerous as to throw a great strain on the machinery: examples in this book are the litigation over registration in Freetown and in Warri in the Western Region, and over flaws in procedure and corrupt practices in Sierra Leone, both in the Colony and in the Protectorate. The administrative problem is that such outbreaks of litigation are patchy and unpredictable. In most places the number of disputed cases about registration, the campaign, polling procedures, and the count is quite small, and can be dealt with easily by the ordinary courts: but sometimes matters get out of hand and ordinary procedure cannot function without intolerable delay. The conditions seem to be set by a combination of high feeling, loose administrative control, and natural litigiousness, factors all present at Warri,[1] in Freetown,[2] and in Mauritius:[3] the actual extent of inefficiency and corruption is of course relevant, but probably legal flaws are always present, even in the best-regulated elections, causing little litigation because the contending parties tend to accept (like companies insuring motorists) a 'knock-for-knock' system.

In these conditions there is perhaps a good deal to be said for the system of electoral *commissions* used by the French. These consist of a person appointed by the administration and persons appointed by each of the parties: there are various *commissions* concerned with the revision of the register, the distribution of electors' cards, and procedure at each polling-station. The British allow agents of the candidates to observe polling and the count, but this system does nothing to share administrative work with the parties and to give them some corporate responsibility for making the election work. French electoral *commissions* are often the scenes of violent disputes: yet the existence of a regular channel of communication of this sort might have mitigated troubles such as those at Warri. It does, however, involve acceptance of the French system of recognized parties; or a movement towards the system used in Britain, by which party agents are recognized by law and are|at work in the constituencies even between elections.

---

[1] p. 50 above.   [2] p. 198 above.
[3] *Report on the Conduct of Local Government Elections in Mauritius* (*Keith-Lucas*), (Port Louis, 1956).

The French system is supervised by the *Conseil d'Etat* in Paris, which is responsible for the legal correctness and substantial equity of French administrative procedure throughout French territory. Certain matters are dealt with by the ordinary criminal courts, but most of the responsibility for supervision lies with the *Conseil d'Etat* and the *Conseil du contentieux administratif* in each territory. This work is in a technical sense admirably done, but is seriously handicapped because the evidence available consists largely of the *procès-verbaux* of the various electoral commissions, not always accurately or clearly compiled.[1] British procedure depends on using the ordinary local courts, reinforced in emergency by the appointment of independent people to act as temporary judges. Evidence is more readily available to these courts; on the other hand, like other British courts, they can deal only with specific breaches of the law, not with wider questions of administrative propriety. Whichever system is adopted, adjudication must in the end become a purely local matter, and respect for elections will decline unless it is buttressed by the tradition of an independent judiciary.

3. Political Parties

Political parties arise where traditional forms of authority prove inadequate in face of a new situation. One factor in creating such a situation has been the introduction of an alien political device, that of mass elections; there are of course many other factors, social and economic, but the formal structure of elections does a good deal to determine the character of political organizations. The parties described in our five studies are not electoral organizations only, but none of them would have existed in its present form if it had not been necessary to fight elections. This is equally true in very different circumstances, for instance in those of the Sierra Leone People's Party, Action Group in the Western Region, and the district political associations in Kenya.

For our present purpose, therefore, we can limit somewhat the immense field of investigation offered by the new political parties. Our problem is 'how has the introduction of elections affected the growth of parties in these five territories?' This question of course involves its converse, 'how has this party development modified the practice of elections?' We propose to take only four heads, out of many which might be discussed: communications and ideology, leadership and organization, finance, and 'tribalism.' These four

[1] André Holleaux, 'Les Elections aux Assemblées des Territoires d'outre-mer', *Revue juridique et politique de l'Union Française*, vol. x (1956), p. 1.

aspects of the problem inter-act, but we can only deal with them consecutively.

(a) *Communications and ideology*. The environment from which these African societies are emerging was one in which travel was limited by the pace of movement possible in difficult country (travel by water played some small part along the coast and the great rivers), individual travel was rare because of its danger, communication of information was limited by highly localized languages and the absence of literacy, mass communications did not exist beyond the range of the human voice, and culture was transmitted by day to day association within the family and village. All these things are going. Both in East and in West Africa the African population (as wage-earners in an exchange economy) travel long distances by train, bus, 'mammy-wagon', and bicycle, over a system of highways designed in the first instance by the colonial powers: they move both as groups and as individuals; mobility and organized education generate a *lingua franca*, European or African, used over quite large areas, and reduced to writing as a matter of common usage; and from this grows a situation in which one man or group can reach very large audiences, through press or radio, or simply by moving about the country and talking in public. These things affect both the nature of culture and the way in which it is transmitted; culture is more widely extended and also more diversified, face to face contact within a stable group is no longer its only vehicle.

The relevance of this to electoral politics is that a candidate or party seeking votes must move, at least partly, in this new environment. Even independent candidates in isolated constituencies, such as existed to some extent in Kenya and in Sierra Leone, must take account of the fact that constituencies are too large to be units of the old culture, and that there are many people even in the villages who respond to themes met with in a larger world. It is possible—and clearly it did happen in some places—for a candidate to stand pat on the support of a solid block of territorial loyalties in one area of the constituency; electoral arithmetic is simple if each local block puts up its own candidate, as each need only reckon the number of his personal following. But any electoral system, even that of simple plurality voting, complicates these elementary calculations. If one block has an absolute majority in the constituency it will be tempted to bring its internal dissensions into the open, so that each faction looks for some support outside. If no block has a majority there is even greater pressure to form electoral alliances. In either case, even within a single constituency a local candidate finds himself inclined, if not forced, to 'stump' the whole constituency (or such parts of it as he can hope to influence), to canvass influential people outside his immediate 'connexion', and to seek for a 'language', or ideology, or set of slogans, which will enable him to state issues in a way intelligible across local boundaries. In most cases, of course, it turns out that the easiest slogan to use is 'out with the white man'; this may happen not because 'black nationalism' or 'Africanism' is so intense that it submerges all other issues, but because there is no other common sentiment above the local level to which to appeal.

The same causes act in a more vigorous way if the stake in the election is not merely success in a constituency (as in Kenya) but a share in the government of the country, as in the two Nigerian Regions. The importance of this stake is most obvious where the programme of constitutional development is based on the British model, which offers control of the government to those who can command a majority in the elected assembly and can then form a cabinet. The French situation is less clear-cut. Under the *loi-cadre*, the reforming law passed in 1956, ministers chosen by an elected assembly are given control over 'territorial' services, but there remain in all territories also 'national' services controlled by the French state, which the local electorate can influence at least only in an uncertain and obscure way through political connexions in Paris.

All five studies indicate, in different ways, how party development may be fostered and shaped by the electoral system. This is perhaps most obvious in the marginal cases. Northern Nigeria is very poor and lacks literacy and communications, so that the existing régime is internally stable enough; but it is involved in elections by the general movement of events in West Africa, and must create an electoral organization for its own defence. That party, the N.P.C., is at present little more than a 'front' for traditional institutions, but its nature would change if it were forced by events into serious campaigning among a wide electorate. The position of the S.L.P.P. in the Protectorate is not very different. But in the south of Nigeria the parties have been forced by competition to use fully the technical resources available, and they have advanced a long way towards their European models. Electoral campaigns in the Eastern and Western Regions (unlike those in Sierra Leone outside the Colony, in Kenya outside Nairobi) can be described quite readily within the framework of British experience: the party manifestos, the broadcasts, the influence of the press, the 'whistle stop' tours of the leaders, the interaction of central and local issues in the choice of candidates and in the search for blocks of votes. The analogy must not be pressed too far: the resources of mass communication are limited, even in the most developed parts of Africa, and meetings in the open in the tropics are rather different from meetings in British school-rooms or at factory gates. But it is worth something: for instance, West African parties set to work in a methodical way to teach their faithful voters how to register their vote correctly: most British party agents would agree that one of the main objects of local campaigning in Britain now is to get the name of the party candidate well into the heads of voters, so that they will know what to do when faced with a ballot paper on which there are printed names only, and not party labels. There are in fact only a limited number of tasks for such an organization to perform within an electoral system run in an orderly way: if resources are available the party will shape itself to its tasks.

It is generally believed that to sustain it a party needs a policy and an ideology, as well as an electoral organization. To put it as Taper and Tadpole put it in the 1830's, a party must have a 'cry'; it must have catch-phrases which encourage loyalty because they indicate attitudes widely shared, and it must state publicly the sort of action which it promises in exchange for votes. Perhaps it ought to have a 'philosophy' too: perhaps not, perhaps parties work better if they are not too scrupulous about intellectual respectability. Of the parties described in the book, perhaps only the B.P.S. aspires to have a philosophy, an indication of the effective existence of an intellectual middle class in Senegal. Elsewhere, there are individual leaders who are highly intellectual, but the number of those prepared to debate acutely about party ideologies is too small to affect the general tone of politics. In spite of this, there is in practice a certain unity in statement, because party policies and party cries seem to be very much the same throughout Africa: 'African self-government', 'jobs for Africans', 'more economic development', 'better education'. This is effective as a programme for opposition, but not for government: when the question of power becomes pressing a potential government must face the fact that it cannot do everything, and must therefore offer more to some than to others. The imminence of self-government tends to force parties back into sectionalism, since they must seek support by promises to effective interests, from the level of villages to that of great towns and tribes. The parties are well fitted to express these ordinary aspirations directly and plainly, but it is not easy for them to combine sectional interests into effective and disciplined action at the national level. This is not easy even for great parties in Western democracies: still less for political organizations with only a short tradition behind them.

(*b*) *Leadership and organization.* This lack of established party tradition is not made good by the existence of strong party organization and the vested interests which it creates. It is easy to exaggerate the strength and competence of the central 'bureaucracies' of British and other Western parties. In the U.S.A. these party bureaucracies are negligible, in Britain they spend more time in magnifying their office than in exercising effective influence. But in these two countries, and elsewhere, there is an established 'corps' of what the French call *les militants*: people who see themselves as the political *élite*, are perhaps seen by others mainly as cranks who have taken to politics for a hobby, as others take to boats, budgerigars, or postage-stamps. The *militants* are an odd tribe, but it is they who perpetuate attachment to the party name, leaders, and tradition; for instance Liberal *militants* in the provinces in Britain survived the virtual disappearance of the Liberal party at Westminster, and they were bid for by other parties in the long-drawn-out bankruptcy sale of Liberal assets.

One can perhaps find traces of such a situation in Africa in a few areas which have a long history of electoral politics, in particular in the four *communes* of Senegal; but the relative importance of these areas is declining, and elsewhere party organization has scarcely existed for more than ten years. In some cases, for instance that of Action Group, the work of the central party office is clearly pretty good, even judged by Western standards, and there is also an inner group of associated leaders. Bodies such as the B.P.S. in Senegal, the Convention People's Party in Ghana, the N.C.N.C. in Nigeria have also some effective party membership spread through the constituencies, and not identical with the traditional authorities there. It is extremely difficult to assess the strength of this objectively; indeed there can be no effective test until independence is realized or is imminent.

Where (as in all these instances) party tradition or doctrine and party organization are both weak, it is natural for a party to make its appeal through the personality of an individual. Given reasonable facilities for transport and mass communications, the impress of individual personality can be transmitted quite quickly through a large political community, and the notion of a person may be more influential than ideology or policy. But the concept of 'charismatic' personality may in this context be the source of some confusion, because it ties together two rather different questions. There is, first, the question of psychology and 'face to face' relations: have some people greater gifts and greater skill than others in establishing ascendancy by personal qualities, such as appearance, charm of voice and manner, quickness, stamina, readiness to take risks, which give them an almost hypnotic influence? There is, secondly, the question of the 'projection' of personality to a large political community, and this is a matter partly of designing or choosing a simplified 'larger-than-life' personality to fit the needs and culture of the community, partly of the existence and control of adequate technical means of mass communication. 'Charismatic' personality does not help party organization unless it is technically feasible to project it in mass communications. The point is illustrated by various parables told in novels and plays of 'personalities' invented out of nothing by astute manipulators. Such a *reductio ad absurdum* is unlikely in practical politics: the effective leader, like Dr. Nkrumah or Dr. Azikiwe, doubtless combines personal ascendancy over an inner circle with astute or instinctive selection of public attitudes and with mastery of the technical resources available. But the personal 'grace' or magic of leaders is in large measure a matter of competent staff-work by these gentlemen and their supporters. In politics personality does not exist in isolation from organization; they are not alternatives but complements.[1]

Subject to these reservations it must be agreed that it is simplest in African conditions to build an organization round a personality: and once this has been done the organization is to some extent captive, as the Nazi party was Hitler's captive, as the American Democratic party from 1932 to 1945 was tied to F. D. Roosevelt, as the British Liberal party from 1880 to 1895 was tied to Mr. Gladstone. These three examples are drawn from very different contexts, to indicate that there is nothing of necessity 'fascist' or 'dictatorial' about this situation; nevertheless, its dangers are obvious. Perhaps the Western democracies are now so familiar with these dangers that they wince too readily at the first symptoms, and deflate potential leaders before they can emerge effectively. In certain circumstances personal leadership may be the best device available; the question then is whether it is to be used oppressively or otherwise.

(c) *Party finance.* In a money economy all these matters of organization depend primarily on money. Naturally we are unable to present any adequate account of the finance of African parties; there is the same gap in almost all descriptions of Western parties. This does not diminish the importance of the subject. Communications and organization are necessary to a party: both involve the use of scarce resources. To some extent lack of money can be made good

---

[1] On this question see in particular the references to 'charisma' in the index of Apter, *The Gold Coast in Transition* (Princeton, 1955). As used by Professor Apter the term seems too vague to be of much value for political analysis.

by the personal devotion of volunteers: but this too represents a contribution of economic resources which is only possible within limiting conditions.

The simplest 'model' of the finances of an electoral party is based on experience of some American city and state machines. Control of election to the assembly gives power to tax, to place contracts, to make patronage appointments: some paid jobs may also be filled at the same time by direct election. A group of individuals pool their resources to win an election—or they come together after winning individual contests. The group is then in power; as long as it coheres, it can maintain its organization by placing its party officials in patronage posts paid for out of public funds, and it can keep its war-chest filled by a percentage levy on their salaries, and also by securing contributions to party funds tacitly related to favours regarding the incidence of taxation or the placing of public contracts. The party is thus better organized and financed than potential rivals; it has the continuous backing of experienced *militants*; it has a good deal of control over electoral machinery too, but it can probably win almost any election by better organization, without bothering to 'steal' it by corrupt practices.

This is an abstract model; no party machine ever worked in so simple a way. The famous American machines often acted less legally (the 'model' sketched is extra-legal rather than illegal); on the other hand they had certain human virtues. They often rendered useful social service to their voters, and they made sentimental appeals to tradition and to the unity of the under-dogs, which were not wholly cynical. Certainly no African party works in this way. But the model serves, as such models do, to bring out some points of interest. It draws attention (in the first place) to the great contrast between poor parties and rich parties, between Kenya and Sierra Leone on the one hand, the two Nigerian Regions on the other, between incoherent and coherent electoral campaigns. It is not possible to fight a national campaign properly without money and organization; and elections, at least on the British model, are futile unless they are preceded by a national campaign penetrating enough to elicit some genuine sentiment about the potential Government. Responsible cabinet government implies organized parties; parties must be paid for by someone. In the second place, therefore, one must face the question—paid for by whom?

In Africa there is generally little chance that they can be paid for by the subscriptions of individual party members; the level of subscriptions possible could not justify the cost of collection and accountancy. The B.P.S. has perhaps the strongest membership organization, but even in this case it might be more exact to say that the party sells membership cards than that it has members. The British Labour party is paid for largely by individual subscriptions channelled through large organizations, the trade unions, which are rich as organizations though their members are poor. Such a development is not impossible in those parts of Africa where relatively strong trade unions exist, as in the Copper Belt of Northern Rhodesia,[1] but the trade unions play very little part in financing political activity in any of the territories we have described. It therefore seems to follow that strong parties must depend for finance either on business organizations or on rich men: and there is no doubt that Action Group and the N.C.N.C. are thus financed.

Who wills the end wills the means. Electoral campaigns must be paid for, and this can only be done through subscriptions to party funds. It is therefore impossible to make such subscriptions illegal: even if this were done they could not be effectively repressed. Nor is it possible to enact any strict limit on the amounts to be spent by parties. Clearly laws relating to specific cases of bribery and improper influence must be applied literally: it is possible to do this without wrecking the party system, because the most important forms of party influence, those affecting legislation and public appointments, are essential to government and cannot be made illegal. But such a relation between the party and the interests may end by corrupting the basis of the régime, because elections become wholly cynical: and it is therefore worth giving some consideration to the only methods of control tried in the West which have had any success at all. These are the legal requirement of publicity for party accounts, as well as for the electoral expenses of candidates; and government assistance, to a limited extent, for the campaigns of all serious candidates, irrespective of party.[2] Neither of these things is easy to work out in legislative form, and in any case opinion rather than law is the main source of control. But even imperfectly applied they have some effect: the first because it establishes formally the principle of public knowledge and discussion about party finance, the second because it recognizes that the campaign is also part of the election, and that the state has some responsibility for this too.

(d) *Tribalism.* Tribalism, even as referred to in this book, is so various a phenomenon that its unity is precarious. On the one hand, what is there in common, to take these cases alone, between the organization of Mandingo, Fulani, Yoruba, Itsekiri, Mende, Jaluo,

---

[1] There are great difficulties even there; see A. L. Epstein's book on *Politics in an Urban African Community* (Manchester University Press, 1958).

[2] Senegal follows the French model on this latter point.

Kikuyu? On the other hand, what distinguishes all these from highly localized vested interests in other countries, such as those of the Highlands and Islands of Scotland, the Breton or Basque lands in France, the French in Canada? Perhaps in principle the difference is more than one of degree, because the tribe is in principle an all-inclusive organization, embracing religion, politics, economics, kinship, and language together: but the tribal principle has been broken through everywhere by changes in economic relations, and it seems likely that in time other relations must weaken too. 'Resurgent tribalism' (Professor Harlow's phrase) is rather a recognition than a reversal of this process.[1]

Yet at present all African parties tend to become tribal parties. This is in part due to determinants built into the electoral systems. Even the richest African parties are relatively weak in central finance, and are therefore greatly dependent on resources made available locally: the central organization is rarely strong enough to crush an independent candidate standing with some local support (the B.P.S. is the strongest party here recorded, in this respect as in others); and in the extreme case (that of the S.L.P.P.) the official party nomination is worth almost nothing. In addition, all the franchises described, even that in Kenya, are relatively wide, and enfranchise a majority who are still embedded in tribal tradition: it is very difficult to approach local electors except by a campaign which enlists the support of local magnates, hammers at local issues, and repeats very simple slogans about tribal loyalty and the wicked ways of strangers. If tribalism is the enemy, elections are partly responsible for encouraging it.

But there is no reason to suppose that strong tribal loyalty is in all cases incompatible with electoral democracy. Elections within a tribe may prove to be as good a way as any of adjudicating about the ceaseless internal quarrels of local communities; elections involving many tribes may in the end help territorial cohesion, because some majority must be found, and this can only be done by a compromise between tribes or by a party cutting across tribes. The difficulties come where there are tribes—such as the Baganda, the Yoruba, the Ibo—too small to form an independent state, yet so much larger than their neighbours that they are bound to dominate them under any electoral system. Nigeria has for the moment found a tolerably free system, by which the N.C.N.C. organizes dissidents in Yorubaland, Action Group does the same in Iboland, and both are interested in sustaining some opposition to the régime in the Northern Region. But it is not certain that this curious arrangement of checks and

[1] See his article on 'Tribalism in Africa', *J. Afr. Admin.*, vol. vii (1955), p. 17.

balances would remain stable in a self-governing Nigeria; and there are at least as great doubts about the balance between nationalism and tribalism in Ghana and in Uganda. On this much of the future of elections in Africa depends.

4. The Future

Up to this point, a political scientist experienced mainly in Western institutions finds himself astonished at the adaptability of the electoral formula: experience about the practice of elections elsewhere seems relevant to elections in Africa, and Africans seem well able to settle into the system and adapt it to their needs. But in the West the system has never been able to stand the combination of intense localism with universal suffrage: it was the extension of the franchise in Ireland in 1885 which in the end made inevitable the extremely wasteful and foolish break between Ireland and Britain, and perhaps the same happened, with less violence, between Norway and Sweden in 1905. No African who reflects on the question doubts that Africa needs larger, not smaller, states: but it will be a political task of extreme difficulty to realize larger unity and at the same time to maintain free elections.

There are two other great difficulties to be faced, those of economic development and of efficient administration. These great problems cohere with that of elections, and nothing useful could be said about the political future unless all were studied together. Any kind of economic development presupposes the existence of a decent framework of administration; this is as true of 'free' development under private enterprise as of 'forced' development within a directed economy. Perhaps 'free' development requires a less elaborate system of public administration than does a directed economy, because the main tasks of the administration are to 'hold the ring', by maintaining public order, business legality, and the social and educational services essential to an efficient working population. But even these are very large tasks: and in a 'free' economy the administration is under an additional strain, because on it depends the confidence of foreign investors, and yet rich companies can scarcely fail to attack its efficiency and integrity by competing for the services of the best men and by using their wealth to attract privileges to themselves. Whichever system is chosen, 'free' or 'directed', the approach to self-government places added strains on the administration, and at the same time weakens its resistance to them. We have pointed out already how fundamental this is to the question of stability in the operation of elections.

Elections are also in other ways reciprocally related to economic development. The idea of the 'free world' links the idea of a particular kind of economic development to that of a political system based on 'free elections'. But nothing disturbs business confidence more than elections which go wrong, by producing chaos or by producing a régime hostile to foreign enterprise, so that the two postulates of the 'free world' system are apt to clash. Furthermore, the economic situation greatly affects the prospects of electoral stability. Steadily increasing economic prosperity makes for political stability, even though there may be vigorous clashes between local interests for better shares of the cake: set-backs, even temporary ones, call the whole system into question, and set going demands for completely new political and economic tactics.

To these complex interactions must be added uncertainties about the distribution of effective military force and of essential raw materials for Western industry. All that the political scientist can say is that the export of elections has not failed yet, and that it has not reached the sort of dead end from which further development is impossible. The whole subject is alive, and it is perhaps more profitable to speculate about what can be learnt than about what will happen.

The outlook for research depends largely on the attitude of the authorities in the emergent states and on the sort of work that can be done in this field by their own universities and colleges. Political research, indeed all forms of economic and social research, are geared into the current political situation, and talk about prospects for research is also talk about political prospects. But given local encouragement, such as has been given in India, what can usefully be done?

It would (in the first place) be a great service if more Governments would follow the Indian example by issuing after each general election a statistical and administrative report setting out what happened, in a form which is kept reasonably stable through a long series of elections. This is not done in Great Britain; it is done in some British territories, but not in others. Where it is not done, the gap has to be made good, rather laboriously and ineffectively, by private enterprise, because basic data of this sort are as necessary to politicians and to administrators as to research workers, and must be put together somehow.

If this were done, it would dispose of one of the functions of electoral surveys such as those reported here, which are in part factual records of a kind useful to historians and for comparative study. But (as we wrote earlier) an electoral survey affords an excellent occasion for a 'first look' at the state of politics in any country where elections are important, and at this stage it would be valuable to have surveys of elections in almost any of the 'emergent states'. But there is no point in surveys endlessly repeated without selection; tactics in research are a matter of relating techniques to problems.

Of the problems not dealt with by any of our surveys, two seem to be of outstanding importance. One is that of elections involving various communities as well as various tribes and interests. The Kenya African elections were in the first instance isolated from those of other communities in Kenya, but this cannot continue, even if the system of separate communal electorates continues. In all the other territories of East and Central Africa 'common roll' is on the agenda in one form or another, and whether it is adopted or not the debate is bound to accelerate the process of unifying the local political systems through electoral campaigning. But common electoral campaigning may be accompanied by intensified communal antagonism; the whole course of events is unpredictable and needs study. To some extent, such study may be easier in the smaller and more isolated territories where communalism is strong, such as Mauritius, Fiji, or British Guiana. The fate of these places does not affect the fate of nations, but they are 'laboratories' of great interest, as well as great charm.

The other problem which might be approached by the method of survey is that of the domestication of elections in territories that have become independent. The process is perhaps almost complete in India, Ceylon, and Burma, and also under a presidential system in the Philippines; but the turning-point has not yet been reached in Ghana, the Sudan,[1] and Malaya, which are still to have their first locally managed general elections. The situation in each of these three very different territories is of extreme interest.

It is clear, however, that there are some problems which the method of electoral survey cannot tackle. Of necessity it looks at the situation from above, from the national level, and it offers no more than a still photograph at one instant of time. To get any appreciation of the situation in depth it is necessary also to look at the way in which electoral politics fits into the social structure at the level of daily life. One method is that of social anthropology, and an important start has been made in East and Central Africa with very intimate local studies of this kind. Nothing can replace this method for the comprehensive study of politics in a concrete social setting, but of necessity it takes time, and can offer only illustrations, not conclusions, about the politics of a large territory taken as a whole. For such larger studies there are various statistical techniques to

[1] This took place in the Sudan in March 1958.

hand, developed mainly in the U.S.A., to a lesser extent in Europe. It is easy to suggest punched-card records of the careers of leaders, sample surveys of the characteristics and attitudes of voters, correlations of political with social and economic statistics. This is easier to suggest than to do, because the management of such techniques is related to language, to the administrative situation, to the availability of skilled assistants. All this is often impracticable, certainly expensive; and it may be easier for the historian than for the social scientist to take the next steps. There is for instance much printed and written material available about the early history of parties and other political organizations and about their relation to other new social organizations, such as tribal associations in towns, trade unions, and co-operatives; the parties must also be seen in relation to the emergence of local men at the top of the administration, and of new administrative devices, such as local authorities, development corporations, and marketing boards. But much of this material is ephemeral and is disappearing, and so is the opportunity of interviewing participants. This too, like so much else, depends on local interest and initiative; a research programme in this field is largely a programme of self-examination, and it will not come to much unless Africans and others directly participant become interested in their own history and in comparative study of their own institutions.

INDEX

Aba, 113, 141, 146, 149, 150, 151.
Abbas, Gueye, 334.
Action Group, Nigeria: formation, 14, 22; developments in, 14–16, 22–23; programme, 28–29; leadership, 29; organization, 29–30, 31, 33, 480, 484; finance, 32–33, 483; as government, W.R., 35–39, 42; in Lagos, 36, 38; dissension in, 41; registration campaign, 47; preparation for election, 53, 54; nomination of candidates, 56; manifesto, 58; accusations against, 59; campaign, 59–60, 61–63; local campaigns, 64–65; party press, 66–69; broadcasts, 71; in Oyo, 78–83; defeat in Oyo, 85; in Warri, 87–94; campaign in Warri, 90, 91–92; nature of, 476.
  In Eastern Region: 107; description, 123; manifesto, 127–30; and press, 132–3; broadcasts, 137; campaign, 141–3; finance, 143; symbol of, 145; results, 156, 157, 473. *See also* Awolowo, Chief Obafemi.
Adelabu, Adegoke, 25, 38–39, 61, 71, 82, 102.
Afolabi, P. A., 81, 82, 85.
African Continental Bank, Azikiwe's connexion with, 17, 38, 124–5, 128 n., 146. *See also* Foster-Sutton.
Afrique nouvelle (Dakar), 368–70, 374.
'A-K' Plan, 427, 440.
Akerele, A., 80, 83, 85.
Argwings-Kodhek, C. M. G.: forms N.D.A.C., 413, 439–40; occupation, 424; 'A-K' plan, 427; director, *Nyanza Times*, 433; opposition to, 441–3; campaign, 444–6, 448–9; defeat of, 450, 461; accusations against, 457.
Asians in Kenya: numbers, 391; representation, 394, 400; 1956 elections, 431.
Awokoya, S. O., 27, 41, 55.
Awolowo, Chief Obafemi: leader, Action Group, 14, 16, 21, 23; in A.G. organization, 32; as Premier, W.R., 36–38, 40–42, 44; on dissolution, 53; accused of dictatorial actions, 58; campaign by, 59–60, 62, 63; broadcasts, 71; statement

on receipt cards, 74; in Oyo, 82; in Warri, 90.
  In Eastern Region: broadcast, 137; campaign by, 141, 145, 147.
Awori, W. W. W., 453, 459.
Azikiwe, Dr. Nnamdi: founder, N.C.N.C., 12, 13; as Premier, E.R., 17.
  In Western Region: in N.C.N.C. organization, 30, 32–33; at London Conference, 36; in U.S., 37, 40; statement on Ibadan Council, 39; campaign, 42, 59–62, 63; on dissolution, 53–54; issues manifesto, 58; broadcasts, 71; in Oyo, 82; in Warri, 88, 90.
  In Eastern Region: influence of, 109; and Foster-Sutton Report, 109–11; press support for, 133, 134, 135; broadcasts by, 137; campaign, 139–40, 147; on results, 156–8; personality, 481. *See also* African Continental Bank, Azikiwe's connexion with.

Babacar Sy, El Hadj, 287, 380.
Balogun, Chief Kolawole, 31, 54, 61.
Bankole-Bright, Dr. H. C.: leader of opposition, Sierra Leone, 181; leader, National Council of Sierra Leone, 187–8, 190; campaign, 209, 211, 212, 217; broadcasts, 222–3; defeat of, 256, 257, 269.
Benin–Delta State, claim for, 18–19, 25, 97; support of major parties of, 29, 57, 91–92; opposition to, 59.
Beoku-Betts, R., 189, 211, 223, 236.
Bloc Africain, 310, 312.
Bloc Démocratique Sénégalais: formation, 315–16; nature, 316, 318, 320–1; demand for self-government, 321; prospects, 322; attitude to *regroupement*, 323–5; fuses to form B.P.S., 325, 334–5.
Bloc Populaire Sénégalais: formed, 325; success in municipal elections, 326; policy, 333; congress, 334, 363; character, 334–5; constitution, 338–9; membership, 339; organization, 340–2, 480, 482–3, 484; finance, 341; conflict over nominations, 342–4; accusations of intimidation by, 354,

356, 384; candidates of, 356–63; newspaper, 370, 373; manifesto, 375; radical outlook, 381–2; attacks on metropolitan government, 383–4; success of, 388–90; 'philosophy', 479. *See also* Senghor, L. S.
Blundell, Michael, 401, 430, 452.
Blyden, Edward: founder, S.L.I.M., 190, 195; campaign, 202, 208, 209, 210, 211, 213, 235, 237; results, 259, 269.
Bo: franchise, 181, 182, 198; U.P.P. in, 205; S.L.P.P. in, 215; candidates in, 230, 231, 238; administrative problems in, 241; results in, 260.
Bright-Taylor, Mrs., 216, 234, 235.
Bureh, Kande, 230, 231, 257, 269.

Calabar, 124, 143.
Calabar, Ogoja and Rivers State (C.O.R.), demand for, 124, 127, 129, 130, 134, 157.
Candidates:
Kenya: Coutts' proposals concerning, 404; government proposals concerning, 407–8; Leg. Co. debate on, 408; nomination of, 422–3; occupations of, 423; experience of, 424; policies of, 429; in Nairobi, 443; in other constituencies, 451–5; difficulties of, 456–7.
Nigeria, E.R.: regulations concerning, 115–16; in Owerri, 150.
Nigeria, W.R.: choice of, 55; independent, 56–57; occupations, 57; in Oyo, 80, 81; in Warri, 88–89; reasons for selection, 98.
Senegal: nomination difficulties of, 343–5; regulations for, 345; party affiliations of, 356–7; ages, 358; ethnic origins, 358–9; birthplaces, 359–60; occupations, 360–2; political experience, 362.
Sierra Leone: campaigns by, 223–7; importance of local connexion for, 225, 226, 227, 228, 230, 259, 260; occupations of, 228–30; of S.L.P.P., 230–2; success of independent, 258–61; successful, 262.
Capricorn Africa Society: in Kenya, 405; 'Capricorn Contract', 426–7, 429, 430, 431, 443, 445, 453, 455.
Chiefs, importance of:
Kenya (and elders), 454 n.
Nigeria, E.R., 142.
Nigeria, W.R., 24, 60. *See also* Oyo, Alafin of; Warri, Olu of.
Senegal, 287–8.
Sierra Leone, 173, 179, 186, 224, 226, 231, 238, 260, 266.

Colonial Times (Nairobi), 433, 435.
Communists, in Senegal, 310, 311–12, 314, 317–18, 327, 329.
Constituencies, 472–3; in Nigeria, W.R., 51–53, 103–4; in Nigeria, E.R., 115–16, 159–60; in Sierra Leone, 180, 183; in Senegal, 297, 298–9; in Kenya, 410.
Corrupt practices: possibilities of, 475, 483.
Kenya: lack of evidence of, 457.
Nigeria, E.R.: accusations of, 147.
Nigeria, W.R.: lack of evidence of, 84, 101.
Senegal: lack of evidence of, 356.
Sierra Leone: definition of, 225; accusations of, 249, 251; petitions concerning, 264–5.
Coutts Report, 402–5, 406–7, 440, 471.
Cummings-John, Mrs. C. A., 232, 253, 257, 269.

Daily Guardian (Freetown), 216.
Daily Mail (Freetown), 215, 217.
Daily Service (Lagos), 34, 66–68, 127; in E.R., 132.
Daily Times (Lagos), 33–34, 68, 127; in E.R., 132.
Dakar: development of, 281, 282; 'Commune', 290, 292, 309; capital, A.O.F., 296; political activity in, 310, 326, 334; electorate in, 347–8, 359; manifestos displayed in, 364; candidates in, 371; meetings in, 380; polling in, 386, 387; results in, 388.
Delta province, W.R., 18, 20, 52.
Dia, Mamadou: elected 1956, 321; demands party fusion, 325, 330; report by, 337; experience of, 362; religion, 363.
Diagne, Blaise, 307, 308.
Diamond mining, Sierra Leone, 173 n., 175, 177, 194–5.
Diourbel, 293, 326, 356, 371.
Disorder and violence:
Nigeria, E.R.: hooliganism, 123–4, 142, 147; preventive measures, 149.
Nigeria, W.R.: measures to prevent, 55; in Ijebu-Ode, 61, 67; lack of, at polling, 75; fears of, 100.
Senegal: provisions against, 354, 386; history of, 379–80.
Sierra Leone: lack of, 251, 268.
Dynamic Party (Nigeria, W.R.), 26, 55, 57, 59, 66.

East African Standard (Nairobi), 428, 435.
Eastern Outlook (Enugu), 132, 134, 138.

Echos d'Afrique noire (Dakar), 367–8.
Economic issues: as electoral factor,
479; relation to elections, 485–6.
Kenya, 426, 428, 429, 448.
Nigeria, E.R.: banking policy, 124–5,
128; N.C.N.C. proposals, 125;
revenue allocation, 127, 130;
Action Group proposals, 128–9.
Nigeria, W.R.: in Action Group
campaign, 29, 62; allocation of
revenue, 28, 63.
Senegal: B.D.S. programme, 316;
P.S.A.S. programme, 371–2, 373.
Sierra Leone, 218, 219, 223.
Education: as electoral factor, 479.
Kenya: United Front proposals, 426;
'A-K' proposals, 428; as issue, 429,
445, 448.
Nigeria, E.R.: 'Universal Primary
Education' as issue, 111–13;
N.C.N.C. proposals, 125; Action
Group proposals, 129.
Nigeria, W.R., 37.
Senegal, 316.
Sierra Leone, 219–20.
Edukugho, Chief Reece, 88, 92, 94.
Egbe Omo Oduduwa, 14, 21–22; rela-
tions with Action Group, 22–23, 77.
Electoral administration, 4–5; of pol-
ling, 466–7, 474–5; staff for, 470;
publicity for, 470–1; adjudication,
475–6.
Kenya: legislation concerning, 409–
11; 'expatriate' voting, 446–8;
polling arrangements, 447, 449–
50; success of, 456.
Nigeria, E.R.: regulations, 113–19;
polling arrangements, 116–17,
121–3, 150, 151–2; administrative
organization, 119; amendments,
148; divergencies in, 149; central
organization of, 153–4; counting,
154–6; costs, 158; recommendations concerning, 159–60.
Nigeria, W.R.: regulations, 43–45;
polling arrangements, 72–75; success of, 98; distrust of, 99–100.
Senegal: history of, 296–8; polling and
counting regulations, 303–5; problems of, 305–6; distribution of
electoral cards, 349–52; polling
stations and staff, 352–4; records
of committees, 354–5; campaign
regulations, 364; success of, 387.
Sierra Leone: precedents, 180; polling
system, 183; district council elections, 185–6; administrative organization of, 195–202, 236–7;
publicity for, 237–41; staff for

polling administration, 241–3;
identification problems, 244–6;
polling arrangements, 246–51;
counting, 253–5; election petitions,
264, 267–8.
See also Franchise; Registration;
Symbols.
English language, use of:
Kenya: a necessity for candidates,
395, 404, 408, 415, 422–3, 444.
Nigeria, E.R.: in press, 132; in broadcasts, 136, 137; in speeches, 142.
Nigeria, W.R.: in eastern provinces,
18, 87; in campaign, 60.
Sierra Leone: in speeches in Freetown,
209; in broadcasts, 221; in posters,
227; a necessity for candidates, 228;
in official publicity, 240.
Enugu, 112; N.C.N.C. centre, 123, 133,
156; Action Group centre, 141;
capital, E.R., 152, 153–4, 157, 161.
European settlers: electoral influence,
3;
in Kenya: numbers, 391; immigration
of, as issue, 428, 429; 1956 elections, 430;
in Senegal: numbers, 282; composition
of, 283–4; in political developments, 309; registration of, 348–9;
as candidates, 359; apathy of, 369.
Eyo, E. O., 151.

Foster-Sutton Report, 17, 38; importance of, 109–10, 161; and N.C.N.C.,
110, 124, 146; and U.N.I.P., 131;
press reaction to, 134; and Action
Group, 141.
Franchise: variations in, 471–2.
Kenya: Coutts' Report on, 402–5;
government proposals for, 405–6;
Leg. Co. debate on, 408; alterations to, 410–11; United Front
proposals for, 425; 'A-K' proposals
for, 427; Mboya's proposals for,
448; discussion of, 457–8; analysis
of, 459–61.
Nigeria, E.R., 114, 121.
Nigeria, W.R.: regulations, 43–44;
discussion of, 104–5.
Senegal: history of, 292, 293, 294;
provisions for, 298–9.
Sierra Leone, 179–84.
Freetown: history, 168, 169; as constituency, 183, 184; registration in,
198–200; meetings in, 207–14; local
candidates for, 230, 231–2, 233;
polling in, 243, 247–8, 250–1; results
for, 256–7; political attitudes in, 265,
266.

PRINTED IN GREAT BRITAIN
AT THE UNIVERSITY PRESS, OXFORD
BY VIVIAN RIDLER
PRINTER TO THE UNIVERSITY